This is a wonderful book. Moving. Honest. Detailed. The stories grip me; they stay with me. I hope many students read this book. Teachers, too. What they learn will help them be better at the changes we so desperately need.

Todd R. Clear, University Professor, Rutgers Law School, author of *Imprisoning Communities: How Mass Incarceration Makes Disadvantaged Neighborhoods Worse; The Punishment Imperative: The Rise and Failure of Mass Incarceration in America;* and *American Corrections*

❦

This wise and compelling book reminds us that reentry is much more than the single experience of an individual leaving prison. An entire community is impacted. By elevating multiple first-person reentry stories, the authors bring these kaleidoscopic perspectives to life. Our understanding of reentry is immeasurably enriched by listening to these voices. Most powerfully, the book asks a heretical question: if we recognized that everyone who has strayed returns home, how would we rethink our approach to crime and punishment? Long after reading the book, that haunting question hangs in the air. Answering that question will also require careful listening to the voices of those same communities.

Jeremy Travis, Executive Vice President of Criminal Justice, Arnold Ventures, author of *But They All Come Back: Facing the Challenges of Prisoner Reentry*

❦

Sharing the Burden of Repair is a must read for people interested in corrections. Through a collection of conversations and listening sessions, the authors provide a unique blend of perspectives to paint a picture of the progressive path that Georgia's criminal justice system has taken towards those under supervision as well as a broader approach to building community. The stories are raw and show both the passion of those in the system as well as the ongoing struggle to shift from a "catch people doing wrong" to a "promoting success" model.

Brian Lovins, PhD, Principal: Justice System Partners; President-Elect: American Probation and Parole Association

When students ask how they can help to end mass incarceration and the political climate that creates and sustains it, I tell them the first thing they have to do is to learn to listen – not to me, but to the voices of those who have survived imprisonment and found a way toward reintegration. So, it comes as no surprise that this powerful and timely book is the product of a remarkable process of sustained listening. These are the stories behind the numbers that make up mass incarceration and they are our best hope for redemption.

Shadd Maruna, author of *Making Good: How Ex-Convicts Reform and Rebuild Their Lives*

This book is a "MUST READ," an assemblage of stories that shares the most comprehensive views on one of the most challenging issues in this century, mass incarceration. While relating the history of Georgia's reentry journey, the book communicates gripping stories that give insight and awareness to any and all readers. It transcends the borders of Georgia. I could hear the theme song from *The Help* movie, "The Living Proof," as each chapter, section, and story revealed another perceptive point of view. This book is not only relevant and appropriate to the common citizen, but to the criminal justice profession, faith and community based organizations, governments, academia, for-profit and non-profit organizations, families, and all impacted by incarceration. And every person and institution in America is impacted by incarceration! My question: "What are we going to do today?" We must work to change the world.

A.J. Sabree, MS, ThM: former Director of Reentry Services, Georgia Department of Corrections; Consultant on Reentry Services, Georgia Department of Juvenile Justice

This work provides a rare, real, and in-depth view of the corrections system from the views of the offender, administrator, and stakeholder. It reveals what is going well, what's not working, and what we as a system need to start doing. Definitely a worthwhile and lasting read.

Michael W. Nail, Commissioner, Georgia Department of Community Supervision

❦

As the title implies, *Sharing the Burden of Repair* invites ordinary citizens into the complex conversations around our current criminal justice system. It makes the point that, even without personal contact with the system, each and every citizen impacts and is impacted by it. The work focuses on Georgia, but the issues are universal.

This is an ambitious undertaking. It is impossible to talk about any one aspect of criminal justice reform without including the whole, as the detailed introduction so ably points out. Thus, over the course of six years, the authors have asked themselves tough questions, and taken them to all actors in the system through listening interviews. The resulting volume is smart, informed and informative, organizing the vast number of issues into interconnected and understandable units.

Sharing the Burden is both a challenge and a call to action for anyone concerned about the individual and social costs of incarceration, especially how to reshape the process to accommodate its ultimate goal: reentry of the majority of those incarcerated back to their communities. OUR communities.

Sarah W. Bartlett, founder **writinginsideVT**, co-editor of *Hear Me, See Me: Incarcerated Women Write* and *Lifelines: Re-Writing Lives from Inside Out*

❦

Sharing the Burden of Repair is an excellent tool to begin meaningful, insightful dialogue about the plight of public safety in our community, dialogue that should prompt positive intervention *beyond* conversation.

Rev. Thurmond N. Tillman, Pastor, First African Baptist Church, Savannah

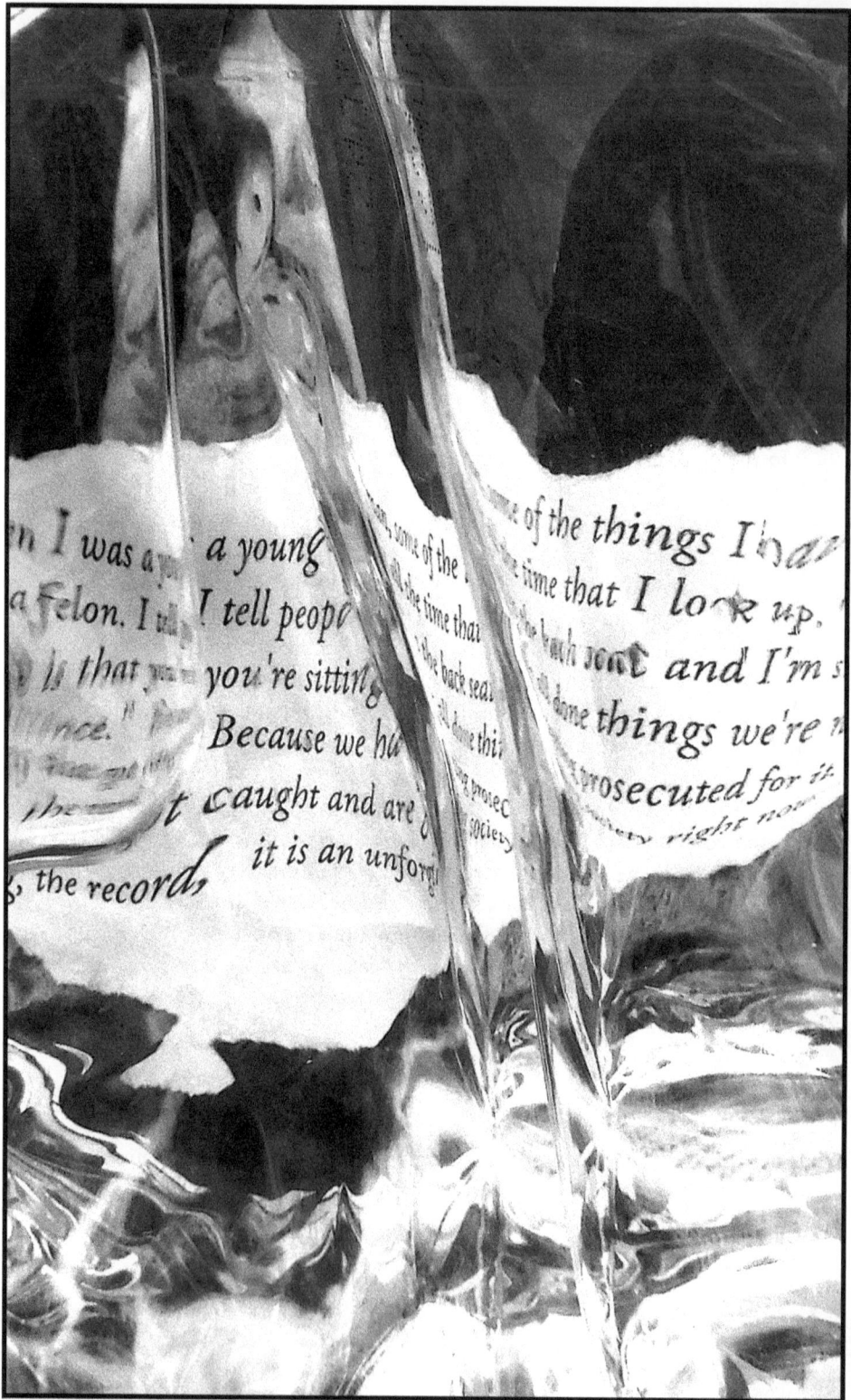

n I was a y... a young... ...some of the... ...me of the things I ha...

a felon. I u... I tell peop... ...all the time that... ...he time that I lo...k up.

...is that y... you're sittin... ...the back sea... and I'm s...

...nce."... Because we hi... ...done thi... done things we're...

...t caught and are... ...g prose... ...prosecuted for it...

...society... ...right now...

..., the record... it is an unforg...

SHARING THE BURDEN OF REPAIR

REENTRY AFTER MASS INCARCERATION

WISING UP ANTHOLOGIES

RE-CREATING OUR COMMON CHORD

CROSSING CLASS: *The Invisible Wall*

THE KINDNESS OF STRANGERS

DARING TO REPAIR:
What Is It, Who Does It & Why?

SHIFTING BALANCE SHEETS:
Women's Stories of Naturalized Citizenship & Cultural Attachment

COMPLEX ALLEGIANCES:
Constellations of Immigration, Citizenship, & Belonging

WISING UP LISTENING PROJECTS

GOD SPEAKS MY LANGUAGE, CAN YOU?
Heather Tosteson

DISCUSSION GUIDE

SHARING THE BURDEN OF REPAIR
Reentry After Mass Incarceration
www.universaltable.org

SHARING THE BURDEN OF REPAIR

REENTRY AFTER MASS INCARCERATION

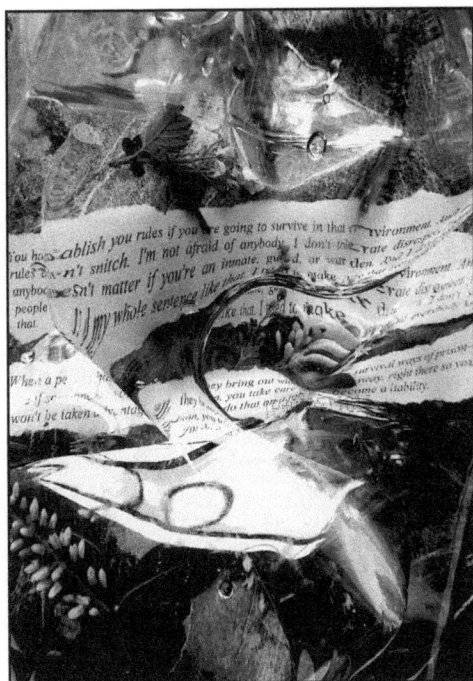

A WISING UP LISTENING PROJECT

HEATHER TOSTESON & CHARLES D. BROCKETT

Wising Up Press

Wising Up Press
P.O. Box 2122
Decatur, GA 30031-2122
www.universaltable.org

Catalogue-in-Publication data is on file with the Library of Congress.
LCCN: 2020937953

ISBN: 978-1-7324514-5-2

DEDICATION

To the memory of Betty Hasan-Amin and to all the thoughtful individuals who have so generously shared their wisdom with us for this listening project.

...be the ones that will...
...at thing...
...ord, ...nforg...

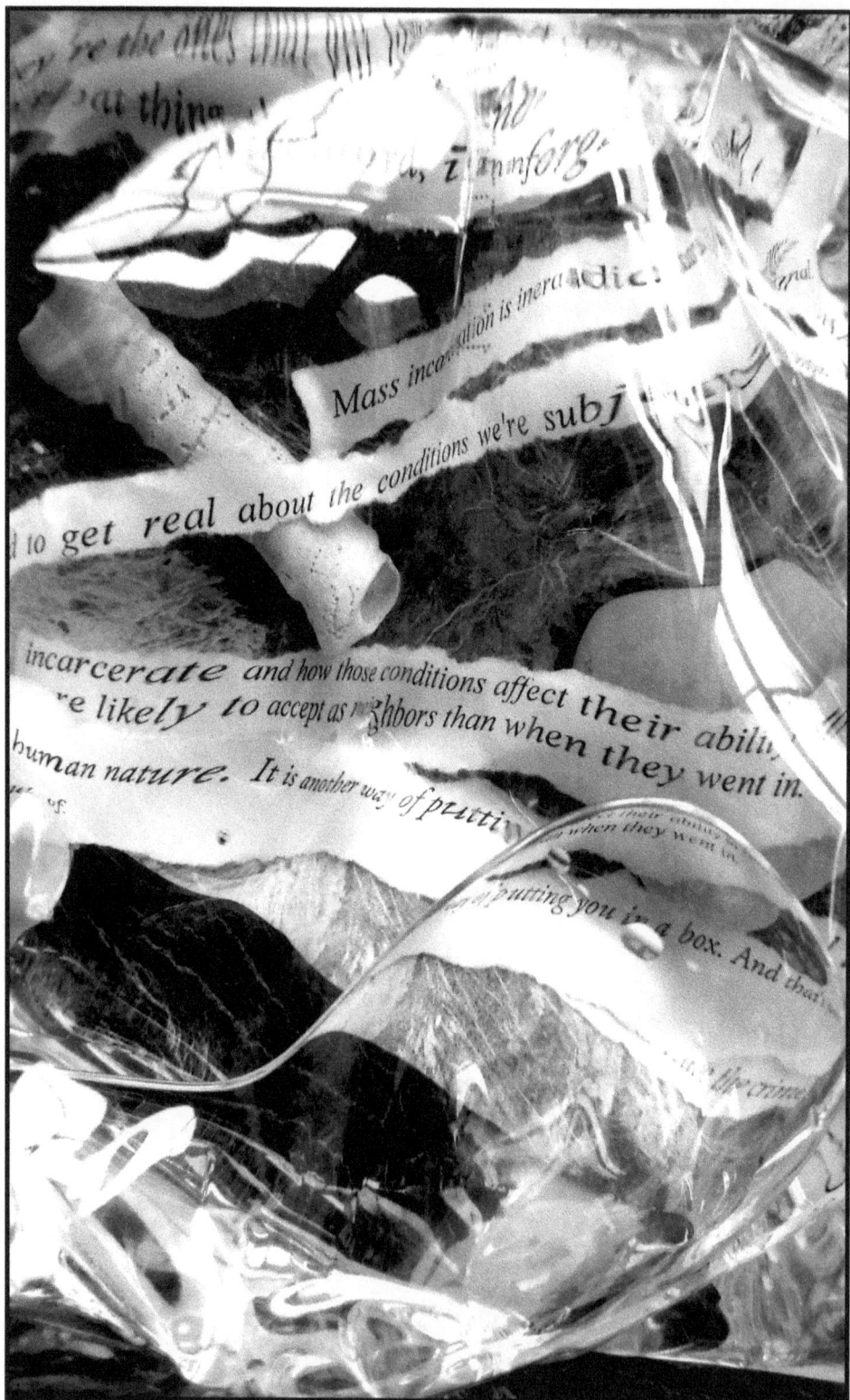

Mass incarceration is inera...dic...

...we're subj...

...d to get real about the conditions

incarcerate and how those conditions affect their abili...
...re likely to accept as neighbors than when they went in.

human nature. It is another way of putti...
...their ability... when they went in.

...putting you in a box. And that...

CONTENTS

didn't want to ... ...nt to se... ...ell so much shame.
from that. Talk... Talk... ...fided in my pastor friends.
want you to co... ...to con... my house. I want everyone
...ut moved me to an... ...place.

need to shift to ma...
reenter and reintegrat...
...able action?

What attitudes need to ...
incarcerated people to reenter ...
socially and morally desirable ac...

...o do was deprogram me. He had to pu... ...o put me...
good. All I knew was the street life... ...je. All I...
...y to get over. That's what you had in ... ...ud in the...
...to have it. But if I had to get over... ...over on...
...as you or me. That was the... ...ntly

FOREWORD

Reentry is here. We simply can't afford financially to imprison at the rate and length we have for the last three decades. But for reentry to be here to stay, we as an entire society need to share the burden. What attitudes need to shift to make assisting formerly incarcerated people to reenter and reintegrate in society a safe, socially and morally desirable action? Why is a commitment to reentry as a stance so important for a highly polarized society? What kind of a system do we create when we think of those who break laws as essentially different from us? What does this attitude justify, what does it protect us against? What does thinking this way do to our character as individuals and as a nation?

This book is the result of a six-year Wising Up Listening Project on reentry in Georgia. Its aim is to share what we learned, to expand, individual story by individual story, our understanding of the importance and the challenges of successful reentry for all of us after an age of mass incarceration. This project has taught us that we need to look more carefully at the stories we use to understand crime—and justice. We need to collaborate on new ones, more complex, nuanced, compassionate ones that make room for both the suffering of the victims of crime and the possibility of change and constructive social contribution on the part of those who have been convicted of crimes and punished for them—stories that understand the reality of both irreparable harm and our capacity for remorse and change. We need to bring these stories under a single roof, hold them all in our hearts if we are to work toward a truly just system—one where we feel assured that our children, our brothers and sisters, our mothers and fathers, or we ourselves will be justly treated if we commit a crime or are the victim of one. This book is one attempt, by common citizens, to do so.

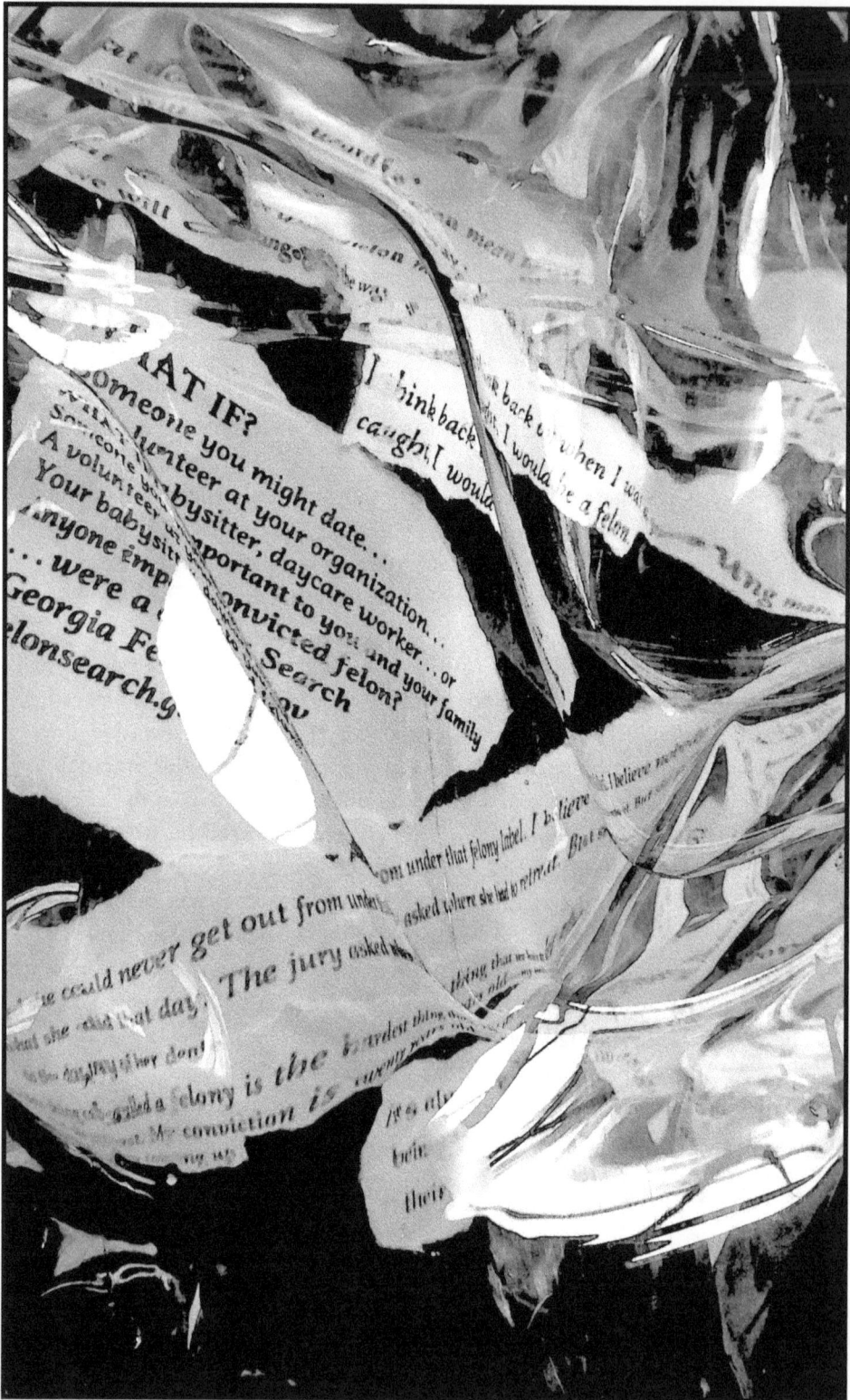

WHAT IF?

...omeone you might date. . .

...volunteer at your organization. . .

...Someone babysitter, daycare worker. . .or

A volunteer important to you and your family

Your babysitter...

...anyone emp... ...onvicted felon?

...were a c... Search

Georgia Fe...

...elonsearch.g...

I think back... ...ack when I wa...

caught, I woul... ...it, I woula be a felon

...m under that felony label. I believe...

...asked where she had to retr.a.t. But s...

...could never get out from under... ...what she did that day. The jury asked...

...aid a felony is the hardest thing...

...conviction is twenty years...

INTRODUCTION

WHAT ARE WE CLAPPING FOR?

In the 2019 State of the Union address, the president announced the passage of a long-awaited bipartisan criminal justice reform bill, the First Step Act. He identified two of his guests as people directly impacted by the bill. When they stood, they received standing ovations. But if one stops to think about it, the applause is as ambiguous as our attitudes toward criminal justice. Another family, earlier, was applauded for having a family member murdered in their home by an illegal immigrant, their presence at the speech providing support for the president's claims that the issue of illegal immigration is inseparable from crime. The two people who stood as exemplars of criminal justice reform were not illegal immigrants. They were black. They both had served extremely long sentences for nonviolent drug crimes. Matthew Charles, the first person to be released as a result of the First Step Act, was serving a thirty-five-year sentence. Alice Johnson, who was granted presidential clemency in June, 2018, after her story came to the president's attention through the advocacy of a reality television star, was serving a mandatory life sentence. Although strong advocates of criminal justice reform, we found the applause unsettling.

Were the members of Congress applauding the now very rare bipartisan support behind the bill? Applauding their own ability to begin to right some clear injustices in federal criminal justice laws, especially concerning racial inequality in sentencing, by placing greater emphasis on judicial discretion in sentencing, community supervision, and rehabilitation? Were they applauding stories of personal rehabilitation *in spite of* unjust sentences? In other words, applauding these individuals' heroic resistance? Or their heroic persistence?

Is it in our best interest as a society to have rehabilitation be an heroic story where the criminal justice system *as a system* is the malignant adversary? Does it help us to ignore or forget that the laws we are righting have had—and continue to have—lasting consequences that individuals may *not* be able to overcome? Or that those in prison, in general, are not innocent—that rehabilitation and reintegration must include a far more nuanced and uncomfortable relationship to individual behavior and societal response that includes an acknowledgement of the capacity for wrong-doing on all sides? Does that awareness deserve applause—or a moment of meditative silence?

What If

In the early days of our interviewing, there was a billboard posted prominently in many of the MARTA stations in Atlanta as well as on the subway cars. The *What If* campaign was designed to gather income for the state through felon searches using Georgia's own databases. It played on our fears. Here is the text:

What If?
Someone you might date . . .
A volunteer at your organization . . .
Your babysitter, daycare worker . . . or
Anyone important to you and your family
. . . were a convicted felon?
Georgia Felon Search
felonsearch.ga.gov

Ironically, the *What If* campaign was rolled out at the very same time that the governor, Nathan Deal, was promoting criminal justice reform, including supporting the *Ban the Box* campaign, whose aim is to give people with criminal records a chance at a first interview by not having to check a box indicating their criminal record on their job applications. The incongruity inspired us to talk with various people involved in both efforts.

But these questions—*What if someone important to you and your family were a convicted felon? What if you were one?*—are valid questions in a country that imprisons more people than any other in the world. Indeed, they are ones as a society we need to embrace—even if they bring us into direct and uncomfortable contact with our own deep contradictions.

At this point, there is a general consensus that we have imprisoned far too many people, far too inequitably, for far too long, in harsh conditions that do not improve them or create greater safety for us as a society. How do we as a society *repair* that damage in a way that builds genuine social trust?

We are not suggesting that most people who go to prison are innocent of the crimes with which they are charged, or that they did not do genuine harm. We *are* suggesting that how we as a society respond to that wrong-doing has great impact on whether there will be genuine social repair. Without that social repair our best interests as a society—safety and social trust and voluntary prosocial commitments—will not be met.

We start with a challenging premise: *A criminal justice system that does not focus on reentry and reintegration at every step in its process, from pre-arrest to final release, is both inherently unjust and unsafe.*

Along with the presumption of innocence, we need the presumptions of growth, remorse, accountability, and change, *we need the assumption of return* if we are to have a system that makes us genuinely, sustainably safe. As common citizens it is our responsibility to make sure that the circle of justice is completed by asking ourselves WHAT IF throughout our criminal justice system: What if *I* were a felon, a victim, a family member, a defense attorney, a prosecutor, a judge, a prison guard, a community supervision officer, a neighbor, an employer, a friend? What, from this position in the system, would feel just?

We can introduce reforms throughout the system—from ending the school-to-prison pipeline, improving education, encouraging diversion, drug and mental health courts—but the reality is that we have already sent many of our citizens to prison for very long periods of time, subjected them to harsh conditions that did not make them more prosocial. How do we make it safe for all of us to have them return now as our neighbors? What do we owe them? What do they owe us? Institutional reform alone will not repair the current damage, simply reduce the future cost. The focus of this book is what relationships we are willing to create with the millions we have already incarcerated if we are, all of us, *together,* to rebuild social trust—individual by individual, community by community.

Our Own What If

Our first inspiration for this project was being the victims of crime ourselves. We live in unincorporated Stone Mountain, in DeKalb County, Georgia, a racially mixed community with a high number of recent immigrants, many of them refugees, an area we chose for its complex and promising diversity. However, soon after moving here, we were robbed of all our computers and our brand new car. We had a security alarm but had failed to set it for a half-hour trip to the grocery store. Because two bicycles were abandoned on the grass in front of our house, it was suggested that the robbers were juveniles. Our car was found in an apartment complex ten blocks from our house several days later. When we questioned the police officer who was involved in its recovery about the safety of our new neighborhood, he answered that the neighborhood wasn't dangerous, although it had some "mischievous" kids. We thought of our new car, of all the never recovered computers we use for our professional work and wondered whether "mischievous" covered our loss.

When we collected the car from a county storage lot many miles away, we pondered the meaning of the CD in the player, a combination of rap and African song, the several McDonald's wrappers. We busied ourselves with improving our security system, adding new motion detectors, installing floor bolts, pounding in signs front and back and sideways advertising the alarm system. Whenever we passed the local high school four blocks away, we wondered if "our" thieves were attending classes or blithely out prowling empty houses. We wondered in new ways about the significance of the county's high dropout rates. What could we do to ensure our safety in the future? What did we want to have happen to "our" thieves? Given the permanent loss of all our computers, a simple "Sorry, my bad," would not suffice. Would having them work all the hours it had taken us to earn the money to buy the computers and car be sufficient? Or would they have to work all the hours *they* would need to work at minimum wages to really understand what they had done? Or did we want to address root causes and make sure they learned to read, finished high school, went to college or trade school (none of which were very probable, much less guaranteed at our low performing high school)?

But what about the unease that filled us every time we heard someone walk across our front porch and pause before ringing the bell? Or the way we had begun to look twice at every teenage boy (and why did we assume they were boys, not girls) who walked too slowly down our street? How could they make restitution for this generalized loss of social trust? A distrust that extended to the police, for whom this was life as usual in DeKalb, indeed deserved only the casual descriptor "mischievous." It was true that prison did not enter our thoughts about potential punishments, but a vague sense of physical threat kept us psychologically imprisoned for several years afterwards, reinforced by the assault on our frail Vietnamese neighbor as he got out of his car in his own driveway, and the three burglaries at the home of the African-American family across the street. We hear that anxiety echoed, magnified many times over, on our local listserv, where every car that pauses for more than ten minutes inspires an anxious inquiry.

A more important inspiration for the project was our friend Betty Hasan-Amin, who participated in another listening project on interfaith understanding and also offered enthusiastic support for our two-year listening project on immigration, citizenship, and belonging. We visited her one day and found her busy writing a letter to then Attorney General Eric Holder protesting the differential impact of our sentencing laws, and, most poignantly, the severe collateral consequences of criminal convictions that now made it impossible for her sons to find good, stable employment. To feel that these bright and able young men, in their early or mid-twenties, would face a lifetime of prejudice and economic disadvantage after she had fought so hard to raise them and open doors for them was an anguish to her. More than that, it was a profound injustice because it robbed her and our society of all the good her sons were able to do for themselves and others. She could not protect them from their own worst choices, nor could she protect them from the inequities of a system that penalized them far more harshly than it would have done if they were white.

As we listened, we understood that others who had not met Betty, who just heard the outlines of her story, would make some damaging assumptions about her and her sons, assumptions that ignored all the determination that had led her, paralyzed and wheelchair bound at seventeen, to complete college, become a teacher, a devoted mother, assumptions that ignored all the care she had dedicated to their upbringing, ignored the potential of these intelligent young men, potential she had cultivated so faithfully and still cultivated, assumptions that were resolutely deaf to her suffering. These assumptions focused exclusively on individual responsibility and ignored the role that we, as citizens, might play in that suffering by countenancing these increasingly harsh laws and their glaringly inequitable social and racial impact.

But what consolidated that interest and concern of ours was a single phrase said in passing by an urbane man we were talking to while doing our immigration listening project. He was a former director of an international school located in Buckhead, the wealthiest section of Atlanta. Retired, his interest had now turned to our slightly down at the heels area of the city with its highly international population. He was considering starting his own non-profit directed towards recent immigrants and one of his ideas was to bring wealthy businessmen down to mentor refugees living in the many apartment complexes. When asked whether these businessmen might also mentor the many young African-American boys in those same complexes (the complexes where "our" thieves probably lived), he answered immediately and without hesitation, "Absolutely not. It isn't exotic."

He's right, of course, the level of crime in our community—and its perpetrators—are *not* exotic. The situations that promote this are not exotic. They are deeply entrenched, seemingly intractable, reinforced subtly and overtly by our institutions as well as our attitudes. Engaging with the issue of mass incarceration and reentry is *not* exotic. It is difficult, implicating in ways that can make us feel very uncomfortable—and helpless. With immigrants we don't feel responsible for whatever happened in their country of origin; we usually assume that with a little assistance they will be able to thrive and climb. They reinforce our best assumptions about our society and our equal right to pursue happiness with a good chance of achieving it in some measure. But with this very *un*exotic question of *endemic* poverty, *endemic* racism, *endemic* violence, *endemic* crime, these assumptions of the power of the individual will are challenged.

We think that accepting that challenge together will make us all stronger.

APPROACH AND SCOPE OF OUR LISTENING PROJECT

Our greatest qualification for this project is that we are *average* citizens— and that provides us with both our social location and the persistence of our interest. We do live in an unusually mixed neighborhood for the south, and we do live in what has been one of the most punishing states in the nation and remains the most highly supervised. Because of our education and our professional experience, we have disciplinary fluency, which helped us gain access within the criminal justice system and, through a review of the scholarship, to locate our interest there as well. But prior to beginning this project, we had virtually no contact with the criminal justice system. That grounding in ignorance was a strength. It allowed us to be open to many different perspectives and a wide range of experiences—to follow our *questions* about the criminal justice system rather than search for confirmation for our assumptions.

We did, however, have three fundamental assumptions that deeply informed how we *conducted* this project. First, this issue mattered to us and it mattered to us *as citizens*. Second, we assumed that everyone we met had something to add to our understanding and that it was our job to listen for it.

We also assumed it was our job to listen in a particular way, one that sought to identify with the flow of good and wisdom in each person we met.

The majority of the interviews and research for this book took place between 2014 and 2016, a period of such intensive listening and reading, and such rapid institutional and attitudinal change, that we are still shaking our heads when we look back at our calendars, our interview and reading lists. But then, three years into the project, we slammed on the brakes. We were beyond exhausted. We had listened for hours at a time to more than two hundred people. We had read more books than that. We had more information than we could process. The tenor of the country had changed. *We* had changed, but we couldn't say how, or how much.

If we had finished writing this book three years ago we would have had a different book. For one thing, we would not have been able to absorb what we'd heard in the way we think is most necessary—heart to heart, with nuance. That took many more hours of relistening. Since we were conducting our interviewing at the height of reform momentum, we also would not have directly experienced one of the greatest and most uncomfortable truths about criminal justice in the United States—its constant oscillation between punishment and reform.

We *have* been able to see some of the important benefits of this wave of institutional reform. However, with time, we are also able to see what *hasn't* changed institutionally or legally. We can also see what some of these reforms may now be asking of us as common citizens if they are to become lasting changes.

Here are questions we now ask:

❧ *Has our move away from incarceration toward diversion and community supervision really reduced the population under control—or actually increased it and brought it closer to home, our homes? If so, what do we, as citizens, have to do to make this shift successful for us as well as for those being supervised?*

❧ *Has this been a decade of unusual bipartisan consensus around criminal reform that will result in relatively small incremental changes rather than a serious rethinking of why we punish so much more than other developed democracies?*

❧ *Will these reforms stop before we address the major structural reasons for the high level of incarceration—and before we address the many very real obstacles to reentry, both formal and informal, that remain? Whose responsibility is it to see this through?*

❖ *Have we reached the limit that institutional reform can do to facilitate reentry—if there is not a substantive accompanying change in public attitudes and commitments?*

Listening in Good Faith

Sometimes it feels like it was the most quixotic of enterprises, this listening in good faith throughout such a difficult and complicated and rapidly changing system. But the question—*Why did we do it?*—is far less important than why so many people agreed to so generously share their own experiences and wisdom with us.

Throughout the system there was a hunger to be heard in the way we were committed to listening, with an expressed intention to identify, to put ourselves in other people's shoes, to see us as much as possible through *their* eyes—and whether we could or not, to see *them* consistently in good faith. We all hunger for that kind of listening and seeing—but especially in the criminal justice system. Although we say that our criminal justice system is based on the presumption of innocence, the reality is that throughout the entire system there is a powerful and pervasive *absence* of that presumption that affects everyone—and an even more profound hunger *for* it.

There are truths and insights that are only possible with a presumption of good faith, ones that are crucial to creating a truly just correctional system, ones that invite us as a society back into safer, fairer relationship with one another. It may be that people like us, common citizens, called by something more implicating and transformative than simple curiosity, who can grieve and hope for *everyone* involved have a crucial role to play in this much needed re-envisioning.

When we think back on the many interviews we conducted, what is most striking is how *likeable* we found the people we talked with. This basic affinity crossed many viewpoints, stances toward criminal justice, levels of education, dramatic differences in life experiences. In an essentially adversarial system suffused with suspicion, this is actually remarkable. It is also important if we are to collaborate in healthy change.

We think our response had to do with a very specific quality of these interviews: We were listening to *identify*, to try to see how someone else understood themselves, their own actions and the purposes and impact of the criminal justice system. They were presenting themselves in their best light. They were being invited to join us in imagining positive change that took their own experiences and their own visions of justice as of equal richness and value.

The impact on *us* of that commitment to listen in good faith was also important. It meant we couldn't disengage or diminish the importance of what we were hearing. We didn't, as we listened, have to judge, reconcile—or even figure out how *we* fit in. Our job was just to hold the person we were talking to steadily in attention. This stance we feel is crucial when we think about genuine reintegration. For the effect of this experience of likeability on us was to increase our *appreciation* of the diversity of viewpoints, our *resilience* in absorbing them—and our *hope* for better solutions as well. The *way* we listened humanized, qualified and tested our thoughts by bringing them into direct emotional connection with the experiences of *real* people, *real* fellow citizens. With this kind of listening we were creating a basket that could hold a wide range of complicated experiences, differing thoughts, strong preferences in a way that created an abundance of possibility, *not* chaos.

This appreciation is crucial if we want to engage in any consistent, long-term way with a system that holds the darkest dimensions of us as a society—from the conditions that create criminal behavior through the criminal justice system that does not, as yet, acknowledge the essential dehumanization we create if that system is not grounded in the possibility of full return. This experience of likeability is important because if we make someone radically, irrevocably different from us, it begins an insidious process by which we eventually dehumanize ourselves as well as them.

REENTRY STORIES

Why do we focus so much on stories in this book—and include so many from different people at different points in the criminal justice system? Because we *think* differently when we think in stories and this way of thinking may be better for the kinds of questions we face when we try to assess and address the harm we do one another. Stories help us *all* think in more nuanced, sophisticated and fluid ways about the many different causes and implications of our actions—the complexity of our motives, conscious and unconscious, the social assumptions and practices that constrain or compel us. When we talk abstractly about government or law or institutions or morals or religious belief, we can forget who made these abstract systems— and why. These systems came out of life, from people not that different from us, as attempts to address real life fears and needs—for meaning, order, safety, connection—and must come back to those real life conditions to be tested, revised—or discarded. The best way to responsibly complete that circle, evaluate that categorical system, is often story.

When asked abstractly what punishment is appropriate for a crime, a jury will choose a punishment that is much harsher than the one they will choose in a trial, after listening to the different stories people are telling and bringing their own knowledge of life to bear. Differing expectations come to light. People can feel when the abstract categorizations of a law don't apply well to the particular harm that was done. Our sense of causality and choice can change too if the jury is diverse enough, enough experience is brought to bear. What we thought was obvious, universal, may not prove to be so. What may look like callous disregard may indeed be so—or it may be genuine ignorance, short-sightedness, a sense of invincibility, or fear and desperation. People may well begin to think beyond those simplistic categories of guilty or innocent to why and what next and eventual return.

The stories we share here are *reentry* stories—conceived and told from wherever in the system people were located at the time we talked with them. Everyone knew our concern was effective reentry after mass incarceration, and people talked with us because they wanted to reflect on the subject, on what made reentry difficult, what could make it more possible. Reentry stories are not retrospective, they are prospective. Their aim is to draw you into the teller's future, even if they explore a painful past to do so.

Only by being able to bear hearing the stories of people who went to prison—what they did, what they were charged with, what they experienced before prison and in prison, how it changed them, and what is required to come back and reintegrate—do we get a clear sense of how effective imprisonment is in creating a safer world for us. Telling those stories, having them heard by people with very different assumptions and life experiences, changes both the teller and the listener.

The same is true for offenders. Only by being able to bear hearing the stories of victims, prosecutors, family members, employers, and probation officers do offenders get a real sense of the pervasive and lasting social cost of *their* actions. This book is designed to increase listening on all sides.

When we say *the system is rigged* or *there is nothing I can do to change the situation* or *if you have the will, you will find a way*, we are telling a *story*. Actions flow from these beliefs, so do consequences. To meet people as they claim the story they are now living and, perhaps, begin to imagine a different one, can change both their world and our own. It begins, as we said before, with a sense of possibility, of *in*conclusiveness. It begins with *How?* It begins with *What if?*

ORGANIZATION OF BOOK

We have chosen to focus primarily on the individual stories of people reintegrating after incarceration and also the experiences of people in community supervision because this is the area of the criminal justice system where the challenges of reentry and reintegration are most alive. Community supervision requires that officers constantly balance support and accountability. The temperaments and life experiences of people attracted to this work have a lot to teach us, as community members, about how we might approach reentry more realistically and resiliently. Their point of view is also crucial because as we move away from mass incarceration we run the high probability of moving toward mass supervision, which creates its own challenges. Indeed, Georgia is the state where this is already the condition—250,000 adults in Georgia were under felony probation supervision in 2018 (1 in 18 adults), a rate triple that of the still formidable rate of the nation as a whole (1 in 55). As community supervision populations continue to grow, we will need to see how this increased presence of criminal-justice-involved individuals in communities affects public attitudes toward reentry. Consequently, the experience of what we call holding communities is also central to understanding the challenge of reentry, beginning with families, peer support groups, chaplains, people providing housing, community reentry coalitions, and employers.

Finally, the current consensus on the need for criminal justice reform is affecting all the different areas of criminal justice, from police to prosecutors to judges to prisons as well as legislators, not always consistently or at the same pace. Our interest here is how an *assumption of return* applied at every step in the process currently modifies, or would modify, our approach to crime and punishment. In our conclusion we explore what we can do as common citizens to re-envision justice beyond the law in a way that incorporates return at every step. We also ask how our criminal justice system would change if, instead of focusing on protecting the privileges of the middle class, it oriented its laws instead toward protecting those most *vulnerable* to crime and to criminal behavior.

I

BY THEIR OWN RECKONING

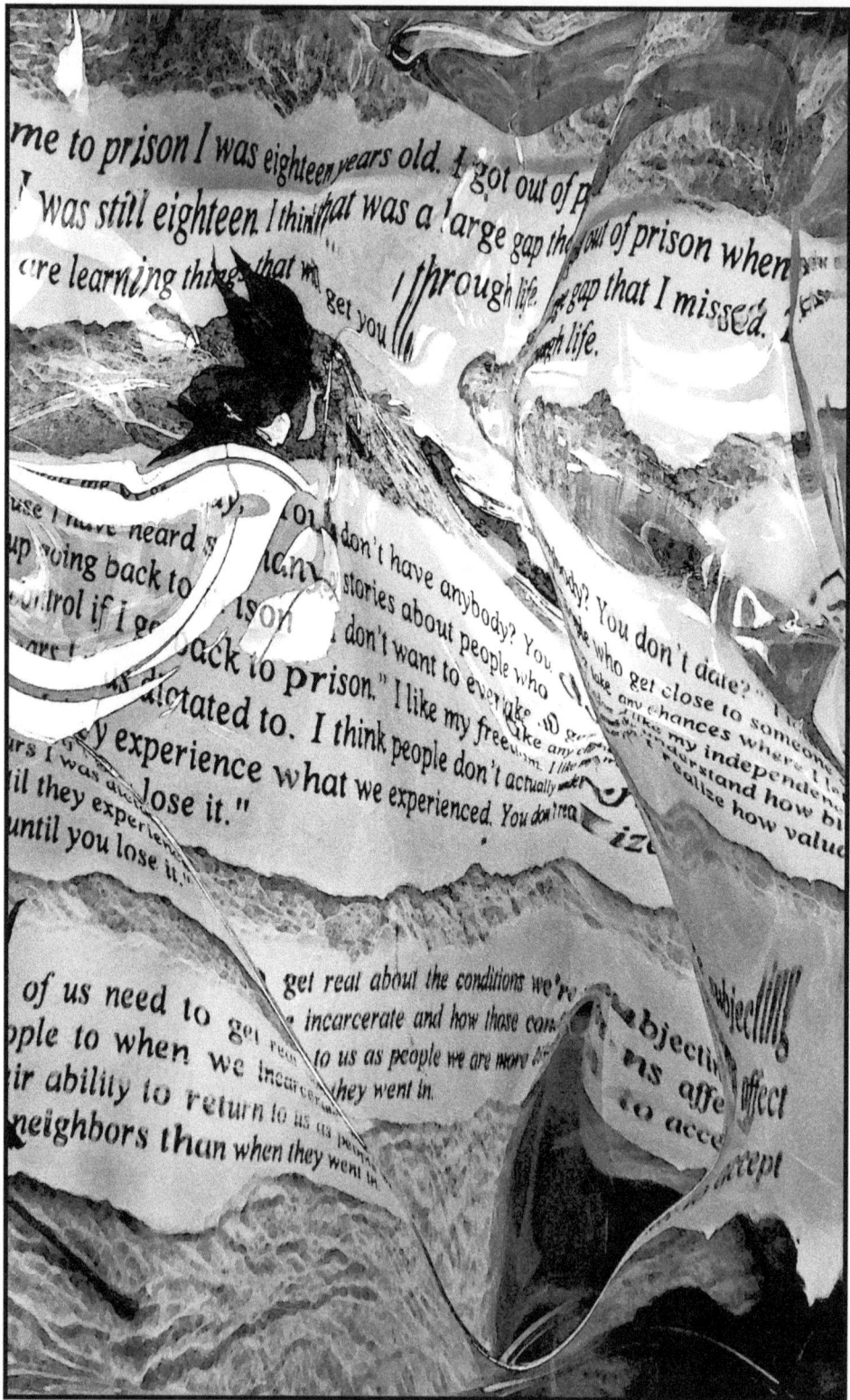

me to prison I was eighteen years old. I got out of p
I was still eighteen I think that was a large gap that out of prison when
are learning things that w get you I through life. gap that I missed.
gh life.

use I have heard s you don't have anybody? You don't date?
up going back to stories about people who who get close to someone
control if I ge ls don't want to eve take any chances where I
rs ack to prison." I like my freed I like my independen
dictated to. I think people don't actually I like how b
y experience what we experienced. You don't rea realize how valu
rs I was lose it." iz
until you lose it.

of us need to get real about the conditions we're bject
ople to when we incarcerate and how those con ns affe ffect
ir ability to return to us as people we are more to acce
neighbors than when they went in. cept

OVERVIEW: DESISTANCE

We talked to numerous men and women who have been convicted of felonies. We planned originally to focus exclusively on people convicted of nonviolent crime; however, most of the people we talked to, especially those we talked to at length and followed for several years, had been convicted of violent crimes. Everyone at some point had been incarcerated, some of them for decades. The time since incarceration also ranged from weeks to almost forty years. The inclusion of violent crime was important because these are the offenses that are most challenging for how we as a society handle reentry.

We start with these stories because any discussion of reentry that doesn't include offenders' own understanding of the causal arc of their life—what they hold themselves accountable for, what they have pride in achieving, what they see as their gifts to society, what they see as society's gifts to them—is not grounded in the most essential elements of *trustworthy* social relation: choice and integrity. We need to understand what being a productive and valued citizen means to them—and to bring that understanding into complex dialogue with *our* understanding of what it means to us. Hopefully, both understandings will change with the encounter.

THE DESISTANCE STORY

Essential Good: The social psychologist Shadd Maruna in his book *Making Good: How Ex-Convicts Reform and Rebuild Their Lives* emphasizes the importance that the story offenders tell about themselves and their actions and motivations is to their ability to reenter society and to desist successfully from crime in the future.[1] This desistance story needs to have at its heart an understanding of the essential good of the person telling the story even as it acknowledges the harm he or she has done. Without this positive core—a sense of personal initiative and affirmation—lasting change is near impossible for any of us.

Turning Point: That turning point, where something shifts and we are able to assume responsibility for both the harm we have done *and* our capacity to change, can come at very different points in our lives. The turning point for Khadijah came on her third imprisonment, when she was running fiercely around a track, surrounded by barbed wire, and said to herself, "My mother didn't raise me this way." At that moment she understood herself as *capable* of doing better—and felt her connection to her strong mother, whom she greatly admired. From this understanding, she could reorganize her life, find the strength to be accountable, find the energy to change.

For Ariif, it came twenty-five years into his incarceration when he could acknowledge his guilt for murder first to himself and then before the parole board. To do this he needed to be able to absorb that guilt in a way that did not label him as forever, essentially, evil and worthless—or the society around him as irrationally repressive. His religious faith gave him the strength to do this.

External Validation: Maruna also points out that it is crucial for that change to be validated by someone with social standing: a prison warden, a chaplain, a judge, an admired family member. This normative labeling power, even from a single person, helps that change stick—because by their acknowledgement they provide a powerful social hope that not only can constructive change take place but that it can make a *social* difference.[2]

So for those of us with the power to define, to meet someone in their new, more self-affirming and society-affirming story, we need to be listening for that flow of good and find ways to respond to it. This sometimes means that we need to readjust our own ideas and instincts about wrong-doing, our desire to label someone as *essentially and forever* other than us, to deny them permanently that core label, good. Perhaps our own understanding of good needs to change—not in a way that denies or minimizes wrong-doing, lasting harm, but one that does allow for growth and change—and essential cross-identification.

BELIEVING PEOPLE CAN CHANGE: WHAT'S IN A NAME?

In another interesting study looking at public attitudes about reentry, Maruna found resistance to reentry was *most* influenced by whether we believe people can change, rather than conservative or liberal values in general. This makes sense, of course. If we *don't* feel people can change, then encouraging reentry means just loosing unreformed—or even more hardened—criminals into the general population.[3]

The idea of criminal behavior as an intrinsic, essential quality is implicit in some ideas about criminal mind, especially those that don't include causal factors—like early trauma, mental illness, poverty, educational deficits, peer and cultural influence. The same is true when people think these situational, social and psychological factors are themselves fixed, immutable, predictive, which can be heard in statements like, "What do you expect given how he grew up?"

As a society we have through our language made that hardening of attitude more difficult to overcome. We constantly link an individual back to the crime as an *essential* identity through the language we use. You can't be an ex-felon. Once a felon, *always* a felon. Technically, this means that you will always have been convicted of a crime that is punishable by a year or more in prison. But for most people, that is not what felon means. The word felon has the quality of an essential, immutable negative identity. That is the fear that the *What If?* ad in the Atlanta metro was playing on.

However, a commitment to effective reentry is based, of necessity, on the belief that people *can* reenter society and contribute to society after having been convicted of and punished for a crime. If we saddle people with names that imply the opposite, we are continually activating an essential contradiction in professed and implicit beliefs.

We can see this tension in the difficulty that people have coming up with terms for the formerly incarcerated that feel accurate and future-oriented: returning citizen and reformed citizen are two currently popular variants.

Because of the intense and pervasive stigma we ascribe to felonies, record expungement is often proposed as a response. But *is* it possible in the age of the internet, when all information floats in a fermenting continuous present, to expunge or suppress criminal histories? Just type in a name on the internet, any name, and you can tell immediately by the sites that promise you information whether there are any legal records available on that person.

Many people we talked to expressed frustration and alienation when they observed that someone who has known them for years, who has based their assessment of them on direct observation of their behaviors, will change their attitudes completely if and when they learn they have a criminal record. "They will never look at you the same again." "You always know." "One day you were trustworthy, and now you're not." The sense of helplessness at this shift is painful to hear. These individuals haven't changed in their behaviors in the length of time these people have known them, but their *essential* identity in the other person's eyes has been permanently changed, damaged.

The potential for an equal relationship now or in the future feels impossible.

Is it safe to ignore any of our histories, just to go on face value, current behavior? What would we miss if we did this? What might we gain? Are we holding people responsible for their behavior or for *our* assumptions about them? How would we feel if some of our most dubious actions from years ago became the primary, the exclusive, way by which people measured our *current* worth? Instead of trying to obscure through pseudonyms or through actively erasing the traces of the records, we may need to reconsider how we *hear* these words—felon, formerly incarcerated—and the specific and unique realities that lie behind them in each particular case.

OTHER IMPORTANT QUALITIES OF DESISTANCE STORIES

There are some other important qualities in the stories people shared, that help us understand the process of reentry.

Shameless: Many of the most successful individuals we met were ones who defined themselves as shameless, meaning they insisted that their entire past was part of who they are now. Indeed they would often acknowledge that the skills that allowed them to reintegrate, to become resilient and trustworthy, were exactly the same skills they used earlier in criminal activities. They—shamelessly—push us to reconsider our definitions and frames.

This is easier to do if the crime was not a violent one. With a violent crime, we often feel it is important for the individual to disavow all possibility of repeating those behaviors in the future. Complete renunciation and transformation are often what we think are needed to feel safe in these cases. But are they?

Prosocial Core: We found it helpful in our interviews to listen to the prosocial core that people who had reentered successfully chose to organize around. Often this came from someone influential in their upbringing, a mother, grandmother, someone who had a clear set of moral standards *and* a particular affection for them *and* an expectation that they could and would meet those standards. Sometimes it was someone they met in prison who saw and spoke to that positive possibility in them—a chaplain, an older prisoner, a warden. Sometimes it was a child for whom they wanted to serve as a model. The important point here is that this was not experienced as an imposed set of expectations, it was a way of *being with* others, a social contract whose benefit they had directly experienced themselves in the form of kindness, higher expectations, and fairness.

I Didn't See It Coming: One of the interesting dimensions of many of these stories, one that can feel disingenuous but is probably accurate, is how often we heard someone, especially someone arrested as a juvenile, describe the shock they felt at their arrest and, even more, the shock they felt at the charges being brought against them. *They didn't see it coming.* Even if they had been dealing drugs, or conducting numerous robberies. Does this have to do with the mental processes of an adolescent? In particular an adolescent attracted to risky behavior? Often their crimes—especially robbery—were committed in groups, so did that peer normalization involve *suppressing* relevant information about the likely consequences? Were they, individually and together, *truly ignorant* of the possible consequences of their behavior? In some cases, prison itself had become normative among their friends or family—so a year or two or five—didn't seem aversive, even if unexpected.

But for others, it was as if a completely different world opened up for them with the prospect of conviction. They experienced an identity crisis. It is difficult to share their shock, but it is important not to deny it since it is part of a particular kind of near-sightedness that is common to those who end up in prison, a near-sightedness or consequence-blindness that doesn't necessarily resolve itself *in* prison. It is a quality that can hamper reentry because it means that some individuals will often be blind to the challenges and demands reentry will place on them as well. In some community supervision trainings as well as reentry classes, the ability to foresee consequences, to develop alternative scenarios both practical and moral, is being emphasized as something that can be taught, that isn't innate. It isn't taken for granted that people know how to *do* better.

Self-Acceptance: Listening back over the interviews with our ex-offenders, what was striking was their resilience, sense of humor—and high self-esteem. This made them very comfortable to be with.

None of the people we talked with were innocent of the crimes they were convicted of, although some felt the punishment far exceeded the crime. Few expressed a strong sense of remorse about the crime itself or its victims. That remorse, more often, had to do with the years and potential lost to incarceration itself. This does not mean that they condoned the crime or would repeat it now. This does not mean that they are not as reliably prosocial as your neighbor.

The absence of expressed remorse was not indifference. Most of the people we spoke with strongly desired never to return to prison. But they were able to absorb the reality of their crime and their incarceration into a larger positive identity that we may not immediately share. There was an awareness of an area of shared reality and see-sawing interpretation that one man who had served twenty years for murder described well: "We want to make the crime less than it was and other people want to make it worse than it was—and the answer is in between. We're not the monsters people want to think we are. But we're not innocent either."

It is hard for any of us to absorb our *capacity* to do profound harm into our sense of ourselves, even harder to absorb the reality of having committed it. To be able to absorb that capacity as part, but not the whole of us, challenges us even further. As a society we want to otherize this capacity through stigma. We stigmatize what threatens our idea of what life *should* be.

The robust self-acceptance of many of the men and women we talked with makes us aware that often when we talk about reentry, what we actually mean is that we want that person to experience the inner constraints most of us do. We want their own self-acceptance to be contingent, conditional. But that sense of self-acceptance on the part of people returning, that they are *not* prisoners of internalized stigma, may well give them the resilience they need to counter the profound, relentless external stigma we expose them to through laws and attitudes, a stigma that we need to reconsider as a society in the face of mass incarceration.

It is not always easy to put oneself in the place of the person telling their story, especially if it includes acts that deeply challenge our sense of safety as well as moral virtue, but it is crucial to an understanding of the true moral weight of an action. More important is to ask ourselves, if *I* had acted this way, how would I begin to square myself with myself, with those I loved, with my victims, with the world around me? Who would need to come and meet me, and how, for these changes and amends I want to make to feel possible—and persistent?

A robust self-acceptance on both sides—one that does not lose touch with the harm that was done, that insists on assurances that it will not happen again, and an awareness of an individual's and a society's ability to move beyond those actions, to make genuine reparation, to consistently choose differently in the future—is necessary for genuine reintegration to take place.

In the stories that follow, we emphasize the causal arc of people's lives as they understand them, but we also group them around various issues that we feel are especially important in understanding reentry. These differences include the kind of crime, but even more importantly the age at conviction, length of incarceration, number of incarcerations, environmental, psychological and social conditions both before, during, and after imprisonment. All of these need to be considered when trying to understand what shapes the experience of reentry for a specific individual.

Endnotes
[1] S. Maruna. *Making Good: How Ex-Convicts Reform and Rebuild Their Lives.* American Psychological Association, 2001.
[2] Maruna. "Reentry as a Rite of Passage," *Punishment & Society.* 13, 1 (2011): 3-28; also see: "Elements of Successful Desistance Signaling," *Criminology & Public Policy.* (2012) 11, 1: 73-86; Maruna, and T. P. LeBel, "The Desistance Paradigm in Correctional Practice: From Programmes to Lives." In *Offender Supervision: New Directions in Theory, Research and Practice*, ed. F. McNeill, P. Raynor, and C. Trotter, pp. 65-89. Willan, 2010.
[3] Maruna and A. King, "Once a Criminal, Always a Criminal?: 'Redeemability' and the Psychology of Punitive Attitudes," *European Journal of Criminal Policy Research.* 15 (2009): 7-24.

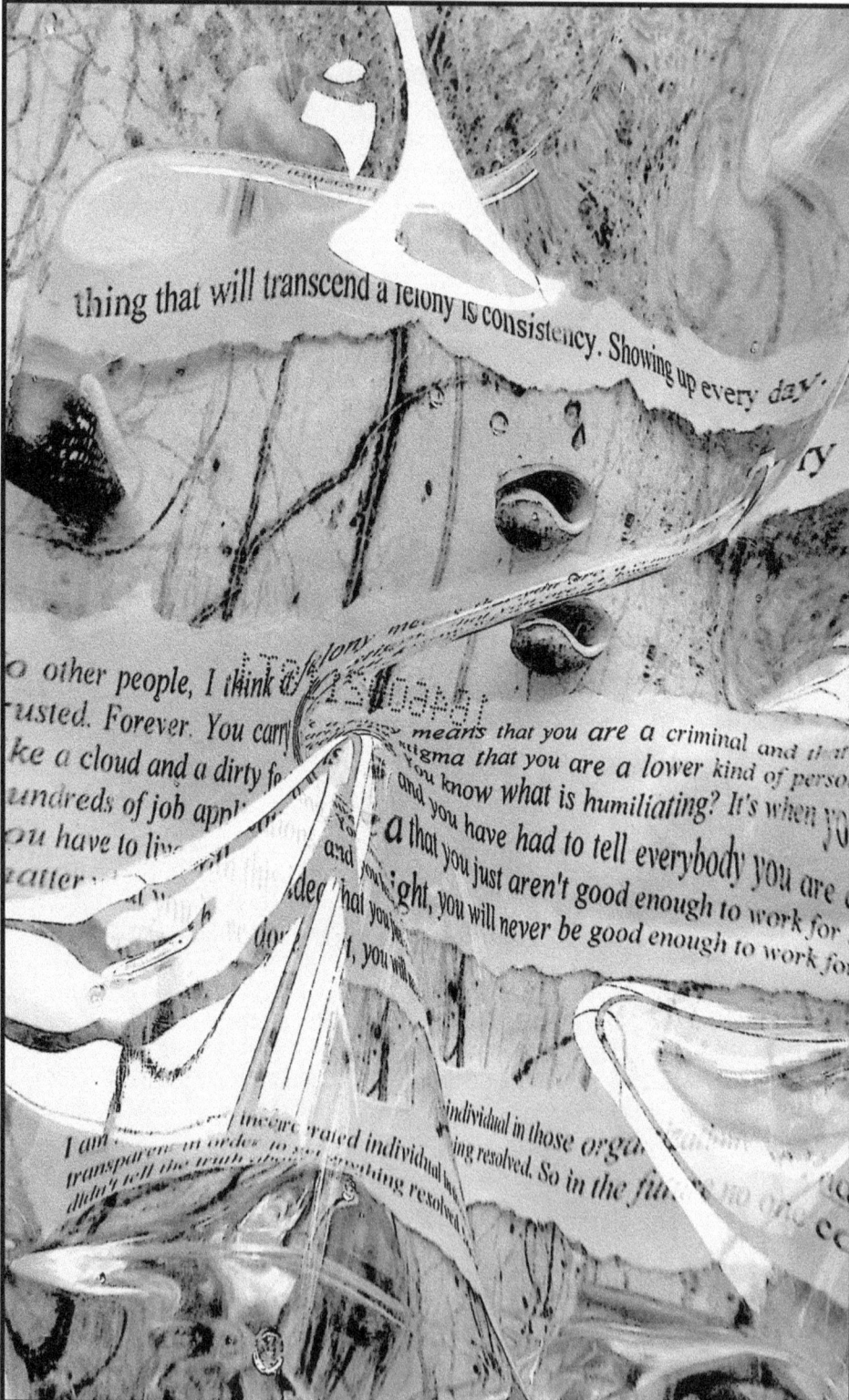

thing that will transcend a felony is consistency. Showing up every day.

...ry

o other people, I think t...
usted. Forever. You carry... means that you are a criminal and that
ke a cloud and a dirty fo... ...gma that you are a lower kind of perso...
undreds of job appli... ...you know what is humiliating? It's when yo...
ou have to live... ...a that you have had to tell everybody you are a...
...atter... ...ght, you just aren't good enough to work for...
...t, you will never be good enough to work fo...

I am... ...incarcerated individual in those orga...
transparent in order to... ...ing resolved. So in the fu... no one c...
...didn't tell the truth about... ...ething resolved...

\(1\)/

THE SISYPHEAN STONE

IVAN

What are you going to do with a guy that will not give up doing right?

We begin with Ivan's story because it speaks so directly to the *lasting* weight of a felony conviction. Even after a relatively minor drug conviction and short prison sentence completed in his late teens, Ivan still faces severely limiting collateral consequences decades later, despite a long history of hard work and advanced education. What is striking about Ivan's story is the disproportion of collateral versus direct consequences of his criminal conviction. This is *not* a reflection of highly punitive sentencing, rather of the laws and regulations, and, even more importantly, social attitudes that work actively to reduce the ability of even the most committed of individuals to engage fully and constructively in our society after a felony conviction. It is hard to imagine many of us marshaling such determination again and again and again to overcome poor choices we made, and paid for, before we were twenty. Even harder to imagine what it feels like to helplessly watch our wives and children assume this burden too.

We first met Ivan when we heard him speak eloquently about the damaging impact of collateral consequences at a breakout session on employment at a Fulton County community engagement rollout for the Georgia Prison Reentry Initiative. Our interview took place at Georgia Works, a non-profit that helps homeless men become gainfully employed. Men live at Georgia Works for up to a year, where they receive housing, support, and are employed at minimum wage for thirty hours a week. Participants are required to renounce government benefits and to stay alcohol free. Ivan was a senior case manager there at the time of the interview.

Ivan's office had a large window looking out on a leafy courtyard and a door looking in on a large common room. On the other side of the common room large plate glass windows revealed clean, austere rooms with neatly made cots. Most of the men were out working, but towards the end of the interview, as the men were returning from work, a quiet hum rose from the common room.

EARLY INFLUENCES

Ivan grew up in Indianapolis, the middle child of five. Ivan's mother was nineteen when she had her first child, twenty-four when she had her last and divorced Ivan's father. His mother worked hard to support them and to keep them together, but Ivan and his siblings spent a lot of time at the houses of other family members. "Not everyone cares about you like your parents would," he observed. "There was a lot of trauma there." His mother too had had a lot of trauma in her own childhood. But Ivan was also aware that his mother loved them: "I never doubted this. I didn't hate the way I was raised. It was just the way it was. I didn't think we were poor."

As Ivan talked, he was clearly pondering again what had influenced his own thought processes as a child. Even in elementary school, he never paid much attention in school and was only interested in art. But he could read well. In middle school, he moved to a new school in a more racially mixed neighborhood and he found himself getting in trouble. "My mom was gone a lot and we were home alone. I was distracted, getting into fights all the time."

In eighth grade, he decided to straighten out and began getting good grades, but was teased for his attempts. "I was tired of being a nerd—fighting all the time because I'm trying to be smart. I decided I was going to be a cool kid." Cool kids drank alcohol and smoked cigarettes. His older brother and sister were cool kids, but expected Ivan to make his own cool friends.

By his freshman year, Ivan was going to a cousin's house every day to drink and smoke marijuana. By the time he was a sophomore he was also selling a little weed to afford his own. He used Dr. Dre to help rationalize the use of marijuana as a natural product. By the time he was a junior, he was going to school only to meet in the parking lot and find someone with weed, doing just enough school work to get by.

Ivan thinks now that his behaviors, including his level of drug use, were on another scale from his older siblings, who were also experimenting. His need for peer approval was higher; he was angrier, and the peers he hung out with were angrier and more violent as well. He may also have been more addicted. As an additional stimulus and complication, Ivan's father, who he had not seen as a young child, now smoked and drank with him.

His mother made numerous attempts to try to address the rebellious behaviors of Ivan and his older siblings, who were all running away from home. She had a sheriff come and talk with them and also other family members, especially her hardworking uncles. But, Ivan was resistant: *In my mind, I'm thinking about my dad and his lifestyle and I'm thinking about what the rapsters are saying and I'm thinking about the other people on the streets and the people in the school who are getting the respect and are considered to be cool and who are black like I am, and I have this other thing going on with people wondering if I am black or not because I don't look—It's a complete identity crisis.*

When he was finally suspended for smoking weed on campus, his mother enrolled him in Job Corps. "It was good but I wasn't ready to change." Job Corps actually encouraged Ivan's delinquent behavior by exposing him to peers who were "still like me, hanging on to the lifestyle." Kicked out after a few months, Ivan decided to go to Chicago to join the gang of one of the boys he had met at Job Corps. However, he received a call that the boy had been shot and killed on the way to the bus station to pick him up. He returned home to find that he was now truly on his own.

STREET LIFE

I just ended up on the streets and my mother said, "You're gonna have to stay there because you can't live here with me because you don't look for jobs, you don't want to live right. So if you want to live on the streets, don't call me and ask to come home because you're not going to." To be honest, I'm thankful that she did that. I know it was tough for her.

It was also tough for Ivan: *Having to sleep outside, having to get on buses to stay warm and be on the streets like that and deal with the harshness of all that, not having a place of your own, it made me start thinking twice. But in my mind, I'm thinking, "I don't mind, I can handle this. I gotta do what I gotta do."*

I would get in fights, get jumped, get beat, get shot at. Guns put to my head. People robbed me. It was so bad that periodically I would think, "Something is not right." I would think, "God, you got to get me out of the situation." I didn't really want to change, I wanted to get out of the cold.

Although Ivan had "a loose commitment to getting things right," when he lost his job by drinking and he saw a man two doors down selling drugs, he thought, "I'm going to take this $40 and buy some crack and sell it." Quickly $40 became $150. At first he was also using, but saw he would never make money that way, so restricted his own drug use to alcohol and marijuana. He was soon able to afford an apartment of his own.

Conversion & Arrest

Ivan was making a lot of money, but his unease was building as well. *I was so high, so drunk all the time it was like a fog. I'm always in this apartment. I'm always selling this stuff. There is always this paranoia and lifestyle where anything goes. It started wearing on me. I just started having this realization that this money means nothing to me, these people who are around me mean nothing. People started looking like they were demons. I started looking like I was dying. I could hardly look at myself in the mirror. I think at this time I was about eighteen and it was just this horrible lifestyle. I tripped on some acid, thought I went to hell. It all started looking like this big world of evil. Everybody was evil, including me.*

One night Ivan smoked crack again and began to realize that he might be an addict, something he didn't associate with alcohol or weed. *People who smoked crack weren't human to me. I had such a disrespect for people who used crack. And here I was using it. I had been selling drugs to twenty-year-old guys who were acting like they weren't users. I am one of those guys, I thought. This is not what I want to do with my life.*

Ivan found himself praying, but also felt unable to change his life. *Two days later I was standing out on the porch and the Sheriff's Department had surrounded my apartment. They came in with ski masks, the whole serve-the-warrant thing. The irony of it for me was that I had peace when they showed up. I thought, "Man, this is over. You don't have to try to run. You don't have to resist. You asked God to help you resist and here's your option to get out of this." My viewpoint of it at the time was, This is an answer.*

The police, who had sent in a confidential informant to buy from Ivan, wanted to know who his suppliers were. They threatened Ivan with spending the rest of his life in prison, made jokes about his being raped. But for Ivan, the arrest had ended his involvement with drugs. *I told them, "I don't care what you say, go ahead and do what you need to do, because for me it's over." I had no interest in talking or telling on anybody. I just knew I needed to get out of it. But when you've been out on the streets long enough and been doing enough bad stuff, you sometimes don't just get out very easily. Most of the people I saw getting out were being killed or getting locked up. I did know that this was my moment to get out. I was in lock-up and I would tell people, "I think God has given me a chance to get it right." They'd say, "Well that's serious. You need to take that serious."*

CONVICTION & INCARCERATION

Arrested in 1996, at eighteen Ivan faced a possible twenty-eight years in prison for carrying a gun, having $1,100 in cash and one fourth of an ounce of crack cocaine in his possession. It was his first offense as an adult. Represented by a public defender, he pled to the most serious charge, dealing in narcotics, and all the lesser charges were dropped. His minister, sister and a friend appeared in court for his sentencing. He feels this show of support positively influenced the judge, who gave him a six-year sentence, four years of which were suspended. He received two days for every day he served, so faced one year of prison time. The judge also gave him an automatic modification after six months if he had no infractions, but warned him he would serve the entire sentence if he messed up. Ultimately, Ivan served only six months before going on work release.

Ivan decided from the beginning of his time in prison to act inside prison the way he was going to act out on the street when he was released—because being in prison was very *like* being on the street. He met people he had run with on the street and people he had spent time with in jail. People could live exactly as they did out on the streets, selling drugs, drinking alcohol, gang banging. *I knew I didn't want that anymore. I thought, "How I live in here is how I am going to live on the streets. I am going to live for the Lord and do right."*

Ivan was helped in his resolve by the incentive of an automatic modification. He knew he was appearing before the judge within months and he didn't want to do anything to mess that up. He was also helped by having what he called his "personal scared straight program," when he was moved to a maximum security prison for two weeks while he was being questioned about a murder in which many of his friends were implicated (although he was not).

Not only was Ivan allowed work release, but he was also released early. He proudly noted how responsible he had been: finding a job, paying his work release and probation fees, going to rehab classes. By the time he was released, he had saved a thousand dollars while making $6.25 an hour. He put money on a car, saved another thousand and bought that car. He got his driver's license and quickly rented an apartment. He earned his GED, studying for it and enrolling and taking the test at his own initiative. In his account Ivan stressed how many of the positive changes in his life came because of inner determination, not external prompting. "My focus was laser. It was not so much I *have* to live right as I *want* to live right."

Reentry

Already, however, the collateral consequences of his conviction were beginning to become clear. He went to church regularly and found support there when he became discouraged about keeping a job. "Every job I got was through temp service, but when the thirty-days review came up to get hired on full-time, they let you go." The only jobs he could keep were construction jobs, but they were always low level: *All my friends were getting these warehouse jobs and then going on to work for Ford. But Ford or GM isn't going to hire you. Any career job you could get that was blue collar you wouldn't get. You certainly weren't going to get a white-collar job if all you had was a GED.*

Ivan was accepted at Bible College, but when they found out about his felony conviction, he was told he wasn't eligible for financial loans. Luckily, a woman in the financial aid office found other ways for him to finance his education.

Given all these setbacks, the support of the members of his church was very important. *They embraced me and supported me and helped me keep moving forward even on days when everything wasn't going so great. People didn't always know what I was going through but I would go over to a friend's house and they would say, "Have you had dinner?" Just little things. People treating me like a normal person. But then there were people that once they found out I had a felony—before they treated me good, but once they found out they wanted to act like I was some dangerous, untrustworthy person all of a sudden. That always shocked me because I would think to myself, "you didn't know it and now that you do, you can't trust me?"*

Acutely aware of the power of the stigma associated with a felony conviction, one of the most interesting dimensions of Ivan's journey is how he has come to understand the origins and implications of that stigma differently over the years. But the pain is always there. *To other people, I think a felony means that you are a criminal and that you can't be trusted. Forever. You carry the stigma that you are a lower kind of person. It's almost like a cloud and a dirty feeling. You know what is humiliating? It's when you have put in hundreds of job applications and you have had to tell everybody you are a felon. When you have to live with this idea that you just aren't good enough to work for somebody. No matter what you have done right, you will never be good enough to work for people.*

After finishing college, Ivan realized he wouldn't be able to use his degree. He entered the construction trade, got an apprenticeship with the bricklayers union, which did accept people with felony convictions. Unfortunately, he also found that he faced intense racism within the union. He was married now and had children, so felt that he had to endure.

After eight years, he was laid off from his job as a bricklayer. When he didn't get any help from the union, he decided to work for himself. This was as much necessity as choice. *I made good money. $32/hour, $27/hour take home pay. I was trying to move up in it but saw I was never going to get anywhere. I was not like them. I was never going to be accepted by them. It didn't matter how hard I worked, how sober I was, how good I was. It didn't matter how many block I put in the wall or how many brick I laid, I was never going to make it in their world.*

Ivan had a truck and bought a snowplow and did anything he could to make money.

But the frustration of not finding a job at his level of education was keen. *Everywhere I would go to find a job trying to do something a college-level person would do, managing or construction management, I would be told no. I spent a year after being laid off, job application after job application, talking to people and nothing would happen. So I started working for myself. . . . To this day, I know I can't work for the federal government. I know I can't work for the state government. The idea that even with the masters degree, there are certain things I can't do, I think it is very frustrating. But more frustrating when you know you've done right and you've worked hard and it all can go away overnight.*

Finally, Ivan found a project management job in Atlanta and moved down, leaving his family in Indianapolis at first. He moved his wife, two sons and a daughter down three months later, only to be laid off.

The next year and a half were a powerful challenge for Ivan and his family. They found a subsidized apartment through a Christian outreach program. He sold much of the equipment from his business to keep them afloat, as well as doing cash jobs using his numerous construction skills. The jobs were of short duration making it difficult to stabilize. His drug conviction nearly twenty years earlier meant that he and his family were not eligible for food stamps. His wife, who had given up her job to move to Atlanta, at some point found a job. Ivan sent out hundreds of resumes with no positive results. His view of the future became very bleak.

I just felt worthless. . . . I remember a point in that time where I felt there was not much hope for me and my sons. I wasn't worried about my wife, she can work, or my daughter. I started thinking, "maybe this is just the way it is for black men." At this time I had gone through school and had done a lot of studying on all this prison stuff because I'm trying to find out why it is the way it is. Because this isn't right. I shouldn't be able to want to work this bad and not be able to do it. That doesn't make any sense to me. I would get Social Security information that would tell me what I was worth dead. I'm better off dead!

Again, church community provided Ivan with some hope and possibility. Ivan and his family became involved in a church start-up. Through this, he found part-time work that eventually led to work at a large homeless mission. He also found a calling through a growing recognition that the challenges he faced were not his alone, but were experienced by millions. He began to recognize his own strengths—a combination of skills, tenacity and deep, optimistic faith—and how these might help others who faced the challenges he did with a criminal history.

Now, all this time, in my heart, all I could think over all these years was, "This isn't right." What could be done? I used to dream all the time. You can make good money working construction, but you have to have a good company to work for. But once you teach a man skills, he can eat. I did that. I survived. You need a wall built, you can call me, I can do that. I can come fix your bathroom. I have skills. I can do things. I have something to exchange and don't necessarily need a "job" to make it. I thought, "Man, if I could just teach guys to do this." But more importantly, if I could teach guys to endure, to persevere, to have character. That's what's kept me.

Ultimately trust in God, belief in God, belief that things were ultimately going to work out—that kept me from going crazy, it kept me from giving up, it kept me from turning back, it kept me from leaving my marriage because I felt I was too worthless to provide anything. I felt all those things, but I just knew one thing: You just don't give up. Where do I get that from? If I look, God didn't give up on me, so how can I give up on Him and believing He is going to do His part, which is take care of me, provide for me?

While working at the mission, Ivan met Bill McGahan, the founder of Georgia Works at the point when McGahan was formulating his ideas for a non-profit approach to reducing homelessness. They shared a belief in the dignity of work, but Ivan emphasized how deeply inter-related homelessness and unemployment were with criminal histories and recidivism.

At Georgia Works, Ivan found a way to use his education in

management and leadership and his numerous construction skills—and also
to speak prophetically back in actions and in words to a society that has made
constructive change so difficult for him and millions of men like him, a way
that speaks through and to values that are foundational to our understanding
of ourselves as a country.

*What I began to see, through study, through school was the impact, the
disproportional impact of incarceration. I said, OK, I'm really pissed off about
this and I'm going to devote my life to changing it. . . . When you do the numbers
and find out a third of your whole ethnic group, people you come from, your
heritage, are being imprisoned, dying off—you start to think what can be done?*

*We talk about inheritance. A poor black kid, what does he inherit? When
he's born into this world, the story has already begun with his parents. He comes
into that reality. He lives in that world. Whatever he's learned, whatever he's
been deprived of, whatever he's been taught, which in my experience, in the places
where I've been and the experiences I had growing up, it teaches you to be hard,
to not feel, to not care. The level of abuse that happens in that environment, the
hardness—this is a long time, these are generations.*

*That is where systemic racism comes in. You know what makes oppression
effective is when you have the oppressed believe that they are never anything better
than what they currently have. It's psychological. If you do what's right, we'll
make it twice as hard for you. Your work isn't rewarded like his work and I'm
going to let you see that so that you know you will never be as good as him and that
you will always be kept at this level. Well, psychologically, what does that do to a
person? You create a culture that says, we are to not be like them. . . . You give into
this mold, this identity: I am to be angry, to be black, a rebel because the system
hates me, wasn't designed for my benefit or my good. Therefore I can never ally
myself with that system, that's my oppressor. We don't know that the trick is that
this thinking is the oppression. To give in to that. To say, we can't do what's right
by the system or by the law.*

Ivan wanted to counteract this fatalism in the work he was doing. *I've
tried to teach these guys that this isn't just about the system or about getting a job.
This is about your character, your ability to endure. I want you to get your human
dignity back. I want you to know you are a man. I want to sit down and hear
your story and be a true witness. Affirm the fact you've been hurt without giving
you an excuse to stay there. I get it, you've been hurt, you've been wronged, you've
been lied to, mistreated, you've even hurt yourself, lied to yourself, abused yourself,
burnt your bridges, just did you wrong. But if you knew every human being who*

walked the earth is just like you—You just need to know you're normal. And that you can come out of this.

Now that we know that is the way it is, let's heal. Let's start thinking differently. Most of the time, people think of it as just what they're going through and they don't matter, they're just a blip. But they're not, they're tied up into someone else's story. I've started thinking this isn't about me, but about the generation behind me and the generation behind them. With my guys, we talk about being self-sufficient and being independent, but see, I really need us to move away from independence to interdependence. We as a people don't rise up alone, we're always in need of the assistance of another. To be interdependent means I have a healthy role to play.

So let's give people an opportunity. That's what we do here. We're going to give that to men, no matter how many times they got it wrong before, because we know that without that opportunity there is no redemption. He may have done it fifteen times, but when he gets that moment of a change, when he gets that moment when he says, "This isn't right. I was wrong. But now I want to do it right."—he needs to be met there. And if we're to be that kind of society, I really believe we would live in the reality that people are people, that they are broken, that they can do great wrong and they can also do great good.

Since talking with us, Ivan has gone back to being self-employed. He is the director of his own construction company that focuses on urban renewal. He also serves on the advisory board at another homeless shelter.

\2/

SHAMELESS:
The Staying Power of a Fully Integrated Story
Tommy, Khadijah

What Pastor Tommy and Khadijah share is a faith that their lives taken as a whole, criminal history openly included, make good sense. The self-acceptance, confidence, and clarity that come with this belief are striking, and are based on their own choices and achievements as well as on something deeper and more mysterious. Their stories give us a more nuanced way of understanding desistance.

"I'm not ashamed," Pastor Tommy said. *When you can talk about experiences that have been detrimental, embarrassing, life-altering things, you know that you are in the process of healing. If I continue to not talk about it, if I continue to keep it suppressed, who am I really helping? You have to get to a point where you take that power back. For me, I need for people to know, this is where I came from—but I didn't stay there.*

"Why did my life take this journey?" Khadijah mused in her interview. *I'm a firm believer that God gives every one of us a journey in life and again we don't necessarily understand that journey while we are journeying, but when you sit down and be still and think about your life and what was done, you can see how it was really necessary. It was really necessary.*

One thing both these successful people share is an appreciation of the gifts of their upbringing and of their own initiative—and a firm belief in the necessity and value of steps. Some factors that both Tommy and Khadijah described as significant in their successful reentry were role models who invited them to positions of equality; strong faith communities that supported them in their reentry, indeed, have come to depend on their gifts and abilities; along with the role of shorter sentences; the freedom to prepare for incarceration and reentry; and better incarceration conditions, either living in an honor dorm or in a minimum security setting. They are both striking for their emphasis on the importance of intentionality. Reentry doesn't just happen, they believe, especially successful reentry; it is created—with effort, the help of others, and a good measure of grace.

PASTOR TOMMY

This is what I've been through, but this is where I'm going.

Of all the ex-offenders we interviewed, Pastor Tommy felt like the one who had most completely integrated the different elements of his life into a continuous story and also the one who had been most intentional and strategic about his reentry plan seventeen years earlier. He is also the first to tell you he could not have done it alone. A small man in his early forties, he has a husky voice and a contagious laugh. At the time we spoke, he was the young adult minister for a large evangelical church on an expansive semi-rural campus in South DeKalb. In one of the many church classrooms, he shared his story with ease, actually with relish because he sees it, in its totality, as a blessing story.

EARLY INFLUENCES

Tommy grew up in Detroit, the youngest of four children and the only boy in his immediate family. The first eleven years of his life, before his parents separated, were stable. However his parents divorced acrimoniously, and his father, embittered, refused to see Tommy until his high school graduation. Although they reconciled at that point, his father's absence deeply influenced Tommy's choices as an adolescent. His father died when Tommy was twenty-one, and he still mourns the years of estrangement.

With his parents' separation, Tommy's living situation became unstable. His mother went to live with her mother, who considered Tommy disrespectful, a problem child, and wouldn't let him live with her. *I just kind of stayed where I had to stay at. My mom and dad separating put a new perspective on my life. It became about survival. So I didn't really have a childhood like normal people. I had a survival childhood. But I never felt deprived. It was just the way it was.*

For about three years, until his mother bought a house of her own, Tommy found his role models on the street. But his goals remained highly prosocial, directed toward self-sufficiency and the well-being of those he loved. This is an attitude that runs through all of Tommy's activities, legal or illegal. *It was very common coming from the environment I was in to be thirteen or fourteen years old and selling either marijuana or crack cocaine or pills. It was just part of the culture. If you didn't have those good role models to reel you in, then you had those street models looking for young men who had no models. It was either at the time joining a gang or being involved in some type of illegal activity, so either way I went, there was opportunity to be involved in some type of circle.*

But peer inclusion and acceptance was not Tommy's major motivation: *What mattered was self-sufficiency, the mindset of being able to provide for the family since I knew my mother didn't have a man around anymore. Then I had sisters. At that time, two of them had already had babies out of wedlock. So my youngest sister, who was three years older than me, she had a baby and my responsibility became taking care of her baby. When I would make money, my whole concept was Pampers, milk, clothes. So, I'm out in the streets, but there is always a reason and it was more me trying to become a provider.*

It just felt like I had to do what I had to do. It wasn't even a sad situation for me. The focus was always on being able to bring something to the table for the family. My sister knew what I was doing. My mom did, but she didn't know to what degree, but it was kind of like the old adage, you don't ask, you don't tell. She knew money wasn't just coming in from a job. I wasn't old enough for a job, so she knew I was doing something. "You hustling doing something? Are you cutting grass?"'

Tommy did not see his activities as criminal: *I was so young at the time, thirteen years old, getting caught wasn't even a thought process for me. I always thought I was going to make money, I was going to be smart about it. So I never, I can't recall me ever having a fear of getting caught at all, at all.*

The description Tommy gives of his street mentors is balanced. He sees them as sharing with him the same survival skills they had found necessary: *They would take care of me, give me money, let me know what to do, what not to do. They kept me safe, absolutely. Even from a standpoint of making sure that school was still a priority. So I guess you could say those were my mentors. They were providing me with an income, showing me everything you needed to know about selling drugs. That was part of the mentoring process. This is what you are supposed to do, this is how you weigh it up, this is how you cook it. Those mentors were about twenty-two or twenty-three years old and I was thirteen, fourteen.*

Tommy's life settled down once his mother bought a house and he was living with her again. He described his mother with obvious affection and respect: *My mom was a great mother, awesome, whatever she could do she would do, but she wasn't going to be that type of disciplinarian. She herself was very law-*

abiding. She did what she could, but she was more of a provider. She worked two jobs to provide, paid all her bills. She was very strong integrity-wise, but wasn't a talker in terms of walking me through decisions.

Tommy described how once, when they were visiting family in Mississippi, he stole a radio from a neighbor boy and his mother, discovering this after they returned to Detroit, forced him to call and apologize and send the radio back. *She expected you to know better. And sometimes you just didn't. So the only people telling you what to do are the guys in the street, and they're just telling you to get you to do what they need you to do.*

Tommy preferred the street to school, but demonstrated his intelligence and determination at the end of the eleventh grade when he learned from a school counselor that given his frequent absences he lacked so many credits he would not be able to graduate with his class. This created a substantial challenge for him, which he met by going to summer school, getting all As, then adding night school to his final year of classes. He graduated on time. In this accelerated and challenging catch-up process, Tommy's horizons widened and he began to consider going on to college. He and his best friend decided to go to junior college, improve their grades and then go on to a four-year college. Always a businessman, Tommy sold concessions for various hip hop and R&B bands performing in and around Detroit during this period.

ACTIVE CRIMINAL CAREER

Tommy did very well his first semester in community college, but in his second semester his best friend died unexpectedly of a heart attack while playing basketball. This loss turned Tommy's life upside down. He didn't finish the semester: *My mind just switched when he passed at nineteen or twenty. He had no children. He'd never got his own place. It brought reality to our situation. The first thing I thought about was leaving a seed because I didn't know if I was going to make it to twenty-one. My girlfriend at the time became pregnant with our son. Because I didn't want to be traveling, I got back into the drug game. When I got back in, I was the one having people work for me. It altered the course of my life. I had a good run for three years. From 1995 to 1998, I was "the man." I was what you call a ghetto superstar. I could buy what I wanted. I had a house over here, an apartment over there. Truck. Cars. Just living the lifestyle.*

Tommy's drug dealing was also a means to a more pro-social end: "When I first got into the business of selling drugs, my mindset was I was just going to get into it until I could save up enough and we could start our own business." The business he and his girlfriend, a nursing student, had in mind was a nurse staffing company. Tommy provided the payroll for the first six months from his drug profits. They quickly began to get contracts with different nursing homes, expanding rapidly from one to fifty employees. He describes their development with a sense of amusement and pride. Within a year and a half, they won a three-year contract to provide services to all the facilities in the Henry Ford Health System. Tommy also folded some of his illegal profits into a restaurant. A month after the stars-studded ribbon-cutting opening, Tommy's business activities, legal and illegal, came to an abrupt halt.

ARREST: Arrested on drug charges, Tommy was jailed in July of 1997. The charges he faced were not for his own substantial marijuana trade, rather he was pulled into an unrelated sting operation. Tommy, at age twenty-one, was facing a possible federal sentence of twenty years. He fought the charges for twenty-two months, while alternately incarcerated in a federal detention center and the county jail, before pleading guilty to a thirty-six month sentence that his lawyer assured him would be reduced to time served. By this time, Tommy was open to a plea because he had experienced a conversion and was eager to set his life on a new trajectory.

In the federal detention center he also began to realize something about the company he was keeping that moved his understanding of his activities from delinquent to frankly criminal: *Everybody caught up on a federal case is in that detention center until they sentence you. People who were doing murder for hire hits. In the next cell was someone who had been charged with cutting up bodies and feeding them to his dogs. Two of my cellmates were two of the most notorious drug dealers ever to roam Detroit. One was so big that he owned casinos in the Bahamas. When they arrested him, they took thirty million from him. They were my cellmates. That was what I was involved with.*

But in the county jail he realized something closer to home. *He* was becoming dangerous too: *Getting arrested and going into county jail, I began running into guys from the neighborhood, guys who had heard of me and knew about me. The first thing that guys would say to me was, "Man, we heard you was rich." I wasn't rich but I was saving—couple hundred thousand isn't rich. Some of the guys saying that were the ones who were responsible for kidnapping guys and killing them. So early on, I got an appreciation that I was so fortunate because I could be dead. I took the attitude, "Man, this is the best place I could be right now."*

Because when you're in it, the drug game, you become a different person. I became a different person. Say for instance I would have found out that someone was trying to harm my family, it would have took me to a different place. I would have become violent absolutely, because it would have been about protecting. For me, that is my number one thing: I am going to protect my family, I'm going to protect me at all costs. So it would have taken me to a different place that I may not have been able to come back from. I wasn't the guy that was going to mess with folks, take from folks, try to harm them, but if you did something to me, now it become a problem. I didn't have to act that out now.

CONVERSION: About a year into his incarceration, Tommy experienced an out of body experience. "The Lord came into my jail cell. It was one of the weirdest things. I literally got saved in my jail cell in bed reading *The Daily Bread*. When that happened with me, it changed how I looked at life." Tommy laughed loudly when he talked about getting religion in jail, then got serious: "This was sixteen, almost seventeen years ago. Looking back on it now, He's done exactly what He said He was going to do."

The guidance Tommy received was very specific. He was going to become a teacher of God's word. He was going to marry his girlfriend, Rhonda, and through the two of them God was going to do good things. And God was going to make Tommy a living example of God's grace, which meant to Tommy that he would always be in the spotlight, meaning there was no way he was going to be able to hide who he was or what he was doing.

Tommy said that after this experience, a great peace came over him, even though he was still facing the possibility of twenty years. *God took all those things off me that had been burdening me. My trust factor in Him was complete. One of the things that was a major burden to me was that I was responsible for the lives and the families of so many people that were getting drugs from me. If you don't get no work, we can't eat. . . . It became a burden just to maintain that amount of money every week. . . . I was literally just doing it now to make sure other people were getting taken care of. I had already done the things that in my eyes I wanted to prove, like being able to purchase my own home, to buy cars. After you do that, it's done. My burdens were all the things that came with being the Connect.*

PRO-ACTIVE REENTRY PLANNING

A year later, Tommy accepted a plea. However, instead of time served the judge told him he would have to serve out the full thirty-six months. After arguing furiously with his lawyer, Tommy, always pragmatic, asked the judge if he could have bond until it was time for him to turn himself in to complete his sentence. The judge agreed. During the nine months that he was out, Tommy implemented the plan he had developed since he had experienced his conversion. Four days after he was released, he married Rhonda. He had observed that most of the wealthiest people in the federal detention center had earned their wealth through real estate, so he enrolled in real estate evening school. He worked daily nine-to-five for his brother-in-law's transportation company driving a van for the disabled. He passed his courses and gained his real estate broker's license. His felony conviction didn't stand in the way of his licensure because it didn't involve embezzlement. Before returning to prison to complete his term, he sold a house and was able to pay off his debts and leave money to help his wife for the time he was away.

Most importantly, during this period Tommy found a church home. This was, second to marrying, the most important of the directives he had received in his conversion experience. *What God had to do was deprogram me. He had to put me in a setting where the foundation was good. All I knew was the street life. All I knew was how to manipulate. I had integrity as far as I needed to have it. But if I had to get over on you, I was going to get over on you because it was you or me. That was the mentality.*

The best thing that ever happened to me was getting out of jail and going to that church. Seeing a pastor love his wife and his children, seeing a man love God unconditionally and trust Him, and love people. Being under a Word that wasn't confusing, it was convicting. It made me have to change. It made me have to look at myself in the mirror. It made me have to become a better man.

This choice demonstrated an interesting and consistent dimension of Tommy's restructuring of his life after his conversion. Despite his own charismatic leadership qualities and organizational ability, he made consistent choices to put himself under someone else's authority who he thought had higher moral standing, godliness. This structure seemed to free him to use his own gifts to the full.

During this interim between sentences, Tommy experienced the power that came from integrating all his experience within this new story. He and his wife, with special permission from federal probation, were allowed to travel to Virginia Beach for a church couples retreat. Tommy and his wife were asked to speak as newlyweds. When Tommy got up, he was completely open, spoke about his ankle bracelet, his current situation, the loyalty of his wife.

When I finished talking, I realized how testimony was so important. There was a line of men wanting to talk to me. They had been through the same thing. And there was a line of women waiting to talk to my wife. This is what the men kept coming by saying to me: "Man, I had to do five years and I never could have shared like that." "I been in ten years—" I'm ministering to all these guys who had been to prison or gone through stuff. She's ministering to their wives. From that point on, the pastor had an idea of what we'd been through and how it spoke to others. The pastor saw into my heart and my wife's heart, and we began serving uncontrollably. Even in prison, I sent letters.

REENTRY

Tommy was sent to a minimum-security prison in Pennsylvania to finish out his sentence. When he returned home, he began a successful real estate company that by 2006 had twenty employees and offices in Michigan and Wisconsin. Ordained as a deacon, he engaged in youth ministry and also became a major supporter of his church, subsidizing the pastor's trips to Africa and Jamaica and brokering the deal for a new church and providing the deposit.

However, when the recession hit, Tommy accepted a job offer in Atlanta, which ultimately involved breaking with his religious mentor who wanted him to stay with the church. Soon after he moved his family down, he realized the job was not going to work out. The message he heard was, "You thought you were moving down for real estate but you're coming for ministry. If I'd told you, you'd never have left because you were too attached." So, along with continuing his real estate activities, Tommy developed a close association with the church in which he now served, acting in numerous volunteer capacities, including being an usher, serving in school, homeless, and nursing home ministries, and as security for the pastor. He began to take seminary classes and was invited on as a full-time youth minister. His wife was also engaged in church ministry. "I'm just on a journey. I don't know where God is taking me or her, but I trust it."

TEACHING BACK

Tommy was clear that openly discussing incarceration and reentry would not be culturally acceptable in his church, although he knew that many families had experience with it. The shame was too great. He did, however, have some clear suggestions about what people could do to improve their own chances of successful reentry: a mentor, steps, and future orientation.

The biggest thing I learned when I got out of prison was that I needed a model and a mentor. A model and mentor give you accountability. We talk about community, we talk about jobs, we talk about housing, but it all really boils back down to the individual. You have to be willing. Acknowledge you need help. Some people don't ask for help until they're drowning. Get a life jacket before you even get in the water. You know you can't read, so how are you going to go to this job when you know you can't read?

There are steps. For most people who have been incarcerated, a lot of them have been incarcerated because they wanted it quick, they wanted it fast, so they didn't know how to take those steps. They wanted to go from A to Z immediately. But it's a process. My life has been sixteen, seventeen years now since I gave my life to Christ. It's been a process. Things didn't happen overnight. They just didn't happen that way.

But as you keep continuing to go forward, never look back. I never looked back. I just explained to people, this is what I've been through, but this is where I'm going. I think that takes the power out of that negativity. There are jobs that are not going to receive you. There are people who are not going to hire you. But create your OWN job, create your OWN business, create your OWN financial freedom. That don't necessarily mean you're going to become a millionaire. If I can just get a lawn mower I can create my own independence. If I can just go out and purchase me something under market and sell at a retail price. Sometimes no one may give you a chance. You have to create your own chances. We have too many opportunities in America not to create opportunities. I went to real estate school. I had to create a job where maybe somebody would not have hired me. For whatever it is you can do, you have to be willing.

Tommy did believe that many of the positive qualities that have helped him to thrive in his life now were present in his life before, and that culture, or environment, was essential in defining their use then *and* now: *Had I not been in the culture I was in, I never would have desired to go out, sell the drugs, be the drug dealer, have the gold chains, have the nice shoes. But because that was our culture, it became part of my fabric. I was in prison with some of the brightest people you can imagine. They ran multi-million dollar corporations. Those same people, if you could get them in positions where they could use those same abilities for good, for righteousness, they will be very successful. The same principles that apply in corporate America, honesty, integrity, loyalty, hard work, those same things apply in the drug game. You're doing illegal things, but these are the things you need to have if you are going to make it.*

Tommy did not credit the criminal justice system for any help with his rehabilitation: *I haven't seen rehabilitation coming from the justice system. For most of the people who have gotten out of prison and rehabilitated themselves, it was a result of them making a decision, the right people coming into their lives, their wanting to provide a better life for themselves and their families.*

The justice system didn't help me at all. There was no training in the prison. I just feel like when it comes to the justice system, they're benefitting more off people being in jail than out of jail. Any time you privatize prisons and you have them on a stock market and you're making money off of them, when you have people in there making thirteen cents an hour, you are profiting off them.

KHADIJAH

That's my conclusion, there was a reason.

The day we met with her in downtown Atlanta near her office, Khadijah, a slim woman nearing sixty, was stylishly dressed in a narrow red checked skirt and black and white jacket. Securely balanced on impressively high red suede heels, she nodded her gleaming shaved head in welcome.

When we talked, Khadijah was a branch operational manager for a large national nurse staffing firm which filled a number of federal contracts. Her responsibilities have expanded since then. At that point, she had worked for the company for fourteen years, moving up from certified nursing assistant to staffing specialist, then from assistant branch manager to branch manager. She liked the blend of skills she needed to use. "I'm wearing four, five, sometimes seven hats. I think it is more soothing for me because I've been here all these years and I'm kind of comfortable and knowing what I'm doing. I'm confident."

She also credited her social skills as part of her success: "I didn't try to prove anything, I just did what I do. I have real good rapport with my clients and those who work for me. ICU nurses. I always believed that when you're nice to people, they're nice to you. People will go that extra mile for you." This was a sentiment echoed by her supervisor, who knew about Khadijah's criminal history, but cited these qualities when she decided to hire her: "This stuff is very old. I'm going to keep you because everybody likes you."

Khadijah emphasized the symmetry in her life now—her work life, which for many years took precedence, was now balanced by regular intensive workouts at the gym four days a week, an evening schedule interrupted only by her regular attendance at biweekly meetings of the reentry support group PIIC (Persons Impacted by Incarceration Collaborative), of which she was a founding member. She also, like her mother before her, began her preparations for Sunday dinner on Saturdays (after teaching a spin class) so that Sunday remained her day of rest although she is a devout Muslim. She ascribed her work ethic to her mother's influence, something she returned to numerous times in her interview.

Early Influences

Khadijah grew up in Brunswick, Georgia in a large single-parent family. Her mother had nine children and also adopted a fourteen-year-old girl with a baby. Khadijah was the youngest of the girls with one older brother and four younger ones. Closely spaced, the ten were in their fifties and sixties when we spoke.

With a smile Khadijah described her mother as "very strict and very hard and she always made us understand the importance of working very hard." This didn't always sit easily with Khadijah. Her mother worked two jobs and she expected her children, when they became adolescents, to work as well. *Just like any fourteen year-old, you want to play with your friends during the summer. I didn't want to get up and go one morning and she told me, "When people hire you, they expect you to be there." That word "expect," it stuck with me and I still live by that today. When people hire you, they expect you to be there. And I added a little bit more—flourishing and doing your job. Not so much because you like to work, but working is innately a part of this culture and you're just expected to do it. It's not even a choice about whether you like it or don't like it, it's just what you do in order to live and provide for your family and for yourself.*

Khadijah emphasized how much she gained not only from her own mother but also from the other mothers she saw around her when she was growing up: *My mother was always there for us. She's eighty-three now. She's still right there, ruling the house and ruling us with an iron fist! I think about my upbringing all the time now. Being raised in one of those large government projects. When you think about it, during those times, everyone who lived in that cul de sac was a large family with a single woman and those were some remarkable women. They were strong, they took care of us. We had the clothes, we had the food. My mother won the best yard almost every month because she plant her flowers very well. My mother, she put carpet on her floors, wallpaper on her walls. They would come by and do inspections and her house was always nice and neat and won the house of the month. They were remarkable women and for me I know that's where I take my strength.*

None of her sisters and only one of her brothers followed Khadijah's path: *I shouldn't have been like Alice in Wonderland. I should have taken a better path, an unrugged path. I took a lot of troubled roads. . . . Even so, I'm the one now that everybody comes to for advice. I'm almost like the oldest of all my mother's children now. I'm the successful one in terms of my career and what it is I know, decisions that I make. God really elevated me through all that I went through.*

INCARCERATION

Khadijah served three prison terms, the first a three-year term in 1974 when she was nineteen or twenty. Then, after a six or seven-year period of desistance, she served two subsequent two-year terms that were revocations of probation sentences, the last one completed in 1994.

She had her three children, now in their mid-forties, when she was between seventeen and twenty. Her mother cared for her children when she was incarcerated. This was unproblematic to her at the time. "Back then, you don't think about it. You don't see the significance of your not being there." When asked if her children's own life choices were influenced by hers, she laughed and said her daughter was a vice-president in a very large bank and they talked three or four times a day—but they did not talk about her absences.

DECISION TO CHANGE: It wasn't until Khadijah's third term in prison that she decided she wanted to reevaluate her life. *Reentry is all about the individual and what they decide. You can put an individual in for thirty years, but if that individual doesn't decide they want remarkable changes in their life, then they won't change. I'm a firm believer you have to change what's inside of your soul. If you don't change what's inside of your soul, then your condition is not going to change.*

For Khadijah, what followed from that decision was, as it was for Tommy, surprisingly clear and specific: *Once you decide to change, that should be it. I don't see making a real significant change while having other aspects of life where bad is entwined in that life. You should just have remarkable things going on. You should be working hard, you should be doing things in society, you should be paying your taxes, you should be helping out with whatever religious group you are in, you should be doing some motivational speaking, you should be trying to impart good information to people you see making mistakes.*

Khadijah laughed when asked whether she made a similar decision in either of her earlier incarcerations. *I didn't even think about wanting to change. That's not what you want to do at that point. And if you have given it a thought, it's only a fleeting thought. It isn't, "This is it. I don't want to do this anymore. I'm sick and tired of being sick and tired." That's not the thought! The whole time you're there, you're thinking, "I wonder what Mary and Jane are doing," and "I'm going to the club when I get home." I wasn't thinking about changing. I was thinking about going back home and having fun all over again.*

READYING FOR REENTRY: What made the difference? Age, primarily. Khadijah was nearing forty. But incarceration was also a time of introspection for her. She was always a big reader. Inmates, she insisted, are students, serious students. She studied the *Koran*, H.G. Wells, the *Bible*. In Pulaski Prison, she was in the honor dorm, where inmates met biweekly with the warden and assistant and deputy wardens. The warden at the time had known Khadijah for years, since she herself had been a correctional officer, so was prepared when Khadijah told her that she needed more than Harlequin romances in the library. She arranged to have more serious books sent from another prison library. Khadijah read during yard call because it was a rare time of uninterrupted quiet. She rejected the idea that prison could ever get comfortable, even if you had known staff there for over twenty years: "Any amount of time in there is in an institution."

What Khadijah found most difficult was having to stand up whenever an officer entered. To her this felt as if she were honoring man, not God. She found it profoundly humiliating. But there was something else that troubled her even more. *Another thing that got to me was that we were required for an hour to do exercise. I guess that's why I'm a runner because I would run the full hour. But while I was running on this track, I was constantly thinking while I was looking at the fence, I was looking at the wire that goes around the fence and that wire was saying to me, "You were so out of control that society had to seat you inside this compound, inside this wire to contain you." That was another great factor to me.*

You are in this position and you know you have to be there. You agree and you disagree. It has nothing to do with the punishment. You have to be punished for whatever it is you have done. The disagreement is with yourself: "I should have known better. My mother didn't raise me this way." So you agree but you disagree.

At that point, Khadijah realized that she wanted to change. *Over the doors of schools in some country, I think it's England, it says, "Know Thyself." Once you know yourself, once you motivate yourself and look at yourself, you have to do better, you really have to do better.*

Khadijah didn't have any institutional help with reentry, but she has an important ability she shares with Tommy and others who have been successful at reentry. She can plan. *Preparation begins when you walk through the door. It doesn't begin when you have six months left before going home. One time when I went back I had been certified as a nursing assistant, so I had that under my belt. Then I became a real student of Islam and I began to study more and read more and develop myself and made decisions. You have to have Plan A, B, C and D. You have to go as far as you can in those plans because some of them are going to fail—keeping in mind who you are, what you've been through, and what marks you have against you. So you think about how am I going to work, and maintain, and worry about this felony conviction on my shoulders.*

Reentry

Once Khadijah left prison for the last time, she methodically followed a plan to build her job skills, create relational stability, change location, and find a community that would help her desist.

She was able to get a job as a nursing assistant with the help of a brother who was also a CNA. She also took a job at Head Start as a volunteer, having been advised by others that if she stuck with it she would probably be hired on, which she was. She began speaking at the alternative school in Brunswick, able through her own unvarnished story to capture the attention of adolescents who teachers had thought were unreachable.

She married her husband when he was released from prison and the two of them, both dedicated converts to Islam, decided to move to Atlanta to live in an Islamic community. They felt the Islamic community provided a valuable source of support because it was accepting of their prison experience and of their desire to live differently now. Khadijah was very clear about the importance of being surrounded by people who live the change you want in your own life: *People who have been through the experience and have decided they're not going to make those mistakes again. Those were the people you needed to stay around if you wanted to sustain yourself and have a different impact.*

She and her husband provide this kind of modeling to others now. *We are examples to our family members, we are examples to people back home who knew us when we were out in the world. We've lived through it, been through it, and we try to impress on people if you don't keep this straight and narrow, you're going to veer off.*

A very important mentor and model for Khadijah was Wajeehah Khabeer, an Islamic prison chaplain Khadijah had become acquainted with during her three incarcerations at different women's prisons in the state. When Khadijah moved to Atlanta, Wajeehah was very ill and Khadijah, at Wajeehah's husband's request, agreed to become one of her personal caregivers. Khadijah visited Wajeehah each evening after she had finished her two day jobs. She knew Wajeehah had other, more regular friends, so felt honored to be involved in her life and care. It was in these conversations with Wajeehah that Khadijah began to realize how important prison work had been to Wajeehah. *Her smile would be there, she would be so happy remembering. And sometimes time would just pass us by and it would go so late in the evening, her husband would come back there and say "Khadijah, you got to go back home. You and Wajeehah, that's enough!"*

After Wajeehah's death, Khadijah went to Wajeehah's husband and told him, *I want to keep Waheejah's work alive because it meant so much to her and she meant so much to me.*

Khadijah has dedicated herself to reentry in several ways. For five years she and her husband provided reentry housing for women thirty-eight years and older coming out of drug treatment. Khadijah's House "had frills, lace, pillows, things women love to have." Khadijah's most successful tenant, still a friend, was a woman who had been to jail eleven times for prostitution but went on to secretarial school and a responsible position. Others were not as successful. This was not a treatment program, it was a first step and Khadijah, with her belief in the importance of individual motivation, was not a hand holder: "I was not going to stand over you."

Her current activities include work with Comprehensive Human Services, a Muslim human resources group she had helped found eight years before that mentored sex offenders through a state contract. But her most important engagement was with PIIC where she was one of the two women who were core members. Her affection and sense of responsibility for the group were obvious.

You could see her two worlds come together visibly whenever she chaired a meeting and gave to others the advice she gave herself when she decided it was time for her to change. It was not about rewriting the past: *Accept the fact that you have in your history what you have. Once you accept that fact, you mentally prepare yourself for rejections.* "*There is really a strong possibility I will not get this job. There is a strong possibility that this will not work out for me.*" *But you also know that in time, if you put a lot of time behind you, all of that stuff will work out in your favor. For example, I have a pardon from the state of Georgia. That means all your rights have been restored—but your record will always be there.*

As a motivational speaker, Khadijah took her former boss with her when she spoke about reentry—because she was the one who took a chance on her. *She gave me the footing I needed to be the person I am today. She gave me a job. By her actions she said, "I'm not judging you for who you were. I'm judging you for who you are right now, and I'm going to keep you."*

\3/

A LITTLE DIRT IN THE WATER
JAMAL, ROLAND

The men whose stories we include here viewed engagement with the criminal justice system as normative, possibly inevitable, but not defining. They grew up moving fluidly between what the sociologist Elijah Anderson describes as "street" and "decent" values. Both value systems had been presented to them as normative, either by their family, peers, or the communities in which they lived. This allowed them to move quickly back out into society, but it also meant that there was less inhibition about continuing to throw a little dirt in the water. Desistance—if described as being scrupulously law abiding—can often feel at odds with economic survival or advancement, and the request to choose one *or* the other, naive.

Jamal and Roland were about the same age. Jamal ran his own trucking company. Roland was an accountant. Neither was incarcerated for a substantial length of time, but both struggled with the economic challenges of felony convictions. Both of them talked at some length with us about the origin and impact of the often discordant value systems they had internalized. Dimensions of their stories that stood out for us were the role of family expectations and responsibilities, the role of education in expanding or contracting their opportunities, how they understand their criminal records, the different ways they had established reentry peer groups, what events had caused them to re-evaluate their choices—and how deep that re-evaluation went.

JAMAL

I always did right and I always threw some dirt in the water. Now, I can't afford to mess it up.

Jamal had forgotten our appointment but when reminded, he showed up without excuses or apologies fifteen minutes later, cellphone and a thick, well-worn leather-bound scheduling calendar in hand, a broad smile on his face. A tall, muscular man in his early thirties with a confident manner, he was talking with us as a favor to a friend. He set his cellphone and calendar beside him at the table. Throughout the interview he received a phone call almost every ten minutes. Answering, he effortlessly shifted into a more professional voice as he talked to potential customers, citing rates for his moving company, consulting the schedule that kept his five trucks and twenty-two employees in continuous play.

Jamal, entrepreneurial by nature, was self-employed by necessity. He is an optimist, announcing early in the interview, "I like to look forward even though you have to look back." Aware of the constraints that having a felony record posed for him, he also seemed relatively philosophical and sanguine about them. He didn't minimize or disavow his earlier criminal activity, he just didn't see a need for it anymore. In many ways he was typical of the oscillating path to desistance from crime that is well-observed in young men, a combination of increasing age and insight. He also reflected the shifting norms associated with mass incarceration—it is both such a broad social reality now it doesn't automatically trigger profound self-doubt or reassessment. It can also be just a stage that one can move out of should the right circumstances present themselves.

Jamal had been able to choose to set his life trajectory on a more law abiding path because he was raised by a devout Muslim mother who lived by a clear set of religious and moral values to which, in general, Jamal himself subscribed: "Our belief system definitely kept us from a lot of things that would have made our lives much harder. So I have to give her all credit for where I am today, for my journeys and all that is good that comes from what I do." His laugh settled the other stuff squarely on his own shoulders. Aligning his activities more consistently with legal codes has been a rational choice for Jamal, not a moral or social imperative, because he was also raised in an environment with an equally clear set of seemingly irreconcilable realities from which his mother could not protect him. From an early age, he had to find ways to integrate them both so that he was not defined as weak or vulnerable.

Jamal believes in leading by example: "I have twenty-two employees, and between them and my brothers, I talk a little, but I show more." At the time we interviewed him, his son was eight months old. He had been thinking about the kind of father he wanted to be: *I do want different for my son. As a dad, I would definitely like to be strong. Not being a friend first, I want to be a parent. But you need to have friendship and trust to have rapport. I do want to have rapport. I don't want to have him not want to talk to me. We're going to live and enjoy life and figure out the best way to do things. We're going to figure it out together. I just want to do it without hurting him. I just don't want him to be a weak man at all and I do kind of see my brothers and my father as weak. Not through a fault of theirs. I can respect anyone for who they are. It's not on me to judge.*

Early Influences

Jamal's father left when he was a very young child and lived several states away, so was not a presence in his daily life. His older brother was gay, so didn't meet Jamal's definition of a big brother who could protect him. *I didn't get any Cliff Notes from my father. Or no path from my mother, God bless her heart. She was definitely in the scripture, a lot of scripture. They say it is for all time, but application is a different story. And there we are. So it's like, let's figure this thing out.*

Jamal grew up in East Atlanta across the street from his religious school, where he made honor roll, and down the street from some of the most difficult projects in the city, where the friends he played with after school lived. As a child he didn't feel that he had many responsibilities, but realizes in retrospect that, with a physically disabled single mother, he probably did: *I just felt, "this is what we have to do, so we do it."* He thought that the attitude and expectations that this developed in him were positive: *"That's why I feel like for kids in school, you don't need to get paid $5 for As. Grades, you're just supposed to do that. And I never got paid. . . . I got my As and I was on the honor roll, so I felt like I got my due recognition for it. You do what you have to do and stay the course.*

But out on the street, the choices Jamal faced couldn't always be answered by his mother's values, neither was the course he was supposed to be staying always clear: *When you get older, things get a little blurred about how do we do this, what direction do we go in, where your integrity is in certain situations. My mother made me a thinker, so I looked at situations. I saw a lot of people making it hard on themselves. But then I had to start asking myself why they were doing it. And then I had to look into it a little more and say, well why are you doing it?*

Jamal held steady jobs from the time he was thirteen or fourteen, first at a golf course, then working in a video game store owned by the father of a friend. He also hawked water, disposable cameras and T-shirts at various events. He described how he combined his activities: *Always just coming up with the hustlers, guys who made it happen. Even after school. That's thirteen, fourteen, that age. Even selling the reefer. An older guy gave me the weed. I asked him for more and he asked. "What did you do with the first one?" I said, "I smoked it." He said, "All right, but I ain't gonna give you no more." So, I smoked half and sold the other half, and came back and he said, "OK." We went from there. I always dibbled and dabbled with that.*

But schoolwork was always done because I knew that I could do that and always please my momma and then I could go and play, whatever. She had no idea I was doing the other stuff. It was two different worlds. She knew the school. But you get out of the school and then there's the neighborhood. Even though I did a lot as far as sports, but when you're not doing the sports, you are definitely in that environment. I feel odd talking about this stuff. It's so long ago.

Dᴏɪɴɢ Mʏ Oᴡɴ Tʜɪɴɢ, Mᴀᴋɪɴɢ Iᴛ Hᴀᴘᴘᴇɴ

For most of his twenties this pattern of balancing out legitimate and illegitimate activity felt necessary to Jamal. The first time it brought him into direct contact with the criminal justice system was his first semester at a private college a few hours from home. *First semester in college, got in a fight and a guy was pistol whipped, and I ended up getting locked up. Some other stuff. Another dude got robbed and I got locked up for that too. I went down to Macon with that Atlanta stuff and lord have mercy got me out of there quick.*

Jamal returned to Atlanta, got an apartment, continued to work at the game store, but also began selling more drugs. Police kicked in the door to his apartment and he was arrested again. *At that time, I had three cases pending— aggravated assault, theft by taking, and possession with intent to distribute cocaine, methamphetamines: two in Macon and one in Clayton. Ended up on probation. Still doing what I got to do, whatever.* He was eighteen.

What shifted the balance of his activities toward the legitimate was not probation, rather moving back home with his mother: "That was woah. Couldn't even function, living with my momma. Thought, let's get back to doing what I got to do." So, Jamal went to a nearby technical college and received a degree in automotive technology and, through the recommendation of one of his professors, went to work at one of the local car dealerships.

Jamal has the qualities of a good entrepreneur and leader, but not necessarily those of a docile employee and quickly had a showdown with the manager and got fired. However, that same day he got himself hired by the company that washed the cars for the dealership, so showed up there the next day for work, getting some pleasure flaunting his continued presence to the manager. He acknowledged the manager's suspicion that he was selling drugs to the other mechanics had some validity. Jamal liked the hustle, being paid by how many cars you could bring in and how quickly you could service them. He liked working with old friends.

But he quickly decided he was better off working for himself, "Doing my own thing. Making it happen." This was made more necessary because the game store he had been working in for a decade finally closed, made obsolete by changes in technology. Jamal started looking at the electronics now in demand: *Started selling electronics wholesale, but at first a lot of it was stolen. . . . That was when flat screens really hit, so a lot of those smash and grabs and blue jean bandits, I know a lot of those guys so at first I started messing with those and then started going wholesale with it, buying pallets of broke or refurbished electronics and that was good. I ended up getting good with a guy who had a little shop and was good at doing repairs. So I had an electronics business and started moving a lot of laptops, GPSs, cellphones. At one end, a lot of it was hot. But over here, there are a couple of warehouses I can go to today with computer monitors and stuff like that. On the entrepreneurial side.*

At this point, Jamal was on non-reporting status with probation, so he could conduct his mix of legal and illegal activities without much concern about getting caught. He never saw it as a risk, indeed, seemed surprised at the question. At this point, he began running guns to New York because the Georgia purchase laws were so much less restrictive. However, a fight with the boyfriend of one of the women who were transporting the guns (the boyfriend wanted to keep one) resulted in new charges of aggravated assault and marijuana possession. But the charges that led, finally, to a term in prison came by chance when probation officers entered the apartment he shared with a cousin looking for his cousin's baby daddy. They found twenty computer monitors, none of which were hot, he noted, but also some bullets, which led to a search that uncovered some guns that he, as a convicted felon, was not allowed to possess. Jamal remained angry that the legal monitors, with a value of thirteen thousand dollars, were appropriated by the officers without receipt.

With these new charges, Jamal for the first and last time was incarcerated.

He served fourteen months in all, the first two months for the aggravated assault, then a year for the firearms charge. He didn't find the sentences unfair.

He preferred a straight prison sentence to a split one: *They could have given me more. They were offering me five years, do two. I said no, I didn't want to be on probation. Because when I had it, I violated a couple of times and got sent back to jail. On one court date, they said five do one. I could have gone home and I would have had four years of probation. Probation was worse. More monitoring, more penalties. Then you got to pay them. It just puts you in a messed up situation.*

Incarceration: Do Better

The period of incarceration was a period of reassessment for Jamal in a way that probation had not been. He began to realize that he had more choices than he had imagined: *It changed things for me. I just had time to sit back and really think, time to look at everything and everyone. Of course, everybody gets spiritual when you're by yourself and get lonely. You read. Lot of people get righteous when they get locked up. I realized how I didn't keep the balance. I always did right and I always threw some dirt in the water. I realized that I was unbalanced. And, furthermore, I don't NEED to be doing anything wrong. I would have had less money if I had kept it straight legit, but I would still have been able to survive.*

The question of survival was crucial for Jamal in his twenties and drove many of his choices. He had seen his older brother running into problems with housing and ending up riding a train back and forth for three days. He did not, under any circumstances, want to end up like that. He vowed then he would do what it took to make sure that didn't happen.

During his incarceration he did reassess his own moral reasoning: *At this point, I thought "Do Better." Whatever you do, "Do Better." Like politicians, it's only wrong when you get caught. But I don't like victimizing anyone, and that's the problem with the hot electronics and such. I didn't victimize anyone but I did. I'm not going in your house. No way I'm breaking in anyone's house. No way I'm stealing anything. But I'll buy it, so I'm still victimizing. Drugs, if that's what you want to do, that's what you want to do. But, ideally, I don't want to do any of that.*

In prison, Jamal also demonstrated his ability to lead, by using his business savvy to manage conflict. It wasn't easy at first: *Did a lot of reading, praying. It weren't nothing else to do besides gambling, and you get enough of that. I always moved, I always moved forever. And there it was, oh my gosh, I'm*

about to go crazy just sitting here and talking to that dummy and that dummy.
And then I started talking to them for real instead of just blowing them off and
keeping it moving. So I did look after a lot of guys when I was locked up. I knew
a lot of people when I was locked up. I knew a lot of people coming and going.
So, I was good.

Jamal was imprisoned in his home county, housed on the floors with
people convicted of murder and armed robbery, which at first didn't feel
appropriate to him. However, being housed with people facing thirty or
fifty-five year sentences made him realize that he didn't want to be in their
position. At some points, half of the members of the pod were in gangs. The
gangs upset the balance in the pod and the level of victimization rose. *But I*
was the one who stood up. So anything happened, that other half of the pod was
going to ride with me. And that's what kept everything cool, everybody could live.
People still got their stuff took, but that was it. Of course, I'm not going to go stand
up for everybody for no reason.

The reason the other half of the pod was going to ride with Jamal had to
do with his approach to being in prison, which did not differ too much from
his approach out on the streets: *I used a lot of my influence to keep peace in*
that pod. You got thirty-two guys in there. Somebody going to get beat up. You're
going not to see eye-to-eye. But then you have some who are preying on others just
because they're weak. You either going to be smart enough and keep out of the way
and navigate it or you are going to be predator or prey. I didn't victimize and I
wasn't a victim.

I had books coming in and I was putting guys onto good literature. We
talking and having good conversation. We playing cards, we gambling. I was inner
store man, I was selling two for threes. I give you a rack of cookies and you give me
two next week. So I was doing that. Stamps, paper, deodorant. And I looked after
my people. We ate good every day. We got the stuff coming in, cigarettes, weed,
lighters, cellphones. Making it happen. But didn't get it off anyone else's back.
Didn't take it from anyone. Made it a win win. We swapping books out from
my pod to other pods. In those trying times, you closer to God and you can build
better relationships, because you can talk, this is you. It ain't about anything else.
Everybody have the same outfit. The difference was this man got fifty-five years,
this man ain't never going home. This man got twelve years. I was only looking at
five years. This was something that kept me in touch.

REENTRY: *I AIN'T THROWING NO DIRT IN THE WATER*

When Jamal came out of prison at the age of twenty-five, he was ready to do whatever he needed to do to stay out of prison. In some ways this shift was easy for him: *My thing is simple. Mine was just about money, I was just trying to make a dollar. Other people do things for no reason, just because its cool, everybody's doing it, to live the lifestyle. That don't make sense to me. For me it's all about business.*

Through a combination of intention and good luck, Jamal's activities shifted decisively toward the legitimate. Soon after leaving prison, Jamal found a job with a concrete company with a primarily Mexican crew. Since most of the workers were not legal, his criminal record was not an obstacle. He quickly made himself useful, buying a pick-up truck so he could run and get supplies, something the other workers could not do legally. He rose quickly. Although less skilled than the Mexican workers, he had the advantage of language and quickly moved into a foreman-like capacity, which he acknowledged was unfair based on skill and experience and led to some resentment. When business slowed over the winter, he started up his own delivery business, running it simultaneously with his work at the concrete company.

Jamal saw the job at the concrete company as essential in getting him started down a legitimate avenue, even at $10 an hour for heavy manual labor. "I could make that work," he said. It allowed him to buy his truck, get an apartment. In general, he feels that having a job soon after reentry is core to being able to revise your priorities.

THINKING LIKE AN EMPLOYER: But the rightness of his actions on the job with the concrete company clearly troubled him, and he kept returning to it at different points in our conversation, trying to puzzle out causality and responsibility. He was ultimately fired, the reason given was problems with morale with the crew, but he felt that it was because he had already started his delivery business and was taking calls for it while at work. He kept trying to decide about the appropriateness of doing this. Granted, there were many periods of inactivity on the construction jobs and many of the men were using their phones. Other members of the crew had different side businesses. Taking the calls didn't interfere with the quality of his work. But he himself defined these as rationalizations that did not sit easily for him now that he was an employer himself. He wouldn't want *his* employees taking calls while they were on his trucks or in his customers' houses.

His account of this first job, his perspective taking, was very different from his descriptions of his earlier jobs or arrests, which all were expressed in the passive voice, doors were broken into, bullets were found on tables, the actor undefined. He was clearly looking at his actions from the perspective of both employer and employee now: *We've been through something like thirty employees. I hire people with records. You have to live and learn on that. Some people are not built for work. Moving is tough, especially when you're dealing with the elements. We definitely don't have the best of trucks, so we may not have air conditioning or heat. But we've got to make it happen.*

Some people just don't work out. A guy is out smoking a cigarette. A guy is out cussing. A guy is out sitting down. Some guys have certain airs about them that allow them to feel privileged. I'm hiring guys and they say, "I should make more money." I say, "Why?" Then they have nothing to say. Others, they're calling up and don't want to work. Get paid at the end of the day and don't want to work the next day. Everybody get paid at the end of the day, by the time the sweat dried off your brow, you're getting paid. Then others, what they do with their money—I'm on to you. I see, the weed man already calling you. You already spent half your money and you haven't got it yet.

The expectations Jamal had of his own employees were defined by the business he was now conducting. They weren't out pouring people's driveways. They were in the customers' homes. This was Jamal's momma's world and its assumptions and rules applied. He realized that building a reliable reputation was key to the success of his company, and he didn't want anything to jeopardize that. No stealing, no opening of boxes. Men needed to show up on time. No drugs on the trucks. A two-strike policy. The first time, you sit out for two weeks. The second time you're out. "I had to fire my cousin," he said.

We're trying to make a name for ourself. And most of the guys understand that. They see that. They know that what I'm doing here is bigger than your pay at the end of the day or my pay at the end of the day. It's a way out. And we're building. A lot of people have seen us grow. Saturday, we had seven trucks running (our trucks and a couple of Budget trucks). We get the job done, we get plenty of referrals. Plenty, plenty referrals.

LEGITIMACY: Once he was fired, Jamal turned his attention to his delivery company full-time. He knew nothing about moving, but learned quickly and in a way that feels very much his own: *I had to get that formula. I had to learn a lot. I would call and act like a customer and ask all kinds of questions. I even had a couple of companies come out to my house and give me an estimate. They never knew. I even got boxes and packed them myself.*

Within five months, Jamal had three box trucks as well as his pick-up. Even with twenty-two employees, Jamal still handled all the scheduling. Now confident of his ability to run his business competently, he found himself able to turn jobs down. "Before, I wasn't ready to let a job go. But now I do. Because good service is more important."

One reason he set the requirements he did for his employees was that he didn't want his trucks stopped by the Department of Transportation (DOT): *DOT pull you over, that's a whole different set of problems. Everything DOT has to be in order. You have to have DOT inspections, you have to have your medical card, you have to have everything. Anything wrong, they'll go through it all and let you know. So you definitely don't want to get a truck shut down.*

It is very important to Jamal that his business be successful *and* legal: *I always did something. Legal. Illegal. Both. I always balanced it out. Always, always, always balanced it out. It was never completely illegal, or completely legal. Even now, it's completely legal, but it's so much red tape, you made it illegal. You know what I mean. It's kind of tough.*

He went on to describe the dilemma he felt he faced: *This company has been my transformation. I ain't throwing ANY dirt in the water. The reason I say, legal and not legal, is my felonious situation. I have everything I need to be legit with it, but— You have to have three different insurances—business, cargo, and vehicle full coverage. Have that. Have to have an office, place to park the trucks. Have that. Have to be incorporated, and we do have an S-Corporation. You have to show them fifty thousand dollars, and I have that. You take all this together and submit it to the state, they're going to run a background check. You fail the background check, you done burnt that company's name and you have to start and do it all over again in another name. I was talking to an insurance guy last week. He told me, "Just put it in someone else's name from the very beginning and you won't have to worry about it." So that's where I am now. But there is so much risk and liability, it's not like saying "Sign for this cellphone." You really can lose money. You can get sued. So that is a lot to ask someone to do. I could ask someone to do it who doesn't understand what's at stake. But first it has to be someone I can trust. And someone who is OK with that.*

When asked if he had talked with a lawyer about this, he said no. He had called the state and sounded them out and felt that this would be the case. He was still trying to decide what to do. He clearly felt he had much to lose—and even more to gain—by finding a reliable, legitimate way through this dilemma. It was clear that he did not want to lose control of something he had built himself and yet this might be his only option, again creating a familiar dualism. The only way to define his business as above board was to define himself as not.

Jamal felt that this company was something that he could give his son, something that would give his child a legitimate option from the very beginning, allowing him to avoid many of the choices Jamal felt he had had to make himself. He also loved his work: *I have no days off. But I enjoy it. It's a blessing and I don't want to go back to anything else, Lord have mercy. I am definitely not trying to go back to jail. And I do understand I could lose it all tomorrow. That's what keeps me going so hard. I mean, I wake up tomorrow and the state could be at the door.*

ROLAND

Marijuana wasn't the problem. The criminal justice system was the problem.

We first met Roland, a handsome, articulate man in his late twenties, at a meeting of the Reformed Citizens Committee of the 9 to 5 union, a group actively working on Ban the Box campaigns in Atlanta and around the state. Roland had quickly become their expert on the minutiae of the Economic Employment Opportunity Commission's reading of Title VII of the Civil Rights Act, which prohibits blanket discrimination of people with criminal convictions because of the clearly disparate racial impact of mass incarceration. We met with Roland and his girlfriend at an upscale mall and housing complex near Georgia Tech to talk further.

Roland had been employed for the last few years as a financial representative in a software firm. He has a B.S. in business administration, a degree he completed during the period he had absconded from community corrections. After graduation, even while investigating MBA programs, especially those that didn't ask questions about criminal history, he decided to turn himself in and appeal his conviction. He served ten months in a work camp. Like Jamal, Roland explained his own experience as one of moving between two worlds. However, his situation differed because his arrest and felony conviction were for drug use, in particular marijuana, which he did not see as a crime.

He acknowledged the challenges of a felony conviction: *Does a felony conviction get in the way? Yes. My crime doesn't relate to anything I do in accounting, but they place you in a bucket and you go nowhere. I never got a call back from a restaurant. I always answer truthful. But companies have a blanket refusal policy. They don't take into consideration the crime, the severity, the time since.*

Roland went back and forth about the justice of his conviction, which had to do with the justice of marijuana laws in general. "Marijuana possession was irresponsible, but morally, I'm still on the cusp. I don't beat myself up about it." He was arrested for possession, not selling, he emphasized, and he had a little less than a pound of marijuana in his possession, a quantity that in New York state, where he spent most of his youth, would not be a felony. In Florida, where he was arrested, possession of twenty grams constituted a felony.

EARLY INFLUENCES

Like Jamal, Roland grew up in a world where legitimate and illegitimate activities were both normative, but in his case these norms were geographically separated. He moved frequently between these norms to rationalize his choice. Most of his life, he lived with his mother, who had moved them to Syracuse, New York when he was four. But he also spent extensive time in Panama City, Florida, where his grandmother, to whom he was devoted, and his father lived.

One thing everyone in his family shared was a strong work ethic. His grandmother, who was the mother of ten or more children, believed in doing the right thing. Work was the right thing. She didn't put such a priority on education because she hadn't gotten beyond grade school. Both his parents also had high, although differing, expectations for Roland. His father's expectations were behavioral, a man who worked with his hands, he expected Roland to rake the yard and *behave* well in school. Roland's mother's expectations were more ethical and abstract; she wanted him to excel on principle. "My mom went to community college when she was pregnant with me. I don't know what instilled it in her, but it was very important to her that I go to college. *Her* parents didn't make it to college."

When he was in eighth grade Roland was sent to live with his father for the first time because his mother felt that she "couldn't handle him." The norms in Panama City were different from those of Roland's life in

Syracuse. He felt he was being tested by the Panama City kids. While staying connected to his mother's aspirations, in Panama City he hung out with very affluent white kids who saw him as intelligent and athletic (marijuana was their connection). This came up later when he observed, *They wouldn't have absconded. On the other hand, they wouldn't have been sent to prison unless they violated five times. They might have gotten sent to drug court.*

Roland observed that some children, himself included, were put in situations where the probabilities of doing illegal activities are greater. He described the economy and culture of Panama City as infused with this kind of opportunity: *Everyone had a work ethic even if they were in the street. African Americans like clothes, expensive $30 ball caps, name brand sneakers, jeans. Girls want these fashions. They want these things now. It entices kids, and they see selling drugs as a way to get them. You have the opportunity to do it. You know the people who use and you know the person who can get it for you and you have the respect to operate. When your family, mother, brother, uncle, are involved, you inherit it. People are selling amongst each other. It's safer to sell to African Americans. If white, the buyer could be a cop. The ideology is "You're going to get the drugs or goods anyway, so you may as well buy it from me."*

Arrest & Supervision

Roland believes he became more vulnerable to the culture of Panama City after he transferred from Morgan State to Florida A&M: "If I'd stayed in Baltimore, it would never have happened." Even so, having used marijuana periodically in high school and in college, Roland didn't necessarily see himself threatening his career ambitions by smoking. "I was so close to finishing. I was in my first semester of my junior year. Everything was in line to finish. I had a wonderful GPA."

Roland was arrested returning from a nightclub, having decided to ride with a cousin and another girl rather than with a "wild guy." He was driving and he says the police had reason to stop the car—no headlights and an expired tag. The police weren't profiling but were notorious for it. The girls "told the police everything they wanted."

Roland has some difficulty explaining how he responded to this arrest. *I knew the consequences, but my life was going so well, in spite of smoking occasionally. I wanted to do what I wanted to do. I was immature. I got into more trouble, more misdemeanors. My grandma had died and I was depressed. I thought I was going to be a felon. I felt I'd lost everything. I smoked even more.*

There was a lawyer, but he just wanted to get paid. They tell you the rules and that you'd get in trouble, but I didn't think that prison was a real possibility. The whole time after the arrest, while I was on probation for the misdemeanors, I slacked off in school.

Roland also stubbornly violated the conditions of his probation. On his original probation, he was allowed to continue to go to school while under community control but did poorly his second semester of his junior year and made a retroactive withdrawal. When he violated his probation at six months, the conditions became increasingly severe. The main problem was failing his drug tests. "But rehab for marijuana doesn't really help. They can't scare you like they do with heroin or crack."

Roland was highly resistant to stopping smoking marijuana. How much of this was due to substance dependency and how much to rebellion against the laws themselves still wasn't clear. "Even when I was in prison, I would smoke," he said defiantly. "Until I *want* to stop smoking, nothing's going make me stop."

He pointed out that he was not alone in his difficulty complying with the requirements of probation, that probation had a 20% completion rate. After his first violation, he was put on house arrest for two years, with a one-year early termination. He felt that this sentence was one that was usually given *to people who are a threat to society. I could have did it, but me being immature—To have your whole life on the line, you can't do it. A complete lack of self-control. But look at the completion rate. I was in my early twenties, very rambunctious.*

Roland alternated between a rational, equivocal analysis of the "crime" and an acknowledgement of the emotionally devastating impact on him of the stigmatizing felony conviction. In particular, as he failed at probation, he felt he was losing the support of his family. *My family was very supportive. They saw I'd gotten in this situation but I was still going to school. My family was proud of me, compared to the kids selling crack cocaine. The fact that I graduated high school and went to college. People respect and admire that. My parents probably expected me to abide by my probation. By this time they were worried.*

After he violated community supervision, Roland absconded to Tallahassee where he lived with his supportive girlfriend, who continued to support him when he went to prison and when he came up to Atlanta to join her after his release. Absconding, Roland definitely felt he was doing something wrong and unrationalizable. "I felt I lost *everything* when I absconded. I had never had that hopeless feeling—but I got a taste of it."

When Roland turned himself in after graduation, he was sent to a work camp. Because his sentence was so short, he was not eligible for work release but did work on public works and also acted as a GED tutor. He spent his time studying for his Chartered Financial Analyst exams.

REENTRY & ADVOCACY

He came out of this experience with an interest in the criminal justice system itself. *I learned the mechanisms, the stages and structures of motions. I paid attention in court. I noticed disparities and inequities. Even though I made horrible decisions, I still saw where they made choices that didn't help with rehabilitation.*

Roland had become very interested in advocacy: *How many people in prison don't have an education? There is a lot of ignorance. Only a few people have the intellect to articulate their thoughts and they wouldn't necessarily sacrifice their time to advocate.* Advocacy also united Roland with a value he shared with his mother: *I've always volunteered, and my mother always volunteers. We are big on service, find it very fulfilling.*

Roland felt that corrections in Florida, in particular, was designed only to punish. The guards, he noted, were paid little and were bitter: *This is the job, this is their life. They are there to make your stay worse. They go out of their way to make you uncomfortable.* He did not address the challenges he posed to them with his stubborn non-compliance. Instead, he felt: *The whole process should be centered on rehabilitation. Punishment is a given. From that moment on you need to focus on rehabilitation. Require that people get a GED, get training in a trade or post-secondary education, and come out with tangible skills and real education. You need people to have hope.*

\4/

THE LOST DECADE
NIER, DAINHEN, KEVIN

MANDATORY MINIMUMS

During the mid-1990s, Georgia passed two laws that greatly increased the length of time people served for violent crimes—and reduced the ages at which they served them. In 1994, Georgia passed SB 440, which allowed juveniles ages thirteen to seventeen to be tried as adults when charged with one of what were called the "Seven Deadly Sins." The peak for adolescent male anti-social behavior—especially crimes like breaking and entering, burglary, and robbery—is this same age range, the peak coming around fifteen. This was followed in 1995 by SB 441, which set mandatory minimums for these seven deadlies, which include murder, voluntary manslaughter, and armed robbery with a firearm, as well as establishing the two-strikes law that sends people to prison for life without parole after two such convictions.

One of the most disturbing trends of the last twenty-five years has been the sheer number of juveniles and men in their early twenties being sent to prison for mandatory minimums. These sentences must be served out in their entirety. They provide no incentives for good behavior. These young offenders often go in for armed robbery and are charged as groups. The sentences are particularly troubling because these young men are incarcerated for the years that are most formative for their adult identities—and capacities. They usually enter prison with deficits in education, skills, little to no job experience, very limited maturity—none of which are reduced by long incarceration. Most of those sentences have been served with minimal, if any, programming and without supervision on release.

To some of these young men, this lost decade has become a rite of passage—but it is a rite that creates a worldview in which the prison experience is seen as normative, *not* extraordinary. Their desire to desist afterwards is what they find distinctive about themselves, even extraordinary. The scale by which they measure competence and achievement is *also* measured by what they have seen in prison—in ways that build a sense of confidence in their abilities that may not be sufficiently grounded in actual practice to see them well through the usual challenges of early adulthood, let alone the additional challenges that follow on a felony conviction. Charismatic authority, rather than skill and knowledge and self-discipline, then becomes alluring. That is something they *have* been able to develop and refine in prison. As is hustling.

Hustle and the Entrepreneurial Imperative: Many of our ex-offenders may have renounced stealing or robbery, but they have not renounced hustle—indeed may rely on it even more than before. Hustle is just good old capitalism under another name. Hustle isn't always economic—it has to do with social capital as well. It is about who you know, who owes you a favor, who needs to be connected. This interest and talent elides smoothly into entrepreneurialism, which, because of all the constraints placed on ex-offenders, is where people are encouraged to focus after reentry—even if it is not a good fit for their temperament. For those for whom it is a good fit temperamentally, it may not always be the safest direction if they don't have legal norms firmly internalized.

Charismatic Authority and Motivational Speaking: Many of the men and women we have talked with define their occupation as motivational speaker, or self-identified chaplain, and serve as consultants to lawyers, juvenile courts, U.S. attorneys offices, and schools on the basis of their incarceration experience. Their professional and economic possibilities depend on their ability to describe their lives as call stories, cautionary but redemptive tales. This both liberates them and locks them into this experience as the one in their lives with the greatest social value. (One of our favorite versions of this, less penitent and more media savvy, is a group of men trying to develop a reality show, Ex-cons of Atlanta.) Many of the people we talked to would take another job, especially a steady one with benefits, if it were available to them—indeed hoped these speaking gigs would lead to that and became increasingly frustrated when they received positive receptions that did not translate into more sustainable employment.

Others would not. The level of acclaim they received in this arena exceeded what they would be able to have working with the few employable skills they have been able to attain during long incarcerations. These are highly intelligent people, articulate and personable, often with penetrating and useful insights into the system that absorbed years or decades of their young lives. Our reservation is that they stay symbiotically attached to the criminal justice system out of necessity. They receive their social authority simply from having survived that system. We feel they deserve more than that—mundane, transferable skills that they can use once those stories are no longer current, when a reformist wave crests and another more punitive one rises, for example.

The three men whose stories we share in this chapter all went into prison around 1995-1996, when mandatory minimums were going into effect in Georgia. They differ in age. Nier, in his early thirties, was convicted at fifteen and received a twenty-year sentence with a mandatory ten to serve, and was still serving out probation when we talked. He entered adult prison at seventeen. Dainhen went in at around nineteen, already a father. Kevin was sixteen when he was convicted, jailed for three years pending appeals, then entered prison. Both Dainhen and Kevin were released in 2006, had been out more than a decade when we spoke with them.

As we listened to their stories, what struck us were the people who served as their role models and mentors, both while they were in prison and when they were released; what programs made a difference; what their different talents were and how they chose to develop them; and what roles self-discipline as well as entrepreneurial drive have played in their reentry efforts.

NIER

Since I have been out I have fallen three times, but I never thought about going back to the streets.

Nier's challenging experience with reentry is probably more typical of children incarcerated as adults under the SB 440 law than others we present. Nier was incarcerated at fifteen on a twenty-year sentence for rape with a mandatory ten to serve. When we talked to him, he had been out about seven years. He and his family were going through a very difficult time. Nier was trying hard to keep his footing. The family car had broken down, setting off a cascade of negative consequences. His wife had just lost one of her two jobs because of the lack of transportation, and he was unable to engage in the occasional work he usually found for the same reason. He felt they had very little social support from either of their families—and mandatory probation fees provided another significant drain on their already precarious finances.

He was obviously feeling the strain. *It's hard, temptation is everywhere. I got homeboys that I grew up with and I see them riding around in Porsches, in Lexuses and I know what they are doing. I am doing it the other way, and it is hard and I be wondering why is it so hard to do good but easy to be bad, easy to be bad and get money out of doing bad. When you do good, the people that good and bad both come against you. The good people don't understand what you doing and the bad people mad because you doing the things that you doing.*

He was determined, however, to find a way through. *Since I been out I've fallen down three times, but I never thought about going back to the streets. I just work my way through it. When you are down and out it really shows you who your friends are.*

Early Influences

Nier grew up in a family deeply involved in drugs. *It was like this, my daddy was a drug leader, my aunty was the candy lady, and my momma was the weed lady.* His description of his introduction to the drug trade was matter of fact: *I started selling drugs at twelve, kept them in a pill box. One day I left them in the house. Went back to get them, and there they were on the table. My mom had found them in my room. She don't cuss me out, she don't say "why you bringing this in my house?" She say, "You are going to have to pay a bill around here." My father was a drug dealer, when I go to him for money he would give me drugs, tell my to buy my own stuff.*

His father died when he was in prison and although he felt responsible for his mother, who was schizophrenic, Nier found it difficult to be around her. *She'd tell me all the time that I won't be nothing. "You a bastard child. I don't know who your daddy is."* Nier didn't want to treat his own three children that way. *I'm trying to keep my family together but if I don't find nothing to do right now I might have to tell my wife to go live with her own mother. Because I am in a situation where I ain't producing money like when I had a car. I don't panic. Because I know God is good, he always listens in some type of way. But it hard. It is going to be hard out here. It's a fight.*

Incarceration, Miss Peggy, & The Secret

At seventeen, after two years in juvenile prison, Nier was put directly into the adult prison population in one of the most notorious Georgia prisons, Alto, where many of the youngest prisoners were housed. All of those we talked to described it as violent and chaotic, with gangs based on city of origin. Involved in a big fight based on these competing affiliations, Nier was put in the hole. Then, because he had a fight with the deputy warden, he was put on high max. "He called me a nigger. I said come into my cell and say that. He did and I hit him." The guards took Nier out of view of the cameras and beat him severely, then put him in the hole. "They beat me up real bad."

Nier was illiterate: "I couldn't even spell cat." But while he was in the hole, an older orderly brought him books. He would look at the pictures. When the orderly asked if he had read the books, he said no. "Why? I see you looking at the pictures." When Nier explained that he couldn't, the orderly, who had been in for twenty years, sat down and started helping him. Nier liked the story of Malcolm X best, because he also came from the streets, illiterate, and learned to read in prison.

During the time Nier was in prison he was fortunate to meet an older woman, Miss Peggy, a volunteer who felt a call to work with young offenders. Even after his release, she remained his most significant source of social support. He described how he first met Miss Peggy and how she gained his trust: *There was this dude next to me, his name was Detroit. Says there was this white lady sending money. He said he was going to write to her and see if he can get some money out of her. She sent him some and he drew a picture of a hand and sent it to her saying it was for her to slap herself with for sending him the money. That weekend Miss Peggy came to see him. She talked to him and then she talked with me. I disregarded what she said. Told her, Ain't nothing she could do for me. This is hell on earth. She said, "Tell me what you need." I said, "I need to see somebody from my family, my grandmother." She took her name and number and the next week she brought my grandmother to come see me. She started bringing her constantly.*

Moved to another prison, Nier again met Miss Peggy who had him sign up for a class she was giving and introduced him to *The Secret* and the Laws of Attraction. Miss Peggy was also volunteering at Hancock Transition Center when he was moved there. *There were no programs in there. The only thing that I had was Miss Peggy. She gave me an outlook, a blueprint on how to think. And I just took it and searched. Don't need a man to tell me how to think. I search. And I search. It is all about the knowledge. You got to want it. Some folks just want to stay with what they got. You need to know that people are going to come at you from all levels to play you. I know the Law of Attraction is true. You attract what you put out. If you think negative, negative things are going to come.*

Nier explained how this emphasis on the positive helped him respond to prejudice:

I know I got strikes against me because of my skin color. It's going always to be like that. Why would I let that hold me down? Don't need to sit down with "They didn't give me the job because I am black." No something else went wrong. They didn't give you the job because you wasn't talking the right way or dressed the right way. I love my culture, I am into my culture, I got gold teeth, wear baggy pants. But at the same time I know that I have to Clark Kent. I know that I need to go shake hands, to get things going for me, that is the way of the world. Need to make enough money for people to be comfortable with me. Learn to play the game.

REENTRY & SUPERVISION

Nier emphasized how much greater the challenges are for someone reentering who was incarcerated as a child. *It's different if you go in at twenty-six, you do ten years, when you get out you know what to do as an adult because you were an adult when you went in. When you go in as a kid, everything is different. There are programs for ex-offenders that were twenty-five or thirty when they were locked up but there is nothing for the kids that were locked up when they thirteen, fourteen, fifteen, sixteen. When they get out, they not getting life skills on how to do things. They out here feeling around blind on how to do things. Whoever is giving them the support, they hold on to. It is crazy because them is the people who are going right back to jail. They don't know what to do, they don't have no skills, they don't know how to get into school. It's a battle if you don't have the family or the support, it pushes you back to the streets, back to where you can find some kind of support. A person has to mentally be ready for the streets when you get out because everything is going to come at you at one time.*

Not only were basic survival needs challenging for Nier, community supervision was as well. In large part this had to do with both the length of his probation—ten years—and also the nature of his supervision. The length of time he was on probation greatly increased the chances of being revoked. Nier had been sent back to jail (not prison) twice, once for a week and once for a month. He saw the financial challenges of the programs probation required as the cause of a downward cycle of both potential reincarceration and financial collapse. *They put you in classes that you have to pay for. I got locked up last year. I had to make a decision, pay my mortgage and my bills, or don't go to work and go to this class—but then my kids don't eat. Don't put no man in that situation because he is going to choose his family over what DOC [Corrections] is trying to do. Crazy, locked up for a class you missed. Meet people in jail you know saying, "What you in for?" "Locked me up for not going to a class that I pay for." They got hooks in you that they can pull any time. They don't care what you are going through, they have no sympathy. The ones that are trying to do right, they hurry you up, they snatch you back in. When you are trying to do something right, its just so hard, you have to prove all sorts of stuff, bring all sorts of paperwork. There was a dude hadn't been reporting for two years and he got reinstated and let back out whereas I had been paying my fees, and I had wife and three kids, but they gave me thirty days. They should at least give some leeway. Probation officers come to you house and they are mad because you are doing good.*

Nier was cynical about the classes they were requiring of him. He believed community supervision's motives were purely financial: *I didn't go to my class about three or four weeks because I couldn't. I didn't have a car. Plus I had to work. I know how my probation officer works, I know she is going to put out a warrant on me. So what I did, I sent $200 to her and I showed up to the class and I paid $300 on the class. No warrant. She lifted the warrant. The money made the difference. As long as you are paying the money they don't even care.*

Nier also objected to the content of the classes. Because he was convicted of child molestation, a relationship with a girl of fourteen, a year younger than he was, Nier is on the sex-offender caseload. He feels the long-term consequences associated with the conviction are unfair. *I am in there with some real old Chesters. Some real child molesters. They talking about having touched a four-year-old kid. I don't want to sit in there but I have to. Telling me how their life messed up. How they are having urges. I don't what to sit in there and listen to that. I was fifteen going out with a girl fourteen—and I got kids at home. Makes my flesh crawl. . . . I don't want to sit around listening to that. I hate sitting around talking about problems. I am sitting there thinking about am I going to get fired from my job. But I pay for this class.*

Miss Peggy remained a constant positive presence in Nier's life and an invitation to a positive outlook: *Right now I don't have any support, but I have Miss Peggy. She will come and check on me, see if I am all right. But I be on my last—about ready to break down myself. It is hard. I hear my wife in the bathroom crying. And I am the man. I am trying to find out what to do without getting in trouble. It is hard. But it's not that hard, something is going to happen, things don't never stay the same. You got a choice. The choices you make is where you go.*

DAINHEN

What I'm learning in life is that anything is possible, you just simply need to find out how to get it done.

Dainhen, another young man who began serving a mandatory ten-year minimum sentence for armed robbery, was not an SB 440. He was nineteen, already a father. He was incarcerated during the same period of time as Nier and Kevin, 1996-2006. He also was sent to Alto, one of the most notorious of Georgia's prisons. His relative success was shaped strongly by two key mentors, one inside the prison, a woman who taught him how to read seriously and to debate, and another on the outside, an ex-offender involved in reentry efforts. He also was aided by the infusion of funding for reentry that was part of Georgia's recent wave of criminal justice reform. Since reentering he had earned an associates degree in marketing and management and a certificate in anger management. Dainhen is strongly entrepreneurial. His skills include public speaking. He wrote a book about his experiences in prison and spoke about his experience on various reentry videos as well. He described himself as "a vital visionary who has used his setbacks and mistakes to add to his purposeful mission."

Early Influences & Delinquency

Dainhen's mother was a schoolteacher, his father he described as "a street guy from Detroit." He described himself as coming from a two-parent home, but his father was both dealing in and using drugs when he was growing up. *We went from having too much to not having enough. To him paying full attention to not paying attention at all. He was just doing the best he could with what he had.*

His parents broke up before he was a teenager. Like a number of the younger offenders, his inspiration for crime was a desire for clothes. *I wanted to be able to buy things like new sneakers. My mom would not let me got to school and have a job. So I started doing "locker research"—I started stealing.*

He felt his marijuana use contributed to his delinquency. So did peer influences: *When you leave a seventeen-year-old to fend for himself to a degree, he is going to come up with the things the people around him come up with. When you give me something to go for, I'm going to go for it full. If we are going to break the law, I am going to rob everybody.*

Dainhen found that he liked the authority he felt when he used a gun: *I found that there was a false sense of power that was given to a young teen with a firearm. I could control this room with a firearm. And make a lot of money. I was somebody who believes he has it figured out.*

He was arrested several times before the arrest for armed robbery that led to his ten-year sentence. Even so, he was shocked when he heard his sentence: *I am thinking, "Why is the air so thin? Why are my knees buckling?" My mom put her hand into my back and she said "Don't cry, you did the crime." When I got back to the cell, I didn't cry but in the shower.*

Incarceration, Book Group & Debate Club

During his first five years in prison, Dainhen gave no thought to changing his worldview or his goals—which were to return to robbing, hopefully more successfully, when he got out. What turned him around was a book club started by Susan Shlaer, "an old, white, Jewish lady," the director of education at Alto. The book group was an attempt to counteract the loss of programming. The experience was transformative for Dainhen. He felt he was being given a key to how the world really worked. "I was reading books but the crazy part, I went to prison for breaking the law and I read books that were about breaking the law." The books they read included *Catch-22*, anything by Ayn Rand, and *To Kill a Mockingbird*.

Ms. Shlaer, she wasn't pushy, she didn't care what I was locked up for. Her whole thing was education, education. She would let us choose the books and just say, "let's discuss them, let's talk about them." We set around in a circle with mean guys, guys with double life [sentences] and we had intimate conversations about the characters, the plot. She would sit there and she would listen. I didn't like the way that I spoke. I spoke with a very deep southern dialect. She told me, "just try reading out loud and try to enunciate your words." So for about four years every book that I read, I read it out loud.

Susan Shlaer's opinion was one Dainhen deeply valued. Sent to the hole, Dainhen didn't care what his mother or the parole board would say, but he worried about the opinion of his mentor. *I thought, Ms. Shlaer is going to kill me. But, she came to the hole, she slid two books in my cell, and I was like, ah man, she still loves me!*

One of the books Shlaer gave Dainhen was <u>Guns, Germs and Steel</u>. He explained, *I read it outloud in the hole. It's a big book! I just wanted to talk to her about the book. I just didn't want her to feel like her efforts had gone unnoticed,* and I didn't want her to feel that I was the kind of person that didn't value what she had given. It's a big book, but when you have nothing to do, the book is nothing.

These books enlarged Dainhen and his companions' worlds significantly. In particular, it made Dainhen think about how he modeled the world, how he believed it worked: *My life was based on a lack of information and reading. I was, you know what, this is how the whole world is working, not just in these United States. But it's not just about a little black boy like me from Decatur, no the world is so much bigger, there is so much going on. We were talking about racism. I could understand how a guy of another race could not see me as an equal because that was how that individual was raised. He wasn't born with that trait, that was something taught to him. If you turn off everything else and you just let me listen to rap music all day and all I see is the things that rap music promotes, then nine times out of ten I am going to try to base my life on that. It is just a matter of having enough information pertaining to the world in order to make a logical decision. Because if I only give you half the information, then it is not a sound decision.*

Shlaer also started a debate club, facilitated by a professor from the University of Georgia, which also provided additional intellectual discipline. *That program, where we were defending the affirmative then the negative, it caused me to not just value research and information, I also learned that it is not always who is right, who is wrong, it is about how you prepare your statement, how you word it, how you captivate the audience with your non-verbal, your eye contact. Now when I go through life, when people are talking, in my mind I automatically start thinking about three main points why that is not true. I question everything.*

The professor would bring in debate teams from UGA and also other schools. Dainhen came away from the experience understanding that *the world is a stage and you are always going to be watched. I can say something that is going to get me shot up or get me invited to the White House. That is the power of words. That is the power of knowing what it is your are talking about.*

The members of the book club and debate team didn't restrict their self-education to these two experiences. They also taught themselves sign language: *Imagine a bunch of killers in a mop closet sign languaging. For weeks on end we would not talk to each other, we would just go use sign language.* They used this group approach continuously to enlarge their verbal mastery: *Whatever book came to us, that we got a hold of, we would give ourselves a chapter test, vocabulary words, we would rip that book apart.*

Dainhen was clear that Susan Shlaer was the person who had had the greatest effect on his life. *She is one of the reasons why I am so gung ho on putting goodness in the world. She didn't know us, she got paid to be there but she didn't have to do this . . . . Who cares about Georgia prisoners? But she did. She said anything is possible and she gave me the tools I needed.*

REENTRY

Because of the influence of the book and debate clubs, Dainhen began to think more seriously about how not to return to prison after he was released. When he was released, he applied to Atlanta Tech, which had a special aid program to help young African-American men attend community college.

Another positive result of the clubs was that within prison Dainhen and other members of the clubs began to develop a positive sense of social identity as "Shlaer's Finest," an identity they continued to share when they left, learning from each other's reentry experiences. A close friend with an ice cream truck encouraged Dainhen to apply his educational loan to more entrepreneurial purposes—buying several moonwalks and an ice cream truck. At the time we talked, Dainhen owned sixteen moonwalks, which provided him with a basic income.

When Dainhen emerged, he had another mentor in Darryl, an older ex-offender known in the prison as "Coach." Darryl, college educated and netted into the reentry initiative, encouraged Dainhen to become certified as an anger management consultant, then hired him on as a case manager on a reentry grant.

Dainhen remains committed to charismatic and entrepreneurial values. He now, because of his debate experience in particular, feels that he has ways to counteract negative opinions: *Your perception of me is just that, just a perception, I can alter it. Your perception of me is in my hands.*

He still believes in aiming high, not just for himself but also for others: *I think a lot of times, especially in the African-American community, you know what we do, we ask our kids, "What kind of work do you want to do when you grow up?" As opposed to asking them, "What kind of business are you going to run?"*

Dainhen is committed to reentry, and helping other people achieve what he has: *They actually pay me to walk into the prison and talk to people. I know that if I mess this up, I mess this up not just for me but for everybody else who gets out of prison. . . . If I do my part then maybe somebody else will have a chance. If I can put goodness in the world and get paid for it then I am winning.*

KEVIN

Getting out and making it wasn't a question. It was just about not accepting no for an answer.

We interviewed Kevin in 2019, several years later than the other men in this listening project. We met him at one of the country libraries, where we talked in an attractive meeting room with a large glass wall looking out on the foyer. It seemed appropriate because Kevin is very open about his life, his criminal record and the hard work it has taken to arrive where he is now. He was dressed in an elegant sport coat of a subdued plaid, a color coordinated shirt. He had arrived in his company truck. Its name *Four Fourty Trucking*, advertised his business and was also an open tribute to one of the most pivotal moments of his life and its paradoxical benefits.

Kevin was one of the first juveniles prosecuted through the SB 440 law in our county. Arrested at sixteen for armed robbery, he was convicted in 1996 and sentenced to a mandatory minimum of ten years. The first three years, he, along with about eleven other juveniles, were housed in the county jail in a special dorm as they waited out their appeals. So part of Kevin has always understood himself not to be a unique case. On the other hand, he does claim unique credit for his successful reentry: *You have to choose to change. That is the bottom line. I will never say prison changed me. I chose to change. I can say that the time I had to sit down gave me time to think about my decisions and how I wanted my life to look, but prison itself changes no one. If anything, it makes you worse. It makes you more criminal.*

Early Influences & Delinquency

Born in New Orleans, Kevin and his mother moved to the Atlanta area when he was twelve because of a reorganization at AT&T, where his mother worked. He found the move alienating. In particular he disliked the feeling that in seventh grade, which in New Orleans had been housed independently, he was back on a closed campus that felt like elementary school. He rebelled and was often suspended. "I felt like I'd grown up and was now reverted to kid again, but I couldn't voice this."

In addition, the family finances were "tight as the skin on a sausage." This was because his mother was both paying rent in Georgia and the mortgage on their New Orleans house as they sought a buyer, although he didn't understand that at the time. He just knew that before they moved, she could get him everything he wanted and now she couldn't: *That's when my crumble start. It started with stealing from the gas station and selling candy and juice at school, drug sales on the weekend. In my mind I'm helping her help me. "Don't worry mama, I'm going to get it." And she worked so much she couldn't monitor me.*

In ninth grade a friend's older brother introduced him to robbing. A counter-balance to his delinquency was his interest in baseball. Playing baseball restricted his engagement in criminal activities, but when he was forced to transfer to another high school in tenth grade after having been caught gambling, he was excluded from sports for a semester. It was during this period that he committed the armed robbery of a local convenience store that led to his decade of incarceration.

SB 440

Kevin and his companion were picked up the day after their robbery. Appeal documents make it clear that neither he nor his mother really understood when waiving his Miranda rights that he was going to be charged as an adult. The only evidence for armed robbery was the assertion of his companion that they had had a gun: *They took us to the station that evening and locked us up that night for armed robbery. No gun, just him saying that I made him do it. Enough for them to arrest us. No real evidence. Nobody got touched in our robbery. I'm not gonna say there wasn't no gun, just that they had no gun. They don't need a gun. They just need someone to say there was a gun. That's enough to charge for armed robbery.*

Kevin, when asked about whether he had any sense of the harm or threat he may have created in his victim, puzzled this: *Most dangerous age for males is between thirteen and seventeen. We live in almost a fantasy world. We can't play the tape all the way through as if, "I do this today, this is what is going to happen tomorrow." So, no, I wasn't thinking about the effects I was having on someone else. It never crossed my mind. It didn't. All that crossed my mind was, "Keep this money, I'm going shopping tomorrow." That was it.*

Kevin was immediately transferred to Panthersville, the local juvenile prison, facing one count of armed robbery. He expected that he would receive the punishment that he'd seen doled out to his peers. Nobody had gotten shot. There was no evidence. *Honestly my situation didn't hit me. I seen other guys get locked up for armed robbery and come back to school in ninety days, 120 days so we was thinking, I'm gonna go to boot camp. That was kinda so brave-like. We kids. In our minds its nothing so serious. It is but in our minds it wasn't. And everybody's doing it. They coming back to school and people are, "Oh, man, you just got out. Okay." We didn't know things changed. The second or third day the public defender came to see me at the juvenile and that was when she broke the news to me I was facing ten years. My heart hit the floor. "Ten! How many?!" I'm thinking about prom, about graduating high school. I never envisioned this. We didn't go to prison. We went to boot camp. We went to juvenile.*

Kevin went to trial and was found guilty. His companion, who was tried with him, testified against Kevin, and the jury found his friend not guilty because of coercion. However, Kevin would not change places with him. Two years later his friend was murdered. "If I'd been let out, it could have been me. It saved me from myself and my environment."

INCARCERATION, SELF-AGENCY & HUSTLE

Kevin saw his stay in prison as having several pivotal moments, some in terms of his ability to survive there, others in terms of his ability to prepare for reentry. He was, luckily, not sent to Alto, the most dangerous of the youth prisons. At his first prison, he established his reputation as someone who could defend himself, something he felt was essential to his safety in prison. *You have to create a reputation. You have to hurt someone the first time they say something. That reputation follows you throughout all the prisons.* He had a number of disciplinary infractions that sent him into solitary for periods of time.

Self-Agency: The next prison, Frank Scott, was the only one still providing some training in trades. They had already gotten rid of college courses. Kevin had earned his GED when in jail because his lawyers had been trying to negotiate a sentence that would require he go to college. At Frank Scott he took a course in graphic arts. He also made close friends with an older man, Tiger, who had already served ten to twelve years of a life sentence. This meant they were facing roughly equivalent times until release. His friend did two things—the first was to introduce Kevin to stocks, which he was able to purchase in prison. Even a small investment meant that he would receive a stock certificate and that he would receive quarterly dividends, both of which symbolized to Kevin that he still participated in the larger world.

The other shared activity was education. The two men decided that after they finished their first trades, they would take another one. Generally inmates in Georgia are allowed to take only one trade per sentence. A counselor told them that they would have to leave and return on another sentence to be eligible for more training. However, they decided to contest the decision and contested all the way up to the deputy warden. They were allowed to take an additional trade. Kevin chose architectural drafting and loved it, in part because the blueprints they made were then used to build real houses out in the world.

More importantly, their ability to protest, to take their aspiration and complaint up the institutional ladder had a transformative effect on Kevin. *That was a pivotal point in my life because I learned then, and this is bad grammar, "Ain't no no." And I felt I broke through the glass ceiling. We were the only ones allowed to take a second trade. Nobody even asked to do it. So we got our second trade and it was like, Yes! There was nothing that could stop me. That was the same energy I got out with. I still had five or six years left to serve but that same kind of energy told me there's nothing I can't do.*

Hustle: Kevin was far from a model prisoner. The same day he received permission to take a second trade, he was caught with a cellphone. He had, as he described it, hustle. *I learned in prison that you can make people conform to what you want if you doing something they want you to. One of the jobs I had, it really wasn't one of my jobs—but I showed up every day and the officers thought it was my job. An orderly needed to clean up the visitation room after visitation. Visitation would let out and I'd go down there and just start cleaning up. After a couple of weeks, one day I didn't go and they were asking, "Why you ain't going to work?" It wasn't my job, but I made it my job and they kept me doing it. I used that. I used to smuggle stuff in. So I'm hustling.*

Kevin made a clear distinction between robbing, stealing, and hustle. *Stealing is cowardly. If you going to rob, you see me take it. We wasn't doing no stealing. A lot of people in prison steal. But you have more of a sense of pride hustling rather than stealing.*

When asked to describe some of the other rules in prison, Kevin emphasized the importance of clinging to your own circle because guards judged you by the company you kept. This was important because his own circle was involved in "personal dealings," which he went on to describe as another form of institutional hustle: "We were the guys who would figure out how to get the officers to bring stuff in." This contraband exchange relied on charm as well as material resources. Kevin was young, bright, attractive, well-spoken. *I was an asset. I was the one they would send to ask for a library pass because it's probably 70% women working in the prison. . . . A lot of them don't make very much money, so a lot of them are open to corruption. Men too.* The mother of his first child worked in the prison.

Eventually, Kevin's activities came to the attention of the warden, who transferred him because of disciplinary infractions to one of the worst prisons in the state, Calhoun, saying, "I'm going to send you so far your mama going to have to catch a plane to come see you." Calhoun was a high security prison. It was very violent. The day he arrived there, Kevin knew it was too much and called his mother and asked her to do what she could to get him moved: "My fear was not somebody hurting me but me hurting someone else. I wasn't afraid. I would have stabbed someone if I had to. I just didn't want to do any more time. That was the reality point for me. I could be like these guys who are *not* getting out."

Kevin's mother had become a founding member of Moms Advocating Juvenile Justice, a non-profit whose aim was to increase the options of juveniles adjudicated as adults—not to evade punishment but to have it be proportionate and more specific to the individual than ten-year mandatory sentences. She was effective at having him transferred.

REENTRY

Kevin was one of the first SB 440s moved to a transitional center, work-release prisons that people can be sent to for their last eighteen months of prison. Mandatory minimums, or max outs, are generally not eligible. Kevin promptly found a job in a McDonalds where he worked until his release. The day he was released, he kissed the pavement before getting in the car with his mother.

Kevin's reentry strategy drew on some of the dimensions of his capacity to hustle, but was also combined with an interest in stability and a willingness to work hard at difficult jobs and move up gradually. He was unable to get any employment in the trades he had been trained for because no one would hire someone with a criminal record. He worked for a while in a hotel restaurant, which he enjoyed, but he left it for a grueling job at Trojan Batteries, which offered him a career ladder and a 401K. *I called about the job every day for a month. My mentality was ain't no no. They say no, my mentality was maybe somebody got fired, so I'll call again. It wasn't no fear of failure because I ain't taking no from anybody. That same courage I had robbing and selling drugs I applied it in a positive way. I am going to take this job. You going to hire me one of these days. I kept calling. All you can do is tell me no.*

He used the same determination on the job, which was hot and physically taxing. He cross-trained for jobs he thought might advance him. He offered to work for bosses so abrasive no one else would work with them: *The same thing I did in prison I did here. My mentality was, I'm not going to wait for you to put me there, I'm going to put myself there. When the opportunity come, I'm ready for it. I didn't understand "showing initiative," I'm still learning. I still have sixteen-year-old mind set. I'm going to learn a new job so I can make some more money. But in management eye, it is "He takes initiative. We like him." Didn't have a name for it. I applied the same hustle to the job. Before I left, I was in management, I was a team leader, I had twenty-five operators who worked under me.*

He felt he learned a lot as a team leader about how to motivate the people who reported to him, finding a different way to talk to each one. He also, once he became a team leader, found his social world changed, the people he looked to for advice and models were in management, not on the assembly lines. One of his colleagues had a trucking company, and he learned from him before starting his own. An interesting piece of advice he was given was never to learn how to drive a truck himself because he would be enticed to step in and fill the gap if there was a problem with his work force. "Does the president of Trojan Batteries know how to make a battery?" his mentor asked him.

GIVING BACK : PREVENTION & REENTRY

One of Kevin's aspirations had been to hire people with records to drive his trucks. At the point that we talked to him, he had made his first hire of this kind and was feeling very positive. Kevin had been doing several other things to help others with reentry. He served as the only ex-offender on the steering committee for the community coordinator in the county's Department of Community Supervision office. Most of them, he notes, have never met an ex-offender before.

He was also working with the U.S. Attorney's office in Atlanta in a six-month program designed to encourage gang members to leave their gangs—Adults Committed to Empowerment Success (ACES). The underlying idea is that they will form a social bond with one another that will help them weather reentry. Participants spend three months in Metro Regional, a transitional center repurposed as a multi-faceted reentry facility in Atlanta. At graduation, each participant was given a personally tailored suit. Kevin shared with them his own experience getting housing—filling out and paying the fees for thirty apartment applications before he found one that would accept him. (He had family support when he returned, living with his mother for several years before he was able to get housing.)

"I'm here to take away excuses," he explains. "One thing that will transcend a felony is consistency. Showing up every day."

\5/

RAISING OURSELVES

ANTHONY

When does it become acceptable to become your environment?

Every time we read the transcript of our interview with Anthony, we pause, amazed at the level of growth and maturation he was able to achieve for himself during the twenty-five years he served in some of Georgia's worst prisons. There is a seeking intelligence here that allowed him to survive a traumatic childhood and equally traumatic adulthood and come out whole. Angry—and whole. Entering prison at seventeen, he made a vow to himself, "You a man when you walk across this. When you walk across this in twenty-five years, you still going to be a man." He did more than that. He came out a moral, humane adult. *How* he built that inner structure is the heart of his story. A tall, handsome man in his early fifties, we first met him when he spoke at a meeting of A.B.L.E., a social change group advocating criminal justice reform.

EARLY INFLUENCES

Anthony's early life was brutal and traumatic. One of fourteen children, he was orphaned at seven when his mother was beaten to death by her boyfriend. Three months earlier one of Anthony's brothers, who had been arrested with two of his other brothers, died when his jail cell was set on fire and he was severely burned. Forbidden to see his brother because he was a child, Anthony remembers his mother and brothers emerging from the hospital room crying. His family believed that the police had set his brother's cell on fire. "And that's when I really started looking at life in this aggressive, fuck-it type mode," he said.

The question of where his anger originated is probably less important than all the many ways it was stoked by his subsequent experiences. After his mother's death, Anthony and his siblings were separated and sent to various foster settings. The one Anthony talked about most was the group home where he stayed the longest. It was his third or fourth placement. He admired the women who started the home: *But when you have that many troubled kids in one place and you don't have counseling, you can imagine what it turn into. I didn't want to be someone who got beat up every week. So I became aggressive.*

He described how they were punished: *They had a long hallway, and if you got in trouble, they would put kids at each side of the hallway with belts and you would have to undress and you would have to run from this end to that end and they would whip you, and that's where my ability to fight came from. I went through that one time. I went and the first boy who hit me, I stopped and beat his ass. And then I ended up having to fight all the kids in the dormitory because the dormitory parents said, "Git him" and so I had to fight all of them. I was about nine.*

Speaking with us, Anthony could clearly see that his aggressiveness had strong environmental origins, but back then he didn't. *At that point in my life, I'm rebellious, angry, mad——but I've lost the reason why I'm mad. I don't remember how my brother died, not on a conscious level. I don't remember how my mother died. On a conscious level it's not there, but on an unconscious level it is. The various abuses, the molestations in the foster homes, they're in the back of my mind. But when I try and analyze my anger, they're not there. It wasn't until I actually was in prison that I understood.*

He was clear that anger is preferable to fear: *Kids should not grow up enraged or in fear. They should definitely not grow up in fear. I would prefer they grow up enraged.* He saw how his aggression evolved and his sympathies narrowed: *I can actually see the transition from being a defender of people. I used to be the type of kid who if I saw you bullying this guy, I'd say, "Nah, fight me." Because I was good at fighting. And I can see the transition from that to "Man, forget it. If he don't fight for himself let him get beat up." I can remember how it progressed.*

The impact of labeling was not abstract to him. At ten or eleven, Anthony punched the father in his foster home and ran away after the man had grabbed him by his penis. When found by the police two days later, he was put in juvenile detention: *The judge labeled me as incorrigible. I'm like ten or eleven years old. So incorrigible meant to me that I had been violated. I didn't know that it meant that I was bad. Because again no one explained anything to me.*

Anthony liked the juvenile detention center. It felt cleaner and more orderly than the foster homes he had been sent to, but by this time,

Anthony's lack of trust was profound and affected his perception of all the social institutions that he came into contact with: *Going back to my mind state at the time: I hate the police because my family said it was the police set my brother's cell on fire, so I've always hated them. I don't trust social workers because in my mind it was all about business. And I don't like secret organizations. . . . I hate them because if you spend time in the foster system you spend a lot of time in the court system because the court has dispensation to allow these people to put you here or there. It was always these secret deals that decided your life. They come out of the room and they shake hands and then they send you somewhere and you get abused and what kind of deal was that? And then they'll find out about the abuse and they'll move you to another place and then another deal will be swung and then the people make you feel like they doing you a favor by having you there. You know, "I didn't have to take you." "Nobody wanted you." dadada. And you going, "And you swore on that deal for me!" So you stop trusting that these people have your best interests at heart.*

DELINQUENCY

Anthony's fighting got him kicked out of several more foster placements, and his schooling suffered. He had never done well in school, although he seemed to do well in sports and in drumming. His illiteracy went unnoticed because in each new school he was placed by age rather than accomplishment. Anthony now realizes that he is smart: *I know that now because I can read and learn anything. I never been to mechanics school, but I bought a book and rebuilt a car. I never studied computers but when people have computer issues, they call me and I say, "Let me read up on it and I'll get back with you." I can grasp things like that. But in school I just never could.*

Sixteen was a pivotal year for Anthony. He dropped out of school, joined Job Corps, served his first adult sentence, next a juvenile sentence, then was arrested on the rape charge that would, by the age of seventeen, send him to prison for twenty-five years.

Job Corps, in his description, was both a wonderful reprieve from some of the strains of his life in Atlanta and a fertile training ground for advanced criminal behavior. He had joined to study electrical wiring and plumbing, and to avoid prosecution for a burglary charge. He liked the mountain setting in Franklin, North Carolina and Job Corps felt similar to foster care, although the young men in it came from up and down the Atlantic coast and were older and more aggressive. His Atlanta peers were cowed. Anthony was not. In the style he had perfected from his foster care experience, he asked who was the baddest dude around and promptly picked a fight—which he won. This established his standing among his peers but had the unexpected, to Anthony, consequence of expulsion from the program. He talked his way back in by agreeing to avoid other altercations because he liked the quiet and cleanliness of the mountains.

But his basic values and lifestyle remained unquestioned. He was not alone. The occasional visits to Atlanta were orgies of delinquency: *Imagine this. A hundred kids out of the mountains, brought to Atlanta and let off the bus with a "Meet us back in six hours." People ended up with life sentences. We were able to come to the city, do whatever we want, get out on the bus and be out of sight for months. For the criminal mind it was a perfect opportunity, so we would come with plans—we're going to rob this, break into this, and that's how we came down to Atlanta.*

On one of these trips, Anthony was arrested for a "snatch burglary." Sent to adult jail, he responded exactly as he had in foster care and Job Corp. "Now I'm in the big boy game. I'm sixteen. I look like a girl, so now its time to man up. So I go in fighting." Anthony immediately attacked the jail inmate in charge of his cell and was put in the hole, a closet sized room with no windows, a hole in the floor for a toilet, a mattress for a bed. He contemplated suicide but there were no means available. His court-appointed lawyer didn't ask his age and he was tried as an adult and was given a year, six and a half months of which he served in jail.

When he came out, he tried to go back to a foster home, but they told him he was too old: *So I'm sixteen, homeless and I have a felony. No skills. Can't read and write. Don't know where my family at. I started stealing everything I could. Petty crime. Breaking into stores. Breaking into people's houses. Got a job helping rebuild this guy's house. I would live in the house while we doing the job.*

He was arrested for one of these burglaries, but this time was sent to juvenile. While there, watching the news one night he heard an announcement that a woman named Annie May had been beaten to death. She was his sister. His girlfriend was able to enlist the help of the chaplain, and Anthony was allowed out for the funeral. This allowed him to meet the rest of his family, most of whom he hadn't seen since he was seven. This reunion simply deepened his involvement in crime: *Two of my brothers had just gotten out of prison that week. One of them had did ten years, the other had did fifteen, and we all got out at the same time. Their mentality no better than mine. The three of us together, we can make stuff happen. You know, I want to be part of the family. I said sure, whatever, I'm down. So I became sort of the enforcer for the family.*

Then Anthony started dating a fifteen-year-old girl, and was caught in bed with her by her irate mother, a police officer. At first the charge was sexual assault, which was then raised to rape. Anthony claims their relationship was consensual and that if in the early 1980s they had had rape kits, there would have been no signs of force. At first he didn't understand the seriousness of the charge: *At the time, I didn't see it as a big deal. The rape was only one crime. They could have sent me to prison for any number of things that I did. I didn't know sexual assault was a major life-changing situation. All that mean is I got me some. But by the time I went to court it was rape. Twenty-five years in prison.*

When it came time to go to trial, just before they began to choose the jury, the judge called a recess and called Anthony into his chambers: *He said, "Look man, you ain't but seventeen. If you go to trial now, they will give you life. Look, go ahead and plead guilty. I'll give you a twenty-year sentence. You'll do maybe five in and fifteen on probation. Now, if you tell anyone we had this conversation I'm going to deny it to my grave." I say, "I understand."*

So we go out there. I pled guilty. He gave me twenty-five year. I'm like, good God almighty, that's not what he said. Remember, I got probation on another robbery, which was another five years. By the time I finished with the court system, I had 165 years total. And I'm mad to death. Can't read. Can't write. But I'm mad.

INCARCERATION & SURVIVAL

In Jackson, the diagnostic prison, Anthony behaved as he did in foster care and jail. He immediately attacked his white cellmate for calling him a nigger, then, as soon as he emerged from three weeks in the hole, he attacked his former cellmate's brother: "It made sense to me. I figure if my brother was there, I would have done the same thing. So I figure, let's get it out of the way."

He was promptly sent to Mount Vernon State Prison, which he described as an old school penitentiary. "They give you the same old speech, 'You think you're bad, we've seen worse. You're not bad. We break you here, we break you there.' Dadada." But more than the hard labor, Anthony's concern was self-protection. He ran into one of his previous co-defendants, someone even smaller than he. Anthony revealed at this point that at seventeen he was only 5'5", with a voice that was still changing, revising all our mental images of his behavior. "But super aggressive," he repeated. He used this aggression to protect his friend from sexual assault—which again sent him to the hole.

But the hole was not the worst place for Anthony, any more than high max and solitary would be later. It allowed him some respite from the need to be so constantly primed to fight. He had been so malnourished that he actually gained weight on the day-old ball of mashed oatmeal, okra, and poke salad he was fed once a day. When released, he immediately got into another fight, went back in the hole and again returned larger and stronger. "It was my trend."

Anthony did not restrict his aggression to fellow prisoners. He described why he attacked one officer: *He was new. Making comments you shouldn't make in prison. Referring to us as a group as "bitches," "criminals," "you ain't shit, if you get out of line, I'm going to—". . . daddadadah. So I'm sitting around looking at the old vets, they just sucking this up. And in my mind, that is slave mentality. And I say, "You all scared of this dude?" Officer is like, "You have something to say?" So I busted him in the mouth.*

When Anthony talked about his fights, he slipped easily back into his mindset at the time: *My situation in my mind was permanent, and I had to remove this threat.* As he spoke with us he viewed his behavior with some detachment and humor, but he also gave the impression that he still felt his choices, given the circumstances, were appropriate. His choices were no longer driven completely by force, however: *You have to establish your rules if you are going to survive in that environment. And my rules are: I don't snitch. I'm not afraid of anybody. I don't tolerate disrespect from anybody—it doesn't matter if you're an inmate, guard, or warden. And I don't steal people's stuff. I did my whole sentence like that. I tried to make sure that everybody knew that.*

After attacking the officer, Anthony was sent to Reidsville, the most notorious of Georgia's prisons. Reidsville was a very different environment and he had to reconsider his approach: *These dudes are killers and I know they are killers. I'm meeting people who been in prison twenty-five years already, two guys who have been there thirty-five years. I'm meeting guys who killed four people and six people. I'm meeting people who killed their family. I'm thinking, "Oh, this is serious. All I got is a rape. Now I have to step my game up." But I don't want to catch another sentence in prison. I don't want a murder charge in prison. But I got to strike fear in these guys in some kind of way or I got to establish a level of respect. And I did both.*

Anthony established respect by keeping his word: *If I told you I was going to be there in five minutes I was there in four minutes and fifty-eight seconds. And that goes a long way in prison. If I told you I was going to do you, you know you're going to get done.*

The other way Anthony established respect was to offer to fight the biggest man in prison, Big Bubba, who was six-feet six-inches and weighed 280 pounds. Anthony explained his reasoning to his opponent: *"If you beat my ass, everybody expect it. If I win, nobody will beat my ass as long as I'm in prison. Let's fight."* We fought and he beat my ass. Last fight I ever fought. This *was the respect thing.*

Another important collateral benefit of the fight was that he started being mentored by a fellow prisoner, Iceman, who was skilled in karate, and served as a trainer for the prison CERT teams. Anthony learned martial arts, jujitsu, karate, and boxing. "I already had heart," he said. "Now I had skill."

Anthony wanted respect from the administration as well. He had earned their fear. By this time he had a history of five assaults on officers: "My rule with the officers was the same as with everybody. You don't treat me with respect, I'm coming to get you." When an officer called him "inmate," he reacted: "Wait a minute. My name isn't inmate. I can never allow anyone to call me that." He ended up fighting two officers, then an entire CERT team: "So, they take me in the elevator and try to beat me but there were so many of them in that little space, they couldn't really hurt me." He was taken to the fourth floor, but protected from the officers who wanted payback by a very old prisoner whom he had helped early in his stay at the prison, who announced, "'You can fight me, but I'm not going allow you to go in and jump on that kid.' So, he saved me," Anthony observed. "I started learning from this. If you do good things for people, they tend to come back. They don't come back right away, but—"

HIGH MAX & SELF ACTUALIZATION

SAFETY: Anthony was put on high max for five years for assaulting the officers: "High max, you spend twenty-three hours in your cell, come out for one hour. But it was cool because now I'm focusing on me." It may indeed be that Anthony was able to develop a measure of insight because when he was in high max he didn't have to focus on physical threats in his immediate environment. He would say that when he came off high max the first time (he went twice, each time for five years), "I was ready in the sense that I knew prison wasn't going to break me."

Anthony also began to be more introspective now that he felt that his safety was more secure: *When you go through prison you go through stages. I didn't know it until I was there. First you have the disbelief—twenty-five years! Then you got the anger. Then you get to the self-pity—Nobody care about me, nobody send me any money. Nobody even know I'm here. You go through that depression thing. And then you say, "Fuck it, I'm going to do me. So what is it I need to do? I'm going to get my body in better shape and I'm going to learn how to read and write."*

LITERACY: Anthony wanted to learn to read and write because without these skills he was not able to act in his own defense in the penal system. For example, when he entered prison, he had a 165-year sentence. A white inmate he met at Jackson, one he had defended from rape (not because he liked him but because he disliked the men ganging up on him), had read about his trial and sentencing and told him to write the Sentencing Review Panel to ask that his sentence be reviewed because the sentence seemed disproportionate for a first adult felony conviction. Anthony didn't feel he could admit that he couldn't read or write, so responded noncommittally. Picking up on the reason for his hesitance, the inmate wrote to the review panel for him. The appeal was successful and Anthony's sentence was reduced to twenty-five years.

On high max, Anthony learned to read by following the advice of a fellow inmate: *He say, "Read something you like. Read a fuck book. There's going to be a lot of oohs and aahs, but I guarantee you'll like it and finish the whole book." And he's right, I finished the whole book! But it made sense. It still makes sense: Read something you like.*

LEARNING: Anthony experienced an intellectual awakening that would be startling anywhere: *So I started reading these books. Then I bought me a dictionary and began reading about different words. Then I started watching the news and really listening to what they were saying and when they said a word I didn't know, I'd look it up. And then we started like little debates about politics and social situations. I'm still mediator. I'm still somebody you don't fuck with. But now I'm becoming more intellectual. Then I find that my favorite subject in the whole world is Greek mythology. Yeah, trip me out! The very first Greek book I read was The Iliad. Then I had to read The Odyssey. Then I had to read Dante. And then Lucretius. Then I got into Kant, a German philosopher. Then Nostradamus. Then I started getting into math. I would study fractions for three months, then algebra for three months, then geometry or trigonometry for four months.*

COMMUNITY: This intellectual drive became, improbably, a shared experience. *We started a class where we were teaching other guys. There were forty of us on high max and out of that only two had their GED. We made a neighborhood challenge. "We got to be here, so lets do something with it. We going to make sure everybody can get their GED." So at nine o'clock we're going to turn all the televisions off (televisions don't go off until 11) and we're all going to study. Whoever is good at whatever subject, you teach that subject. And the rest of you going to shut up and learn something. My theme was math, so I taught math on Monday. Another guy was good in history, and he taught history. We did that for months. Then it was about time for some of us to start coming off of high max, so we said, look we got to take that test. But we agreed we were all going to take it at the same time. So we called the schoolteacher over and everyone passed except for one person.*

CHARACTER, CRIMINALITY, ENVIRONMENT

Anthony began to wonder what it was that led some people to prison and others not. *I started looking at my environment—this guy's locked up for child molestation, this guy's locked up for double murder, this guy killed his whole family, I'm locked up for rape. And whenever we got to debating, I would say, "Look, we all came from different environments, but we all ended up right here. How the fuck is that possible?"*

"What do you mean? We all got caught."

"Yeah, but we different. You went to school, you went to college. You had a mama and daddy." *It never made sense to me how all these people with different personalities and different situations ended up right here. So it had to be some common thread. And then it was, I'm just like these dudes. I'm aggressive. I'm selfish. So I saw those things as what brought us to this fucked up place. So, yeah, I saw them as character flaws.*

This line of inquiry brought Anthony into conversation with the warden and the prison psychiatrist. One day Anthony stopped the warden as he passed the solitary cell in which Anthony was confined and said, "My mind isn't right in the sense that I can't understand: What makes me different from Ted Bundy? What makes me different from Charles Manson?"

"I don't know, you need to talk to a psychiatrist," the warden answered.

"Can you arrange it?" Anthony asked.

"I'll see what I can do." No psychiatrist appeared, so Anthony persisted, in his usual tactful fashion, the next time he saw the warden. "Hey Warden, I try to respect you as a man. But if you can't honor your word, you're a bitch."

"Who you calling a bitch?"

"Your actions are bitch-like. Because as a man, if I tell you I'm going to do something, it's done."

The psychiatrist soon appeared. He told Anthony he couldn't put him on the caseload because he wasn't officially classified as mental health. Anthony told him that was a matter of opinion but that he just had some questions and needed answers: *Every month you all come by our cells and ask us these simple questions: "Do you know what today's date is? Do you know who is the president of the United States? Are you OK?" And everybody here passed that test. But man, guys over here are throwing feces on each other. That can't be normal behavior.*

The psychiatrist said, "In this environment it is."

"See, that's one of my questions," Anthony went on. *When does it become acceptable to become your environment? I've been raised around criminals my whole life and for some reason I don't really fit. I've never done drugs, I don't drink, I don't abuse women. But I'm a criminal. How did that happen?*

So the psychiatrist started to give Anthony books to read about socially deviant behavior, showed him how psychological profiles of criminals were done. Anthony read but nothing felt like it fit his situation. Not until he read *The Odyssey* for the third time. The excitement he had felt at the time was still vibrant in his voice as he described that moment of insight: *It was when Odysseus had got so arrogant he stood up on a mountain and said, "I, Odysseus, conquered Troy." It made perfect sense to me then. Because I had made my whole life about me. My mom died when I was seven. I hadn't thought about her since I was eight. My brother died when I was six and I hadn't thought about him. That's when I started thinking, "I got to start bringing other things into my life. I've got to start being more empathetic toward other people's situations." It was already there. I think it is for everybody. But it can be forced out by hardship or circumstances, and I allowed it to be forced out.*

Anthony described why he felt the psychiatrist himself was only unintentionally helpful: *He was helpful without knowing he was helpful. His ignorance was helpful. Like I asked him, "How would you know if you was insane?" He said, "You wouldn't." I said, "Exactly." But he didn't understand. So I said, "So if you were insane, you would think you were sane and everybody else is crazy." He said, "Yeah." So I said, "So I'm not insane because I don't think the rest of you all is insane. I just think you all live life in a way that's totally foreign to me. So I don't think you're crazy. But I'm talking to a guy next door who is totally crazy because he think we all crazy except for him."*

ANGER MANAGEMENT: Anthony was required to take both anger management and substance abuse classes, although he never used drugs. He defined his own issue not as anger management but as anger abuse. Anger management was the closest he could come. But he objected when the instructor told him they needed to get away from "learned emotions, like anger and rage." Anthony disputed him, saying, "No, if anger was an emotion it would have to be innate. The behavior expressing anger would have to be learned." The instructor kicked him out of class, but later, taking a refresher training with the psychologist who developed the course, the instructor brought up Anthony's objection and the psychologist told him that Anthony was right. Anger was innate, its expressions learned. So, the instructor apologized to Anthony and gave him his certificate. Anthony accepted both, but told the instructor: "Man, if you only talk to people you agree with, you're not going to learn anything. You got to have that outside agitator, you know."

The instructor, impressed by the whole interchange, told him he was going to be OK. Anthony objected: "Right. I have twenty-five years in prison, I have nowhere to live, no education, no money and no family. How am I going to be all right?"

"You have logic," the instructor told him. "You're going to figure it out."

"And that's how I did my last ten years, " Anthony said.

FAITH: Anthony spent much of his remaining time in prison focusing on his spiritual life. He was drawn to Islam for three reasons: "Number one they were all black men and I needed to see that black men can do something other than what I had done. And in Islam you have to study, it's a requirement, and you are going to be tested on your knowledge and there is code of conduct and a code of ethics and I thought I needed all three of those."

But what he felt was the greatest contribution of his interest in Islam was that it exposed him to other religions as well: *You have to study so I started studying about Christianity and Judaism and Hinduism and Buddhism as well as Islam, and I came up with the conclusion that the Bible is one chapter in that big book, the Koran is another chapter in that big book, so that helps me expand as far as accepting other people.*

MENTORING: Anthony also started mentoring younger inmates about how to survive in prison: *I tell them, It's simple, man. This is prison. You're going to be here a while. Here's what you do. Don't snitch. Don't borrow money from anybody you don't think you can beat in a head-up fight. And never ever compromise your principles. Principles are like rubber bands, the more you stretch them, the weaker they get. So never ever, not one compromise. The best way to establish a solid core is to establish a solid body, so I would teach them how to work out and then I'd tell them, "A body is designed to carry something bigger, so now let's work on your brain."*

PURPOSE: Anthony had some advice for Corrections about how better to prepare people for reentry while in prison, especially the importance of positive expectations. Corrections, he said, like the military, breaks people down but, unlike the military, fails to build them back up: *It does a great job at destroying you but don't replace it with anything. If you come out just thinking "I got to survive," that's when you get back into what you were doing before. I had a great expectation when I came out: I'm going to succeed without causing other people detriment. People said how? I told them I don't know, but it won't be from sucking from people who don't have anything to give.*

Anthony pointed out that prison encourages negative emotions by depriving people of purpose: *The only emotion you really need in prison is anger and rage. That's all you need. You have to be ruthless and you have to stay mad at something. That again is a failing of the prison system: There's nothing to feel good about.*

Purpose gives us a sense of time and of future: *Once you give a person a purpose that regulates their time. You have no sense of time in prison. You have no sense of tomorrow or next year. If you have no sense of tomorrow, you have no expectations, if you have no expectations, you have no plans, you don't have a future. And that's how you spend every waking moment in prison. And then you come to society and that is the same mentality you deal with. When you see people out here robbing and killing, they have no sense of time, they have no plans. Society creates that when you totally disenfranchise people.*

Now a homeowner, Anthony pointed to HUD as an organization that helped shape and promote purpose. *Some organizations understand this. Like HUD, the housing thing, they understand this. I don't know if it was on a conscious level or if it was just happenstance, but once you establish a foundation with a person, HUD mandates certain things for a person. You have to be in a house for five years, so that's time. You have to maintain a house, so that's a purpose. So, I'm asking, did they luck up on this philosophy or did they read Kant?*

REENTRY

Anthony had been out of prison for six years when we talked to him. He was in a stable relationship, had stable housing and a steady job. On a personal basis he helped other people who were reentering and also worked with A.B.L.E. to help reduce structural barriers to reentry by such actions as Banning the Box. He was proud of what he had accomplished and was determined not to return to prison.

He still faced challenges controlling the expression of his emotions, especially if he felt he was being treated unfairly, but those expressions almost never involved physical violence although they often involved active, furious defiance. "I've been in prison twenty-five years. It was hard at first for me to maintain a job. I still had attitude. I was still defensive and argumentative."

Anthony obtained a union job at FedEx by applying online. A woman in Pennsylvania interviewed him. He immediately told her he had a history, but she asked him how old he was when it happened (sixteen) and how old he was now (fifty) and told him she would take a chance on him if he had a clean drug screen and a clean driver's license. He knew he wouldn't have gotten the job if he had applied directly in Georgia. He sometimes felt exasperated because others didn't work as hard as he and his co-worker Carlos, both ex-offenders with strong work ethics. But Carlos reminded him, when he was tempted to quit, "Bro it's not even about you. What about the next dude getting out of prison looking for a job and they use you as an excuse for why they won't hire him?"

Anthony identified two significant systemic barriers to his reentry: being listed on the sex offender registry and, more troubling, probation itself.

SEX OFFENDER REGISTRY

One of the difficulties with the constraints of the sex offender registry and sex offender probation is that they treat everyone as if they were an active predatory pederast, so the level of surveillance is formidable. This is especially difficult if the actual act was having consensual sex with a girl a year your junior. Even though a judge had informed Anthony that the extensive state probation surveillance conditions for sex offenders didn't apply to him because his conviction predated them by fifteen years, he was registered on the federal sex offender registry because it was retroactive by thirty years.

There is a psychological impact to being on the registry that exceeds direct surveillance, which Anthony expressed poignantly. In his mind, listing on the sex registry effectively barred him from having children: *The best I can tell you is I never molested a child in my life. I hate having this sex offense because when I first got out of prison, all they talked about was stay away from churches, stay away from daycare and they said it so much and they bring so much authority behind it—like I'll send you back to prison for life—that I started to think, "Maybe I am a child molester." And I started avoiding kids.*

And then I thought, "This isn't even life." If you take away the political, the economic aspect of how we're living, life basically comes down to growing up, having kids, or if you can't have kids, watching other kids grow up. And that's the sense of time and purpose. I love watching kids, I love hearing them giggle. We live in a townhouse in a cul de sac. Across from us is a subdivision. You can hear kids playing, laughing. I leave the windows up so I can hear. But I think, I can't even indulge in that cause I'm registered as a sex offender and they have me so scared.

It lasts forever. Forever. I don't have kids. Shandra, my wife, she knows I would make a great father. But I can't. I don't want my child up under that "Did he touch you?" That's one of the real barriers for me.

PROBATION

But even more challenging to Anthony was his relationship to probation—one that he believed, with some objective confirmation, was designed to push him back into prison. He felt that their actions and attitudes were, like prison itself, exclusively focused on breaking him down, proving that he was innately criminal. He was determined to prove them wrong. This struggle started as soon as he was released:

When I first got out of prison I had forty-eight hours to report to probation. Remember, I don't have a car. I don't have any money. But I got to get there. So I get there. He says, "How things going?"

I say, "They're OK. But I don't have any place to stay. I've been gone for twenty-five years. I don't have any money. I don't have a job."

So this probation officer, this protector of the public interest, says to me, "I don't give a fuck. You can live up under a bridge for all I care, but just give me the address of the bridge you live up under."

Anthony was determined to prove his officer wrong: *The next time he saw me, I had a car. The next time he saw me, I had a job. The next time he saw me, I had two cars. And the next time he saw me, I had two cars, two jobs, and a house. So each time he saw me, it was like I didn't give a fuck either. So he started telling his supervisor, "Anthony is too arrogant."*

At the beginning they had me so scared. I would walk down the street and people would come up to me and say, "You just got out, didn't you?" "How you know?" It was my whole persona. I go into a store and I'm afraid to touch anything, even if I want to read it. I said, "Fuck, they making me into what they want me to be."

So I went into there one day and—again I don't recommend this to everybody—the probation officer begin every meeting the same way, "Now you know we can send you back to prison, right?" Every month. Every month. So one day, I just said, "Fuck you. Do what you're going to do." He said, "Huh?"

"Man I work two jobs, I bought two cars and I bought a house. I'm engaged to be married. Nigger, I'm doing better than you. What the fuck am I trying to do running around trying to live up to your expectations for me for?"

So he called his supervisor. This is how they decide to break you. They come in, they got their hands on their gun. "Who is it?" Now I have seven probation officers, with guns, standing around me. "We could send you back to prison."

I say, "Man, like I told him, fuck you all. Do what you going to do." The head probation officer, they call him chief, he say, "What's your judge name? I'm going to call him." I say, "That mother-fucker dead. He fucked up my life and died. I don't give a fuck about him. I don't give a fuck about you. You not going to make me what you want me to be. I ain't going to be no homeless, begging bum scared out of his wits because you niggers" (because there won't nobody but black men around me) "want some power. Now I'm going to live my life or you can send me back to prison."

They sent me home.

Anthony had gained the enmity of his probation officer. So when sometime later he had to leave his apartment on short notice on a Friday evening, even though he informed his officer he was leaving and would call him Monday to give him a new address, the officer first thing Monday morning had a warrant sworn out for his arrest. (The rule is you must inform your officer of a change of residence before moving.) Anthony spent $4,800 to hire a lawyer to represent him at a probation revocation hearing "because I don't have any rights in a probation revocation hearing." But Anthony was not without support.

The probation officer said, "He quit his job and we don't want him to. We want to revoke two years." The judge say, "OK."

They say, "We hear rumors he's using drugs, he's staying out all night partying."

But if you have a lawyer they have to let him speak. My lawyer said, "Your honor, my client works two jobs." (I work at the Kroger warehouse 1 a.m. to 12 p.m. the next day, then go home, shower, eat something and go to a part-time job at FedEx for two and a half hours, then I go home, shower, eat again and go to sleep and get ready for the night. I did this every night for seven-eight months.)

My lawyer say, "Your honor, my client has never used drugs. You can test him now."

The supervisors from both my jobs came to court. My ex-girl came to court. The first person that gave me a job came to court. The judge was so mad, he finally gave me a turn to speak.

I said, "Your honor, the probation department is not trying to help anybody reenter or acclimate to society. Their job is to take my manhood, take my self-esteem, take my pride and stomp on it and make me desperate enough to go back to prison." Then I started to tell him about the things they were saying and doing.

The judge was so mad, he said, "From now on Mr.L__ you never have to report to them again. If they want to see you, they have to come to you. And if you're not there, they have to call and make an appointment with you."

Anthony's challenges with probation continued and put a heavy toll on his relationship with his partner. *Before we even got into a relationship, Shandra and I went out and I said, "Listen, I'm a good person. And I'm a good man. But there are going to be outside pressures on our relationship. The question is going to be if you can handle them. You're going to say yeah, yeah right now. But I explain to you, precious, they going to come from the police, they going to come from the probation officers because they know that one of the main ingredients to keep people from reoffending are strong community ties, personal relationships, and a job. They can't just go into the jobs anymore and say, 'I'm just coming in to see about Anthony. He's under probation care.' And then they'd fire you. They can't do that anymore, so they go after the relationship."*

My probation officer right now calls Shandra almost every week and asks her, "Are you OK? How is Mr.L __?" And Shandra says, "Why that woman keep calling me?" And I tell her, "Her job is to create outside pressure on the relationship to the point you want to break up with me."

Now Shandra beginning to understand it. One night, about one o'clock, we both asleep and the police come and bang on the door—boom boom boom— and we got three floors. So on this particular night we're on the third floor. I go downstairs. There are about nine police cars there. With their lights on. They hiding behind walls and the bushes with their hands on the guns. "You Anthony?"

"Yes."

"Just checking to see you're home."

"What the fuck?" There are nine cars out there. "Why you all doing this?"

They just walk off.

The next day, we went to the police station and made a complaint and they ain't been back but that's the kind of outside pressures I told her were going to come because I know how this system works. It is not designed to help me stay in society.

Anthony when he started his interview emphasized that what he really wanted to achieve through his story was to have "the emotional content of reentry to be exposed." The reasons for some of these actions will surely be differently interpreted by probation—some are from their point of view simply procedural requirements they have no control over. With the new Department of Community Supervision, which has a more rehabilitative stance, the abusive nature of the interactions has probably toned down considerably. But these procedural requirements do have relational costs that work strongly against effective reentry—ones that Anthony has described vividly—and that have practical costs for us as a society. As stringently as Anthony asked himself in prison whether criminality was innate or learned, we have to ask ourselves, if *recidivism* is innate or learned—and, if so, who is doing the teaching?

We are richer for having in our midst someone with Anthony's resistance, which is also resilience, intelligence, insight, passion for self-improvement, and a defiant and noble commitment against all the predictions, all the odds, to living a richly productive life *without causing detriment to others*. Anthony's anger remains a powerful challenge of him and those around him, especially those tasked with monitoring his reentry. But what would we as a society have lost if he had ever agreed to take himself at society's estimation as stupid, worthless, unwanted, and innately bad?

❨6❩

NEVER TOO LATE: FREQUENT CYCLERS & DESISTANCE
JOE, MARILYNN

Much frustration and defeatism accompany the reality of repeated recidivism. Chronic, low-level crimes can dramatically damage the quality of life for residents. They fray people's sense of safety and community, destroy trust and patience. An enraged Kasim Reed, when mayor of Atlanta, formed a frequent-offender commission to look at the issue. The commission is revived periodically, mayor after mayor, whenever outrage is great in the wealthier parts of the city. Recidivism is an issue that often sets police and prosecutors at odds with an urban judiciary they think too lenient. In Reed's case, the mayor was particularly incensed about a specific magistrate judge who he felt was unduly permissive, publicly chastising him by name. This was intriguing because we heard this judge's name soon after in a very different context, as one of the people who played a pivotal role in helping Marilynn turn her life around. Another judge, known as "Hanging Hancock" by many of the people we talked with because of his intolerance for crime and most especially *excuses* for crime, particularly black on black crime, unexpectedly played a similar role in the life of Joe. Both Joe and Marilynn's stories invite us to look at recidivist careers a little differently, making room for genuine hope.

Given the length of their criminal careers, the turn arounds of Joe and Marilynn are striking. Both stopped in their late 50's—but their changes in behavior and attitude and purpose were not driven exclusively by age. They were *met* in their desire to change, even with seemingly intractable patterns of recidivism.

JOE
I had to change all my thinking

Joe has a wonderful sense of style. He always showed up for support group meetings and for interviews with his outfits beautifully coordinated from his Muslim kufi hats to his colorful shirts and his tone perfect shoes. There is a vitality and unforced charm about him that make him feel deeply trustworthy, a valid impression and also an improbable mystery, one that he willingly pondered during our interview.

"From 1970 to 2002, I never spent more than twelve months out of prison," he said. "I have more than thirty-five felonies on my record." He thought he has been treated easy by the criminal justice system—and by society. Inexplicably released ahead of time on several sentences, he also was given the easiest jobs in prison, "never out there on the roads." "My children love me to death," he said with a puzzled smile. "Go figure."

Policemen shared his bafflement at the positive turn his life had taken: *A policeman stop me now when I'm driving, I know he will come back from his car with a puzzled look on his face and ask, "What you been up to these last ten years?" He'll have checked my record and will see there's been nothing these last twelve years, no arrest, nothing.*

Joe, at fifty-six, turned his life around, contrary to even his most loyal advocates' predictions. He gave up heroin and cocaine, began work as an addictions counselor with a group that focused on pretreatment for homeless, HIV-positive individuals with addiction problems.

At sixty-eight, when we talked to him, Joe was vigorous, muscular, unlined. His body showed little visible toll from his long addiction. Perhaps his extensive prison time protected him, reducing his access to drugs and their depleting effects, we suggested. He quickly rejected the idea: "Some of the strongest stuff I shot up, I got in prison, stuff you can't even get on the street."

Oddly, given the strength and longevity of his addictions, none of Joe's convictions were for drugs. They were all for theft of one kind or another. None were violent. "It they was, I'd be there now," he said matter of factly.

How and why Joe came out and stayed out, working steadily and contributing constructively to society after a thirty-year pattern of habitual recidivism that put him in Georgia state prison eight times and federal prison twice wasn't, he insisted, explained by his getting sober, rather by changing his thinking, which he believed to be the root cause of both his addiction and his criminal behavior. He invited us to think about causes and consequences a little differently as well, favoring something less linear and more vivid, faith-filled and bemused.

EARLY INFLUENCES

Joe described his childhood as happy, secure, and relatively privileged for a young black boy growing up in the fifties primarily in rural Georgia. Joe was born in Atlanta, the oldest of four siblings and the only boy. His father never lived with them. When Joe was six, his mother decided he would be better off in the country and sent him to live with her sister. Joe's aunt raised him from age six to sixteen. He didn't feel abandoned by his mother because she visited often, and he would go to Atlanta to see her.

His aunt worked in the home of a wealthy family, the Nolans, working sequentially for both father and son. The Nolans were very appreciative of Joe's aunt, who was their cook and nanny. "They treated me real nice. I'd eat there, watch television." The racial divisions weren't as sharp as in Atlanta: "Racism was real prevalent, but I played on the same street with white kids."

Joe was always a thrill-seeker. "I learned how to shoot pool real good. Gambling, hustling, I was really good. That's how I survived." He was also a talented athlete and was invited by a scout to go to a farm school for a semi-pro team when he was fifteen. He had his mother's permission, but broke his arm a week before he was scheduled to go.

By high school, he was completely disinterested in school and was getting locked up for gambling. His aunt's employer would call the jail and tell them to let him out. "I was kind of omnipotent," Joe observed. He kept getting in trouble and going to jail. By the time he was fourteen or fifteen, he was accustomed to having a hundred dollars in his pocket. "I could throw dice, cheat with cards. I was known for that. Hustlers saw potential in me and taught me about crooked dice and we would win money together. I had a taste for it." He dropped out of school.

Mr. Nolan began suggesting that he might be better off back in Atlanta. The job prospects Joe saw weren't many and some he flatly rejected: "I wasn't going to work in the fields. Some people drove trucks or worked in grocery stores, but most of them worked in the fields."

Crime seemed more profitable. He was already an experienced thief: *I started stealing at an early age. I would sell bottles and make money. I would take bottles from the back door and then take them back in the front door and sell them. I would sell the store eggs. Sold them and then stole them back. The man there would stutter, "By the time you're twenty-one, you're going to prison."*

It was when Joe began to question some of the more basic structures of society that his problems with law enforcement increased. When an African-

American girl was shot by police and paralyzed, Joe openly asked, "Are we just going to let people shoot us and not do something?" Word got back to the police and they went to Joe's aunt and told her, "Get him out from down here."

Joe began to engage more seriously with the criminal justice system. His aunt's employer was no longer able to protect him: *They placed a theft on me and put me in juvie. Mr. Nolan said to let me out. It was a kangaroo court. But I was friends with all the white guys. We played together. The sheriff's grandson came to court for me, so they had to turn me loose. But Mr. Nolan told my aunt, "If you don't send him back, they'll do something to him."*

CRIMINAL CAREER & INCARCERATION

Back in Atlanta, Joe did not go to school. His mother had very limited education herself, but Joe described her as a very hard worker. Joe wasn't. He began drinking heavily and going out to clubs. His first serious brush with the law came after he started fighting at a club, and in the ensuing melee, his best friend was shot and killed. Joe was locked up for "malicious mischief" but felt his friend's death was his fault. From that point, he began to get seriously caught up in drugs. He began serving his first prison sentence in 1970 and continued with less than a year between sentences for the next thirty-two years.

Joe could never complete probation, but in prison he was an ideal prisoner. He received parole several times because of that. When he was in federal prison, he was allowed to work outside the walls, one of the very few allowed this privilege. Joe described why he and prison were a good fit: *I was always obedient in my conduct. I could always do the right thing when people watching. I call that people pleasing. Prison was a way of life—I was comfortable in prison. I had soft-shoe jobs—I cut hair, was a dorm orderly. It was my comfort zone. I knew that's not where I wanted to be, but I made the best of it.*

CONVERSION & RECOVERY

Joe's attitude toward his constant recidivism began to change in 2002 when he was introduced to Islam. "I began to see my life a little different. My understanding about who I was and what God was like changed." This became clearer to him after he returned to prison in 2004. At this point he had converted. Brother John Mohammed, the Muslim prison chaplain who had introduced Joe to Islam said to him, "Sometimes when I see you coming back, I wonder about the message I'm giving you."

Joe's response was interesting, and had to do with people pleasing and also something more: *It hurt me to think he was downing himself because of me. I told him, "Mohammed worried about his people too. God gave the message clear. It was not the message that was the problem, it was the vehicle." But he stuck by me.*

Joe stuck by himself as well, with some recidivism: *When I got out in 2004, I was doing some stuff and I made my mind up. I knew Muslims out on the street who had changed their life. I went into treatment. I knew drugs were not my problem. My problem was my thinking. If you don't figure out why you using—if you don't change your thinking, your thinking will change you. Islam had changed my thinking. I went to Narcotics Anonymous. A guy there said, "You won't make it." But if someone says I can't—I stayed clean for six months just to prove it. Then I spent three days getting high.*

Joe began to understand recovery through Islam: *The Koran says, "Come not to prayer intoxicated." We are caliphs, caretakers. My life is entrusted to me. I was not a good custodian. A brother asked me, "Do you love yourself?" I said yes. But he answered, "You can't love yourself and try to kill yourself at the same time." I was disobedient to God. God's mercy extended over me. I had to change all my thinking. I could see all my thinking was bad. When I left drugs, I never committed another crime. If I change my thinking, I change my behavior, and I change my outcome. I began to hate crime.*

Stealing was a way of my life for me, but I never thought of the person I was stealing from. I thought of myself as a Robin Hood but I was stealing because I was an addict. It was when the first car I ever bought was stolen, that I realized the impact. My NA sponsor said, "Now you can see." I probably caused people to lose their jobs by what I did.

Joe identified other areas where his thinking began to change. In prison, he had been a bit of a Lothario, writing many lonely women who, when he was released, would take care of him. He began to see that "People are not objects. You can mess up a lot of people. I was just lying to them."

His sense of causality was distorted by drugs as well: *When you start using drugs, they numb you. You stop feeling. You become hard. There's animalistic stuff. Urinating in the street like a dog. Something has really happened to you. Living in an abandoned house, you get mad at the police for stopping you from living in that mess. When I got clean, I realized that it was my thinking. Last time I went to prison, it was because I had a stolen car with stolen stuff in it and I was driving*

*on a one-way street. On my way to prison, I was thinking that the only reason I
was going to prison was because I drove down a one-way street!*

Joe found that as his thinking cleared, emotional clarity returned: *I
began to understand the person I was—a human being that breathed and felt and
cared about people. I wasn't taught to mistrust people or steal. My aunt raised four
or five kids on twenty dollars a week. I never went hungry. It was imbedded in me
to do the right thing. I had covered that up. What got into me was the guidance
about what I am here for. I knew I could do better, that the outer reflects the inner.
Conscience was awake in me, but you got to listen to it. God isn't going to tell you
to do something detrimental.*

Another reason that Joe may have turned his life around at this point
was that he did not want his mother to die while he was in prison. *My father,
aunt, cousin and niece all died while I was in prison, and I never could go to the
funeral. Last time I was out my mother had cancer and I prayed, "Please God
don't let me be in prison when my mom pass." And I wasn't. My mother had
Alzheimer's. She couldn't talk. She had throat cancer and a laryngectomy twenty-
one years earlier. But when I did get out, she remembered I was her son. My sister,
who took care of her all those years, she said, "She love you more." I told her, "I
gave her more trouble." We all there together with her the day before she died. I
was free. My prayers were answered.*

Reentry

Through his drug program, Joe became involved with a group called
Recovery Consultants of Atlanta. They were responsible for outreach to the
homeless population, providing HIV testing and prevention and treatment
for men and women. The first time he went out, Joe showed that he was
very effective at reaching the population: "We come from the same place,"
he explained. "In one day, we got more people off the street and in treatment
than anyone else had in a month."

They began to focus on pretreatment since there was difficulty getting
people into detox if they were homeless. Pretreatment was designed to help
eradicate barriers between the individual and treatment, getting them food
stamps, IDs, testing for TB and HIV status, and providing drug education.
Identifying the right program to send them to was, "Treat right, not alike."

At this point, Joe faced his final challenge. He had a misdemeanor
charge in DeKalb County, but because of his record it was raised to a felony,
so he was again facing ten years, this time for theft by taking. Because he was

in treatment and also working with Recovery Consultants, Joe questioned the sentence: *I walked in with the understanding that they were going to give me ten-years-do-eight, but then it change to ten-years-do-seven, to ten-do-one, to ten-do-six-months. I had an advocate saying I was in recovery and was eleven-months clean. Judge Hanging Hancock said ten-do-one. I raised my hand. "I got to go to jail?"*

"What makes you think you deserve probation?" the judge asked. "I earned it," I told him. "I walked into this courtroom. I got a job. The work I do, people turn their nose at, working with HIV and the homeless. I am an asset."

He gave me six months in jail. That was March 21st. That day they hired me to be the first Resident Manager for the program. I turned myself in that Friday. I was out August 6th and went to work. In September I was at the White House representing guys in recovery. They served me. George Bush was there.

GIVING BACK

Family: Paying back was important to Joe. *I took so much. I hurt a lot of people. I have three grown kids. None of my children have criminal convictions. I just went to my granddaughter's recital. I keep her sometimes for my daughter. My son is married. He has no biological kids but he raised three kids. Maybe because his father wasn't there for him. Everything you do affects others. I have a sister who is a University of Georgia graduate. She came to visit me and told me, "I never talked about you when I was in school. I was around people who were telling about their brothers' successes. Who want to tell people your brother is in prison, living in abandoned houses?" Now she wants to tell everyone about me.*

Peer Support: Joe was one of the founding members of the reentry support group PIIC. Joe thinks of PIIC as a place where people can come to find shelter, food, clothing and "a place where people look like them." He also felt that they could play an important role in reducing the culture shock associated with reentry, helping people reduce institutionalized behaviors that weren't helpful: "You need to understand that people who may rush by you and jostle you in the MARTA are not trying to disrespect you."

Joe mused on the different responses people have to felony convictions: *In the Masjid, people don't want you to talk about your past. It's over. Who you are now is what matters. You never hear a grounded Muslim giving a confession. But in society as a whole, they never stop looking at your past. Politicians, the law. I can get arrested now, and they can see the whole record.*

Institutional Support: Completing probation was a major triumph: *I was* *on ten years of unsupervised probation. When they cut the ankle bracelet off, my probation officer, she's a police now, brought eight to ten police down to the Gateway to see me. I reported every month on time, paid money on time, never tested positive. Three years ago, they told me, "You don't need to report no more." I started walking out and I broke down and cried. I had never been able to follow rules on the street. But I completed probation.*

We were able to observe in the following years how Joe successfully handled multiple stressors, most importantly losing his job at Recovery Consultants because of the expiration of the grant he was employed under. The discipline he discovered in himself held; he maintained his sobriety, and after a year of unemployment again found several jobs as a substance abuse counselor. During that challenging period he continued his work with the PIIC support group and also informally volunteered his services as a counselor with people at his masjid whose families had members with addiction issues.

Judge "Hanging" Hancock

Several of the people we interviewed had appeared before Judge Michael Hancock, a semi-retired Superior Court judge when we talked with him. He had gained his nickname of "Hanging Hancock" from defendants because of his reputation as a strict no-excuses judge. We asked the judge if he ever got the sense from male black defendants that he as an African American might be more understanding and lenient with them. His response was emphatic: "It does not work with me." In fact, precisely because he had "encountered some of the same experiences they have," Judge Hancock believes "we do more harm than we realize in terms of giving folks excuses" or maintaining "low expectations."

Young defendants facing this distinguished-looking older judge probably don't realize that he came from difficult circumstances himself. Judge Hancock grew up in rural northeast Georgia. At the age of nineteen he was already a father, living in a two-room shotgun house, using the back porch as a refrigerator in the dead of winter. He bought a cheap coal-burning stove with a crack in it that would send soot particles into the air. *I would go to work and to school with specks of soot on my clothes and smelling like burned coal.*

As a teenager he knew life on the streets and some of his friends from that period did do time in prison. Judge Hancock gave major credit to his mother for helping him to stay on the right path, raising him with "the Bible in one hand and the switch in the other." He also benefited from a supportive extended family, including one aunt who "started teaching us before we went to school." It was this emphasis on education that "kept the fire burning and is what gave me the motivation to charge on and get on through school."

Because of this background—both his growing up years and his service as public defender—Judge Hancock felt grounded in his judgments: *I know the games. I talk the language and I know the mentality. I have not too much patience with folks who come in and right off the bat say, I do bad things because of prior circumstances or because my mom or my dad is a drug addict and I have been a latch-key kid. I don't buy into that.*

This did not mean that Judge Hancock was a believer of "lock'em up and throw away the key." Speaking of lengthy imprisonment, he pointed out that "it gets to a point where its effectiveness is lost and bitterness is bred." Consequently, he has "never liked the idea of mandatory minimum sentencing." As a judge, *There always is the hope anybody you sentence is going someday to see the light and turn their life around. But it makes it less likely the longer they are confined.*

MARILYNN

I wanted to work. I wanted to have a career and retire.

When we spoke with Marilynn she was in her mid-sixties. We first saw her in action in the spring of 2013 at a meeting in Atlanta of the Reformed Citizens Committee of the 9 to 5 National Association of Working Women, an organization dedicated to achieving economic justice for low-income women who are directly impacted by employment discrimination. Marilynn, a chapter organizer, had started the committee some years earlier to address employment discrimination against the formerly incarcerated. She had just succeeded in having a Ban-the-Box ordinance passed in the city of Atlanta after a two-year campaign. The governor was about to announce an executive order that extended the ban to state employment applications. Dedicated to lasting change, Marilynn wasn't satisfied. She wanted to start a statewide campaign that would allow other major cities to do the same as Atlanta and also lead to legislation making the executive order into law. She was envisioning train-the-trainer sessions in the cities with the largest populations of formerly incarcerated: Macon, Albany, Savannah, Augusta. By the end of the meeting, everyone had an idea of what they needed to do to lobby people in DeKalb County to complete its Ban-the-Box initiative, what the larger statewide campaign was going to look like, and how they might expand this to private employers. Most importantly, each of them had offered to take a part, large or small, in making this happen. They were all invited into a group photograph to seal their participation; Marilynn, with laryngitis, stood in the middle smiling confidently.

In the years since our interview, Marilyn joined forces with former Soros fellow Xochitl Bervera to found Women on the Rise, an activist group of formerly incarcerated women. Their latest cause has been closing the decrepit Atlanta jail, a goal they accomplished in June 2019 through a multi-faceted campaign that dramatically reduced jail populations.

Marilyn didn't hesitate when asked if these skills were ones she had also used in her long criminal career: *Sure. What I did was take the skills, the conning, the scheming, whatever you do in the illegitimate life and flipped them over and used them in a positive life. Those are same skills—organizing, lobbying, planning.*

What was striking with Marilynn was the combination of fierce and unapologetic survival drive and an equally tenacious yearning for middle-class stability, which found its expression in a desire for the most prosaic and basic building block of that life—stable employment: *I didn't want to be behind the bars or behind the fence. I wanted to see trees. I wanted to work. I wanted to have a career and retire. Not be working like I am now on a mass incarceration campaign. But I wasn't allowed to. If I told the truth, there went the job. I always knew once they do the background check, it was over. It was scary. I was always under false pretenses. I was always waiting for someone to lower the boom. That's why I'm so transparent today. I don't have to worry. There will always be options. I do believe I can get a job now. My background is my background and I've learned to make my background be an asset to me rather than a liability.*

EARLY INFLUENCES

Marilynn grew up in the Old Fourth Ward in Buttermilk Bottom, which she described as the first ghetto in Atlanta. She and her mother weren't close. Marilynn's mother was black, but Marilynn had lighter skin and hazel eyes. Her mother told her, "Ever since you were in the world, I had my head down." Not only was Marilynn seen as a source of shame, she was also a source of deprivation: *Mother didn't receive welfare because she was accused of sleeping with a white man. So she had to work two jobs. I rarely saw her. Not only was my mother shunned, I was shunned. I couldn't play with the girls, but I could play with the boys. So I grew up sexually abused, verbally abused, and emotionally abused.*

Marilynn was raised primarily by her grandmother, who taught her to steal. On Fridays, they would meet Marilynn's grandfather with his paycheck at the grocery store. Marilynn would ask for things in the store, and her grandmother would say, "OK, but get rid of it before we get to the counter." This created a sense of both secrecy and entitlement. As Marilynn described it, laughing, "It mold me to think I could have anything in there, just had to get rid of it before I got to the counter." That she was *taught* to steal is a very important point to Marilynn and one she returned to several times in her interview.

CRIMINAL CAREER & MIDDLE CLASS ASPIRATIONS

As a juvenile, Marilynn was arrested for shoplifting. Since she hung out with the boys, who were often doing things, "my juvenile record look like my adult one." She never finished high school. By the time Marilynn was eighteen she was in prison. Her daughter was nine months old when Marilynn first left her.

Marilynn was only in prison for nine months the first time. When she came out, all the girls she had gone to school with were getting work, nice jobs, at department stores or the phone company. Marilynn wanted one too. *I would go and fill out application after application. At that time it wasn't the box, but they would ask, "Have you been locked up?" I say "yes" and, once I did, I didn't get a call back. Even as a teenager, I volunteered with the city of Atlanta because I wanted a job so bad. But they didn't know I had a record. I had a girlfriend who worked in budget and planning. She knew I had one, but she let me volunteer because she knew I wanted to work. So then I started lying. I got eighteen jobs in my life, but I lied to get those jobs. Once, it might have been the Sheraton, they waited to do a background check. Some jobs will wait until they want to hire you permanently. When they saw my record I was terminated and that would throw me back to a life of crime.*

She went back to prison when she was twenty-two, and she would return four more times, the last time when she was fifty. She turned her life around successfully only when facing a seventh conviction about six years later. Her sentences were usually two years, of which she served a year or less.

The longest time served was twenty-seven months. Most were for shoplifting or domestic disturbances. Her last incarceration had an arbitrary quality to it, but may also reflect a general frustration with the intractability of recidivism: *That one-year sentence was because I have a record. Some judges say, if you are a convicted felon and you come before them for any reason, whether you are guilty or not, you will serve one year just because. I served that one year in Cobb County just because.*

Marilynn was honest about the rewards she saw in crime, and also the tension she felt between her desire for a more conventional life for herself and her family. *Being a career criminal, even if that isn't what you want to do, you embrace it. This is your support, this is your stability. This is the way you take care of your kids. This is the way you take the vacations you enjoy; this is the way you live in luxury like people who got money and take vacations on the job. It's the same thing. Except I stole the money to do it with. Some things I did, I did enjoy the luxury of.*

I used to walk around with this purse and there was nothing in it but money. My first crime was simple shoplifting. But from twenty-one it was all about going into peoples' safes and getting money. In a month's time, twenty or thirty thousand was nothing for me to steal. Especially the first of the month. And I may only have stole twice a month. But all I stole was money. But when I was getting arrested, I stole clothes. I think my last arrest was for stealing eighteen thousand dollars worth of jewelry.

I did pretty well, but I got caught, so I didn't do well enough. I've had a couple of grocery stores. I've lived in five-bedroom homes, I've had BMWs, I've had show dogs, I took trips, I flew my kids to different places to concerts. So I did pretty well. But I often thought, when I get to the age I am now, "I ain't put nothing in Uncle Sam's pot. So what do you do?"

REENTRY PLANNING

Along with her thieving, Marilynn still applied for jobs and kept them until her background caught up with her. She was getting tired of going to prison. In her fourth incarceration, she began to think seriously about what she was doing and why. "I do want the money I have, but I don't want to come here. So how do I do that?" she asked herself. She wrote a course, "Reversing the Cycle of Incarceration," which included everything she herself needed and which she now teaches to others.

So I wrote that program, and when I got out I started following it. When

I got out I wanted employment, but I didn't want McDonalds, I didn't want Burger King, I didn't want minimum wage. But then I had to think about, I've been to prison four or five times and they didn't pay me a dime. I didn't choose the position I had in prison. I had to start to incorporate that. You develop a great work ethic because you are going to be at work and you are going to be on time. You get structure because you are told what to do every hour of the day. You are instructed. Organizing. Everything is neat and everything is clean. After that go round, those are the things I started using to help me.

So now I'm not looking at no prestige job. I'm looking at any job where I can say I am formerly incarcerated. All I'm looking for is a job where you accept me and let me be this person with this background. And that was really hard for me to find. Because there are not too many people who are going to hire a formerly incarcerated individual. Especially for me, I've been to prison six times. Maybe have like twenty to thirty felonies. Don't know how many times I've been arrested, never counted them."

The turn around was far from immediate. Marilynn was incarcerated two more times.

BEING MET IN HER DESIRE TO CHANGE

What did have an important effect on Marilynn was the decision a magistrate judge made when she came before him facing charges that could lead to a seventh incarceration. She described it vividly:

I was about to go to prison my seventh time. They offered me five years and I said, "No, I'm just not going back to prison." So the DA said, "Look at your record, you have to go back."

"Well, that's what I need you to do, Take a look at it and not send me back."

She said, "I don't see no other way."

I said, "Can I talk with the judge?"

She said "No, you have to make your transactions here with us." But when I got in front of the judge, I asked him could I talk to him and he said yes I could.

So I told him just how I felt: "I've been to prison six times. I don't know how many times I've been arrested. But what prison did for me was introduce me to new crime, or it made me contemplate on how to do the crimes I've done better when I come out."

"So what are you suggesting?"

"I need some type of program, something that can lead me to a job, something that can bring me close to a job so I can break this. I already have skills for

resumes, but I couldn't get that leap." It was Judge Lovett. He told me to have a seat and he come back to me.

He said, "I haven't offered you anything yet. The DA offered you five do one."

"I don't want it."

"Do you want what I'm going to offer?"

"Yes."

"You don't know what I'm going to offer."

"But I think you're fair."

"You know what, I just went in and read your record. I'm not sending you back. I see where you've been back to prison six times. I see where you've been arrested. Same thing over and over and over."

"And that's what the seventh time would be."

"But I don't know what I'm going to do with you right now. So have a seat."

There was a guy walking through the court and he called the guy over and then the guy came over to me and he looked at my hands and said, "Well, you're not a crack addict."

"My addiction is trying to live, trying to survive."

"But the only way I can take you is if you say you are drug addict."

So I said, "Judge Lovett, I'm a drug addict." So I went to Fulton County Accountability Court. Its just the same with finding a place to live. If you're not a drug addict or HIV, if you just have a background. They can't take you. So you have to tag one of those on.

Judge Lovett is a very fair judge. I sat in his courtroom after that several times and watched him. I went back this year and gave him a portfolio of everything I've done since he gave me an opportunity.

Working Openly, Finding Traction

What really changed Marilyn's life pattern was receiving a job with her criminal history out in the open: "Since June 16, 2009 when I got the job with First Step Staffing, I haven't committed another crime," she said proudly. First Step Staffing hired formerly incarcerated people, but they had to be homeless. Marilyn, however, kept stubbornly returning to their orientation until the fourth time when she was offered a job of eight hours a week at $6.35 an hour. She quickly turned those eight hours into 39.75 hours.

Marilyn also found the organization 9 to 5, "or it found me." When she read their mission statement, she knew it was the place she was looking for.

She worked as a volunteer, then joined the Board, then became co-chair. At that point, Marilynn felt ready to share her own experiences of discrimination because of a criminal history.

I said, "Guess what, I'm formerly incarcerated and I've been discriminated against for forty years. I feel like one of the children wandering in the wilderness. And I need to start this campaign right here. Your mission says all type of discrimination against low-income women. I make minimum wage."

Marilynn talked with the national director, who was aware of Marilynn's record, but perhaps not of its extensiveness. She said that if they could find enough people interested, Marilynn could begin. Marilynn promptly found thirty formerly incarcerated women who were interested and began her work on Ban-the-Box.

It was important to Marilynn to be transparent about her criminal history in her employment and also in her advocacy work. At one point in her work with 9 to 5 she was invited to a Mayor's Roundtable with the national director of 9 to 5. She was anxious about going: *These are the police that locked me up. I can't sit here and act like I don't have a record. They actually wrote me a script. I said, "I can't go in and say all of this. I need to let these people know that because of my being born in poverty and minimum wage, I was taught to steal. Once I let them know I'm formerly incarcerated and was taught to steal, I can read your script. Could be one of those polices sitting in the audience." Once she allowed me to say that in front of a lot of dignitaries, that was my opening to come out of the closet.*

Since then transparency had become even more important to her: *I am the formerly incarcerated individual in those organizations, so I have to be transparent in order to get anything resolved. So in the future no one can say, "Well, she didn't tell the truth about this."*

PARENTING

One of the consequences of her life pattern that Marilynn had not been able to turn around was its impact on her children: *My children seem to have followed my route. My son is in Cobb County jail right now. My girl been home a couple of years. She committed federal crimes. My son committed state crimes. In my absence, they took they own route. Once I started to get a handle on my life, I couldn't reach back and make them do what I wanted them to do. And I learnt something from that also. Because I used to have to say, "Do as I say, not as you see me do." But truth is kids do as they see you do. And I can't blame anyone but myself.*

With my son, I tried to reach out to him because I am now transitioned over and he's still doing things. I keep reaching out to him. "It's not easy, but you got a mom now who can help you. Let me help you. You've got to stop. You may have to live in a shelter. You may have to stand in a soup line."

But the way I think now, I would rather be broke, hungry, than to be locked up. I don't never want to do that again. But he wouldn't listen. Now he's reaching out to me, but I say No, because he trying to dictate to me. I know what it takes. He wants to go to an outpatient program and I know he need to be in an inpatient program where you can be structured where he can learn some skills. He never had a job. My son is forty-two, he can read and write, but he may not know how to fill out a powerful resume so someone will even look at you. Those are the things he needs to know. He needs to know how to articulate his background to an employer. He needs to take those skills he learned in prison and turn them into a positive. He needs to be able to say: "I learned how to cook in prison. I learned it well. I learned it every day. I learned it supervised."

What Marilynn would most like her children to experience is the state she experiences now: *Even with all the money I had, I'm more content today than I've ever been in my life. With what I make, I'm not paycheck-to-paycheck. I have money left over to do things if I want to do them. I pay my bills on time. But the main thing that keeps me content is I don't have to leave my home and say "I'll be home in a little bit" and a little bit might be two years. When I leave home now, I'm going to work and I'll be back at four o'clock. That in itself is the most peace that a formerly incarcerated person can have. You never have to worry about, "Ma'am, come go with me."*

\7/

UNEXPECTED BENEFITS: LIFE CONFIDENCE
ADIL, ROSE

We assume that prison time is a universally negative experience, but for some people it allows for life-changing shifts that increase a person's confidence about their ability to face inner or external challenges they had not imagined overcoming. The reward for Adil was literacy, for Rose, sobriety. Whether this change was the result of anything positive in the system or just happened to take place in that setting, the change was significant enough that it deeply colored their understanding of their prison experience.

Although both Adil and Rose were convicted of violent crimes—robbery, burglary, and possession of a firearm during a robbery for Adil, and aggravated assault for Rose—they are highly unlikely to ever commit similar crimes, indeed are gentle people. Their stories bring up two issues that recur in different forms in other stories. The first is how their systems distrust limited their efforts at their own defense. Adil felt there was no difference ultimately between the interests of the defense attorney and the prosecutor so never shared his story. Second, how law enforcement in Rose's case is often called in to reinforce personal vendettas in ways that can suddenly and unequally criminalize behaviors that are, in a given context, within *community* norms.

ADIL

Good came out of it. No pressure, no diamond. Now I can read a book to learn.

Adil's grandmother, a friend of ours, brought him over to talk with us, and, after listening for a few minutes, made her way out to the porch to commune with the late spring afternoon and leave him free to speak unfettered. Their relationship was obviously fond. Adil, a tall, athletic young man with a soft voice and a contagious laugh easily and undefensively shared his story, which he revealed he had never shared with anyone in the criminal justice system. The lack of systems confidence reflected in that reticence, which is deeply rooted in his own personal experience but also a more general cultural stance, probably affected Adil's interactions with his schools as well as with the criminal justice system. We talked to Adil about ten months after he had been released from prison in Virginia. He was on eight more years of probation, monitored in his home state, Georgia. He had been imprisoned at nineteen and was twenty-six when we spoke.

EARLY INFLUENCES

Adil was the middle child of five. His older brother and sister each had a different father. Adil and his younger brother and sister shared the same father, who left the home when Adil was in PreK. He understood his role in the family to be a unifier: "I want everyone to be OK. I don't want anyone to be worried."

Adil grew up in Atlanta suburbs, within a relatively small area geographically that felt large to him because of frequent moves and changes of schools. School didn't hold his attention. His father was a street merchant as were many of his father's twelve siblings. They provided Adil with his models: "They taught me everything. They molded me into a business-minded person." Adil's still not sure if his father graduated from high school, "he was not around enough to ask him," but he clearly saw education as irrelevant to his own goals and his abilities: *When I was young I was chasing the money. I had the opportunity to go and get everything wholesale. I went to school just to sell. In elementary school, candy; in middle school, clothes. I was making more than the average hourly rate as a young kid. I was thinking I don't really need the school I could just pursue the business. I was not understanding, it's not just about the money. It's about what's in your head.*

This indifference to school was also due to Adil's learning difficulties: "I had a hard time reading. I didn't want anyone to know. You feel everybody know but you." Adil stopped going to school when he was around fifteen or sixteen. He was in a regular high school, but his frequent absences meant he needed to make up many credits. He was sent to an alternative school, one where they let you keep trying until you got your diploma. Pregnant girls, young boys in the juvenile justice system attended. Adil quickly did not.

DELINQUENCY & SELF-SUFFICIENCY

Adil's weakness and his strengths determined where he turned his attention: *When I was little, I got into some trouble—empty apartments. Older, I was selling clothes and chasing for bigger money. Selling drugs, selling stolen goods, everything. It didn't matter what it was, it was just money. As a family, we had what we needed but sometimes it was hard. To take some of the stress off her, I thought, "I'll get my own shoes." I would only tell my mother about the legit.*

I took a market and ran with it. In a neighborhood, if you watch and every ten or fifteen minutes someone is asking for marijuana, then I'll get it and make me a profit. I'm not trying to hurt nobody. What people ask for, I get it. That market is open. Being young and it's in your face, you're going to jump into it, especially if you're not old enough to get a job.

At this point, Adil began to get in trouble with the police and developed an arrest record. But it was for something he didn't expect, selling clothes, and had a paradoxical effect: "The clothes were fakes. The cops bought them, then arrested me. I thought, well, if they arrested me for that, why don't I just sell stuff that isn't legit?"

CRIME

These activities are not what sent Adil to prison. One weekend a favorite cousin invited Adil to Virginia, his father's home state, to attend a family reunion. Adil went, intending to buy clothes to resell in Georgia as well. After a weekend of family festivities, Adil, his cousin, and his cousin's younger brother went to Virginia Beach to meet up with some girls. When they arrived, they realized that the scenario at the hotel was different from what they expected. There were two men in their late twenties with the three young women, ages sixteen to eighteen. The men wanted to buy some drugs, and Adil, ever the broker, said he knew where to get some.

But something else was getting triggered in Adil. He became convinced that these older men meant to harm the girls. As he was telling the story, he laughed at his response to his reasoning, although he didn't question the reasoning itself. He continued to feel the girls were in danger, and this prospect was deeply threatening to him: *I got little sisters. They trying to get these girls high so they can do things. I decided I was going to ruin the party. I decided to go back and rob them so they won't have any money to do anything with the girls. I know it don't make no sense but it seemed like the right thing then.*

We came back and told them we couldn't find drugs. But they sent for the girls. In my mind I know it isn't right. I know girls who had drugs and never came back in their right mind. I'd never robbed anyone before. I'm always trading, but no robbery. But I felt something was going to happen to the girls. My cousins just wanted the money. When we robbed them, I didn't even count the money. I just put it in my pocket.

Adil did look around for video cameras and saw none. He returned to Atlanta and assumed their crime had gone undetected. But his younger cousin was caught using the stolen cellphone and gave up their names. His older cousin laid the blame solely on Adil.

Adil never shared the motivation for his crime with his public defender: "The court of law don't go off on emotion. It's only if you did it or you didn't." He had watched *48 Hours* to see what it was safe to say. He'd watched enough to see that public defenders talk with the prosecutors, which means you need to treat them as if they *are* the prosecutors. "They say keep your mouth closed until you see a lawyer. But I couldn't explain that part to *anyone* the whole time I was locked up."

ARREST & PRE-TRIAL INCARCERATION

Adil spent much of his three years of incarceration in the Virginia Beach jail waiting for his case to be resolved learning about the law the way he did most everything, by closely observing the world around him. When he first came in, a detective told him that if he confessed everything, he could get ten years rather than twenty to twenty-five. But Adil already knew the range was five to twenty-five. The public defender told him that because he had never been in trouble before, they could get some charges dropped. But Adil also observed that 97% of the cases in Virginia were resolved by plea deals because otherwise you would receive the maximum sentence if you lost at trial. He was aware he was not even from Virginia, which he thought made him more vulnerable.

His public defender made a motion of discovery and Adil realized that his cousin had laid the blame for everything on him and had also incriminated his own younger brother. Even though his victims were coming to court high and drunk, he knew his cousin would go against him. Although there was no physical evidence, he realized that "In Virginia all they need is just word of mouth. You got to prove that you *didn't* do it." So even though he was a first offender, Adil decided that he had no choice but to take a plea. People told him that he would probably receive five years. "I was prepared for anything they would give me. Because I did it. I didn't *tell* anyone of course, but I knew I did it."

The felony charges were reduced from thirteen to three: robbery, burglary, possession of a firearm during robbery. Adil was given five and a half years, including time served, which meant that he spent two and a half years in the Virginia prison system, one year in diagnostics and the last eighteen months in regular prison, which had more space and programming. This proved important because something life-changing had happened to Adil while he was awaiting the resolution of his case. He had learned to really read.

Collateral Benefit: Literacy

When I got locked up in jail, you were always waiting. Waiting to go to court, waiting on your next meal. Sitting and waiting. I picked up a book. I had never read a whole book before. I liked it. I was learning more and more. It come to me, like, "Man, I can grab any kind of book. I might can't spell but I can read." I understood that the only difference between people is what they know in their head. Only difference between me and a doctor is the books we read. So it means I can do anything, be anything. I went on a learning spree. Didn't focus on one thing. If the book available, I'd read it.

Now literate, when Adil went into the regular prison he was ready to take advantage of what opportunities he could find. *They say prison is for you to correct yourself. They not forcing anyone to correct themselves. They not helping you. In prison, same thing as on the street. Some trying to do right and some not. Prison is just a business. They keep you alive is all.*

But there were programs in brick masonry, carpentry, plumbing and horticulture. You could get transferred from one prison to another one to take a program you wanted. Adil went in to prison with a positive attitude, ready to absorb what he could: *For many people, it hurt them to be taken away. But for me, I think, I'm alive, I'm going to change. They not here beating us, killing us. You got opportunities. People with twenty, thirty years or life, they don't see the end of the tunnel. And people with shorter sentences, they still overwhelmed. But, I'm not going in here and waste it. For the time I'm here, I have the opportunities. I got to get out of here, be up to par. I'm getting older. The world is moving, I got to be moving too. I got a family behind me, a good support system. They didn't feel it was me. I got into some trouble, but I thrive in getting into difficult situations and getting out.*

I see more opportunity doing legitimate stuff now. I read so much. In the prison system, the world seemed so big because you're in this small place. But it's the same thing out here. Same people, just dress differently.

Reentry

Adil was living with his grandmother in Atlanta because the transportation situation was better. He worked at a fish restaurant whose owner his grandmother knew. He said that now that the pace was faster, he was reading less but wanted to study more. At one point he was considering enrolling in an extremely expensive for-profit college. We introduced him to an excellent program at Atlanta Technical College that was focused on getting young black men, with or without criminal records, into college by actively reducing obstacles to the application process and allowing them free, grant-subsidized study. Impressed with the program, Adil enrolled, but then did not attend, to his grandmother's dismay.

Economic self-sufficiency would always be the most immediate goal for Adil. School might never feel like the most direct route to it. He was concerned about being able to pay his monthly $33 probation fee, getting a phone, a car. He regularly saw his probation officer, but never talked with her, to her frustration. He felt she assigned him to drug and alcohol classes just to try to have some influence. "I don't talk with her. I don't tell her anything. She ask me why I never talk back. I thought I was just doing time." Adil didn't object to the terms of probation: the fees, keeping out of trouble, not leaving the state or county without permission of the judge. He just was not going to trust them with any personal information. Probation was proving flexible, allowing him to spend months in Virginia helping his father take care of his dying grandfather.

The reason he knew he wouldn't go back in the system were his strong family ties: *When you young, you don't really see the support you have. Now I have time to think about it. My brothers and sisters don't realize the support the way that I do because I've seen both sides. I'm mostly kicking in with my family. It was hard on them. I'm the man in the middle, holding on to everyone.*

This is a role he played in prison as well: *I sit and observe, putting myself in everyone's shoes. Someone get hungry and everything go down. Where they next honeybun coming from? They can't function right. I observe and analyze and then I make a joke about us all being hungry, like it was nothing, and then it won't escalate.*

Adil realized that there are stereotypes about men who have been to prison that he didn't feel were accurate. His own sense of himself as a good person remained unchanged, if anything, reinforced. *I met so many guys not really on the street, just caught doing a little something. Not no beast. Nine times out of ten, they a normal person did something to try and make money to help they family. Most simple thing, possession of drugs. No kingpin, just some little dude. Felony is bad, but it didn't change the person. Still kind-hearted. Anybody can go to prison, but that doesn't change who they could be.*

ROSE

Rehab by itself wouldn't have worked. . . . From then on I weighed it, drink or go to jail.

Originally hesitant to talk with us, Rose was one of the few people who asked to use a pseudonym. In her early fifties, she looked much younger, an effect emphasized by her voice which was soft and high, retaining something of a child's sense of wonder, even though she spoke of difficult things.

Rose grew up in Columbus, Georgia, the third of four siblings. She moved up to Atlanta when she was twenty-four, some years after her mother had moved there, and studied to become a certified nursing assistant (CNA). The mother of two children, she worked steadily as a CNA for nearly twenty years. She had good jobs, at Southern Bell and Kaiser, but sometimes lost them because her drinking interfered and there were days she "wasn't able to get up and go to work."

Arrest & Conviction

When Rose was thirty-nine, she was arrested for aggravated assault in an altercation with a neighbor. *A lady jumped on me and I picked up a stick. The lady told the police a lie, that I started it. She had beat me up before real good. They put me in a police car, I was still yelling, drinking.*

Rose was convicted and given five years probation. She was getting ready to leave the apartment complex when a second altercation occurred. *The same lady said something to me, and I picked up scissors. I was upset because I had already been to jail. I picked up the scissors but I didn't touch her. It was like she was picking on me because she know I was a drunk and just decided to pick on me and I wasn't thinking right. She was a mean lady. I cussed her out, but in our neighborhood we cuss people out and it don't mean nothing.*

The angry neighbor told Rose's probation officer about the altercation, and the probation officer served a warrant and moved to have six months of Rose's probation revoked. Rose went to jail, where she was informed she was facing a second charge of aggravated assault and that probation was trying to revoke all five years on the first conviction. Rose's public defender told her he was going to ask for three years of prison time. Rose was adamant that that was too much time. "In my head, I hadn't done anything wrong. When you be drinking, your mind is altered."

She refused a plea of five years, concurrent, and was sent back to jail where she languished without a court date for many months. She thought that this was because the public defender was frustrated with her. Rose had a cousin call the judge and request a court date because without it the public defender "was tired of fooling with me." She waited another four months for the court date. The Sunday before, the public defender came and told her he was going to do a plea of five years, do one. Rose agreed. One reason Rose fought the longer prison term suggested by her public defender is that she didn't want that long a separation from her family, especially her grandson, who was only three years old at the time.

Prison & Rehab

In court, the prosecutor tried to get all five years of her original probation revoked. But the judge listened when Rose asked to go into a rehab program, Phoenix Alliance, which had been suggested to her by a fellow inmate who with Rose was part of a support program provided in the jail, New Beginnings. The judge gave Rose a one-year prison sentence, six months for revoked probation and six months on the new charge, with four years of probation to follow. In all, Rose served about eighteen months, including the six month rehab program she entered immediately after serving her prison time. She was forty-two when she returned home.

She relished her sobriety: *I wish it could have happened earlier. It made me change my life. There is a difference in all my relationships. My mom is so proud of me. The legal system made me stop drinking. I thought I was going to drink until I died. Because I couldn't stop on my own. Once I stopped, I asked myself, "Why was I doing all that drinking?" I couldn't answer. It had me by the neck. Along with cigarettes. I ended up stopping cigarettes too.*

Rose experienced the most institutional help, oddly, from the much maligned Fulton County Jail, which offered GED, conflict resolution, and a New Beginnings programs. She was very loyal to the New Beginnings program and regularly celebrated Christmas at the jail with the women who were now in that program, along with other women alumni. She maintained friendships with women she met there, especially the woman who referred her to Phoenix Alliance and also was instrumental in her meeting Miss Ann (discussed below) and finding employment on her release: "We're close. We were both able to turn our lives around."

Reentry & Employment

But her criminal convictions posed very serious employment problems for Rose for many years despite her sobriety and her positive work record. Her probation officer tried to help. She sent Rose to the Department of Labor's collaborative program with Corrections, TOPPSTEP, which Rose did not find helpful. She filled out fifty or sixty applications. She couldn't get employment through formal applications because they all asked about criminal history. One office told her directly that was the reason she wasn't considered.

The first steady job Rose found came because a CNA staffing agency application did not ask about a criminal record and the company didn't do a background check. They needed employees. Years later, her background came to light: *They told me I needed to straighten it out but I couldn't work for them anymore. They felt bad. They knew I came to work every day, but they had to go by the book. The state sent the agency a letter that told them they weren't supposed to employ anyone with a felony, so they had to let me go. I had been working for them five or six years.* Rose worked for Miss Ann for five of those years. Miss Ann was very upset about losing one of her best caregivers.

Over the next five years, Rose worked by word of mouth but she also applied twice for a pardon, receiving it the second time. However, she noted that this still meant she had aggravated assault on her record and many employment agencies saw that and immediately refused to consider her. She had tried to get her record expunged, but was not eligible because she has two charges and she pled guilty. "They look at aggravated assault and think I am a monster." She had written on her applications, "Please let me explain," but was not given a chance to.

However, some agencies would hire people with criminal records, especially if customers encouraged them to. Five years later, when Miss Ann changed her staffing agency, she specifically requested Rose as her CNA. The agency approved Rose now that she had a pardon. There had also been, in those five years, the beginning of a change in the political climate with a lessening of the institutional stigma for criminal histories. Rose now had letters from two state agencies—the Departments of Community Health and of Behavioral Health and Developmental Disabilities—supporting her fitness for work.

Rose still puzzled the relative justice, and the intractability of stigma surrounding criminal convictions, particularly hers. Agencies, she observed, were more willing to hire, but most nursing home facilities and hospitals would not recognize a pardon. "Before I got a felony, I worked in a nursing home. There were people there who were *not* nice people, but they don't have a record. A person with a record who has learned a lesson, they won't give them a chance."

She also noted that although theft prohibited you from working in the medical field, if you have a DUI, "right out the door, they will hire you" because it is nonviolent and not theft. She realized that, even fourteen years after her release, she would always have difficulties seeking employment because of the two aggravated assaults.

FAMILY TIES

Rose felt that "God cleaned me up for my grandson." He was eighteen and lived with her. Rose's grandson ended up in juvenile court at the end of ninth grade because his mother "just decided she didn't want to take care of him. She said she was scared of him." Rose received a call from the juvenile court asking her to take temporary custody of her grandson because Rose's daughter was having her own substance abuse problems with marijuana and was going to be incarcerated for two years. By the eleventh grade, her grandson was on the honor roll.

Just a few days before our interview, Rose's grandson had called her from Alabama. He was on a school tour of colleges sponsored by his high school and was calling from Alabama State University. He was signing a college acceptance form. He sent her a photo. *He came home, he was so excited. He kept saying, "Grandma, I'm going to college!" I told him to calm down, but he said, "I've been in juvenile and I'm going to college!!!!"*

\8/

PRECARIOUS BUT PERSISTENT

Fareed, Eloise

Reentry isn't ever a done deal, something you can put behind you once and for all. The persistence of collateral consequences means that when you lose a job, or housing, the next job or housing may be a long time coming. These consequences are particularly challenging for people who have served long sentences and are returning to society later in life, especially if they have been relatively successful in their reentry efforts for years and then suffer a reversal of fortune. Fareed and Eloise successfully faced such challenges during the two year period we followed them, showing us just how precarious stability can be and how hard won and deeply rooted their commitment to living a law-abiding life had become.

FAREED

It's been a struggle being free but any day being free is better than any good day in prison.

We interviewed Fareed in his large home in a well kept and spacious suburban housing development set out in the country about an hour southeast of Atlanta. He described it as a "bougie neighborhood," where the neighbors didn't speak to each other much. He had built the house a few years after leaving prison, at the beginning of a new marriage, now ended. When we talked he was living there with one of his sons and his grandson. His reaction to the house, a combination of pride and dismissiveness, was expressive of that ambivalent history.

Before we began, Fareed read the interview questions carefully. Looking up, he said they sounded positive. He had been a paid participant in a doctoral study, but there he was asked to talk about the experience of incarceration itself. He had found the interview upsetting. He liked the interviewer, a young woman about the age of one of his daughters. He didn't like the subject. He didn't think that he would feel that way about our questions because they were about his life after prison. He had been out for eleven years at the time we talked. In our conversation, we actually spent most time on his life before prison rather than his life after, which provided us with a deeper appreciation of the shifts in norms and practices that a commitment to a legitimate lifestyle had required of him.

The incongruity between the tidy suburban surroundings and Fareed's story, which included ten years as an Atlanta drug king, added a slight tilt to our worldview. We had never met someone who had regularly worn three guns holstered to him, especially one who mentioned it as a casual aside: *I had some idea that I was some big bad dude. I had an image. I thought I was some commando type. But I never used them. Even when I went to prison, the guys in there come up to me, "You Wolf? The image I had was this big crazy man. But you not like that."*

EARLY INFLUENCES

Fareed's parents were members of the Nation of Islam. Fareed was the fifth of eight children. He divided his childhood into three parts. The first was a period of relative stability in Newark, New Jersey, where he was sent to Islamic school from the ages of eight to twelve. Then, for the next two years, he entered a period of rapid moves and puzzling, often uncomfortable culture shifts. First, his father moved the family to a farm in South Georgia near the Florida border owned by the Nation of Islam. For Fareed rural Georgia with its dirt roads, long rides on a school bus, and public schools contrasted poorly with New Jersey where he had a bike and was able to earn as much as $70 weekly doing odd jobs at local stores. Here money was scarce. Working on the farm, he made only $10 every two weeks. Public school was a full rather than a half-day. Within the next year and a half, the family moved five more times between Miami, Newark, and the Georgia farm, ending up in Miami, where Fareed again went to Muslim school.

At fifteen, Fareed, who had skipped two grades, graduated from high school and started junior college. He was intelligent, but completely unprepared for the social challenge of college. At first a straight A-student, he began hanging out with the older students and dabbling with drugs. Failing, he soon withdrew from school. His parents had separated by this point, and Fareed and the brother closest in age were expected to be able to live on their own, although his mother allowed him to live with her for a year.

Hustling & Scamming

During these years, Fareed took up his father's trade, selling "slum jewelry"—costume rings and watches that he bought for five dollars and sold for thirty to fifty, telling people they were real. Fareed saved enough money to afford an apartment and a car.

In 1980, Fareed's older brother died at the age of twenty-three of an overdose. Fareed's father, whatever other illicit activities he engaged in, was an observant Muslim in this area and never used drugs, smoked, or drank alcohol. Fareed's father, concerned about Fareed's own drug use, convinced Fareed to move to Atlanta where his father now lived.

Fareed moved, but continued hustling: *We had started another business by then—selling fake gold bars and fake diamonds. I would fly to Ohio, Pittsburgh, Seattle, Portland. I wasn't but nineteen years old. I would take a plane, rent a car, stay in a hotel room for a week and come back with eight or ten thousand dollars in my pocket. We would look for stores with big cars, Cadillacs or Mercedes, where it looked like someone had money and then go in and ask for the boss, ask if he wanted to buy gold.* Fareed had one real gold bar and a real diamond that he would show them as bait, then switch out after the sale. Although not directly stated, the implicit understanding all around was that the gold and diamonds were stolen.

First Arrest & Incarceration

In 1982, Fareed, now married, was arrested and charged with theft by deception on two or three cases of selling gold bars. He didn't see this as problematic: *They had this first offender act. You get probation with non-report, so I accepted that, but I never accepted that I wouldn't keep doing what I was doing. So I had this probation, and went about my own business.*

Indeed, he didn't necessarily see the activities as illegal. He was arrested again that year in both Florida and Georgia for similar activity. This time in Georgia he was offered two years of prison time. *I just couldn't understand. "Why you giving me two years?" I was in my early twenties with a baby coming. I thought, "with all this crime going on, why are you doing this? I'm not hurting anyone with this fake stuff."*

The prosecutor threatened Fareed with a ten-year sentence if he went to trial. Instead, Fareed fled. "I ran out of the courtroom, I said I had to go to the bathroom and I just disappeared. So I was a fugitive from November 1982 until I got caught in Florida in 1983." Part of the reason for Fareed's decision to abscond was that his wife was expecting a baby in six weeks. He continued his scamming in Florida, but did not get apprehended. In 1984, he finally pled guilty to the outstanding charges of theft by deception and was incarcerated in a Georgia prison for six months. "I did six months inside and six months parole. Six months was hard to me."

SCAMMING TO TRAFFICKING

Fareed had some vague intentions to do differently when he was released. He did not like prison and did not intend to return. He planned to work for his father's wrecking service and junk yard. His wife disagreed. "My wife said if I don't hustle, she would leave me. She wasn't going to be with 'a grease monkey.'" She suggested Fareed take up dealing drugs. "I'm thinking, wow, I just got out. I don't know. I got six months on parole. I have a young son. But my wife said if I loved her, I would do this." Her brother, who had been Fareed's co-defendant on the earlier fake gold bar case, was now selling drugs and offered to become partners with Fareed, putting up the money while Fareed did the selling. However, dealing drugs was not part of his own family legacy. "I didn't look up to drug dealers. I thought they were scum. Who sell drugs and kill your own people? That's totally messed up."

He conquered his own reservations quickly: *Once I decided to do it, it was a whole other story. I'd tell myself: "I'm not forcing nobody to come take it. People going to buy it from somebody else, why not me?" This was my justification to myself. Don't worry about the morality of it. It's just about you getting money. That was the beginning of my real life of crime. It made me unravel through my whole life. I think I lost a lot of moral identity. Hustling, yeah, you find somebody, they taking something off you too, but I'm the one taking the real risk. They think they getting something for nothing. But when you selling drugs, you got to look up the ramifications. I didn't look up the legal system.*

So Fareed, still on parole, was provided with a pager and a pistol and went to work. He oversaw packaging the cocaine and managed the crew sent out to sell the drug. *I would drive to my dad's shop and throw on these overalls and do whatever he need me to do, pick up a car, go take a car to the junk. My pager go off, I would go in my car, make my delivery and come back. Did that through the whole six months on parole. I went off parole, I never went back to his shop. I was a full-fledged street drug person.*

Within a year, he and his brother-in-law had a falling out, but Fareed continued in the drug business. He saved his money and by the end of the year had about twenty thousand saved, and he and his wife moved out of his father's house into an apartment. He began to buy fancy equipment for his car, stereo and rims for the wheels, that signaled his occupation to the world. He also became a womanizer, like this father.

He pondered the nature of his father's influence on him. *I had a lot of respect for my father. I thought the world of him. My dad dropped out of school in eighth grade. He was raised in the country on a dirt road. His mom had twelve children. He showed me how to make money. He always dressed good, had a nice car, had businesses. On hindsight, I think he might have set me up for failure, but at the time, I thought he did pretty good.*

In the ten years that he was an active drug dealer, Fareed never caught a case except for the one that ended his criminal career. Fareed assumed a street name, Wolf. He found a reliable distributor in Miami, who brought him ten keys a week on credit, half of which he could sometimes sell just driving down the street. "That was the game. I had a long journey."

During this period, Fareed led a double life. He owned various legitimate businesses to launder his profits like his father had: a beauty supply store, a car wash. He paid taxes. He got out the vote for Jesse Jackson. He joined the NAACP. *I looked like the average successful citizen. I called myself legit. I knew I wasn't legit. I was embarrassed for the people on the street to know my name was Fareed.*

He liked the veneer of legitimacy but also liked hanging out at strip clubs, especially Magic City, in downtown Atlanta. It was his informal office, all his crew hung there. *I had horses, jet skis, motorcycles. Everything I did, I did kind of elaborate. I had big parties, birthday parties. We would all fly to Miami together, first class. Rent two Cadillacs, go out to the clubs. I thought it was something real fancy and good until the feds came and indicted me.*

FEDERAL INDICTMENT AND SENTENCING

Fareed was indicted April 22, 1993. "It was like the whole world went *whoooosh*." Fareed was in Arizona vacationing with his children when one of his co-conspirators, whose house was being tapped, called and "they recorded him telling me what he did, what he want to do, what happened. Later that night, they raided his house and found a little over a kilo of coke, $75,000 and a pistol. That was the immediate downfall." Fareed, along with sixteen other people, were charged with a continuing criminal enterprise, a charge that carries a life sentence. "They had me on the news, and I thought, 'These guys aren't joking.'"

After hearing the news Fareed went to stay in a hotel where he was paged by the DA who told him that if he gave himself up, the consequences would be lighter. However, the lawyer Fareed consulted told him it would cost at least a hundred thousand to represent him if he did so. *Seems like they always catch you at a bad time, one of those hard dry times, and all I had to my name was about a hundred thousand. When the DA called me back, I said, "You going to have to find me." He said, 'We do that, it will be harder on you." I said, "Do what you have to do." I threw the pager away. Gone.*

He spent a year as a fugitive, moving rather boldly between New Jersey, Atlanta, and Miami, visiting his children, his father, girlfriends. He says he was shown on America's Most Wanted, and a woman in Miami finally turned him in for the reward.

INCARCERATION & PREPARING FOR REENTRY

As soon as Fareed was taken into custody, he reverted to his religion. He insisted on being called Fareed, refusing to be identified by his street name, even in court. Ultimately, his sentence was much lighter than the threatened life sentence. Because he pled guilty and agreed in principle to cooperate with the government, he received a fifteen-year sentence, which was further reduced by another five years when two people who were associated with him pled guilty a few years later and their pleas were credited. He also attended a 500-hour drug program, which reduced his sentence by another year. In all, Fareed served seven years and nine months. This felt long but not unbearable: *I can't fathom doing thirty-five years. I've been the squeakiest clean guy since. I have dreams about prison.*

During his incarceration, Fareed tried to maintain his ties with his five children: *Once I got sentenced, I knew I would be coming home. God can give you an answer. I tried to establish a relationship with my children from inside. Writing and calling. Their moms would bring them. One I didn't know was mine until I got out. She was twelve when I got out.*

He now feels that however difficult prison was, it saved him from something worse: *It was hard. When I think about the whole events of prison, the thing I can recognize now, I didn't recognize then: Prison probably saved my life. Usually that lifestyle, somebody kill you or you die of some thing.*

Fareed used his time in prison productively. He told us he had a briefcase in the house with about fifty certificates he had earned in federal prison, which offers far more programming than state prisons, especially Georgia prisons. He attended classes in accounting, bookkeeping, home design, carpentry, upholstery cleaning, paralegal, real estate law, and house inspection among others. Fareed was also a popular speaker with all the Islamic communities he found inside.

REENTRY

When Fareed was released in 2002, "reentry wasn't around." He felt he received very little family support. His father and his two younger brothers had died while he was in prison. His one surviving brother, who had worked with him selling drugs, had been sent to state prison for manslaughter in 1986. Added to the same federal indictment as Fareed, he was released from federal prison in 1999. Fareed's nephew was released soon after. So family resources were heavily strained by the time Fareed was released. One sister allowed him to live with her for three months. He married his second wife a little over a year later. He and his wife built their house in 2005, and divorced about five years later. He found steady work as a housing inspector, a trade he had learned in prison.

GIVING BACK

A very important turning point for Fareed was joining the PIIC support group in 2009: *When I found that group, I stayed with it. For me, it's about giving back. This is my call. My eternal self told me you got to pay for the deeds that you did. I was an animal. I was bad. This is how I assess myself. Here is a guy who was raised different, who was raised good, and you come out and sell drugs and didn't care about your community, didn't care about your people. So I have to make amends to society due to God forgiving me. I still want to be in heaven, not hell. I'm still paying and repenting for my previous sins. I don't know when I leave this earth, but I want to have a good mark, not my past bad mark.*

Fareed and his brother also engaged in prison ministry. He talked proudly about how they were both able to walk into prison through the front gates, right through the metal detectors "like the guards." Wearing their Volunteer Associates badges, they often spoke with the Islamic communities in the prisons. He shared that when he had recently spoken at Jackson diagnostic prison, one of the guards actually gave him the keys to unlock the door to the meeting room. He described himself as Aaron to his brother's Moses, but obviously had his own call to motivational speaking. He had an internet radio show for some years where he shared his sermons. He also joined PIIC members when they spoke at various prisons to encourage lifers.

FAMILY

Fareed was proud of his five children's accomplishments. One son had a masters from Georgia State, his oldest daughter was married with two daughters, his youngest daughter was in college, and, to his great pride, his middle daughter had just been sworn in as a lawyer.

His relationship with his first ex-wife remained challenging: *Even when I did my criminal activity, I felt I was living a double life. I never wanted to bring it home. My wife knew, encouraged it, but then didn't like it. She went on to college. Helped to raised the kids. But she never want to forget what I did. Other people remind me I wasn't that bad. I say, "How can you glorify crime?" I am my own worst critic in a way, but when I look at the change, I know people can change.*

He and his daughter, the newly minted lawyer, often ran together, and were both training to run in the annual Fourth of July Peachtree Marathon, along with his ex-wife and one of his sons.

STIGMA

In our interview, Fareed expressed his frustration at society's unwillingness to forgive or forget. The two are clearly linked. He applied for a pardon in 2009 and received it in 2011, with all rights returned except firearms: "I can run for office, be a notary public." Like a number of people we talked to, he was very disappointed and frustrated that a pardon has no standing with employers or people in general. *That we have this felony is the hardest thing to let go. Mine is twenty years old. My crime was in '94. I still get background checks and it still come up. I say, hey, I got a pardon, how is my background still affecting me? What my background have to do with what I'm doing? What about the twenty years since then? When is enough enough?*

When asked what importance he felt other people gave a felony conviction, Fareed said: *Some people have the idea we're not even human beings. When I went to visit the prison, a guard said, "They just some damn animals." He don't know I ever been there. He think he talking to someone from the free world. I let it fly. They talk about America being a melting pot. I think of it like God is marshaling us together. Whether we like it or not, we are being pushed together so we can become more welcoming and learn something about each other.*

EMPLOYMENT

When Fareed was released, he worked steadily as a home inspector until the crash of the housing market. From that point on, employment was a continuing challenge. After we talked to him, he lost his house as well and spent two very difficult years looking for stable work. After taking a CDL course in another state that was open to someone with a criminal record, he finally found employment as a municipal bus driver in Atlanta. When he returned to the support group some months later, he seemed relaxed and deeply content. "I just wake up every day now at peace," he said. "I drive around giving thanks to Allah."

ELOISE

After eleven years of reentry, I turned around and it was a blank space. Nobody offered to help.

Originally, Eloise told us she didn't think she would be eligible for our listening project. "All my crimes were violent," she said, holding up our original call for participation. "You say here you interested in nonviolent crime." She offered to do whatever she could to help. As she stood there quietly in the elegant red dress she had worn to a meeting earlier in the day where she was representing PIIC, we quietly conceded to the growing realization that we couldn't restrict our project in that way.

Eloise has a charismatic warmth and beauty that quickly pull you in— and a raw power that keeps you on the alert. Eloise was one of the few women who were part of the core membership of PIIC, and the only one who had served sentences for armed robbery equivalent in length and gravity with the men. She was incarcerated for twenty-seven years in total, with sentences of ten, twelve, and then five years. There was less than a year between the incarcerations—just enough time to birth two children in addition to the one she had before her first incarceration.

We interviewed Eloise twice, once in the summer of 2014 and again in the spring of 2016. The first interview took place at Eloise's lovingly furnished townhouse apartment in the city of Carrollton, an hour west of Atlanta, near the Alabama border. There were large stuffed sofas and armchairs in the living room, flowers and decorative soaps in the guest bathroom. It was as if every surface had been caressed, made inviting. On the wall of the kitchen divider hung framed photos of her mother and her children. "This is my mother. Isn't she beautiful? She couldn't love me," Eloise said.

She proudly focused on the photos of her children. Later it came out that she was alienated from them, a reality that she struggled, sometimes successfully, to accept. She began the interview talking about the impact her incarcerations had on them: *I feel that I disrupted or maybe even destroyed three beautiful person's opportunities to be normal functioning participants in society. The way I did that was by making choices to go to prison. And the consequences of those choices—the children have nothing to do with me. They are not to be blamed. But I can see, interacting with them, how their lives could have been different if I had been there. There can be no justifiable reason for bringing a child into the world if you go on to abandon them.*

Early Influences

Eloise had a keen sense of dramatic delivery and an appreciation of the drama of her own life. She often referred to herself in the third person. We were swiftly drawn in: *I was born dead, I was born breeched. I think that was the last vestiges of real deep segregation, color segregation, and I happened to be dark and for some reason my mother couldn't love me. She told me that happened the very day I was born, when the doctor told her I was dead. They laid me on her chest and she moved me to the side. She told me that. And my aunt validated it.*

Eloise's childhood was impoverished and brutal. Her father came back from World War II with post-traumatic stress: "I don't know what happened in New Guinea, but he would wake up and he would strangle you." Given Eloise's dark skin, he felt she was not his child. Both her parents became alcoholics. She described their situation as "no job, no education, no love." They lived in a single room "with two beds, four children, and two adults."

At the age of nine, Eloise was sexually molested by an older woman who had befriended her and would often feed her and have her stay at her house. This betrayal still haunted her: *She really really put the nail in the coffin on trust. I already couldn't understand why my father was so mean and beat me all the time. And my mother was so unkind. There was so much for a little girl to sort through. There was too much. I'm giving you the build up of mistrust, hatred, and the making of an animal.*

Incarceration, Boundaries, & Insight

Eloise experienced further sexual violence when she was eighteen and brutally raped. "After the incident, I became mean. I allowed a defender inside of me to keep me from losing my mind. And I didn't care what I destroyed." She married and had a child. When her husband went to prison and her mother passed away, Eloise began to steal food from stores. She met up with some people who "seen I had a heart and I was mean and also knew I was hurt and brazen, and that was a perfect mixture right there to put a pistol in her hand and turn her loose." This led to her repeated armed robberies and prison terms.

As Eloise would be the first to say, she had serious trust issues. But she was also able to feel deep gratitude for the people who had a positive influence on her. She described a number of women who helped her during her time in prison. They gave Eloise skills, insights, and boundaries to help tame some of her rage.

The most important was her friend and lover Lisa, with whom she had a long relationship, revived whenever they were in a prison at the same time: *I was involved with a person who taught me how to love. If you notice, I ain't said anything about love yet because I didn't know anything about love. Lisa was seeing in me what I couldn't see in myself. I was trying to survive in prison because I didn't have family help. She had means, but she also had love. She had been loved and she shared that with me. I stayed in that relationship almost twenty years. Through her reaching out for me. Her and her family provided for me. She encouraged me to go to school. She encouraged me to be the best woman I could be. And she often told me, "You so beautiful." That opened a door inside me to want to help others. In prison, the girls would come in and they were so young. You can do things in your youth that you can't correct. I began to be a mentor to the young ladies in prison. I would hear so many Eloises. Even the little mean ones, I mean really mean.*

Barbara LeBow, a playwright who taught in the prison in the 1980s, encouraged Eloise to write plays and to act: *She helped a person named Eloise outside of herself, through drama, to get a glimpse of her self inside. That opened the door to self-discovery. From that I learned what you do is not who you are. A person does bad things but that doesn't mean they are a bad person. She was one of the people who wrote the parole board and helped me get my pardon. She knew me in my rage and anger.*

Chaplain Susan Bishop, a long-time prison chaplain, was also influential: *She always accepted Eloise. I've known her thirty-five, almost forty years. She is a selfless person and when she is interacting with you that is exactly what she is doing. When she listens, she listens. She has a compassion. She will build a relationship to where she can be honest with you. She will say, "Eloise, now look, I want you to think about what you just said. Do you think that was right for that action?" She gives you an opportunity to look at it, and she will tell you the truth and not placate and tell you what you want to hear.*

Eloise admired the chaplain's ability to maintain boundaries: *As long as I'm doing right, she right there with you. When you're not right, she won't have nothing to do with you. Point blank, simple as that. That was fair. You can't cry "Lord a mercy" when you're in the wrong.*

Eloise had a similar appreciation of the warden and head of security: *They were straight up. They didn't play no games. No favoritism. They didn't feel sorry for you, there was none of that. It was all about prison but they were fair. They had the capacity to do it right.*

These women all held a clear set of expectations of Eloise, ones that in time she felt confident she could meet.

REENTRY

By the time she was in for her third prison term, Eloise was older and tired. Her friend Lisa had died. Her last sentence was much more troubling to her because she felt she had been set up by members of her own family. She felt she had burned her bridges with all her children. In February, 2005, when Eloise left prison for the last time, terrified, she spent her first night in a bus station. She called a friend who had been released, and the friend, a middle-class white woman who had been in prison for forgery, opened her home in Carrollton to Eloise, who lived there until she found a job and the apartment.

EMPLOYMENT & SHIFTING EXPECTATIONS

Eloise was finally able to find a job nine months after release with the help of a new program, Take 5, sponsored by the Department of Corrections and led by A.J. Sabree, then director of Reentry Services. Eloise was hired by a large wire factory in Carrollton. She worked there for eight years and was proud of having progressed from $12/hour to $20/hour.

But the clarity of expectations and boundaries that she responded well to in prison was lacking here, and the social and negotiating skills she had learned in prison did not serve her well. Indeed, the most basic assumption she had about the job, that she was hired on her own merit, was also called into question. When she was injured because of faulty training, she wrote up her grievance as she had been taught to do in prison. She asked for a meeting with the managers and administration, and presented her grievance: *Remember I told you, that's what I did in prison. I would write people up. They did me wrong and you have to understand I have been done wrong in my life and I have a habit of not letting you just do me any kind of way. But I didn't show out or become obstructive. The manager said he would get back to me.*

That very night A.J. Sabree and B.J. Blair were knocking at this very door. "You are never to do that, Eloise. You have to communicate through us." It was a deal they cut. I was not to complain and I complained by having the meeting.

Eloise did speak up sometime later because she felt she might get physically injured: *I told them the machine was tearing up. I knew my limbs were in danger and told them about the machine. I had moved into an area where there were only men and they didn't want me there. They knew what was going to happen. They knew about that machine. They knew eventually I would get hurt.*

As she feared, Eloise was hurt by a malfunctioning machine, had unsuccessful back surgery, and ended up being terminated in 2012 because she was on permanent disability. She is both very proud of her tenure at Southwire and confused about what could have been done differently. The day we talked she was thinking about something Sabree had said in the last support group meeting. As she recalled, he said, *"When a person has been to prison, they bring out with them the survival ways of prison—like if someone do you wrong in prison, you take care of it right away, right there so you won't be taken advantage of. But if you do that on a job, you become a liability." I was a liability there because of speaking out.* Liability was clearly a painful label for her.

Teaching Back

Employment: When Eloise returned to prison as a volunteer to talk about reentry, she was at a loss about what to say about employment: *You do what you have to do to keep the job, yes you do. But what do you do if someone's violating you and you can't say anything? You can walk away, you can quit, you do have that option, but if you can't find a job, what do you do?*

Perspective Taking: Eloise felt that ex-offenders had no chance to de-program after prison. She felt that more effort needed to be made to understand the individual needs and abilities of people leaving prison so that employers and employees can have a more accurate idea of what they are both getting into. She felt that in prison all those years, "you left me to chance." Prison should be a place where people had a real opportunity to change. Since it wasn't, she felt it was irresponsible for the Department of Corrections to release people directly back into communities, relying only on the good will of churches and volunteer groups. *We are not barred from any community. It's just not fair to those who haven't committed crimes. Look at it from that perspective. It's not fair to have someone like me come and live by you and you not know that.*

Sitting with the Facts: Some years after leaving prison Eloise wrote a very blunt memoir that her friends in the support group discouraged her from publishing. "People don't want to know that stuff about you," they told her. Eloise went ahead anyway. "No matter what has transpired in your life, the factual truth is what is going to help you. If you can't deal with the factual truth, you are never going to move forward in life." The book makes uncomfortable reading at times, especially scenes that describe the volatility and suppressed violence that she could still demonstrate, especially toward family members, when her hopes and expectations weren't met. But Eloise said, "I just wanted to get it *all* out of me. I wanted to leave it behind."

Stigma: One of the last things Eloise said in our first interview proved remarkably prophetic of the challenges she would face in the following years. When asked what she thought felon meant to other people, she said: *It depends on who you are talking with. I've been in this dwelling for nine years. And my neighbors, I wouldn't just go and knock on their door and tell them I been in prison all those years for armed robbery. But if in some way we were in conversation and there was a need for that to be disclosed, I would but only if I felt safe to do it. I know how the world is, I know how the world looks at you. You can't even get a place to live, let alone convey anything to a neighbor. We can't even get a place to live unless there is a measure of compassion. And that is wrong by all standards.*

HOMELESSNESS

Two years later, through a quixotic set of events, Eloise lost her beloved apartment. It took her a number of difficult months to find another one. Given her home's obvious importance to her, this was a period of maximal stress. In those months, when she came to PIIC meetings, her hair and dress were haphazard, her attention distracted, the frustration and raw anger at her situation barely reined in. She didn't want hospitality, she wanted a secure base. She refused to gloss over her intense feeling of displacement. "If you got no key to the house, you homeless," she asserted in one meeting.

But then, some five or six months later, Eloise glided in to chair the meeting. She wore a sleek, pageboy wig, a fur coat, boots. She had found an apartment. The owner, now her friend, was a hair dresser, and Eloise was helping her out occasionally in her shop. Once Eloise was securely settled in, she spoke to us about this difficult experience and its unexpected and most welcome resolution. It had clearly tried all her social ties, exposed assumptions or expectations of others and of herself that weren't met.

Eloise's homelessness began with an impulsive good deed. Over the previous year, she had befriended Rufus, a man in his sixties newly released after forty-six years of incarceration. We first met Rufus, distressed and disoriented, at one of the first PIIC meetings we attended. He couldn't recognize the neighborhood he had grown up in. He was troubled by lack of respect on the subway, but realized, as he poignantly said, "I don't know anything. I just got to be a sponge." He lived in crowded transitional housing with nineteen men, a situation he described as worse than prison. He confided to Eloise that he was tired of living with all men. However, he was on disability and couldn't afford anything else. Following the model of the friend who had helped her when she first got out, Eloise told him he could come and stay at her apartment.

Unfortunately, Rufus brought bedbugs with him from the transitional housing. When Eloise informed the landlord, he asked where they came from. This put Eloise in a dilemma because it was against the policy to have anyone staying there who wasn't on the lease, but she reluctantly told him about Rufus. The owner was actually quite reasonable. He said she could stay if she paid for the renovation required, which would run about a thousand dollars, but if he had to pay for it, she would have to leave even though she had been a perfect tenant. Eloise did not have the money and took the only choice she really had, throwing away all her furniture and putting her televisions and washing machine in storage.

Rufus returned to his bed bug infested transitional housing. Eloise was understanding: *With him being locked up for so many years, I'm not sure he even know what they were either. You don't have bedbugs in prison.*

She had no time to plan, and did not have the money to rent an apartment, so began to live out of her car, going to stay in a hotel when her disability check came in, then going back to her car. "That went on from July to October and that was the most horrendous part of my recovery. It was unbeknownst to me, the can of worms I opened trying to help somebody."

Jobs, housing and relationships are the three key elements of successful reentry. Loss of one often challenges the others. At times like this, what we can realistically expect of others isn't always clear—to us or to them. Eloise felt let down by many people during this period, especially her companions in reentry: *I found no help with reentry. None whatsoever. A couple of people when my money was short, they would let me come into they house and spend the night or I would come in and clean up their house for a night's stay.*

She did find help in an unexpected place, from the women in the reentry ministry at Peachtree Road Methodist Church located in Buckhead, the wealthiest and whitest area of Atlanta. (This church has a close connection with the prison chaplain Susan Bishop). Eloise was very appreciative of the group: *They were talking to me every week. With them I was able to be weak and to say, "I'm afraid. I don't know what to do." When you don't have money and you really don't have friends—They would allow me to come to the church and we would meet so I could offload and get enough strength to go on. There was a group of them.*

She also struggled with her sense of general betrayal and the need to claim responsibility: *Nobody is responsible for my upkeep but me. To be accountable for my freedom, I'm still responsible for Eloise. And knowing my situation . . . but there is a God and with the help of those women, I got this place.*

The basement apartment that Eloise had found was in a nice housing development in a small town some forty-five minutes from Atlanta. She had a separate entrance, and the large plate glass windows in her living room and bedroom looked out on a wide lawn shaded by tall trees, with an inviting small bench and a bird feeder. Although more sparsely furnished than Eloise's prior apartment, this one was also very clean and decorated with care, obviously a cherished space, fast becoming a home.

Eloise almost refused to take it because she was insistent that the owner know about her background before she accepted. This provoked much debate with her support team—a debate that encapsulates many of our contradictory attitudes about reentry.

They was so tired of the way I was living that they just didn't want me to say something that would blow the opportunity. I said, "I will not go into that lady's home with this record and my past without her knowing something."

"Well let her get to know you first."

So there we go, we're lying by omission again. I have been living with a free conscience ever since I been out of prison. I have been able to tell the truth. Walk with my head up. Now, you are asking me to live in lies. I may as well pick a pistol up and go and rob somebody. Of course I'm not going to do that! I'm just giving you an example.

"'Neither of you have allowed me to come into your house and you know my situation. Would you like me to do that to her? You know my situation and she don't. Do you think it is fair to go into that lady's home?"

They said, "All right. We'll go back and talk to the Board again."

Oh my God, they mulled it over, they mulled it over. After about a week, they said, "Eloise, just take it easy when you tell her. And don't mention your book."

Eloise did tell the owner all about her background—although possibly not about her book. When she had finished, the owner said, "Eloise, I won't judge you, but I will help you." These words were balm for Eloise. *And that's what she did and that's what she do. I love Ann as my friend. We have our boundaries. I'm the renter, she's the owner. I respect her property to the utmost. I respect Ann to the utmost.*

Eloise was still trying to make sense of the experience, especially where her disappointment was valid, but more importantly, whether it is sustainable or useful. Ann clearly felt like an answered prayer. The women from Peachtree Methodist supported her steadily in her time of trial have her gratitude and loyalty, but they did not invite her into their homes. Although she may be disappointed in her brothers and sisters in reentry, they remain "part of my freedom and my stability. I can't let them go." She did want to share this part of her story because she knew she was not alone in it, that there are some stories of reentry that are far more successful than hers, but that her challenges—with family, job, and now housing—are also an important part of the more realistic and grounded story of reentry that we all need to share, with its limits, disappointments, and moments of unexpected grace.

\9/

BEARING THE MORAL WEIGHT OF MURDER
Omar, Kathleen, Kevin, Ariif

Several of the men and one of the women we interviewed were convicted of murder and were reentering after having served one, or more, life sentences. Murder, for many of us, however much we enjoy murder mysteries and cop shows, is the crime we *don't* want to know very much about in our personal life. Certainly not face to face. We don't want to put ourselves in the murderer's mind, then or now. It is difficult for any of us to come to terms with our capacity for violence—and we all prefer to have that awareness buffered. However, a commitment to real reintegration asks that we—as well as the murderer-who-has-served-his/her-time—*both* explore and shift our preconceptions, explanations, and expectations. The best way to do that *is* face to face.

Some probation and parole officers told us that they find lifers, especially those serving sentences for murder, the easiest individuals to supervise when they leave prison. They have been incarcerated for a very long time. They don't want to return to prison. They have often used their time in prison more constructively than people with shorter sentences. There is also a feeling that many of these crimes were passionate, never-to-be-repeated ones, an aberration not a pattern.

In this chapter we look directly at what may need to shift in the stories ex-offenders tell *and* in the stories *we* tell *about* them for us to feel we can safely live together again. In its simplest terms safety is based on a sense that the murderer can feel the preciousness of life—ours in particular—and the enormity of having taken one. They must show active remorse.

However, there is a problem with this "simple" expectation: It is *very* difficult for any of us to really feel the harm *we* do. We can certainly feel the harm others may do us. But we tend to minimize the impact of our own actions—and to explain them in terms of *our* motivations, not their impact on the other person.

When these natural dynamics are applied to something like murder, they can feel callous, dangerous, almost monstrous. In Victim-Offender dialogues, for example, facilitators keep repeating to the participating offenders that this is *not* about them, it is about the victims, about answering *their* questions, meeting *their* needs for an explanation for an act that has torn their lives apart, challenged their faith in the world. Often the victim's expectations are *not* met by the dialogue itself. Victims want to know why. They want to know that the offender *feels* the full extent of their pain, its expanding circles of implication. This need can go unmet. The offender can't explain, or the explanation in no way makes the loss more comprehensible, possibly even less. Although the dialogue itself may disappoint, the process doesn't. What is most important to the victim finally is feeling supported by the facilitators of the dialogue and by the act of claiming their *own* need to understand, to get access to the mind of the offender. In this sense, the receiving community, especially following reentry for violent crime, has a similar need to understand, to make comprehensible.

What we, as potential neighbors, need to know when someone returns from prison after serving a sentence for murder is not necessarily that they have empathy for their victims but that the man or woman now knows enough about themselves, and has the self-control, never, under any circumstances, to kill again. This is what we, in many ways, are listening for in everything they tell us. The answer may be there, but it may not appear in forms that we recognize—forms that have nothing specifically to do with the crime at all, nothing to do with specific remorse.

In the four stories we share here, that assurance can come from how they define themselves now, the number and depth of their social ties, their definition of themselves as *fundamentally* good, with an essential identity not defined exclusively or even primarily, by this one terrible act. Their path to that understanding may never reference the crime itself, rather the many years and the many consistent prosocial choices that followed.

We need to think when—and why—we sometimes want to ascribe to people convicted of felonies in general, but especially those who have committed murder, an essential, immutable, *negative* identity. Once a murderer, *always* a murderer. Does this insistence, this labeling, really protect us? It minimizes or actively negates all the prosocial choices the individual has made both before and after that crime. It is from those *positive* choices, the awareness that he or she has the freedom to choose them, that real, lasting change will come.

As you read these stories, we invite you to ask: Would I feel comfortable having this person, now, as my neighbor? We do feel, for various reasons, that each of the individuals included here will desist from crime. How they indicate this commitment is different in each instance, but it is important for us to meet them at that place of desistance *by their own reckoning*, for that is why they will make good neighbors now.

OMAR

I am determined not to give up because too many people depend on me to do right.

Omar, imprisoned at nineteen for fourteen years for armed robbery, kidnapping, and murder is now a frequent spokesperson for groups promoting reentry, including the Georgia Department of Corrections and more recently the U.S. Attorney's Office in Atlanta. A handsome man in his early forties with an endearing demeanor, he has recently published a memoir distributed through Amazon. In 2018, to his deep joy, he finally received a pardon.

Omar's charisma isn't tied up with heroic rebellion. It has to do with something more poignant, a belief that the good he does will bear fruit. Since he was sentenced at eighteen, Omar has done his best to play by the rules of the system to which he was consigned—but the rewards of that behavior don't carry far enough beyond those walls to guarantee him stable work or housing, both essential to self-sufficiency and a sense of manhood. His frustration sometimes breaks through—just enough for him to feel trustworthy, making it clear that, with all his gentleness, he knows the cost and value of the choices he's made *and* that he wants these choices to count in exactly the same spirit he made them, in the hope of full constructive return and participation in society.

EARLY INFLUENCES

Omar was raised by his grandparents in Alabama until he was about ten. His mother had been in high school when he was born, and she went to Atlanta to work, bringing him to the city after she felt sufficiently established economically. He remembered his grandparents' home as warm, filled with people. He adored his grandmother: "She taught me what it was to love people. She planted many positive seeds." A schoolteacher, she always had students and children over on the weekends. His grandfather was a farmer, hard-working, hard drinking, and prayerful. His grandmother cared for a number of her grandchildren, at least five by Omar's account, who were sent to her by her children. He had two aunts and an uncle who also lived there.

At the same time, some negative seeds were being planted. From an early age, Omar was being taken out by his uncle and his cousin to shoplift. He found this exciting and fun. He thinks his grandmother knew what his uncle and cousin were doing—but not that they had involved him in it. These negative influences became stronger when he arrived in Atlanta. His mother had rented an apartment that she let her younger siblings live in with Omar during the week while she stayed with her boyfriend. He stayed there because of the better school district. She may have been unaware of the level of alcohol and drug use and gambling and fighting that went on. She was, Omar said, a provider. Not necessarily a mentor.

Delinquency

Although Omar did fairly well in elementary school, by eighth grade, at which time he was living alone with his mother, he was having trouble. He was a popular boy who felt "my mom could not afford the necessities to highlight my popularity." He had friends in the neighborhood who were selling drugs, and he was attracted to the money. Omar felt that if he had been allowed to play basketball his life path would have been different. He made the team in ninth grade but was told he couldn't play because of his grades. Instead of improving them, he dropped out.

He strongly felt the lack of male mentors. His mother's boyfriend shrugged at Omar's behavior: "You got to let him be a man. You got to let him find out for himself." Omar felt that mothers taught their daughters, but they didn't do the same with sons. And it was easy for a man to reject another man, however young and in need of mentoring: *Bitterness came with that. She paid more attention to her mate than to her child. I wanted to make her happy, but I lost that somewhere. I think my mother loved me to death, but she just didn't know the difference between being a parent and a provider. She was not on top of things like homework. She wanted a life.*

At fifteen, Omar caught his first jail charge for stealing athletic jackets and shoes. Between the ages of sixteen and eighteen, he was in and out of juvenile for robbery, terroristic threats and carrying a pistol. He didn't necessarily define himself as delinquent, *I never got into the drugs or drinking like my uncle and cousin. They were wild, abusive. I never thought I'd live that life. But I couldn't control my anger.*

CONVICTION

On February 5, 1993 Omar had an awakening. He was in DeKalb jail facing possible life sentences with twelve major felonies for armed robberies and aggravated assaults. This was before murder was added to his charges: *It was like I woke up but it was too late. For once in my life, it was real. I realized it wasn't the life I wanted to live. But I didn't think I was ever getting out. I was saved in jail. I was desperate for a change. I thought they might see I wasn't involved in murder, but they dropped murder charges on the guy who did it and put them on me. There were times I thought of suicide. I'd rather die than do all that time.*

Ultimately, Omar received a sentence of eighteen years rather than a life sentence. "A lot of things in that case didn't add up and I think the judge knew that." For Omar, the difference between eighteen years and the twenty-five years associated with a life sentence was profound. "Eighteen years felt livable." He left a child and a pregnant, angry girlfriend saying, "How could you leave me like this. You left me with these kids."

INCARCERATION

Like many of the other men we talked with who were sent to prison young, Omar was sent to Alto. *It was one of the worst prisons. It had an infamous reputation. A hellhole. I had just turned nineteen. It was a whole nother world. I thought, "You really need to play your cards right." Guys were getting stabbed, raped, pimped, their heads broken. I wasn't like that. I thought, "You have to be strategic. You have to be mindful of people you associate with, have friendships with. This is about survival. This is real."*

When Omar entered prison in 1994, there were still educational programs available, and that allowed him to structure his life at first. He was given a kitchen detail for the first year. He planned the next year to begin alternating between a college program and a trade program, taking each for two years, which would account for most of the seven years until he was eligible to be considered for parole. However the next year, Parole increased the length of time to serve before eligibility from seven to fifteen years—and the college program was dissolved. Omar began "to lose himself," in his case by fraternizing with the female staff.

What changed his attitude and his strategy was being put into a highly structured dorm with strict rules—pants had to be ironed and creased, boots polished. He attended nine months of classes. He thrived with the discipline, became a leader, and stayed there almost two years before reentering the general population. From then on he became involved with the church, choir, and self-help groups such as AA, NA and Family Violence, which were the only programs then available in the prisons. He particularly liked Bible study because it allowed him to interact with volunteers from the outside. However he insisted, "No program work. *People* work. You have to face your problems."

By this time, the prison was trying to do better with juveniles incarcerated as adults, not immediately putting them in with the adult population. Omar became a mentor and enjoyed the role: "I felt like I was looking after my own son."

Omar was very popular with the staff at the prison. They praised him to his mother, sought different jobs for him that they thought he would like. "Making the right choices made people meet me." He identified the qualities that would make him do so well throughout his time in prison. "I learned how to do it through the system," Omar agreed. "I treated the officers like they were humans." One correctional officer said, "If we had more inmates like Omar, I could work from home." Indeed, he was transferred because the warden felt the lines between Omar and the guards were becoming blurred.

Omar was transferred to Al Burris, a prison dedicated to juveniles. Omar continued his mentoring work through the chaplaincy department. The behavior he was modeling was also becoming an essential part of his identity, which he understood most clearly when he violated it. Just before he was transferred, he had gotten into a fight as he and one of his mentees were walking to the cafeteria. His mentee told him, "I don't want to see you fighting." Omar felt shame. "I felt terrible. I *could* have avoided it. My pride got in the way. The kid and I are good friends to this day, but when he said that, it *crushed* me."

Eleven years into his sentence, Omar was abruptly transferred in the middle of the night to the Atlanta Transitional Center. He was delighted at his relative freedom. He had his own clothes, not a uniform. There was a payphone. He could see his sons in the living room, sit on the couch. He became involved in a church program.

A year later when Omar learned he had been passed over for parole and would have to wait three more years to be reconsidered, the warden, who thought highly of him, told him. "I can send you back, but I prefer to keep you here. Let me fight this one out."

Omar also became very close to the transitional center chaplain, to the assistant warden, and to the man who taught the Bar Association reentry classes, Edward Menifee, who facilitated motivational speaking engagements for him at different juvenile courts, high schools, and middle schools. He became part of a choir that toured the state.

In 2007, Omar finally received parole. He went out on work release, working at the same battery factory that hired Kevin (in Chapter 4). He was able to buy his son his first phone, excited finally to be able to provide for him.

REENTRY

MOTIVATION: Omar was exceedingly aware of the impact of having been incarcerated from an early age: *When I came to prison I was eighteen years old. I got out of prison when I was thirty-three, but I was still eighteen. You come to prison and everything is preset for you. There are responsibilities you just don't learn. I found myself making the same mistakes an eighteen or nineteen year old would do. Just this year I said to myself, OK, you have to mature twice as fast. You are forty years old and have been out almost seven years, but really I'm only like twenty-five years old. I had to battle a lot when I got out of prison. I didn't have a chance to be settled. I had to battle the sex offense stuff, battle a living place, battle losing a job. You have to allow yourself to learn those things. It has been difficult but I am determined not to give up because too many people depend on me to do right.*

SEX OFFENDER REGISTRY: The day Omar was scheduled to leave the transitional center, he reported at the parole office ready to rent a condo in a fairly upscale suburb of Atlanta. However, he was told by Parole that this would not be an acceptable address because Omar was listed on the sex-offender registry. "I had only fifteen minutes to find a place to live. I had served fourteen years and ten months. How could this happen?"

The reason why Omar was listed on the registry was because a new Georgia law said that if there was a minor present during the commission of a crime for any reason, then you must register as a sex offender. There had been a minor in a house that Omar robbed. With the help of a volunteer chaplain, a room was found for Omar in a halfway house for drug and alcohol addiction within the small time-window he was given. He experienced a very different reentry from what he had planned and saved for.

Luckily, Omar had strong advocates for many of the challenges he faced. Due to the advocacy and expertise of the Southern Center of Human Rights he was taken off the sex-offender list two years later. However, at that same time, his job at the battery factory ended when the factory laid off its third shift during the recession. Omar persisted. He studied full-time at DeKalb Tech to get credentialed as a heating and air (HVAC) technician. Andrea Shelton, a lawyer who had been inspired by her own brother's incarceration to form a prison ministry, Sheltering Heart, and who had helped Omar find housing when he first left the transitional center, now came up with a suggestion for how to help him professionally. "Would you consider going back into the prison system?" she asked him. Omar's mentor, Chaplain Nix had recently died. She and Omar went to the warden with the proposal that Omar take over his responsibilities at the transitional center, with a part-time salary provided by the non-profit. The warden enthusiastically agreed. When we interviewed him, Omar had held the position for four years, coordinating all the religious programs and self-help groups: *My transition was successful because of the people around me and also because of the decisions I made. It still needs to go back to the person——how bad you want to be successful. But that's not enough. You need other people.*

That mix is well illustrated by the surprising confluence on interests that accompanied his finally being removed from the sex-registry: *I came off the list because they changed the law. Same judge that signed me off the sex-offender list was the DA on my murder case. Crazy. Judge Gregory Adams. I had the opportunity to sit down with him. I had followed his career in the newspaper, and I couldn't stand him. He didn't even research his case because I ain't killed nobody and I got eighteen years for that, but when I looked on the paperwork and seen who signed off on it—*

And maybe two weeks after I got signed off it, I seen him at the mall. I went up to him and said "You probably don't know me but you were the DA on my case and I just want to let you know how God brings things back around. Once upon a time I didn't like you but now I thank God for you." When I graduated, he actually was on the committee at the school and watched me go across the stage and he was probably thinking, "what about this guy, he's showing up everywhere!"

Another important reintegration experience for Omar was meeting the family of the man who he was convicted of killing during a robbery: *One great opportunity I had was I was able to meet the family of the victim. They embraced me and they forgave me, even though they believe I didn't do it. They have it in their heart, just as I told them, that I didn't do it. The mother and I, we've had breakfast, we've had dinner. That helped me out a lot. I want people to see that there was a person who was willing to forgive. For men who have changed their life, that is an energy boost, a reason to keep going forward and to keep striving. Because she is encouragative. She tells me everything is going to be all right. She gets mad if I don't call. She reminds me so much of my grandmother.*

EMPLOYMENT: Employment remained a challenge every time we spoke with Omar. The first time we heard Omar was at the Fulton County rollout of the Georgia Prisoner Reentry Initiative (PRI). He spoke at the close of the plenary session, talking about his time in prison, his work as a chaplain, and then mentioned his current job search. Afterwards, he was surrounded by well-wishers, some with job leads.

When we interviewed Omar in the chaplaincy office at the Atlanta Transitional Center shortly after, he was relaxed, gracious. He was sitting behind the desk once used by his mentor Chaplain Nix and the comfort and authority that he felt in this setting was apparent. As he talked at length about his struggles with reentry, he was sitting in a place where the sharp edge of these persistent challenges was blunted by the knowledge that here he was valued and was doing valuable work. But he was also bleak. He was unemployed again. He was in his forties and still living with his mother.

Almost two years later, at yet another PRI rollout in an adjoining county, Omar sat beside us, listening restlessly to the same speeches, the same appeals by various people eager for inclusion—and for funding. All he wanted was to get to the speakers table to talk to the director of the Governor's Office of Transition and Reentry. "I need to talk, I need a job," he said jumping from his seat and forcing his way toward the speakers, an energy quite different from that we'd experienced when we'd interviewed him at the Atlanta Transitional Center.

The last time we saw him speak, two years later, Omar was part of a panel discussion organized by the Atlanta U.S. Attorney's Office. The lead federal prosecutor had had his own moment of enlightenment when someone he had convicted called him years later to ask for help with reentry. Suddenly the puzzle pieces connected, and the prosecutor was seeing a different pattern entirely, one that included the responsibility for return. So he had commissioned a video, *RELEASED: When Does the Sentence End?,* and had put together a well-rehearsed panel of eloquent formerly incarcerated people to speak after it was shown. When Omar spoke, he was blunt. All this progress on reentry didn't apply to offenders convicted of violent crimes. Employment remained almost impossible to find. Housing too.

With the help of another member of the panel, he later wrote his memoir and in 2018 was featured in the column of a local newspaper sharing the welcome news that he now had a pardon. That, he said, should make it possible for him at last to be employed. In his mind it was the same as record expungement or absolution.

Even when *that* hope dims, we believe Omar will continue to desist for the same reasons he gave for why he was able to weather prison: "I didn't *want* to be in prison. I love my kids. I built my relationship with God, the way my grandmother taught me."

Why, we wonder, do we as a society *want* to make it so hard for someone as committed to right living as Omar, whose goals are simple and laudable— self-sufficiency based on the use of a skill, like heating and air, that will allow him to provide for a family?

Omar's frustration about collateral consequences came out most clearly, oddly, in a meditation about the limits put on ex-offenders' ability to possess firearms. *When I first got out, I thought, man I don't even want to get near one. But now, I'm thinking about the culture that we stay in. For some of us who stay in certain environments you want to be a man who protects. . . . At the end of the day, I'm a man that wants a family, that wants to be able to provide for a family. I want to be a man that protect his family. Why should I be prevented by something I did twenty years ago?*

KATHLEEN

My crime was emotional and should never have happened. It does not define who I am, but society allows it to label me forever.

Kathleen was the only person we interviewed who asked to remain anonymous and did not want to be interviewed in person; instead, a writer herself, she sent in written responses to our questions. She came to our attention at a reunion called *Sisters into the Light* in honor of longtime prison chaplain Susan Bishop. Kathleen was obviously popular and highly respected among these women. At that point, recently released, she had plans to start a publishing house to help formerly incarcerated women share their stories. In that first year of reentry, she published eleven books of her own—novels, children's stories, self-help, and several works making the Bible more accessible—most of which she completed during her time in prison. She has published none since that year.

Kathleen chose to return to live in the community where she committed her crime. She was both bitter and content about her reentry experience: *It seems most expected me to fail until I proved them wrong. But none of that has changed the joy and love I feel for my Savior and for my life. I am so grateful and love the new me and I am willing to work hard and be humble in this new life as I have learned the secret of being content.* The life that fulfills her includes *walking my dog in the woods morning and night, writing to my friends in prison, enjoying my friends at work and church, and going out to eat. That is the simple life I lead now.*

CRIME & CONVICTION

Kathleen pled guilty to voluntary manslaughter in the death of her mother, who was in her late eighties at the time. She was given a sentence of twenty years, eleven to serve and nine on probation. At the time she corresponded with us, she had been out for more than a year on parole at the lowest level of supervision. She was scheduled to start probation soon.

Kathleen's crime was met with astonishment at the time it was committed. She was a popular high school English teacher, whose students thought highly of her. "She seemed like she loved students more than anything else in the whole world," one of her students said. Her parents were visiting and in an argument with her mother, she hit her mother several times with a hammer, then pushed her down a flight of stairs. Her remorse was immediate. She went to seek the help of a neighbor who was a nurse, then called 911. When the ambulance came, she was found covered with blood, curled in a fetal position near her mother, sobbing. Her mother was comatose. When her mother died six weeks later, the charges against Kathleen changed from aggravated assault to felony murder. The voluntary manslaughter plea felt satisfactory to the prosecution.

One of the volunteer chaplains who had started her work around the time Kathleen entered prison described the heart-rending level of despair and contrition she felt, how she had spent several weeks under suicide watch. Those images of her provide a context for her own responses to the challenges of reentry.

Her history provides another. She described a childhood laced with trauma, including the death of two brothers in one year, when she was six; one due to drunk driving, the other due to encephalitis. Her two remaining older siblings left home, as did her father, and she was alone with her mother: *My mother went crazy and abused me terribly. Besides beatings and enemas, I was locked in my room most of the time. When I got too old for that, she would just take things away while I was at school: clothes, toys, books, my dog. After a very painful incident, I stopped talking for a year. That was third grade. But a teacher introduced me to God and I believed after that I had an angel for a friend. I found solace in the woods, riding my horse, drawing, and writing. I still do.*

Kathleen was alienated from her parents for a long period of time. She left home at seventeen and spent twenty years in the west, where she married, raised two daughters, and taught high school and college for twenty years. Divorced after seventeen years, she came to Georgia in her early fifties and earned a PhD. Ironically, the visit by her parents from their home in the northeast was an attempt to heal the distance between them. When reached by reporters immediately after the incident, her older sister's immediate response to the incident was to say, "She's a wonderful person who made a huge mistake." This interpretation may not have withstood her mother's consequent death. At the time she corresponded with us, Kathleen said her family of origin would have nothing to do with her. Her daughters lived in different states, so did not provide a measure of social support either.

Reentry

Kathleen did, however, have chosen family in her neighbors across the street, an older couple who went to the same church. They understood the context of her crime: "They also met my parents and saw how mean they were so they understood more about what happened." The couple remained supportive of her throughout her time in prison, visiting and sending packages, and provided her with a place to stay when she was released. At the time she wrote us, she was living with them again. *We are friends/family/confidants/caregivers all rolled into one. I clean their house and solve problems with computer and Kindle or phones or anything else. Mary just broke her hip and I have been doing a lot for her.*

But the experience of reentry was far from smooth: *There was the euphoria of freedom, the outdoors, the food, the cell phone, and I got a puppy. Then there was the reality of no job, not able to teach again, no apartments would let me rent, no bank would approve a loan to buy a house . . . terrible. I couldn't even get a crummy job and I worked everyday on it.*

Even more painful than not having a job was having one that stigmatized her deeply. A Baptist preacher offered her a job as a janitor in his church in a city an hour away. She had corresponded with him while in prison about his radio broadcasts. She accepted and moved up there, but found the situation unbearable: *People at the church were critical of me being an ex-felon and said I shouldn't be able to clean the school rooms. They wouldn't let me teach a Sunday school class. I helped with English in the citizenship program and the homeless program but it was a lonely job and I felt so scorned and unwanted. I hated being a janitor because it seemed so valueless. I found a Bible study of ladies at a Methodist church that was awesome and a lake trail to walk with my dog. Other than that I was so sad that some days I would just lay in bed and feel like I was sick with the flu.*

She returned to live with her elderly friends. *I finally just decided to end all that and go back even though I had no job because at least I felt like a person with respect and I felt loved. It was a good decision. I healed and went back to job hunting.*

Kathleen started volunteering at a church-run consignment shop that eventually offered her a job. She ran into stigma there as well—but unlike the congregation at the Baptist church where she had worked before, the prejudice she experienced was not intractable. *At first they told me I would never get a raise, or use the phone or computer, but later they saw how good I was and I started training all the Goodwill people and translating and I got a raise. Now I clean the building and their church and I make plenty of money and I love my schedule. I also have lots of friends there and it feels like a family. They are all so accepting of me and never bring up the past, nor do I. That is what I am most pleased about concerning my reentry: I have a place I belong, feel comfortable, and I have a life again because of the stability there.*

TEACHING BACK: Kathleen remained angry at the general absence of institutional or social support for reentry: *The criminal justice system has in my opinion been nothing but negative and seems to expect the worst. Parole treated me like a serious criminal when I just wanted to start life over and be normal again. Before I left prison they said I had parole, then I didn't, then I did with only two weeks notice. Drove me crazy. I asked a lawyer about getting my crime expunged and was laughed out of the office. I got no help on finding work and no positive encouragement. I had a terrible time getting a driver's license too. People in government seemed to enjoy the idea of making me fail. The only challenge I feel now is patience to endure the rest of parole and nine years of probation. It seems like overkill to me and I'm ready to just have a normal life. I do everything I am supposed to but there is no reward. It is just punishment but never a reward.*

But broader social stigma and resistance were even greater obstacles: *I found no help from any organizations. I tried to get help from the local Baptist church and got no help for jobs or counseling. Some people actually laughed at me in interviews when they saw the felony on the application. It was hard to reenter society as a convict when I never felt like one and assumed I would be accepted again as a good person. One bookstore that knew about me from the newspaper accounts said I couldn't work there as it would hurt their business. Your friends may share their love for you but only enjoy your positive attitude and not your problems, and your associates just want to see you do a good job at work and expect more out of you than other employees so you have to try harder than you did before the crime.*

People at work assumed I would be a problem trying to use the computer for illegal purposes or stealing even though I have never done an illegal thing in my life. I am free of any addiction but they assumed I was an addict and would bring in drugs. The police assumed the worst. People interviewing me feared me and were never kind. The bank and anywhere I went for help wanted to keep their distance. I only got a good response from one person at work who had a nephew on death row so she understood that I was going through hell. No one in my family wanted to help me.

The reasons for Kathleen's bitterness and anger have to do with her own understanding of the nature of her crime, which was traumatic in its origin and tragic in its consequences: *I think the hardest thing about reentry was that I have never thought of myself as a criminal. The reactions were a shock to me since I assumed I would return to the respect I had since I am still a good person and I was always a good teacher. Once people get to know me at work, at church, or anywhere, they are 100% kind and friendly. Even more than before prison because they are respectful of what I have endured when before they didn't know.*

KEVIN

I always feel I am going to get there, not always be a second class citizen. In my <u>*mind*</u> *it's going to change.*

Kevin arranged to have us meet in an elegant room in a spacious, bright conference center for a large regional technical college, located in one of the counties just outside the Atlanta metro area. He is the conference center manager. The center focuses on workforce development.

A handsome blonde man in his early forties with a strong, engaging Georgia accent, the word Kevin uses most often to describe his situation is blessed. He is blessed to have caring and considerate colleagues at the conference center. Blessed to have the job at all. Blessed to have family and friends who supported him through his fifteen-year incarceration for a life sentence for murder and on his release. Blessed to be able to use the knowledge and experience acquired in prison to help others reenter, both with housing and workforce skill development. Blessed to be free.

What we took away from the interview as a lasting memory was the intensity of his regret about the murder of his close friend. But the interview began with the sleight of hand that had been necessary for him to secure this job that he valued highly and that made good use of his obvious charm, his knowledge of the target audience, and his strong administrative skills. He liked the job because his boss was off site, so there was no micromanagement but constant contact. After prison, Kevin had a strong aversion to feeling controlled, but he liked to collaborate.

The job was suggested to him by the director of admissions at the college, whose own son was incarcerated. He had met Kevin at the transitional center where Kevin was living while he worked at the governor's mansion. He knew Kevin was college educated and had been teaching GED at the transitional center and throughout his many years in prison. He encouraged Kevin to apply for various job openings in their adult education department. What allowed Kevin to be considered was his adherence to the letter, not the intent, of the application form. Asked if he had committed a crime in the last seven to nine years, he could honestly answer no because he had been incarcerated for more than the last nine years. He could honestly answer that he was not on parole because at the time he filled out the form he was still in a transitional center so was technically still incarcerated. "When they did the background check, there was nothing you could find on me. I'm blessed."

Most people he worked with knew about his record: *I had a supervisor and she felt it was her duty to share it with everyone. I could tell when people learned. They were either really kind or they were stand-offish. But there is always a change, I promise you.* At the time we talked, several years later, Kevin had very good relations with everyone he worked with directly. They lunched together, visited each other's homes.

The people who were most resistant to his presence were people in the police academy located in the center: *We were having an event, and a woman involved asked me to help her move some things that were in the police academy. So I walked back there and we were picking up trays of coleslaw. The director of the academy stepped over to me later on, "This isn't personal, but I don't want you near the police academy. I can talk to your supervisor if I need to, but I just want you to be aware that I don't want you in the police academy." When she said that, it took me back. You know you want to feel that you are as good as the next person. You want to think people are going to forgive you.*

This was not the only occasion. *We were working another event, and I had a clipboard. One of the ladies was asking who had it. Another woman later told me she heard someone from the police academy say, "The killer, he has the clipboard." But I still kill them with kindness. Every time I see them, I speak to them. I refuse to let them get the better of me. I think they have seen my dedication and hard work. I think they have maybe changed. At least they speak and say good morning now.*

CRIME & FORGIVENESS

The response of the members of the police academy to his criminal record is reflective of a basic problem in our adversarial justice system: *This whole legal concept that you can't say your sorry because that will be admitting guilt, I have trouble with that. If you're a decent human being, you want to be able to look at someone and say, "I'm sorry, I'm so sorry." You want to be able to hug a mama and say, "I'm so sorry. I'm so sorry." And they wouldn't let me do that and I think about it because you always want to tell that family that you're sorry.*

Kevin was raised on Saint Simon's Island, on the Georgia coast. His family was large, cohesive, of moderate means. He worked his way through the University of Georgia. He was particularly close to his mother, and remained so all her life.

The murder occurred shortly after leaving college, at Kevin's apartment after a night of drinking and partying. The story he tells has many of the characteristics of a trauma narrative constantly relived—vivid sensory detail and a timeless, engraved quality that needs to unroll from beginning to end. Very early in our conversation, Kevin shared it: *I made this one bad decision, big mistake, and it is totally my fault. I was out partying with friends and I accidentally killed one of my friends. He was a wonderful person and there is no excuse for it except my being young and stupid and drinking and partying. We got in a fight. We had gone out with a couple of girls and one of the girls was at the house. I had just moved into an apartment. The AC had gone out and we were trying to get the windows open. We were scraping the paint out. He had a butter knife and I had a steak knife. He pushed me and I ran behind him and I had the steak knife in my pocket and I put him in a headlock and when I shoved him, the knife in my pocket went into his heart. I can't change what people say. They said he had defense wounds on his hands. It was totally my fault so I'm not changing that. If I hadn't chased him and if I hadn't been drinking and stupid, he would still be alive. So I'm totally responsible.*

He told me, "Kevin, it feels like blood spurting." The girl was driving and I had him in the back seat on my lap and I'm trying to get him to wake up and he wasn't waking up. I was probably doing more damage than being helpful but I didn't know it at the time. And we got to the hospital and she ran in to get the nurses and doctors and they came out and I helped them lift him on the gurney and I was telling them, "It's all my fault. It's all my fault."

And they contacted his mom and we talked on the phone and I was telling her, "It's all my fault. It's all my fault." I was telling her she needed to get down here and she said there was no way. They lived in Virginia.

I was so crazy at that time that they gave me a sedative. I remember the police officer came to get me. He didn't put handcuffs on me or anything. He asked me questions, then he said he had to take me back to the hospital to do a drug test. I still can't believe he's dead and am saying, "There's no way he's dead."

So we went back to the hospital and the police officer said, "I'm sorry but they're going to make me put these handcuffs on you." I'm still stressing out about everything. I'm not thinking anything about jail or prison. That's not even crossing my mind. We went back in and I told him, I still can't believe he's dead. So he took me all the way down to the basement and talked to someone in the morgue and they told me to open the bottom drawer and there was a bag in there, so I unzipped the bag and he was in there. That's when reality hit.

With something like that, which is so traumatic, you're not thinking correctly, you're not thinking about jail. It was the least of my worries at the time.

My mom and brothers and sisters came up from Brunswick, a three-hour drive. They had to wait to get a Superior Court judge a week later. Home for six months before trial, I still never thought about going to jail. I guess you think, "I'm not a bad person, they're not going to send me to jail. It's not like I intended to kill him or anything."

In appeal documents, it appears that the crime was more violent than Kevin can absorb, that the knife went in with more force and required more force to withdraw, that there were defensive wounds on his friend's hands. Kevin is, of course, aware of the differences. "You always want to make it less bad than it was, and other people want to make it worse—and the truth is usually in between." The story Kevin tells is the truth he can live with. He does not minimize the tragic loss of his friend's life or his part in it. What he refuses to assume is conscious malicious intent—or an essential, irreversible negative identity.

Kevin so strongly believed that it was an accident that his lawyer did not directly relay a plea deal for involuntary manslaughter. It is not clear Kevin would have accepted a plea deal at that point anyway. He was charged and convicted of felony murder and received a life sentence, which in 1994 when he was convicted, was twenty-five years with parole eligibility after seven years. In 1995, the time until parole eligibility was doubled, to fourteen years.

Kevin described how for the first couple of years in prison, he would dream about his victim, who in his dreams was still alive. Kevin would tell him, "Go and tell these folks you're alive. They think you're dead. You need to tell these folks you are alive."

But the family of his victim as well as Kevin's own family, struggled over the years about forgiveness. The father of the victim came to visit Kevin soon after his son's death. After he talked with the DA, the father's attitude changed. Before the trial, Kevin's family visited the father. The visit may not have gone well. Kevin felt his own family was so concerned about him, they might not have shown enough concern for the father. However, the father called the warden at the first prison Kevin was sent to and asked to speak to Kevin. The warden said that this was the first time he had ever allowed this, but if Kevin wanted to talk to him, he would allow it as long as he was in the room. There was a lot of crying. The father was trying to reconcile, just as Kevin probably was, some of the claims of the prosecutors and the autopsy report findings with Kevin's account.

Fifteen years later when Kevin's parole eligibility was approaching, Kevin's aging mother tried to visit the victim's mother in Virginia but was refused entry. This visit probably combined genuine remorse and concern for the victim's mother and also concern about the approaching parole decision for Kevin, where victims are allowed to speak against parole.

INCARCERATION

Prison was a traumatic and then a hardening experience for Kevin. He found people abrasive, frightening. He explained the hardening process that took place over several years by describing an incident early in his time in prison: *I remember we were out in the yard and some guys were shouting and this officer saying, "If you all don't shut up I'll make you stay out there all night long." It was December in Savannah and that can be cold. It was raining. A white guy said to those shouting, "Why don't you shut the fuck up." I didn't think anything about it, just thought it was an argument and once we went inside this would be over. But I went inside the building and I see these guys come up to the guy who had told them to shut up, they beat him with a chair. There were about five or six guys. And this was a white guy and these were black guys jumping on him. I wasn't looking at the color, this was just what it was. I had never seen that before in my life. You look at my charge and say, "Well you just committed a murder how can you think that this is something you haven't seen?"*

I'm trying to get people to stop it. They are not going to get involved in it. But, this guy doesn't deserve to be beat to death. The guys who are doing the beating are looking at me now. I'm very new, only there two or three months. Everybody just steps back in their room and look at me like I'm crazy for standing out there. These guys weren't even in our dorm. They had snuck in to beat him up. I was staring at the officer behind the glass, trying to force the officer to look at me so he can see in my eyes that we need help—because I couldn't bang on window or it would draw their attention. So one of the guys said, "You say one word, you'll be next." So all I could do was just stand there and look. When they finally got enough, I went in there and looked after the guy. His eyes were all black and blue and he was bleeding and I took care of him.

I realized six or seven years down the line, I had become one of those people who kept inside their doors—that I stepped aside, that I wasn't one to get involved. When you first come in, you go to help like you would outside, but after awhile you're immune to that. You back up and stay away from things.

Kevin was lucky to receive steady support from family and friends throughout his time in prison. When he was overwhelmed, his friends would remind him he would not be in there forever. Most of the prisons he was sent to were close to his family, and his mother would visit weekly. If he was moved to a new prison and she was unable to see him for awhile, she would just drive around the prison, consoled by knowing that he was inside.

Another thing that made Kevin's incarceration manageable was that he always believed he would get out: *I think those appeals always made me think, you're going to go home. You're going to go home. That this wasn't a permanent situation. And throughout my entire incarceration I never once believed that I wasn't going home.* His toughest year was his seventh, when his father died, then his parole was set off for another eight years because of the change in the law—and then his stepfather died.

His coping strategy was to keep constantly busy. Generosity also helped. One thing that Kevin's mother taught him was to treat people *better* than you wanted to be treated. He understood his situation was different from many of his incarcerated friends: *They couldn't call home. They didn't have money for the commissary. It made me more empathetic. I could brighten someone's life by giving them something. You see poverty, the lowest of the low, and it makes you see how blessed you are. I used to work for a furniture company, and I would open stores. People would come in with a Department of Corrections ID, and I would just throw their applications away. Ignorance led me to do things I am ashamed of now.*

In prison, he found inmates were the most helpful to him: *Some guys are decent, creative, kind. This world is mirrored there. They are a little more violent, and more honest about how they feel.* Chaplains were of some help, and some corrections officers were kind and some were "awful, rude, unkind, tormenting." He admired those officers who were not afraid to speak up, who did what he had tried to do his first months in prison, insist that there was a code of conduct for officers as well that was based on basic decency.

Kevin spent two of his last years in prison working at the governor's mansion, which is staffed by prisoners. At first Kevin wasn't interested when his warden suggested he let himself be considered for the privilege because it meant he would have to move. "Prison is traumatic," he repeated. "*Any* change in prison is traumatic." But the move proved positive. Living in the transitional center allowed him to acclimate to all the changes that had taken place in the years of incarceration, and also to see the attitudes of different governors toward the work staff, the difference between tolerance and genuine acceptance. For example, Governor Nathan Deal made sure his chef was paid wages similar to what he would make in the free world.

Reentry & Giving Back

Kevin was, as he recognized, very lucky to find a good job even before he left prison. He has been lucky in several other ways as well.

SOCIAL TIES: Kevin's mother died the year before he was released, but Kevin had supportive siblings and life-long friends as well as supportive colleagues at work. His friends did not label him by what he had done. During his incarceration, they had visited him in prison, written letters, sent Christmas cards. His siblings were so supportive he sometimes found them smothering, which was why he decided not to move back to his hometown.

The longest lasting effect prison had had on Kevin was a wariness of emotional intimacy and a need for control: *I push people away. I have some people I spend some time with. But I was forced to live with so many people and I had people who had so much control over my life—when I watched TV, what I watched on TV, what I could eat, when I could eat, when I used the restroom. A woman asked me yesterday, "You don't have anybody? You don't date?" I told her, "No because I have heard so many stories about people who get close to someone and they end up going back to prison. I don't want to ever take any chances where I let someone control if I go back to prison." I like my freedom. I like my independence. For so many years I was dictated to. I think people don't actually understand how blessed they are until they experience what we experienced. You don't realize how valuable freedom is until you lose it.*

HOUSING: Unlike the usual experience, finding housing for Kevin was easy. He found his first apartment with the help of a colleague, who introduced him to her brother who had an apartment to rent without mentioning his criminal record.

Kevin was excited by his current situation that allowed him both to be open about his own record and to help others reenter. A wealthy local man whose son was incarcerated in Arizona for vehicular homicide had decided to turn an old mansion in the town square into a transition house for men who had been incarcerated. He made Kevin the resident manager, which provided Kevin with housing: *Our mission is to help guys who have been gone a long time and have lost everything. Nineteen or twenty years old when they go in and have been gone for twenty or thirty years and they've lost their moms and their dads, and their sisters and have their own lives.* Kevin, working with a local pastor and a woman active in community outreach, was developing the entrance criteria and program links to make the place effective for rehabilitation as well as housing.

TEACHING BACK: Education was key to the changes Kevin wanted to see to improve reentry. The conference center housed a large national work skills certification program in which Kevin was involved. He also served on the board of a regional workforce commission where he could lobby to open some of this training and education to people with criminal records. Many of the people on the commission did not know he had a criminal background: *Every time, we cross people who have been incarcerated off the list of people eligible. Sometimes I'll bite my tongue, other times I'll speak up and say, "Well can't we—" and they will get quiet, then say, "It's not us. It's the employers. They don't want anyone with a background." That's one of the number one things we need to address. Employers need to be educated.*

Kevin felt that the biggest obstacle to reentry was adequate, credentialed skills training while in prison. If people were offered courses, like culinary art, that had no associated accreditation, they were useless on release. Many prisoners are required to get GEDs, but there are some people who will never be able to earn them. He wondered why they weren't being taught trades, like welding, that might have real world usefulness. He summed up the challenge he saw as, "If you take a drug dealer who is able to earn $200 a day dealing, *how* can he learn to do something else to support himself?"

He also described all the ways prison actively worked against all the social skills that are equally necessary to getting and keeping a job. Prison taught you not to shake hands, not to approach anyone, never to speak unless you were spoken to. It educated you in how to be *anti*social. How, he wondered, did you begin to undo that?

ARIIF

The greatest high in my life is to be a sober-minded, God-conscious human being. Just to have your faculties, to be able to think.

Ariif had a daunting reputation in prison. From what we gathered from comments made by members of PIIC, he was at one time seen as dangerous, incorrigible, and, simultaneously, a source of hope and inspiration. "If *Ariif* could get out—"; "If *Ariif* could make it out here—" When this was remarked on, Ariif looked genuinely puzzled. "A reputation?" he asked and shook his head. We found it difficult to believe too since the respect he had now was so obviously based on very different criteria. A tall, muscular man then in his late sixties, he was measured and thoughtful in his speech, quietly confident in his bearing. He often wore a Muslim prayer cap.

Ariif served a total of thirty-three years in Georgia prisons, an eight-year sentence in the 1970s, and twenty-four years on three consecutive life sentences, from the early 1980s to 2006. He spent five years of his first sentence in administrative isolation. A few years into his second sentence, he escaped and was a fugitive for a year and a half before turning himself in. He was released when he was sixty. At the time we talked with him he had been out about seven years, his sentence commuted so he was no longer on parole.

Since his release, he had worked for the Georgia Department of Transportation as a traffic signal technician, a skill he learned in prison. He has become a supervisor since we interviewed him. He had married his childhood sweetheart and was working on his BA in business, which he has now completed. His greatest aspiration was to continue his studies and earn his doctorate. "Knowledge is power," he said. "You can carry it from the cradle to the grave."

EARLY INFLUENCES

Ariif's mother was fourteen and his father sixteen when he was born. He was raised primarily within his mother's family, particularly by his grandmother, who encouraged his parents not to marry because she thought they were too young. His mother was the middle child of eight. The relationship between the maternal and paternal families was supportive and Ariif moved back and forth easily inside the village that raised him. When he was twelve he went to live primarily with his father, stepmother and four half-siblings. Both sides were made up of hard-working, church people. His maternal grandmother and his aunts and mother were all factory workers. His father was a truck driver and his paternal grandmother had a beauty salon. Education was not of such a high value. However, Ariif was a good student, also a good athlete and finished high school, which was seen as a significant accomplishment.

He then joined the Air Force because he had an uncle who had served and he was impressed by him when he would come home to visit. Ariif also wanted to escape: "I wanted to get away from the conditions I grew up in. I wanted to detach myself from that."

Ariif was posted to Germany in 1965, and played competitive sports, including professional ball, all over Europe. He worked first as military police, then changed to aerospace security technician, which involved securing nuclear devices. He took continuing education classes.

But it was the range of social and cultural values he was exposed to that had the greatest effect: *I enjoyed being exposed to other cultures and people. I learned I was naive about most things. It made me grow up and take responsibility for myself. I was a good observer and listener. I went to many countries on leave. Most of the countries were more progressive than the U.S. They didn't have the racial strife. I had a fondness for jazz and there were a lot of African-American artists in Europe. I knew Richard Wright and James Baldwin had been there. Dizzie Gillespie, Yusuf Latif.*

Growing up, Ariif had lived in a mixed-race working class neighborhood where white and black children played together on the streets but did not visit each other's houses. He didn't understand this as segregation until some white policemen picked him up when he was ten as a joke and told him never to cross the train tracks.

In Germany, he had friends of both races and many nationalities: *I learned to speak a little German and Spanish. I was fascinated by people. I had African friends. One from Nigeria taught Swahili at the University of Cologne. We all loved jazz. I was bitter about all the stuff going on back in the States, Martin Luther King's murder, the shootings at Kent State, but it was totally different in Europe, more comfortable.* His friends also exposed him to weed, hash, and harder drugs.

First Crime, Incarceration, Activism

Except for Ariif, the impact of broader social forces were rarely mentioned in our interviews. In Ariif's case, the shift from the broader horizons of Europe to the racial constriction of Atlanta contributed to his anger. So did his use of drugs. Honorably discharged from the Air Force in October, 1968, he was incarcerated for armed bank robbery and assault by January 1970. He was given a life sentence, which at that time was eight years served: *How I got there in my head . . . I was frustrated by stuff in society. One of my high school friends approached me. I had taken the civil service exam and had worked about a year in the post office. I quit because I was associating with street hustlers. I liked the fast money; the challenge, risk and excitement turned me on. I had no sense of direction.*

Ariif was sent to Georgia's most infamous prison at that time, Reidsville. During the time he was there the *Guthrie v. Evans* case was tried, which exposed the inhumane conditions in the prison and put it under federal supervision for over twenty years. These suits included complaints about medical and psychiatric care, substandard conditions including plumbing, sewage and fire hazards, unconstitutional disciplinary practices, guard brutality, racial discrimination in work assignments and discipline, verbal abuse, infringing the rights of Muslim inmates, the lack of educational and vocational activities, and interference with the mail. The consent decrees agreed on in 1978, late in Ariif's stay, included stopping unsupervised bread and water diets.

Ariif described these conditions more concretely: *It was a horrible experience. There were two or three deaths a month on average at Reidsville. Blood on the floors and the walls. Hundreds of men lived in open dormitories, knives were common. There were people screaming from being stabbed to death, rapists. It was a segregated institution. They kept white inmates on the east side and blacks on the west side. There were no African Americans employed as guards. There were race riots. Administrative people would give weapons to white guys. It was barbaric.*

A group of African-American student activists from Clark University, The Harriet Tubman Brigade, brought in educational material for them to use. An article published in their newsletter, *The Link,* connected the race struggle going on outside the prison with the struggle inside the prison system. Ariif began to apply this idea to his own situation and began to understand his incarceration—and his rebellion against it—as part of a larger political struggle. He began to hold political education classes with other prisoners around basic concepts of unity, about their own lives and families. He also began to organize work stoppages and hunger strikes to protest the terrible prison conditions: *I was naive enough not to be afraid. I organized people around events to improve conditions. I felt I had to. It was dangerous work, but if you tolerated the conditions, you were in danger anyway. We wanted to be treated like humans.*

At one point we heard Ariif describe himself during that period as a "proud convict": *I used to stand up for my own rights, politically educating people and passing materials around. We encouraged people to stay away from institutionalized behavior like gambling and just the crazy crazy stuff there.*

He read ferociously. And he had time to do so, because for the next five years, 1972 to 1977, he was held in isolation. In some ways, this was terrible, but it also protected him: *My father was of the opinion that he could help me with Parole if I was a model prisoner, but being a model prisoner in Georgia at that time was not the way to go—because the prisons had no standards. They could care less about protecting the few rights you retained. It was a gruesome, ugly, vile, violent situation.* During this time of isolation, along with occasional family visits, he was allowed visits—and reading material—from the Harriet Tubman Brigade, which supported his sense of mission. The ultimate success of the lawsuits, which put Reidsville under federal supervision for twenty years, also gave him a sense of validation and agency.

Unsurprisingly, he left prison angrier than he went in.

RECIDIVISM

Ariif was out only three and a half years before his second conviction, what he called "the magic number for recidivism." Chemical addiction had a lot to do with his return. He had sobered up a little in prison, but he was in strong denial about how strong his addictions were. Once he came out, he began using cocaine again: "I convinced myself I could control it. I could just snort it." He then started mixing it with heroin and injecting it.

He also returned to the same friends, the same activities. He was deeply involved in the drug culture. The murder was of a peer, "part of a street code mentality, that gave me creds from people." He then returned to the same prison culture he had left—this time with three life sentences for armed robbery, aggravated assault, and murder. But he was not the same: "I had become harder. I took someone's life. I am not proud of that. It is something you can never get back."

Ariif was harder but also more responsible: *Returning, I was at my lowest point. I could see how devastating my conduct was to my family. I knew they were decent people. These were choices I had made. I was devastated that I had allowed myself to be entrapped by the criminal justice system. I had looked at my activities as a rebellion against the establishment. But they were self-destructive. Certain truths slap you in the face. I did this to myself.*

He was alone in absorbing this truth. His father had supported him through his first incarceration, but had told him, "I'm going to be there for you the first time. But if you get in trouble again, you're on your own."

ESCAPE, RESPONSIBILITY, GROWTH

This self-accounting became too difficult, and four years into his second sentence, Ariif escaped from the prison in downtown Atlanta and stayed out for eighteen months: *I was undone about being back in the system, so I ran. After I came back to prison, then I became sober-minded and began to do a lot of self-inventory. I came to grips with some of the realities around me and in me. I reconciled to the fact you need to know who you are as a human being. I had to reclaim my humanity.*

Intellectual Grounding: Ariif began reading extensively and also assimilating and integrating what he was reading. "I became a voracious reader the first time I was in, but it didn't penetrate." He was interested in the political implications of the philosophers he read, including Karl Marx's *Communist Manifesto*, Hegel, Kant. "I wanted to know what they had envisioned for mankind." A book that had a lot of influence was Frances MacDonald Cornford's *From Religion to Philosophy: A Study in the Origins of Western Speculation.* This book, first published in 1912 and republished in 1957, was for Ariif a book about the importance of consciousness and conscious existence: *I wanted to live with that consciousness. I found it liberating. I read everything that allowed me to become a better thinker—Herbert Marcuse, Erich Fromm's Escape from Freedom and The Art of Loving, Maslow's hierarchy of needs, Pavlov and operant behavior.*

Islam: Ariif's interest in Islam came in part because he was "always open to spearheading things that might change general living conditions." The Muslims in prison, especially at Reidsville, had been involved in protesting and improving conditions there. They also sent chaplains into the prisons, people like A.J. Sabree, who had helped defuse and improve the situation. *I was attracted to the prayer. It had a natural rhythm, like pulses of life five times a day. If you can think on God a minimum of five times a day, you are going to change. I could appreciate the result it had in transforming guys who had no sense of direction.* Ariif also liked that Muslims believed that there was no compulsion in religion and that everyone was encouraged to study, to learn.

In time Ariif became an amir, what they called a prison imam: *It took some years and learning. Most of the guys I associated with who were Muslim, the teachers and outside imams and the amirs, they thought of me as being reasonably intelligent, and when I began to express myself about what I was learning about the faith and when I continued to show some growth, they liked associating with me and having me on committees. I was very active inside the system in the Muslim community.*

Ariif's faith had various positive effects. "I choose to be objective and a man of faith," he said. "If I do right by myself and other people, God will bring blessing." This belief helped Ariif accept responsibility for the murder he had committed. This acknowledgement is made much more difficult within our system because it means that you are relinquishing your right to appeal. "I fought my case for a few years through the court. But you know you did the crime, and you need to own up to God." He was also able to tell the parole board he accepted responsibility and wonders if that had any effect on their eventual decision to give him parole. Whether it did or not, its impact on him was essential for his own growth: "It helped me to free myself from this horrendous act. I learned God's mercy exceeds His wrath."

REENTRY

After Ariif had served twenty-two years on his three life sentences, he was eligible for parole review. He was denied and was set off for eight more years. He challenged this decision because his crimes had been committed when other parole rules were in effect. Before 1986, people with life sentences were reviewed annually for parole eligibility after they had served seven years. Later rules have continually expanded the amount of time to be served before consideration and also have given the parole board the freedom to set people off for eight years before reconsidering. However, a lawsuit, *Akins v. Snow*, had established that these harsher terms could not be applied retroactively. So Ariif, whose crimes preceded these new procedures, was set off two years, then reconsidered annually.

He believed his release was facilitated eventually by the intervention of the warden at Central Prison in Macon who came there in 2006. The warden had been a correctional officer in Reidsville when Ariif had been there. When he saw Ariif, he said, "I've been keeping up with you." He asked him when he was coming up for review again. Wardens have the authority to weigh in heavily on your release from prison. "Keep your nose clean," he told Ariif.

By this time, Ariif served as a teacher's aide, ran self-help groups, was a vice-president of Jaycees and Alcoholics and Narcotics Anonymous groups, and was active in the Islamic community. The warden told him, "We use you old guys to control the young guys."

Ariif emphasized that preparation for reentry takes place while you are still inside, that you must fight continuously not to become institutionalized: *There was not one day that I was comfortable with it. I would lie down at night and say, "Peace, all things in God's time," but there was not one day I was comfortable with it.*

Ariif found a job quickly when he received parole. At first he married a young woman he had met while incarcerated, a relationship that didn't last, then lived with his father, who at this point was highly supportive. His ten siblings have done well, and include a college athletic director, a small business owner, and an accountant. They too were supportive. He attended the Atlanta Masjid, whose congregation included many people he grew up with. He found that people he knew before he went to prison were often the people who were most accepting—because they had a sense of him that was larger than his criminal history.

Since reentering, Ariif had actively worked to make reentry more possible for others. A founding member of the support group PIIC (Persons Impacted by Incarceration), which held monthly support groups for formerly incarcerated people, he often provided sage, unsentimental advice. He also provided sex-offender counseling and support services to people under supervision through Comprehensive Human Services, a social service agency where he is Assistant Director of Support Services. He travelled frequently with other members of PIIC to some of the worst prisons in Georgia to encourage men who have no hope of leaving prison, an increasingly large proportion of the prison populations. "You don't know what the future will bring," he would tell them. "Laws change. Look at me. No one expected me to get out."

When asked about the significance others give to his criminal history, he said: *If they don't know, they treat you as an equal. If they do know, they often don't want to associate. Sometimes they are forgiving. But stereotypes, even in a family, are "people never change." For the most part, I worry about what I can control. I focus on living responsibly. Choices come with consequences.*

\10/

SEX OFFENDERS

Ostracism in perpetuity—is it necessary?

It is difficult when one has intimate, life-long knowledge of the profoundly damaging consequences of child sexual abuse to listen in good faith to the nuances in the stories of sexual offenders, or those society has defined as sexual offenders. It is also necessary. Because sex offense is one area where we most actively use the power of broad, relentless social stigma to prevent any possibility of repetition—and also any possibility of reentry or reintegration. If that power is being transferred to us as citizens, then it is our responsibility to use it wisely.

Sex registry has been federally required of the states since 1994. Two years later Megan's Law mandated public disclosure of individuals identified as "potentially dangerous sex offenders." In 2006 the Adam Walsh Act mandated a new registration structure at both federal and state levels with a three-tier system based on crime severity with different requirements for each level. Over this period all states also extended registration requirements to juveniles convicted in adult courts of sexual offenses. Most states also have done the same for children adjudicated delinquent of sex offenses through their juvenile systems.[1]

The 2006 Walsh Act also broadened the scope of what is considered a sexual offense (and thereby requiring registration as a sexual offender), including even public urination and indecent exposure. Similar expansion has occurred in recent years in state after state. With the broadening of what is considered criminal sexual offending, sex offenders have become the fastest growing category of state and federal prisoners. Consequently, their proportion among the prison population is climbing, varying among the states from 10% up to close to 30% of all prisoners.[2] The estimates of the numbers on sex offender registries keeps growing as well to over 900,000 in 2018.[3] In Georgia, the total number on the registry in 2019 was 32,223, increasing annually by about 1,400. Of these, 27,483 were unincarcerated.[4]

Maps and addresses of sex offenders are available, indeed our local newspaper publishes a map every Halloween. As this practice implies, many people interpret your presence on these registries as proof that you are a predatory pedophile. It also implies that the usual sexual predator is someone you don't know, when 86% of sexual violence victims know their perpetrators.[5] It also assumes that stranger predation of juveniles takes place in the residences of predators, which is also not true. However, these assumptions and fears infuse our society and are exacerbated by the registries. Courts are beginning to define sex registration as a continuing punishment, in part because of the breadth and severity of the stigma that goes with it. It is almost impossible to find housing if you are on the registry. Work is also difficult.

RIDE-ALONG

Convicted sex offenders are primarily male. They cross the whole economic spectrum, which was evident to us on a ride-along in our home county with Thomas Hare, who had recently been promoted to assistant chief in the Department of Community Supervision, to visit people on his prior sex-offender case load.

We visited a small run-down house a mile from where we live, where we were met by an elderly man's very pregnant granddaughter who described the stroke that had just sent him to the hospital. His physical state made the supervision requirement that he have no contact with children under eighteen irrelevant, while the number of family members regularly in and out of the house made its enforcement difficult.

Our next visit was to a suburban development to the south of the county, where a man, convicted of possessing child pornography, was now on probation after having spent a year in jail. His two dogs barking vigorously around his feet, he shook hands firmly and smiled broadly. He had just gone on a job interview, an architect friend of his checking out beforehand whether there were any schools or bus stops within 1,000 feet of the employer. His wife was now the major breadwinner. He was hoping that the job would work out; his unemployment was adding strain to their marriage. He wanted permission to visit an old friend in North Carolina.

In another suburban development a few miles north, we visited a man in his late twenties who worked night shift at a hotel. He had served two years in prison, had recently completed treatment, and was now facing fifteen years of probation for having molested an eleven-year-old boy he was babysitting. His partner came out to visit with Hare as well. Officers standardly interview spouses and partners.

In another city on the far east side of the county, we visited a man in a condo complex who was under house arrest and wearing an ankle monitor. He also had been convicted of possessing child pornography. His wife, a schoolteacher, was pregnant with their first child. He was able to go to church, look for a job, and go to band practice, but he wanted to go to the grocery store because "he didn't want his wife to have to lift things." He couldn't find a lawyer to go to court and make the petition for less than $1500. Hare asked if his therapist was helping with this. Hare was suspicious because his wife was a second grade teacher still actively teaching, so was lifting things all the time. Helping his wife with the grocery shopping was probably the least of this father-to-be's real challenges. Supervision requirements forbid supervisees being in contact with anyone under eighteen, even their own children, unless permitted by court order. They also forbid their possessing photographs of anyone under eighteen.

Going north, we pulled into a parking lot for a hardware store. Hare was careful to avoid visiting places of work, so called this supervisee instead on his cellphone. The man answered promptly, from a boat on a nearby lake where he was out fishing. Hare arranged to see him another time. The man was on lifetime supervision because he openly said he still fantasized about his child victim. "Not quite a predator," Hare said, "but he makes everyone uncomfortable."

As we drove past a car wash, Hare mentioned that one of his most successful supervisees worked there. They had had to apply for special permission for him to work there because it is was closer than 1,000 feet to a high school. The man was now a manager.

We also visited a split-level house in a subdivision in the far north of the county, bird feeders on all the trees, the home of a high school teacher accused of sliding his fingers into the waistbands of his female students' jeans, and under the elastic of their underwear. He was out running errands. His wife, recovering from hip surgery, was not able to come to the door. Hare spoke to her briefly from the stoop. Community supervision officers are allowed to come at any hour of the day or night to the homes and workplaces of sex offenders and search the premises.

Another man in an elegant garage apartment located closer to the center of the county, an Alcoholics Anonymous sponsor, was saying good-bye to one of his mentees, whom he was going to invite to his church. He had been incarcerated for four years for sodomy and aggravated assault with a woman, an encounter he insisted had been consensual, perhaps complicated by drugs. He had been out of prison a decade, still attended therapy although it was no longer required, and had a successful job as a search engine optimizer, a job that he could do from home. His mentee had also been on Hare's caseload. Both men complimented Hare on his recent promotion.

Viewing from this distance, the front seat of an unmarked car with the engine running, or out on the lawn, politely shaking hands, created a different experience from just reading a record of the crimes. There were real faces. Homes. Back stories. The bird feeders stayed in our mind, as did the second grade teacher expecting her first child, the old Sears catalogue with photos of young boys in underwear that fascinated the man in the fishing boat and made all those who supervised him, from officer to judge, uneasy. But the experience we had talking directly and at more length with people enduring the long-term collateral consequences of their sex-offender status created far more complex responses.

INTERNET EXPLOITATION
DARREN

One morning we were awakened by a desperate call from a mother in New Orleans. She had somehow located our listening project on the web and was trying to see if we or anyone we knew might be able to help her son, Darren, who lived in Georgia. He needed a job, was terrified of losing his house. He had accepted a plea deal at the encouragement of his lawyer. The felony charge, sexual exploitation of minors, would not require prison time, rather a five-month incarceration in a probation detention facility, then probation for a year and a half. It also included registering as a sex offender. He hadn't understood the implications. Neither had his family.

Thomas Hare explained on our ride-along: *A lot of people take pleas like that and don't fully understand what it means to be placed on the sex registry, what the proximity restrictions are going to mean. Your house will be put on the registry, and a lot of people don't like that, so they will make them move out. And when they come to us for intake and we tell them these things, they say, "Nobody told me in court."*

Darren's mother described all the steps she and her son had already taken to try and improve his situation. A college-educated IT worker with ten-years experience who owned his home, he was now in danger of defaulting on his mortgage—and terrified. He had left one job when charged, lost another job when convicted. The owner of a small private firm had tried to hire Darren on release from the detention center, but all his other employees threatened to quit if he did. Now Darren, with little income, faced a year and a half of probation, court ordered therapy at $40 a week, fines of $2500. In ten years, if he remained crime free, he could petition to be removed from the registry. Until then, how would he survive if every job search implied he was a dangerous predator?

Darren's mother was desperate. She firmly believed in the innocence of her only son. She and her husband had given their son the $100,000 to post bail. But her husband had been laid off a year ago, three days before he turned sixty, while he was recovering from salivary gland cancer. Their income had fallen from a $100,000 a year to $2300 a month. She was sixty-one, trying to pick up any jobs, for example online and focus group surveys, to bring in income. She didn't know what else she could do from Louisiana. The probation officers were kind, as were the sheriff's deputies who checked on her son monthly. They were worried that he would forget to celebrate Christmas. She was worried how any of them were going to survive after that.

Darren himself described how he filled out ten applications a day at TOPPSTEP, the Department of Labor's program for returning citizens. He'd received fifteen job offers, all rescinded when employers received the results of the background check. Someone had suggested he contact a disbarred lawyer who had embezzled in Miami but now had a successful church in his area. When he talked with people at the Governor's Officer on Transition and Reentry, they bluntly told him, "We know no success stories of people with sex offenses."

The newspapers told a different story from the mother, of a young man, perhaps one with delayed emotional development, whatever his intelligence and level of education, who had made his neighbors increasingly uneasy because he hung out in his home with sixteen-year-old boys playing video games. The boys all denied there was anything going on, even one boy who was found with marijuana said Darren hadn't given it to him. But Darren *had* impersonated a teenage girl on the internet and encouraged teenage boys to send his alter-ego nude photos. This was the charge he ultimately pled to.

JUVENILES CHARGED AS ADULTS
NIER, ANTHONY, GENARLOW, OMAR

Juvenile sexual offenders rarely recidivate, yet they have often been harshly punished. Both Nier and Anthony, whose stories we have already shared, were juveniles when they received lengthy sentences in adult prison for sex crimes. Laws in Georgia have since changed such that their sexual encounters would now only be considered misdemeanors. Instead, Nier, at fifteen, received ten years in prison and fifteen on probation; Anthony, at sixteen, twenty-five years in prison, down from 165 years.

Nier described his crime in this way: *The girl was one year younger than me. Her mom was letting me stay with her but the mom was on drugs. I went to get her drugs . . . she got me locked up. From my background in and out of juvenile, things like that, they just gone and railroaded me.*

Anthony described his this way: *I started dating this girl. At the time I didn't know who she was. She was just cute. Her mom caught us in bed. Because she was DeKalb County police and she walked into her daughter having sex, the mom pushed it to rape. I expect her daughter said something, when she pushed her, about my making her. But I'd been to the house a number of times and she knew we was dating, so it wasn't a date rape. We were in her mom bed. If they would have did any type of check like a rape kit—they didn't do them then—they would have seen there was nothing forced, no clothes torn, no scratches, no forced penetration. But they didn't ask.*

For both these men, the supervision conditions associated with being identified as a sex offender on top of very long prison sentences felt unjust. When they were boys, Anthony and Nier were both defiantly delinquent, also deeply deprived. People were clearly fed up and angry with them. The choice to charge and convict them on sexual charges, especially given their ages, was driven by the fact that there were angry, and in the case of the mother in law enforcement, empowered parents on the side of the victims—and sexual crimes provided prosecutors with the longest sentences.

Georgia's juvenile sex offender laws gained international attention in 2005 with the trial of Genarlow Wilson. He and four other teenage boys were arrested for engaging in multiple sex acts with two girls, ages sixteen and seventeen. A videotape made by one of the teens provided the evidence.

Wilson refused the plea bargain taken by the other boys, believing he had committed no crime. He was convicted in 2005 of aggravated child molestation, receiving a sentence of ten years in prison.

Fortunately for Wilson, the conviction received substantial critical attention and a number of people took up his cause. The following year the Georgia legislature passed what is commonly referred to as a "Romeo and Juliet" amendment to the law. Consensual underage sexual activity is still illegal but if both are no older than eighteen and there is no more than four years between them the offense is downgraded to a misdemeanor.

There was another important aspect to this story. The prosecutor in this case, Douglas County District Attorney David McDade, made multiple copies of the sex tape to defend his position in the face of mounting criticism, showing it to lawmakers, reporters, and even a talk show host. As one of McDade's critics pointed out, "there's no exception to the child porn laws that says prosecutors may distribute child pornography if they're trying to salvage their reputations."[6]

An oddity in Georgia's Sex Registry law is that kidnapping or false imprisonment of a minor puts you on the sex offender registry. These charges are often associated with armed robberies where a child just happened to be somewhere on the premises and was never the focus of the crime. This is what happened to Omar. The sex-offender label created far worse collateral consequences for him than his murder conviction. The law was changed in 2012, driven in part by the Southern Center for Human Rights' advocacy for Omar. The modification in the law allows people who had a kidnapping or false imprisonment charge without any sexual offense or attempted sexual offense associated to petition to be removed from the sex registry. This charge has continued to interfere with a number of reentry efforts, according to community supervision officers we've talked to. Since armed robberies are one of the most common charges of juveniles tried as adults or of young adults, these additional consequences have had a serious impact on their ability to find work or housing, especially because these petitions are both costly and slow.

COMMUNITY RESTORATION

IRVING
I was brought back to be a blessing.

We were introduced to Irving by Aakeem, a lifer and an SB 440, who together with Irving developed a successful inmate-initiated mentoring program at Telfair Prison. (Aakeem's story is shared in the family chapter.) Irving had been out of prison for about a year and a half when we talked with him. He lived in a town near the coast with a large army base. He was a small man, in a suit a little too large. He had a low rather husky voice. We met at a coffee house in town and sat in armchairs in a small conversational alcove, talking, over background music and bustle, about very difficult things.

Irving's story is unusual because of the level of social support he received both during his prison term and in his reentry and seems to promise something very unusual for a sex offender, genuine social restoration.

Irving grew up in Long Island, joined the military in 1980 after finishing high school. He married after training. He retired from the military after he came back from Korea, nearly thirty-five years ago. He was always active in music, participating in, organizing and directing choirs. In Korea, he was the coordinator for all gospel music services at the military bases. When he retired, he created a community choir. He was also employed as the first case manager for the city's Next Step Homeless Program for three years before his arrest. In 2004, he was convicted of child molestation and sentenced to ten years in prison. He was released in 2014, with five years more on parole. Now in his early fifties, he and his wife were separated. Their three children, young adults, were all successfully independent.

PRISON

Irving was lucky to receive a high level of social support while in prison: *My family, pastor, and my pastor friends all came to visit me all the time in prison. The prison chaplain invited the pastors to do worship services in the prison. This was support from people I knew. They remembered the good in me.*

He personally did not receive harsh treatment from other inmates as a sex offender: *I have seen cruel treatment of sex offenders, but I never experienced it—no threats or taunting.*

GIVING BACK: PRISON

In prison, Irving was active in the chaplaincy department from the beginning: *preaching, choir president, giving workshops on choir etiquette, music ministry. The chaplain gave me carte blanche.*

Telfair prison at the time Irving was sent there was a very dangerous, closed, high security prison: *I was a medium risk. People kept asking why I was there. I believe God's divine purpose was for me to be there. I wouldn't have been able to do as much as I did in another program. We helped bring peace to that prison.* At that time, especially in 2009/10 when he and Aakeem developed their mentoring program, *young men were coming in in droves. Life sentences had increased from fifteen to thirty years. There were stabbings, gang riots, uprisings.*

Aakeem developed a proposal for a mentoring program, Young Men on the Move Mentoring, that Irving wrote up for him and helped develop. Aakeem at that time was Muslim, Irving was Christian. Both were leaders in the faith and character dorms, and their program was interfaith: *The administration was looking for something different. Because it came from inmates it was more appealing. The wardens agreed when we told them we had more credibility "because you're not walking in the shoes we're walking in."*

Their first meeting drew 126 men; eighty signed up for the program. They created five groups based on length of time left to serve and found two mentors for each group. Each mentor created the curriculum for his own hour-long programs. Irving led the group with men with four years or less to serve and concentrated on reentry: *My sole mission was to get those guys into a mindset that prepared them to go <u>home</u>. They allowed me to put together a curriculum for reentry that went beyond materials from the Department of Corrections. We met once a week.*

I wanted a setting where you could talk about issues you're not comfortable discussing. In prison, all you have is concrete floors. Except in the administration building. The classroom I chose was a blue room, with blue walls, carpet, furniture. I wanted it to feel like a place we could have teas. A safe haven. I thought it was necessary to take them out of the prison environment even if only for an hour or an hour and a half a week so they could express themselves without hindrance.

We spent time identifying triggers. Personal development stops when you go to prison. If you go in as a teenager, even if you're thirty or forty, you're still in that same mindset. <u>Unless</u> you are forging forward, unless you surround yourself with the right people, programs. It was awesome to feel they felt safe with me. I was forty to fifty at the time. They had no fathers. I felt that they were my sons. Aakeem kept impressing on me and everyone, we're a <u>family</u>—regardless of religions or gang affiliations. I took that in. I have two sons, the oldest thirty and the younger *twenty-four. If ever my sons were incarcerated, I would want someone to take them under their wing.*

Reentry

Irving felt that the Department of Corrections was cavalier about reentry. *They only talk about reentry three months before you get out. People need to have someone walk through the <u>community</u> issues with them. The reentry programs in prison look good on paper. I went to a workshop on the COMPAS assessment. But none of that has any credence to it. They should have had a place for me when I got out. Three weeks before I was leaving, the counselor asked me, "Where are you going to live?" I said I didn't know and she said, "I'll categorize you as homeless." They just give you a $25 card, nothing else. There's no accountability to it.*

Irving spent the last two years of his incarceration at Dooly Prison where he continued his interest in reentry. He wrote out by hand three copies of a reentry curriculum he had developed and sent them to the directors of the local reentry coalition in his home county as well as to the mayor of the city. The first response was disappointing: *When I got back here and I was homeless in a hotel, I called the chairperson of the coalition. The first question he asked me was, "Irving, why did you come back here?" It hurt me. He has a child who is incarcerated but he didn't understand. So, I took it as a personal mission to educate him on reentry. Now he is the poster child for reentry at county, state, and regional level. But we had to have that conversation: "This is the reason I came back: I was mandated to return to the county in which I was convicted. I didn't come back out of choice. I didn't come back because I wanted to." That has changed with the criminal justice reform, but at the time I was convicted that was one of the terms.*

Forced to return to the community where he had committed his crime required something of both Irving and of the community that may be very important for both—and for us if we want to begin to imagine what restoration after sex offenses could look like. Irving had clearly thought about this a lot: *There has to be a healing piece in this reentry process. My crime and conviction were highlighted because of my position. It pulled people apart. Some said I didn't do it, others that I did. I went away for ten years. Time has a way of healing, of touching people's hearts. I went away for a reason. I'm not going to make little or light of what has happened in the last ten years. The victim and his family, they have suffered. My youngest two kids were getting ready to go to high school when I went in. I was sheltered on the inside. They were on the outside.*

It was difficult. They made it through only with the grace of God and my wife. I look at what my victim went through as well. What I did affected a vast number of people. I am human, but I can't afford to mess up. What I've found out is that there is a sense of forgiveness. I had a community choir. I was all over the community. But this community has a forgiving heart.

His wife's forgiveness was especially important: *My wife believed in me. I hurt people really bad. I self-punished. I didn't think there was forgiveness for what I was convicted of. But I kept hearing restoration. It took a long time for that to resonate with my spirit. My wife said, "Irving, everyone has forgiven you." When she said that, it took a weight off. I began to walk in my forgiveness. I don't believe my victims have forgiven me. I would love to have them do that. But if not, I can still go on.*

The overt social support of his pastor friends helped as well: *When I first got out, I didn't want to see anybody I felt so much shame. I had <u>hurt</u> people. I had to break loose from that. Talk. I confided in my pastor friends. One of them said, "Come and see me. I want you to come to my house. I want everyone to see I'm inviting you to my house." That moved me to another place.*

Very active now in his church, originally he was wary about joining: *It took me seven months before I joined the church. My pastor helped me in my restoration. If I hadn't had that, I wouldn't be able to survive. I went every Sunday for six months after I returned before I joined the church.* When we talked he was serving as an usher, in the men's chorus and church choir, and on the ministerial staff.

Irving talked as well about the importance of continuing therapy, one of the many terms of the very strict supervision required of sex offenders. At first he objected because he had received therapy in prison. However, he now felt that continued weekly therapy had been crucial in his reentry: *My counselors have been so supportive. My first therapist told me, "The more you talk about it, the more you will heal." I needed to get it off me. For ten years, I was never able to share. I did <u>irreparable</u> damage. This was part of my restoration. To share it in order to be able to help someone. My crime is different, but I want to be able to help others.*

Giving Back: Community

Irving has found his call in helping others who face similar reentry challenges to his own—and has become indispensable to other people who are doing similar work with the homeless and the formerly incarcerated.

When he was homeless after his release from prison, Irving found housing in a center started by an eighty-two-year-old wheelchair-bound psychologist, Dr. Kirk, who had previously run healing centers in Europe and Australia, and had started this healing center for the homeless a decade earlier. After living in one of her houses for awhile, Irving went to her and offered his skills and talents as a volunteer. When she accepted, it felt like divine intervention.

He had tried to get employment but people wouldn't hire him because of his record. If he was already working, as soon as they received the background check, the told him they couldn't hire him. *My crime will never change. Every time you do a check, it will come back the same. But I have changed. I had to build my trust back in this community. It was like walking on eggshells. I knew everything was OK, and I also knew I was being assessed constantly.*

Dr. Kirk opened her heart to Irving. She made him her administrative assistant, responsible for running the men's shelter: *She looks past my past. She gives me opportunities she wouldn't have given her own son. I'm entrusted with day-to-day operations of Kirk Home for the Homeless. People have put things in my hand, responsibilities and leadership and ministry, I never thought I'd see again. Dr. Kirk opened a whole world for me.*

Irving began to offer life-skills classes, spiritual guidance, and offered a more structured environment for the men living in the shelter. He invited them to accompany him to community events and encouraged their participation in community service projects. He conducted grant research and grant writing. One of those grants was to refurbish a house that would meet the standards for state subsidized reentry housing.

My whole thing right now is reentry. I can get out of sorts; I will find myself slipping. God will remind me. "You can't afford to slip, you can't afford to mess up because you are holding up somebody else's blessing." It hit me like a ton of bricks. Because someone is depending on that house, finding a refuge in that house, depending on making contact with someone who has been down that road. The coalition that we have in place, I love all of them, they all love me. But there's a distinct difference between their day-to-day livelihood and my day-to-day livelihood and so I'm drawn to those guys who have come out and are looking for some resources and are looking for some support. I'm drawn to them. There's a kindred spirit. So God told me, "You can't afford to mess up."

When asked what it was that encouraged him, he stressed that it was the little things. *A smile, last night a hug. People know what my crime was. They know what my punishment was. And then when I see them, it's like nothing happened. They will come up and hug me, say, "It's good to see you. Where you been?" I'll say, "I been away for awhile." The chief of police, I ran into him at city hall yesterday and he said, "Where you been?" "I been away for awhile." He said, "Welcome back. We've missed you." He'll never know what that meant to me. I knew him because I ran the homeless program before I went in. It's just those small things, it's the small things. When I'm leaving the office, Dr. Kirk says, "Give me a kiss before you go, Irving." Everybody doesn't remember only the bad. They know the potential that lies within. There's still so much more to Irving. I do know I've been brought back here to be a blessing to somebody.*

Eɴᴅɴᴏᴛᴇꜱ

1. Human Rights Watch, *Raised on the Registry: The Irreparable Harm of Placing Children on Sex Offender Registries in the US.* HRW, 2013, pp. 16-18.

2. M. Gottschalk. *Caught: The Prison State and the Lockdown of American Politics.* Princeton University Press, 2015, p. 199.

3. E. Horowitz. *Protecting Our Kids? How Sex Offender Laws Are Failing Us.* Praeger, 2015, p. 51; S. Yoder, "Why Sex Offender Registries Keep Growing Even As Sexual Violence Rates Fall," *The Appeal.* 3 Jul 2018.

4. Georgia Bureau of Investigation. "Georgia Sex Offender Registry."

5. National Center for Victims of Crime, "Statistics on Perpetrators of Child Sexual Abuse."

6. A. Tuck, "Genarlow Wilson's journey from prison to Morehouse," *Atlanta Journal-Constitution.* 18 May 2013; R. Balko, "Good riddance, Mr. McDade," *Washington Post.* 14 Apr 2014. McDade resigned from his position in April 2014 under mounting charges of improper use of public funds. The Georgia legislature refused to apply the reform retroactively. In October 2007 the Georgia Supreme Court ruled on Wilson's sentence, finding it "cruel and unusual" and "grossly disproportionate." Wilson graduated from Morehouse College in May 2013.

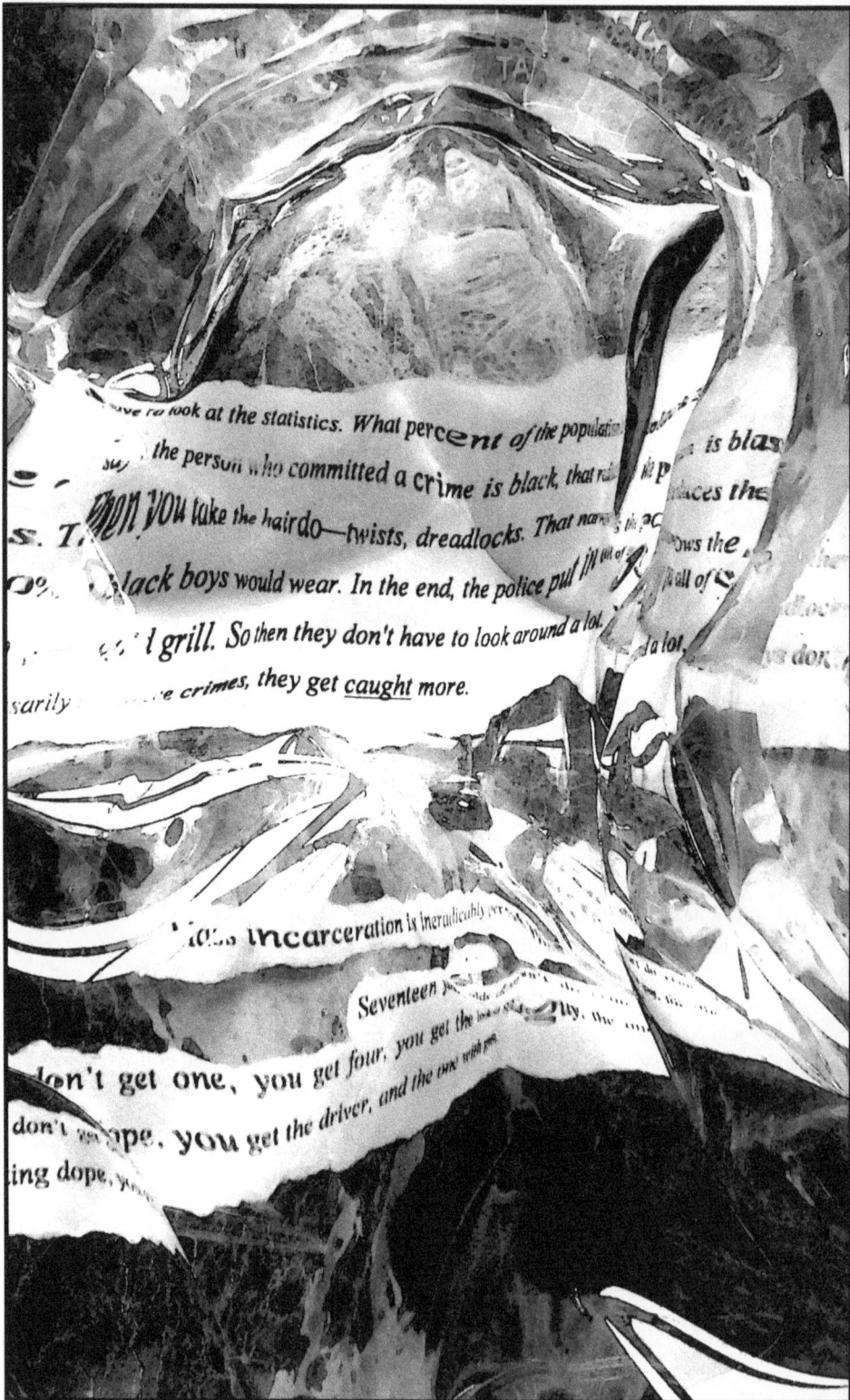

...ave to look at the statistics. What percent of the population... ...is black

...su... the person who committed a crime is black, that r... ...places the

s. T... ...hen you take the hairdo—twists, dreadlocks. That na... ...ows the

...0%... ...lack boys would wear. In the end, the police put i... ...all of...

...s... ...l grill. So then they don't have to look around a lot... ...a lot...

...sarily ... ...e crimes, they get <u>caught</u> more.

...oss incarceration is ineradicably per...

Seventeen ...

...on't get one, you get four, you get the...

...don't ...ope, you get the driver, and the o...

...ing dope, y...

II

THE BROADER CONTEXT

\\\\//

MASS INCARCERATION IN NUMBERS

The skyrocketing incarceration rates of past decades in the United States have placed it at the top for *all* of the countries of the world. Figure II.1 shows the six countries that had the highest rates for the most recent year available from the relevant United Nations agency, along with a number of other countries valuable for comparison.

Figure II.1. Imprisonment Rates: Highest Countries & Selected Others

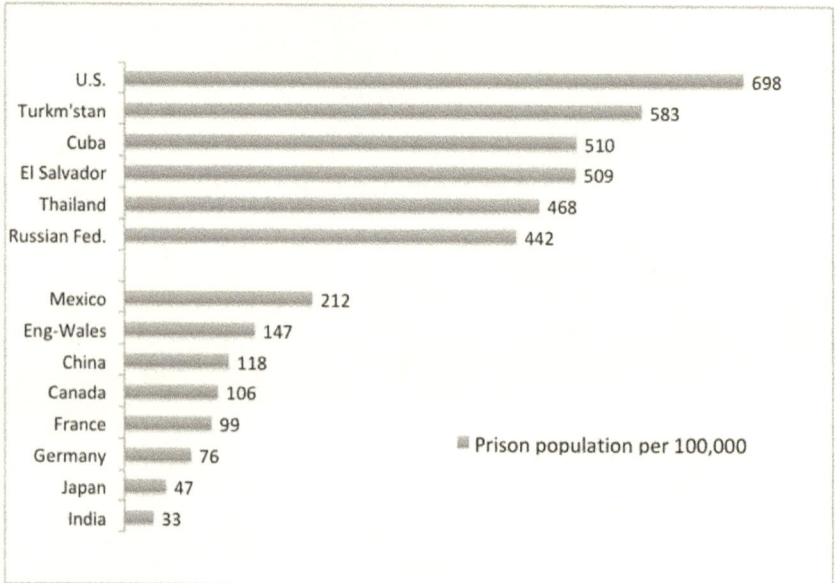

Source: United Nations Office on Drugs and Crime, "Homicide Counts and Rates," *Global Study on Homicide*. 2013. Web. Excludes tiny countries.

MASS INCARCERATION IN THE UNITED STATES

The number of people incarcerated in the United States exploded in the 1980s, continuing to sharply increase for about another two decades, as shown by Figure II.2. Federal prisons, which are for people convicted of violating federal law, hold only a minor portion of all inmates. Instead, most offenders are convicted of violating state laws and are held in prisons run by each state. Jails are usually administered by counties, typically incarcerating people waiting trial who are denied bail or, more likely, can not afford their bail; inmates serving shorter sentences (such as under a year); and offenders waiting transfer to state prison. States also run separate juvenile justice systems, including youth residential facilities. Because the federal prison population is so much smaller than that of the states, Figure II.2 plots the two against separate population scales, states on the left vertical axis, the federal on the right (jails not included).

Figure II.2. Imprisonment Rates: Federal and States, 1978-2016

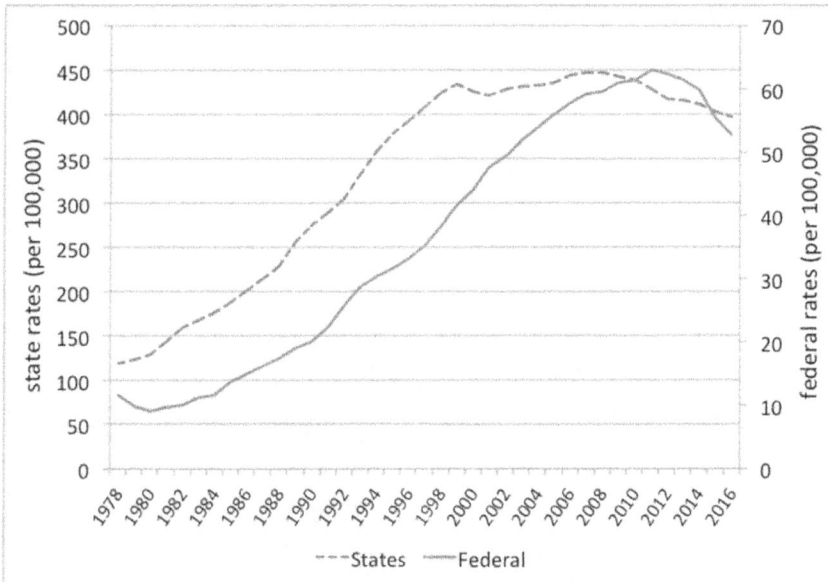

Source: U.S. Bureau of Justice Statistics. "Imprisonment rate of sentenced prisoners under the jurisdiction of state or federal correctional authorities per 100,000 U.S. residents, December 31, 1978-2016." Generated using the Corrections Statistical Analysis Tool at www.bjs.gov.

Georgia has long been one of the states with the highest imprisonment rates in the country. Indeed, across the time span shown in Figure II.3, Georgia's rate averaged 92 points above that for all states combined.

Figure II.3. Imprisonment Rates: Georgia and All States, 1978-2016

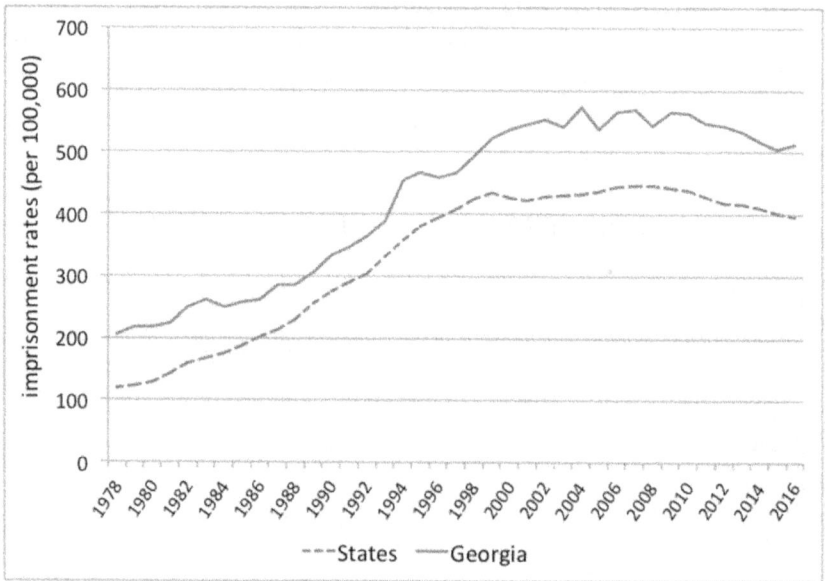

Source: U.S. Bureau of Justice Statistics.

All states share the pattern in recent decades of increasing rates of imprisonment and incarceration (the latter adds the local jail population to the state prison population), but there are enormous differences between them. Figure II.4 shows some of these striking differences, giving the four states with the highest incarceration rates in 2014, along with the four with the lowest.

Figure II.4. U.S. Incarceration Rates: Highest & Lowest States, 2014

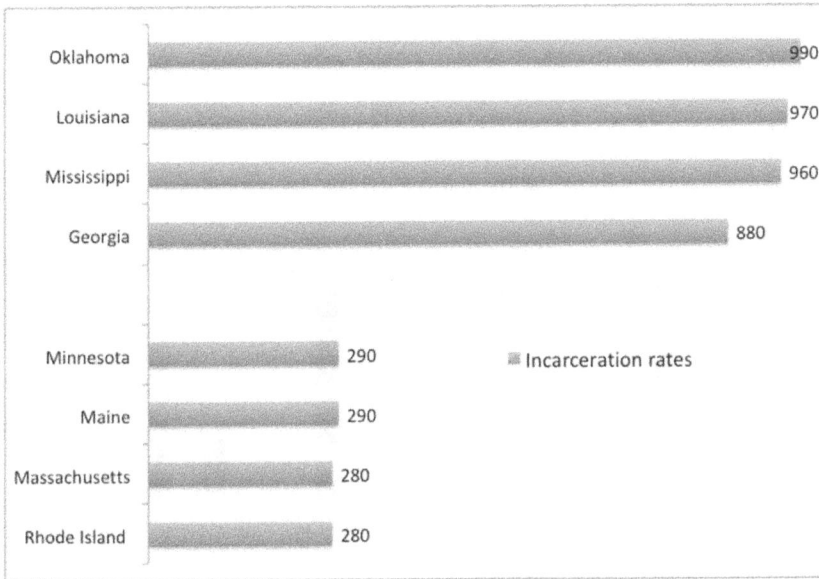

Source: US Bureau of Justice Statistics, "Correctional Populations in the United States, 2016."

The regional differences cannot be missed. Three of the four states with the lowest rates are in New England with the fourth another far northern state. Conversely, the four states that incarcerate the highest percentage of their citizens are all found along the southern half of the country (as are the next four).

Racial and Ethnic Disparities in U.S. Prisons

The issue of race is a central feature of mass incarceration in the United States. In Figure II.5 it is readily apparent that African Americans have been greatly overrepresented among the U.S. prison population (combining both federal and state). Black inmates were slightly more numerous than white inmates in 1990 and 2000 and essentially about the same in 1980 and 2010, even though blacks are a much smaller share of the overall population than are whites.

Figure II.5. Racial Makeup of United States and Its Prisoners, 1980-2010

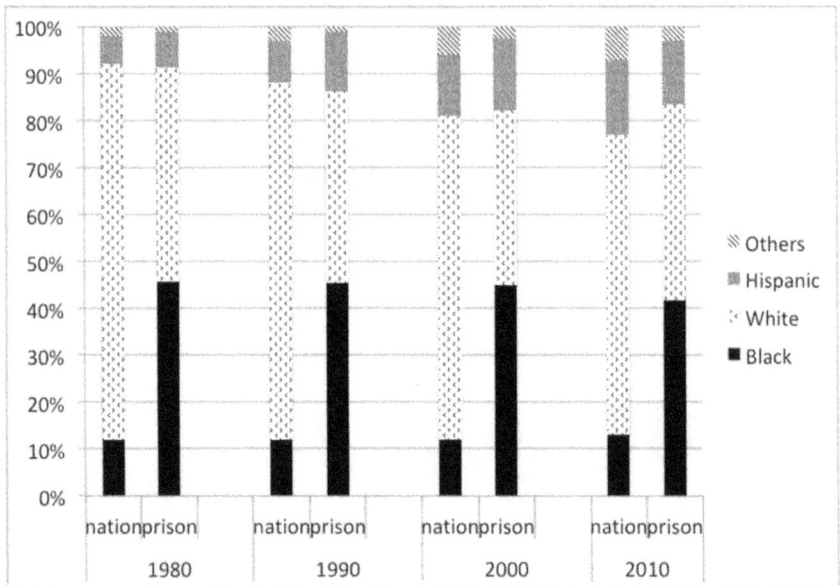

Source: U.S. Bureau of Justice Statistics. See methodological explanation in Addendum..

The states with the highest rates of African Americans in their prisons in the early 2010s, when the national average was 1408 (per 100,000), were Oklahoma (2625), Wisconsin (2542) and Vermont (2357); Georgia was thirty-eighth (1066). The relative likelihood of imprisonment for black residents of New Jersey was 12.2 times greater than that for whites (nationally it was 5.1). Georgia's score of 3.2 was actually the third lowest in the country after Hawaii and Mississippi. The same trends also held for Hispanics, although the disparities compared to whites were not as great.[1]

Still, there is a substantial racial imbalance in imprisonment rates in Georgia. As Figure II.6 shows, the peak occurred in 1990 when the percentage of African Americans among prisoners was 2.4 times greater than in the general population whereas whites were under-represented by half. The imbalance then slowly dropped across the next two decades due to both a slight decline in the percentage of blacks among inmates at the same time that African Americans as a percentage of the overall state population has been climbing. An additional explanation for the decline has been a shift in drug arrests in

Georgia—fewer blacks are being convicted for crack cocaine related offenses while more whites are being convicted for methamphetamine offenses.[2] As a consequence of these changes, the percentage of African Americans among new prisoners in the state fell eight points across the decade through 2018.[3]

Figure II.6. Racial Makeup of Georgia and Its Prisoners, 1980-2010

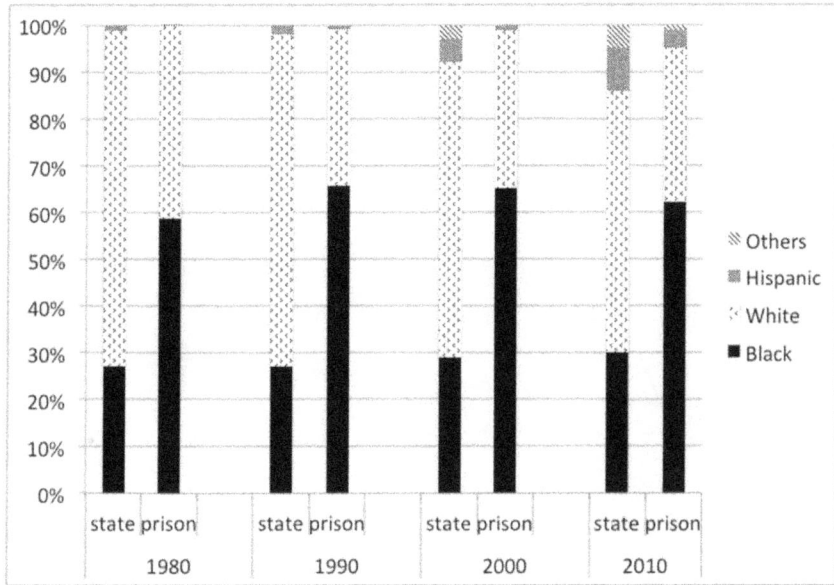

Source: U.S. Bureau of Justice Statistics. See explanation in Addendum.

Mass Incarceration as Crime Reduction Policy

With incarceration rates throughout the United States rising sharply in the early 1980s, the natural question is whether there had been a corresponding increase in crime rates. The answer is an unambiguous yes. This raises a second crucial question that we answer below: was mass incarceration an appropriate response to rapidly rising crime rates that then succeeded in bringing those rates down?

THE RISE AND FALL OF CRIME RATES IN THE UNITED STATES

Figure II.7 shows the trends across more than a half of a century for both violent and property crimes for federal and state levels combined (taking into account population growth). Clearly there was an immense spike in both, especially the violent crime rate, which by the time it reached its peak in 1991 was 4.7 times greater than it had been in 1960. However, crime rates then fell, cut in half by 2012 for violent crimes and by 2015 for property crimes.

Figure II.7 Violent & Property Crimes Rates: U.S., 1960-2018

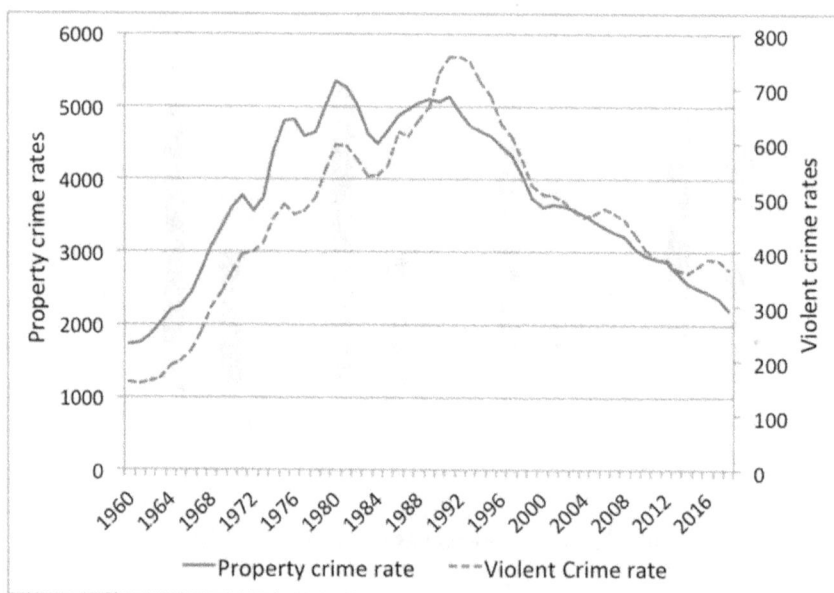

Source: Created from *Uniform Crime Report* of the FBI. See explanation in Addendum.

Georgia features the same overall patterns for its crime rates. Both increased about fivefold and then dropped steadily, with the violent crime rate cut in half by 2011 and property crime by 2014.

Figure II.8. Violent & Property Crime Rates: Georgia, 1960-2018

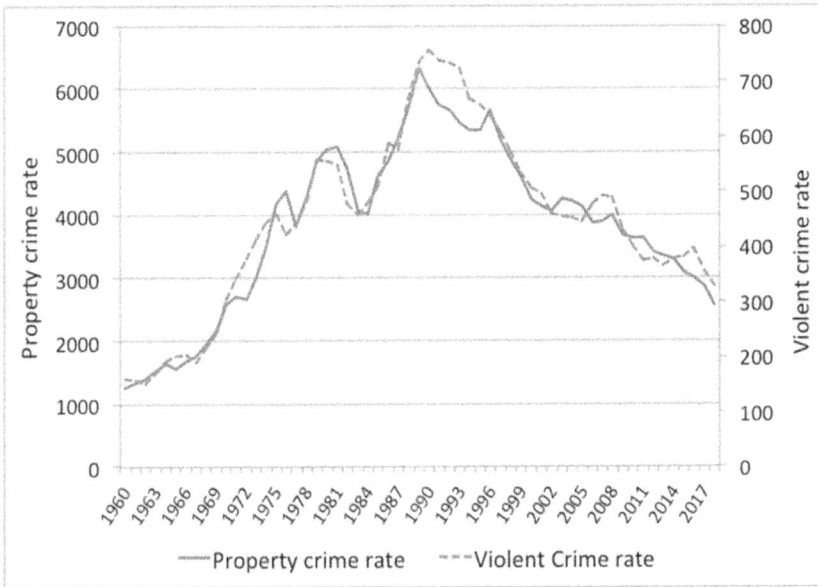

Source: Created from *Uniform Crime Report* of the FBI. See explanation in Addendum.

Drug offenses are not included in the FBI crime indices because of the impossibility of gauging their occurrence—if person B were to sell an illegal drug to person A, who is going to report the crime? Consequently, the measure that is used for drug offenses is arrests. In a typical year, drug abuse violations (unlawful possession, sale, manufacturing, etc. of a controlled substance) are the most common form of arrests at the state and local levels. The most common among these offenses is marijuana possession.[4]

As Figure II.9 shows, drug arrest rates for the United States more than doubled during the 1980s and then after two drops reached their peak in 2006. Although they have since been falling, the rate of drug arrests in 2017 remained about twice what it was in 1980. A rural Georgia county (Dooley) had the distinction in 2016 of having the highest proportion of marijuana arrests among all of its arrests (almost 55%).[5]

Figure II.9. Drug Arrests Rates: United States, 1980-2017

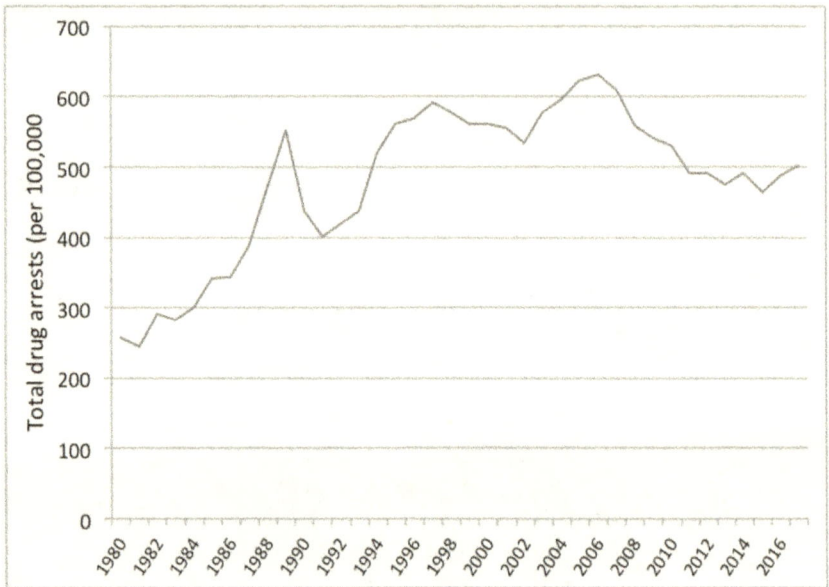

Source: Created from *Uniform Crime Report* of the FBI.

DID MASS INCARCERATION SUCCEED IN REDUCING CRIME?

The eventual drop in crime rates in the United States following years of unprecedented growth of mass incarceration has been the largest and longest decline of crime rates since the beginning of the twentieth century.[6] The all-important question is whether mass incarceration can be credited—and justified—as a success in the fight against crime.

Figure II.10 begins with 1978 when crime rates were near their peaks following their alarming climb from the early 1960s. Soon the imprisonment rate began its steady two-decades escalation. However, when the crime rates turned and began their steady fall in the early 1990s, the imprisonment rate had reached only about a half of what would be its eventual plateau a decade later. In other words, even if we were to claim that mass incarceration did play an important role in bringing down crime rates, it still was far more excessive than necessary for that purpose.

Figure II.10. Crime & Imprisonment Rates: United States, 1978-2016

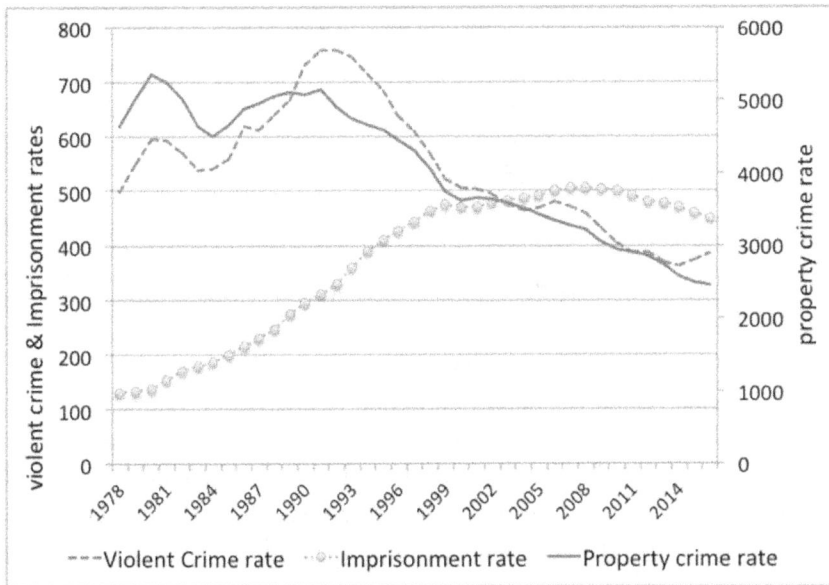

Source: Figures 1.2 and 1.7.

But, even this grants too much to mass incarceration as a crime reduction policy. From his authoritative analyses of the subject, the noted statistician William Spelman concluded that the massive increase in incarceration accounts at most for only about a quarter of the drop in crime.[7] This conclusion is re-enforced when the U.S. experience is compared to that of other countries, as shown by a number of studies.

The most compelling comparison is with Canada, which shared the crime wave that began in the early 1960s as well as its later sustained fall. What was not shared was the approach to incarceration. Between 1960 and 2004 the incarceration rate for Canada (combining federal and provincial levels) only fluctuated between 80 and 120 (per 100,000 people), ending at about the same point where it started (around 100).[8] In contrast, the comparable U.S. rate was about 3.7 times greater in 2004 than its 1978 starting point.

Looking at the broader body of studies that compare the United States with other countries, researchers conclude, "it is no longer reasonable even to hypothesize that crime patterns can be explained in terms of punishment policies or imprisonment rates."[9] How can this be? The very short answer—

but one to be amplified throughout this book—is that much crime is not based on a rational calculation of costs and benefits.

Instead, the best explanation for both the rise of the crime wave and then its decline is demography. It is well established that the age group from which criminal behavior is most likely is youths between ages fifteen to nineteen, followed by those up to about twenty-four.[10] The escalation of crime rates directly corresponded to the decades when the huge post-WWII Baby Boom generation was supplying an historically large number of youths in their prime years for offending.[11]

A related driver was the increase in drug use, a factor also associated in part with the teenage and young adult years of Baby Boomers. Then, the expansion of harder drug use, such as cocaine and heroin, brought additional crime to support expensive habits. With harder drugs also came violent drug markets, particularly in urban minority communities.[12] Some observers also emphasize the role of politicians (such as Presidents Richard Nixon and Ronald Reagan) inciting the public for their own political gain. However, the most rigorous and recent analysis finds that worked for them because of pre-existing direct links between crime rates and political opinion.[13]

Demographic change most likely also accounts for the subsequent fall in crime rates. Throughout the affluent democracies, the proportion of the population with the greatest propensity to commit crime (fifteen to twenty-four) has fallen.[14] In contrast, there has been a corresponding increase in the share of people older than forty-five, that is, in people "well equipped to provide social control of youths and young adults."[15]

ENDNOTES

1. A. Nellis, "The Color of Justice: Racial and Ethnic Disparity in State Prisons." The Sentencing Project. June 2016.

2. B. Rankin and A. G. Sheinin, "Fewer Black Georgians Sent to Prison," Atlanta Journal-Constitution. 02 Aug 2014.

3. Georgia Department of Corrections, "Inmate Statistical Profile," 2010, 2018.

4. T. Dorsey and D. J. James, "Drug and Crime Facts." U.S. Bureau of Justice Statistics.

5. C. Ingraham, "Where the War on Weed Stills Rages," *Washington Post,* 15 Apr 2019.

6. F. E. Zimring, *The Great American Crime Decline.* Oxford University Press, 2007, p. 196.

7. C. Haney. *Reforming Punishment: Psychological Limits to the Pains of Imprisonment.* American Psychological Association, 2006, p. 7.

8. C. M. Webster and A. N. Doob. "Punitive Trends and Stable Imprisonment Rates in Canada." In *Crime, Punishment, and Politics in Comparative Perspective.* Ed. M. Tonry. University of Chicago Press, 2007, pp. 303, 311.

9. M. Tonry, "Why Crime Rates Are Falling throughout the Western World." *Crime and Justice.* 43, 1 (2014), p. 53. Also see in the same volume: G. Farrell, N. Tilley, and A. Tseloni. "Why the Crime Drop?" and T. Lappi-Seppälä and M. Lehti, "Cross-Comparative Perspectives on Global Homicide Trends."

10. D. P. Farrington and R. Loeber. "Two Approaches to Developmental/Life-Course Theorizing." In *The Oxford Handbook of Criminological Theory.* Eds. F. T. Cullen and P. Wilcox. Oxford University Press, 2013, p. 229.

11. R. Rosenfeld. "Changing Crime Rates." In *Crime and Public Policy.* Eds. J. Q. Wilson and J. Petersilia. Oxford University Press, 2011, pp. 575-576.

12. Rosenfeld, "Changing Crime Rates," p. 576.

13. P. K. Enns. *Incarceration Nation: How the United States Became the Most Punitive Democracy in the World.* Cambridge University Press, 2016.

14. Another possible factor has been the removal of lead from the environment. B. B. Boutwell, et al. "The Intersection of Aggregate-Level Lead Exposure and Crime." *Environmental Research.* 148, July (2016): 79-85.

15. E. P. Baumer and K. T. Wolff. "The Breadth and Causes of Contemporary Cross-National Homicide Trends." *Crime and Justice.* 43, 1 (2014), p. 278.

that i you talk to people with respect and don't take away ... dig

worst thing you can do is take way a man's dignity.

they talk. 'You got to be the stupidest such and such and ... Such ...
now the nothing be ... you can't say nuttin. They' ... you ... In the situ...
you to S ... Something so they can lock you up, but I ain't never pa...

... we can with what we have and never lose sight that a ...

... to me, I ... had to tell him, "You sent me to ... me
But it came to me, I ... went and looked at the pape ...
a waiver because you wel ... er and I just showed you ...
How it's a year and a half ...

III

COMMUNITY SUPERVISION
A Foot in Both Worlds: Control to Reintegration

Every probationer, I have I ask, "Who cares about you?"
And they'll say, "Nobody."
And I'll say, "Until today."
Now they can't go through life saying nobody...
...de the difference in every case I've supervised

\\ \/ /

INTRODUCTION

SIDING WITH SUCCESS

Because community supervision takes place here, where we live, at the intersection of institutional, individual, and community accountability, it can't avoid some of the deep contradictions in our attitudes as a society towards punishment and reentry, and neither can we. When people are supervised in the community, the questions of harm, punishment and restoration and our roles in them are live, complex—and in our face. We may oppose mass incarceration in principle and in practice, we may question the length of sentences, the harshness of the conditions under which people have been imprisoned, but that does not necessarily translate into a desire to have people reentering from prison, or people under supervision in lieu of imprisonment, as our neighbors, our employees, or our co-workers.

We can learn a great deal from those who have chosen to work at the heart of these tensions, and this re-evaluation is necessary because as we move away from mass incarceration towards more diversion courts and probation, we increasingly become a country of mass supervision instead.

Georgia is far and away the national frontrunner for the number of people on community supervision and has been for years. Georgia's rate of probation and parole is four times higher than the national average. One out of 18 people in Georgia are under some form of correctional control, primarily probation. Not only is the number of people involved high, but the sentences are often very long: the average length of probation sentences in Georgia is 9.5 years, and 15 years is not uncommon. The number of people under supervision has grown steadily even through the years of criminal justice reform. The number of adults under felony supervision in Georgia in 2015 was 180,000; by 2019, the number had grown by over 45,000.

However, Georgia's changing approach to community supervision is also one of the strongest success stories in its criminal justice reform effort. These extravagant supervision numbers make this both a significant accomplishment and a necessity.

We were given unusual access to Parole and then to a new Department of Community Supervision (DCS) during this period of rapid criminal justice reform, beginning in 2014 and continuing through 2019—which provided us a fascinating glimpse into institutional reform as well as an in-depth exposure to the daily realities of probation and parole officers. Consequently, in this section on community supervision we have two stories to share: First, the story of *institutional* change that has helped establish community supervision as a stand-alone practice and philosophy. We are particularly interested in what shared qualities in the people involved in this remarkably rapid institutional reform helped make it successful. Secondly, we share a longer and more intimate story about the daily realities that face individual officers and offenders as they negotiate the complex dance of accountability and support that makes up the actual *practice* of community supervision, a perspective and set of competencies that are valuable for all of us as we hold more and more individuals in the community as they serve their sentences. That story focuses on some of the key differences between rural and urban supervision.

[Sources for this section: pp. 326-327]

DIFFERENCES BETWEEN PROBATION AND PAROLE

Although DCS provides the field supervision for both parolees and probationers, and all officers are now cross-trained in their different procedures, historically the two forms of supervision have been quite different in culture, size, and practices. The basic academic requirements for parole officers and probation officers are identical, a college degree, usually with some academic training in criminal justice.

The Georgia State Board of Pardons and Paroles controls clemency— who is released early from prison and/or who is killed by the state. They are a much smaller institution than the Department of Corrections, and they have much greater control over who they release. Consequently, it is far more likely that a restorative approach will originate there. Caseloads can be managed by controlling when and under what conditions prisoners are released. Parolees are highly vetted for changed behavior and readiness for release. Prosecutors, victims, families, wardens can all weigh in on the decision. Parole in Georgia had given its field officers a high degree of autonomy on deciding when and to what degree to institute sanctions on parolees, so officers have had a greater sense of agency and responsibility.

Probation is a more complex institution with many more players. Judges decide whether people are given probation and probationers remain accountable to the court in which they were sentenced. Probation officers do not have the autonomy of parole officers. Changes in probation conditions must be approved by the sentencing judge and also the DA and defense attorney, all of which reduce the sense of agency of the officer. Probation is often served in lieu of imprisonment. This remains a significant threat to people who have never been to prison. However, if sent to prison to serve out their term, release from prison is determined either by parole eligibility or by serving out their term, independent of behavior. Some judges control for this by giving an individual both a prison sentence and also a long probation sentence to follow. Readiness for probation, however, is not part of the assessment from a maxed out sentence.

The number of people on probation is orders of magnitude greater than those on parole. The administrative and supervision structure of probation in Georgia, shaped by the culture of Corrections, encouraged a "fortress mentality" where probationers had to report to probation offices. There the behavior of officers could often mimic that of corrections officers in prisons, since Probation served as a career advancement for many corrections officers.

One effect of these differences is that during the merger of field services, DCS lost many active parole officers, who were daunted by the significant increase in caseloads, made worse by the increased bureaucratic complexity of probation and the consequent loss of autonomy. Many of them returned to Parole in new positions as investigative officers. Probation officers found their relative increase in autonomy with the unification more attractive. However, four years into the new structure, half of current DCS officers have begun their careers using the new combined field services approach, so these tensions are resolving.

\1/

INSTITUTIONAL & PHILOSOPHICAL REFORM
I think we've just given people permission to practice in the way they have wanted to all along.
Michael Nail, Commissioner, Department of Community Supervision

THE CREATION OF DCS

In 2015, as part of its criminal justice reform Georgia created a new agency, the Department of Community Supervision, which combined field services from Probation, Parole, and Juvenile Justice felony probation. The agency also has oversight over misdemeanor probation, which is conducted by private for-profit agencies. The intention was to centralize and standardize supervision practices. This was a major undertaking, prepared for in part by various earlier reforms in both Probation and Parole. Given the enormous size of the Georgia supervision population, especially probation, and the differences in the institutional cultures of Parole and Probation as well as of their practices, the consolidation process has been remarkably efficient, highly motivating for staff, and has allowed the development of a distinctive philosophy for community supervision that is at odds with that of much of the criminal justice system, particularly corrections.

This extensive reorganization and reform has provided a structure in which a more positive, relational and socially-contextualized form of community supervision can be practiced. The new agency's unambivalent statement that they want to see people succeed on supervision—radical in the context of the generally punitive stance of the criminal justice system—weights the see-saw of accountability and support firmly on the side of support. Their motto, "One Officer, One Family, One Community," acknowledges the intersection of interests involved in community supervision.

This approach counteracts the usual individualistic bias of corrections and of the criminal justice system in general, an approach summed up in the booklet on reentry distributed in prisons with the motivational statement: *Reentry Begins with You.* This is a troubling but accurate assertion in prisons stripped for years of almost all programming, in highly punitive states, like

Georgia, with great racial, economic, and educational inequalities. Now, Michael Nail, the commissioner of DCS says, "When I was a young officer, I thought the relationship was just between me and my probationer. How dumb was that!"

The major changes that are the results of this restructuring and reform are:

◈ *Basing officers primarily in the field rather than in offices.*

◈ *Making extensive use of communication and GPS technology to cut costs.*

◈ *Standardizing supervision conditions and procedures whether people are on probation or parole.*

◈ *Using evidence-based practices that improve efficiency and effectiveness, including concentrating supervision on people who are most likely to recidivate, and actively trying to reduce the length and amount of supervision for those who are not likely to reoffend.*

◈ *Taking a strengths-based approach to supervision, emphasizing the use of incentives to improve compliance, from the regular use of positive feedback to reducing fees, shortening supervision, or removing people from active supervision entirely when appropriate or possible.*

◈ *Cross-training all officers on both parole and probation procedures so they can supervise people in both systems, increasing continuity of supervision and flexibility of staff.*

◈ *Training officers on the soft skills needed for a more responsive, community-focused form of supervision.*

◈ *Improving resources for reentry, such as community coordinators, housing and prison in-reach specialists, and more addiction services through the system of Day Reporting Centers.*

Effectively combining, standardizing, streamlining, and refocusing the field supervision activities of three agencies within two years, along with the activities of the short-lived Governor's Office on Transition and Reentry, required meeting the challenge of what David Morrison, director of field operations first at Parole and then at DCS, has described as a "30,000 foot perspective, seeing the whole picture, everything coming at you from different directions—budgetary, legislative, political, and media—and still get out and lead from the front, get out in the field."

The temperament, experience, knowledge, and commitments of the people directly involved in this restructuring, in particular that of its first and current commissioner, Nail, were crucial in their ability to lead from the front, claiming from the first the intention to be "the national leader for innovative and progressive community supervision." If praised directly, Nail would immediately look around him to share the credit, but so would those he works with, which is part of why they have been successful.

We look at the development of this new agency through some of those traits because they are also traits needed to be successful as a community supervision officer. We are also interested in the synergy between these qualities that helped make the transition possible and make us hopeful about its continued success.

Transparency And Social Trust

We first met with Michael Nail in 2014 when he was executive director of Parole. We had mentioned to a former Parole Board member, Robert Keller, then assistant director of a newly formed Governor's Office of Transition and Reentry (GOTSR), that it was nearly impossible to talk with people in Corrections or Parole. He simply said, "Call Michael." We sent Nail a description of our project, and he immediately agreed to talk with us—and to have other members of Parole field services talk to us as well.

Nail is burly, short, bald—and welcoming, always with a wide smile and an accent that is pure Georgia. He is on a first name basis with staff and officers. One of our first questions to him was why he was so unusually open. His response defines an understanding of corrections that is strikingly different from what we often encountered elsewhere in the criminal justice system: *If you can't explain your business, then you should not be in it. Folks deserve to know. You always say you wish people knew what you were doing, but if you don't take the time, you can't connect. When I came into the business in 1989, there was a bumper sticker: "Corrections is everybody's business." I believe that. Too often we just want to bring people in when we want something. But it can't be all take, asking for help only on pieces we want you to see. How you let people in and who you let in tells a lot about you. If you want to control the situation, that's not a relationship. I always tell people: If I know, I'll tell you. If I don't know, I'll tell you. If I know and won't tell you, I'll tell you that—if safety and security is not at risk.*

As an example, Nail described his response to a highly critical article about Parole—which was to invite the reporter on a ride-along with a parole officer, telling him, "What you printed hurt, but it will also help us improve." He added with a smile and a shrug, "The natural instinct is to defend against the criticism, but then you won't learn."

This level of social trust is essential if you are going to base your activities within the community, where your officers will be entering homes, interacting not only with the people they supervise but also with their families, neighbors, members of the surrounding community, especially if you are going to be asking for their support and confidence—and often their resources. Transparency is also essential when trying to combine the activities of several agencies of very different sizes that have sometimes had competitive relationships with each other.

A Taste for Complexity

What seems common sense in the abstract, like combining similar activities across agencies, can be complex on many levels, from the political to the procedural. Before taking over the creation of this new agency, Nail had several experiences of rapid institutional consolidation that helped prepare for this larger enterprise. A decade or more earlier, under Commissioner James Donald, he helped integrate the previously separate probation and prison divisions of the Department of Corrections, which involved becoming cross-trained in the practices and culture of both, an attempt to create a complementary rather than competitive approach. Although originally at Probation, the complexity of prison operations appealed to Nail, and he found himself shifting over to prison facilities management, which he described as very complicated and difficult—and interesting.

Nail also learned some broader lessons about the difficulty of trying to integrate contradictory missions: *When you share probation and prisons, they are in direct opposition to one another. Prison, your role on paper is to keep them in. In probation, your role is to keep them out. It is difficult for one agency to lead two missions. With probation, I loved being able to be proactive. But with prisons, so much is reactive. Probation saw themselves as the red-headed step-children of corrections, with 5% of the budget and twice as many offenders. In this new role, I was going to make sure enough credit went to Probation. But it didn't matter how hard I tried to do that. If you are talking about an important probation project, that conversation will end quickly as soon as there is a security emergency. The dynamics of 24/7/365 is so different from probation.*

Along with his nuts and bolts understanding of prison management, Nail took a commitment to cross-mission understanding with him when he moved to the Georgia Board of Parole as their executive director. He began asking parole officers how many had been in a prison. Only about 10% of his officers had, and usually only for a final hearing or a meeting. "Here in parole we are responsible for transitioning offenders. How can we do that if we have never been in their environment?" Nail asked.

He began to require that new recruits spend a week in a prison before beginning their parole training, a week spent on the floor with the guards, not trailing the warden. Nail often emphasized the difference between a tour of the diagnostic prison, Jackson, which he likened to visiting a model home, with visiting a prison unannounced on a Friday night—a far more accurate measure of what is actually happening in the prisons. The prison immersion program was so successful that experienced officers asked if they too could participate.

PRECEDING REFORMS IN COMMUNITY SUPERVISION

There were two important successful reform initiatives, one in Parole and one in Probation that preceded, and prepared for, the creation of DCS.

PAROLE: VIRTUAL OFFICE

Parole in 2011/12 was driven to a rapid, extensive and innovative reform in its supervision practices, moving its parole officers into virtual offices in the field to save money on office space and also to get people where they needed to be—out in the communities. They had a three-year plan in place to make changes, but faced with a large budget cut, they implemented the shift in a single year. Cars were equipped with computers and printers. Officers were given the autonomy to structure their own work hours, allowing them to better balance home and work. They also began to use technology extensively: voice monitoring to reduce the need for active supervision for low-risk offenders; GPS monitoring to do the same for higher-risk offenders; and teleconferencing for revocation hearings, thus reducing travel costs and improving efficiency and officer safety. These changes were nationally recognized for their innovation and pragmatism.

The experience created a sense of confidence and accomplishment for the people involved. David Morrison, a few years later, still described it with a sense of awe: *With all the money saved, we kept all personnel, no one was laid off or furloughed. We realized implementation would need to be different in different places, so we gave people that authority. It was an unbelievable feat. I can't believe we made it—got out of the buildings, copied and shredded all the documents, got the new equipment, did the training. Certainly there was apprehension about doing it but it would be hard to find anyone who doesn't like it. Officer morale is up. There are people who like autonomy who don't want to be micromanaged. The younger people loved it—the freedom, technology. It was a huge recruitment tool for us from Probation.*

Probation: 10-Step Framework

The Department of Corrections also instituted a substantial probation reform, *The 10-Step Framework*, to bring it in line with current best-practices in supervision, many already in use in Parole. Initiated in 2009 and implemented in 2011 to 2013, the reform carefully followed the reform strategies described in PEW's 2008 report, *Putting Public Safety First*. Again the impetus was primarily economic. Georgia Probation had a supervision population of around 150,000, which translated to 1 in 13 Georgians. Steps taken to increase efficiency included ranking offenders by risk in order to focus supervision efforts and resources and, like Parole, using technology, especially voice monitoring, to help supervise probationers. Steps focused on improving procedural justice included encouraging diversion and accountability courts, developing a position for an officer who could advise the court about effective sentences and alternatives to incarceration, and developing a uniform sanctions matrix that allowed probation officers to make more uniform and prompt decisions about sanctions without always having to go back to court for a judge's approval. A more rehabilitative emphasis included refocusing the Community Impact Program from a warrant-serving program to one that focused more on prevention, for example identifying resources for high-risk probationers. To aid in reentry, an effort was made to improve the movement from prison to community supervision by focusing on pre-release preparations. All of these changes were in line with the focus of the broader criminal justice reforms of that period. However, this was a top-down, think-tank-to-administration effort, and the level of buy-in from actual probation officers, especially given the high volume of cases, was less clear.

Governor's Office Of Transition, Support, And Reentry (GOTSR)

An example of a less successful prefatory institutional step was the Governor's Office of Transition, Support and Reentry, created in 2013. Originally planned as a six-person office whose focus was to be on developing more community support and community resources for prisoner reentry, it rapidly metastasized, with the help of numerous grants, into a stand-alone agency that meshed poorly with existing agencies. One of the biggest criticisms we found from our interviews was that so much money and effort were expended on creating an institution that few resources were finding their way to the people who were actually reentering—which was the original mission. A major problem was that most of the people leading it had no direct experience with either corrections or community supervision. Although well-intentioned, and encouraged by foundations, it was a top-down effort with very little buy-in from people already on the ground, nor benefit to them. Absorbed into DCS, several of its initiatives, for example providing community, housing and prison in-reach specialists, have proved successful when more tightly integrated into the activities of supervision officers.

QUALITIES KEY TO SUCCESSFUL REFORM

The success of these probation and parole reforms built resilience, competence, and confidence for greater consolidation and reform. In Parole in particular, confidence among field officers themselves came from a knowledge that people came first, that *their* buy-in was essential.

HIGH EQ—PEOPLE FIRST

A number of people in community supervision, including Nail, comfortably identified themselves as higher on EQ than IQ, a social intelligence that is core to effectiveness in community-based supervision at all levels, from leadership to administration to active supervision. It was a major contributor to their success in different ways.

PRACTITIONERS FIRST: Those responsible for directing the changes were clear from the beginning that their success depended on the knowledge as well as motivation of the people who did the actual work of supervision. "Here is the real source of success for a good leader: listen to the folks who are doing the job, they know what is working, what isn't, and how to fix it," Nail said of the earlier parole reform.

This was also true of the larger reform that resulted in DCS. All the leadership team had direct experience in community supervision, and that experience drove key choices about where to focus their attention. Staff buy-in was considered the core element in the restructuring. Early consolidation efforts focused on improving staff training—crucial as officers were now expected to be able to function in two different reporting structures. Improving salaries and reducing active caseloads were also used as early measures of success.

Perceived Fairness and Inclusion: One of the biggest challenges of bringing parole and probation officers into one unified agency had to do with the big difference in scale of the two agencies, Probation being almost six times larger. Perceived fairness in choosing who would be on the administrative team and who would be regional chiefs was a delicate issue. Parole regions and judicial circuits needed to be reconciled, but then someone needed to be a coordinating chief responsible for being the connection to the community. Chief officers from both agencies could apply. A high EQ solution that was to some extent a product of necessity proved to have unexpected benefits in several different directions.

During this period of criminal justice reform, there had been a concerted effort to increase community engagement around issues of reentry. So the decision was made to have community leaders be part of the interviewing teams that selected the new coordinating chiefs. Expanding the selection panel opened the process up, improved transparency, reduced inter-agency tensions, and allowed the community to have real input—changing the accountability dynamic in significant ways that grounded the One Officer, One Family, One Community commitment.

Clearly Defining Success

Nail described the particular challenges of community supervision in this way in an early interview when he was still at Parole: *We used to say in community corrections that you have to have a balanced approach—law enforcement and treatment—and I subscribed to that for years. But it is better to think of "blending," which then depends on the unique circumstances. For some offenders you never need to exercise a law enforcement role. You've got to do more than give people an opportunity to change—it is also your job to do everything you can to facilitate change. Sometimes it sticks and sometimes it doesn't. But we are there to help them transition back, not to impede that but to facilitate that. That is our job. If you don't like that aspect of the job, then you are in the wrong business. If you like locking people up more, then you need to move to law enforcement. Or others, who let cases go too long before intervening, maybe should move to social work or counseling. What we need are people who know how to blend effectively.*

Blending support and accountability with a clear *dominant* commitment to a positive outcome is the major emphasis of DCS supervision policy. In its quiet way, it is quite radical inside the criminal justice system to say unequivocally, *We want you to succeed.* Recidivism is often the major measure for supervision. This is actually a very blunt measure. Other success indicators were quickly added to emphasize a more positive, reentry-focused approach. The most obvious one was to see successful completion of supervision as an *accomplishment.* As in the case of Joe in an earlier chapter, community supervision can be the first external expectation someone has ever met. Other indicators included were the time it took to fail, in other words taking into account the length of desistance, as well as supervisees *efforts* toward reentry, such as participation in treatment programs, finding stable employment. Current measures of success also include the number of officer/supervisee interactions, residential stability, and the percentage fulfilling community service, drug screening, financial and administrative obligations.

INSTITUTIONALIZING INCENTIVES: The emphasis on incentives has practice implications, which were quickly folded into the procedures for the department. Less than a year into the consolidation process, in an interview with Nail and Scott Maurer, assistant commissioner of DCS, the conversation focused on developing an incentives matrix to use with the more conventional sanctions matrix. Guidelines were provided on how to apply tested methods of supervision that promoted desistance and modeled prosocial behavior. Desistance was clearly defined in the guidelines as something that took time and effort: "The process of replacing criminal behavior and associated anti-social identity with prosocial characteristics including personal recovery, learning to live a life of progressive value recognized by the individual and her/his community."

Even though the evidence-based literature has been emphasizing the effectiveness of positive reinforcement for years, positive reinforcement can feel at odds with an enforcement orientation. One way to reduce the tension of this attitudinal shift for officers was to *require* positive reinforcement. The individualization of both sanctions and incentives was emphasized, with a four-to-one ratio of positive to negative rewards being documented as carefully as sanctions. As a way of engaging supervisees in their own change process, officers were asked to provide their supervisees with a survey of the incentives and sanctions and to ask them to identify those that were most effective for them personally: for example, in terms of rewards, the relative importance of verbal recognition, curfew changes, or reduced reporting; in terms of sanctions, the relative aversiveness of travel restrictions, informing family of failures of compliance, or going to court.

Legislating Incentives: In 2017 in one of the last criminal justice reform bills of the Deal administration, SB 174, DCS was given legal ability to apply an incentive structure that would help reduce the cost and extent of supervision. They were allowed to front-end resources in the first years of reentry when people are most likely to recidivate and focus them on people at greatest risk to recidivate, and to reduce supervision on those who didn't need it, thus increasing *their* likelihood to be successful as well. People who had successfully met all supervision requirements for three years could petition to have their sentences ended, thus addressing the problem of excessively long probation sentences. After two years, nonviolent offenders who had met supervision requirements and paid their restitution could be moved to non-report, thus dramatically reducing active supervision cases. Individuals successfully completing supervision or treatment received certificates acknowledging their accomplishments.

Tools for Success: Soft Skills Training

The qualities that people gave as necessary for a good parole officer almost all turned on social skills. Morrison's list included "level headedness, patience, compassion, common sense (this is big—everything is not black and white), autonomy and discretion, grounded, thick skin, realize there will be failures and also that everybody is not bad, and genuine—that is really important." Jasmin Hill, a DCS district director, added to the list: "Integrity is probably the one quality that can't be taught. Honest. Fair. The *desire* to be a role model, to demonstrate prosocial behavior people may not have seen before."

These qualities are to some extent innate but can also be encouraged by training. They can be reinforced, or diminished, by institutional culture as well. A course on enhanced supervision skills has been so effective and popular with experienced officers as well as officers in training that the entire agency is being trained in it. An important assumption of the course is that many basic EQ and reasoning skills need to be *learned*—and gives officers methods by which to facilitate that learning in themselves as well as in others. A primary role for officers, as Hill pointed out, is to *model* these skills in their own behavior, using them to relate to the people they supervise and to help their supervisees develop these capacities in themselves 'in order "to have better relationships, sustainable connections with people who are going to support their recovery."

Just seeing some of the qualities that make it difficult for offenders to be compliant with supervision—the inability to plan, impulsiveness, lack of self-discipline and accountability, limited empathy—as modifiable with teaching, practice, and encouragement, has, by their own accounts, increased the optimism and patience of officers and thus the quality of their relationships with the offenders. "I no longer have a headache after I talk to someone," one experienced officer told us. It also helps with efficiency, which is crucial in this job. More clearly defining the needs of offenders, especially in terms of their importance for recovery or desistance, can help officers triage their heavy case loads, allowing them more readily to decide, with limited time, where to focus their energy to make the biggest difference in their *relationships* with the people they supervise.

This training also includes having officers wear body cameras so their interactions with supervisees can be reviewed, which promotes this basic value shift from enforcement to facilitation. As Morrison pointed out to us, we behave differently when someone is watching—and our behavior changes in the direction in which we know we are being evaluated. This is particularly important in a field where people are often trained to be hypervigilant and quick to aggression, or who just find themselves frequently in circumstances that naturally provoke hypervigilance, which is especially true of urban supervision with its very high caseloads. To de-escalate has to be an intentional, institutionally supported effort. More recently, additional training in procedural justice has been piloted, emphasizing the importance of respect, comprehension, fairness, and agency in interactions with supervisees.

Efficiency/Pragmatism/Competence

Pragmatism, or common sense, and efficiency are especially valuable in community supervision. Being organized was a quality uniformly listed as essential. This has led to the ready adoption of technological innovations in supervision in Georgia and also explains the acceptance of an evidence-based approach, where you use tested methods and continue to test them for their applicability to the concrete challenges you are facing. Should political administrations change and attitudes toward punishment and reform oscillate again toward harsher stances—you are more likely to be able to preserve these more incentivized approaches if you can show that they actually lead to success, especially success that is directly related not just to desistance from crime but also to increased social participation.

Homegrown / National Horizon

Almost everyone we talked to in community supervision was a Georgia native, so it is interesting that the vision of DCS, which has broad agency buy-in, is to be _the national leader for innovative and progressive community supervision._ One experience that fostered that aspiration, and also tested its feasibility, was Nail's involvement in a three-year Harvard Executive Sessions on Community Corrections, that drew together several dozen scholars, activists and practitioners in community corrections to assess current realities and future possibilities for community corrections. Although occasionally frustrated by the failure of the sessions to be adequately grounded in the realities of practice—e.g., legislative constraints, limited financial resources, overwhelming case loads, limited or non-existent community capacity for treatment, or community buy-in—Nail also found the sessions pushed his thinking. An important result of the sessions was a national consensus statement on community corrections, a consensus that provides support and validation for many of the practices now being implemented by DCS.

The consensus can be summarized as Less is More. Broadly endorsed by leaders in community corrections, as well as by criminal justice associations, prosecutors, criminal justice scholars, and industry leaders, these recommendations reflect the changes already implemented in Georgia. They include reserving community corrections for those who really need it; limiting the length and the conditions of supervision to those that really meet sentencing objectives; using incentives, including early discharge, to encourage compliance; reducing supervision fees; and using those savings to provide community services and support to people under supervision.

Because today over four and a half million people are on probation and/or parole throughout the United States, other groups, for example Fair and Just Prosecution, have even more expansive suggestions than the Executive Sessions consensus statement to help shrink this number. Most of these suggestions focus on shortening probation periods since the evidence shows that most violations occur within the first year of release. These suggestions include limiting probation after incarceration to one year in most cases, or terminating longer sentences after a year if someone has been compliant for a year, limiting supervision after jail to six months, not penalizing alcohol or marijuana use, and not incarcerating for technical violations. Again, many of these suggestions are already being tried, formally or informally, at DCS.

Across the country, the growing concern about mass supervision among community supervision practitioners themselves has led to the formation of a national consortium of concerned active and former directors of supervision across the country, EXiT: Executives Transforming Probation and Parole. They call for a "smaller and more focused footprint" that will "promote development and success rather than trying to find failure." They are concerned supervision at the scale and in the form it is now being practiced is a "tripwire to imprisonment, creating a vicious cycle of reincarceration" that disproportionately affects people of color. In particular, EXiT would like to see probation used only when necessary, be as brief as necessary and tailored to the actual needs and goals of the individuals—an approach Nail, a signatory of the effort, describes as "one size fits one." They would like to eliminate racial inequality in supervision and end supervision fees and incarceration for technical violations. Their community engagement platform emphasizes the need for systemic change, procedural justice, and involving justice-involved individuals as equal partners in systemic change.

CALL /VISION

Many people we met in community supervision, especially those who made it a life-long career, felt a strong affinity from the very beginning to the essence of this difficult practice—the ability to bridge very different realities, to bring justice full circle. Nail said, simply, "I knew I could make a difference here." It was also a difference he felt was worth making, a conviction, shared by many people we talked with, that the voice and perspective they are introducing into the criminal justice system and into the larger society is a much needed one.

Common sense, genuine, non-dogmatic, tenacious, this perspective has a social vision inherent in it, one that is best summed up by the term *melioristic*—the belief that, step by step, the world gets better and that we can be part of that change for the better, that as a society we are *all* engaged in a desistance process. This change is not restricted to the individuals supervised but also encompasses the correction systems and the underlying social forces that influence our behavior and our opportunities. It is best measured by actions and consequences. And by the concept we heard several times of "owning"—owning your hopes and intentions *and* owning your circumstances.

Nail summed it up this way: *I believe in consequences. If you do this—*

there are going to be consequences. But I also believe that whatever the price is for an action, once it is paid, it is paid. A parolee is no longer an inmate. And when they are discharged from parole, they are no longer a parolee. As a society we said if you do this, here is the consequence—but when you pay the price, you've paid the price. Shouldn't we all be about second chances? There go I but for the grace of God. . . . Any one of us could be in that position. And because they are paying that consequence, that does not mean that their family has to, that relatives and friends have to. But, unfortunately, you might as well imprison everybody associated with that individual because they are in prison, it is just that they are not behind the fence.

It is unfortunate, but sometimes we are a society that builds ourselves up by tearing others down. I'm not sure why. Give the man a chance! We will have inmates that work on all the training they need for a certain license—barber, welding. They have been trained, but when they get before that licensing board, they will be denied. No one will say they were denied because they were a convicted felon, but that is why they were denied. When do you realize an individual has paid their price, that they paid the price that we set on them as a governmental authority? When does it end? Why do you have to carry it to your grave?

Jasmin Hill, now a district director, spoke to us when she had just become the first DCS coordinating chief for DeKalb County, early in the reorganization process. Her background was in probation. At that point she was thinking about some of the community resistance she was experiencing. Her work as a coordinating chief often meant asking for material assistance from those very communities that have been most inequitably affected by mass incarceration. A difficulty in asking for help is that people associate probation primarily with enforcement not support: *I'm not sure whether it's legislation or policy or procedure that keeps us from saying that we're helping people. We need resources—for domestic violence, parenting, substance abuse—as a way to get there. I have to find those resources because I need something I can give my officers so they have an answer when people ask for help. They—communities and offenders—can't believe we're here to help them if we're not addressing issues and gaps in the community.*

Faced with resistance by community members to having people reentering or under supervision living in their community, she said bluntly, "These people are going to be here and live in *our* community. We are *all* citizens of Georgia."

She went on to explain the source of her own commitment to a job that felt challenging and sometimes thankless: *I'm the one here who is dealing with the people who don't want other people to be their neighbors. We don't have an island to put them on. They have paid their debt and they have to live somewhere. The reason I do this, I believe in all people. I told the people I supervised, the difference between you and I, you made some wrong choices. I have a son and a daughter, and I know what it is to care for them. I try to impart that to my officers: This is someone's son, daughter, father—just like yours. Some will grasp it and have more fulfilling careers. Some will never see it. I ask them: "Then why are you in probation? Why are you in parole?"*

Like most people in supervision, she also emphasized that community supervision has a corrective mission as well: *It is not all about helping. Some of it is punishment and retribution. Probation is an alternative to prison. It is not designed to make their lives easy. Personally, I would go to prison if I had to choose. Probation is hard.*

But she also felt that life demanded this kind of commitment. If probation is hard, life is harder. She said of her young offenders who talked too much about the adverse conditions of their childhoods: *As adults, they must take ownership of their lives. I listen to all their whining. My dad left. I was assaulted. Then I ask them, "What does any of this have to do with what you are going to choose to do tomorrow?"*

This question in no way evades the question of larger social responsibility: *When I came in I was young and without a family. I was excited about giving back to the community, but I didn't fully grasp what that entailed. As I worked, I saw life as I'd never seen it before, people who don't know people who have worked. I'm thankful for my life, fearful for what is to come. I'm concerned now that I am a mother with what will be the experiences of my children. If we're not one community, how will my children be divided or separated in society's eyes? It makes me want to work harder, do more, fight longer so it can be a just system, a system that is only dealing with offenders we're scared of, not those we're mad at.*

When asked what changes people would like to see in the criminal justice system, particularly in terms of reentry and rehabilitation, the answer was remarkably consistent: Address the underlying societal and psychological causes before there was any contact with the criminal system at all.

Nail said bluntly: *I still don't think we start reentry soon enough. It has to start with the very first engagement with the system. I would say it starts with arrest. Until as a system we recognize that, we are going to pay a price. Young people up to twenty-five return to prison at a rate twice greater than the rest. If they are already in, you are waiting too late to be talking about reentry. We pour all of this money into the adult system. But we know from research if a child has a parent that is incarcerated, if it is family of four, there is 75% chance one of them will go to prison. How often do we go in parolee's house and they have a child? How many opportunities are we missing to have a positive impact on that child? We miss a lot.*

David Morrison emphasized that one part of this melioristic vision is a sturdy form of compassion, a commitment to the essential dignity of another: *I went into college thinking "lock them all up and throw away the key," but you start learning about it and then you start working with it and you realize a lot of the people have never had a positive influence in their lives. They never had a leg up. They never really had a chance. They are still human beings, and it is the right thing to do to treat them like human beings. You learn quickly that if you talk to people with respect and don't take away their dignity, it will keep you from getting hurt. The worst thing you can do is take way a man's dignity.*

Nail, when asked what quality he would like to see remain with DCS whenever he left, said without hesitation: *The fundamental care philosophy. We have made a caring culture here. We do the best job we can with what we have and never lose sight that we are here to provide people with the means to change. DCS is not probation or parole. We have transferred from a control system to one where the bottom line is <u>Do we leave people better</u>? Their success is <u>our</u> success.*

CHALLENGES

The major challenge that DCS will face is the enormity of the task. In the first three years of its existence, its supervision population had grown by 25%, but its budget only by 13.7%. The last, the only, pay raise was in 2017 as part of an across-the-board raise to all law enforcement.

An essential question is whether these improved supervision processes can actually reduce the probation/parole population. The answer at present is no. This is due to both the high number of people still being put on probation and also the length of the probation sentences, both of which are out of their control. Even it they can reduce the proportion of people under active supervision, that doesn't mean that the total number of people on a correctional leash has been reduced. As long as people are on supervision, the threat of incarceration still exists. One of the arguments against long supervision is that it increases the chances of revocation on technical reasons and also arrest on other charges. It also reduces chances of employment, since sentences are still in effect, and the stigma of being a felon persists. It also reduces full social participation because as long as someone is on paper, they cannot vote.

Limiting the growth of the community supervision population is an issue that has not been sufficiently addressed yet. Probation is the major driver of growth. Limiting the growth of the probation population rests with prosecutors and the judiciary—unless legislation is passed that gives authority to the Department of Community Supervision or some other body to reduce the length of probation and balance local sentencing disparities. The judiciary in Georgia in general still favors very long probation sentences and has not yet bought into the broad Less is More consensus on community supervision. Prison sentencing disparities, which can be great across counties, are evened out in Parole by the Parole Board's sentencing matrix, but that does not occur with probation sentences. Parole can also control the number of individuals it releases. Control over probation, however, is broadly dispersed among the judiciary and prosecutors, and there is no coordination across counties in terms of the overall growth of the state probation population. Theoretically, its growth is unlimited. Two significant perverse incentives promote probation growth: Prosecutors often run on their conviction rates and probation fines go back to the originating county. (Supervision fees, much smaller than fines, do not go to DCS, rather directly to the state treasury.)

Criminal justice reform seems to go in waves and is heavily dependent on who is in office. The previous governor of Georgia, Nathan Deal, was, and remains, a passionate advocate of criminal justice reform, especially of reentry efforts. The current governor instead emphasizes enforcement, which tends to privilege resources for prisons rather than community corrections.

In addition, public opinion about the community's role and responsibility in reentry and restoration has not changed at the same pace as criminal reform efforts. Without that attitude shift, the added presence of more offenders within communities may increase opposition rather than tolerance. We do think that observing community supervision officers in practice may help with the necessary attitudinal shifts that can allow us as community members to become more comfortable keeping justice-involved people within the community instead of exposing them to the more brutal experience of Georgia prisons, an experience that rarely makes them safer for us when they return.

\(2/

RURAL SUPERVISION

M.O.R.E: MAX-OUT RE-ENTRY

DCS officers' participation in the M.O.R.E. program unfortunately ended in October 2019, to the deep disappointment of the officers involved. The reasons given for the decision were in large part economic and also reflected the different priorities of a new administration, which put more focus on enforcement. However, the program and the approach demonstrated by these dedicated M.O.R.E. officers is so intrinsic to effective reentry, especially for people who would otherwise be released directly into the community, we are pleased to begin our account with them.

The M.O.R.E. Program

In 2012, concerned about the higher level of recidivism among max-outs, the Georgia Council on Criminal Justice Reform suggested to Parole that they try and create a program for these individuals. The M.O.R.E. program started up in 2013 and in 2015 received a national award from the American Probation and Parole Association for Excellence in Community Crime Prevention.

The M.O.R.E. program was designed to provide some level of assistance and supervision to those in Georgia's prisons who are ineligible for parole (statutory max-outs) or because the parole board has refused them parole. These inmates are usually released without any restrictions—or supports. Max-outs sometimes are nonviolent offenders serving shorter terms, but they also include those serving long mandatory or life sentences for violent crimes. At its most dramatic, this can mean that someone in a maximum-security setting can walk straight out of solitary into the larger society with nothing more than a bus ticket and a gift card for $25. It doesn't matter whether they have a place to go, whether they have any means of social or financial support, whether they have drug dependencies, difficulty managing their anger, or limited abilities to read or to plan.

Max-outs are clearly not a problem restricted to Georgia. The Pew

Foundation reported that between 1990 and 2012 the number of max-outs in 43 states rose from 14% of inmates to 22%, with 115,372 inmates unconditionally released. In Georgia the percentage is double that. In 2015, max-outs made up 42% of those released, and 46% in 2018. However, Georgia has been a leader in trying to find some solutions that make release for these individuals safer both for them and for the communities they enter.

We spoke in 2015 with Barbara Neville, who was then director of the M.O.R.E. program. Her career had covered many facets of court and field probation as well as parole, including being a hearing examiner and administering the Residential Substance Abuse Treatment program. Originally trained as a nurse, Neville had an unapologetically rehabilitative stance toward supervision. When, as a probation officer she sent a young woman yet again to a residential substance abuse program instead of prison, the judge asked her, "How many times are you going to do that?" "As long as it takes," she answered. This attitude came through in the explicit expectations for M.O.R.E. officers: "The goal of the M.O.R.E. program is to assist in ANY way possible in order for the resident to prepare for reentry."

Neville, a calm, warm woman, described the qualities she felt were needed to be successful as a M.O.R.E. officer. First of all compassion, then curiosity and creativity, an ability to think outside the box. Also an ability to handle culture shock because this job put the officer directly inside a prison environment, for the transitional centers are work release centers that are still very tightly controlled. The differences in approach and culture were remarked on by both M.O.R.E. officers we talked with.

The person who would be most successful as a participant in the program, Neville felt, was someone who "never had a disciplinary report, has a vocational skill, has some family—and knows where his birth certificate is." However, these men and women may not be the ones who most need it. Assignment to transitional centers in general is based on needs not readiness for reentry. These are the prisoners who, according to risk assessments given at the beginning of their incarceration, were most likely to become burdens to the state on release because they did not have housing, skills, a family support system, might have mental or addiction issues, or be a registered sex offender.

Neville recognized this was also the case for many M.O.R.E. participants: *For the M.O.R.E. program to reach out and actually touch these inmates before they end up on the streets with nobody to talk to other than somebody in law enforcement looking to put them back in prison—that's the most beneficial. There are some with thirty years in prison, no visitors, no money, no job, no skills. You can even max right out of segregation.*

The M.O.R.E. program identified individuals who would max-out in twelve to eighteen months and reviewed their files carefully. If these individuals were free of serious disciplinary reports, did not have severe mental illness, were serving a nonviolent offense or first offense for a violent felony, and there was space in the transitional centers, they could be placed in a transitional center if they agreed. This allowed them to begin work release, preferably near where they intended to live. During 2014, 500 inmates were put in the M.O.R.E. program; 241 successfully completed it and were released during that year. Another 42 inmates who originally were denied parole were reconsidered and granted parole, which allowed them to leave prison early and move out into the community under parole supervision. However, this is a small number of the max-outs in any year. Overall, only 12% of the overall annual prison releases go to the thirteen transition centers in the state. M.O.R.E. participants made up a small proportion of this subgroup.

When at the transitional center, M.O.R.E. participants were under the supervision of a special parole/DCS officer who worked inside the transitional center, and provided them with some of the services that parolees receive when they leave prison: help finding employment, housing, substance abuse treatment, or mental health services. Because they could work from the transitional center like the other residents, M.O.R.E. participants were able to earn and save money for their release. The cost savings for the Department of Corrections were considerable: for each day that someone was in a transitional center under the M.O.R.E. program, they saved the state $12.51, and those who paroled out through this program saved the state $46.87.

M.O.R.E. IN PRACTICE

In 2015 and again in 2019, we visited and talked in depth with two experienced M.O.R.E. officers, Melanie Scarbrough and Buster Johnson. Both officers were located in areas that were quite rural, helping us to understand the important differences in the experience and practice of community supervision from urban and rural perspectives, both for the officers and for those supervised. The main difference is how deeply the rural officers are embedded in their communities, which affects how they understand and practice their jobs and naturally aligns them closely to the *One Officer, One Family, One Community* commitment of DCS.

Melanie Scarbrough

Melanie Scarbrough worked as a M.O.R.E. officer at two transitional centers located in prisons near each other in the mall infused area north of Atlanta where suburbs dissolve into more purely rural landscapes. She described the area as bifurcated, economically and racially, either middle class or very poor and in public housing. Phillips Transitional Center, associated with Phillips State Prison, is a male facility. Arrendale Transitional Center, associated with Arrendale State Prison, is farther north and is a female facility. More of her cases were at Phillips TC. Because of the more rigid reporting structure in the Department of Corrections compared to community supervision, we did not try to meet at the transitional center, rather met at several restaurants in the area.

Tall and blonde, in her forties, Scarbrough seemed very at home in the world and people responded to that instinctively. She didn't see anyone in a vacuum: we all come with families, communities, systems in which we are embedded. This awareness empowered and oriented her: *I'm aware when I'm arresting someone, you're not just arresting them, you're arresting a whole family. I love reentry because of this. You affect one person and you affect many.*

Her broad, contextualized social awareness came from her personal as well as her professional experience. Scarbrough grew up in Toccoa, a small town in the mountains a little farther north, where her father was the police chief. She was aware that they had a certain standing in the community, one that came with positive expectations.

Her mother, raised in a Christian home "where people didn't drink or cuss," had three brothers who went to prison. "It's not always the family that leads to prison—in their case, it was drugs and alcohol." Her uncles were not violent. Her last surviving uncle was in prison for meth trafficking at the time of our first interview. "My mother prays for him every day."

In her career, Scarbrough worked in welfare agencies as well as with probation, and parole. Going through the University of Georgia as a young mother, she earned her BA in sociology and criminal justice while working nights as a 911 dispatcher for a rural county, a job she still held along with her job as a M.O.R.E. officer. Her first job after graduation was with the Department of Family and Child Services (DFACS), where she worked first in foster care and then as a forensic child abuse investigator. "Yes, it was difficult. Yes, I took it home with me. If you didn't take it home, something was wrong with you." She then worked as a felony probation officer for six years before transferring to parole, where she worked for six years as a M.O.R.E. officer before returning to field supervision when the program closed.

She believes if we work with reentry in mind, recidivism will be less: *Some people can't be rehabilitated. They just don't get it—or they are mentally ill. But on average, you can work with people. If we focused more on that, it would be better.*

This positive attitude may come from her embeddedness in the community so that she is able to see the changes taking place over longer periods of time. "Most of my work is in the area where I live. It's efficient. I can go to Walmart on a Friday night and see everyone on my case load." Her son, she noted, had learned not to say anything when she ran into someone. "He *sees* my respect."

The families she saw in her work in community supervision were often the same families she once worked with at DFACS. She had people in probation and parole who she had supervised in foster care. At her son's school, parents on her caseload would come up and speak with her, introduce her to their own parents and other family. She saw these interactions as important for developing broader social and institutional trust. Other people would see the parents interacting with her and think, "Oh, she's not so bad." When parents had a question about their own case, she answered but brought the conversation back to what they had in common—their children. "Personally, I think, wasn't it *great* that they were there at the school for Field Day or Honors Day."

Children would ask her if she was going to come by later and see their mama: *Children don't need to be intimidated. If the conversation's difficult, I make sure to talk away from them. I take them aside and explain about my uniform and my weapons and my vest. I tell them their mama or daddy just needed some time out and now I'm helping them get it back together. I don't want to make a bad impression so they won't trust the system.* The system, as she saw it, was not just corrections, but school systems, welfare, police, judges, lawyers, employers, churches.

The qualities she identified as essential for any community supervision officer were all crucial to building social trust. As an instructor in the DCS basic training program for new officers, she told the students, "Your best weapon is your mouth." She added, *You can teach anyone to shoot a gun, but people have to have something inside themselves to be good officers. They need morals, good values. They are going to do right even if no one's looking.*

Respect was the most important element she brought to her corrections work: *I've arrested a lot of people. I've never had to fight with anyone. If you respect people, don't belittle them or talk down, they understand you have to sanction them. I tell them, "You didn't follow the rules. This is the bad part of my job, but I have to do it." They might ask, "Am I going to jail?" When I say yes, they ask, "Can I get some stuff together?" and I tell them yes. My chief once said, "I can't believe you told him he could do that—he won't show up." But he did. People do. In some ways, it's a parent thing.*

Respect has long-term benefits. Scarbrough described a time when, stopping at a station to buy gas, a man she had known from DFACS came over to her car. She had had to remove his children, but he had come over to tell her proudly that he had gotten his children back from foster care, that his daughter was now in college. *Even if you take someone's children away from them, if you treat them with respect, they don't hold it against you.*

These qualities she felt were even more necessary as a M.O.R.E. officer: *The superintendent at the transitional center said he was going to start calling me Mama Scarbrough. I don't mind. Many of them do need parenting. These guys and girls are very needy. When I walk through the doors in the morning, they surround me. I tell them, "Just let me put these bags down first, then I can listen to you." You need to be compassionate and patient. They need a lot of direction. You need to be passionate about your job, which is to be a counselor, nurturing. Hear what they have to say. Tell them, "It will work out." But you have to be genuine. That's crucial. They're better people readers than most.*

The reasons that these M.O.R.E. participants were so needy, she felt, was that many of them entered prison so early they failed to grow up. Their maturation stopped with incarceration. They had few boundaries. They didn't understand that while time stopped for them, it had gone on for those on the outside. She gave two examples of how she tried to broaden people's perspectives so that their expectations for reentry were more realistic.

In the first case, a woman who had been imprisoned for fourteen years told her that she wouldn't be needing a job when she was released because she was going to live with her boyfriend, who had raised her daughter throughout her incarceration. Scarbrough asked her directly, *You think he's been faithful all these years, waited on you? Life went on. He raised your daughter alone all those years. Consider all that before you depend on him.*

It took several months for the woman to reconsider her plan, but one day she came to Scarbrough and told her that she was getting money together and asked for help looking for an apartment. She told Scarbrough: "I had to think awhile about what you said. I think we should date again, get to know each other. I need to re-establish a relationship with my daughter. I've only exchanged cards and phone calls. I don't <u>know</u> her."

Another example, holding some personal relevance given Scarbrough's own very busy schedule as a single mother working two jobs, concerned a man on her caseload she let use her phone to call home. He had been locked up for ten years. On the phone, he was arguing with his wife, telling her what to do with one of their kids. When he got off, Scarbrough spoke to him bluntly: "*I'll tell you something as a mama. I'd have trouble taking direction from someone who left me for ten years with four teenagers to raise on my own. I'd think, 'Who are you to be telling me what to do?' You can't do that. You can call and <u>ask</u> her how she's doing. You need to <u>earn</u> respect with your kids and wife.*"

He said, "I didn't think about that—"

"*If she had left you and <u>you</u> raised those kids, how would <u>you</u> take it? You can be supportive and sympathetic, but not dominating.*"

One of the most important dimensions of Scarbrough's style was her belief that people are teachable—and that you need to hear what it is they need to learn. She emphasized the importance of basic life skills. In some ways, that was the focus of the M.O.R.E. program—and of transitional programs in general. For people leaving prison, she would define one of those basic competencies as addressing the consequences of institutionalization. She tried, when she was doing intake, to try to understand the specific impact of incarceration on an individual. How well were they sleeping? Where did they feel most disoriented—for example, learning how to use an automated bus pass after thirty-two years in prison?

One of the first and most important skills they needed to learn was de-escalation: *Prison is not the free world. Many of these men do not know you can walk away from conflict. They don't know how to resolve conflict in a nonviolent way. They need rewiring.*

She described a man who was angered that other men going out for work were allowed to wear shorts in the summer heat, but he was being required to wear long pants to get on the prison van that would shuttle him to his work. He had objected strongly and the transitional center guards had put him in handcuffs. Scarbrough asked to speak to him alone. She reminded him that he could always pull sweatpants on over his shorts and remove them when he got to work: *In the free world, we are not free to just cuss other people out. Sometimes here in the free world, we just have to eat crow.*

Telling the story, she reminded us of the enormity of that statement: *But you don't eat crow in prison. In prison you can't say you're sorry. He started crying. I told him, "Tell Sarge you need to talk to him." He apologized, and they took the cuffs off. He told me that he felt like less of a man, but I told him he was more.*

Other behaviors that were a constructive deflection of aggression in prison, like filing grievances, needed to be modified as well. Their world was larger now. She would tell men, *I want your important grievances heard. But if you don't receive your dinner in ten minutes in a chow line, that's not worth a grievance.*

One way she had found to bring the men she supervised into a mutual relationship that drew on their own prosocial inclinations was to ask their advice about raising her son: *I reach them by telling them I'm a single mom with two jobs and am raising a fifteen-year-old boy. I ask them, "What do you think I can do to keep him from being where you are?" They usually talked about television and music, that I should monitor those.*

There were challenges to modeling this prosocial stance inside a transitional center, especially in a male one. At Arrendale prison and by extension at the transitional center, women have more programming: they can be part of a local fire department, a choir that performs around the state, train as dog groomers, and earn a theological certificate. Although there is trades programming at Phillips prison, at the transitional center programming for men is limited to GED preparation, AA, and church services. More importantly, the atmosphere in the women's transitional center, with its mirrors, hair dryers, and toiletries, speaks to the goal of performing well in the "free world" in a way the men's transitional center, often without soap or toilet paper, does not.

In addition, the male center is dormitory style with fifty men to a dorm: *This can be very hard for those guys to handle. One guy was upset because his bed was in a blind spot, so everyone gathered around his bed to smoke and use drugs. He had been in prison thirty years and he didn't want to go back. But if you were to move him, they would think he was a snitch. I had to tell him to hang in there for the first thirty days, after that we would be able to move him.* For someone trying to make a transition toward sustained prosocial behavior, those first thirty days are key.

More challenging was the difference in tone used by the M.O.R.E.

officers and the corrections officers inside the transitional center. The tone of a center, in her opinion, was set by the head of security not the warden. If he or she cursed at or belittled the staff, the guards in turn would do so with the inmates: *In corrections, the major concern is safety, keeping order, keeping peace. I understand that a lot of effort is needed to do that. But how do you treat people? Not just shouting orders at them like they are cattle. A good example of the difference is that in parole or probation, we call people Mr. Johnson. In corrections they call them subject 95821.*

As a whole, for anyone who has worked in corrections, there is a clear us and them. Corrections officers need to stick together, to have each other's back. They need the bonding. But you can treat people like people and still do your job and run a safe transitional center. Even when the residents get disrespectful, we need to be respectful. You can use a sense of humor. For example, one time we were trying to get something set up in the employment center and people were coming up and tapping on the windows and doors. I got on the intercom and announced, "Unless you're bleeding, dying or throwing up, don't call because I don't know what I'm doing. Just give us some time to work this out." And then nobody bothered us.*

The corrections officers noticed that the men mouthed off to them but not to Scarbrough. She explained why: *The carrot is more powerful than the stick. The guards tell them, "I'm going to make sure you go back to prison." But I tell them, "They can't send you back to prison without my approval. But I can also do things that can help you. I can put in for you to go home early, to be put on parole. I get to say if you get a chance to go to another TC if this one doesn't work out."*

Scarbrough's list of what people needed to have pulled together to be able to have a good chance at a successful transition include a Social Security number and birth certificate, steady employment, savings of at least $1,000, stable housing (preferably not with a mother or girlfriend). They needed, if possible, a valid driver's license, because there was little public transportation in the area. They also needed to have been free of disciplinary reports for the period they were in the transitional center as a sign of prosocial commitment. With employers, she felt that being under supervision made people more employable. She could tell the employers to call her if they were late, she would check on them, assure that they were regularly drug screened. She felt her involvement improved the level of trust for these men and increased the chances that employers would continue to employ people from the M.O.R.E. program.

She divided her M.O.R.E. participants into three main categories, each with different needs: In order of difficulty—lifers, sex offenders, and young men with ten-year mandatory sentences.

Lifers, who are required to spend six months in a transitional center before release, were by far the easiest. They did not want to return to prison. They had received the most trades programming in prison. In general, their greatest challenges were adjusting to the changes in society after being incarcerated for decades. *Before I came to work with probation and parole, if I talked about lifers, I might have said throw away the key. But you meet men who have served twenty-seven to thirty years for a bar fight. They have served their time. My idea of even some of the most heinous crimes have changed. If that person has really changed, they are not the person they were when they committed the crime. I respond to them as the person they are now. You can't harbor hate in your heart forever.*

Public prejudice against sex offenders made housing one of their most pressing concerns. Most of them were employed, but many were not able to leave the transitional center even with substantial savings because they couldn't find a place to live. In Georgia, anyone on the sex registry cannot live within 1,000 feet of a church or school, but, as Scarbrough pointed out, Georgia is the Bible belt with churches abounding. She tells people that the men have jobs, that they are bringing much needed money to poor counties.

Her work in child welfare made these cases challenging: *Because of my DFACS work, I'm aware of the lasting consequences of these acts. But I don't think they get what it means to those children, how it lasts their entire lives.* She did feel that those who could be open with themselves and with her about their crimes—something they often could not afford to do in prison—were more likely to be successful in reentering.

Another challenge is that listing on the sex registry is usually, in community eyes, equivalent to being branded a predatory child molester. However, people are on it for all sorts of other reasons, as discussed earlier. This could mean that someone who went to prison at fifteen for robbery where a child was present, even after serving his sentence, would never be able to see his own nieces and nephews graduate from school or attend family functions. These restrictions, especially if not appropriate to the actual crime, made social reintegration much more difficult. "As an officer, how do you address the prejudice?" Scarbrough asked.

The group she found most troubling were the ten-year mandatory minimums, usually for armed robbery. Many of these were SB 440s, young men who went in at about seventeen, like Kevin, and came out in their late twenties. *So you were raised by wolves, I tell them. The only influences they had in prison were their peers and correctional officers who changed over constantly. No relationship with a mentor. No counseling because they can't keep counselors because of pay and caseload. No programming. Eight years of nothing. They need to know how to do life. I have a hard time with them. They were in gangs in prison. They're harder to reach. But if they ever trust you, they're just kids. They need the nurturing. Cooking classes, parenting class, along with employment classes are not a waste of time given how young they were going in.*

She found that one of the biggest obstacles to successful reentry with this group was their failure to grasp the severity of their crimes. She felt they had difficulty acknowledging guilt and responsibility. A consistent measure of trustworthiness for Scarbrough was the ability to understand the impact of your actions, whatever the crime. These young men were not there yet. She called them out when she felt they were conning her, "Don't pretend to be what you're not. Try again." She felt sometimes their parents, especially mothers, helped them make excuses. "Many of them are mama's boys—and the mothers want to think they were less involved than they really were."

She described one young man whose victims protested his presence at the transitional center. "He probably doesn't realize the impact of holding a gun on that man and woman. *They* haven't gotten over it." She overheard this young man talking to a chaplain and minimizing his involvement, claiming he had only been the driver when he had actually been a gunman and active in the kidnapping: *Later, I called him on it. They need to understand I know. They need to be honest about what happened. Honest with law enforcement and honest with their families. They don't need to tell everyone, but they need to be honest with themselves and with their families.*

She found that lifers, perhaps because of their distance in time from their crimes, were more able to be honest. She described a man who had served a life sentence for kidnapping. The story as he told it was comic: stealing a car from a used car lot because they had stolen computers they now needed to transport, a woman from the dealership tased and in the trunk, escaping. As he said, "a life sentence for being dumb." Scarbrough found him trustworthy because his account matched the one in his record almost word for word: *I respected that. I told him so. And he said, "I may be joking in the way I tell it, but I'm not joking about the crime. It took me about seven to ten years for it to sink in that I was serving a life sentence. Same amount of time it took to sink in how terrible that would have been if it were my sister."*

The man she was speaking with now was not the man who had committed the crime. Making this distinction meant paying special attention to the present, what actions provide the current basis for trust. Scarbrough recalled how as a parole officer she had supervised two brothers who had both received life sentences. She had read their legal files, which ran thirty pages or more. The crime they were convicted of was horrific. But she told her chief that she wouldn't hesitate to take a nap on their sofa. Her chief looked dubious. "I told him that I trusted them. I knew they wouldn't hurt me. The crime was horrific, but they weren't those people anymore."

However, a recent experience was haunting her. She had read the file of a woman preparing to leave prison after serving a life sentence, who had been fifteen when she was sent to prison. She had been part of a gang and had engaged in the kidnapping and extremely sadistic torture of a girl her own age with whom she had a relatively minor disagreement, a crime that extended over a week. Now, twenty-five years later, an articulate, poised, middle-aged woman, part of a prison choir, she was maxing out, preparing for reentry. But the crime was not impulsive. The dissonance was deeply disorienting for Scarbrough: *I felt sick. My own son is fifteen. He would never do anything like this—ever. I asked myself, Why do I do this? Maybe I shouldn't have been nosey? How do I separate who she is now and who she was then? I try to judge from where they are now. But how does someone do something like that and then talk to me like a regular person? I hated that I asked myself, Why is she even coming in here, asking me a question? When I ask guys what I did that made a difference in their reentry, half the time they tell me, "Just your believing in me."*

She was right that her ability to have confidence in the men she works with was part of her particular gift for supervision. She described how one of the counselors at the transitional center was obviously frightened of the men in the center, saying, "I'm not taking any of them in the van with me. What if it breaks down?" Scarbrough responded, "It's in how you treat *them.* They like me. I expect they'd guide the traffic and help me change the tire."

She thought that this core respect was essential if people leaving prison are ever going to have trust in the system. "To have trust in the system, you have to feel we're not out to get you." But to have this trust she was trying to build stick, the community needed to meet those returning half way. In some ways she saw her own role as consistently modeling that stance for <u>all</u>

members of the community, whether a resident of the transitional center, a correctional officer, a potential employer, an apartment manager, or for her son when shopping together at Walmart on a Friday night. Clearly, it is not always easy, but therein lies its value.

Buster Johnson

Officer Buster Johnson has been a parole officer for over twenty years and worked in the M.O.R.E. program at Smith Transitional Center in Claxton since the beginning of the program in 2013. Before that he was the sole parole officer for surrounding Evans County, a position he holds now as well. Then his caseload averaged 85 parolees and he was responsible for all supervision, including mental health and sex offenders.

Claxton is a town of less than 2,500 located in a rural, economically depressed area off the highway from Macon to Savannah, which we have come to call Prison Alley for the many state prisons located in its vicinity. Claxton's major claims to fame are fruitcakes and having been the only place where a meteorite was known to hit a mailbox (Dec.10, 1984, auction price $83,000). The major employer in town is Claxton Poultry, which we discuss more in our chapter on employers. All residents of Smith Transitional Center, a minimum-security facility, are expected to work at the poultry plant, which is across the highway. When not on their work shift, the residents are expected to be in the transitional center, which has a capacity of 213 residents. Men are transported in a van to the grocery store since there is no public transportation. Indeed there is little of anything in downtown Claxton except an attractive post office and town hall, many thrift stores, and the Claxton Fruitcake salesroom.

In the fall of 2015 we met with Johnson and then with his M.O.R.E. graduate, Michael, in a conference room on the second floor of city hall. Johnson, a relatively small man with a carrying voice that combines authority and warmth, cheerfully greeted the receptionists like old friends as we entered the building. He had greeted us similarly when we pulled into the TC parking lot.

Some months before we came to Claxton, we first interviewed Johnson with his long-time colleague Mike Bobo, then chief of parole in the nearby town of Jessup (now a DCS coordinating chief), when they were attending a week-long Victim-Offender Dialogue (VOD) training session. In one of the practice sessions at that VOD training, a session that involved interrogating a possible sexual offender, it was possible to watch Johnson shift into enforcement mode, with all the changes in voice and stance that requires. It gave us a clear sense of his range. How he blended these two parts of his role, support and enforcement, was a little different from Officer Scarbrough, but equally effective.

This theme ran through our last conversation, in 2019, when Johnson was taking a deep breath, having come off three extremely busy months serving double duty as the M.O.R.E. officer for both Smith Transitional Center and Coastal Transitional Center until a new officer was appointed there. Coastal TC, located in Savannah an hour away, has an official capacity of 213, but was at 270. His caseload had included thirty-four at Coastal and seventeen at Smith. As with Scarbrough, Johnson's ability to personally influence the decision about early release was a powerful incentive for the men he supervised. When we talked, he had made four successful recommendations in the past two months for men previously denied parole.

Supervising at Smith with its rural setting and single employer, and Coastal, with its urban setting and broader range of potential employers posed very different challenges. The main challenge at Smith was that jobs at the poultry plant were grueling. The only alternative was enrolling in a CDL program at a local vocational school, but for that men needed a valid driver's license and no drug record. If neither of those worked, a resident would have to be transferred to another transitional center, if there was space, or back to prison. Security was tighter and morale lower at Smith. The correctional officers at Smith, Johnson observed, still thought of it as prison, not a *transition* center. Many correctional officers were looking for jobs elsewhere.

At Coastal, control was lighter and morale higher. Men were able to find their own jobs, even beyond the sixty-three listed potential employers. If a particular job didn't work out, men could fairly readily find another one. They were able to go out on their own to the grocery store on passes. For a time they had been allowed to take public transportation or walk to work, but that also meant they could walk to their old haunts and possibly take up their less salutary habits. The solution was to require them to pay out of pocket for private transportation, adding a monthly $70 transportation fee to the $90 they already paid for room and board, thus making saving for release far more difficult on minimum wage. For Johnson, the many different shifts that the men worked meant he had to extend his own hours until ten at night in order to be able to meet with them. However, he liked the variety of locations and range of challenges he was facing.

One major difference he noted was that the M.O.R.E. program tried to locate people near their homes so that when they left they would have a community they could engage with and a job they could continue. Corrections, on the other hand, felt that people would relapse into their prior criminal behavior if they were located too near their homes, so they tried to fill the transitional centers with individuals who would move away from the community on release. Resilience and focus were more necessary if you took the M.O.R.E. approach. Johnson thought that if a man had nowhere to go, it was best for him to stay where he had a job and where he had experienced supervision, however briefly, so knew there was some support. For locals, especially those with drug problems, returning home posed challenges. "It helps maintain sobriety not to know any of the drug dealers in the area," Johnson said. However, if families said they would support the individual and help him get back on his feet, he supported return.

Johnson shared several stories about the vulnerability of people at the point when they were first released from a transitional center. Recently, a man had disappeared only two weeks after he was released from Coastal TC. A warrant was sworn out when he did not report for parole. Johnson tried to call him, then went to his residence. He was strung out on drugs: *We'll continue him on parole, but put him on a curfew. We're letting him sit in jail awhile to get sober, then we'll get him some treatment. The new M.O.R.E. officer is going to do an interview and find out what drugs he's on, then make her recommendation. We can't get him into the Salvation Army because he needs to have six months left on his sentence and he doesn't. We may have to put him on outpatient with random drug screens, and if that doesn't work, up the effort.*

This kind of dramatic relapse was not uncommon. The year before Johnson had a parolee leave the transitional center with $10,000 saved: *The week he got out, he spent all that money on drugs. Luckily he had paid his rent so he had a place to stay until we could get him into a drug center. But he lost his job. You can't see that coming. He wasn't using at the TC. I've had guys who work well for months, and then they binge. One guy stole the security television from a hospital to pawn!*

Johnson's resilience to setbacks of this kind had developed over time: *When I started this job, I thought I was going to change lives—but that just isn't realistic. All I can do is my job. It doesn't do any good to hurt myself over it. I don't take it personally anymore. When I first started, I was taking it personally, very personally. I've grown up, and I know it's not me, it's their decisions. All the counseling in the world, sometimes it doesn't take. But in parole we give them every chance before we send them back to prison.*

Johnson enjoyed facilitating that extra chance. He had recently spent several days driving a recent parole release from the TC around to various towns in the area to find housing—and then spent another few days doing the same to help him find employment. Given the absence of public transportation in the Claxton area, this assistance was crucial. It is also part of the M.O.R.E. expectation that officers help in *any* way possible.

Johnson was particularly encouraged by a pilot training program to improve reentry readiness that the Department of Corrections was testing at Smith. It made use of the first thirty days, the classification period when residents are usually keep on site, to provide classes on job interview techniques and guided discussions on employment to help create more realistic and focused expectations about the kind of jobs they wanted and what they could reasonably expect to earn. He felt these classes would help men both find a job that suited them and help them stick at it.

Johnson reminded men that there were many actions they could take while at the transitional center that would help them. For example, they could earn Performance Incentive Credits (PIC points) that could reduce their tentative parole month by a full year. They could take a defensive driving course. They could take other programs. Even good behavior could earn them credits. "I encourage them to do community service, building up hours, resume, reputation." He felt that the younger men in particular were not taking advantage of their opportunities.

Four years before Johnson had taken the Enhanced Supervision course that is now being required of all DCS officers and found his own practice greatly changed by it. The biggest benefit of the course, one that he found very helpful to share with the men he supervised, was simply that we have control over the choices we make, and we can make them more deliberately. It is an approach that encouraged second chances, and always came with the risk of failure. He noted that corrections officers relied almost completely on external controls: *It's like, "Step out of line and I'm going to put you back in line." They don't have interactions, they just dominate. But we need to ask a guy, "Do you <u>understand</u> what you're doing? Do you know the consequences?"*

Johnson talked about where he felt the enhanced supervision approach made the greatest difference: *It didn't change my practice or how I handle my cases. But it did change how I deal with violations and how to deal with problem solving—by giving the problem back to them and helping them find the solution in a way that is affirming and is asking them to grow. When you are dealing with discipline, you say, "I'm disappointed you did this. What do you think are the consequences? Do you want to change? Will you give me your* <u>*word*</u> *you'll not use for a week?" When you see they are clean for a week, you affirm, by asking, "How did that feel? Do you think you can continue? Can you give me your* <u>*word*</u>*?" You make it part of a relationship.*

The biggest difference the course made for him was he now saw that fostering good choices, good judgment was a teachable skill. He emphasized the role of writing in helping people think before they acted: *I had this guy test positive. Parole remanded him—sent him here to the TC as a second chance before going back to prison. I asked him to write down why he was using, what it was doing for him, and the consequences, the things that were not good about using. Also, why I should give him a second chance. I gave him three days. In three days, he handed me this letter. It was a really thoughtful response.*

Johnson also recognized when a more directive response was required. There were times when external constraints were needed, for example when there was the potential for domestic violence. Johnson described a situation when someone with mental health issues was released from Coastal TC: *When he first came out, he and his girlfriend were always fighting. I told him, "You don't need to have contact. It's a volatile relationship." I told him* <u>*no*</u> *contact. I found out he was still having contact, and I called the cops. I told him, "I'm going to have an administrative hearing. You're not listening." I pulled in the chief and we told him, "If this continues, you're going to end up in prison. It needs to stop." Far as I know, he's had no further contact with her. He's getting mental health counseling. He has a job. He's going in the right direction for now.*

Another time when a parolee beat his wife, the wife called Johnson. She had photographs of the abuse. Johnson went to the Parole Board and applied to revoke the man's parole and send him back to prison, but the wife didn't want him to go to jail. When he was released, he intended to go back home, but they told him he couldn't until he had counseling. "Sometimes, you have to protect people from themselves," Johnson said.

Johnson shared two stories of successes that give him great pleasure: *I find my career gratifying. I enjoy what I do. I know there are 10% we can't do nothing with, but for at least 90% we're seeing positive change. In Evans County, one young lady is doing fantastic. She's not on paper, working at McDonald's.*

She told me, "My dad ended up back in prison." I've dealt with her dad on many occasions, he's still hooked on cocaine. She used to be bad on cocaine herself, but she chose, she made a decision. I asked her what might have made a difference. She said when she was on parole with me, I stayed on her constantly, I had her go to the classes.

Another success story concerned someone who was at Coastal TC but had settled in the Claxton area. He was now a manager of a Burger King: *They were training him to be a manager while he was still on paper. Soon as he was off, they gave him his own store to manage. He has been off paper for a year and is still doing fantastic. He's even offered other guys at Coastal jobs. His goal is to be able to buy a Burger King.*

When asked about the community's response to having men from the TC decide to stay in Claxton, Johnson said: *I think the community has mixed feelings about the TC and the YDC [youth detention center]. They're happy when guys hang around, but not when they blow up. In Claxton, the community sees the repercussions of the ones who come out and don't keep a job. Community and law enforcement only see the ones who aren't successful.*

He saw himself as having an important role to play in increasing acceptance: *I'm known in my community. They come to me before they go to law enforcement if they think parole is involved. They're quick to come to us because they can see we are trying to work with the guys.*

In Johnson's view community acceptance *has to do with the attitude of the person, and not the offense itself. In a small town, everyone knows what you did. They know your family. This is different from a city. But even in a small community, a man has to earn that trust, earn his place.* This effort created a positive reinforcement cycle. As Johnson acknowledges, *officers put more effort into those who are trying.*

The challenge of what to do with those who weren't trying, who were still doing wrong was difficult, especially understanding the interplay of individual and systemic factors: *I feel that society has gone so far that we don't know how to deal with people who are doing wrong. We only know how to put them behind bars. In Evans County, it feels like going to prison is not a big deal now. In Claxton, people are waving at you after you get out. I think it has to do with the way you grew up. I see families coddling. I come to the parents' house and the guy is still in bed. Why isn't he out there, looking for a job? A lot of guys on parole think they won't get caught, so continue to do what they got caught in regards to. It's not the action itself that bothers them, it's the getting caught.*

He was particularly troubled by a recent effort by various men to pimp themselves to married women at nearby Fort Stuart. They had made up cards advertising their services and were distributing them. Johnson asked them, "You really think that's right?" The men said, "Well, the women have a choice." Johnson reminded them that the soldiers at Fort Stuart were trained to kill. "But all they think is, *as long as I don't get caught. There's no inner morality here.*"

One activity that had absorbed Johnson and given him much satisfaction in the last four years was his work as a facilitator in prison-based Victim-Offender dialogues. When he first was training for this and thinking about how it might affect his supervision practice, he said, "I didn't know there was closure—just a step forward." The importance of acknowledging guilt and responsibility was one part of his VOD training that Johnson had brought more deeply into his own supervision practice: *The men often act like they feel like a victim to society. They say, "I didn't do anything wrong." It seems like prison is no longer punishment in society's eyes—or in theirs. It's an initiation into manhood. That's what it feels like with some of these guys.*

This lack of an inner compass is clearly something Johnson refused to take for granted: *In prison, it is all about me. What I can get. These guys don't care about one another or anybody. I see that the younger they are, the more trouble you have. But in society in general—who is setting the good example? I don't see it there. Guys are following examples they see—and making wrong decisions. Will society fix this? I don't know. There is such a "me" attitude. If you can change that, it would change a lot of things.*

Johnson did have suggestions about what might make community supervision more successful. First, of course, was to reduce the very high caseloads that prevent officers from being able to get much done. Second was to reduce the economic barriers to reentry and reintegration. He was encouraged by the recent changes that DCS has been able to make so that supervisees were only paying restitution *or* supervision fees. His suggestion was that judges take into account how long it would take someone realistically to pay restitution and divide it over a longer period of time. Like many, he felt inability to pay was not a reason to send someone who was otherwise compliant back to prison.

One quality of Johnson's, which Scarbrough shared, was a fundamental kindness. He observed, "You can get a feel for who will make it. Someone *cares* about them." He clearly is willing to be that someone as the following story of Michael, a M.O.R.E. graduate and parolee, demonstrates. But what was most interesting was Buster's insistence that this kindness not be seen as exceptional. He saw showing favoritism as destructive to his effectiveness, so the kindness which was so intrinsic to him became a stance, a communal commitment, one that we, as community members, can learn to emulate.

Since the closing of the M.O.R.E. program, Johnson has returned to field supervision and has a caseload of 235.

MICHAEL
This, what I'm telling you here, this is my testimony.

Michael, a tall, thin man with long graying red hair pulled away from his face in a ponytail, a bandanna across his forehead, shared his life story with us across a big table in a conference room on the upper floor of the Claxton City Hall. He did so at Johnson's request, but this conversation wasn't simply an act of courtesy. When Michael spoke there was an inner pressure—to speech, to clarity, to seeing the patterns in his own life. He talked rapidly and without break for several hours—until Johnson came in to remind him it was time to leave for his nine-hour shift at the poultry plant, which ran from 5:30 in the evening until 2:45 a.m.

Michael began his story with what he saw as the crucial event that led to the acts that resulted in his incarceration in his forties. From Mississippi originally, Michael, at eighteen, married a young woman from south Georgia because of an unplanned pregnancy. He saw this as an act of responsibility, not love. His daughter was now in her mid-twenties. He also had a younger son. He had returned from a two-year stint in the Navy to find his wife pregnant by another man. He claimed the child and raised him and obviously cared for him deeply. He and his wife had an understanding that the biological paternity of the boy would be kept a secret. However, when they were divorcing, his wife presented this information to the court in order to prevent Michael from having visitation, even if it meant foregoing child support: *When I read that, saw it was public knowledge, the bottom dropped. I lost my job, my car, my house. It didn't matter. I got in with a crowd that didn't have nothing.*

Clearly there were other factors active here. One was how drug use contributed to Michael's downward slide. Some of his jobs involved chronic toxic exposures, for example a job where he repainted used tires using a gallon of paint and four gallons of gasoline. He also often felt socially isolated. He described living twenty years in his wife's hometown, where he always felt ostracized by her family: *My in-laws never took me serious. All they saw was a stranger. There was never the respect of a family member. I was my own island. It didn't take long for that island to crumble.*

There were also significant errors of judgment. His period in the Navy in his mid-twenties included nine months in the brig for a series of almost comic misadventures that made him AWOL. He was ultimately given an early release: *I loved boot camp, but not the squadron. I felt like I had a bull's-eye on my back. Everyone was aiming at me.*

The events that led to his prison sentence also had a comic side, which Michael, with self-deprecating humor, acknowledged: *Never hire a blind man to be a lookout for anything. I was the lookout but without my glasses for two burglaries of unoccupied buildings. We ran out into the fields when we saw people coming. I was glad to be at the jail after we were caught, I had tired myself out with the running.*

Defended by what he described as a "public pretender," he received three sentences. As a first offender, he received what would be an unbelievably harsh sentence in Atlanta, but for south Georgia it is far from uncommon. For burglary of an unoccupied building, he received a twenty-year serve-ten prison sentence, with a twenty-year probation sentence to follow. He also received a five-year prison sentence for damage to property. He was eligible for parole for both prison sentences after he had served a third of each, five years in all. Michael served his sixty months in prison on the two sentences "with a two-week vacation between them." However, given the twenty-year probation sentence, "I will be a senior citizen before I come off paper."

The two-week reprieve was due to a bureaucratic error and highlights key differences at that point in time between attitudes in Probation and Parole. It also demonstrates important dimensions of Michael's own character: diligence and self-sufficiency. After Michael had been in prison for twenty months, he received notice that he was being released on parole. However, he could not be released without an address. During the eight months Michael spent in jail awaiting trial, a minister had come to the jail weekly and he had given Michael his card. So Michael gave the minister's name and address, and when Parole called, the minister told them to send Michael on. The minister housed Michael in the church, where in return for lodging Michael cleaned the church building of the all black congregation. Michael heard that the local poultry plant was hiring, and three days later, he had a job there.

When he received his first paycheck two weeks later, Michael promptly went to the parole office to pay his fee. The people at the parole office were confused. "Why are you here?" The error was on Parole's side. They had granted him parole for the five-year sentence, which was the only charge that the prison had received for him. Michael's twenty-year-do-ten sentence hadn't shown up in his file.

He was told to go to the probation office where the reception was far more hostile. "What are you doing here?" the officer yelled. "I'm going to get you on the first bus back to prison." Michael was upset at the response. He had simply followed the orders he had been given: Give us an address, leave the premises, report to parole, find a job. He was upset that his compliance went unrecognized by probation: *So, when free, what did I do? First thing I did, I got a job. I was only out two weeks, but it was long enough to get a paycheck.*

The parole officer was considerate and apologetic. "He asked me to put my hands behind my back for the handcuffs. He told me, 'I went to bat for you and so did the minister, but they're sending you back.'" Before Michael returned to prison, the minister shook his hand and said, "I've been to the jail week after week, and you are the first person who got the message—that I would be there for you." But Michael retained both fear and anger about the treatment he received from the probation officer.

The next several years of Michael's sentence were spent at a county work camp. "The food is a *lot* better. You get to go out of the camp and go to work during the day." He was assigned maintenance and then helped refinish the lawyers' office in a county courthouse. He obviously took pride in the work. When he heard about the Smith TC where he could again work at a poultry plant, he was interested. Because at this point he had served 20% of his ten-year sentence, he was eligible.

At the TC, Michael was determined to do well: *You're in control when you're inside. You have two choices. Screwing up—or not. You are the only person who can determine if you will make it. When they throw you in that plant, they throw three dangerous things at you: women, alcohol right down the street, and drugs everywhere. There they are, the three necessary evils, front and center. But I had set my mind. I was a disappointment to my mother. My going to prison was a total shock for my family.*

When Michael left the TC, he decided to continue to live in Claxton and to keep the job he had at the poultry plant. He didn't want to go back to the town he had lived in most his adult life: *Going back to that little town, people know everything, and you have no job. Where are you going to stay?*

Everybody who knows you can't stand you. But coming out here you could have your trailer, your <u>home</u>. And you have a <u>job</u>. The whole process is about change. Change everything if you're going to be serious about it.

Although Michael had been drug free in prison, before that "cocaine and marijuana were my constants." Johnson assigned him to take a drug course—and hand delivered his certificate of completion. Michael also took a course in life skills through the probation office, where he was taught how to get more in touch with himself and how to evaluate his needs better: *There was a lot of reflecting: What got you where you were? What got you where you are now? Where are you going next?*

Michael was proud of his job at the plant. He was a floor man: *All the meat dropped, that's my responsibility. I have a dolly that carries fifty pounds of meat. I walk all night long down the five lines. A revolving circle. I'm supervising with a squeegee.*

Michael had "*hometized* myself. I go to work and come home. I buy groceries on the weekend. The more you associate with anybody, the more likely it is to get in trouble." He walked the forty-five minutes to and from work, which meant he arrived home at close to four in the morning. His ten cats were his major source of companionship: *They're like my DVD. I can sit and watch them for hours. When I come back from work, they're in the window watching for me.*

Johnson mentioned in our conversations, as have other community supervision officers, that isolation is one of the biggest hazards for people coming out of prison. They are so afraid of going back, they cut off all social contact. Michael described Johnson's advice to him: *He told me that I was a contributing member of society, but not social. "You need to get yourself a church,"* he told me. *"You're not letting nobody in." In my mind, that was right. The more people I let in, the more danger. It's all a matter of association. If a buddy of yours says—you could melt. So <u>no</u> entertaining.*

Michael's relationships with various family members were complex. The one family member he had been consistently close to for much of his life was his maternal aunt, who had died the previous year. She was the only one who wrote him regularly while he was in prison and had helped Michael and his mother reconnect while he was in prison.

One day, two years before he spoke with us, Michael had received a call from his mother, who told him her cancer had come back. This news disturbed him greatly. It also set in motion a series of social interactions that had made a tremendous difference in Michael's life: *Every third Saturday, a church comes and sets up a roadside ministry with a free breakfast. I stopped. It shook me, this news about my mother. I wanted my mother's name to be put on their prayer list. I had a long talk with their pastor and a lady outside the church. Every Sunday the church prepares a free breakfast. They invited me to come to that breakfast. I went and personally said my mother's name in the prayer. When my mom found out I was going to church and put prayers in for her she asked, "Did hell freeze over?"*

But now I <u>run</u> the breakfast ministry from 5 to 6 a.m. I have the keys to the building. An inmate convicted of burglary! That is <u>my</u> kitchen. What happened was it was all volunteer, each one responsible for food for a month. But then a woman who was wife to the veterinarian here, she said, "We're going to appoint someone to run this kitchen. We need a constant. We'll pay them." I said, "Can I throw my hat in the pool for consideration?" I had made no secret of my past. Lots of Saturdays I had helped them pass out food.

I was telling Mr. Johnson one day when he picked me up in the rain and took me to work, "you could almost say this was a master plan." I joined the church and was baptized this August. They know me. Know my wrongs and know my rights. The community sees me too. The people at the church did everything they could after my mother died. They tried their best to help me make it through everything I was going through. Half of them didn't know about my past and didn't care.

Michael was philosophical about the relative challenges of having a criminal record. He felt that because his time in prison allowed him to become sober, "I've had more good than bad from it." He didn't feel that his record interfered with his employment possibilities as much as it might for others: *But I'm not going to be dishonest. I want them to know. They need to know who I am, not who I used to be. The person I used to be, I don't know anymore. He's long gone.*

One strong concern Michael had was that he might have to go back to where he used to live to serve out his probation sentence. To transfer his probation to Claxton, he was told he would have to return to the town where he originally lived and interact with the probation officer who had so harshly returned him to prison years before. When he called, the probation officer said, "You out? You need to come and see me face to face." Michael was afraid that if he went there, he would never be able to come back. Johnson reassured him this would not happen: *Mr. Johnson said, "Don't worry. I'll put you on the bus, and I'll come get you when you come back." But I want this man permanently removed. If someone is destined to see you fail, there's nothing you can do. That is the mind set throughout the system of corrections officers. I used that as my motivation. When I go back by the TC, I smile at them. I want them to see me. I like the view from this side of the razor wire.*

Michael's life was precariously balanced economically. He had not always walked to and from work. Until recently he had ridden a bicycle: *We work a lot of Saturdays. They give us an attendance bonus. If we work 44 hours, we get an extra $47. You build your budget around it. They let you know on Thursday. But then one week, that didn't happen. So, my bike was the first thing to go. I don't blame anyone but myself.*

Michael told us how after work, from 4 to 4:30 in the morning, he now regularly met at McDonalds with a man from the church to do Bible study. The study companion was working on preparing his own testimony. Michael told him about planning to meet and talk with us. *And then, you know, I realized, this, what I am telling you here, this is my testimony. I give credit to that man up there for everything that has happened to me.*

When we talked to Johnson a few years later, we learned that Michael now worked at the local Dairy Queen as a fry cook. He had gotten sick and because of extended medical issues lost his job at the plant. He was not making as much money as he used to, but he remained involved with the church. Johnson still saw Michael's life as a success story. He has not gone back to drugs. And he did go and see his son get married.

RURAL RIDE-ALONG

CASEY BARKLEY

The first thing we learned about Officer Casey Barkley was that she was as flexible as she would later prove knowledgeable. The officer we were scheduled to meet for an early morning ride-along out of the LaFayette DCS Office had broken his elbow the evening before when out with a warrant-serving team and was unavailable. She comfortably took over his duties, explaining that she usually conducted the ride-alongs for the office.

Arriving after a long drive from I-75 through very rural and sparsely inhabited north Georgia, the DCS office on the outskirts of LaFayette had the look of a prosperous brick suburban house, with its five dormer windows on the second floor, the lake and long lawn leading up to it. It probably began as a bank building. Down the slope was another more modest white house that served as the counseling and Day Reporting Center for the district. The LaFayette DCS office provides community supervision for four counties in the far northwest corner of the state—Dade, Catoosa, Chattooga, and Walker—ranging from very rural to more suburban/urban ones that form part of the greater Chattanooga area. LaFayette, the county seat of Walker County, has a population of around 7,000.

Unlike some of the bleaker waiting rooms we had visited, this one felt bright, a little church-like with its wooden benches. The bulletin board listed various churches with assistance programs. Its bathroom had colored soap and air freshener. The receptionist provided us with a pen with flower attached to sign in.

DCS MERGER

As a replacement was identified and duties were sorted upstairs in a back office filled with files and computers, there was a discussion between the three women in the room, an assistant chief, another DCS officer and Officer Barkley, about how long the officers had served on average and whether the merger had proved more challenging for those from probation or parole. The conclusion was most officers there had served about six and a half years, but everyone in the office now, except Barkley, had come from the probation side. She was the only parole officer who stayed after the merger: *It was a very big transition, especially for parole. There are lot more probation cases than parole cases, so when we integrated caseloads, I went from having 80 to 100 parole cases I knew very well to having roughly 100 probation cases and maybe 10 parole cases. And they didn't have a training program to learn the other side, so you just kind of had to do it on the fly. So that was an adjustment. But it made me learn it quicker that way because I did have so many probation cases that were violating. So I learned it quicker than most people did.*

There is different sanctioning we can do with parole versus probation cases. If someone is on parole in Georgia it doesn't matter where we take them to jail. If it is a probation case, we have to take them to their sentencing circuit. So that was an adjustment. The major differences I had to adjust to were that with the Parole Board, I knew what I was going to get for what. If I told an offender they were going to get a specific sanction, they were going to get it. With probation if I'm having to take it back in front of a judge, I don't know what that particular judge is going to do that particular day with that particular offender. So two different offenders with the same violation would get two different sanctions and that makes supervision harder to do. We have four counties in this circuit, so we have to deal with four courts—four judges.

When Barkley joined parole in 2014, it had already gone virtual, so she began her career in community supervision trained in their new, field-based approach. Before that she had been a police dispatcher. In her time as a parole and then DCS officer, she had supervised in all four counties, and had supervised about 400 people overall. When the two field services merged and numerous vacancies occurred, she assumed responsibility for field training for new officers, but retained relationships with those parolees she had previously supervised: *Even when I didn't have a caseload, my old offenders would still contact me when they needed something. I was going out in the field with my trainees—so I would continue to help them then.*

Barkley enjoys teaching and teaches firearms and defensive tactics at the basic training for new officers. She also teaches how to serve warrants and, because she focused from the beginning on mental health and crisis-intervention, she was being pulled into teaching enhanced supervision, and, soon, would be providing trauma-informed training. There was a take-one, teach-one dimension to these trainings as a way of increasing the rate of dissemination across the state. Even in her choices of what areas to serve as a trainer, Barkley demonstrated the foot-in-both worlds approach common to most of the current community supervision officers: *I like training. I definitely enjoy it. We care about the community and want to do good for people, but we also have that little adrenaline part that we like to be able to take care of. We like the excitement. So from the officer standpoint I like teaching about safety, but I also like training them on how to talk to someone. There are some who come in very timid and that can be a problem from the officer's standpoint, and others want to come in with guns blazing, and that is a very big issue as well. You need to be able to talk.*

When asked if she had someone who had served as her mentor or model, she described someone who had the balance she admired: *He was my chief and my field-training officer on parole, but he's retired now. Chill. Straightforward. Treated them like they were somebody. If it was time to go hands on or raise your voice, that's what you do. But once it's done, it's done. Once the handcuffs are on, talk to them like they are somebody again. Tell them why we have arrested them. Tell them, "This is what we're going to do to address this situation. This doesn't mean you're going back to prison, you may just need time out. We're still working with you, we still care about you, but this is the situation and we need to address it." This always spoke volumes to me. They <u>are</u> somebody. They have an issue, whether they want to address that issue or not is not your job. You can't <u>make</u> somebody want to change. You can offer them the tools and address the violations as they come, but they are still somebody and treat them like somebody.*

NEW MODELS OF SUPERVISION

This insistence on treating people like they are somebody helped modify the impact of what she called "old probation" on probationers and parolees, a resetting of expectations which was necessary for a more relational form of supervision where mutual trust is important. This resetting of expectations began by putting more emphasis on honesty than obedience: *They don't trust us. With that old supervision style in probation and in parole, the older officers would just lock them up. So that is what they expected to happen, regardless of whether they told the truth or not. So they would lie just to get out of things, and same with parole. I tell them, "I'm going to be as straightforward with you as I can. I'm not going to lie to you because I don't expect you to lie to me. And I don't tolerate lying. You tell me the truth, no matter how bad it is, I'll try and work with you." They're hesitant to accept this at first, and they'll lie, and of course I'll have to address the lie. Me, as a mother, that helps me. I can detect when people are lying to me. That mom radar runs deep. But the more and more I'm honest with them, the more they start to trust me, and the more honest they become with me. That is the biggest game-changer in their supervision. They feel like they can talk to me and they feel like I am invested in their supervision and in their wanting to change. Then they begin wanting to seek out those resources I have in terms of employment and substance abuse—and they are actually getting the help that they need.*

This trust, and the relationships that build from it, increased the influence she could have: *Especially when they have begun to trust you and they know you care, they don't want to disappoint you. They'll lie because they are afraid of the disappointment, not necessarily the consequences. One guy I supervised for years, I was able to get his in-patient treatment paid for. He got out and had backslid, and that just broke his heart—to* tell *me that he had backslid more than that he actually used. They get invested in you if you have had them for some time.*

Another dimension of this insistence on seeing the people you supervise as somebody was not reducing someone's whole life to a single act. Barkley saw this as the distinctive function of community supervision: *I think what helps me and what distinguishes us from other law enforcement is that we get to know the person and not the crime, the conviction. People look solely at the conviction and not the person, but we get to know the background. When I have a case—like my murder and sex-offender cases—I would read the incident report. I would read the polygraphs. I would know the background and the why. I would talk to them and ask them why they did something. It's not that it excuses the behavior but you at least start understanding their perspective, why they did it. It's more humanizing.*

Her embeddedness in the area reinforced this attitude. She grew up in LaFayette and had long-term relationships with some of the people she ended up supervising: *To me this is the best of both worlds if you want to be part of law enforcement and also want to help someone who is going through a tough time. When I began, I supervised the area where I grew up, so I had a lot of people on my caseload that I went to high school with. So that was something where I knew their home life beforehand, so I knew why they were in the situation they were in. I was able to relate to them a little better and provide them with the services or the sanctioning they would need for that. It was always interesting to see that aspect. I have also supervised where I live now. So I have had my kids' friends' parents on my caseload. I'm still kind of dealing with that. I was coaching cheerleading for my daughter this past year and I had two offenders and I had to coach their child. That was one of those lines I had to deal with—they would come and ask me about their supervision during practice and I would ask them to wait until practice was over.*

This social familiarity also influenced which regulations she emphasized and where she exercised discretion: *I'm like as long as I'm showing you respect, you show me respect I don't care if you call me Ms. Casey, that doesn't bother me. I grew up with a lot of these people and they learn your first name. But there are some officers, they'll ask what is your first name, and the officer will say, "Officer." That's old probation—old corrections. If I feel you are doing it as a disrespect tactic, I might address it there, but I try to call each person Mr. or Mrs. and do the same thing I expect you to do for me.*

We discussed the differences between DCS offices we had observed—especially some urban ones which had had a correctional feel—where the officers berated individuals for wearing hats, confiscated cellphones: *If I ask you to take your hat off, it's because I think someone is concealing something. That's old probation again. They'll make rules like you can't bring your cellphone in the building. I don't enforce that. I like them to have their cellphones honestly. If I think you're lying to me or you're violating, I'm going to search your cellphone. People forget to delete a lot of things of their cellphones. I caught one person coming in—I was told he had left the state without permission. He was lying to me about it, so I told him to hand me his phone. And there were pictures of him on the beach on the date he had left the state along with his hotel confirmation. So, I said, "You are lying to me." Why would I take away a very useful tool just to prove a point, just to show who's in control?*

They will know who is in control. Your demeanor will tell who is in control. There's no need to be a jerk about it. Treat them like they're a human being and they will treat you with a lot more respect. These people, I'm going to their houses, where they have the upper hand. Why would I want to be a jerk to them or be disrespectful to them in an office and then go to their house where they have their buddies, where they have the upper hand?

Ride-Along

On our ride-along, it was interesting to watch Barkley walk her talk. Our first and over-riding impression was how isolated being a community supervision officer is. An officer is alone in her car with a list of people to see, driving long distances along empty country roads accompanied only by a GPS that is frequently bewildered by the haphazard numbering on mailboxes. Residences can be few and far between and they can range from spacious and well-kept trailers to decrepit ones, large new farmhouses to small, aging suburban ranch houses.

Most of Barkley's cases, like the majority of the cases in the area, were people on probation for drug charges, primarily methamphetamine, either possession or trafficking. There were also some aggravated assault, burglary: *Usually my worst offenders are my best cases. They have been in prison for a long time, and they know what prison is and they don't want to go back.* She found high-risk offenders, who were seen monthly, more compliant than lower-risk offenders seen at three-month intervals. However, risk level didn't determine her approach: *As far as I'm concerned, these are all convicted felons and I need to treat them with the same level of caution and safety.*

Field visits are intentionally unscheduled, although officers learn the work schedules of the people they supervise to increase their chances of encountering them. Barkley will also go to their place of employment to make contact if the company is open to that. Some of the large employers actually receive funding for hiring people with criminal records: *That's good for us in getting people employment. The issue can be there are a lot of convicted felons there that have a drug problem, so it may not be the best place for people to work because they will be around people who can get them in trouble.*

On this ride-along, Barkley was introducing herself to people being transferred to her caseload as their new supervision officer or introducing herself to people who were just beginning supervision. In both situations, the major purpose of the visit was to clarify expectations and define priorities. She came across as confident, brisk, reasonable, responsive.

The first man we visited, Michael, was someone whom she had supervised on and off since she began her career in community supervision, usually as part of her mental health load. She had sent him back to a probation detention center or prison three separate times in the last five years. A paranoid schizophrenic, he was on probation for meth possession and aggravated assault charges. He tended to use meth to self-medicate. He was, at present, not supposed to be working or driving so she was quite sure he would be home. His trailer, situated in a large yard, was well-maintained.

Barkley remarked that Michael was usually very neat, so if the environment was disordered, if there were dirty dishes or clothes lying around, that would be a sign that he was off his medications. She rapped loudly on his bedroom window with the side of her large pocket knife, and Michael came to the door. His living room was immaculate. A middle-aged man, he was soft-spoken and gentle. He sat on a living room chair. His partner stood in the hallway looking on. Barkley liked the partner because she will get in touch with Barkley if there are problems. In general Barkley liked talking with spouses or girlfriends to keep a line of communication open. It is also a requirement with individuals under high-risk supervision that an officer speak with "a collateral" every month—this can be a friend, family member, neighbor, or treatment provider. The relationship between the couple was of long standing: *She just tends to leave when he gets under the influence because he will get to thinking people are watching him and talking to him through his television. Then he starts acting out and getting very violent.*

When asked if she ever felt anxious being out here by herself, Barkley said, *He's made me anxious before because I didn't have cell service and I normally don't have a radio, so I have no way to contact anybody. But I've taken crisis intervention training, mental health first aid, ESP [Enhanced Supervision Practices] and am an ESP peer coach.*

Several of the cases on her supervision load were ones where drug use and mental problems were intertwined. One of the most common indications of this was hoarding. This was clear at the trailer of another probationer, one with a long history of drug use and trafficking. "He used to be on the Drug Task Force list for trafficking, But not this last year, which is a good thing," Barkley said. His current charge was for burglary, but the case was tried in Gwinnett County, near Atlanta. This meant that should he violate his supervision, his officer would need to apply to the Gwinnett court to issue a warrant.

She expertly guided the car across a narrow eroding dirt bridge with deep gullies on either side, then edged up the slope toward his trailer. After parking, we skirted the abandoned car and refrigerator in the middle of the parking area, nodded at the three small caged dogs in the yard to the right. The garage was filled with numerous sets of rusted body building equipment and a caged rabbit. No one answered the back door. On the porch, a huge dog in a cage too small for him hunched, snarling, behind a large BEWARE OF DOG sign. Barkley, undaunted, having knocked on all the windows with her penknife, just shrugged, "Well, he must be at work like he said."

As we pulled out she observed: *If it is just clutter, it is usually mental health and they're off meds. But here it is: The more clutter I have, the harder it is for you to find my cocaine! Some officers, if it is just gross, they won't search. Others like me will have latex gloves and Germex. I'm gonna search it.* In this case she thought the clutter was now habit, not camouflage: *But some people, it's just how their parents were and they don't see the issue.* The animal hoarding, all the miserable caged dogs and the rabbit, she saw as mental health. Dogs did not concern her. Roosters were another matter: *I'd rather deal with a dog any day than an angry rooster. There was a forty-pound rooster at one of the houses I used to supervise near one of the chicken plants. It was like it was part turkey.*

We stopped at a large prosperous farm, where two large cedar houses were set close together, separated by a parking lot. Stopping at the first, we encountered a woman in her pajamas who directed us to the other house, where her brother-in-law, the probationer we had come to see, lived. When Barkley asked how he was, she said sullenly, "I think he is doing all right. I just don't trust him."

The house we were sent to was large, well-furnished, with numerous all-terrain vehicles stored on the porch. We woke the probationer's sleeping wife, and then met him, coming in from the garage. Barkley told him he might be ready for call-in supervision and asked him to come into the office the following week. Later in the car, we discussed why his sister-in-law might not trust him. Barkley answered, "I don't know why. Which is why I'm going to bring him in and drug screen him before I put him on call-in status." She thought his offense was theft, not drugs.

She went on to talk about the impact of recidivism on families: *It's interesting to talk to family members of offenders, especially repeat offenders. There's a lot of hurt there. There was one offender and I've worked very closely with him. He was a high-ranking Ghostface member. He's in in-patient treatment now. He came to a church here recently to testify.*

[Ghostface is a white gang that began in Georgia prisons but has now moved out to neighboring communities. Its members are now found primarily in the four counties that are covered by the LaFayette DCS office.]

I got very close to his wife and his mom. They would talk to me about him. They love him and would do anything for him, but they would be the first ones to call me and tell me if he was not doing right. We had a long discussion about the hurt of him constantly messing up. He missed every Christmas for the past ten years because he was in and out of prison.

I had to work a lot with him. His first violation with me was a positive drug screen and he had to get through that part of not telling me the truth. He was flushing his system and he thought I didn't know, when of course I did. After we got over that hump, he would talk to me, but he would get himself into situations where he was at the wrong place at the wrong time and ended up getting aggravated assault cases. And we had to work through that and when he got out we had to start working from scratch all over again. His family loved him and wanted him to do right, but there was a lot of damage done that he had to work through. So it was good to see him giving his testimony in that in-patient treatment and his family there supporting him and seeing that he was actually doing better and they were starting to mend those fences.

One of the more interesting and thought-provoking visits concerned a man, James, who had recently been released from prison after being in and out of prison for sixteen years on a cocaine charge, possibly with some probation revocations involved. James was at home but in a back bedroom when we called at his mother's trailer where he was currently living. His mother was sweeping the floor as we arrived, and she ushered us in warmly. She introduced herself by her first name, Mary. She called out to her son to let him know we were there. She then proceeded to tell us proudly that her son had been the first African-American quarterback at the local high school. This had been his first Christmas at home in many years.

Barkley moved toward the back of the living room to wait for James. When James, tall, quiet, composed, emerged from the bedrooms, he went to shake her hand, but she immediately put her hands behind her back, saying, "I don't shake hands. It's just me."

Mary put her broom down, clearly offended. "What is this with not shaking hands?" she asked. As Barkley talked with James, Mary extended her hand to us to shake, which we did. She continued telling us about her son, that he was highly intelligent, that his old coach had helped him find a job, how everyone in town knew about his athletic prowess.

Mary clearly felt she had done all she could to try to protect James. Orphaned at seven herself, Mary had been raised by her grandmother who had lived until she was over a hundred in the trailer still situated farther up the hill. Mary had done everything she could so her own children wouldn't feel the same sense of abandonment she had felt at the early loss of her own mother. "But your children have to make their own mistakes."

While we were having this conversation, Barkley was finishing her conversation with her new parolee. "You being paid with a receipt or under the table?" she asked matter of factly. "Under the table," he replied. "Just have your boss call me so I can put down that you are working," she said.

Later, discussing the meeting, Barkley explained: *That was the first time I met him. I don't know if you heard what I said to him. I told him I was pretty laid back but I need to be able to find you and I need to make sure that you're not lying to me. But do as you're told to do and let me know if you need anything. And he's one of those who understand that. You have to learn how to present yourself to each individual offender because you can't talk to one offender one way and do the same way to another offender.*

When asked, Barkley explained that her refusal to shake hands was something she had been taught in training. As a relatively small woman, someone could throw her off balance if she did so. It was hard to see how that would have been the case in this low-key domestic situation. She seemed unaware of the racial implications of her choice in this setting, although the mother of the first African-American quarterback at the local high school clearly was not. The population in these counties is 90% white, but the towns have a larger proportion of African Americans, which is reflected in the racial make-up of their probation populations.

In another spacious and well-furnished trailer belonging to his parents, a man in his thirties recently released from prison spoke with Barkley about meeting his probation requirements. He needed to enroll in an in-patient drug treatment program within the next few weeks to meet the terms of his probation. He wanted one where he could earn the privilege of going out to work because he needed to pay for the costs of treatment himself. He also wanted a center where he would be permitted to smoke. Barkley had several recommendations.

At yet another trailer whose entrance was impeded by a carport filled with seemingly random objects, a woman brushed away a curtain as she opened the door. Attractive, blonde, with a pageboy haircut, she looked a little like a 1950s housewife. She apologized for the chaos; they had had an electrical fire. Her husband, the probationer, was in bed. From the doorway to the trailer, Barkley introduced herself as his new officer. He and a friend had a construction firm. Barkley asked for a letter of employment from his "employer." His previous officer had let him go out of town for vacation and for jobs. Would that still be possible? he asked. She told him that as long as she was informed beforehand, it wouldn't be problematic. In this area, at the corner of Georgia, Alabama and Tennessee, interstate travel is usual.

Driving down a winding forested road, Barkley recognized someone pulling out of a driveway who was on her caseload, so stopped her car and called out to her. "Alice! Just who I want to see!" They decided to talk right there along the side of the road. Barkley ran through the standard questions: *Are you using illegal substances? Are you abiding by the conditions of supervision?* Barkley let Alice know that she thought that she might qualify for monthly call-in status. She asked her to come into the office the next week and bring her papers to verify her official termination date. "Are you on Social Security yet?" Barkley asked her. "No, not yet," Alice answered. "Let me know when you are, and I'll stop the fees," Barkley told her as they went back to their separate cars.

In a small residential neighborhood at the edge of LaFayette, we made our last stop of the morning to share some good news with Martha, a woman who had been on Barkley's mental health caseloads in the past. Martha held the door half-closed as she spoke with Barkley. On probation for eight years for possession of hydrocodone and aggravated assault, Martha was now eligible to go on non-report on both her counts. She seemed surprised and pleased at the news—and quite ready to close the door as soon as she received it. Behind her mountains of hoarded clothes loomed.

SB 174: SUPERVISING THROUGH INCENTIVES

It was clear that many of the changes in supervision laid out in SB 174, particularly efforts to reduce the burden of supervision by making it shorter and more specific, moving people to call-in or unsupervised status whenever appropriate, were being implemented frequently here in LaFayette. This was significant given the extremely long probation times often given in rural counties like these, although the length of sentences appears to be diminishing with the rapid rise in cases. Barkley observed: *Five years ago you would receive a sentence of ten to fifteen years on probation for a simple possession charge. But because the numbers have sky-rocketed as much as they have, the sentences have really started to go down. They get three years for a meth charge now.*

Supervising someone with a three-year sentence was often more difficult than supervising one with a fifteen-year sentence: *There are a lot of these people who have been on probation and parole their entire adult life. It is nothing for them to do six months or three years. It doesn't bother them. It doesn't affect them at all. Some of them just go back because that is their family in a sense. That's what they know.*

The current law says that after two years, if an individual on probation owes no restitution and has no felony convictions, they *must* be placed on unsupervised status. To some extent this is an administrative measure to reduce the unworkable number of cases. However, Barkley was ambivalent about this from a rehabilitation standpoint: *It doesn't matter if they have had a revocation of their probation or not. So they could essentially be offending right now, using drugs, and we would legally have to put them on unsupervised if they don't have a new felony. That's where I don't feel the law works in our favor.*

However, she was highly in favor of incentives that she felt contributed to constructive reentry. She described what she saw as a responsibly stepped progression for the woman she talked to alongside the road: *For people like her who has not had a violation and has done very well—she never tested positive and I could always find her—we try to give them a little more freedom and responsibility. That's why we have the call-in status. If she does well on that, we can eventually put her on unsupervised, which means she wouldn't even call. Then she is on probation and every aspect of her conditions still apply but we don't come and see her unless we get information that there is an issue or she gets arrested for a new felony or violent misdemeanor. And then, if she is still doing well, she has no revocations, and after three years she's done everything she needs to do, we can get her early terminated. So we do have things in place so if we see she's doing really well we can cut out those long sentences.*

Barkley held out the possibility of early termination as an aspirational goal to most of the people she supervised. She walked them through the steps described above, with unsupervised as "a glimmer of hope" at the end. She also described how she was trying to actively apply these incentives to different stages of a combined parole and probation sentence for someone with an extremely long drug sentence: *For one parolee, I did a commutation request. I supervised him back three years ago. I put him on call-in. I told him even if I'm not your officer in two years, come and find me and I will put in a request for you to have your parole commuted—because he was on until 2035. And then he has ten years of probation after that. He had several trafficking charges and manufacturing drug charges, but he got on parole and he had no violations, no positive drug screens. He had been a model parolee. Even during the time he was on call-in status, he would be contacting me, "Hey, I'm calling every month just to make sure there's nothing I need to do." He kept in contact with me for those two years. He texted me and he asked about commutation, and I submitted it and hopefully that will be accepted by the Parole Board and that will take all his parole years off and he can start his probation early. And if he does well for three years on his probation, I can request an early termination of his probation. He is in his late forties. He served a long time, ten to fifteen years in prison. If these reductions weren't possible he wouldn't be off paper until 2045. For him, I don't feel he needs that long a time. He's doing very well. He has a high-paying job. He works for an electrical company. He's had the same employment since he's been on parole. He's maintained the same house. He's very much a model citizen. So, I don't feel he should be on paper that length of time. He learned his lesson in prison.*

We also discussed the opposite side of supervision, the decision to revoke: *I will do everything I can to work with the offender. I will give them out-patient drug treatment if it is a drug problem. I will give them a more intensive out-patient. I will do in-patient. I will exhaust all efforts before I revoke somebody. If you need a job, I'll get you one. If you need a place to stay, I will drive you to homeless shelters, I will find somewhere for you to have a hotel stay until you can get on your feet. So, if I've exhausted my efforts and I'm working harder than you are for you to do a successful life, then it is time for you to go back to prison for a time and reassess your life. I don't take it lightly because I do believe everyone deserves a fair shot at having a change in their lives, I know change does not happen overnight.*

Another question we have asked a number of community supervision officers is what they do to assess the impact of prison itself, particular how it might affect reentry. In the story Barkley shared with us, we could see the importance of early identification of trauma for more successful reentry. She may have been more sensitive to this because of the training she has received around mental health and crisis intervention. She also felt that being a female officer made it more permissible for the individual to express his distress.

On a day when she was on officer-of-the-day duties, meaning that she handled the processing of everyone coming into community supervision from prison, probation detention centers, or residential substance abuse treatment, she saw a man who was clearly in crisis: *Most people aren't really affected by our prison probation centers. But this man would not make eye contact with me. You could tell he was about to cry when he was talking to me. He was very distraught. I started talking to him. "I've never been locked up before and I don't want to go back." There was something that happened to him there that he didn't want to tell me but you could tell it really bothered him. That offender hadn't been ordered to go to mental health assessment, he was ordered to do substance abuse. But he seemed like someone who really needed to talk to someone, so I suggested it and he said, "Actually I would like to talk to someone." I took him over to our counselor and got him an emergency session with her for mental health, in a one-on-one, not a group setting too. Because he was one who said, "I really don't want to be around people." He was married, so I got it so he could have marriage counseling if he needed it. I do think it is true that people are more willing to talk to me compared to some of the bigger men.*

There may be other reasons that people are more willing to talk to her. As we were returning to the DCS office, she pointed out a young man walking by the road and waved at him: *He does community service with us. He's very intelligent and does art, and he learned that I have an art degree—in studio art. He found that out and got to talking to me. He's trying to turn his life around. He's very interested in creating a free program for kids that focuses on art and try to get them out of the situation he was in as a kid. He keeps messing up on his supervision but you can tell he is very passionate about it.*

With someone like Casey Barkley, committed to seeing the whole person, not just the conviction, it sounded like he just might succeed.

\\3//

URBAN SUPERVISION

URBAN RIDE-ALONGS

The urban ride-along with young DCS Officer Eric Crider through southeast Atlanta in the spring of 2019 brought back memories of one we went on several years earlier out of the South Fulton parole office with Officer Tom Andris. The officers were both fairly new, both idealistic, but there was a striking difference in how much institutional support they felt, which strongly affected their own sense of competence and agency—and their sense of the ultimate value of what they were doing.

Tom Andris

Tom Andris had been working as a parole officer for a little more than two years when we met in 2014. He had only worked in South Fulton, the most challenging area in the state. Previously, he had served in the National Guard for nine years as an infantry squad leader, serving tours in Iraq and Afghanistan, while completing his college degree in political science at Georgia College and State University. Over the active years of our listening project, we would have other conversations with Andris, whose interest in victim-offender dialogues led him to move into the Victim Services division of Parole as a program manager for several years, facilitating victim offender dialogues and developing other activities that improved the sense of restoration for victims, including those victimized in prison. He has now moved from Atlanta and works as a special investigator for a national firm providing security investigative services to government.

Andris said he usually made his visits in the evening in order to find people at home—daytime visits were not very productive. The ride-along itself mainly involved knocking briefly at small brick homes where people would only talk through a half-closed door, circling large apartment complexes where more than half the inhabitants had felony convictions, knocking futilely on doors in other apartment complexes and sliding a card in along the floor, and one longer visit at a halfway house, where we talked with a tired man in his fifties, newly released from prison, who just wanted to get back home to Macon, so wanted his parole transferred there if possible. He didn't look like he would ever have the energy to reoffend.

However, we had a long, earnest conversation preceding our drive that explored the gap between what Andris had imagined his work would be like and what it actually proved to be. It began with what he thought would be the basis of his identification with the men he supervised: *As a veteran I've experienced a lot of the same reentry challenges that a lot of felons have. The whole idea of being picked out of one world and thrown into another world, isolated from the world that you know, from your family and friends, missing holidays, missing birthdays, missing funerals. They go on living their life while you're stuck in this little bubble that isn't even the real world. They're institutionalized, and in the military you can get institutionalized too. There's jargon, there's lingo. They tell you what to eat, when to eat, when to shave, how to shave. You wear uniforms every day, there's a regimen. You're surrounded by barbed wire—and it's a deadly atmosphere too.*

And then, when I got out of the army, even though I was still working on my degree, I still basically had no education, no car, I was still living with my parents. I had no job. I was an infantryman, so I really had no tangible skill. My skill in the army was to go on patrols and hunt down the enemy. Employers aren't really looking for someone like that. The only difference between me and them I felt was that I had some money in the bank after my deployment, which I used to get a car, to get an apartment, to finish my degree, to take myself further. As a sergeant, I had counseled soldiers. I would have to reprimand and figure out how to correct it. I really felt that matched what parole was doing here too because you develop a strategy to survive in that isolation that may not translate to the real world. While you are in the military or in prison, you set up a goal: I am going to get this job, I know someone who knows someone who can get me this. Then you get out and you realize that job has been gone a long time—and you don't even have a car to get to that job. The thing that you held on to to help you believe you could get through that moment is now not there. And then everything really starts to crumble. They stumble at that point.

However, Andris found that as a parole officer, he had to adjust his expectations of both the behavior and the thought processes of those he supervised. His own experience with criminal behavior was restricted. He was aware that he had been sheltered in his upbringing in a fairly wealthy, white suburb where the biggest crime was stealing a golf cart. If as a boy you and your friends entered an abandoned building, police would pick you up, warn you, then give you a ride home: *I really had no notion of what a criminal lifestyle is, or why someone becomes a criminal, or how they get stuck in the criminal cycle until I started this job. I used to just think they were rational thinkers. A logical person would say, I don't want to rob a bank because I don't want to do so many years in prison, or I will speed because I can afford the $200 fine.*

What I discovered was that no matter what race or home background they come from, they are not rational actors. There's something that's misfiring in their head, it doesn't click with them that if I do X, the consequences will be Y and Z and they will be very severe and I won't like it. It happens all the time here. I will tell them, "To stay out of jail, you have to come and see me on Monday. It's as simple as that." On Monday, they don't show up. I don't even get a phone call. You would think a rational person would be camped outside the door in the morning and would be blowing up my cellphone. It's like, what gives? That is the most surprising stuff: I can say go right, they'll go left; say it's light, and they'll say its dark. Some are just messing with you, but for the majority of them, it's just not clicking.

He found the younger men who had been given five-year sentences for armed robbery, spending only one or two years in prison, were the most difficult to supervise. They immediately went back to the streets, rejoined gangs, their time in prison serving primarily to enhance their street cred. "It didn't click."

What Andris saw as most crucial to success was a full-time steady job that allowed men to pay their fees, establish a routine, contribute to their families, especially if they could stay drug free. "But if they lose their job, get stressed, start using drugs, have relationship issues, they're going to look to crime just to make ends meet." He also saw that when someone lost the person who was providing their core family support and accountability, for example a mother, sometimes they would begin to take on these roles themselves.

Parole had by then made the transition to virtual offices, and Andris appreciated the additional flexibility and autonomy of the change. "It would be hard to work 9 to 5 again. I like working from home, on my own schedule, managing my time." He saw his co-workers only two or three times a week, but was calling and communicating with them every day. He would need to coordinate, ask other officers to accompany him, if he needed to arrest someone for drug use and send them to jail. Time-management skills were essential, he emphasized.

But time-management skills were not enough to handle the serious demands of the case loads, which differed from other areas in the state because of both the challenging quality and the density of the parole population. In 2014, in South Fulton where there were 1,100 parolees under supervision, there were ten officers. Two of them supervised sex offenders, so had case loads of forty, the others had case loads of over a hundred, compared to the state-wide average at that point for parole of seventy to eighty. The turnover rate of officers was high, seven officers had left and five or six had been hired during his time there. This was particularly challenging because with the extensive vetting Parole did before hiring and the officer training, it took almost a year to select, train and bring an officer up to a full caseload. The turnover also damaged the continuity of service—and possibility of relationship—with parolees.

In this office, you can't wear that counselor's hat. You can't learn their background, get a handle on those risk factors. I would like to have that dimension. Here, it is more law enforcement. The numbers drive that. You have one hundred people to see. Your highs require a visit a month, your standards once every three to four months, your specialized twice a month. You have twenty business days to get this done, along with serving as duty officer, handling transfer requests, administrative hearings, preliminary and final. And then there are the housing and the employment and the collateral family calls.

You are set up for failure. The chief said, just do forty visits. See your specialized and your highs once a month. The computer sets the risk level. Sometimes it's off, for example two of my specialized are old ladies who spent twenty-five years in prison for murder. One is deaf and the other blind, but they want them on electronic monitors and visited twice a month. There is a lot of burnout here compared to other districts. Sure, I could change districts, but everyone knows this is a high profile district, and if I want to get promoted . . .

These challenges were alive to Andris because that week the nightmare event that most worries Parole had tragically happened: someone on parole supervision had committed a murder. With that, suddenly all the overworked parole officers felt vulnerable. They understood that it was an officer, not an administrator, who would take the fall. So their chief's tacit acknowledgement of the impossibility of meeting the official standards of supervision was just that, tacit and deniable. All of them would be held to that impossible math.

In a later conversation, Andris described what he felt would make the role of parole officers easier—stop asking them to assume primary responsibility for providing access to all the social services that a parolee needed. He suggested creating a committee made up of representatives from major employment and social service agencies that could meet with individuals as they returned, thus providing a much greater network of employment, housing and service referrals and fuller mental health assessments than any lone parole officer. This is now part of the responsibility of the housing and community coordinators that have since become part of DCS.

Andris also wanted to fold in a victim-offender dimension: *There is another element to this committee that I wish could manifest itself, and that is the idea of the community holding the offender more personally accountable for his crime than just whatever sentence the judge was required to hand out. It's a concept at the core of Victim Offender Dialogue. So not only would this committee provide services to the offender, but it should also be a moment when they get to express how the offender's crime impacted them personally and impacted the neighborhood. It would be great for a victim or a victim's advocate group to participate so that they can express the grief, anger, or forgiveness to the offender. I can't think of a better way of giving an offender an opportunity to "make amends" for what they did than to be included in the "network" we call society and turn their life around.*

Eric Crider

Unlike Tom Andris, Eric Crider did not bring into his work a different set of institutional expectations and experiences. He entered DCS a few months after college. In some ways you could see him as a pure product of the new DCS philosophy and training methods. He saw no difficulty absorbing and applying the very different procedures that guide parole and probation: *Unlike some of the older officers who were here before the merger, for us it wasn't a parole brain adjusting to probation or probation brain adjusting to parole. It was all new and you were learning it all together.*

A poised, positive young man, who looked even younger than his twenty-four years, Crider majored in criminal justice at the University of West Georgia, like many of the people we spoke with from Parole and DCS. He considered enlisting in the Navy, but at the suggestion of a friend, applied to DCS: *I wanted to get into something where I could help. In all law enforcement, there is an opportunity because you're dealing with people, but I feel like probation and parole, it's one of the few jobs where your job is to try and keep people out of prison and on a better path. I'm not saying that street enforcement's job is to put people in prison, but it is their job to keep the public safe and doing that sometimes involves that. But in our job, keeping the public safe involves getting that person away from a criminal mindset to a more adjusted role in society.*

When we went on our ride-along, Crider had been working for DCS for a little more than a year, and had been supervising in his current location for three months. He had an even more formidable caseload than Andris, but at that point did not appear daunted: *Typically Tuesday to Thursday, I'm out in field. I see people early in the month with a more fixed schedule. That gives me a chance late in the month to go after people who move around a lot. I have just under 200 cases—191 of them under active supervision. I see some of them every ninety days, some of them once every thirty days. It's all based off their history. A positive drug screen moves them up in the rating system. I have 45 who have to be seen once a month. 130 have to be seen every couple of months. The people I see once a month, I keep up with better. The group I see less often, I try and work it to where . . . I don't want them to think that ninety days to the day he'll come see me again. Sometimes it will be sixty, sometimes seventy, sometimes it will be forty.*

Turnover remained a problem, but one he felt was being addressed: *It's such a big area and right now we have three certified officers on our team. But we have one who is about to graduate basic and one that is about to go into basic. So in about three months, we'll have five active and certified officers and then our numbers will come down. We lost a few officers, one transferred and one was terminated.*

The area of South Fulton we were canvassing is made up of single-family residential homes, some of them on large lots, others in small suburbs, an area much less dense than the area we visited with Andris. The first house we visited was a two-story home set back on a wide lot. There was a large U-Haul in front of it. There were cars in various stages of repair or dismantlement beside the garage and in a thicket of trees to the left of the house. The man we spoke with, Mr. D., was small and very muscular. He shook my hand. His front teeth were white and long, but he was missing all his back molars on both sides. When he was asked how his children were doing, he said he couldn't understand what changes a girl's body goes through. His daughter, eleven, had started to have her period—and he didn't know or want to know how to deal with it. He gave a mock shiver.

Prison was all right, Mr. D. responded. He had been in for five years.

But he didn't plan to return. He was now thirty-seven. "I have too much in my life—my kids, my work—to be going in and out anymore."

His girlfriend, who was the necessary collateral contact, said that they weren't going to be changing houses, meaning they weren't going to move in with her mother. Rather, they were looking for a place of their own, although neither of them seemed to have a sense of urgency about this.

One of the special conditions of Mr. D.'s probation was that he finish his GED. He was having trouble with the math. Crider, who was good in math, offered to help *if* Mr. D. asked for it. Crider, as he left, listed the specific days that he would be available to help, *if* he was asked.

Crider saw his approach as having been influenced by the enhanced supervision techniques he learned in basic training: *Yes, I see it as my job to actively give people choices to help build a better relationship. Put yourself in their shoes. Understand what they're saying. Don't just go and see him and then put him away until next month. Understand that he needs a little help with that GED and reach out, get him the help he needs so he knows, OK, I can count on him. He's not just here to check off a box. He's here to help. Then, if he makes a mistake, he'll let you know—I've had offenders who will call me and tell me, "I went to a party the other day and this and this happened. The police were called. They didn't arrest me, I just wanted to let you know." It's an accountability thing. If they are willing to call you to admit something happened, they're getting to a point where they understand that they shouldn't have let that happen. They're not always going to be on supervision. So if we just month to month say do that, do that, then when they get done they haven't learned a lot. But if we can get to a point where we move toward accountability, move toward respect, then maybe when they are off supervision those things still stick with them.*

The next house we visited was in a small suburb with closely spaced houses, some of them neatly maintained, one at the end of the block with mounds of clothing and furniture on the front lawn as if an eviction was in process. The woman we were visiting was in her late twenties or early thirties, a young mother on probation. She was small, very thin, attractive, dressed in a black shirt and pants and wearing several gold necklaces, including a crucifix. She shook hands warmly and opened the door to let us in the house.

All the shades in the open living and dining area were drawn over the picture windows and the door to the carport. They were white so there was a luminosity to the dimness that matched the glow from the aquarium on the kitchen counter. Large mounds of clothes covered several chairs. She and

Crider talked about the JPay app, which can be used to pay supervision fees and fines, but did not seem to be working for her. He gave her the code, then said he would drop some papers by so she could pay that way if she needed to. She went to hunt for the receipt forms her aunt was going to use to formally document her employment. She worked for her family, who owned twenty-two houses. She refinished the floors. Once she returned with the forms, she asked if she could speak with Crider further outside the house.

She was concerned that her twin brother, who was living with her, was becoming more aggressive. "It used to be just us but now I have my little girl and he resents the attention. He wants all my attention. That's why he's kicking in my bedroom door." She played a video of her brother kicking open the door. "I have many more," she said. But he was her *twin* brother, and without her house, he would be homeless. On the other hand, she couldn't have him there with her daughter when he was behaving this way. She thought that drugs and HIV contributed to his behavior. She thought he was very angry about contracting HIV.

She had filled out a Temporary Protection Order (TPO), but knew her brother would go berserk when he received it. Asked if she had somewhere to go, she answered, affronted, "It's *my* house." Crider persisted, "If you needed to go somewhere until the situation was under control, is there a place you and your daughter could go?"

She identified her sister's home some distance away. He assured her that if that should happen, he wouldn't move her case there but would keep her on his caseload. He also suggested that she contact the Grady Hospital Crisis Assessment Team if she really felt her brother was losing control. He assured her that if her brother called *him*, he would let her know. She was particularly worried because she was the one on paper, so any contact with law enforcement might jeopardize her supervision conditions. "But he is the one who needs to go to prison."

When we returned to the car, Crider shared his perspective: *You don't want to belittle a situation, but you just have to take things with a grain of salt. From what I know about her and seeing the video I feel like that is a realistic situation that needs to be handled and she is doing the best she can with the temporary protection order. That's why I suggested the Grady crisis unit.*

This is something I have to explain to people who are on supervision—that if you call someone and an officer comes out to the house and sees felony probation on your record, they are automatically going to be a little more suspicious of you.

So, you have to take extra steps. Like I said to her, do the TPO. If he shows up again, keep your daughter away from the situation. That way, if it is an emergency situation, she isn't even involved. The good thing is that in two weeks if it pops up on my computer that she has a family violence charge, I'll have a little background. I can go talk to the judge. I've reached out to judges before to keep my people from getting revoked because from a judge's point of view, here is a sister beating on a brother, end of story. Sometimes they don't know the backstory.

The next man we visited, Mr. T., lived with his mother in a tidy house whose porch was hung with many wind chimes. There were two small yipping dogs that Crider had him lock up before entering the house. We entered the living room, well-furnished with three large red sofas. Mr. T. was a body-builder and trainer, his shoulders about three times the width of his waist, but he had a warm smile and gentle handshake. His mother was out, which meant there would be no collateral meeting for Crider's records.

In all these encounters, Crider would stand with his hands holding both sides of his collar and ask each supervisee the same questions: *Have you had contact with law enforcement? Have you used illegal substances? You know you can't change addresses without letting me know, right? Or leave the state, right? Anything else you want to share?* In retrospect the posture was probably to aim the body camera that was used to help train officers.

Again, there were fine points about the JPay system. Again, Crider offered to drop off paper forms. Mr. T. did have several questions to ask. He wanted to know how much notice he needed to give before traveling to the Dominican Republic. He was only allowed to travel to countries with extradition treaties, he was told. He also asked about travel in the U.S., which was possible with pre-notification, an address, and a reason.

When we asked about his sentence, he said he had served five years straight in prison for theft, he was charged with aggravated theft although he hadn't been part of the aggravation. Now he had fifteen years on probation. He had been out for about three years, but had recently returned from six months at a detention center. There were two incidents that were bothering him. One had to do with riding in the car with his mother in a nearby city. She was pulled over and they both had to show their licenses and when his showed he was on probation, they wanted to revoke him. Just because they stopped his mother. Could they do that? he asked. The other incident was more serious—the cause of the time he had just spent in the probation detention center. He worked as a bouncer in a club and had accepted a ride home, but there were drugs in the car, which were found when the police stopped it. Mr. T. said he didn't know they were there, but because the drugs were loose, ownership couldn't be determined so the police held everyone in the car equally responsible.

But what really upset Mr. T. was his treatment during his five years in prison, in particular the absence of useful programming. He was moved through three or four prisons in those years. At Tift, the DOC administration campus, he learned how to use four forklifts and wired fifty police cars—*but they wouldn't give him certification for what he learned and the work he did.* "If I had that certification, I could have gone to OSHA and gotten certified and had a job as soon as I left," he said. When he had insisted with DOC about the certification, they said he was only working for them, and then moved him again because of his complaints.

He felt that fifteen years was too long for probation, that it kept making him vulnerable to more charges, like the traffic stop with his mother. This felt very unfair because he was trying to do everything right.

Crider explored some of the dimensions of the Mr. T.'s complaints when we returned to the car: *His original meth charge was a very high amount. His co-defendants were aggressive, but he wasn't. But he got a similar sentence to them. You can tell from seeing him that he looks like someone who really has his stuff together. You can tell it is frustrating to look ahead and see the fifteen years. He's probably going to be someone who is eligible for early termination, If they have been doing good with no trouble at all, they can be put on unsupervised after two years—don't even have to call in or pay in.*

Why it's so hard is that he was doing so well, but with that new arrest, we can't put him on unsupervised. If he were to hurt somebody, the public is going to say, "Well he already got a new charge, why did you let the reins loose?" I don't think that will happen with him. I don't think he's going to reoffend. I feel he has a good head on his shoulders, but it's a struggle. He claimed to me that he wasn't aware that the drugs were there. I believe him. But I understand the officer who pulled them over. It would be hard to sort out.

Our last visit of the afternoon was with a man living with his mother. This meeting had been announced ahead of time because the man had children he needed to pick up at school. He and Crider discussed ways he could continue to work as a musician without breaking the rules about drug exposure. He had tested positive for THC, but claimed it was due to secondary exposure because others were smoking in the recording studio. He now told Crider that they had made a rule that no one could smoke grass in the studio. He checked with Crider to see if he could go to Florida with his group when it performed. Crider gave permission: *When he comes in to get that travel permit, he'll be drug screened again. If he can manage to do what he's doing and stay out of trouble, I'm not going to put too much pressure on it. Me and my supervisor already talked about this: If it comes down to my giving a little slack because I'm trying to build a better relationship, I will be able to explain that.*

On our ride to the station, Crider mused about the balance of control, support, and accountability he was being asked to maintain: *I like helping people, but on the other hand, I'm on the arrest team. I serve warrants at people's houses who have violated. I'm here to protect and help them, but I am also here protect the public. If they are going to do things that endanger other members of society, it is my duty to see that they don't hurt other people. That's how I've always seen how it holds together. You're helping the clients but you're also helping the public by either helping the clients reintegrate or keeping them from further hurting you.*

Typically for me, it is: This is your probation. I'm going to help you when I can. But this is your probation. You're going to make decisions and I am going to react based on those decisions. If you do what you're supposed to and you respect me and don't lie to me or mislead, then I'm going to respect you and I'm not going to be all over you for stuff I don't need to be all over you about and we'll be fine. If you don't do what I ask you to, if you don't do what the courts ask you to do, if you start getting in trouble or start making it difficult for the people around you, then I'm going to get stronger and stronger and harder and harder. I say it all the time: "I'm not threatening you, but this is how it is going to be."

As we are getting out of the car, Crider described how balancing the demands of his job with his personal life was sometimes challenging. His fiancée had already told him on more than one occasion not to pick up his laptop at nine at night, and had called him on the tone of voice she had once heard him using with a parolee (they had been talking over the phone as he entered the DCS office building). "I was coming to the assistance of one of the receptionists. He was talking back to her. I couldn't let that stand," he explained. "I told my fiancée that this was just part of the job, something I had to do."

SAFE ENOUGH: AN OPEN QUESTION

Putting officers in the field, so they meet people in their communities, in their daily lives is an important improvement in community supervision. Officers are able to learn far more about the people they are trying to help desist. On our ride-alongs we could see how effective this was.

However, all the officers when we rode with them gave us a bulletproof vest to wear. They themselves had vests, tasers, guns, and handcuffs. Indeed Crider, who is very fit but not very tall, wore his firearm in a thigh holster because the combined weight was too much to wear comfortably around his waist. We found ourselves asking officers, "How afraid *are* you of the people you supervise?" We're not suggesting that this is an easy question to answer. But it is a very relevant question for any community member because we must believe that if someone has been put on community supervision they are considered *safe-enough* to live and work among us. If officers, in how they structure their offices and in their dress, seem to contradict this assumption of safe-enough, the result is increased anxiety and intolerance in communities. This is especially troubling in communities that have already experienced inequitable surveillance, prosecution, and incarceration. The discomfort can be directed either at the officer or at the person being supervised. Given the reality that at present Georgia has compounded mass incarceration with mass supervision, one can't help wonder what the effect of sending out highly armed officers at all hours does to community cohesion and the commitment to reintegration.

Discussing the issue with Michael Nail, he provided some background about how community supervision officers came to be armed. This was not the case until 1994 when, during the Summer Olympics in Atlanta, there was a shortage of law enforcement officers, and probation officers, since they were certified law enforcement officers, were armed and brought in to support police. They were then reluctant to give up their weapons. This was the period when the large wave of highly punitive legislation was taking place. Parole officers also historically have not been uniformed or armed, but requested both uniforms and tasers when their duties were redefined as being completely field based and they moved to mobile offices. Nail is committed to the safety of the officers, but recognizes the basic contradiction.

We do continue to ask: *Are* guns necessary on regular field visits, unless an officer intends to issue a warrant or make an arrest? If officers feel that they always need their guns and body armor, then how do they convey to the general community that those they supervise are people safe enough to live among us and capable of positive change—with adequate support and accountability? Are they instead presenting people with the image of someone who is a constant, incorrigible risk for *us*? A risk an officer faces once every 90 days but expects us, as neighbors, to take on every day?

MENTAL HEALTH AND SEX OFFENDERS

EPIFFANY HENRY

*I think probation is a caring business. You can get all the education you try to get, but if you truly don't connect with the individual or if you don't care, they won't be successful. And **I** care.*

Although Epiffany Henry has now left DCS to work on probation programming in a municipal court, her voice and perspective remain one of the most resonant we encountered and highly reflective of the current commitments of DCS. We spoke with her in the fall of 2015 just as DCS was combining.

When Henry, a tall attractive woman in her early thirties, said, *I care,* it was obvious from her voice that she meant it. She could also demonstrate it concretely to each of her probationers with an astonishingly detailed knowledge of their specific circumstances. Given her position as a probation officer, she knew she was saying something with much broader implications; she was inviting her wary probationers into a more consistent and assured relationship with what had often felt like an implacable and indifferent system whose only intent was to punish and control. A strong believer in the ripple effect, she was aware that just as behind every probationer there is a family, behind every probation officer there is a very large system with people like her in it who could prove helpful to them. She wanted to have her probationers open to that possibility, however startling it might be.

That is one thing I take into probation, that as a probation officer, it took a village to get me where I am and to keep me where I am.

Every probationer, I have I ask, "Who cares about you?"

And they'll say, "Nobody."

And I'll say, "Until today."

I tell them, "I care about you and your family, and I am going to do everything in my power to help you successfully complete probation. But do understand, I am going to do it the right way, the way the judge told me to do it, but I care."

When they know you care, that gives them the inner drive to do a little more, to push. Even when they've done something they shouldn't have, they'll call and say, "I failed you. I'm sorry. I was trying."

Now they can't go through life saying nobody care, because me as an officer, I care—and thankfully that has made the difference in every case I've supervised.

Henry was clear that caring in itself wasn't enough. Reliable behaviors on the part of the officer were also needed—so were reliable goals: *Not only do you have to care, you have to be fair, firm and consistent. With my cases and in my dealings with probationers, I tell them my expectations up front, so they know what to expect. Then when something happens, they already have the "I care" component and they also know to expect what the outcome is going to be.*

I recently had to issue a warrant for a guy who received a new charge and he didn't understand and he said, "Henry, you know I'm out here trying. I'm doing what you expect of me." And I told him, "You're absolutely right, but I have a job to do. I'm under oath by the court to handle your case as I would handle any case that violated." However, I have no trouble going before the judge and saying, "This is what I know. This is what he was doing."

I was able to recall for him everything he has told me. He was just baffled, and it calmed him down and he was like, "All right, I get it. I understand you're doing your job."

To fully appreciate this story, it is important to know that Henry has an eidetic memory, able to recall both faces and conversations with extreme accuracy, a capacity she said was very helpful in her work (and also occasionally overwhelming). It may have contributed to her sense that seeing the *whole* story, sharing the *whole* story, individual by individual, was crucial: *I think that's where the difference comes in. Yes, they violated their probation terms, but they're human and <u>they'll need someone to vouch for them.</u> I think that's where in our field you can drop the ball. Because if you don't become their advocate to tell the <u>whole</u> story to the judge when you get the opportunity, that's where offenders lose faith in the system.*

Establishing some measure of trust in the system was one of the most important roles Henry felt she had as a community supervision officer. She saw the probationers' distrust as having far reaching causes, ones that to some extent she shares. She thought her role was to provide an important counterbalance: *When you understand that dilemma that you have in front of you and you put that on your shoulders and you realize, I can't go back in history to change what happened. But I can affect what goes forward. And that's what I tell every probationer because I do understand. I do a lot of reading and I watch* *a lot of documentaries and I realize this criminal justice issue stems as far back as slavery. So when it goes down generations and it becomes patterns to not trust police, don't trust the government, don't trust doctors . . . I can't change that. I'm part of that. But what can I do <u>now</u>?*

I tell every probationer, "I apologize if you feel this system has failed you. There is nothing I can do to change that. But what I <u>can</u> do from this day forward is to educate you on what you need to do as a probationer. I'm going to make sure you understand that. I can be your officer today and you wake up tomorrow and I may not be your officer because things change. But if I give you the basic understanding of how to maneuver through probation, how to follow the rules, then if you do these things, you will be successful. This is <u>your</u> life and you need to care about it more than I care about it."

So if I am clear with each probationer, consistent with every probationer, teaching them the rules, what the department expects of them, what the judge expects of them, go over what they actually agreed to in court—to me, that's what makes them successful. Probationers may think I'm giving them more of an insight of their case, or doing more, but I'm actually doing exactly what the department says to do. It's the tone. Two people can say the same thing, but it's the <u>way</u> that you say it and the <u>time</u> that you take to say it that make the difference. I have had several probationers who even when they finished probation were afraid to walk away because they say, "You are the first person who truly cared and made me accountable and finish something." So I think the way to fix the system is not to play into the stereotypes. We have to understand what we're up against and how to go forward just being . . . transparent.

One of the challenges Henry faced in building trust was the triangulated nature of probation. She was creating a personal relationship with each probationer, but she was also subject to the expectations and procedures of the department, and those, in turn, were subject to the wishes of the judge in charge of the case: *You have to understand you're just a small piece of it, a very small piece, especially when you can only do so much for a probationer. You have your beliefs about what is best for them, the department has standards of what we should do for them, and with those two components, if they get before the judge, the judge has the final say so about what actually happens to them.*

Some judges will take probation's account into their opinion when making a verdict. Some don't care. You never know unless you have dealt with that judge, dealt with that county. But you have to tell the probationer that at the beginning: "You are at the mercies of the court and if I have to take you back before the judge,

I can't account for what is going to happen with your case. "

If you have that transparency, then if that probationer or prisoner has to go back to prison, when they come out, because they're gonna come out, and you may have them again to supervise, but when they come out they're going to understand that it wasn't you that sent them back, it was the judge. And that helps a lot.

Her own interactions with judges, particularly in court probation, were positive: *Judges respect consistency and in my opinion they respect officers who understand their job and do their job well. Sometimes probation gets a bad rap with judges because there is a huge turnover rate and then you begin to see officers who don't care about their job. When I was in DeKalb, the judges would make it clear that they could tell by how warrants and notes were written the officers that knew their jobs and the officers that didn't.*

Given the complexity of the dynamics in this intrinsically triangulated situation, her passionate desire to make a difference, and the complexity of the cases she supervised, previously mental health, then sex offenders, Henry returned often to the definition of her job: *You have to always remember: Why am I here? To service the Court. And to ensure that the offender does exactly what the judge ordered him to do. However, doing that I also have the duty to them, their family, and my community to rehabilitate them and teach them how to live out here so they won't go back into the prison.*

Mental Health

We became interested in interviewing Henry when we observed her before and during a felony mental health accountability court session in DeKalb County. Elegantly dressed in a suit, papers in hand, she quietly talked with various men sitting on the benches outside the courtroom or standing looking out the large windows. She made eye contact, carefully reviewing their information before they appeared before the judge. It was clear Henry knew each of the men well, discussing in detail their medications, their doctor's visits, their compliance with their terms of supervision, and letting them know what she would present to the judge. Her tone was warm but matter of fact. You could see each of them expand a little in her attention.

When it became possible to talk with her a year later, after the formation of DCS, she was working in South Fulton doing sex-offender supervision. However, her passion for mental health supervision was clear, and she used insights drawn from it to understand supervision in general as well as her current responsibilities.

Henry graduated from Auburn University with a degree in criminal justice. Her first job was at a youth detention center in Alabama working with juveniles with serious mental illness, and she found she loved the challenge of working with those with mental illness. Coming to Atlanta, she worked as a caseworker with an organization that provided services to families whose children had mental illness, many of whom had experienced crimes or violence. Wanting to use her criminal justice degree, she then entered felony court probation in the Stone Mountain judicial circuit where she quickly found herself drawn to the mental health court Judge Cynthia Becker was starting. Her supervisor saw her interest and aptitude for it and assigned her there. Not formally an accountability court, it was created to respond to Judge Becker's observation that many of her probationers had underlying mental health issues that interfered with compliance and needed to be addressed.

After a year, Henry asked to be given a caseload of field supervision as well because she wanted more direct interaction with probationers. She was told she would need to relinquish her activities in court probation, but she requested that she be able to keep her mental health court cases. Although this was an uncommon request, she asked them to let her try carrying both for ninety days.

At the same time, the Department of Corrections was creating a new position for specialized mental health probation officers in response to a year-long study they had conducted to see how many probationers were being sent back to prison on technical violations. Of these cases, two thousand had mental illness and the reason for their non-compliance was usually that they were not taking their medications. Revocation in these cases was very expensive because the Department of Corrections was responsible for their medications and treatment when they returned to prison. It also had consequences when they were released again, because their SSI benefits were cut off as soon as they entered the prison and could often take months after release to come back on—a delay which could cause another cycle of non-compliance and revocation. The role of the newly created mental health probation officer was to try to identify and respond to the reasons for non-compliance in those with mental illness before revocation took place.

Henry was made one of the first mental health officers, her supervisor explaining, "You were so adamant about keeping those court cases, I knew you would be a perfect fit for this caseload." She and the other mental health officer in the circuit had reduced caseloads of forty to forty-five cases to allow them to focus more on these more demanding cases: *I adopted all the mental health court cases and then any new individuals flagged as suffering mental illness. My duty was to go and see them at home besides just seeing them at court and to speak frequently with the doctors.*

Henry was able to use her own experience in mental health to shape the job, requesting that they have treatment team meetings and teaching the other mental health specialist and the supervisor how to read treatment reports.

Again, education was core to how Henry understood her job: *My goal with mental health probationers was to educate them on their illness. A lot of them began by saying, "I'm not crazy, so I'm not taking this medication." So educating them on what the mental illness was, how the mental illness affected them, and how they could be successful with that illness was needed. Understanding your role is a very important part of a mental health caseload and understanding how to properly direct the offender because a lot of times the probationers would get so comfortable with me they would start veering off into therapy sessions. I would preface the conversations with, "Understand, I am not professionally trained as a psychiatrist or therapist. We may have to stop the interactions here so I can get you the further help."*

Georgia was the first state to have specialized mental health probation, so the assumptions it was based on were still developing. One of the basic assumptions that Henry questioned was that mental health cases could be stabilized sufficiently enough to be included in a standard caseload. This idea came from what she believed was a basic misunderstanding of mental illness: *With mental health, you have to understand their behavior cycles. That was one of the things that I thought was funny about how the department set up the position of mental health officer position. It was kind of understood that we would have the cases 180 days if they were coming out of prison, ninety days if on probation. Your job was to get the probationer stable, and then request that they be moved to a normal probation caseload, which for a standard officer is often huge. The idea was that this would keep the mental health officer's caseload down.*

The department's way of measuring stable would be housing, taking meds, and being connected to services (meaning they know where to get the help). But if you have worked in a clinical setting, you understand stable is a lifelong journey. You may be stable as long as I have you, but something as simple as me giving you to a new probation officer can make you unstable because you have to build trust with that probation officer. You may become depressed and stop taking your medicine. Just because you know where to get the help doesn't mean you are going to get the help.

The dimension of mental health supervision that she thought would be most useful for all probation officers was de-escalation: *If you learn how to de-escalate an offender, even if they don't suffer from a mental illness, I think a lot of situations can be combatted. If you realize the severity of how much they are actually losing by going back into the prison system, rather than just a "You did this so I'm going to get you back" response. There is so much we can do as officers to either intervene when that escalation is happening or before they have to go back before the judge, when they could end up back in custody.*

SEX OFFENDERS

There were other dimensions of mental health supervision that Henry found particularly applicable to her current work with sex offenders. Indeed, a number of the individuals on her sex-offender case load had diagnosed mental illnesses as well: *There is something that made you sexually offend someone. There is a disconnect there. I have several on my caseload who suffer from serious mental illness. When I start to talk to them I realize that they themselves were victims of a sex crime when they were young. Dealing with that trauma is how they became a perpetrator on someone else.*

But there were also some distinctive differences in how she related to these cases: *You just have to be more stern, more visual in your approach to your caseload as a sex-offender officer because you have so many dynamics going on. You have the mental illness component, but they will be completely compliant and you can't get blind-sided by that because they are sneaky and could be doing something else. You have to read the details of their indictment so you will know what to look for if you go out to the home because they may still have those same patterns. You have to learn the state guidelines as far as proximity. You need to know those parameters, and you have to go out and measure and make sure. And you also have to have the ability to turn it off because you are hearing and seeing so many things that you could get burnt out really easily.*

What she liked about these cases is also what she disliked: *The mental illness portion—because when we go into the proximity rules and the stigma, those are triggers. What I would normally do with a mental health probationer, try to build them up and instill hope into them, you can't necessarily do with a sex offender because they may have no other option but to be homeless.*

She pointed out that there is no common demographic for sex offenders: *About twelve of the sixty men are homeless. One of my probationers has a house that costs a million dollars. Some have well-paying jobs. Some are going to try and better themselves and some are not. It's all about the hope they have in themselves, their identity. Some you can instill that hope and they will go out and get a job.*

One difference in her supervision style was that she did not feel comfortable engaging in the same level of advocacy she did for her straight mental health caseload: *I can't vouch for what they do beyond my seeing them. You don't want to get to the point that you ask somebody to give them a job and God forbid they sexually offend.*

I try to get the sexual offender to understand why the community might be reluctant to hire them, get them to try and look at the other side. I always start out with, "What is one of the worst labels you can have in life?" They often say, "Being a sex offender." And then I ask, "If you were not a sex offender and you had a business, would you be willing to hire sex offenders?" Their answer is usually no.

My next step is to say, "You probably feel you are worth more than what you may get, but having something is better than nothing. Understand what you're up against." I always tell them, "You only need one yes. You're going to get a hundred no's, but you are going to get to that one yes." A lot of time when they hit desperation or despair, you can just reiterate this to them. "Try, just try. You're up against that stigma and you're going to have to prove until the day you die that you are rehabilitated."

Henry drew on her own faith to foster hope in these men in the face of this daunting stigma and a system of supervision and of collateral consequences so onerous that it seems to set them up for inevitable failure: *I ask them, "What is your identity? What do __you__ believe you are? You have this label for life, but what do __you__ think you are? Are you going to let this label stop you or are you going to be successful and push?"*

I tell them, "You have to think outside the box if you're going to live because this label isn't going anywhere, the community's ideas aren't going anywhere. Change your ideas of what __you__ believe you are, and then we'll see where you are." Some of them start their own business, like a car wash. So there is a lot of coaching them, trying to build them up but still being firm with what the court wants them to do. With some it works, with some it doesn't. They continue to be homeless. That's the part where it is hard for me.

In the face of troubling, unanswerable questions, she returned often to her job definition for clarity: *You have to remember what your job is, which is to uphold the order of the court regardless of how you like it. I asked a public defender one time, "How do you defend someone who you know is guilty of* *murder but you're trying to get them off?" She told me, "It is my job to uphold the Constitution, not to get into the particulars of if they did it or not." It is not my job to get into how the law is written, it is my job to carry out the order of the court. In doing that, I carry out that order with <u>care</u> for the offender.*

COMMUNITY: THE RIPPLE EFFECT

Henry had a strong feel for our interrelatedness, one that was central to her own experience of the world and how she approached the question of reentry and reintegration for her probationers: *When I look at a probationer, I don't only look at them, I am thinking about the family that is behind them. If I teach you better ways of handling a situation, my theory and hope are that you will take that to your family. If you're a father and I teach you how to be accountable to probation, and how to be more professional in dress, and how to look at yourself as somebody, possibly you will instill that in your child. And if I teach you how to talk, maybe you'll learn how to talk to that teacher when you go to the school dealing with an issue with your child. It's just so much bigger than what is in front of you and you just have to have that mentality and <u>want</u> to help. It goes back to caring. You have to be in the caring business.*

Her approach was very similar to the one then starting to be explored in the newly formed DCS's "One Officer, One Household, One Community" approach. She was excited about the new approach but thought it might be problematic for some officers who had not thought of their work in these terms. She wanted this new focus to lead to a more individualized approach to supervision: *My hope with the new wave is that we become more interested in how to help them truly reintegrate into the community and not have this cookie cutter way of supervising offenders. For example, "They need to get a GED, they need to get a GED." That may not be the number one thing they need right now. You might go to their house and they don't even have power on right now. Someone who can't read, who never excelled in education, is not thinking about getting a GED, they need power and food in the house. So, I would like to see the new wave of community supervision help them truly reintegrate into the community.*

She also thought that it was difficult for communities to wrap their minds around community supervision and their role in it as well: *Once we realize it is going to take all of us to solve this problem, we'll all be better off. We've hit on the stigma, the jobs, the education, the trust, these are community issues. Law enforcement can only do so much. When the community realizes that it is a more important factor than any probation officer or any judge or jail or prison, we will have a better system. You as a shop owner, you're going to have to be willing to hire a convicted felon. Allow them to live in your neighborhood, be your neighbor.* Her own early experience and the lessons she had taken from them influenced how she approached the questions of individual and structural responsibility. She understood her own success as a shared commitment between her and her community: *I also grew up in a housing project. My mom was on government assistance. I grew up with gangs beating guys right outside my front steps, going to school with girls pregnant in the sixth grade. I grew up with all of that. I knew several people, even family members, who went to prison or jails because they were tied up with crime or drugs. I just had a drive that I didn't want to be a part of that. I wanted to be the person on the inside to try to stop it, to show them a different way, a better way. Because I knew there was one, but somebody had to believe in you and you had to take that belief a step farther and believe in yourself to change.*

The difference for me is that I had a village wrapped around me. My kindergarten teacher followed me to twelfth grade. She instilled in me each year, you will be in the top ten in your class, you are important. I had cheerleading, dance teachers, coaches in my life. God has always put someone in my life to remind me that I am worth so much more than what I have in front of me. And not everyone has that. So if I can make you feel you are important and that you matter, maybe you will make the next person feel important and that they matter.

I definitely saw that ripple effect in my family. I grew up with both parents. My mom was very young. She had my older sister when she was sixteen, me when she was nineteen, and my younger sister when she was twenty-one. My dad was in the military and we all, me and my sisters, were the first in our family to go to college and finish. None of us had children while we were in school, no pregnancies, none of that. And the difference between us and our family had to have been our community connections, it had to be that village that wrapped around us. I got things from my teachers and my coaches that my mom and dad couldn't give me. I feel it is my goal to do that because had it not been for the community aspect, I can't honestly say that I would be here.

Henry emphasized that what separated her from the probationers she supervised was something that can ultimately unite them: *I tell probationers, "There is just one thing that stops me from being on the other side of the table like you. It doesn't make me any better than you. I just decided not to do the crime. I could very well be in your shoes. I know exactly where you come from. But I wanted something better for myself. Just because your family did this and you come from that, doesn't mean you have to do it too."* A lot of time the offenders think we came from the silver spoon and we have no idea of the reality of what life is really like. When they find out about me, they think, well, this officer is really just like me but she decided to do something different. It stops the excuses.

But Henry also recognized the shaping influence of community, especially if someone knew no alternative. She described the vertigo of this experience humorously: *I use as an example, when I went off to college, I thought I was special because I didn't have a baby. Then, on campus, I saw these thirty thousand other students who didn't have children. My idea of being special was based on my community until I fell out of that community, then I realized that's not special, that's abnormal what is happening there.*

She also understood that you can't remove race, or the profound systems distrust that racial inequity has created from the criminal justice system or community supervision: *Do you know that statistically there are now more people under supervision in our country than there were slaves on plantations? When you hit on how the laws are set up and when you go into the prison and you see the vast wave of people who are not educated and had so much potential and could have been so vital to the community and you start to wonder how did this happen and whose goal was it for us <u>not</u> to be able to tap into that promise? I don't know whether that was anyone's goal but how <u>did</u> it happen?*

Henry shook her head: "When you bring up the race card it erases the bigger issue and then where are you? We travel around in circles and nothing gets done." However, she also understood that increasing trust in the system could save lives, black lives, on both sides. "The question of trustworthiness is huge in the black community," she said. She used this potent example, one that had special salience for her because she had recently married and her husband was a police officer: *I tell my probationers specifically now, more so than when I started, "If you get pulled over by the police, you do it." That's where the core trust issue is with the black community about policing. That's why we're seeing so many murders. A lot of offenders do not have a trust in the system on the latter end, when they get before the judge, so they take the law in their hands on the front end and do not realize that is <u>not</u> the time to plead your case. You could very well die when you're trying to plead your case. Wait until you get before the judge. And they're saying, well it won't matter when I get before the judge, so I'm going to try and stop it on the front end. You can't take justice in your hand when the officer is trying to do their job. It's not the time or the place.*

By her own practices as a probation officer—the care she showed for each of her probationers, the education she strove to give them about how the system worked, her clear and confident expectations—Henry was trying to convey, individual by individual, that within that court, within that system, there was a real possibility they might find someone who understood the importance of considering, like she did, their *whole* story. With care.

OLD PROBATION: PRAGMATISM AND BURNOUT
Deon Allen

At the same time we spoke with Henry, we spoke with Officer Deon Allen, also a probation officer in South Fulton. The DCS merger had taken place but there were no significant changes on the ground yet. Allen was cautiously optimistic but also frustrated and tired. In some ways, he felt he had fallen into probation and couldn't find his way back to what he felt was his true calling—teaching. He grew up in Ohio and went to college on a football scholarship, majored in education, but didn't finish his degree. He worked throughout this time in juvenile corrections, so when he moved to Atlanta in 2004, probation seemed a good fit. He had thought he would be doing court case-management but had always been in the field managing high-risk offenders. With ten years in, he was more experienced than many other urban field officers and probably exceeded the average longevity for South Fulton, a notoriously difficult area.

For the last four years he had worked in the Community Impact Program (CIP), a collaboration between probation, parole and the Atlanta Police department, roughly modeled on the Savannah Impact Program. CIP in Atlanta did not have the Savannah program's emphasis on services and employment. It had been mainly a warrant-serving unit focused on establishing authority and safety in communities. It was responsible for events like the one described by Anthony (in Chapter I. 5) when his house was surrounded by armed officers calling out his name loudly enough to wake his neighbors, just checking that he was there. Allen did note that in line with the broader criminal justice reform efforts, CIP in the last few years had begun to focus more on reentry. It now included a mental health counselor, and was being absorbed into the Prisoner Reentry Initiative, with more focus on rehabilitation than control.

The caseloads boggled the imagination. When he began in probation, he standardly had 150 to 300 cases. Only 150 of those were supposed to be active supervision, but the number was always higher. Now, as someone doing high-risk/specialized supervision, he was supposed to be carrying a caseload of 40, but it was actually 70.

Experience had made Allen dubious about the preventive power of supervision: *No matter how many times you see them, it won't stop them from doing what they're going to do. If a probationer commits a crime but reports to me as required the next day, I won't even know.*

Even so, Allen also felt it was possible to identify probationers who were going to be successful. One probationer he was sure was going to be successful first lived with his sister when released from prison, but quickly got two part-time jobs, and within a month had rented his own apartment with his brother, within three months owned a car. "I knew he was going to be a success because he had a plan."

He also could predict who would probably fail: *Others have no goals, they are not looking to do right. If they are disrespectful. If you give them referrals and they don't take them. You can even tell them, "You're going to be locked up again in three to six months." But they don't see that they are doing it to themselves.*

Allen was clear about the economic demands and challenges of reentry. He saw these economic drivers as the most important factor in reentry or recidivism: *Society expects us to undo. They expect us to work miracles. But, society is not offering them a chance. If they can't get a job, or an apartment, they go back to what they know in order to survive. They have families they need to feed. For most of them, the family member who was out is the one has been taking care of the family needs. And also for their needs in prison: the money for phone calls, commissary, the gas to go to and from the prison for visits. When the offender comes out, he is still drawing on that family member for probation fees, restitution. The clock starts as soon as they are released.*

Allen saw employment as key to successful reentry. A pragmatist, he was dismissive of a probation effort to increase job readiness that made men come in four days a week to listen to motivational speakers: *These people don't need that. They don't need to find the money to get here every day. Some people never had an interview. Some people never had a job opportunity.*

Instead, Allen admired job training programs that resulted in actual employment and promoted groups that met those basic economic needs for his probationers. He cited one through a local church that was six to twelve weeks in duration, then offered people paid positions. For some of the men he supervised, this was a first in their lives. He described the frustration of one participant: *A gentleman, tattoos all over his face, been living on the street all his life, drugs all his life—he made it through the first three weeks, but when they asked him to prepare a resume, he had nothing he could put on it.* Allen also positively mentioned Georgia Works (the even longer, residential program Ivan was involved with), where one of the first people to graduate had been on Allen's caseload. *They teach them how to work with many tools. Place them all over the state. This young man was in a gang and trying to get out. He moved to Augusta for his first job assignment.*

Temp agencies also provided employment, but men needed to apply in outlying suburbs to be considered, even if their placements would be in the city. However, as we heard again and again, temp agencies were rarely a long-term solution because men were rarely hired on permanently. Certain crimes made if difficult to find employment, even with a reduction of stigma: *People are more open to employing people now. Employers are more willing to hire a murderer than theft by receiving. No one is going to hire if it was financial identity fraud. In the past, it was really just a blanket no. Now they're willing to give a person a chance, but they're still very skeptical of theft.*

Allen was encouraged by the new emphasis on resources, especially housing. He described how he and other officers had welcomed in a housing coordinator, identifying the apartments that were already open to renting to people with criminal records. Through the housing programs sponsored or credentialed by Parole and Corrections, more apartments were lifting the ban on renting to felons and, with institutional encouragement, were waving the application fees.

Allen wondered, as had Mr. T. on our ride-along, why the work men did in prison couldn't be acknowledged: *All the renovation done at Tift was done by prisoners. Why couldn't they do that here on English Avenue—rehab some of these houses? It could create housing for them. And the community could see what they were doing for themselves and for the community. We need to be putting more money into rebuilding these communities in the first place.*

Overall, Allen thought additional resources were far more important than supervision in facilitating reentry. His experience validated the commonly employed rule of thirds. Out of a caseload of seventy, about thirty to forty were serious about reentry. Of those, about half could do it on their own, half could do it with support. The others were hampered by substance abuse, mental health, or the absence of any support system. As we heard again and again, 80-90% of the people returning from prison are testing positive for drugs, usually marijuana. He felt that the easy access to drugs in prison was driven in part by the economic desperation on the part of the corrections officers: *It boils down to dollars. Someone is offering you more money than you are bringing home. If you don't feel you have anything to lose, why not?*

The fact that probation officers had not received a raise in six or seven years rankled, especially if one was at an age where it was difficult to move over to another field. With the creation of a new agency, only upper management was getting a raise, he observed. (This pressure was relieved somewhat two years later with a general 20% salary increase for all state law enforcement.)

Probation officers are more engaged with the judicial system than parole officers, directly seeing the impact of judicial decisions. As someone committed to second chances, one recent judicial decision Allen had directly observed in court really troubled him. Allen described a young college student who had gone to a club one night. One of the dancers claimed the young man took her money, and the bouncer hit him and made him give the young woman money. (It was not clear from the story whether the young man actually had taken her money.) The young man left the club and went to his car. As he was approaching it, the bouncer began walking the girl to her car, which was parked next to the young man's. Thinking the bouncer was coming back for him, the young man shot at him. He immediately ran across the street to call it in. (He forgot he had his phone on him.) *But the judge didn't take into consideration that he was disorganized. Or that he didn't try to flee. He was sentenced to four years in prison for a first offense. If he was a repeat offender, he'd get two years. I don't understand that. Here he is in college, trying to make something of himself, and the judge cuts it off just like that. I see repeat offenders cycling constantly. Why was that judge trying to waste that young man's life?*

URBAN ADMINISTRATION: SITTING ON A POWDER KEG

Cory Beggs

I'm one of those who believes we need to be very critical of ourselves to make our agency better. And sometimes that requires us to make hard decisions and talk about hard things that make other people uncomfortable.

We talked with Cory Beggs three times, in three different settings, and the content of our conversations reflected those differences. Our first conversation, which took place in our home office where he graciously arranged to meet us, was more intimate and meditative and focused on the philosophy of supervision he had developed working in small communities in North Georgia. The second conversation, held soon after the merger, when he was selected DCS coordinating chief for Atlanta, took place in the decaying and very bleak probation offices on Sylvan Road, where he took us on a tour that began by pointing out where probationers regularly stashed their guns before stepping over potholes and cracks in the parking lot to enter the building. At that point, he was strained not only by the challenges of urban supervision, and the merger, but also the dysfunctions of the GOTSR initiative, which spoke to but did not meet the urgent need for additional resources. Our last conversation took place in their new office in downtown Atlanta. We focused on recent accomplishments—and the problems, now understood as perennial, of working at such daunting scale and complexity with limited resources.

In our opinion, Beggs may have the most difficult job in DCS, especially for an essentially contemplative man. It isn't clear that it helps him to talk about the challenges, but over the years of our project he has been very generous with his time. Beggs is a man who likes to think about history, ideas, but all our conversations inevitably returned to numbers and logistics. As the DCS coordinating chief for the Atlanta Judicial Circuit and Fulton county, the county in Georgia with the highest number of people under community supervision, numbers and logistics are inescapable, bedrock. The last time we talked to him, in the spring of 2019, in what he described as a snapshot of a constantly changing dynamic, the total number of supervision cases in Fulton was 18,000, only 8,000 of which were currently active supervision. (The total number of supervision cases had risen 4,500 in four years.) Beggs had a staff of 76 officers to oversee these 8,000 active cases: 58 field officers; 15 specialized officers for high-risk, mental health and sex offender supervision;

and 3 officers at the Day Reporting Center. Of these 18,000 cases, two-thirds were nonviolent crimes, the remainder were violent crimes, usually repeat offenders who often had several probation sentences running concurrently. The average length of service for his officers was three years, six months, but if you removed two experienced officers, the average depth of experience fell by almost a year. A third of management was brand new.

Beggs brought up, then tried to repress, the thought that this position—which he had filled for five and a half years, twice as long as any of his last three predecessors—might be professional suicide. His predecessors had all been heading into or were already in retirement but Beggs was in his mid-forties. With the consolidation of probation and parole field services in DCS, movement to upper management is less rapid than before. Promotion has often served as a method of retention for highly able officers. The suggestion that the extreme challenges of this position, the lure of complexity itself, might be serving the same function for someone as dedicated as Beggs was met with an exhausted smile.

RURAL SUPERVISION

Beggs' understanding of the promise of community corrections was deeply shaped by his first position as chief of probation in Blairsville, a peaceful mountain town in the North Georgia mountains. His college major was adult education, a perspective that also strongly influenced his understanding of community supervision. Beggs's wife worked for the Department of Family and Children's Services (DFACS), so in many ways they served the same population. The community was small enough that they would have to go to the grocery shop at midnight if they wanted to be sure to avoid running into someone on their caseloads. In contrast, in Atlanta, he had never seen anyone on the street that he'd seen in the office.

Beggs was very proud of the performance of his Blairsville office. With a probation population of 350, they had very high compliance numbers and few warrants. Probation fines are a major burden for many, and Beggs would encourage people to make a good faith effort and then would advocate for them in court. They had 86% collection rates. They never had a compromising situation during a revocation, the point when a probationer is most likely to become aggressive. His office had no turnover, providing continuity for probationers. *Everyone knew each other's cases. It was a big family. We also had rapport with the general population, which is how you get a high compliance rate.*

This rapport extended to the judges. Beggs was a strong supporter of the possibilities of the POSS officer, introduced in the 2013 probation reforms, even though it did not catch on throughout the system. POSS officers were to work directly with judges, DAs and defense attorneys to structure and individualize sentence conditions so that they would best serve a client.

However, Beggs also became very aware of the perverse incentive structure behind probation fines, especially in small towns: *In Blairsville, the sentence for the first meth conviction was fifteen years of probation, plus a fine and drug surcharge. The total usually came in just under $1900. That is difficult for a struggling family. We would amortize that over half the sentence—eight years—to give wiggle room on the other end. We had a system where we had a local bank account and deposited the money there. We kept a reserve of money in the account and whatever was over that reserve we would return to the county. Then we switched to central banking and we wanted to have a zero balance—money comes in and goes out. So we cleared out the account and sent out massive checks. Union County got $85,000 cash. So they got into fine collection, began to think of it as a viable form of income. The county commissioner said, "We received $85,000 in June, why not the same now?" We had to demonstrate how that wasn't possible. But smaller jurisdictions do use probation fines to fund projects. The smaller the community, the more viable the fines are as an income source. That's why in small areas probation operates as a very robust part of the criminal justice program. People know if they don't comply, they will face serious consequences—a very long time to serve. Larger jurisdictions are not looking at fines as any part of their budget.*

One concept that Beggs shared, which we have found useful and explore later in the book, is the idea of middle class bliss—a view of the world that is maintained by denying the complexities of the larger society. As he began to work with the probation population, and his wife with DFACS, they saw things that they had never seen: *It's hard to find your balance when you realize that people don't live like you, that you can't generalize from your position. In Blairsville, what we saw was multi-generational: grandparents, sons, children. The question becomes: How do we break the cycle?*

For Beggs, even though he works on probation and reentry, the answer as a society is to put the resources at the front end, not the back. This came up often when he talked about reentry, especially about how to address recidivism, which was a chronic conversation and consternation now that he was in Atlanta: *Need creates risk. People don't want to invest in prevention. But* *the implications on the back end are tremendous. A couple of years ago, $1 of every $18 in the state budget went to corrections and the schools were short-changed. Our children were short-changed. I ask people to help me work myself out of a job. I'm good at what I do, but I want us to address the needs at the front end.*

Two personal experiences in Beggs's own life shaped his understanding of key goals and challenges of probation. His grandfather's life grounded his aspirations. With only a third grade education, Beggs's grandfather gathered enough technical skills that he came to manage the water system in his small community. Beggs's father in turn would become an engineer. Beggs believes in the importance of upward social mobility, but also acknowledges that it is something that is systemically as much as individually constructed—through education and economic opportunity. So how to bring this attitude into highly disadvantaged communities with high unemployment, where the major economy is informal and often illicit, and where many individuals have no skills or education to build on and also lack the soft skills needed for employment, such as time and anger management—in other words, into typical probation populations—is an open question.

A close relative's trajectory grounded his fears, which were about the generalized, expanding loss of social trust that can accompany repeated drug convictions. At our last interview, Beggs mentioned that his relative, now a five-time convicted felon, would be in prison until 2032. In our first interview, five years earlier, he mentioned his frustration that, after four drug busts, numerous burglaries, his relative's immediate family still insisted on blaming society for his convictions, rather than his own drug-driven behavior. Beggs felt their denial of his addiction made them ignore the warning signs that could have led to intervention and treatment. Instead, they blamed the criminal justice system, and, beyond that, the government as a whole. They had come to believe that "everyone from the government is crooked." Beggs wondered if the social conditions of their own childhoods, growing up poor and with limited education, colored their responses and interpretations. What he did know was that he, and the work he did, was caught up in their net of distrust—and that this broad systems distrust would make reentry and rehabilitation more difficult for people he knew and cared about personally.

SYLVAN ROAD & DCS TRANSITION

The second time we spoke with Beggs, he had been selected as the coordinating chief for the new combined DCS Atlanta office. The only chief in the state with two chiefs under him, this was an important position. He was meant to be the public face of the DCS. But how could he communicate the complexity of urban community supervision in a way that would inspire confidence? "Sometimes it feels like you're sitting on a powder keg," he said bluntly.

In our last conversation, four years later, the reasons for that frustration were even more clear. As soon as probation and parole consolidated there was a large personnel exit, primarily from the parole side, because of the additional caseloads and also because probation's court-based procedures seemed impossibly complex: *We have twenty Superior Court judges in Atlanta. When you would say, well this judge will do this—but this judge won't—I could see the level of frustration just boiling over with those officers. For parole everything went straight up—and parole officers had the backing of the agency. What parole officers had to understand about probation was you have to get the DA's office involved, then you have to get the Public Defenders office involved, and then you have to get the judges involved. Then there were the smaller mechanics—Clerk's office, where you pull the paper work, and Court Administration, which produces the paperwork. All the moving parts: you could just see them tune out.*

There are some states where they merged the two systems, they got rid of the parole piece. They still paroled people, but then they dropped them straight into probation and let that portion start. They didn't keep two field supervision systems up and running. I personally am not proficient in parole. I couldn't go through its whole process. But I can negotiate the whole probation system. It's very familiar to me. I know how to work stuff through that. But new officers look at it, especially here in Atlanta, and it has so many moving pieces, it is overwhelming.

The size of caseloads, and the inability to control them, also factored in: *Parole managed level. If they got too many cases, they would commute. But they kept one level. So caseloads remained the same throughout the life of an officer. We had a lot of probation officers who went to Parole for that control. When we merged together, we went to thirty-three vacancies, just like that. We were struggling just to keep the warrants issued on the cases we needed to.*

This situation was made more complicated by the various ways that Probation had tried to manage its levels—levels which it does not control. The consequences of their choices were becoming clear a decade later: *What they did ten years ago when Probation was under Corrections was put everyone who was on a standard level of supervision on contact status, where they just had to call in once a month and pay a fee. Once they did that, administration said you could give an individual officer 500 call-in cases to supervise. They didn't bring in extra officers; they just changed the procedures to cap the manpower. Atlanta was the only office that did this, because of our volumes—we had 8,000 people on contact status. When we combined, supervision changed, with DCS deploying officers into the field. Problem was that they didn't add any officers. We suddenly had 8,000 more active cases to supervise.*

The average caseload is now down to 150 or 160. We have gone through two hiring freezes. Every time the budget has been balanced on the back of labor. It's like quicksand. You start sinking slowly. And when you lose more and more officers, you go down quick.

We do a lot of employee disciplinary action. But what I look at is that these officers would be incredibly successful anywhere but here. It is just an unrealistic workload. And as an agency, we've merged, but we haven't shed outdated policy. We've added body cameras and we've added ESP—the principles behind it are perfect—but it doesn't relate to the realities of the caseloads.

At the beginning of his time as coordinating chief, Beggs also felt caught in the middle with the GOTSR initiative. Atlanta CIP over the years had developed quite a large community base, all of whom came to the table, facilitating networking, but GOTSR, eager to establish itself, was trying to establish its own independent community network, and in the process alienated established allies: "There was no promise of money, but people in the community thought there was money. Even ones at the table were walking away when it didn't show up." Over the two years of its existence, GOTSR had mushroomed from five to over sixty people, and seemed like a jobs creation program—but only for new administrators, with little benefit to long-term consortiums like CIP or to DCS, or to returning citizens or to community providers. Lines of authority and communication were so unclear or tangled, that the GOTSR community coordinator for Atlanta wouldn't talk to Beggs or share resources with the community supervision officers, who were the ones who most needed the community contacts. This was intensely frustrating. However, in our last interview several years later, Beggs emphasized the contributions that the housing and community coordinators, now fully integrated into DCS, were making.

The Long Haul: A Different Animal

The last time we met, Beggs proudly gave us a tour of the new Atlanta DCS Office and Day Reporting Center. It was bright, freshly painted, expansive. "People don't dread coming to the office anymore. At Sylvan Road, we were pulling raccoons out of the ceiling," he said with a laugh. Beggs had designed the building, which included a large open area for the officers to come in and work at desks when they weren't out in the field, many adjoining conference rooms, and small interview rooms where officers spoke with supervisees through clear bulletproof plexiglass. Beggs included the barrier because these interview areas opened into the officers' own work area and Beggs thought the officers, armed in the field, needed to have an area in the office where they could remove their vests, feel safe and decompress.

He listed the areas where he felt the greatest sense of accomplishment. Foremost was their rapid and comprehensive shift to a very different supervision model: *The biggest thing we've done is we went from a caseload-based supervision based on risk level to a more localized geographical supervision model. We flipped over 13,000 offenders from one supervision model and splashed them over the officers and within a month we were up and running. It took us four months to get to that point, but when we got to the point to pull the trigger, we did it. That was a huge project.*

Now we have officers working zip codes. With this, we garnered a little caseload stabilization. Officers were able to build rapports with offenders—and they also built rapports with communities. So some of them know the resources in that area, and some of them know the other law enforcement officers that work in those areas. That increases public safety ten-fold. That has been the biggest thing.

We now have a lot of projects where we are re-engaging with the community. Re-engaging with the judges, with the DA's office. But working in Fulton County is like working with an amoeba, it is always changing, we are always trying to figure out what we're going to see next.

However, it was difficult to explain the balance between individual accountability and support distinctive to community supervision to others, and thus what constituted success, especially when working at such volume. Beggs touched on this question in various ways during our last conversation: *Parole is a very needs-based supervision model, but probation if pushed can turn into a check-box system. You have a list of conditions on a sentence. If you hit this, this, this and this, you're done. The courts like that. They're moving cases too. We all jam cases through, we don't make meaningful and impactful sentences that will bring any sort of rehabilitation around. I hate to use this word, but it is an industry. If you look at the court system—if you asked the DA's office when was the last time they thought about reintegration or reentry . . .*

Beggs described the challenge he felt recently trying to respond to a question the DA's office had asked, "What do you guys do well?" *My answer to him was "We address needs. We're dealing with individuals, and each individual who comes to us has different needs. They even respond differently to different punishments. So, we spend a little time with them talking about those aspects of their lives to try and find out what is the best route with this person. A need today may not be a need tomorrow and it may be a need again later on, so I can't tell you categorically what we do." He wasn't receptive to this individual approach. I think he was looking for a sound bite. But what I look at is, we address needs because needs create risk.*

Trying to understand and communicate the differences between rural and urban probation is a challenge, one Beggs can't evade. He needs to be able to articulate it to help his urban officers get a clearer sense of what they can and can't be expected to accomplish: *People will say, "Probation is probation is probation." I disagree with that. I have seen it in rural and urban settings. When we first came together, I started saying, "You need to do a workload analysis because I've worked in both rural and urban areas and the policies you're pushing out . . . it's not one size fits all."*

In Blairsville you have judges that give probation officers absolute power and people are scared to death of going into the system. We had a lot more compliance. I used to joke that in the winter we never issued warrants because everyone was cold and under a rock. Down here you've got these massive caseloads, you've got a very active population, a very non-compliant population, a population that is very gypsy-like in a tight area. Problem with zip codes is you can move three streets down and be in another officer's jurisdiction. So you are still hopping around.

The volume of cases and level of reoffending mean that Atlanta defines compliance differently from other districts. Beggs acknowledges this and the tension it can create with other areas of the state—but also finds it necessary: *We don't arrest for positive drug screens. We don't arrest for a lot of technical issues that in other areas of the state they do. If somebody comes to Fulton, gets on felony probation, then is transferred to a rural area, at the first positive drug screen, they are wanting us to issue a warrant. That's not the way we do business here. It creates opposition in the state. "Atlanta just does what they want." That's what I hear all the time. "Atlanta just does what they want. They don't take anybody serious." But our level of comfort with technical violations is different than it is across the state. Sometimes I think if we can just get them through without committing a new felony offense, we have done 90% of what we were supposed to do.*

As I get older, my tolerance for certain things—I've never used any illegal drugs in my life, but I'm getting to the point where if they want to smoke marijuana, I don't care. I'm starting to mellow out on such hard-defined rules. My grandparents and my parents talked about theft, and my brother works in loss prevention at a big box chain store and he's getting more and more frustrated because they are not prosecuting some of these cases. And I look at him and say, "46% of the cases that are going before the judges are violent offenses. Theft from a box store is the least of their concerns." But the box store is the victim and I'm now having to prioritize the level of sin that is occurring against the community. A 2009 Pew study says that with some of these property crimes, it's cheaper just to keep them out in the community and deal with the costs out in the community than it is to incarcerate them.

A phrase that Beggs was trying out, one that related to the volume, the feeling that criminal justice, and supervision, were an industry in Atlanta, was *judicial economy*. What was important was to keep the system moving. This question was especially important because of the high level of recidivism in Atlanta, and the level of overlaid probation sentences. Repeat offenders, when their repeat offenses hit the wealthier parts of the city become big news in the local paper. This activated the DA. Recently, he had come to ask whether the individuals now on unsupervised supervision needed additional supervision. The 2017 law, SB 174, that institutionalized various progressive community supervision practices, allowed any individual under probation supervision who had not committed another felony, whether or not they were compliant with any of the other terms of supervision, to go on unsupervised status. That meant 3,000 individuals were on unsupervised status in Atlanta.

Beggs agreed in principle about the advisability of more supervision, but not in practice: *With the number of cases going through and our trying to retain some semblance of judicial economy, in Fulton County we move cases as quickly as possible. We're not willing to stop and say, "This is a gentleman we need to look at and let's prosecute this to the nth degree because he has obviously not learned his lesson." You just don't stop the system.*

Defense attorneys may have a good case, but they won't fight it because they'll be looked at as someone who will stop the judicial economy piece. We charge high and then we come in low with reduced charges just to get it to the other side. Cases that would carry long and arduous prison or probation sentences in other parts of Georgia just don't exist in Fulton County. There are many sentences, but not long ones. Most are capped at five years. When you run across one that is longer, that person has done something to agitate the criminal justice system here. Or the officer showed up to court or something occurred to make that more egregious. It may be the judges were using best practices, but I think it was just the economy. I don't think it was that they were trying intentionally to say these are the best sentences for us.

Recently, responding to public outrage about recidivism, the DA was interested in using probation revocation as a way to prosecute new cases by recidivists. However, this would disrupt an intricate balancing act being played out between DCS and the local jail. Beggs tried to explain: *Right now about 70% of the probation revocations are held in Fulton County jail. The jail court in Fulton processes about sixty to ninety per week. This allows a relief valve for Fulton county jail, which has been under a federal mandate for overcrowding. If you run ninety people through each week, in three or four weeks, you've released 360 people. When we do this, there is no representation from the DA. We handle those revocations in front of a public defender. We take out all the stuff—no new charges, only move forward on technical. Rarely is the person given more than jail time, possibly a probation detention center or RSAT. If cases do get routed in front of judges, they can revoke anything up to the expiration date of the sentence, which could be significant time. The DA wants to shut down jail revocation and route all that traffic through judges. But when you route another sixty to ninety people through the Superior Court judges—who would all tell you they are tired to the bone—it slows the process down. The judicial economy process is gone.*

Beggs likes difficult problems. The one he chooses to take on now is providing support to the personnel in his office: *I think I've switched from worrying about offenders to worrying about personnel and helping them do their jobs. What I learned in moving through these rural and urban jurisdictions was that case-load ratios mean nothing; they are not a good measure of what an officer does every day. What I wanted to understand was what did the work really look like, boil it down to a time-task analysis: These guys have this number of cases. Contact takes this amount of time. Each task takes this amount of time. From this information, let's build realistic caseloads. This approach lost traction when SB 174 came in because they thought caseloads would be cut by the unsupervised project. It didn't shake out as many cases as we thought. When people have fifteen active cases, all we are doing is terminating a docket, not taking a person off supervision itself.*

Then we have high profile cases. If a murder occurs, and media hits, those cases become the object of scrutiny all the way up the command. In small rural communities, an aggravated assault is once in a blue moon, a murder is once in an eclipse. But here we send up two aggravated assaults just since we've been talking here.

Beggs understands that developing a realistic set of expectations is crucial to being an effective and trustworthy leader: *These officers were trying to do the best they can, but they are always robbing Peter to pay Paul. They look at me to say what's important. And I ask that question and I ask that question and the answer I get is, "Everything is important." Leadership-speak in business would be to talk about not over-extending, about expanding in a way that is equitable and profitable. But government tends to say, "Yeah, we can take it. Yeah, we can take it." And then we take all these bits and pieces and don't do anything really well. Goes back to that DA's question: What do you do really well? We survive.*

The idealism and commitment that underlie Beggs twenty effective years in community supervision quickly surfaced again: *People do need to have a sense of purpose. You don't get rich in this job. But you have to find your purpose within the purpose. I think working with officers is my purpose. In that personal accomplishment book: I designed this building. We had a small team and we pushed all that old stuff into a geographical model of supervision and put it out there equitably for each officer to have. I loved those projects. I loved seeing the immediate product out of those.*

I'm constantly asking what can we do better, what can we change, how can we change it. A lot of people might say, "Let's just hit the brakes for a second—" I joke with my wife: The amount of work I do down here at work, if I could translate that into entrepreneurial adventure . . . But I'm just not a risk taker.

SUPPORT SERVICES:
PRISON IN-REACH AND COMMUNITY COORDINATORS

When embedded in and integrated with DCS field services, the key support functions of the Prison Reentry Initiative have provided much needed resources for officers and supervisees, as Beggs noted. These positions are not law enforcement, rather social services broadly defined. Some of the individuals filling these positions were formerly incarcerated, others have had no prior contact with law enforcement or prisons. We talked to two highly capable women, Sharon Almon, a community coordinator based in DeKalb County, and Melanie Barker, a prison in-reach specialist based in Macon, to learn about their motivations and experiences.

An image we took away from both of the interviews was the delight each woman took in the quite different computer programs that helped them do their jobs. In both cases, we were called over to look at their screens to see ourselves what information they could access—and what their colleagues and field officers could access as well. This was part of the effort to reduce the siloing of information and contribute to a "seamless transition" from prison to supervision and then, possibly, into the larger community.

It has now become a requirement in Georgia prisons that each prisoner will have a reentry plan, the ones for those with higher risks and needs facilitated through the DCS PRI. The PRI program is voluntary for prisoners with scores of 5 or over on a NextGeneration assessment of risks and needs. The program is limited to those who are going under DCS supervision, either as parolees or probationers. A consequence of the PRI effort is that within Corrections itself some of these same services are being expanded to all prisoners who are reentering.

On entry into prison all prisoners are assessed as to their risks and needs and given a preliminary reentry plan that decides the programming they will receive in prison. About a year before leaving prison a more detailed reentry plan is created that focuses primarily on housing, employment, and addiction or mental health services. For high-risk PRI eligible prisoners that plan can be developed with the help of a prison in-reach coordinator. In those seventeen counties that have PRI, the plan is then forwarded to the community coordinator so the community coordinator can start identifying what community resources might be able to meet the individual's need for housing, food, or clothing when they are released.

PRISON IN-REACH COORDINATOR: MELANIE BARKER

The Macon DCS office is located in an office park on the outskirts of the city. It includes a Day Reporting Center, so when we came up there were a number of people chatting outside on the sidewalks awaiting the start of a class. There was a positive energy in the clean, bright waiting room. As in all DCS offices we visited, the offices themselves are used by various officers, since so much of their time is spent in the field. We casually appropriated one.

Melanie Barker is basketball tall, with an athlete's build. The daughter of teachers, she decided early that teaching wasn't for her, although social services were. Her interest in reentry was of long standing. In college, for a project she wrote a practice grant application for funds to reduce recidivism.

Before joining the PRI project, she worked in workforce development, especially with fathers and child support, and then in DFACS. As a mother herself, she found working with vulnerable children too trying. "I couldn't separate myself from the cases." Also, as she said several times, "Children have no choice. With adults, they can choose, whether they know it or not." She was very interested in how to engage and support that sense of choice and agency.

Of the various jobs we learned about, hers felt like one of the loneliest, although it obviously gave her great satisfaction. She was rarely at the Macon DCS officer unless she was meeting with their PRI community coordinator. Barker was assigned to work inside three prisons, each with a distinctive character. Pulaski, one of the two main female prisons in Georgia, had large mental health and sex offender populations, but also fairly extensive programming. Central, a large male medium-security prison in Macon, with open style buildings for the main population and also sex offender and mental health camps, had a garment factory and a Braille transcription program. Montgomery was a small work camp "in the middle of nowhere" where male inmates worked at a poultry farm or upholstery company, and also did work for local governments. Central, because of its proximity, served as her "home" base. Although she usually had a corner she could claim at the various prisons, most of her work, she said, was done at her own dining room table. Overall, she had 130 cases, although the goal was 100. Most of her cases were at Pulaski, which she tried to visit once a week as she did Macon.

Barker had a clear definition of success: To have someone she had worked with have a reentry plan in place when they left prison—and seem hopeful, grateful and motivated. Her work with these high-risk individuals began a year earlier when she identified them through the Scribe program as having a risk score of 5 or more on the Next Generation Assessment they were given when they entered prison. The parameters of risk she used were age, arrest history, mental health, drug use, and trauma, all of which increased the risk of reoffending, balanced sometimes by more protective factors like education, employment, and peer-family influences. She then gave these individuals an orientation to her program and how she might help them. Often the first response was negative: *At first, when we share the risk assessment, they think we are not being nice, that we are predicting their failure. I like being able to explain to them that we're there to help them bridge the gaps. But trying to get rid of the stigma is hard.*

She laughed at the almost byzantine descriptions originally developed for what is called TAP 3. Although now reduced from twenty pages to three, it was still baffling to most people. She preferred to draw a simple diagram instead. But the material in the plan was clearly valuable: *This is the point where it all comes to life for me. Here is where we have specific goals: transportation, necessary documents, a place to stay. This document can list appointments someone has when they leave. This document can go with them if they are transferred to another facility, can follow them over to DCS.*

Working in a prison and not being part of the prison staff created a steep learning curve for Barker. At first she didn't realize she would be working in a prison. She had briefly visited prisons when she worked at DFACS on child support and would have to go and get DNA swabs from men. But now she was in the environment for extended periods of time: *At first I was scared, uncomfortable. Very isolated—there was no one else doing my job and everyone else in there was accustomed to prison employment. It was baptism by fire. I had a stereotypical inmate fear just walking through the compound. The guards were apathetic. It didn't look like they were in authority. They were just doing their twelve hours and going home. When I first started, they put me in an open dorm with two hundred men surrounding me and one officer in a control room. Walking back from the dorm with an officer, I dropped my keys and an offender was hollering at me. I thought to myself, "You will have to handle this or leave this job."*

At the encouragement of someone who had been formerly incarcerated, she went to the deputy warden and asked to be situated with the counselors: *It was the same thing with counselors, there was a lot of pushback at first, but now they see that I am making their jobs easier.*

Her comfort increased with her experience: *Very rarely have I had an aggressive interaction. The men are very receptive, respectful. That helped a lot. I do feel it is important to be inside the prisons. Now it is all more balanced since I am working more closely with the community coordinator on the outside. I'm OK where it is now personally. Neither here nor there, a little linked, a lot isolated.*

Given her positioning, Barker didn't feel as if she was an integral part of DCS, in part because this job was created originally through GOTSR when it was a stand alone entity, and also because she was not a community supervision officer and rarely saw or socialized with them. When asked what inspired her, she talked about the inmates she was helping: *I love talking to people, hearing their stories. The greatest reward in my job is bridging the gap between being in and out. This is a forgotten population. People ignore it because they can. People don't get what it is like in prison.*

The general public has <u>no</u> *idea. My friends and family, I will sometimes hear them say, "If the judge had just locked him up." I want to say to them, "Just locking them up doesn't change anything. PRI does." And then explain why. When people ask me about prison, what I tell them is based on their existing opinion. If they think prison is a terrible place, I tell them about the programming, the skills, the workshops. It's certainly not perfect. They are behind bars. If they think prison makes you better, I emphasize that locking people up* <u>doesn't</u> *change people.*

PRI COMMUNITY COORDINATOR: SHARON ALMON

The DeKalb County office felt much less welcoming than the Macon office. Situated near various bus lines, in a complex with different public service agencies, it still felt isolated. The office itself had the fortress feel of what Officer Barkley described as "old probation": People slumped in their chairs. Signs warned you not to eat, not to use a phone. The officers hectored the men they called up, ordering them to remove their hats, not to use their phones, although it was not clear how they should be occupying themselves except staring at their hands. There was no reading material. When ushered into the back offices, what stood out was the weapon detector, the men standing with their hands on the wall being patted down, and the many empty offices. The empty offices were in part because officers were in the field but also because, like the other major urban DCS offices, turnover was a challenge here.

Still, the assistant chief and the chief we talked with were both very open, personable, welcoming, clear about the challenge the merger had created in the sense of losing all of their parole officers within months because of the caseloads. DeKalb is second only to Fulton in the number of people it supervises. The chiefs were clearly delighted to have Sharon Almon working with them.

Warm, elegant, attractive, enthusiastic, Almon is a dynamo—and the skills she brought were much needed. Almon had worked for many years in workforce development, both in Illinois with Catholic Services focusing on single female head of households, with a particular emphasis on increasing their access to education, then for many years in Atlanta with Jewish Family Services, specializing in workforce development for adults and displaced workers, managing large grants and rising to be director of career services.

Almon said that when she came for her DCS interview and walked into a waiting room filled with young African-American men, all between eighteen and thirty years old, the mother in her clicked on. In some ways this surprised her because she was very old school—"lock them up and throw away the key"—about crime. But she was also familiar with the needs of this population and had specific ideas of how to address them and, most importantly, already had the contacts needed to do so. "I knew I could bring people in," she said. "I don't need to know law, I just need to know needs."

Three years into the position, she had built their database of resource providers from nineteen to 170. Her secret: "I never take no for an answer." These providers helped meet the reentry needs identified early in the PRI process: housing, employment, substance abuse, and health care. She had built up an advisory council of twenty-five people who provided contacts and resources in law, public and private workforce development, dental and medical providers, employers, and even a successful ex-offender now engaged in peer reentry counseling, Kevin, whose story we included earlier. She was clear she needed more employers and more landlords.

Almon was adept at bringing in needed services at little cost—and many times bringing service providers directly to the DCS offices for easy access. For example, once a month, a county workforce development van came for a full day with thirty computers that people could use to work on resumes. Employment counseling and soft skills training were also provided. One morning a month, the county health department brought a van that provided blood pressure screenings, and a free ninety days supply of medicine for those who were newly released. They could sign people up for Affordable Care health insurance as well. A dental practice was providing free dental care to twenty-five people a year. Almon also organized job fairs with the three organizations most involved in workforce development, Goodwill, DeKalb Workforce Development, and the Department of Labor. As she said, employment was key because fees began accumulating the moment people left prison. She was interested in identifying employers and kinds of employment that provided a livable wage and a career path.

When Almon showed us her database, she described how, when she received information from one of the prison in-reach specialists about someone returning to the area and what they had identified as immediate needs, she would be able to identify providers for them. In addition, this information was directly available to the DCS officers as well, so they could provide it to the supervisees. Before, field officers were individually responsible for identifying employers and housing providers, so to have someone with real skills in this area assume primary responsibility gave them more time to focus on the other needs of their supervisees.

Although Almon spoke emphatically about the need for a second chance, and seemed indefatigable in her quest to find effective resources to help people reenter, some of her responses reflected an underlying tension between the two functions of community supervision, support and accountability. She had great camaraderie and shared purpose with her coordinating chiefs, past and present. However, it did not appear that she had a great deal of direct interaction with PRI releases themselves. She was careful to have us hide purses before we went on a tour of the DCS offices, and assured us that none of the people under supervision were ever allowed there. She was sure that her officers would protect her should that ever happen. How much this was a reflection of the overall tone of this office, which felt like it hadn't yet made the transition from the fortress mentality of old probation, or of her own fears was not clear. Kevin, now on her advisory council, was the first ex-offender with whom she had had any sustained interaction. She was obviously very impressed by him. However, in many ways a direct knowledge and comfort with the population she is helping is not needed half as much as what she does have: a strong administrative capacity, a thorough knowledge of and access to social welfare institutions and organizations, and an ability to draw in the resources of the more privileged parts of the county. She also has formidable determination. As she said, "I never take no for an answer. I take it as an opportunity."

The reentry resources identified by the PRI are focused primarily on high-risk offenders, and are only for those who are released to supervision, either through parole or probation, but as we have mentioned, some of these activities now have been more broadly adopted through Corrections, particularly the provision of key documents, like birth certificates, Social Security numbers, and drivers licenses, so max outs can also benefit. Almon's community resource database is available to all DCS officers in her office. If a max out were to call her office for support, she was open to sharing referrals.

COMMUNITY-INITIATED PROGRAMS
Savannah & Macon

In terms of sustainability and genuine reentry collaboration at the local level, two programs that we do not discuss at any length here stand out, one in Savannah and one in Macon. The Savannah Impact Program (SIP), started in 2001 and was ended in 2017 due to a serious municipal budget crisis. We visited there for a day in 2015 and found the program impressive in itself and also in its influence on other programs developed across the state. Those Community Impact Programs (CIP) instituted by Probation and Parole, lost something in translation—and it is what they lost that stands out about SIP—the engagement at the local level. SIP, a "community reentry collaborative," was located in and funded by the police department and its purpose was to focus on high-risk and at-risk adults and juveniles.

SIP was not a top-down initiative. It originated in city government with the strong support of the city manager, and its focus quickly expanded to providing the practical reentry support for those at greatest risk of recidivism. This support provided classes but more importantly included creating an employment program that could lead to people being qualified to compete for municipal jobs. The building they worked in had been refinished by their own work crews, allowing the city at large to see how these individuals could contribute. As Lieutenant Ramona Famble, then the director, said: "People can see our guys out there making a difference. We provide skill building, social redefinition, and family engagement." Their efforts also expanded to active prevention with at-risk youth, folding in workforce development and an internship program. The vulnerability of the program was where it was located in the municipal structure—which was under law enforcement. Police, when faced with a serious budget shortfall, felt the program was peripheral to their law-enforcement mission and belonged under social services.

The Macon Reentry Coalition, which has been active since 2007, evolved through informal collaboration by various federal and state probation and social service professionals and non-profits as well as the mayor's office and Department of Labor as they tried to address the reentry needs of the populations they served. As its executive director, Kevin Mason, a federal probation specialist, said, "I got tired of failures. I changed from trying to chase failures to chasing successes. Doing that, my job changed from solely supervision to one trying to provide services and resources. We needed to find those resources." In that search for resources, he found that he was developing a large email list, which then developed into a more formal collaboration. Its strength remains its networking agility, quickly matching needs and resources. Their longevity is helped by having an effective coordinator, funded by federal probation, who is able to organize meetings and facilitate communications between members. What has made both of these coalitions viable for long periods was the level of perceived need in the communities themselves—and a desire to meet it.

\4/

DAY REPORTING CENTERS

We were interested in learning more about people who were having trouble with community supervision, so asked to speak to some of them. This allowed us to learn more about Day Reporting Centers (DRC), one of the graduated series of community-based sentencing alternatives that DCS uses before supervision is permanently revoked. The advantage of the DRCs is that people remain located inside their communities. Participants are able to work if they are employed. Most of the people who are assigned have problems with substance abuse and are non-compliant with the terms of their supervision. The program lasts between a year and a year and a half and has three steps: Six months of detox/behavior stabilization, six months sobriety/employment, then six months of aftercare. We spent time talking with participants in Atlanta, then, some years later, visited a rural DRC in LaFayette for comparison, where we talked with a counselor about the course sequence and attended one of the cognitive change classes.

OFFICERS' PERSPECTIVES

Katrinka Glass—DRC Origins

Katrinka Glass, a longtime officer at Parole, was the director of the first pilot DRC, established in the 1990s in Atlanta and then went on to help establish centers around the state. After that, until her retirement in 2013, Glass directed Risk Reduction Services within the Department of Corrections, which provided similar substance abuse and cognitive change programming to incarcerated men in the years immediately preceding their reentry.

The idea for the centers came from then executive director of Parole, Beth Oxford, and George Braucht, the parole officer and licensed professional counselor who has been active both within the supervision community and beyond it in the area of substance abuse counseling and credentialed therapeutic housing for those leaving prison with addiction problems. Glass said she felt she was chosen to be the director for the Atlanta center because she was known as an officer who could work effectively with both Parole and

Corrections, whose administrations were often antagonistic.

What Glass found so positive about the DRCs was that they were able to really integrate treatment and supervision: *As part of our research we looked at other day reporting centers across the country. The difference in what we did here was that supervision, the law and order part, and the programming were under the same roof and we held hands. It was very very integrated. I can remember when I was in parole as an officer and we would send people to drug treatment, but the communication was terrible. Officers had to go once or twice a week themselves to be able to monitor attendance and drug use. But when we brought officers and counselors in the same house, it was magic. It was wonderful. Counselors were doing drug tests. Officers were teaching classes. Everybody was cross-trained.*

We would sit down and eat lunch and there was nothing I didn't know about you, that the officer didn't know, that the counselor didn't know. So there was no game playing. When you had an intervention or hearing, the counselor and the officer were both there. You could do good in one area and terrible in the other area and that's OK as long as those areas are talking to each other. You could say, "Well, he's been good in class, passing his drug tests." "Well, I went by his house last night and there was this six-pack by his chair." Or the counselor doesn't know his wife left him, or he's not living at that house, or he has a girl.

Glass emphasized the expanding levels of social trust that evolved at both the institutional and community levels. They received help from the state Department of Labor and Atlanta public schools. Community organizations also stepped up: *We needed help with MARTA passes so people could get to class. I went to someone from the NAACP in DeKalb for the tokens. She wasn't even in our county. She said, "We'll help, but we want to see what the real deal is. We're going to talk with these guys. I'm going to get the real story while I'm over here." She would come and sit in classes. And they loved it, and we had the best relationship with them. She helped with graduations in her personal church. So community is responsive if you go about it the right way. I never asked for help that I didn't get it eventually.*

An even more important level of social trust was the one they were able to build up with families of the men and women assigned to the DRC: *You have to have transparency. You could not believe the difference once we brought the family in. They could see the entire operation; they could ask anything they wanted to. They stopped looking at us like, "Oh, you locked my son up" to "Oh, you better listen to her." It was almost like we were an ally, not an adversary. Once you got that buy-in from the family, family was there all the time.*

Glass describe the changes that working in this kind of setting made in her own views of offenders: *I began my career as a police officer. I was very black and white. My mother had been a binge drinker but had never been in trouble with the law or anything. I didn't associate my mother with that element. When I finally got off the street, got out of uniform, I just assumed that when somebody went to prison, the whole family was just bad. That there were problems with the entire family. I am a little embarrassed to admit this, but I was stunned when I saw the number of very decent families that had family members in prison. I didn't know anything about drug treatment or alcoholism.*

I went to trainings and took classes. I wanted to be in the know with what my officers were doing. It totally changed my whole paradigm. It was seismic. I started looking at people individually and I was thankful I didn't have those problems myself.

I loved working at the DRC. I guess I screwed that up so bad they sent me downtown to do the entire state!

ROBERT WILKERSON—RURAL DRC

The DRC in LaFayette is a pleasant white building with several large meeting rooms and small offices for the four counselors responsible for sixty-four program participants. Robert Wilkerson was a relatively new counselor at the LaFayette Day Reporting Center. His background was in adult education. He had moved to Georgia a year earlier from Missouri. He grew up in a small town where the prison had been the major employer. He had spent much of his career working with 4-H developing and implementing an interesting program that focused on the children of the incarcerated, who can be highly isolated by stigma as well as by the absence of their parent. They brought 4H classes into the visiting rooms of prisons, focusing on improving parenting and leadership skills in inmates, then included the children in 4H programs outside, with the intention of increasing their integration in the larger communities. He helped plant these programs in several other states, in state, juvenile and federal prisons as well as jails.

Wilkerson was still getting used to the content and extent of his workload at the DRC, so could ably describe the syllabus of the highly intensive Phase I, which was focused on detox and behavior stabilization. This involved four hours of classes Monday through Friday. Classes included Motivation for Change; Moral Reconation Therapy (MRT); a parenting class; a recovery skills program (Matrix); a Department of Labor class that covered resume writing, job search and interview skills; a course on life skills; counseling with a significant family member; forty hours of community service; and thirty consecutive days of clean drug screens. Phase II, focused on relapse prevention, included Matrix, and MRT classes, staying clean for sixty days, and completing the rest of your community service. He observed that many people came in having been told the program was terrible and that it set you up to fail, but after a few weeks settled into it.

Some people were there because they didn't want to go into a residential substance abuse treatment program. Trying to get clean and stay clean in place added the challenge of changing established social habits and companions at the same time that you were changing your addictive behaviors and thinking. On the other hand, if one were able to make all these changes, the chance of being able to sustain sobriety in the long haul was higher.

In the Moral Reconation Therapy class of twenty-five that we visited, five participants had come from prison, twenty were probationers. The youth and high spirits of the participants were striking. Most were in their early to mid-twenties. They were reporting on their progress on their current step in their moral development workbook. Several of the young women had relapsed in the past week, but when asked if they were sure they wouldn't relapse again, said they were 100% sure that they wouldn't, although they did not necessarily share any steps they were taking to address the reasons for the relapse. Their good intentions, and their level of confidence in it, were heartily supported by their peers. The older men in the class, who had already taken the course several times, were more restrained in their enthusiasm.

Kinetta Hamilton—Urban DRC

The Atlanta DRC is now located in the attractive new DCS offices, but when we visited, it was located in the grim Sylvan Road facility. Officer Kinetta Hamilton, a DCS officer who worked with the Atlanta DRC introduced us to three men under supervision who were currently assigned to the DRC, each with a rather different story. Each of them was on parole. Before our meeting with them, Hamilton described the purpose and value of the DRC programming and also her own approach to supervision: *The people we're taking you to see at the Day Reporting Center are people having problems with substance abuse. We like to send them there because they also learn some life-changing skills. Some are working, some have families. The reasons they give for using are often that they're stressed—by their work, their families, sometimes by parole. You'll hear some say they don't have a problem, it was just a one-time thing.*

The problem with a lot of our offenders is their thought process is like it was before they were arrested or locked up. Some have been incarcerated so long their thought process is in prison. So we put them in this program to help their thought process so they can get out of the, "Well I'm a convicted felon and I can't get a job." Yes you can. We have a lot of people on parole and a lot of them are employed—with very good jobs. Once we get them out of their negativity, then we can work to get them where they need to be.

Hamilton had been a parole officer for three years, before that she worked as a juvenile correctional officer. She found the transition fairly easy: *I had to get used to not being in an enclosed environment. Going onto their turf was different. Not uncomfortable, different. I personally always go to every house as if it is the first time, whether I have been there fifty times. That keeps me from being comfortable, because in this job you never want to get comfortable because you never know what these people have up their sleeve. You never know what happened the night before. That's how I operate. It just keeps me on my toes.*

Her vigilance made her aware of vigilance in others and may have added to her awareness of the importance of building, rather than assuming, trust. She talked about how she went about assessing the possibly traumatic impact of incarceration on some of the men she worked with, an issue she didn't think should be taken on directly: *You do have some people that will discuss what they witnessed in prison, but for the most part, because most of them are so guarded and have trust issues, it may take some time to open up. We have people who never open up and people who open up from day one. It's really about trust and I've noticed a lot of them have trust issues so a lot of that information is harder to get out of them. That's why I take the conversational route. That's why I like to talk with the family because you'll get a lot of information out of the family versus the offender, and the family kind of gives you insight on how they were before, some of their triggers. Things we wouldn't get from the offender. But because we have the family on our side, it kind of helps us to know the person.*

Hamilton felt that the most important determinant of successful reentry was family support: *I always try to encourage family support. When I go to a house for the first time, I try to interact with everybody. I want the family on the same page because I feel if you have the family behind you, you're more willing to put in the work. Everyone I've seen who has been positive, they had their family behind them. They didn't have a pity party, and that is what we see a lot in parole. But you have been given a second chance and you need to take it. People who have been successful didn't do that. They asked, "What do I need to do? What can I do not to end up back in prison?"*

One of the biggest things that I witness with males are kids. "I don't want my kids to see me back in prison." "My kids are young and I need to be here for my kids." I've had people tell me that they have sons going into their teens and always into things, going down the wrong path, and they didn't want them to keep on that way. But it was one of those things where you can't do what I say unless I'm willing to do it too. When I saw their kids were their motivation, I would use it as well. It was a reminder, "You said you wanted to do this for your kids—Let me remind you that your kids need you."

This emphasis on family is one she carried into her interactions with the people on her caseload as well: *When it comes to my caseload, I treat everyone the same because it could be one of my family members. Everyone has family members who have been in and out of jail. I didn't know anyone who had been in as long as the people I deal with. It was usually like county jail, so something minor. So, I treat everyone with respect. I talk with them. Its not so much a question and answer session as a conversation, because I feel you get more out of them if it is a conversation.*

PARTICIPANTS' PERSPECTIVES

DEANIE

Each of the men we talked with posed a different challenge for supervision. The oldest, Deanie, was in his fifties. He was small, soft-spoken, amenable in a way that didn't necessarily build confidence. He had been in prison six times since he was seventeen, beginning in 1982, when he served three years for robbery. His other five incarcerations had been for cocaine and marijuana, and ranged in length of time from a year to four years. His latest incarceration, which had ended in 2014, was for 42 months, with five years of parole to follow. When he talked with us, he had been on parole for two years. He felt his sentences were fair. "Honestly, I do. I was never convicted of a crime I didn't do, and the times were proportionate. I understood the consequences."

He saw a difference in parole since he first went on it in 1985: *Then, you mess up, you go back. There was a change in attitude in parole beginning in my forties. They are not focusing on trying to incarcerate. Now, you mess up, they say,*

"We'll give you another chance." Maybe it is because of the over-crowding.

He felt Hamilton was a good officer: *She's doing her job and being concerned with your welfare as well. I never had a parole officer who was unfair. Am I discouraged by going back to prison so often? Slightly. It depends on how much you put into keeping yourself out.*

Deanie was knowledgeable about the various programs designed to help returning offenders, and felt parole should know about them and tell people about them, for example, federal bonding programs and record expungement. There was a program that put you in a class for four weeks then put you on a job.

He himself had had great jobs in his life, often with benefits, Mainly working forklifts in warehouses and on construction sites in Atlanta and down at Forsyth. "There are opportunities to get that job. Go in with an open mind, be a people person and a hard worker. Be on time and stay late." These were work habits learned from his parents. "My mother and father were hard workers. My mother had one job for forty years; she just retired. My father was the same way."

When he was in prison this last time, he worked constantly as a fork lift operator in a warehouse in prison industries. "I have never held a job that long." Now his job situation wasn't as good: *I don't have a job now. I had one, but it wasn't permanent. It ran out. I wound up slacking on the job. But if I had kept on—now I'm struggling. You never know when you will get work. It is frustrating. The bills are piling up. It can make you lose focus. I am able to tough it out—but only for a minute.*

In prison he also received programming. He was placed in a residential substance abuse treatment program, took Motivation for Change, and a reentry course that taught him about job applications, interviews, and resumes. "People in prison lose touch with the real world. They need help with things like the latest phones."

He appreciated that the DRC program kept him occupied. It gave him structure, and helped him learn more about his actions and his attitudes. He had just come back into the program, having stopped coming several months before "for my own reasons." If revoked, he figured he could go back to prison for ten years, "But I'm not worried. I don't have the mindset. That life is in the past." For one thing, people cared about his staying out. His daughter, who was twenty-two, wanted him to stay out. He was the only one in his family, close or extended, who had been to prison. He had friends who had gone to prison, but usually only once or twice. "I know very few who have been bouncing around in and out."

Deanie was assigned to this program for a year, 8:30 to 4:30, with a 7 to 7 curfew. He also had to pass his drug screens. That was why he was in the DRC now: he hadn't. Again, though, he asserted that there was no problem: *I'm not afraid of being revoked. The path I'm going now is straight and narrow. I have gone as long as three or four years without using. I can do it. I will do it. It goes back to the will to change. There were things before I wasn't willing to give up. But you get to fifty and you just get tired. My stomach can't tolerate it any more. It helps to take a look in the mirror. There are very few years left. That kicks in. The mind thing, it goes in and out. Just being in for all those years. Trust plays a role too. You have so many people who believes in you and you have let down so many times. If they don't see me, they assume I am incarcerated again. When you have those boring moments, you have this idea of being around people drinking and smoking. It's possible to have a good time without doing those things.*

Deanie concluded, a little plaintively, "But I like NA/AA. I enjoy talking with people about my experience. . . " A condition of the DRC drug treatment program was that it forbid talking about past use or glamorizing drug use—a constraint he clearly found taxing.

NAPOLEON

Napoleon was twenty-five. He had come out of prison a month before and was immediately assigned by Hamilton to the DRC. This was his first prison sentence. He was convicted of residential burglary and sentenced to twenty years, serve five. He has spent ten months in the county jail, then four years in Telfair, one of the toughest prisons in the state. He didn't feel that the sentence was fair because it was his first time, he had had a clean record. However, he had refused to take a first offender plea because if he messed up, he could be charged again under the same sentence. He was now on parole for eight months, then would begin his fifteen years on probation. All the men in his family, father and brothers, were on probation. He was the only one who had gone to prison.

He didn't think the parole sentence was unfair and wouldn't mind the probation sentence if he could have Hamilton as his officer because "She's OK. She works with me."

The terms of his parole were that he had a 6 to 6 curfew, he couldn't fail his drug tests, he had to report to the DRC from 8 to 12, then he worked at a warehouse from 2:30 to 11:00. He appreciated that Hamilton had been flexible with the curfew to allow him to work, which he had been doing since he was released. "She just said bring the schedule and changed my curfew." He saw the DRC program as a waste of time. "I have no drug charge. I have no drug problem." He was tested within thirty days of release and thinks they found traces from prison use. He had thirteen months more in the DRC program.

Napolean was resentful but compliant. He had already taken all the classes in prison: *They want me to be in this class because I had a dirty urine. I can't afford not to because I don't want to be revoked. I won't stay out after curfew. I will make sure I'm not around people with drugs or guns.*

He lived with his mother and sisters and felt he had good family support: "They want me to stay out." However, they expected him to help pay the bills. "That's killing me, paying the power bill." His brother at that time was in the Probation Detention Center for sixty days. His brother was a first offender and had a ten-year sentence.

He felt the terms of his parole were fair, except the 6 p.m. curfew and the way they called at crazy times like 3 a.m., using voice recognition technology, to make sure he was there. He did understand that the consequences of not meeting the parole conditions was going back to prison and he didn't want to go back.

He was eager to finish parole and get onto probation because probation would only return you to prison if you caught another felony charge and he was sure he could avoid that. For other probation infractions, "They'll only give you eight to fourteen days in the county jail. I've been on probation lots of time. It's not going to be a problem." Even if he were revoked on parole, it could only be for eight months—and he could do that as well, but it was possible to keep out of trouble if he stayed with his girlfriend and away from his homeboys.

Napoleon knew many people who had been incarcerated. Indeed, it was probably more difficult for him to name people who hadn't been: *Except for my mama and sisters, they the only ones who's never been. My dad just got off probation. My brother got off. My dad is in and out of jail. Of all my friends who went to prison, they all went back. I'm trying to be different. I don't want to go back. All my friends have felonies. So until I'm off parole, I have to keep away from them or I'll go straight back to prison.*

One reason that Napoleon resented being assigned to the DRC was that he had already been put in a Residential Substance Abuse Treatment program while in prison, had taken the Motivation for Change and Early Recovery Skills programs. Smoking all the time? we asked. Yes, he agreed, but it wasn't a problem.

The threat of being returned to Telfair Prison was truly aversive, but to release the aggression he had used to survive there was also difficult: *Telfair was a closed prison. People there had a lot of time. Everyone had knives. I been like that for four years. I'm only out a month. After prison, you need to let go of attitude: "Around a wolf, be a wolf. Around a sheep, be a sheep." I will defend myself if I need to. I'm still waiting to see what your next move going to be.*

What his attitude now should be wasn't so clear to him. He had changed with prison, and his friends had changed with age: *We not like teenagers. I was thinking it be like it was when I left, but now everyone married with kids. Still smoking and drinking, but all the stealing and robbing, not doing that anymore. When we was fifteen to nineteen we was doing it all the time.*

Napoleon did have goals for himself. He wanted to better himself, earn money, get his barber's license, finish his GED. He thought his participation in the DRC program would prevent him from doing this. But Hamilton was very clear that Napoleon needed the DRC, for his emotional and moral development as much as his drug dependency: *He is one of those people who never thinks he's doing anything wrong. He doesn't get that it is against the law. His drug use is the issue. And he feels that because he's not hurting anybody and its not a crime against anybody else, that it's OK. And we try to get him to realize there are victims in this—like family because you have to continue to go through programs like this and you continue to run the risk of going to jail. He doesn't get it.*

He tries to talk around it. What we try to do as officers is show him another side to it because he's like a lot of offenders: they have a one-track mind to where they only see it through their eyes. So we try to show it through the eyes of their children, or through the eyes of their spouses, or their moms. Once they realize that other people have to deal with this, sometimes they take it more serious. But some are harder to get to than others.

My thing is he's trying to do whatever he can to get out of the program and I think he needs to successfully complete the program to be able to successfully do anything he wants to do outside of it. Being in this program it is possible for him to get his GED and go to barbering school. If he chooses to work and not go to school, that's on him. But I'm not going to allow him to go out. If he doesn't complete the program, he won't complete barbering school; he'll just go back to doing what he was doing. When we put people in the DRC program, often they see it as a punishment. We give them the information we have on it, but a lot of time they don't want to listen. If he had listened, he would know he's going to be better off as a person. He'll have more tools on his belt.

But he makes a lot of excuses. Once he realizes that instead of making excuses he can do something to change his situation, everything will fall into place for him. He just has to want it. I can't want it for him. That's why you were getting the answers you were.

MARCUS

Marcus's story has stayed with us because it combines the complexities of early incarceration, addiction, complex trauma, and institutional errors. What makes his story poignant is the potential lost. We have no real idea what would shift the balances here, what would allow him to fully commit to change. Clearly there were real systems failures that made if more difficult for Marcus to trust that anyone in the criminal justice system has his constructive reintegration as a genuine goal. There were also actions, resistances, interpretations on Marcus's side that make him a headache, most obviously his chronic, stubborn and intentional marijuana use.

Marcus was incarcerated for eleven years, from the time he was eighteen, for armed robbery. He was released on parole in 2010, so had been out five years when we talked with him, with two technical revocations to a probation detention center. Time warped frequently in his account of his life and experiences. What is hard to capture in any linear account is the intimate weaving back and forth of causation, consequence. It is easy to miss Marcus's growing edge, those poignant, half-buried, crucial possibilities.

Marcus had a clear grievance that he wanted heard. Hamilton had chosen him to speak with us for that reason: *I thought he'd have more to say than the others. He wants someone to play the sympathy card with him. When I say sympathy, I don't mean feeling sorry for him, but that he needs his officer to understand, almost a "put yourself in my shoes" kind of deal.*

But, as Marcus had observed, he wasn't going to get that at parole: "They all tired of me over at parole." Hamilton shook her head at the suggestion that with her understanding of Marcus, perhaps she would be a more effective officer for him: *He's a headache. He has trust issues. He feels like everyone is going to do what the previous person did. It's hard to deal with somebody that has that mindset because you feel like everyone is against you. He won't talk to his officer in a manner where it will benefit him. He just needs to sit down and talk with his officer.*

At that point, Marcus had had so many officers, it was difficult to pinpoint which one might be at issue. Hamilton seemed to agree that Marcus might have a point: *Sometimes for us as officers, its harder because we're not in positions where we've ever lost anything. We don't have kids we've lost contact with, we haven't had to start over. We're not trying to be in a situation where we don't care. You have some officers that might not be able to sympathize because they just don't know the feeling.*

But Hamilton was open to some suggested programmatic supports for Marcus, for example readmission into the Fatherhood Project: *If that is something that is going to help him, I'll do it. We can try. I'm one of those who if it is going to put you in the right direction, I'll push you even if it will take you out of your comfort zone a little bit. You can't be afraid to change for the better.*

Marcus's Grievance

"You got to be the stupidest parolee in the world," his parole officer had exclaimed when Marcus reported to him after a long absence—and tested dirty, again, for marijuana. *You know how they talk.* "You got to be the stupidest such and such and such and such. . ." *I couldn't say nothing because you can't say nuttin. They'll put you in the situation where they want you to say something so they can lock you up, but I ain't never had nothing to say. But it came to me, I just had to tell him,* "You sent me to jail for nothing. You had me sign a waiver because you went and looked at the paperwork and you felt you knew I did it. Now it's a year and a half later and I just showed you I was found not guilty by a jury." *He was wrong.*

Dirty urine or not, Marcus wanted some acknowledgement of the personal cost of that false identification and false charge—not only on the part of his parole officer but also on the part of the police, DA, and judge.

This is how Marcus explained his grievance, which he returned to several times in our conversation, the recitations having the vivid but rote quality of a trauma narrative: *I went with someone and they mistake us for someone who had committed a theft somewhere. I went to trial two months ago. They went and seen on tape that I wasn't the person Clayton County was looking for. But I went and did eight months on that thing.*

Parole said they didn't care. It was the fact I was incarcerated and I had that charge. I think that should change about parole because I ain't even able to sue and I lost a lot of money on this. Everything I built on with my son, my house around the corner, I lost in those eight months and I'm still down from it now.

I'm thinking, if you're supposed to help somebody, why you giving them a waiver to go back to prison because in your mind they did it. That's what my parole officer told me, "You did it."

"No, I didn't do it."

"Well, sign this six-months waiver anyway because you shouldn't have got arrested."

I did two months in Clayton jail waiting on a bed and then six months in all on the parole violation. After I got back from doing my eight months, I had to come home and go back to trial every month to Clayton County jail courtroom. I had to keep hearing the lies they were telling about me and their telling me, "Go ahead and take the year they're trying to give you."

And I just did a year! Why would I do that when I know I didn't do this crime?

And I had to spend $60 a day going there and coming back because there was no MARTA bus. $30 going there and $30 coming back.

And my own public defender and the judge were lying to me and telling me to take time for something I didn't do. They had to go and see at the jury trial that it wasn't me. Jury could see it right away from the video.

It was a lot on my shoulder. I'm not able to sue nobody because I don't have the money to get a lawyer. I feel I should be able to get back what I lost from doing time in jail. So, like that's a problem. I lost my apartment and my car. So when I got out I didn't have nothing anymore. I just got out to nothing. And it started stressing me. So I started back doing marijuana. I can't get my old job back and I started smoking weed when I was bored. Not to sit here telling you no lie.

Right after that my parole officer came to me and said, "You dirty. You going to jail." But see, I went and did a couple days in jail. And now I came back because I was dirty again. So now I'm here at the Day Reporting Center.

Marcus had been earning good money roofing and barbering before these setbacks. He felt that he lost more than employment or confidence in the justice system—he'd lost much of his personal support system as well: "The only people who haven't given up on me are me, my son, and my wife."

FAIRNESS & INSTITUTIONAL TRUST

Marcus's keen sense of injustice about the latest charge against him differed markedly from his thinking about the relative fairness of the charges that originally sent him to prison. He went to prison for armed robbery. His five-year probation to follow was for aggravated assault. Marcus felt both his parole and probation sentences were fair because the alternative in each case would be more prison time and anything was better than that. However, he mused on the relative fairness of the armed robbery charge: *If everyone else getting the same time for robbery, I guess it's fair. I never had a gun in none of those situations. I guess it was a brick. Or a BB gun. I never meant to go kill nobody or hurt nobody. But how the law set up, I'm no different from no one else. But looking at the* <u>nature</u> *of the crime, it wasn't fair. I think you should be sentenced by the nature of the crime. Someone should look into the case and see what really happened. I mean did he try to kill someone? Was it over $2? I think one of my case was about like $2. I hit a guy with a brick. He stay in my neighborhood. DA made it armed robbery. I thought it was more like reckless conduct. We were out gambling, throwing dice, whatever. That dude, I hit him with a brick and for that it was armed robbery. Ten years.*

The probation was actually for me hitting the dude with the brick, so that's the five years. It's fair because I could be doing five years in prison. As far as the armed robbery part. . . . They say I took money from the dude, but I never went nowhere that night. There was a big fight, but me and him, we waited on the police to come. He said he was going to call the police and I said I don't care. I ain't think it was going to be armed robbery because when you going to rob someone, if it was going to be armed robbery, you go with the intention you going to take their money and I ain't went with intentions like that. I thought it should have been reckless conduct because we was all out drinking and such.

When asked if he felt he would have any trouble with the man he attacked, since they both lived in the same part of South Fulton, he said immediately, "No, I'll walk the other way." When asked if he would like to make amends to the person he attacked, he said without self-consciousness: *I did. Same day of my trial. I was in a small holding tank and he in another little holding tank. I told him, "G, I'm sorry. Don't do it." I was trying to get him not to go in and give his testimony. But he was only mad because of his head because I hit him on his head with a brick.*

Marcus was also clear that he would not engage again in the behaviors that led to his criminal conviction and imprisonment: *I think my choices came from trying to be slick. I always analyzed it and always thought it was me trying to be slick. Trying to pull things off. But that right there was the big no no. I be looking at ten years—*

He said firmly, *I been done changed those behaviors. I never ever in my life* *thought about trying to rob another person. Or <u>looked</u> at another person like I wanted what he had. So I have <u>changed</u>. For real.*

FAMILY SUPPORT

His father, who was not there when Marcus was growing up, was a support for the years when he was in prison, providing money for his prison account. But his father did not support him as he fought these new charges and Marcus felt that absence keenly: *I felt like he betrayed me when I was just in jail on that recent charge because everybody kept saying "He keep going back to jail." or "He did it and such and such." So nobody want to pay my bond, which was $240. A friend of mine ended up doing it. So I just haven't spoke to my father since then because I felt like none of them believe in me. Like none of them done went to trial with me when I went to choose my jury trial. I felt like he let his guard down on me. You know how you give up on somebody.*

Even though his mother did come to his trial, Marcus didn't necessarily feel she was a support: *Now, I ain't going to say my momma give up on me but I look at it like that cause I don't bring no drama her way.* This is not purely protective of his mother, but also of himself, which he acknowledged: *That's another reason I don't have a good relationship with her, you know, because—well, I want to patch it up because I'm in this program—but when I was smoking weed and drinking a lot, I tried to stay away from her and protect her from looking at me in a certain way. Unhuh, judging, like yeah—like when I couldn't get no job, and she look at me like, "You don't <u>want</u> no job"-but I can't <u>get</u> no job. So I'm going to stay away from you, momma, so we won't have no problems like that.*

Marcus laughed at his reasoning. Although it did throw doubt on his claims that his marijuana use was simply because of the very real stress he felt at a wrongful charge, it also revealed how much Marcus felt the loss of the positive regard, and more importantly, the *hope* of his parents, however reliable—or unreliable—they had been in his life.

DRUG ADDICTION - PAROLE SUPERVISION

Marcus was less clear about his willingness or ability to stop the drug use, which was not part of his criminal conviction, but was now threatening his parole status. Marcus acknowledged that he had a problem with substance abuse: *Because I couldn't stop when they told me to stop.* But he claimed that before the recent challenges, he had it under control. *I was maintaining. I was staying under the radar. There was nobody know about me. I wasn't giving him no problems—*

Staying under the radar was a very important principle for Marcus.

From the beginning of his time on parole, Marcus tried to keep his distance from them: *I will say this, I never went parole way. I won't say they never gave any help, I never seek any help from parole. For one, I was using marijuana. If you using, parole the last people you want to be around. You just want to like live your life and get away from them. Because you don't feel you need no help. And you want to keep on getting high, whatever you using. I use marijuana. Let's say I'm scared to call in each month because I'm scared he will say, come on in and take a drug test. But not calling in, that's trouble by itself—*

This wasn't actually the first time Marcus had been at the Day Reporting Center he revealed as we were talking about ways that he might "rehab himself" since he felt that no program could do so. Sent there some years earlier in his parole, again for marijuana use, he was assigned to the Fatherhood Project. However, both the Fatherhood Project and the Day Reporting Center required that he be clean, which he wouldn't—or couldn't—do: *I didn't want to stop smoking marijuana or abide by the parole laws, so I just left. I let the police come git me whenever they come git me.* Marcus felt it was more efficient to do six months in a detention center than a year of counseling. *I did six months and I came home and I didn't have to worry about anybody worrying about me anymore. I flew under the radar, smoked weed, do what I wanted to do.*

COMPLEX TRAUMA

Being left alone was important to Marcus. Not returning to prison was too. The cost of staying out now was being clean and Marcus wanted to—but he couldn't guarantee it because sometimes his mind did things: *It's just things can go wrong in your own head sometimes that will make you disregard not using. And that's what happen to me and that's the reason why I'm in trouble now. I couldn't shake what was in my head, you know. I came up through a lot coming up as a kid, you know. I still be having—you know there be summat that be coming up, summat that's buried up under the surface, you know. I went through a lot as a four-year old, probably as a three-year old, you see what I'm saying.*

When asked what kinds of things he experienced, he went on: *Like watching my mother get beat. By my father. Him beating me. Beating me in the face with an extension cord. Like stuff was in the newspaper. Like I had to leave him and maybe go to a foster home for like two years. I had to leave them because my mother wouldn't leave him and they said either I would have to be there and he would have to go, so they chose to put me there. So I went through that and my grandmother had to come and get me and I had to stay with her. Like I broke up with them for a long time because DFACS say I couldn't go there. A dude try to hit me with an axe at a young age. My step—that somebody my momma chose to have, you see what I'm saying. In and out of juvenile—*

In addition, the program brought up some of the traumatic dimensions of incarceration itself. When asked if he might think about attending a support group of ex-offenders, Marcus said: *I already told you I don't deal with many people out here. When you been locked up as long as me, your circle is limited. I don't even know how to deal with the big group I'm with here. I don't even know how to connect, you know, for real with nobody. Like my momma. I love these people but I done did so much time away from them, it's like I don't even go see her like I supposed to, like a mother—you know, a son supposed to. I just don't connect good. Because I'm so used to being like in a one-man cell. I been in a one-man cell as long as I been out of prison, you see I'm saying.*

When asked if he felt safer in a one-man cell, he thought we were referring to prison: *It will never feel safe. I don't know why they tell you that. People come in you room whenever. Officers will let em in and do something to you the same way they can out here on the street. I never felt safe.*

When asked if he felt safe now, he said: *I always feel safe on my own. I'm a loner, we can just say that. Say I won't be doing nothing to anyone out here and—never think about doing anything. The only thing I be doing is the marijuana.*

Marcus knew that he must get through this program if he was to help his wife and child, but he also realized it separated him further from his extended family: *I stay away from them for the most part. Not my mother, but my other family. They do a lot of weed. I stay away from them. Plus I work a lot.*

Besides posing the temptation of marijuana use, Marcus's family also was unable to give him any clear models of people successfully completing parole. His two brothers had both been to prison but were out now. *Everyone I know, they go back to jail. They never stay out. They come out on parole and some kind of way they be back in. They like me I guess.*

COMPETENCE & GROWING EDGE

We agreed that Marcus might have to be his family's first parole success. This was not as far-fetched as it might seem because self-reliance was an obvious value and a source of pride for Marcus. For all his self-doubt and reticent presentation, Marcus had a strong sense of confidence about his ability to support himself, which he began to do at seventeen. "I do multiple," he said proudly. "I can do anything. Cleaning. Roofing." Learning how to barber in prison, he eventually provided haircuts for prison staff. He was also trained in roofing at Coffee Correction Center. While at the Day Reporting Center he was working demolition in the evening because he could combine it with his programs.

He also wanted to be there for his son and wife. He knew they wanted him to succeed. He and his wife had just learned that she had diabetes and an enlarged heart. *So it's like, whew, I wish I could get rich some day so she don't have to worry about it.*

When we asked Marcus what he was giving back to his own family now that he was out, he said: *Being there. Ain't nothing like just being there. See my little boy just three years old. Me and his mother the same age and whenever I go and get locked up it's hard on her, hard on her. But when I'm there, it's instant comfort. And I like watching my little boy grow. I've been enjoying watching him grow.*

INSTANT COMFORT . . . For Marcus to know himself in this way was no small thing. It may be where we all need to begin. Again.

SOURCES

GEORGIA REPORTS
Georgia Criminal Justice Reform Council Reports. 2011-2018.
Georgia Department of Community Supervision. *Annual Reports.* 2015-2019.
Georgia Department of Corrections. *Justice Reinvestment in Public Safety.* 2011.

SUPERVISION PRACTICE
Carter, M.M., R. J. Sankovitz. *Dosage Probation: Rethinking the Structure of Probation Sentences.* National Institute of Corrections. January 2014. Georgia Department of Community Supervision: Types of Offender Supervision.
Crime & Justice Institute, National Institute of Corrections. "Implementing Evidence-Based Practice in Community Corrections: The Principles of Effective Intervention," 30 Apr 2004.
Lloyd, C.D. and R.C. Serin. "Agency and outcome expectancies for crime desistance: measuring offenders' personal beliefs about change," *Psychology, Crime & Law.* 18, 6 (2012): 543-565.
Nail, M. "Overview of Georgia Reentry and Creation of the Department of Community Supervision," National Conference of State Legislators, *Legislative Summit,* Boston, MA, 7 Aug 2017.
Rempel, M. "Evidence-Based Strategies for Working with Offenders," Center for Court Innovations. Bureau of Justice Assistance, U.S. Department of Justice. April, 2014.
Serin, R.C., C.D. Lloyd, L.J.Hanby. "Enhancing Offender Re-Entry: An integrated model for enhancing offender re-entry. *European Journal of Probation.* 2, 2 (2010): 53-75.

COMMUNITY CORRECTIONS REFORM
Lutze, F.E., et al. "The Future of Community Corrections Is Now: Stop Dreaming and Take Action" *Journal of Contemporary Criminal Justice.* 28, 1 (2012): 42-59.

Pew Charitable Trusts:
> *Probation and Parole Systems Marked by High Stakes, Missed Opportunities.* 2018.
>
> *MAX OUT: The Rise in Prison Inmates Released Without Supervision.* 2014.
>
> *One in 31: The Long Reach of American Corrections.* 2009.
>
> *Putting Public Safety First: 13 Strategies for Successful Supervision and Reentry.* 2008.

Harvard Executive Sessions:
> Still, W., B. Broderick, S. Raphael, "Building Trust and Legitimacy Within Community Corrections." 2017.
>
> "Toward an Approach to Community Corrections for the 21st Century: Consensus Document of the Executive Session on Community Corrections." 2017.

Exit: Executives Transforming Probation and Parole:
> "Statement on the Future of Probation & Parole in the United States."
>
> "Statement on the Future of Community Corrections." 2017.

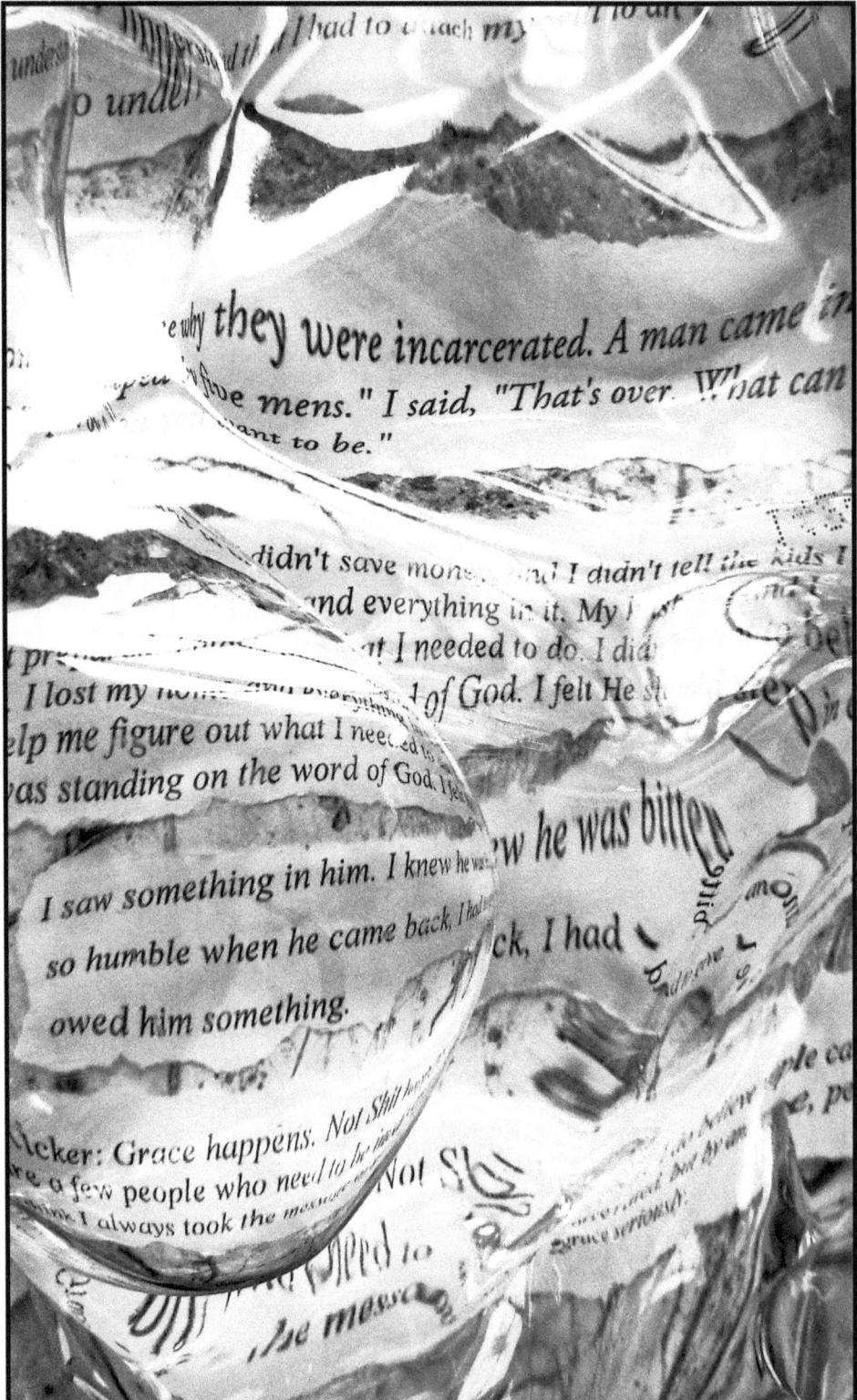

understand it I had to teach my... To un...
o unde...
o unde...

e why they were incarcerated. A man came in...
five mens." I said, "That's over. What can
...ant to be."

didn't save mon... ...nd I didn't tell the kids...
...nd everything in it. My...
...t I needed to do. I did...
I lost my ho... ...of God. I felt He...
elp me figure out what I need...
as standing on the word of God. I...

I saw something in him. I knew he... ...w he was bitten
so humble when he came back, I ha... ...ck, I had
owed him something.

...cker: Grace happens. Not Shit h...
...e a few people who need to be in...
...I always took the me... ...Not Sh...
...eed to
...he mess...

IV

HOLDING COMMUNITIES

He was scary, but away.

I can't do this

ra of the sheep.

People don't understand that everybody intimate. You can't hold your mother's away from you.

mother's

able to forgive yourself, that rig

right here is a breath of fr

you're guilty, don'

don't lie and say you're innoc

Believing hi

him, that makes me just as gui

would lose my love.

❧ 1 ❧

FAMILIES

Incarceration sentences families as well as individuals, reshaping their lives for the length of their family member's sentence, changing their relationships with each other and often with the world around them permanently. Families are also the ones who carry primary responsibility for reentry. When we talk about sharing the burden of reentry, it means sharing it with families as well as the individual who served the time. To do so, we need to understand more about some of the costs we as a society impose on them. We talked with a number of family members to get a better idea of what challenges they faced during the incarceration of their loved ones and also when they returned.

JUST THE WAY IT IS

SIERRA & ALTHEA

One of the experiences we had that gave us a sense of the global shaping impact of incarceration was taking a ride down to Milledgeville, Georgia from Atlanta on a bus filled with women and children who were visiting their fathers, husbands, and sons in the several prisons that surrounded the town. All the women were African American. These trips were sponsored by the Atlanta Open Door Community's Prison Ministry with the participation of churches in Atlanta that provided the bus and the driver and in Milledgeville, First Presbyterian, where the women were treated to an elaborate lunch before being dropped off at the Riverbend and Baldwin prisons for the afternoon. The talk among the volunteers and the clergy in the church, all white, was about mass incarceration, but that wasn't a topic of conversation on the bus.

The women on the bus talked about the people they were coming to see or had just seen. The conditions that led to these visits were seen as personal, particular—but not uncommon.

On the way down, a composed and very bright girl of about three, Sierra, sat quietly with her mother for the hours-long bus ride watching videos on a small portable player, whose colors coordinated with her hair beads. They were coming to visit Sierra's father at Riverbend, a for-profit prison. They came nearly every month if her mother's work schedule permitted. Sierra's father was in for fifteen to twenty years for aggravated assault. He had already served two years in the DeKalb County jail and one year in Riverbend. They didn't, at that point, think about his getting out.

Sierra's mother and father talked every night. The phone rates at Riverbend had gone down recently from $4.75 to $2.50 for fifteen minutes but at Baldwin, the nearby state prison, the phone prices were $15 for fifteen minutes. It was difficult for Sierra's mother having her husband imprisoned because they used to share childcare: he worked at nights and she worked days as a pharmacy tech. "It limits your professional life," Sierra's mother said. She had to turn down a better paying job at Walgreens because the hours were more erratic and she had no one to pick up Sierra.

She thought the length of the sentence her husband was serving was unjust. It was for aggravated assault, not murder or robbery. Even the DA expected it to be reduced to time served, not 20 do 15. She felt that the reason the sentence was so high was that the lawyer they had paid $5,500 to defend him had also been defending a man who shot his wife, a local DA, at the same time. But an appeal would cost $15,000, which they did not have.

If nothing changes, Sierra will make this trip monthly until she is at least fifteen. This experience will become part of the fabric of her life. Every year, over 14,000 children in Georgia have a parent returning from prison. Nationwide, the number of children with an incarcerated parent increased from about 1 in 120 in 1980 to 1 in 28 in 2008 and to over 11% for black children.[1] The expanding circles of implication of that reality for us as a society are staggering.

On the return from the prisons, Althea, who used a walker because of an unsuccessful surgery, described her own son's situation. She had busily crocheted all the way down, and continued crocheting as we talked. Her son had married a woman with six children whose three oldest sons, ages seventeen, sixteen, and fourteen, did not want a stepfather around. One day, the stepsons attacked their stepfather, stabbed him, hit him with a tree limb. The next year, after the oldest stepson told his friends that he was the man around the house and his friends could stay whenever they wanted, the mother and stepfather filed an eviction notice, and the stepsons attacked their stepfather again. In this fight, they included another friend. Althea's son pulled out a penknife during the attack and stabbed the stepson's friend. The boy died three days later.

Althea's son was charged with malice murder, felony murder, and aggravated assault. He had a jury trial but the DAs were already angry because the judge had given him bond and refused to put him on a leg monitor. The jury didn't find him guilty of malice murder and didn't want to find him guilty of murder, but the judge told them they couldn't convict him of involuntary manslaughter. The jury didn't know he would get life, his *natural* life, Althea emphasized. Althea felt that juries had a right to know the sentence ranges someone faced when they convicted someone.

What troubled her most was that the long criminal histories of the stepsons, especially that of the oldest, which included stabbing his own mother, were kept out of the trial. (Althea's son had no prior criminal record.) The stepson was now in jail charged with drug possession, manufacture, and distribution with no possibility of bond. Her son's wife had filed for a divorce, then stolen Althea's identity, so Althea had reported her to the police and the DMV. "I can ruin my credit rating on my own." Althea was intent on improving her own health so she could go and cut timber off some land she owned in North Carolina so she could afford an appeals lawyer for her only child.

Althea had not been able to see her son for his first ten months at Jackson because the counselor had never filed the form for family visits. "He never apologized. All he had to do was push a button to submit the form. He said he was waiting to hear from brothers and sisters. But my son is an only child." She was relieved she had been able to see her son that day because he was going to be taken for gallbladder surgery the following week. At the prison she had had to wait for over a half hour to see her son, so she had gotten up and skated around the waiting room with her walker. Althea had a keen sense of style. She changed her wig daily, from blonde to red to black. "But my son always recognizes me," she said with a warm laugh.

HELPING HANDS

SHIRLEY

Our very first interview for this listening project was with Shirley, who we heard speak at a human rights conference about the lasting impact she felt incarceration had on one of her younger sisters. "I feel she could never get out from under that felony label," Shirley said at that meeting. Her sister, as a young woman, had been convicted of involuntary manslaughter in a tragic incident with her stepson, who was close to her in age. She actually received a light sentence, but something in her changed with this, some hope went out. This clearly still saddened Shirley. "I believe nobody blamed her for what she did that day. The jury asked where she had to retreat. But she persecuted herself to the day of her death."

Shirley, a warm, highly efficient women who ran her own homecare agency named, appropriately, Helping Hands, had stepped up repeatedly for various incarcerated relatives. "My sisters and brothers keep asking if I've given up my halfway house. My husband tells me I'm helpful but I set a lot of conditions—you can be sure I do." She is helpful, not a push-over. She was a middle child of eleven, many of whom were, like her, high performers. Shirley also had two brothers who were incarcerated, one for drug possession (crack), the other for consensual sex with a minor, as well as two nephews, the children of the sister she was openly mourning. She was less understanding of the behaviors, and incarcerations, of her nephews, beginning in their early twenties. However, she felt her sister's crime, conviction, and especially her sister's failure to rebound, her choice to define herself by the crime and conviction and to associate primarily with people so labeled, shaped her nephews' attitudes toward authority.

Her exasperation did not mean she was unwilling to serve as their port of reentry or a source of support when they were doing time. Laughing, she showed us a letter and commissary list from the nephew who was currently incarcerated. He was complaining that she hadn't sent him enough money for a nice pair of sneakers. She did regularly provide him with money and correspondence, as she had with her brothers. Indeed, several other inmates in her brother's prison in Alabama had asked if she might correspond with them as well. She was clear that there were behaviors and choices on the parts of each of her relatives that had contributed to their going to prison, but she was also unwilling to refuse them a second, or third, or fourth chance. This nephew, for example, "from the time he was a child couldn't sit or achieve short term goals, couldn't follow the rules, was always looking for the quick and easy, and couldn't control his anger." So, help involved establishing rules. Shirley was willing to take him in for a year—with a contract: "He needs to tell me why he should come, realize this house is full of rules, that he has a curfew, an obligation to report, and must find legitimate work." She had done this earlier with her brother who was the crack dealer. She wouldn't have done it if he had had addiction.

This rigorous helping stance seemed to be of a piece with the determination that made sure that she herself graduated from high school, worked hard in a bank, returned to college in her forties when she realized that the absence of a college degree hindered her professional advancement, then started her own business. Her commitment had a religious dimension too. She saw what she did as a ministry. When we talked about reentry and community participation, though, she did not generalize from her own attitude and behavior. People didn't want to talk about this at church she said. Shame was a great barrier. They also did not, as she did, see the level of incarceration in the African-American community as having a systemic as well as personal dimension.

WHAT DO WE CALL THIS?
COLEMAN & CLAIRE

At the same human rights meeting where we met Shirley, we also met Coleman. When he heard us describe our listening project, he said loudly, "I'm the proud father of two felons, you can talk with me." We met him and his companion in activism, Claire, in Asheville, North Carolina at a local bookstore and found a set of sofas to settle into for our conversations. His younger son, Devon, had been convicted of selling LSD when he was nineteen and was sent to prison for two years. Both the prosecutor and the deputy sheriff were shocked by the harshness of the sentence for a nonviolent first offense. Coleman thought it was because the judge and the lawyer had a personal animosity. However, this son responded well, earned his GED and also took additional courses in art and comparative religion. Because of his age he was sent to the Path Youth Center, a prison for younger but dangerous inmates, where he used these same skills that led to his conviction, his gift for gab and slickness, to help him negotiate between gangs in the youth center. He was then sent to a drug rehab program at Duke. He received trustee status and then work release. Coleman saw the drug use as a right of passage and clearly felt that the criminal prosecution and especially the incarceration were unnecessary. Reentry had been fairly unproblematic. His son now worked in an Asheville restaurant where many of the staff had criminal records, a setting that actually allowed them to move beyond the labeling that can be so debilitating.

Coleman's older son, Nathan, on the other hand, had been convicted for assault and received a mandatory seven-year sentence because a weapon was involved, four years of which were served in prison. Nathan was already on SSI because of mental health issues. His father found it more difficult to talk about him in a blithe counter-culture way. Nathan had become involved with a white Neo-Nazi gang when he went in to prison, which explained some of his tattoos.

Claire spoke with us about her own six months in a federal prison for civil protest and about a friend, a nun, who also had been imprisoned for her activism. Claire clearly had great admiration for the religious resister, how she was able to organize the women in prison, help them improve their conditions. However, when she heard Coleman trying to explain Nathan's behavior in ways that were similar to those he used for his younger son, she said, simply, "Nathan scares me. His behavior. All those tattoos. His aggressiveness." Coleman fell silent, the pain on his face speaking for him.

However, overall, Coleman felt that the structure of prison had helped Nathan, in particular it had kept his older son on his meds. Reentry for Nathan was more difficult because he was only given a month and a half supply of meds, doctor's visits were cancelled, and Nathan went off his meds and restarting them proved difficult. Unlike his brother, Nathan was ineligible for food stamps because his felony was violent. Housing and employment were also issues. Devon had tried to help his brother with both, but Nathan was unable to keep either. Nathan had a conflictual relationship with his partner—co-dependent domestic violence is how Claire described it—and was going to be in court the next week on that issue, although he was very attached to his two sons. Coleman saw the loss of the prison structure as an independent stressor for someone like Nathan because of his mental health problems. "The system," he pointed out, "doesn't distinguish between healthy and unhealthy."

Coleman had raised his sons as a single parent since they were eight and ten, and their primary relationship was with him and with his family. He felt he grew closer to his sons through the experience, especially because of the letters they exchanged. Coleman said, "When they got out, my family didn't know how to treat them. But I think we're all in prison one way or another. For some of us, the bars are just farther apart."

Trying to use the frame of civil resistance to explain crimes that were impulsive and violent is something we encountered several times with white parents and partners. A close friend of ours, a law-abiding professional woman raised Mennonite, whose son served fifteen years for rape, would begin every conversation about her son by describing how her own father had gone to prison as a pacifist during World War I—then stop with a look of bewilderment and loss.

Another woman we met at various Stop Jim Crow activities in Atlanta had become an active participant in the movement after falling in love with a neighbor with substance abuse problems who was incarcerated in a Probation Detention Center for six months for probation violations. We talked to the couple together soon after he had been released from the detention center, and they were positive about his release. He was going to live with her, rebuild his life with her help. She spoke of his time in detention in terms of unjust prosecution. However, within months after release, after he had resumed his drug use and robbed her, her definition of his behaviors and her tolerance of them changed dramatically. She wrote us, sharing her range of responses.

> *The last time I saw John, he was sloppy drunk and running away from me as I was following him in the truck [that he had stolen the week before], the driver's side door flopping open because he'd trashed the truck and it wouldn't close. It was crazy. But at least satisfying to get that truck back, even if it is a pile of junk now that I will have to sell for next to nothing. He has nobody to turn to other than his druggie friends. His family long ago gave up on him. I have no idea where he may have gone.*

> *All I can think is how there MUST be something good to come of all of this. John has plunged me into debt that I may NEVER pay off, but then again I feel grateful for having my eyes opened to the horrible injustices meted out every single day to those unfortunate enough to come under the control of the criminal justice system. I feel grateful that I have learned in ways nobody could have EVER explained to me just how powerful addiction can be. And I feel driven to somehow enlighten the powers that be that even though programs like RSAT (which John went through) are a step in the right direction, it is a total waste of time and money if there is not equal follow up during the stressful re-entry period.*

LESSONS LEARNED

VIVIAN & VIDA

Vivian, the mother of twin girls, was incarcerated for four years on a fifteen-year sentence for aggravated assault and aggravated battery. Her daughters were thirteen when she went in, eighteen when she returned. We talked with Vivian and then with her and one of her daughters, Vida, about the impact of incarceration and the challenges of reentry for each of them and for them as a family.

We first met Vivian and her daughters at a wonderful annual celebration, Sisters into the Light, organized by long-time prison chaplain Susan Bishop for formerly incarcerated women, most of whom had been part of the successful, touring prison choir Bishop ran at Arrendale Prison. The event was hosted by a large, wealthy Methodist church in an upscale area of Atlanta. After the luncheon, many of the women performed, individually or together, as a tribute to Bishop. Vivian, who has a beautiful voice, sang a solo, while her daughters looked proudly on.

The second child of a teenage mother, Vivian was raised in her grandmother's home in a large extended family. She remembered her grandmother as warm, but her mother, especially as she grew older, was distant. At ten, Vivian was expected to be a primary caretaker for her two younger siblings. She described the living situation as crowded, and herself as shy: *I was always by myself. I had a big imagination. I was more interested in what was going on in my mind than what was going on outside. That still is true. As a hair stylist, I'm always envisioning how someone will look.*

Her father, who Vivian clearly adored, went to prison when she was three and returned when she was ten: *I remember going to see Daddy in prison. I remember him coming home. I was a daddy's girl. I can't say how it made me feel when I was younger. Awesome. He was so smart, creative, always there. He picked up his life right away. He started a clothing business.*

She had worked for the post office for thirteen years before the assault took place. She was completely dedicated to her daughters, and, most particularly, to providing them with ways to express themselves. She encouraged their sense of social activism and agency. In some ways, her own explosive violence may have been a reflection of how deeply she had suppressed her own desire for these same qualities—voice and agency.

We talked about how Vivian had, and had not, prepared herself and her girls for her incarceration. After the attack, Vivian understood the seriousness of the event and called the police herself when she returned home: *I reconsidered as soon as it happened. I was immediately sorry. I didn't want to feel I was a killer. I felt bad for the extent of her injuries. I hated that I had hurt another sister.*

Her lawyer told her that she could expect to do prison time given the severity of the injuries. He said they would appeal but that she would have to go, but didn't think it would be for that long: *The reality was, I was not prepared. I didn't save money, and I didn't tell the kids I was probably going to prison. I lost my home and everything in it. My husband and I separated. He couldn't help me figure out what I needed to do. I didn't want to believe it was going to happen. I was standing on the word of God. I felt He should step in and fix it. It took me time to understand that wasn't my choice to make. About the incident, I could have gotten in the car and left. I remember the judge telling me he was going to give me what the DA suggested, fifteen to serve five. I didn't cry. I smiled to everybody. I didn't have a breakdown moment until I saw my babies. I just wanted to get somewhere where I could think. That was crazy, but that was all that went through my mind at the time: I need a place to sit and think. I needed to think about how they felt. From that time on, I was in total peace. I knew I was going to be OK. My biggest frustration was being separated from my girls.*

Like several of the women we talked with, Vivian felt prison had definite social benefits. One was, most literally, having her voice heard and honored through her work with the choir. She studied cosmetology. She also enjoyed being a mentor for younger women through the Kairos program because it helped "to be able to be a mom to women close to my girls in age."

Most importantly, she developed close supportive female friendships that gave her a sense of community: *Prison gave me the sisters I needed. There's a lot you can't say in regular life, but in prison, you can get real close. I found women I could pray together with, say anything to. I am still able to call and talk to them. They get it. They keep me up and moving and able to work.*

Vivian received substantial family support during her incarceration. Her daughters lived with her mother while she was in prison. Her brother brought her daughters up to see her regularly: *My family would made sure I had money and that my kids were taken care of. My mom and brother and girls were all so encouraging. They were always excited to see me. Always giving. They wrote me and sent me pictures. They came every two weeks, and I found it hard but helpful. I needed to see them. If I couldn't, I would make calls, write letters. They would joke with me, "We be getting ready to see you, but you be gone." That was my work with Kairos and the chapel. My mom was totally different as a grandmother. She apologized to me that she was always asking me to take care of my younger brother and sister, that I had to be their second mom.*

However Vivian's husband distanced himself not only from Vivian but also from his daughters during this time. Vivian was more understanding than their daughters: *He could have helped me more and with the kids. He was in depressive mode, not doing much of anything. Our girls—we had always provided for them, so to hear he wasn't doing that was painful. I understand he was angry about my not being there and that just being around them and doing those things was painful. But the girls were angry with him and still are. I understand that incarceration impacts everybody and impacts everybody differently.*

Vida spoke about how her mother's incarceration had impacted her: *I don't recall my mom ever being a bad person. She was always the sunshine of the group. I was confused. I had questions toward the other person. My mom explained that she was at the wrong place at the wrong time. It was kind of vague. Most people agreed with her actions as far as being respected—she was standing up for herself. I never had had my mom away from me. People don't understand that everybody is incarcerated. When you visit, you can't be intimate. You can't hold your mother's hand. You don't realize you need it until is taken away from you.*

Vida was very intentional about keeping her relationship with her mother open, making sure to write her honestly about the challenges of her own adolescence: *I never wanted to keep secrets from her. Even when I knew I had to make smarter decisions.* But she also understood that she and her sister needed to develop their own inner drive and motivation: *My mom always wanted to __do__ things for us. But now I had to put my big girl panties on. My mom had always been that example; she had set the standards for us. My sister and I talked about all of this a lot. I was determined to keep myself motivated in school. My sister and I battled back and forth in school. I missed my privileges. But I learned to be more responsible, motivated, and independent. Now I know, "If Vida don't do, Vida won't get it."*

Vida found it difficult to live with her grandmother, who she felt was not sufficiently supportive of her mother or of the stress the sisters were going through. Vivian explained: *You know she loves you, but you can't tell if she is __feeling__ that love. I felt the closest to her when I was in prison. Then she could be openly caring. Now that I'm back, it's totally different. I can't say its bad, but it's not good either.*

Both mother and daughter shared their experiences with the adjustments of reentry. Vivian emphasized that reentry was a time of return and also of reassessment: *I realized I didn't have to start where I left. I didn't have to go back to that marriage, that home. That was a relief to me. Family makes you feel you should be where you used to be. But growing means you can pick and choose.*

However, it isn't all about individual choice. Vivian had been changed by her time in prison; her daughters and her mother had been changed by their time apart as well. Vivian found the return very challenging to her own sense of independence: *The most challenging thing is living with my mom. I don't have my own space. I share a room with my daughter. It is like putting me back in a prison situation, just having to room with someone else. My mom will say, "This is my house." For years I had my own home. It is hard to get out of the prison mindset—being closed in and not having enough space of your own. Prison showed me you don't need so much. But that keeping you confined unless someone allow you to leave—coming home, it felt the same.*

Vivian's mother did not understand her choice to leave her marriage, although her daughters did. Their parenting styles differed. Vivian had always been close to her girls and now wanted to spend all her free time with them when she wasn't working two janitorial jobs or trying to get her cosmetology license reinstated. She wanted to get to know who they were now, but her mother criticized her for trying to be her daughters' friend. She didn't see it that way. Her daughters were not the girls she had left behind. Now they were young women. They were dating. They were used to doing on their own, deciding on their own what they wished to do after finishing high school. Vida wanted to become a cosmetologist like her mother and then go into the military, while Vera wanted to go directly on to community college.

An important dimension of Vivian's tension with her mother and of her core hopes for her daughters had to do with voice and agency. This also directly impacted how they all understood the causes and implications of Vivian's crime. Vivian had actively encouraged her daughters to speak up. "Closed mouths don't get fed," she would tell them. "If I speak it into existence, it is mine." This hadn't been Vivian's own experience, but it was what she wanted for her daughters. When she was a child, she was expected to be quiet. The night of the altercation, Vivian was on the way to pick up Vida from a leadership program that emphasized public speaking and social change.

How Vivian understood her crime, how she was able to explain it to her daughters, how they were able to make sense of it, all revolved around the issue of how and to what degree you defended your right to respect. Vida said: *At first I thought it was unfair. When the judge let me speak at the trial, I said I didn't understand why it was only my mother who was going to prison, when it was the other woman who started it.*

Vivian agreed, in part: *At the beginning it felt unfair. I was doing what*

I was teaching them to do: Stand up for yourself and defend yourself. Don't be bullied. Somebody hit you, you hit them back. I was raised that way too. Raising my girls, I didn't understand how to explain it. "Mama on your side, but if you wrong I tell you." I realized later that I didn't want them to be fighting. Vida was in an altercation at school, and I told her, "My girls don't fight." Even when this incident happened I didn't say I was right. In prison, I found myself getting angry with a couple of the ladies. I had to regroup, go to my room and pray. Pray and cry, pray and cry. Pray, "I don't want to be that angry, to be controlled by anger."

When asked whether she would respond differently to similar provocations now, Vivian laughed and said, "Oh, I'd never fight back. I'd just fall to the ground and play dead." But when Vivian was asked about what changes she thought were needed in the criminal justice system, her answers echoed these questions about the necessity, and limits, of voice and self-assertion. She wanted formerly incarcerated people to be able to vote. She felt a woman protecting her child should never get prison time and felt the laws around this were unjust. She had been incarcerated with many women who had been abused and who had been sentenced to twenty years to life for responding to that abuse with violence of their own. "How do you put people away for protecting themselves?" she asked.

In her personal life, she felt that having been labeled a felon meant that most people would always hold her at arm's length: *It's almost as if you are a bad person. They won't say it but you can feel it—that not being trusted. It's an all over thing. I'm not ashamed; I like to tell people. I don't want their pity.* But, this loss of trust was a major reason for her decision to divorce; she felt her husband would never trust her again. She felt that her father had been able to retain his self-esteem after incarceration. She found that men were more able to understand her crime. She did distinguish men who were interested in her *because* of her incarceration from those who wanted to know her as a person. These men often had been incarcerated themselves, and they were teaching her that reentry takes time, that she needed to be patient with herself.

Years later encountering some legal appeals available online, we read a more thorough description of the assault itself, triggered by parking lot rage, in which it appeared the attack was far more violent than our conversations with either mother or daughter indicated. Both women in the altercation were encouraged to withdraw by their companions. However, when the other woman spit on the ground near Vivian, Vivian attacked the unarmed woman with a knife and stabbed her repeatedly, cutting her on the face, neck, and back of the arm. Her victim required fifty-five stitches. However, it is also true, as she said, that she immediately understood the seriousness of what she had done, called the police when she came home, and preserved the weapon for them. The extent of the violence added another nuance to our understanding of these conversations about self-respect and how we defend it—especially that it did *not* feel exceptional or worthy of mention by either mother or daughter, and that just the *idea* that a knife, rather than fists, was involved could so radically change our own understanding of the crime as well.

WHO IS PAYING THE PRICE?

CYNTHIA & TONY

Thirty years ago, when she was nineteen, Cynthia went out one evening with her sisters to a restaurant and met and fell in love with a handsome and personable restaurant manager about a decade older than she. Tony told Cynthia before he married her that he had a criminal record. That sentence, long served, has haunted them both all the days of their marriage.

In 1974, not quite sixteen, Tony was imprisoned in south Georgia for stealing a go-cart with only three wheels. He was so naive, he had gone back to the owner to ask for the missing wheel. Tony was sentenced to zero to six years under a permissive program for juvenile offenders that allowed for early release on the basis of good behavior. However, sent to an adult facility, traumatized and angered by the setting, Tony's behavior did not allow for his early release. Instead, he spent twelve years in prison.

His description of the experience is haunting: *At fifteen it was all about survival every day. At twenty-seven it was still about survival of a different kind. I never felt I'd get out of the mental prison I built. It took me years to get out. I thought I'd be a criminal in my mind for the rest of my life. It might have been more acceptable to just be a criminal. But it never felt right to take that position spiritually. My inner prison was protective, at its center it had a little piece of humanity, of hope, and that kept me pressing forward. The only place lower was death. The only place I could go was up. This was my only little light in that abyss, in all that fear generated by shame, guilt, getting kicked in the teeth, being discriminated against—that this was other people doing this to me. It was about understanding the penitentiary system.*

Tony, the oldest of five children, four of them boys, was raised by a very religious single mother. After his incarceration, his mother's pastor encouraged her to say she only had three sons. Because of his mother's evident shame, Tony felt when he was released that he could not go home until he had earned a pardon, which would take him five years. Years later, he would say, "A pardon is worthless, wouldn't buy a dime." Now, if he were going to advise someone, he would tell them to forget the pardon and concentrate on building relationships, that they were what changed prejudice.

Articulate, thoughtful, and charming, Tony is now the holder of a bachelors degree in psychology and a Certificate in Reentry Leadership from Wheaton, where he was a Charles W. Colson Fellow. Tony described how he had to intentionally socialize himself on leaving prison, how he had to learn how to eat, how to speak, how to make eye contact again, how he bought and read newspapers so that he would have something to make small talk about.

He said he wasn't bitter, but that it had taken a lot of work, that bitterness was a default mechanism easy to fall into: *With every job application you have to relive the crime. Prisoners ask me how I have stayed out for twenty-nine years, and I tell them God is my forethought, my destination, where I want to go. When I look in the rearview mirror, what I pay attention to is how far the penitentiary is from me, I pay attention to the distance.*

Over the years, Tony learned when going for interviews to always take a photo of his young son and his beautiful wife and to show it to potential employers: *I said, "Help me to help them. They didn't do anything."* This would *shift the focus of me to someone doing for others.* This wasn't manipulative. The love of Tony's wife and son were crucial for Tony's own resilience and emotional maturity: *My wife was awesome. For the first ten years, I thought she was enabling. She was tired of seeing me kicked in the teeth. But I needed to do it from my own self-will. She stood by me. I could be very mean but she stood by me. She saw in me what I couldn't see in myself. My son was the same way. I began to understand that I had to attach my will to an emotion bigger than myself.*

But this did not mean that Tony ever felt the work was done: *I don't feel like I've made it. People still discriminate. Twenty-six years later, I took a test to be an insurance agent and aced it—and was turned down because of my record. People still treat me as if I don't belong. I usually don't respond to that. I keep going. You can't change people, you can only change how you respond.*

Over the years, Tony made reentry his professional focus as well as his personal reality. His own experience shaped his understanding of what is required for genuine reintegration to take place. He felt all lasting change was based on emotional connection, that the emotional foundation of an individual's reentry was unique to them. Because one thing prison *is* successful at doing is creating a lasting hatred of control, Tony thought you could not lead or guide someone who was reentering, you could only accompany them. They had to discover in themselves that emotion that was bigger than themselves. All you could do was inspire with your own story, communicate through your story.

One of the interesting dimensions of Tony's approach was his focus on the debilitating and distorting power of shame. When we first spoke, we met across a large conference table in a large meeting room in a very large, very white Baptist church located in a very white suburb of Marietta that Tony and his family had recently joined. He was helping develop a ministry for families with an incarcerated member, what he called the hidden congregation. He felt the pain was the same whether you were African American or white, but that you couldn't stand in a white church and ask, "How many of you know someone who is incarcerated?" On the other hand, it was expected that someone who was African American would know people who were incarcerated. He also felt that with a white person, people usually asked what circumstances had caused the behavior, thus denying personal responsibility. African Americans, on the other hand, were often just angry at the individual who had been incarcerated, ignoring larger causal factors.

Although on the surface a paradoxical choice, joining this church also helped Tony and Cynthia, especially Cynthia, resolve the shame that was at the heart of their own lives. When Cynthia shared her own story, shame was at its core: the shame Tony felt at exposing her to the very real collateral consequences of his prison record. One of the most painful stories Cynthia shared was how Tony, the day of their wedding rehearsal, had second thoughts—not for himself but for her.

Cynthia met Tony seven years after he was released from prison. She didn't know until their engagement that he had a criminal record: *He was the first person I had met with a criminal history. When he told me, it felt kind of scary, hard to explain to my family. I didn't know if I was supposed to be scared. To run away. Growing up, I was just told, "You don't deal with men in jail." I was scared what other people would think, that they'd try to talk me out of it. But I knew I wanted to love him, marry and have a family. I was happy. I was really in love with him.*

I didn't say much to my mother, but I had an aunt I was close to who had had dealings with incarceration—her father and brother. She said, "You don't want to wonder what if—"

On the day of the wedding rehearsal, it was late, and Tony went out and just sat on the sidewalk. He was wondering if he should have me be part of his life, knowing the challenges but not knowing how to explain them to me. When his mother went to talk to him and asked him if he wanted to marry me, he said, "You don't understand what I'm going to put her through."

Tony spoke of Cynthia having enabled him in the first decade of their marriage. Her intention was to empower and protect—and, if she could, release him from the prison in his mind: *It was hard for him to trust because he was always a loner. Everything he knows, he taught himself. Learning how to write and type. I never gave up on him but it was hard to get him to know I would never give up on him. I really saw there was something unique about Tony.*

But Tony was also vulnerable. Cynthia described how, if a job failed, Tony, unable to find another easily because of his felony, would sometimes just lie on the couch for days in dark depression. The more stable breadwinner in the family, working at the same firm for over twenty years, she tried to protect him from knowing their financial situation: *I had seen Tony knocked down so many times. He would tell me, "Cindy, this record will always be with me. I just have to keep pushing along, proving to people I'm better. Turn this pain into purpose." I tried to be so behind him that I made decisions without talking to him. I was trying to do for him. Even if he had talent, it was hard to get jobs. That box. It has no time limit. If he marked it, they wouldn't hire him, and if he didn't, they would let him go. I made financial decisions, bad decisions trying to do the right thing. I thought we could start a business—because he couldn't work. I made the decision we could do it, and we couldn't and we lost the house. The recovery was long and slow, but it taught me he was not as helpless and vulnerable as I thought he was. He was knowledgeable. He could have helped me if I asked. Even though what I did, I did for him, it made things worse.*

Tony himself was similarly protective of their son. He didn't want him to know about his record, refused to take jobs where that information could come out. Cynthia did not tell her own mother for a long time after they were married. "Tony protected us by staying low."

We observed over the two years we saw them what it meant to them to be able to release that shame, to stop lying low. Cynthia described what it felt like to have Tony speak at their new church about his background, how afraid she had been to go into the church and watch the video. But people came up afterwards to talk to them with sympathy and interest and, most important of all, with respect. In a white church. *In our previous church, we couldn't tell anyone. It was very hard and scary to share here. Before I had shared with people I thought were friends, but then they wouldn't talk to me anymore. I was sad and mad. I thought, "Neither of us know that person. He isn't here anymore." So it was very scary to share the video. But it took a great burden off our shoulders. Now it isn't a secret.*

When our son was in ninth grade, we finally told him. He was good. He said, "You're my father. I know you're good. Why does this matter? I know who you are."

For fifteen years, it had only been the three of us. We started opening the door. Tony got involved in what we're working on now (a workshop with the North American Mission Board). We are meeting people we couldn't dream of meeting, and meeting them because of his perseverance. We felt such isolation and shame and loneliness and guilt. But see who we are now! I love the strength we show, our not acting like victims, our being able to help others. This was jail for the family as well. I was mad because Tony was mad. I just wanted to share his state.

It wasn't only Tony who had found his voice. Cynthia had as well. We heard her speak in a training session for the outreach program being developed through the North American Mission Board. For the first time she could be honest about the cost to her of these years, what it had meant to her to share the burden of collateral consequences imposed by the larger society, the conflicting emotions and loyalties she felt as she saw the persistent impact of stigma on her husband and, by association, on her. Emotions that, out of love and loyalty, she was reluctant to acknowledge, as she was the pain she herself felt.

We wanted our pain to become a purpose, to create a place where we could feel safe. No judgment. Where we can walk with someone in a place of dark and turmoil and hold the light. This ministry is a safe haven. We can share our stories. It takes the focus off you if you see your story helps someone else. Then you see you are healing. When Tony asked me and my son about sharing our story and my son said yes, I was scared. But the morning they were going to share it, I felt proud and at peace. It was the first time I had seen the video. Just to hear Tony talk about his time there, it just changed my life totally. Now I see that God has brought me through all of this. I had felt such shame at the thoughts I sometimes had: "I shouldn't have married him." "He's helpless." But my understanding of grace has grown. I can't control my thoughts, but I can control my actions, how long I keep those thoughts.

Although originally very excited about being hired on at the short lived Governor's Office of Transition and Reentry, Tony's optimism about being part of the more institutionalized reentry movement began to cool about a year later as he saw that it would not lead to his having a place in it that felt of equal standing with those without criminal records. When we talked with him at yet another community engagement meeting where energies and expectations were being raised without any funding to back them, he talked about the low morale in the office. In another conversation, asked about the award he had received from Al Burris (the prison that houses younger prisoners in the correctional system) to honor his thirty years of successful reintegration, he was clearly ambivalent. He was presented with a clock that inmates had made out of recycled cardboard: *It felt great but not from the perspective of winning a trophy or race. It was good from the perspective that they had made the clock, that they could take throw-away and make something so beautiful. But that they will get out of the penitentiary with no idea how to use that skill set to move forward in the world—that felt like a tragedy.*

Tony had worked so hard to be on the other side, to be seen for his free-world accomplishments, his degrees, the reentry programs he was trying to develop. But here his standing was based, it could seem, simply on his not returning to prison. When he had worked in prison ministry, it was his message that was the focus, his intellectual authority. Now, it was as if that haunting ancient history had itself become the focus, and his adult accomplishments the background. At this point, his employment felt unreliable and he was very concerned that someone in the new DCS would object to something, anything, he had said. He had been called boisterous. He wondered if we could censor all the hours of our interviews. He didn't feel he could control the video they were making of him: *They can tell my story from whatever perspective they want. I have only one, a reintegrative story, about having been knocked down consistently and having to develop a mental prison with bricks of shame and guilt and collateral consequences. Breaking free of that prison is harder than breaking out of brick and mortar.*

He was also upset that he was being reassigned from the administrative offices and his next position was to be a prison-outreach specialist, someone who would help make sure that men leaving prison had the minimal documents they needed to begin looking for work. He was going to be located inside a prison: *Inside the penitentiary, no one knows if I am friend or foe. The COs and the inmates both distrust me on a consistent basis. I feel like I'm never going to arrive, never learn how to do, there is this constant fear of job loss.*

But the most troubling concern of all was that as he and Cynthia continued looking around for a house to buy, they had recently applied to rent an apartment—and had been turned down because of his felony conviction: *It is forty-two years since I committed that crime. I have a full pardon. I work for the Department of Community Supervision. I have a masters degree. We both have salaries. Cynthia, got mad. "When is enough enough?" she asked. They told her the ban held for a hundred years. But I didn't even react. I'm* used *to people doing that. I can't stop it. I know that I can choose my responses. But inmates aren't taught how to respond to adversity. They're not taught how to react. You can't ask people to keep doing this if there is no possibility of success. Society has a responsibility in this arena.*

His last sentence can be heard as an assertion, an open question, a prayer.

360 DEGREES: FAMILIES SHAPED BY INCARCERATION

AAKEEM, JACQUELINE, ERICA

ARCHETYPE OF HOPE

Aakeem's reputation preceded him. Several people suggested we talk with him, including a probation officer at the Clayton Juvenile Court who had heard him speak there about how families could prepare juveniles for entry into adult prisons, as well as by Danny Horne, who had been director of chaplaincy in the Department of Corrections and now held a similar position in the Department of Juvenile Justice.

The day we heard Danny Horne refer to Aakeem as an "archetype of hope" we were at a program, "Connecting the Dots: Saving Our Youth," presented at Emory University. It was funded by the Barton Child Law and Policy Center, a group at the law school that focuses on juvenile justice, especially the fates of juveniles sentenced as adults. The program's purpose was both to promote Aakeem's work and put it in perspective. Along with Aakeem, we heard from Danny Horne; Stephen Reba, director of the Appeal for Youth Clinic at the Barton Center; and Dennis Francis from the Metro Conflict Defender's Office, an auxiliary public defenders group, which had several times called Aakeem in as a consultant.

The program was opened by Horne, who met Aakeem at Telfair, a very difficult prison, when Aakeem was developing the peer-mentoring program to help bring down the level of violence with Irving (as discussed in Section I, Chapter 10). Horne explained why someone like Akeem was important both within the system and outside it: *Everyone wants to be connected with someone who has gone through hell and emerged a human being, who has been able to create hope out of boredom and the purposelessness of human existence.*

Stephen Reba had spent years appealing the life-without-parole sentences given in Georgia to juveniles tried as adults. In 2005 the U.S. Supreme Court in *Roper v. Simmons* declared imposing the death penalty for a crime committed by a juvenile under the age of eighteen unconstitutional. In 2012 in *Miller v. Alabama* the Court ruled mandatory life sentences for juveniles unconstitutional and then four years later made the ruling retroactive. Appealing and litigating such cases in Georgia is how Reba had met Aakeem, who had been convicted of murder when he was sixteen. Aakeem was sentenced to life with parole, but it had seemed with all the deferrals that parole might never come. Reba and his clinic had strongly supported Aakeem's petition for parole. Reba in his remarks spoke of how encouraging Aakeem's story was, given that 95% of the SB 440s the clinic had been able to successfully appeal had since returned to prison. Aakeem was now close to the key three-year recidivism marker.

Francis from the Conflict Defender's Office described Aakeem as having dogged determination—and an ability to get judges and even DAs excited about reentry. Francis's office was called in to help public defenders when a second defense attorney was needed if several people were being tried for the same crime but their defenses conflicted. He often had to tell the young men, many of them seventeen or eighteen, eager to go to trial, that the evidence was bad, that they were much safer pleading and taking a long sentence with the possibility of parole than going to trial and receiving a sentence without that possibility. "They don't understand that I am trying to save their lives." Aakeem was proof that accepting a twenty-five-year sentence wasn't equivalent to accepting a death sentence, that a full life after twenty-four years incarceration *was* possible.

What preoccupied Francis most was the number of children these juveniles were leaving behind. Almost all of them had at least two children, some five or six. He emphasized the broad social implications of fatherless generation upon fatherless generation. His caseload was exploding with boys ages thirteen to fifteen being prosecuted, in groups, for armed robberies. "They are vulnerable to dominant personalities in the neighborhood." He needed Aakeem to talk with the jaded prosecutors, to get them to see that each kid was special, his circumstances unique.

Aakeem was being consulted as an expert. The Georgia Department of Corrections was Aakeem's institute of higher learning. Now in his early forties, married and expecting his first child, Aakeem was trying, with the help of his mentors, to jumpstart a career as a consultant on what he knew best: successful survival of the Georgia prison system. He had developed courses on preparing your child to go to prison and on the health and well-being of the family while a member was incarcerated, how they should not let themselves be controlled by guilt. He suggested that families establish subjects for discussion during visits—books, movies, current events—so that the interactions were substantive. On that day at Emory, he also had good suggestions about how to distribute the financial costs of reentry throughout a family system. He had an important lesson for those who administered prisons or were focused on creating change in them—one that echoed Francis's comment: There are leaders Aakeem said, and there are followers. Focus your efforts on the leaders. If they change, the others will follow. It was clear he knew to which group he belonged.

Aakeem was attended by two young men, videographers who were going to join him in creating a set of teaching videos based on his experiences. They were his maternal cousins, both of whom had also been incarcerated. At some point toward the end of the audience discussion, Horne added that it was helpful to have a mother as determined as Aakeem's. As Jacqueline, a small, fiery woman spoke up, Aakeem looked a little above her head. He had acknowledged his pregnant wife, a program manager at the Department of Juvenile Justice whom he had met when he was giving a lecture there. His wife had nodded silently. But Aakeem's mother wanted us to know that this was her story too. No one is an island or is raised in a vacuum. Success has deep roots.

For twenty years, she had spent her weekends visiting Georgia prisons. She had told Aakeem early on that this was his college, and she expected him to dry his tears and take advantage of every course that was offered. She had lobbied to move him from prison to prison to make sure he could get any training available in the program-deprived system. When we asked if she would share her story, she immediately agreed. Aakeem's sister, who had sat silently through the talk, also agreed to talk with us but said, "You know, we didn't grow up the way he implied. We're middle class." It was true, when talking about young offenders, Aakeem had described an archetypal childhood of deprivation and allowed the audience to make a natural association. It was not that simple.

AAKEEM'S STORY

Aakeem described the crime that sent him to prison as the crime of someone misled by older companions, someone who aspired to acceptance in an all white environment by imitating the gangsta behavior culturally ascribed to young African Americans: *I was the only black in the high school. I could do the work, but the white high school only had a stereotype of a tough black. I was validated more by the street. I gained friendships when I acted that way. There was the thrill of the images on the TV and on video. Those behaviors looked like fun. It fed the idea that we were invulnerable. It led us to rob a store.* He felt that the strict behavioral limits set by his mother, a devout Jehovah's Witness, increased his social isolation and vulnerability to these distortions.

He described how, in juvenile prison, where he was sent until he turned seventeen, the seeds of his reformation were planted by a librarian who told him that if he continued the way he was going he would be dead in a few years—but that *her* boys went to college: *Miss Collins was like the lady in* Poltergeist*. She took me aside and she said, "I'm watching you and you're going to die in this place or you're going to leave and come back and die in this place if you don't get your act together."*

However, he left soon to go to adult prison, leaving behind Miss Collins and her group. He was sent to Alto prison, and his description of it echoed that of other young men like Omar and Dainhen: *It was the second worst prison in Georgia. No one trained me to move myself into an adult prison. When we walked up the steps, men were choking and raping on the steps. There was an officer on the top step and the bottom step and they didn't do a thing to stop it. "You should have stayed home," they said. I didn't own enough of myself to stand up for myself. It was predator or prey. I fell into the culture. There were rapes, stabbings on a daily basis. It was like nobody cared.*

For the next seven years, Aakeem accommodated himself to his environment. Later, he would conceptualize the "life course" of a prison sentence in seven-year segments, a time frame that followed the periodicity of his parole considerations. In this first stage, the only important thing is assuring your physical survival: *If I went home in seven years, I would have gone back in for selling dope, cooking dope, hotwiring cars—for the criminal education I got inside.*

Miss Collins, the librarian, would write him several years later, at

Aakeem's mother's request, and tell him that she had heard that he had lost himself in prison, but that she knew he would be able to turn his life around. Aakeem over the years proceeded to do so. Much of this development was self-initiated and was organized around how to develop and refine his intrinsic charismatic authority—also how to interact effectively in the prison system: *You have to escape prison before your body does. A judge can only give your body parole. I began to think beyond prison. I went to bed before they told me, rose before they told me.*

Aakeem studied the speeches of Martin Luther King for their rhetoric. He listened to NPR daily to maintain a sense of the larger world. He converted to Islam, and chose membership in the strictest of Islamic sects, the Salafists, saying that he needed the very strict discipline they provided. He told his mother that there were no Jehovah's Witnesses in prison and that he would be physically safe if he joined the Muslims. One of their conditions for his conversion was that, after fifteen years of denial, Aakeem must be honest with his mother about his culpability in the murder for which he was convicted. Aakeem told his mother that he had not told her because he was afraid he would lose her love.

Aakeem began to use his charismatic power systematically. Miss Collins had told him, "You have to find a way to stand out for good things among the thousands." Aakeem could inspire his peers. Prison administration observed and quickly tried to harness this ability: "The wardens started to use me as a tool. I got sent to so many prisons to get them cool: Telfair, Autry, Rogers. I was to help quell group conflict, in-fighting." Aakeem wanted to get some personal benefit. He knew how useful he was: "If you can *quell* things, you can also rile them." Wardens were aware of this. He would ask, "After I do this, you going to ship me?"

Ultimately, his charismatic ability worked to his benefit. When Rogers State Prison was facing a strike, the warden asked Aakeem to intervene. This was part of a larger prison strike and slowdown affecting several other prisons as well, but Rogers produced much of the food for the whole prison system through its farm and canning operations and dairy, beef, and pork production. A strike there would be devastating to the system as a whole—and to the professional career of the warden. Aakeem said he would do it but only if the warden recommended him for parole the next time it came up. Aakeem called all the gang leaders together and said, "If we riot, we're going to lose what we have." He was the first one to go back to work there.

Aakeem was turned down for parole twice more. The second time was the most painful for him. He responded by creating with Irving a peer-mentoring program at Telfair. The prison was in chaos because of the number of young men being sent there with life sentences, all furious and hopeless now that the Parole Board had extended the time before eligibility for parole to thirty years. Aakeem's behavior, intelligence, and effectiveness there caught the attention of people like Reba and Horne.

The warden at Rogers kept his word and recommended Aakeem for parole. A warden's recommendation can over-ride a negative Parole Board decision, so they rarely use this power. The warden had a long talk with Aakeem before he did so. "You grew up in prison and you're slick," the warden told Aakeem. "You have to let that slickness go." He told Aakeem he had made a recommendation like this only three times in twenty years. Aakeem was approved the next time he came up for parole. When asked what Aakeem thought the warden meant by slick, he said, *I knew how to maneuver in prison. Why wouldn't I? I'd been there from fifteen to forty years old. He meant let go of the barter and trade, let the hustle go, don't try to swindle, cut the corners.*

Aakeem was released to a transitional center near Atlanta, where he said half the men didn't work, just smoked weed. He got a job immediately. Aakeem lived first with his father in DeKalb County because he was banned from returning to Gwinnett, where his crime had taken place. His grandmother then signed for an apartment.

Since his release Aakeem had focused on developing a consulting career, creating a family, and starting a church. His wife was Christian and encouraged him to convert from Islam and plant a church under the umbrella of another pastor. We visited them several times at their first church, Cultivators of God Impact Temple, where his wife was as active in running the service as Aakeem, although he did the preaching.

Aakeem at an intellectual level—and the very practical level of spending twenty-four years in prison—recognized the gravity of his crime, but in many ways it provoked less emotion than the feeling that in juvenile prison he had experienced emotional abuse because the female guards there played with his romantic feelings. He returned to this numerous times in conversation as a deep grievance. It made sense then that he chose, on release, to fall in love, marry and create a family with someone from the juvenile prison system who saw his intrinsic value as a human being and as a man.

JACQUELINE: We're Reaping What You Sowed

Jacqueline provided a more complex view of Aakeem's childhood. When we talked to her she was living in an attractive house that she and her current husband had remodeled. She made her living now remodeling houses, but had worked for many years at BellSouth. She spoke quickly and dramatically, with attractive directness.

Jacqueline, born and raised in Brunswick, a tough coastal city, was the oldest of five. She had been responsible for her siblings growing up. Her own family upbringing was perfused with violence. Her major concern when she went off to college was that her siblings keep their father from beating their mother. Her mother ended up joining her in Albany, her children facilitating her departure at gunpoint. All her siblings ascribe their college educations to Jacqueline's example. Even though she encouraged her mother to leave her father, Jacqueline retained her affection for him. He was a bootlegger and some years later was ambushed and murdered. She remembered how at his funeral they had to put a box outside the church for everyone's firearms. He died when Aakeem was five or six. She said that Aakeem and his brothers admired their grandfather enormously.

Aakeem did not have the same admiration for his own father, in large part because of his intense bond with his mother. Jacqueline's marriage to Aakeem's father, which lasted two decades, was tumultuous. The more educated partner and with a stable job, she was often absent at work. She would often get violently angry at her husband for his infidelities, the infections and the social shame they caused her, and would attack him physically.

Aakeem was not the young innocent that some of his own stories implied, she said. Aakeem was the third of five children, but always their natural leader. By the time he was thirteen or fourteen, he would stay out for days, sometimes a week at a time. When asked where he was, he would say, "Taking care of my business." He chafed at the strict limits her beliefs as a Jehovah's Witness imposed, or tried to impose, on his life. However, he was deeply bonded to his mother. He would give her money after her fights with his father. When she hit him because she was so frustrated with his delinquent behavior, he would just stand there crying, saying he was sorry. By fifteen he had dropped out of school.

Before the police came to arrest Aakeem for murder, they had an officer who had gone to college with Jacqueline call and talk with her. "He was the leader," she was told. "Guys who are twenty-four are following him. You have to let them come in and take him." Aakeem cried out to her as he was being carried away at five in the morning. The strength and anguish in the bond between the two of them was still alive in her telling—not just in Jacqueline's description of his arrest but also of the second trial (the first ended in a mistrial), when, after the verdict was announced, Aakeem turned and cried out, "Mama" and she fainted.

The trials themselves were traumatic. The anger of the community was high. Aakeem was seen as a remorseless predator child. Aakeem's case was in the papers every day. The KKK drove by on motorcycles and called Jacqueline "that nigger bitch." Her brothers came over to protect her. The children had to have police escorts take them to school. Police had to put guards around the neighborhood.

For fifteen years, she remained convinced of Aakeem's innocence. Everything she did for him, the weekly visits, the use of her retirement funds for his defense, the constant calls to prison wardens, were predicated on a belief in his innocence. When, at the insistence of his Muslim mentors in prison, Aakeem told her that he was responsible, she felt an expanding sense of betrayal. "Everyone knew, the lawyer, my husband . . . they all knew."

She thought about the victim, an older woman cashiering at a small convenience store: *She was somebody's mom and sister. I wonder if they think about Aakeem. I think he tried to contact them. If had known that he was guilty, you wouldn't have seen me in that court. I wouldn't fight for the others. You do the crime, you do the time.*

Jacqueline did not pour the same resources into the defense of Aakeem's younger brother, who ten years later went into prison to serve eighteen years for aggravated assault, or into the defense for her older son, who served briefer time for a more quixotic robbery attempt with a plastic gun. She and her sisters, all-college educated with good careers, all law-abiding, have pondered why all their sons, not only her three, but their three as well, ended up in prison. Their daughters have not had problems with the law and all have stable jobs. Jacqueline's own two brothers as well as her brothers' sons have not had trouble with the law either.

Jacqueline was, as Horne noted, a formidable advocate for Aakeem in prison. She made sure he was moved to enough prisons that in time he would have studied six different trades. She advocated for him at the Parole Board. She felt her son was being used by the wardens—without adequate compensation. It was she who made sure that Aakeem, after a bureaucratic transfer, was returned to Rogers Prison as promised. The warden had kept up with Aakeem after his release, and has called her to say, "Mom, I'm so proud of what he's doing. Tell him to keep making me proud."

Her understanding of her son's story now distributes responsibility differently than before: *My sons gained something. They are determined not to go back. It is not the life they want to live. It was hard for them. Harder for us. We're reaping what they have sown. We spent dollars for them to eat, dollars to go and see them, time to go and see them, time keeping pictures up to date so they would feel their family was there, that was important to them. We bought Aakeem a car.*

I felt like a victim myself in my marriage. I made my kids victims. Now, I would just have left, but I couldn't then. Aakeem thought, I'm not going to be a victim. He wanted to be a leader rescuing us. When he was staying out all night, he stole a car. They arrested him. I told them to take him to jail, I wouldn't get him out. I thought he would hit the wall. But in there, he was leading everybody too.

It was only when he was a Muslim that he admitted his crime. It was after he had been a long time in. If you're guilty, don't lie and say you're innocent. If you take a life, you have to pay for that. Believing him, that makes me just as guilty. He tells me he didn't tell me because he thought he would lose my love.

Acknowledging Aakeem's guilt, she began to wonder about how safe she was around a murderer: *I wondered, will he kill us. Even when he came to spend the night, I locked the door. He would say, "Mom, I love you," and just cry. "Can I ever make it up?" I told him, "Just make this life better from this day on."*

When Aakeem was preparing to be released from prison, he asked his mother whether she was going to hold a party, a big family reunion, for him. "Why should I do that?" she asked. Instead she taught him how to use self-checkout, open a bank account. *He hadn't ever done any of that, it was like teaching a baby. At the Chinese buffet, he was going to take his plate up and wash it himself.*

ERICA: *Why Does It Always Have to Be About Him?*

Erica, small, bright, soft-spoken and self-contained was the youngest child in the family. Now in her late thirties, she lived with her husband, a firefighter, and her twelve-year old daughter in an attractive house in a quiet suburban development. She was a devout Jehovah's Witness, perhaps even more committed than her mother, as was her husband.

She had played the role of her mother's supporter much of her childhood and young adulthood, as her mother fought, divorced, remarried and then divorced her father again: *I sat back and watched a lot as a child. I was the mediator. Even now, I'm the last one to go to sleep. Hypervigilance. My mom and dad fought often. My mom was the perpetrator of the violence. My mom grew up in a very violent home. Her father was very violent. All the women in the family, my aunts too. They're all quick to fight. I have it too. Luckily my husband doesn't have that energy. My daughter has never seen us argue.*

She lived in the same county where she had lived as a child, a county from which both Aakeem and his younger brother are permanently banned. *They thought of us as a bad family. They would have banned all of us if they could.*

Aakeem often pointed to their isolation as the only African-American family in their schools as a contributing factor to his behavior, but Erica felt the adjustment wasn't that hard. She easily learned what was expected of her. She also pointed out that as a Jehovah's Witness, you are meant to experience yourself as set apart from the society around you, so the racial isolation simply was part of a larger stance toward society in general.

She remembered Aakeem as a kind older brother, a protector. She had positive memories of going to visit him in prison: *We saw him so often, I didn't think of him as so far away. We all went together to see him. It was difficult, but we were excited going. We had good conversations. I was in charge of the money for the vending machines. We never talked about what happened in prison. I would watch prison shows to find that out. He'd come out and look OK. No scars, a fresh haircut, his shoes polished. He did that for us. Now, when I hear the real stories, I say What?! I have a feeling he didn't tell us then because he didn't want us to follow him in. He was very upset when Shannon went in.*

Erica was also very upset when her brother Shannon went to prison ten years after Aakeem. Shannon was her closest sibling. They were in the same grade in school:. *Shannon's imprisonment really affected me. We stayed close throughout his entire incarceration—going to visit, calling, sending money. With Shannon, I was older. I had my own apartment. I could visit without my mom and dad, we could keep our relationship.*

She still felt that Shannon was unfairly harshly prosecuted because of Aakeem's crime and reputation. Shannon at nineteen or twenty was in an altercation with a peer, both of them were armed. He received a twenty-year sentence for aggravated assault, the DA insisting he serve eighteen and that he be permanently banned from the county. She is actually prouder of Shannon's accomplishment's in prison than Aakeem's, perhaps because they are more translatable to the world outside the prison. Shannon became a firefighter and was highly regarded by everyone. Now released, he is a locksmith.

Her husband was able to accept her family history and not define her by it: *When I started dating my husband, all three of my brothers were in prison. It was hard to tell him, but he offered to go with me to visit them. I asked him what made him want to see my brothers, and he said, "If you have all these issues, and you still seem fairly normal, who am I to judge you for what your <u>brothers</u> did?"*

Erica was still troubled by one event during the trial, one that was widely reported in the newspapers. She was with her older sister and her sister's daughter at a break in the trial. She was trying to amuse her niece: *In the courtroom, I remember looking at the other family and not even having remorse because I believed my brother didn't do this. We were in the hall waiting to go back in. I made a gesture with my hand, like a gun, and said "Pow! Pow!" I remember going back into the courtroom. The podium was so high. The judge barred me for the rest of the trial. I thought that was why my brother was convicted. I was actually relieved when I found that Aakeem really did do it because it <u>wasn't</u> my fault that he was convicted. Why did I do it? Just being bad, mean. I was thinking it was just a joke. I wish I had a chance to apologize.*

She mused a little more on the sense she had made of her brother's crime as a child and the sense she made of it now: *For a long time I believed like my mom that Aakeem didn't do it. I thought it was a race issue. There were two other boys with him, both white. One did no time at all, and the other fifteen years. I felt it was racially motivated. Even more motivated if he was made the trigger man. But looking back, it doesn't matter about race.*

Aakeem was following stereotypes, but not <u>family</u> stereotypes. He was gentle, kind as a brother. If you were in trouble, he would cover for you, he would fix it. The way he is now is the way he was before.

Of course I think there were causes for all my brothers. Guns. The company they kept. Their choice of friends. I never say Aakeem went because of my mother or dad. It was because of the outside world. That is why I stress with my daughter to be skeptical about who she associates with. It is easier to be influenced by the bad.

Even though she was protective of her daughter, Erica brought her daughter with her to prison visits so she would know her uncles when they came out. But, like her mother, knowing that Aakeem had in fact committed the murder did give her some reservations, especially about allowing him around her daughter: *At first I was skeptical about my daughter being alone with him. He understood. The first time I let her go out with him, she came back saying, "Uncle Aakeem was like being with Daddy." Aakeem does for her what he wasn't able to do for me.*

Unlike her mother, she doesn't feel resentment towards her brothers and what it required of her and other family members to support them through those many years: *I have no judgment. They did their time. Why point fingers? We sent money, letters, we came to visit because we wanted to. It wasn't obligatory. They owe me nothing.*

As we were leaving, Erica shared a recent event that had been very meaningful to her and to her whole family. Her brother Shannon, who is now married, had fathered a child from a brief relationship while he was in the transitional center. He had refused to marry the mother but wanted to claim paternity and paternal rights, in particular he wanted visitation rights with the child, to share in his physical care. The mother, perhaps angry at the absence of relationship, wanted to block the visitation request. She wanted to block it on the basis of Shannon's criminal history. *The judge said, "If he wasn't incarcerated for child abuse or child molestation, it is irrelevant." When told that Shannon had only recently been released, the judge said, "The baby is over a year old, so it isn't that recent."*

I felt sorry for the mother. Behind Shannon sat his whole family, three brothers, father and mother. My husband had come in his uniform, he knew this was so important for me. She didn't have anybody. She wanted to condition visitation on child support, but Shannon was saying he was willing to help <u>care</u> for the baby. The judge rejected the argument that a man was unable to take care of a baby or a small child. He kept saying, "You will be able to see your child sooner than you think."

That was the first time any part of the criminal justice system has ever had anything good to say about our family.

Endnote

1. S. Wakefield and C. Wildeman. *Children of the Prison Boom: Mass Incarceration and the Future of American Inequality.* Oxford University Press, 2014, pp. 31-32.

‹2›

PEER REENTRY SUPPORT GROUPS
A. J. SABREE, HAZEL HORNE
PERSONS IMPACTED BY INCARCERATION COLLABORATIVE (PIIC)

For almost two years we attended monthly support group meetings of the *Persons Impacted by Incarceration Collaborative (PIIC)*, a group of formerly incarcerated men and women that was formed with the mentorship of A. J. Sabree. The core administrative group included a number of people whose stories have been shared here—Khadijah, Ariif, Dainhen, Eloise, Joe, and Fareed. Many of these individuals had been incarcerated for very long periods of time, so they had known each other, for years, in a very different context. There was another monthly meeting of the PIIC executive committee, where they concentrated on exploring how to increase PIIC's reach and influence. Several of the men travelled frequently to various Georgia prisons to talk with Lifer's Groups. Khadijah and Eloise spoke at the women's prisons. The monthly support groups were open to anyone who wanted to come. Meetings were held in a classroom in a large, attractive building on the campus of Atlanta Technical College. Some individuals drove significant distances to get there.

A.J. SABREE: Reentry Begins with You

A. J. Sabree, who we had first heard about through the African-American Muslim community, was very open to speaking with us when we first met him at a large faith-based reentry meeting held down at the Georgia Department of Corrections (DOC) headquarters an hour south of Atlanta in Forsyth. He invited us to a PIIC meeting that evening. This openness to our listening project was a striking contrast to the response of people currently in Corrections but was consistent with Sabree's own commitment to reentry.

PIIC grew out of Sabree's thirty-year career in DOC, where he served as a prison chaplain, assistant director of chaplaincy, and then, for a decade, as director of an over-arching department of reentry services that included chaplaincy, risk-reduction services, and community reentry. When we met him, he had recently retired from DOC and was serving as a reentry consultant to the Department of Juvenile Justice (DJJ), helping create reentry centers in their prisons. He was in his early sixties. Since leaving DOC, he had lost a hundred and fifty pounds, but photographs of him during his time in DOC showed a substantial man with a commanding physical presence. It was easy to understand how he could have been a core member of the Imam W. D. Mohammed's security detail. Many of the members of PIIC had known him when, as a young imam, he came in to some of the worst prisons and helped them effect change. Sabree is slow spoken, with a stutter that precedes and adds gravitas to his thoughtful comments. He, like Rev. Hazel Horne, provided a crucial link between PIIC and the larger community.

Sabree also connected us with several people recently retired from DOC who could talk with us freely about their work in reentry, including the retired Commissioner Allen Ault. Sabree's relationship with DOC was complex. He knew that his religion had impeded his career, was told this directly more than once. On the other hand, he had been able to rise administratively in the system and was able to make changes that were valuable to him and to those who lived in the prisons. His commitment to reform of the prison system had very personal origins, ones that he shared at PIIC and with us.

As a young man, he had been involved in various illegal activities, primarily selling drugs, but was never convicted. His younger brother, with whom he was very close, followed his example. However, his brother was caught, convicted, and imprisoned for twenty years. Both men are very bright—Sabree mentioned that his brother had tested as having the highest IQ in the prison. They came from a law-abiding family that valued education. A psychologist who was asked to see his brother before the trial told their parents that they should keep Sabree away from his brother because he was a pathological influence on him. "I had become cold," is how Sabree described it. But the psychologist's description of him troubled Sabree so deeply that he began to turn his life around. He became very involved with the Nation of Islam, especially with the rise of the more moderate W. D. Mohammed, and began visiting the prisons. Sabree found Islam attractive "because of its social theology and its discipline—and like Roman Catholicism, it was ritualistic and sacrificial. It helped me cold turkey stop what I was doing."

Sabree had a great sense of guilt about his brother's incarceration and whatever influence he had on him, a guilt he said he had never shared with his brother until after his brother came to one of the PIIC meetings. But Sabree talked often in those meetings about the dangers of becoming cold. Sabree was clearly deferred to in the PIIC meetings, but he usually kept silent until the close, when he would react to what he had heard, summarizing and synthesizing the themes of the evening in a way that was usually both cautionary and motivational. He identified the emotional and social challenges that were intrinsic to reentry, the temptation to fall back on habits that may have worked in prison but did not work in the larger world.

Sabree came into the prisons as a change agent, not necessarily a provocateur, at a time of great turmoil: *From the beginning one of the questions for me was how to impact change without standing on the outside advocating— how to get inside and influence change,* is how Sabree described his intentions. When he first went into Reidsville, it was about to face a federal take-over. There were large numbers of prisoners in open dorms, and knifings were common. Sabree as a chaplain began to invite the leaders of groups together to start a conversation: *I understood the language and the mindset. I had reformed from the street, so I understood criminal thinking. I could kind of engage, offer them something different. Also, you can't just put the responsibility for change on the staff. The staff run the prison at the pleasure of the population because they're outnumbered.* Sabree helped the prisoners organize an Inmate Unity Committee. They asked to meet with the administration. At first the warden objected, but 800 inmates insisted on meeting with the administration and the dialogue began. Having developed a reputation as someone who could work with both prison groups and the administration, wardens requested Sabree's presence throughout the prison system.

This work quickly brought him to central headquarters where in 1988 he became the assistant director of the chaplaincy program. He strongly advocated a pluralistic, multi-faith perspective among the 150 full-time clinical chaplains: "Chaplains don't go there to provide services for a particular faith group, but for all offenders." His approach also made him an ideal candidate in the early 2000s to develop a reentry sensibility in the Georgia prison system as attitudes toward reentry nationally began to shift, a project to which he dedicated the last decade of his career at DOC. In 2007 he wrote an article laying out how he saw reentry philosophy infusing the system.

At that time, no one knew what reentry services were—and they *left me alone to chart my way. I could see reentry was going to be the biggest thing in corrections. Reentry begins at the first point you touch the system and continues after release. I knew it couldn't be piecemeal, it affected everything: policy, the culture of corrections, the culture of community supervision, the programs that would contribute and be effective. Risk reduction, vocational education, volunteers, community engagement, they all fell under reentry. I was Commissioner James Donald's person for change. I had to go around and say all that to the program people, tell them, "You can be part of something that will leave a legacy." It took a long time for the leadership to get it. My gift was that I could sell it. I can <u>sell</u> reentry, make people believe in it. I can approach it from many different perspectives. I'm humble on it. I feel I am receiving help from something greater than myself. And God is bigger than the challenges.*

Sabree's dedication to PIIC was both a matter of personal loyalty to the group of men and women in it and a professional commitment to bringing justice full circle: *Martin Luther King used to say the hottest place in hell was saved for those who maintain neutrality in a moral crisis. This is a moral crisis.*

Sabree talked at some length about the particular hopes he had for PIIC: *Life is always going to be a process—a process to get where God wants you to be. The people who have done best started the process before they got out. You can be free of prison even if they <u>don't</u> let you out. Once you get to a certain point, the system can't hold you.*

What are we looking for here? Everyone is at different stages. It takes a lot for me to give up. I want everyone to have <u>another</u> chance. I do know when I hear someone convicted to criminal mindedness. They may have been in for forty years, but they will still commit crime. They'll tell you that. But the majority of people just don't know how to deal with barriers and challenges. They give up and revert. They don't have all the tools they need. Expectations are put on them that are not normal to them. You can't function all the time as a well-organized group if you have no training in group dynamics. In PIIC, I don't try to talk about that, I try to demonstrate it.

Over his career, Sabree had quietly gathered numerous academic credentials—in clinical chaplaincy, criminal justice, as a paralegal, a real estate agent, often without letting anyone he worked with know. When we last spoke with him he was studying for a PhD in criminal justice. These degrees were a reflection of his intellectual curiosity, his desire for career advancement, and also a crucial counter-balance to the constraints he felt inside the system—they provided him with that inner freedom and self-determination that he was dedicated to helping members of PIIC cultivate. He and his wife also raised eleven children during that time, probably embodying the same message.

REV. HAZEL HORNE: *Lift into Life*

Another regular member of the support group, Reverend Hazel Horne, had also known most of the core members of PIIC during their time in prison through her prison ministry. Small, elegant, with a soft voice that sometimes verged on the unearthly, Horne had seen more than most of us, and for longer, and was still charged with hope. Horne pastors a small, New Thought church in southeastern Atlanta, Jesus Christ Center of Truth, and has had a prison ministry for decades. She often attended meetings with Dorothy Parker, who shared her prison ministry, and with her teenage grandson, Robbie, whose challenges often provided a focus for all the hard won wisdom of the PIIC members.

Our first personal conversation took place at her small white church set in one of those leafy Atlanta suburbs that shift almost instantaneously from large contemporary apartment complexes to vistas that look like a bend in time, as if we were back in the farmland of her challenging, resilient childhood.

Horne remembered with great warmth her childhood in south Georgia, where her father was a sharecropper. They lived without electricity or running water, but with abundant aspiration. She remembered standing in their front yard and watching FDR drive by on his way to Warm Springs, the hope that his presence engendered in a young black girl in south Georgia, the way her father removed his hat in respect. She also remembered the anger she felt when her father, working in the field, felt obliged to take off his hat to the white man who owned the land. She also remembered the chain gangs that came by once a month to work the roads, how when her father heard them approaching he would send Horne and her brother out to draw water from the well and gather food from the kitchen. There, with the guards and the guns, they would serve the men. "We would drink out of the same gourd," she said.

Her father had a fifth-grade education, and made educating his children his priority. Horne and her two siblings all finished high school early. At seventeen she went to Chattanooga to attend a Bible college, working during the week on Lookout Mountain, tending the children of a wealthy couple. There was still a steely anger in her voice at the memory of working for people who could not even care for their own clothes.

Horne decided early in her life that she was going to care for lost or abandoned children. She had been profoundly shaped by the story of her father's abandonment by his own fifteen-year-old mother. She took him with her on a bus to Atlanta and when a stranger on the bus complimented her on her son, said, "You want him, take him." The man, not knowing what to do, took the child to his boarding house and kept him locked in a closet while he worked. (The boy was ultimately found and raised by one of his maternal aunts.) "I only wanted the children nobody else wants," Horne explained.

Horne said she married because she thought she had to if she wanted to foster children. After she and her husband adopted two children, they divorced because he wanted children of his own. When we talked, Horne's two adopted children had both died quite recently, in their early forties, within eight weeks of each other, the daughter of a chronic illness, the son from complications of an operation. She was clearly still mourning them, especially her daughter who had shared her ministry.

Over her lifetime, Horne also fostered fifteen children, mostly informally. "I would go out and check my porch to see if anyone had been left there." She found two brothers, abandoned for five or six days, eating out of the garbage and took them in and raised them for twenty years. One of them died of sickle cell, the other was in prison for meth. He had put her on his visitors list saying, "You're the only mother who has been there for me." Horne also took in the children of several women who were incarcerated. She took in three children of a Nigerian woman who was sentenced to thirty years. The children all finished college. She also took in the two children of a woman who spent several years on death row.

Horne started a prison ministry in 1978 because her brother "had started going in and out." He had "started taking things." She originally went into a prison with Reverend Barbara King's church group, in part to look for her brother. Although she didn't actually find him, she kept returning. "He was pulling me there. Every week I was showing up. I left my children so alone." Her brother died in 1979, but he had managed to send her some money before he died with the wish that she continue her ministry. She took his wish seriously and began to study and was ordained by King. Horne began her ministry at the prison near Stone Mountain where her brother had been held, a community at that time known for its intense racism and as the home of the KKK, as she noted. In time, her ministry expanded to other prisons. She was the first woman chaplain to enter notorious Reidsville.

She described in her soft, imperturbable voice how in the prison men would fight over which religious groups could use the chapel. She insisted they see it as a place where God did not encourage divisions. No one had an exclusive claim on God. "God is going to bring the ones here that need to be here," she told them.

She called her ministry *Lift into Life* because she saw that as her mission, to lift up the men she visited. "I told them, what you did yesterday doesn't say anything about where you are today." Horne didn't say this in a sentimental way, as this story she shared made clear: *A man come to me in the chapel, he was real upset. He told me, "I was raped by five mens last night." I said to him, "Well, that's done. What can I do for you today to help you be the man you want to be?"*

This same ruthless realism and care informed her fostering as well. Mothers might not return for years. Children needed to focus on the here and now.

One story she returned to often was that of the woman who spent time on death row. She had a beautiful voice, was known as "the songbird of the south," and sang in the choir developed by Chaplain Susan Bishop. After her sentence was commuted and she was released from prison, she still felt her children, from whom she had been separated for eleven years and who were now nearly grown, were better off with Horne. However, her son could never accept this, even though he had a home with Horne. "Why my mother not want us?" he asked. He thanked Horne for all she had done for them. At eighteen he died by drowning, and Horne wondered if it was suicide. She returned to the story because it obviously troubled her. It showed the limit of fostering. He *had* received her love, but she felt it couldn't compensate for his profound sense of abandonment.

With her grandson Robbie, who she brought to PIIC, Horne faced a similar struggle. She was raising Robbie along with a girl, Tia, about the same age, very bright and resilient, who Horne had taken in when she was six days old because her mother failed to bond. Robbie also was deeply troubled by the rejection of his mother, who had raised him until the age of five then sent him over to his father to raise. Robbie was as jealous of Tia as he was of the children who lived with his own mother right across the street from him.

Grieving the death of his father and fearing the possibility of losing his older brother to prison, Robbie was becoming delinquent, a subject of great, and unifying, concern to PIIC members in the two years we attended meetings.

The last time we spoke with Horne, she and Robbie were taking refuge in a hotel because a fire caused by faulty wiring in the stove had nearly destroyed her home of sixty years. She described the situation calmly, including as almost an after thought that Robbie's older brother was currently in the hospital with several shots to the abdomen. She thought they were revenge from a spurned boyfriend. He would be fine, she said. They would be too. Her house was insured.

PERSONS IMPACTED BY INCARCERATION COLLABORATIVE (PIIC)

Each meeting of the support group began with someone on the executive committee reading the mission and by-laws in full. The responsibility for moderating the meeting was passed around between members of the executive committee. The content and attendance of each meeting varied quite widely. The moderator raised questions of interest to him or her personally, as well as responding to concerns of the people visiting that month. Sabree and Horne and her colleague Dorothy Parker were almost always in attendance as the representatives of the larger community, as were we, the only white participants. The year before they had a doctoral student in criminology observing. The regular participants seemed comfortable with this observation. Newcomers seemed to take us for granted.

Another regular participant, Miss Y, was not reentering herself. In fact she was a prison guard. But her husband was serving a twenty-year sentence, and since her own twenties she had been active in providing reentry housing. She had taken the prison guard job in order to better understand the conditions her husband and other prisoners faced. Her perspective was an interesting blend of her roles—spouse, landlady, guard, parent. She clearly felt that order in the prisons was in the best interest of the prisoners as well as the guards. She several times acknowledged that her own children questioned her insistence on maintaining a relationship over decades with an absent father they hardly knew.

Since most of the core members had been imprisoned for very long periods and knew Sabree throughout his career in the prison system, they sometimes liked to tease him about his past. Terry liked describing him to newcomers as a firebrand preacher in his youth. Terry himself had been imprisoned for over thirty years on two murder convictions. He is a very bright and charming man, highly literate, now in his sixties. He and Ariif are good friends, but where Ariif had been a proud and resistant convict, Terry was a socially adroit one, learning how to shape the prison context to him as much as he shaped himself to it. In prison he had become a Braille translator. Now that he was out, he had reconnected with his childhood sweetheart, and used his language skills to edit books and develop various movie projects. He particularly enjoyed reading to children at the elementary school his nephew attended.

Dubraye, known during his criminal career as the jerry curl bandit, spent over twenty years in prison for bank robbery. While in prison he had his come-to-God moment, and from then on served out his prison sentence combining a call to ministry with being an effective businessman and "keeping store." A strong believer in the prosperity gospel, now he helped Horne with her church, developing his own gifts as a preacher, worked regularly, and sold slimming tea in his spare time. After leaving prison, he was married briefly to a woman whose own son had been incarcerated and who had been active in developing a support group for mothers with incarcerated children. Divorced, Dubraye attentively cared for his own aging mother until her death. He was also active in developing a reality show, Ex-Cons of Atlanta, which he hoped might air soon. He felt there would be a large audience for it, and that they could easily develop franchises in Detroit (his home town), LA, and Washington, DC.

The very first PIIC meeting we attended was one of the most interesting, creating a context in which to understand the ones that followed. The first person we met was an older man who walked around saying to himself and everyone around him, "I don't know anything. I have to be a sponge." He had been incarcerated for forty-six years. He was disoriented physically as well as sociologically. He could not recognize the area he had grown up in or the behaviors of the people he met. He realized that the anger he felt at his own disorientation would be dangerous to him, and was trying to talk himself down with Ariif's help.

This meeting took place the evening after the core PIIC group had all gone together with Sabree to one of the first large meetings on reentry during the height of Georgia's criminal justice reform. They had gone to introduce

PIIC to a larger audience and were energized by what they had seen.

One of them, Darryl, college-educated and formerly incarcerated twice on drug charges, had developed a career for himself managing halfway houses for those released from prison with mental health issues. Darryl was also now strategically embedding himself in the reentry movement, something made easier by his middle-class bonafides. He actively mentored, and employed, Dainhen, whom he had met in prison. When Darryl arrived an hour into the meeting, he was extremely upset. As he was coming over, he had been called by the Sheriff's Department in the adjoining county. A prisoner had been released from prison who was clearly psychotic. They didn't know what to do. He had been left in front of the jail. They couldn't hold him, but they didn't dare release him either. They wondered if Darryl could do anything to help them. He had gone over there and arranged to have the man placed in one of the transitional housing units he used to manage. "All that talk," he said. "That's just what it is. Talk. On the street, psychotic with no meds. *Nothing has changed.*"

Sabree, slipping into almost a dream state, began to describe several scenes from his time as a prison chaplain that still haunted him: Having to leave Eloise and other women in a decrepit women's prison ankle deep in water, the guilt of going home to his own dry house at night. Eloise, who had experienced the water lapping around her, seemed unfazed by the memory, but clearly it was a pivotal image that would never leave Sabree. Nor would watching a psychotic inmate, who was starving himself to death out of paranoia, being coldly shot to death by prison guards as he madly started climbing a barbed wire fence. That evening these disturbing images were triggered by the very prospect of a more humane approach gaining traction—and the doubt that that traction would hold. Reentry, we quickly realized, involved trauma for those who experienced the prison setting from the outside of the bars as well as for those who experienced it from the inside. The almost sanctimonious optimism of the faith leaders at the conference needed to be balanced against harsh realities that had not yet changed, and possibly never would. In many ways, this was the purpose of Sabree's closing remarks at the end of each meeting. Too much hope was as distorting as too little.

PIIC members need to give back, and one of the topics that would energize them highly was the idea that young boys might follow in their own footsteps. Horne would often bring in her troubled grandson, Robbie, who was acting out dangerously. He had at one point lain down in the middle of the street spreading his arms and legs as you would to make a snow angel, claiming he wanted to die. Another time he had set fire to a school bus and was facing charges of arson. At the PIIC support meetings, Robbie was always well-dressed, responsive. He couldn't identify what was driving his aggressive behaviors. His tennis shoe had been scuffed, someone had offended him. But the members of PIIC had a clear concern about where this behavior could lead him and all of them would chime in, providing him with suggestions about how to control his behavior. He relaxed and expanded into the attention, leaving the meetings walking tall, beaming.

Another time, Joe brought in his nephew, who was sixteen. Joe was furious at him. His nephew had waved a gun in front of his mother, Joe's sister, and threatened suicide. His mother had wrestled the gun away. Joe was most angry because his nephew had endangered his own mother. Joe, who had a long history of drug offenses but no violent crimes, was furious at the potential for violence. When Sabree probed Joe's nephew about his ambitions, he said he wanted to be a successful rapper and take care of his mother. Sabree suggested that it was important to always have about a hundred plans for success and routes to them, just in case one or another didn't pan out. It helped reduce frustration. A few months later, his nephew acting up again, Joe again infuriated, insisted that he would like to see the boy incarcerated, only prison would put some sense in him. The support session involved talking Joe down.

In other sessions, conversations turned on the temptation to return to crime when all the ways you were trying to reenter legitimately felt blocked to you: "A person got to eat," the visitor said. Several times men raised concerns about their own sons and the fear that they would follow in their footsteps. Relapse was always a concern. One job loss could send you back to baseline— facing all the prejudice, all the frustration all over again. Having numerous plans was a helpful hedge against frustration, so was never becoming too secure. Sabree mentioned several times how his brother, who had become a successful computer programmer, working for a company for decades, now faced job loss because the company had been bought out and the new company forbid employing anyone with a criminal record. Here today, gone tomorrow. *Whatever* you do.

There were an interesting couple of sessions when a new woman, Manisha, came to the PIIC meeting asking for help with reentry. She was a cycler, had been since she was a teenager, had rarely spent more than a few months out. She was attractive, ingratiating, seductive. She just had no idea how to stay out, she said, looking slowly around the room. The women in PIIC took a hard line, the men were more solicitous. Horne was caustic but stood back and watched. Her colleague in ministry, Dorothy Parker, kept reminding Manisha that they had reviewed much of the material on reentry in prison. Oh, Manisha said, but it is so different when you're out.

Everyone, however, took a protective posture toward Johnny, a large, muscular man in his fifties who had been incarcerated for forty-six years, since he was ten years old. He had gone to prison for murder because he had killed a man who was attacking his mother. In prison, he had been ordered by other prisoners to kill someone, "so I did what I had to do." Horne, who had known him in prison said he had been beaten up a lot there because he was so young. He kept trying to hang himself, but he told Sabree, "I ain't hanging myself to kill myself, just to get attention." Johnny was married but the marriage was not going well. The wife, according to Horne, "Marry him, but he can't stay with her. When he has money, she gets under him for the money. A lot of the men get married in prison. Johnny is thinking until death do us part." Childlike in his directness, Johnny was hyper-kinetic and walked for hours every day.

Once, a middle-class professional couple came to try to understand what their son, who had been convicted and was soon to be incarcerated, was going to face in prison. They had read *The New Jim Crow*, wanted to discuss their son's situation in terms of systemic racism. PIIC members saw that as irrelevant to the daily challenges of prison life.

The only other person who explicitly raised racism as a topic was also a middle-class participant of the group who came often in our first year. He too had been inspired by *The New Jim Crow*. He was a deacon at a large, historic Congregational church, home to many of the faculty at the historically black colleges. He had a plan to help formerly incarcerated men build housing for themselves. He asked the group to pray that he would receive millions for this effort. He often would ask people, "Who hurt you?" A question that rarely received an answer.

A lasting image we have of the potential influence of PIIC involved a panel, "My Journey to Freedom," which they presented at the Hillside International Truth Center, Rev. Barbara King's church. Ariif, Eloise, and Terry all shared their thoughts on what was needed for successful reentry.

Terry, whose mother and grandmother had died while he was in prison, described PIIC as his family. He said: *Change has to begin while you are behind walls. People fear the unknown. If you don't have a model of legitimacy, faced with a choice, you will lean toward the familiar. The system is mighty, but God is All-mighty. A lot of people didn't expect me to be standing here today.*

Ariif talked about the social and financial impact of prison on the family, and how he had to move from a systemic understanding of his situation to a personal and spiritual one: *In the military, I faced bigotry. I developed a hard side. I reasoned to myself that the crime I committed was because there was so little tolerance for African Americans. You have to confront yourself in prison, come to terms with yourself. Your preparation for release begins inside. I realized something in life was bigger than me. As I developed my faith, it allowed me to navigate in a more sensible way. When you wake up, you realize you still have your faculties, you return to a sense of right and wrong.*

Eloise shared her insights as well: *I was twenty-seven years in the Georgia prison system. My greatest struggle was Eloise. My greatest struggle is Eloise. I had a dysfunctional upbringing, but my biggest problem was Eloise. There comes a time when you have to take responsibility.* She also invited the audience to take responsibility as well. *There are people in prison who have good in them. You have to see how this plight affects you, how recidivism affects you. You need to get the system to understand they need to do their part, like we do our part.*

The audience began to ask questions. One speaker was a guard in the federal prison, had been for twenty years, and emphasized how she had tried to treat people like human beings. Other women brought up what you should tell children who had a parent in prison, how parents could re-establish relationships after long absence.

When someone asked how he handled the frustration at being a felon, Terry said, *Go outside and scream as if being scalded, listen to my music, call my friends from PIIC. We are no more or less than anyone else. We're all children of God trying to find our way.*

Horne stood up and introduced herself and said, *When I went into Reidsville, they asked, "What a woman doing here?" I knew I had to go where God sent me. This is what I have to share: Never stop loving. Love is a river. It continues to flow. You can put all kinds of things in a river, but the water will find a way. Never turn your back on them. If you call me at four in the morning, Hazel will find a way.*

\3/

FAITH COMMUNITIES & REENTRY

SUSAN BISHOP, FURQUAN MUHAMMAD, THURMOND N. TILLMAN

The question we have held in mind as we returned to our interviews with members of what we would call holding communities is *What do people who can absorb wrong-doing have to teach us?* The community-engagement dimension of Georgia's reentry efforts has focused on faith communities, most specifically Baptist ones, and primarily African-American ones, to resource and reinforce the reentry effort. One assumption inherent in this approach is that communities most damaged by mass incarceration have the greatest interest and commitment to reentry and that black churches will form a natural source of support because of their religious convictions.

However, having attended several annual Faith Leaders Day gatherings held by our county DA's office with predominantly African-American pastors, we question the assumption that communities most affected by mass incarceration are always the most open to reentry—or even should be. Crime control and self-defense were these pastors major concerns for their communities and congregations. Indeed, participating in a video practice designed to train officers to distinguish when to respond aggressively and when to de-escalate, it was notable how quickly many of the pastors (as well as the DA) opened fire.

On the other hand, many of the longest lasting, indigenous reentry efforts we have encountered have been developed and sustained by chaplains, pastors, and imams who have a strong identification with those to whom they minister and whose commitment comes from their religious faith. Hazel Horne and A.J. Sabree in the prior chapter are prime examples. We describe here three people who have had a strong influence on many people reentering from Georgia's prisons as well as on those systems themselves: Chaplain Susan Bishop inside the Department of Corrections; Imam Furquan Muhammad from Masjid Al-Mu'minun, who in the past thirty years has served as a volunteer chaplain at over thirty-five Georgia prisons and jails; and Rev. Thurmond N. Tillman, pastor of First African Baptist Church in Savannah, whose engagement in criminal justice and reentry concerns have shaped his ministry for decades.

CHAPLAIN SUSAN BISHOP

When the women sing, it is a transcendent moment for them—and for everyone else too.

Susan Bishop has chosen to spend more than thirty years of her life primarily behind bars, but the first time we met, she was dressed in a colorful, flowing wrap and we sat out in the sun in front of a small restaurant in Decatur musing on her life choices and the transcendence of music. It was one of her teaching days at Emory's Candler School of Theology, and her expressive side was in full view. She was aware of the difference.

When asked what people didn't understand about her job, she answered: *I had to go to a fancy lawyer's office recently for a deposition on a completely different matter. I waited in this splendidly furnished office in downtown Atlanta, big views. I thought, "People really do work in places like this." I go behind razor wire every day to work. My work world is so different from the average person. The wire, the keys, the doors clanging all the time. This is what it must feel like for people in reentry, like me in that lawyer's office. It was such a poignant moment.*

Chaplain Bishop liked to talk about the choirs she has developed in the Georgia prisons over the many years she has worked there. These have been a source of support for inmates and for her: "You can create a sanctuary for creativity, even in a prison—but it's not easy." The choirs she has created have provided this kind of sanctuary: *I find it very rewarding to help women rediscover gifts, pieces of themselves, abilities and skills—things that got pushed aside in their need or drive to survive. With me as a musician, I notice if a woman may have a magnificent voice or plays an instrument. I like when I can help them rediscover through this a past and better time, when they were on track. When you are singing or creating, there is no place for worry, obsessing. It is a transcendent moment. When the women sing, it is a transcendent moment for them—and for everyone else too.*

Bishop came into prison ministry after earning a masters in music education and a masters of divinity through Candler in 1975, a time when her denomination, Southern Baptist, didn't yet ordain women. After working in a work-release program for women, then a psychiatric hospital, she began working in a small prison camp in Milledgeville, where she began her first prison choir: *The chief of security there was already taking the women out to sing at her church. I started refining the music. There were about fifteen women in the choir. We went out once or twice a month to churches. The more we got out, the more we were invited. We were the Colony Farm Gospel Choir. The warden was bothered, but he tolerated. He knew the chief kept it all very tight.*

In 1986, the choir, with twelve inmates, was invited to sing before 20,000 people at the Southern Baptist Conference: *One woman, she was on death row, had a sterling high soprano. She sang a solo and there was a standing ovation. Everyone was moved. They allowed her son and daughter to come and see her. Her son came running up to her after the performance and hugged her. "You just tore them up, Mama. You just tore them up!"* The choir also sang for the hometown opening of *The Color Purple* and were allowed to watch the movie with the audience. (This is the same woman whose story Rev. Horne shared with us from a different perspective. Alice Walker's activism on her behalf helped in her release.)

Bishop then went to Metro Prison, where she was the first female chaplain of a male prison, working with the first female warden of a male prison. Again she started a choir. However, belonging to a prison choir involves many behavioral criteria, which were more difficult to ensure in the male prison: *I would choose my choir and then I'd go check their files. Sure enough, I'd have lost my whole set of first tenors. It made it difficult. So we didn't get to perform outside as much as I have been able to with the women.*

Since Bishop had gone up to Arrendale, her woman's choir there, "Voices of Hope," had become an important outreach tool for reentry efforts. Commissioners of Corrections had brought it to public notice, as did Governor Deal. The Arrendale choir had made several recordings: *They see it as good PR and also helpful for management because the women are better behaved, and it helps with reentry because the women can see the world, be seen in it. You have women who have been incarcerated twenty to twenty-nine years out in the community and appreciated. It is limited interaction, but it is interaction. The experience does something for the congregation and for the women.*

We attended a performance of the Voices of Hope choir at First Corinth Missionary Baptist, a church in west Atlanta. The church had an existing prison ministry and a high level of musical ability in its own choir and in its congregation. The service was carried by song. To see the prison choir, the First Corinth choir and the congregation all singing together was moving. Something powerful and lasting changed for the better on all sides when the prison choir soloist moved up and down the aisles singing,

Mama drug me
to church.
Mama drug me
to Sunday School.
She said, M____,
this the only drug
will see you through.
You don't need to sniff it
up your nose,
you don't have to shoot it
in your veins . . .

People reached out just to touch the soloist's hands, and she reached out in return. There was a yearning and a welcoming there that spoke clearly to the possibility of return.

Equally importantly, the effort of earning a place in the prison choir had been a vehicle for insight and change for participants in ways that help them prepare for reentry. Exactly when that change happened felt mysterious to Bishop: *To have an aha moment, I think you have to be ready for it. I don't know what makes anyone ready. Usually there's something they want to do.*

Bishop discussed one woman's oscillating journey and the role that participating in the choir played in it. She had a very good voice, but was ineligible for the choir because of her disciplinary reports. Bishop told her if she could go six months with no reports, she could join the choir. It took the woman a year and a half and two setbacks to meet that behavioral standard.

After her second setback, she came to Bishop and said: *"Give someone else that space. They will be able to travel."* I told her, *"No. That space has your name on it. Vocally you earned it. Now behaviorally you need to earn it."* So she was in the choir for almost a year before she could travel. Now she's really really changing. Many of those issues that troubled her are dropping away. She doesn't need them any more. It's been a year now. I find this often. Once someone's started changing, they start changing deep down and things fall away.*

Before she retires, Bishop would like to see college education return to the prisons. To further that possibility, she and Professor Elizabeth Bounds at Candler created a Theological Certificate Program for inmates in Arrendale Prison. They also included the prison as a site for Candler's contextual education program—increasing divinity students' familiarity with the distinctive demands of prison ministry. The day we visited Bishop inside Arrendale, we spoke about these programs in more depth as well as other programs developed by the chaplaincy program to help mothers stay constructively engaged with their children.

In the prison, our conversation focused more on control and requirements than transcendence. The banging of doors, the clanging of keys, the steady stream of voices were all evident as we talked. The theological students who had come that day from Emory were now spread out around the prison, several in the mental health unit, others in lock down, some in diagnostic, some in a faith and character dorm. Bishop wanted them immersed: *They need to figure out how to carry on a conversation with someone who is psychotic, someone who you can only speak to you through a small flap in a locked door, how to fit their conversations in between counts and chow, how to minister to the staff as well as the inmates—because how the staff feels determines how the day will go for the inmates as well.* The students also needed to understand the importance of restraint: *This is not necessarily about being liked. About making someone feel good. The long-range goal is what is ultimately in the inmate's best interest. For some people, being told no is the best thing that you can do for them.*

The Theological Certificate program also involved behavioral constraints for participants similar to those for the choir: Good behavior for six months before entering the program and throughout the year. If not, they were taken out and had to start over at the beginning. As with the choir, the number of people applying to be in the program was three or four times its capacity. Bishop felt the program built practical and social skills essential for reentry: community building, communication, writing, religious tolerance.

She also felt that everything that happened in prison helped prepare for reentry: *Coming to terms with their addictions, their desire to live on the edge of excitement, their grief, or past trauma and abuse. All those behaviors that resulted in their coming here will happen again if they don't understand them.* Of the negative behaviors, she thought continued substance abuse was most predictive of recidivism.

Bishop felt chaplains had an important role to play when women <u>did</u> return to prison: *It is critical to have someone who believes in you, who is willing to be an anchor. In the prison system that is not easy to do. I've been around longer, or as long as, any other chaplain. I see women coming in who have been in several times before. I see them in roundup and I think, oh no, they're back, and they look at me and I see they feel that. They feel shame and need: I don't want the chaplain to see me; I need the chaplain. They know I'm not going to turn my back on them. I say, "It's all right. We'll talk later."*

You know what I mean. "You're still here. Maybe God's still here." I don't think never, I think not yet. I have a bumper sticker: "Grace happens." Not Shit happens. I do believe people can change. There are a few people who need to be incarcerated, but by and large, people can change. I think I always took the message of grace seriously.

Another chaplain at Arrendale had focused on the needs of incarcerated mothers to stay engaged with their children. Along with weekend and holiday visitation, there was a special Children's Center one Saturday a month. To participate, women attend an active parenting class and a group meeting and must have no disciplinary reports. The setting was more like a daycare than a prison. The children were fed breakfast. Women could see newborns they last saw in the hospital, could feed them bottles. Bishop described one day when they brought in two teachers from the community who held mock parent-teacher meetings with the women and their children, then had the mothers write their children's real teachers to introduce themselves and begin correspondence. They also arranged to link the mothers and the teachers by phone for real-time parent-teacher conferences.

SISTERS INTO THE LIGHT

When asked what change in social attitudes would make the biggest difference for reentry, Bishop answered: *It would be to take people individually. We have so many stereotypes. Just to let each person be who they are, currently who they are, would be an important step. Who of us is the same at thirty-six that we were at eighteen?*

We attended one event she inspired that did exactly that—for her and for the women she had worked with over the years. Annually Bishop organizes a reunion for her choir graduates with the help of different groups. The year we attended, Peachtree Methodist Church in the wealthy Buckhead area offered to sponsor an all day reunion with luncheon for Bishop and the graduates of her choir. It was held in a large luminous meeting hall, with beautifully set tables, a delicious buffet.

The fifty or more women who came were all excited to share what they had been doing. Some had segregated their prison experience from their current lives out of concern for stigma and rejection, either for them or for their children. In this setting they did not. This event allowed for a coherence that was helpful, allowing them to claim what they had gained from the relationships they developed in prison and to highlight what was working in their lives now. They shared memories and appreciations of Chaplain Bishop.

Women sang, singly or together. What was most interesting about the event was that it did not have the feeling of a charity event. The women attending were appreciative of the care with which the event had been organized, the church women were impressed by the talent and community they saw. They were all able to claim the fullness of the present, a crucial dimension of genuine reintegration.

IMAM FURQUAN MUHAMMAD
We have always had a reentry ministry. It is called helping people.

Imam Furquan Muhammad of the Masjid Al-Mu'minun has been volunteering in Georgia prisons since 1975. All his work is volunteer. When asked how he began, he said, *They needed an imam. There was an Islamic man in prison and the warden told him he could get services if he could find a member of the faith to come. I had no background check problem. I was squeaky clean.* His services from the beginning were open to people of all faiths and races. He also started providing staff and officials information about Islam, particularly about the more international Islam that was being practiced among followers of W. D. Mohammed.

He emphasized that a prison chaplain needs to be open to people of all faiths: *All the people in there are human beings. I don't go in pushing Islam. An inmate, facing death, I tell him, "You can get a Christian if you want." Usually he will say, "I just want a man of the cloth. I just want a chaplain." Sometimes Christian chaplains come behind asking questions. But anyone pushing a religion, his own mindset is wrong.*

He felt prisoners were sometimes transferred to other prisons if they converted, especially Caucasian converts to Islam. "But Muslim speaks to the condition of our heart. You don't become one because its popular or gives you more security." However, he did acknowledge that "Muslims safer in prison because people don't mess with Muslims." He ascribed that to the conflation of two qualities. Gang leaders who came into prison sometimes converted to Islam and other inmates "see *gang* leader, not Muslim." One of his roles, then, was to reassure the prison authorities that the version of Islam practiced by people in the prison was "real" Islam.

Imam Furquan was himself a convert. One of eleven children, he was raised Baptist and became a Muslim in his mid-teens. He had heard of the teachings of Islam and asked his parents about it. They didn't know, so he read the Koran, but it wasn't the Koran itself, rather the contradictory behavior of the Christian people around him that drove his conversion. "People were claiming a church but selling liquor and having girlfriends. It made me assess what I was claiming." He was inspired by the congruent behavior of Muslims he saw at the YMCA near his home, the discipline they showed in their physical exercises, their prayers, their demeanor. Islam to him was about character. His parents supported his decision. He didn't intend to become an imam. "I was just studious and people noticed."

He thought that Islam might have more success in reducing recidivism simply because of the discipline its practice requires, the praying five times a day, which makes you time conscious, and the fasting for the thirty days of Ramadan, which is practiced communally, over a billion people all over the world doing it together.

When we interviewed him in 2014, he saw the prisons as little more, sometimes even less, than warehouses: *The feed them and clothe them but send them out like they were. They can't read, can't write. They don't treat their medical conditions.* An important part of his role as a chaplain was just to respond to inmates as people. If someone asked for help on health, he would check with the medical team: *I don't think any people should be treated like an animal. It may be my history. I see people in there with disabilities. Disabilities they got in prison.*

He felt that it was a mistake to indiscriminately stigmatize everyone who went to prison: *Most people see people in prison as losers. Everyone believes people who go there are all guilty. Good people can be guilty of being in the wrong place. People can be guilty of getting caught up in something.*

Furquan thought time in prison was not necessarily negative, it could be a time of insight: *It is sometimes a blessing. The U.S. is a temptation. Prison is a place where you get out of the rat race. You have time to think. Sometime that period is not as ugly as you think. I'm surprised at the number of people who went in a racist and came out with that changed.*

He did question the prisons' refusal to let ex-offenders return and talk with other inmates: *It doesn't make it easy for models to come in. What matters is that they can be seen as reformed, new creatures.*

He stressed that effective reentry was a choice. When people were getting ready to leave prison, it was their own responsibility to put themselves in places where temptations were less. He told people, both in and out of prison: *You can't practice reentry like an island. Your job is to be aggressive and come to the mosque. When you come to the mosque, you will get help. Bypass the masjid, and that is help you'll never get.*

The help they will get is pragmatic: *The masjid has always had a reentry program. We call it helping people. Putting people to work. Waxing the floor. Doing other jobs here. We don't use federal funds. There are only two ways to make money—legal and illegal. When you fix to make it so hard—people kind of get in survival mode. There are people with lots of skill, but they can't get a job. People will tell you, "I got the money, but I can't rent." The institution used every one of your skills at the institution—but you can't use them when you get out. People think everyone in prison is so stupid, but I've seen a ship built of match ends.*

We got to do a better job to help these people. A man's going to get out, and say, "I was going to do right." But his family has written him off. He can't go to anyone. He can't get work. When it's cold, it's better in prison. I do believe people deserve a second chance. Women who go to prison, <u>they</u> are never forgiven.

Imam Furquan found his prison ministry rewarding in its real world consequences. He could be in a grocery store or gas station, and someone could come up to him and say, "I remember you. You changed my life. I've never been back to prison."

He was clear that churches and mosques needed to do better for the families of people who are incarcerated: *When an individual goes to prison, the whole family goes to prison. Visitation is limited by distance. The family pays the costs of lawyers and sending money to the prisoner. Phone calls are so expensive, $8 or $12 a call. Religious houses of worship can help by helping you get to your incarcerated family member. Churches should have a visitation ministry. They should ask, "Is there something we can do?"*

HEALING COMMUNITIES

Healing Communities was the major community-engagement effort employed by the Georgia Prisoner Reentry Initiative. In practice, this was one of the least successful of the reentry initiatives. Churches were contacted and engaged in training sessions which resulted in their putting a decal on their churches indicating that they were friendly to people reentering. Other than having a more positive attitude, it was not clear what the decals meant, either to the congregations or to people coming for assistance.

The model was developed by Harold Dean Trulear with the Annie E. Casey Foundation to be used for juvenile offenders and their families. It describes itself as interested in reintegration, not just reentry, as more of an attitude shift than a program designed to help reintegration become the norm. Its aim is "to mobilize the relational capital—both abilities and infrastructure—of the faith community around the specific individuals returning from incarceration." The phrase "returning citizens" was coined by Trulear because it "recognizes the citizenship of the formerly incarcerated and their belonging in the community itself." The program appeals to the values of forgiveness, redemption, reconciliation and healing that are "common to congregations in distressed neighborhoods." When focused on juveniles and supported by non-profits, this model makes sense. As communities we don't want to lose our youth and need to acknowledge the broader social conditions that they have had no hand in making.

But, for the state to ask the faithful in communities most damaged by mass incarceration to "pay the price" of restoration is far more problematic. This focus on recruiting faith communities in disadvantaged neighborhoods to help resource state reentry efforts exploits for the *state's* benefit those communities most negatively affected by inequitable *state* prosecution, as well as by the social conditions—poverty, lack of education, violence, and racism—that so clearly contribute to criminal behavior. We can't help wondering whether it would be better to focus that request for resources on those who have been disproportionately *advantaged* by that inequality—the ones whose sons and daughters have often gone unprosecuted, unsaddled by the lasting stigma of a felony conviction, the damage of incarceration.

Many of these themes came up in our discussion with Reverend Thurmond Tillman, who has been party to various reform efforts over the years, including the Governor's Interfaith Council designed to expand on criminal justice reforms.

REV. THURMOND N. TILLMAN
What are we doing to prevent the second strike?

We spoke with Rev. Thurmond N. Tillman at First African Baptist Church in downtown Savannah, the oldest black church in North America (constituted 1777), where he had been pastor for over thirty years. He has been actively involved in reentry throughout his professional life, as was his father before him. In the 1970s his father, a pastor in Brunswick, Georgia, served as the chairman of the board of what was then called the Department of Offender Rehabilitation (now Corrections) when Allen Ault was commissioner.

Tillman is tall, elegant, with a ready sense of humor. He is deeply engaged with the complexities of reentry—and comfortably outspoken about its importance to the larger society. He earned a bachelor's degree in sociology and criminal justice. He then experienced a call to ministry and went on to study at Morehouse School of Religion and the Interdenominational Theological Center in Atlanta. At the same time he had an internship with the Atlanta Diversion Center, and when he graduated became a probation officer there, then became a senior counselor at the diversion center in Albany. He decided, "I didn't want to work for my dad," which ruled out working in Corrections at that time given his father's position on the board. So he worked in a management position at a poultry plant before being called to be pastor at First African Baptist Church. He had thought he might continue to work in a diversion center in Savannah, but the church wanted a full-time pastor.

Tillman brought his commitment to criminal justice into his church, where he has been a strong advocate of giving formerly incarcerated people a second chance: *What people ignore is that 97% of people return. They think we would be safer if they were locked up, safer if they were locked up forever. But if you send someone to prison for ten or twenty years and they are coming out with no rehabilitation, a stranger in a culture that has changed while they were gone, they need the care of being taught and trained to get along with people. But a lot of people don't want to take the time to bring them along. And they don't really want to share where they have been. But it is difficult to get out and make it without community.*

The situation that has concerned Tillman the most and has inspired much of his activism is how to reduce recidivism. This concern crystallized around the Seven Deadlies (SB 440) and Second Strike (SB 441) laws passed in Georgia in 1994 and 1995. SB 440 allowed children as young as thirteen to be tried as adults and defined the Seven Deadlies while SB 441 established mandatory ten-year minimums and a penalty of life without parole for a second conviction of a crime of equal severity.

What concerned Tillman was how the laws threatened to increase, not reduce violence: *I kept writing Governor Zell Miller asking him, What are you doing to prevent the second strike? What if someone serves ten years without parole for armed robbery? You come back to the community. No one wants to hire you. You've been exposed to a lot of violence in prison. Even if no one hires you, you still need money, for food, child support. You're going to turn to what you know—armed robbery. But next time it will be life without parole, so how do you make sure your victim can't testify? Now you're more violent. You think, if I kill, it will be the same punishment.*

Tillman suggested that churches go into prison before people were released. It was possible to know who these SB 440s were and where they were returning. It was possible to intervene at that critical point: *When a church or a faith-based community wraps their arms around a person who has been incarcerated, his family and others are more likely to give him a chance. It removes some of the shame.*

This wrapping one's arms around an ex-offender was not a sentimental gesture. Tillman saw this support as a form of mutual accountability. Several chaplains told us they don't want to know what someone had done, that all that mattered was who they were now. Tillman's concept of a responsive community was different: both the individual and the community needed to consciously absorb the reality of wrong-doing. This idea resonated with that of the restorative justice Circles of Accountability and Support (COSA) developed in Canada and now used in some states in the U.S.

My concept is if we embrace this person as they are, knowing what they've done, that person is more likely to change, more likely to do right. The more we can do something like COSA, the safer we are. It is better to know who is sitting by you. If it is a purse snatcher, you make sure to keep your purse on the other side. If it is a child molester, you sit next to him and make sure he doesn't associate with children. I don't think everyone needs to know, but some people need to. It will help them not reoffend. I don't worry about labeling. People are always labeling, but it is usually based on gossip not facts. We're all always falling short, so there's no label anyone can have that makes me better than somebody else.

In 2003, Tillman began a campaign, Hundred Black Churches Connected, to create a network of churches that might begin to intervene with individuals imprisoned for a first strike at the point when they left prison. The churches could wrap their arms around them and help them make a successful transition. This was just about the time that the first of the SB 440s would begin maxing out. Tillman focused on churches in the coastal region of Georgia. He told a self-deprecating story about how he identified the first young man to be released under the Seven Deadlies in Savannah and called his family to say that he would pick him up. "But they had it all taken care of. He never had any more problem."

Other reentering individuals felt the church was the whole answer. Tillman wryly described a man sitting beaming through a 7 a.m. Bible study as if they were old friends. When Tillman went to speak with him, he said, "I came because you all going to help me. The Bible says God will supply all my needs, and you represent God."

The faith of this man was admirable, but not altogether well-founded. The assumption that reentry will find a natural constituency in the black church is questionable. African-American churches are often highly intolerant of crime and of people who commit crimes. Again and again in our interviews, we heard pastors and chaplains and imams talk about how families do not speak about their incarcerated family members at church.

One of Tillman's challenges was to address the resistance and prejudice of the pastors he was trying to engage around reentry. He described how, when he talked with a pastor about taking a COSA approach in his congregation, the pastor said, "I can't do that. I'm a shepherd of the sheep. You're asking me to welcome in the wolves." The following Monday, he called to apologize. Tillman wondered what happened over the weekend to change his mind, whether he had asked on Sunday how many people in his congregation had been incarcerated or had a family member who had been.

Once Tillman created a line-up of young men at another pastors' conference held at his church. He handed out a checklist to the pastors and asked them to identify who was a married, never incarcerated father of two, who was a murderer, who was accused of murder in self-defense, who spent two years in jail awaiting trial, who was waiting to be tried for a second strike, who had a father and step-father in prison. "The point was that any one of these men could be in your congregation. No secrets. It was better to know." They never identified the murderer, someone who Tillman fondly referred to as his spiritual son, and who now had a successful landscaping business and drove a Mercedes.

Tillman did observe that the only churches that became involved in the One Hundred Churches Connected were churches whose congregations already included people who had come back from prison.

Tillman wanted to harness the significant buying power of the African-American community to support African-American entrepreneurialism and also support those who were most needy in that community. Although a Healing Communities coordinator, he was a little caustic about the use of decals to identify them: *Any house of worship has a symbol—and that symbol* *already says that it is a safe place, or should be. Where we need to put those decals is on <u>businesses</u> that hire the formerly incarcerated—and encourage people to shop there. The decal could identify community-responsive businesses.*

He saw employment as key in many ways, not only providing a livelihood but also actively transforming stigma: *What I'd like to see is a company that was owned and operated and staffed by returning citizens. A community-responsive business. One where when people purchased from it, they realize they are part of the solution. One where people could see that the formerly incarcerated were contributing to the betterment of the community.*

But entrepreneurialism wasn't the only solution, training factored in as well. He described a successful joint venture he began with a restaurant owner in Savannah, the late Roy Thompson, who happened to sit in on a meeting Tillman was having with men who had recently reentered. The men were complaining about employment, and at first Thompson objected saying that jobs were available in Savannah. The men talked about how, a month after being hired, they would be fired when their background checks came back. Tillman had several houses that he was trying to rehab to house people in the community. Thompson took the houses over from Tillman, hired a contractor to oversee the rehab work, and then hired only returning citizens to do the work: *It was a learning experience. The men didn't have to be perfect. They were learning on the job, getting better, and the assumption was by the next project they would be more experienced.*

Unfortunately, all this took place just before the crash of 2008, so the houses did not make the profit they needed to fund the next venture.

This emphasis on employment, and the responsibility we have as a society to respond, is something Tillman is not hesitant to bring up in many different settings. At one point the Department of Corrections (DOC) was starting an employment initiative, Take Five, to encourage large employers to hire returning citizens. Tillman was on an advisory committee and was at a meeting that was designed to persuade various business executives to participate. Tillman turned to the DOC representatives and asked, "Why can't the state hire them too?" The representative said, "We can't hire them to build prisons." "Well why not state contractors then?" Tillman asked. "You could see the businessmen were thinking the same thing: *You're asking this of us, but you won't do it.*"

The challenges of reentry are many, and racial bias is an important one. It begins before arrest, in the different ways we define a crime. An example

Tillman gave was the different responses to two crimes by juveniles. In one, an African-American boy at a local high school shot another boy, supposedly one who had bullied him. Even after the victim was dead, "the boy was still clicking [the trigger] and kicking him." The boy was taken to jail, charged as an adult. Two months later, a white student at a white high school took hostages at a media center: *At the conclusion of the standoff, we never saw his image. He was taken away to Georgia Regional with mental problems. But that other boy, the one who kept clicking and kicking, he obviously had mental problems too.* These differences also exist in the exposures that make people vulnerable to criminal behavior, for example early deprivation or exposure to violence. Tillman quoted a juvenile judge he had heard at a recent conference on juvenile crime who said, "Children do not commit crimes, they commit delinquent acts. Their minds are not developed."

Another challenge is the level of trust and maturity that are needed to desist from crime. Tillman described how his church had tried to wrap its arms around a young man who was convicted of murder. He had received a sentence of thirty-five years. While he was incarcerated, his court-appointed attorney successfully appealed, and, after the young man had served five years in prison, his sentence was modified to five years of incarceration and twenty-five years of probation. He was released and was to report daily to the probation office. He was arrested on a technical violation because he had associated with another person with a felony, and DOC petitioned to revoke all his probation and send him back to prison for twenty-five years.

The judge told them to talk to Tillman first, and when Tillman came up with a plan that included ankle monitoring, shelter, attendance at First African, and monitoring by Savannah Impact Program, the young man was released. He joined the church the second time he visited it. He was baptized and the congregation put their arms around him—something Tillman wasn't sure they would be willing to do since he had various tattoos over his face, including a large one on his forehead: MOE—Money Over Everything. Two men in the congregation were assigned as mentors.

But the young man had the impression that his ankle monitor would be removed on a certain date. He kept mentioning this, and people ignored it. He became depressed when this didn't happen, so four days later decided to cut the monitor off and go visit his girlfriend. He disappeared for thirty days and would not receive calls. This meant that when he was arrested again, he would be returned to prison for the full length of his sentence.

As Tillman told the story, you could see that he felt responsible that he hadn't picked up how frustrated the young man was, but he also felt deeply frustrated at how to reach a mind so focused on the immediate moment that it could not weigh the momentous consequences of his actions. When we talked, a year after the event, the young man was still in jail waiting trial. Tillman, visiting, would tell him he was lucky he was still in jail, not prison. The young man had psychological issues, he mused. He should have been on medications. Someone should have heard, and dismantled, his faulty expectation about when the ankle monitor would be removed.

But the story that moved both of us beyond tears was his account of something that had happened only a week before. A juvenile judge in Savannah had organized a conference on community safety and had brought in two interesting groups from California, boys from Home Boys Industries and from the Robeson Scholars, a group of young men who were part of the Reintegration Academy at Cal Poly Pomona, a program started by the political scientist Dr. Renford Reese to create a prison-to-school pipeline for the formerly incarcerated. One young man in this group, Semaj, was strikingly eloquent. In and out of juvenile justice as a teenager, he had been heavily mentored by another program, the Brotherhood Crusade, wrapped in their attention as Tillman suggested, then connected with the Reintegration Academy. A few months before, Semaj had spoken to Congress and had met President Obama. Hearing the young men speak in Savannah, Tillman asked them to come and speak at his church the following day, Sunday.

The police chief was at the service. The juvenile judge was there. However, when the young men came to the church, they came without Semaj. He and some of the other boys had visited the tourist walk near the harbor the evening before. Boys from the local projects came up and talked with them and invited them to come and see where they lived. But as they came into the projects, the boys turned on them and asked for their wallets. They pulled out guns. Semaj and his companion ran, but Semaj was shot in the arm and the back. The bullet shattered his spine. He learned a few days later that he was permanently paralyzed.

Semaj's responses to this event were both moving and disorienting to some. Semaj's first desire was to speak with the boy who had shot him. He had become fascinated with restorative justice in his college studies, and was instinctively applying those principles now. "I understand how he was thinking," he said. "But until you talk to the person, you really don't know why. I don't want to be quick to judge. I hate being judged."

When we visited with Tillman, Semaj had recently been transferred to the Shepherd Center, a spine and brain rehabilitation center in Atlanta, and Tillman asked if we would visit with him there. When we visited Semaj, he vividly described what Tillman meant when he talked about the importance of a congregation, or a society, wrapping their arms around us.

I never felt so much love as I felt in the hospital. Everyone at that forum [On Community Safety] have kept up with me. Rev. Tillman came and saw me two or three time a day. Anytime I have a problem, I can call him. He prayed every night with me and my mom. The same with the men that mentored me at the Brotherhood Crusade. When I got out of juvie, they gave me five mentors who focused on different things, education, goals, going out and talking to people. They would call my phone every day. I was still pushing them away a year later, but they helped change my belief and behaviors.

And Dr. Reese he's my role model. He said, "If someone spit in my face, I'll wipe it off and walk away." He made me see, there's nothing you can't do. He saw something in me, I didn't see in myself. When I came to that campus, I knew I wanted to stay there. Because I was leaving a culture of dysfunction. Once you get out of that culture you can breathe, think, excel. If there is no good around you, how can you do good?

Semaj was determined to return to Savannah and to continue his violence prevention efforts. He had discovered the power of his own voice through his public speaking. When a few months earlier he had met President Obama, shaken his hand, Semaj had thought, "If I can shake that man's hand, I can do anything." Savannah was a place where he already had used that voice and could continue to use it.

Tillman continues to organize church leaders to combat youth violence in Savannah and encourage reentry, individual by individual. Semaj did return to Savannah and started a non-profit, F.I.R.E.—forgiveness, introspection, respect, education—to help reduce juvenile delinquency and violence.

When asked what changes he would like to see in the criminal justice system, Tillman's two suggestions focused on broader social empowerment and restoration. He wanted communities to have some power to police themselves, to define what they needed from an individual in terms of safety and repair—without always saddling the person with the long-term consequences of involvement in the legal system. The other, just a little tongue in cheek: make ex-offenders judges.

\(4)/

RE-ENTRY PARTNERSHIP HOUSING

PATRICIA BENNETT, MR. A., MR. M., MR. I.

The Re-Entry Partnership Housing (RPH) program was developed by Parole and Corrections to provide temporary food and board to people who would be approved for release on parole if they had housing. This program is designed to stabilize the reentry process and also to reduce prison costs, since subsidizing housing in the community is cheaper than continued incarceration. Landlords, reluctant to rent to people with felony convictions, especially if they are unemployed or sex offenders, are more likely to provide temporary housing with these guarantees. The RPH program contracts with approved housing providers for up to 180 days, more typically 90 days. The program has been expanded to include people on probation and also felony accountability courts. Individuals are supervised by a community supervision officer or an accountability court. (Parole/DCS has also created a registry of approved housing [THOR] that certifies residences for returning citizens who simply need a clean, safe, structured environment after leaving prison—or more intensive settings that incorporate treatment for addiction. Individuals or their families must pay for the cost of THOR housing.)

To learn more about transitional reentry housing and the experiences of men in their first month or two after release, we talked with Patricia Bennett, whose organization, Empowering Men and Women on the Move for Re-Entry, provides RPH housing in the Atlanta area. We arranged to visit one of the two apartments that comprised her program. They were located in a large complex in South Fulton, accessible to public transportation, although about an hour by bus from downtown Atlanta. The range of housing in the area was striking, from abandoned, rotted houses to handsome and spacious newly constructed homes. The apartment complex itself was large, well-maintained. The two, two-bedroom apartments used by the program were in adjoining buildings so the men could eat together. There were four men in each apartment.

We first met Bennett at PIIC meetings when she came to ask for some people who might work for her concessions business at the local baseball stadium. She had expected her residents to participate, thinking it would provide them all with needed funds, but she found her residents were not eager to work there and certainly not eager to work as energetically as she expected. She thought that PIIC might be able to find her more dedicated workers.

Bennett, her trustee, Mr. M., who was a former resident, and two current residents, Mr. A. and Mr. I., talked with us. Bennett had first run reentry housing for women, which she partially subsidized with fundraisers, but she found that she preferred working with men. The women were too needy and manipulative, there was too much emotional noise. Men were more straightforward. (Her trustee, Mr. M., looked a little dubious about the greater tractability of the men.) It was also more financially stable: RHP housing was guaranteed by the state.

When asked why she had become interested in reentry and especially reentry housing, Bennett described her admiration for her own mother, a probation officer in New Jersey. She had clearly developed her own speaking style from her mother, even her own children noted this. She expected to be obeyed. She said, "The challenge is we are dealing with people who are broken. They don't know why they keep returning to prison."

Although the men did not have to work during this time as a condition for housing, they were all on either probation or parole, so supervised by DCS officers and must meet their expectations. Bennett did not have a choice about who came into her program, except that her program did not accept sex offenders because the complex forbid them because there were children living in the apartment complex. She would accept one homeless juvenile release at a time. The men were provided with two meals a day (prepared by the trustee, the menus not open to discussion) and had to follow a four-page list of rules and regulations that covered smoking, stealing, fighting, drugs and alcohol, guests, television, attire, drug testing and room checks. "We can't choose the people," she said, "but we can set the rules."

Bennett would go to the Greyhound station, but only the Greyhound station, to meet the men when they came in. However, she would take them at 4:30 in the morning to the free Mercy Care clinic for the uninsured and homeless to make sure they were first in line when it opened at 7 a.m. There the men could receive free medical, dental, and psychiatric attention for a year.

She had only positive things to say about the parole officer who supervised her residents: *I can call him or text him. He will come over and talk to one of the guys. Even at midnight. I've seen some of these probation officers talk to them like they are under their shoe, but there's nothing you can't talk to him about. He's good at working with this population. He says, "I let you hang yourself."*

Bennett was thinking about trying to find a five-bedroom house with two and a half baths to use instead of the two apartments. Zoning, however, was a problem: "You can't plop a reentry program just anywhere." The apartment complex would allow tenants with felonies, but they wanted a program to vouch for them. She talked about what participants in her housing program wanted—something RPH provided—someone to vouch that the program wasn't shifty, wasn't going to take their entire SSI check.

In terms of the attitudes of the residents, she said, *The men are angry about everything. They don't know how to turn the penal system off. They need to know they are out in society now. Nobody is going to have a pity party for you.*

She found the younger men the most difficult: *They give us a run for our money. They need motherly love. It's like when you go in so young, you're coming out a fifteen year old, even if you're forty. Every two seconds, you're saying something to them. You can't move that in ninety days.*

Employment was an issue. Some men were looking for it: *Ones that are in for a short period of time, they can go out for work. Those who were in a long time, they get frustrated, find it hard to adapt. They need to be guided. They don't know how to conversate. A couple of the older guys, they don't leave the apartment. Some of them have never had a job.*

The men who were present shared their rather different stories with us. The oldest, Mr. A. was fifty-nine. He had been in prison this time, his sixth, for nine years. Never for a violent crime, only burglary. As we were both studying a dead insect on the table, trying to decide whether it was a flea, fly or mosquito, whether to acknowledge or ignore it, he told us that this time he intended to stay out. "I have great-grandkids. I'm tired for real."

Besides, prisons were falling in quality: *The prison system now is really really thin. It used to be a corrections facility. They have nothing to offer you anymore. They used to have trades, like upholstery, every kind of trade, but they ain't got nothing to offer you anymore. Now they (the inmates) just sit up in the dawn thinking about something that they can get into. For real. I used to work at Georgia Military College. They don't have that anymore. I was always minimal security—she can tell you, she has all my papers. When I was up at Hayes, I worked at the landfill. I'm a heavy equipment operator. Stopped it because they thought people might escape, go meet up with their girlfriend.*

Mr. A. had been released from prison two months before, and had another month of subsidized housing. He had his next step planned. A week or two before release he would return to the area where he grew up, some distance from Atlanta, and sign up at a poultry plant, live for awhile at his niece's house. She was raising her half-brother, her father having passed, and still seemed to hold out hope for her uncle. "My sisters are wailing on me. They keep throwing my past at me. Throwing barbs. But my niece is standing by me." Delicately, Mr. A. picked up the unidentified insect and dropped it to the floor.

The trustee, Mr. M., described how he had originally objected to Bennett's many rules: *When I was first released, I had a hard time with curfews. Then I saw they helped. If you're out at night, bad things can happen. When my ninety days were over, I moved out to another apartment with some men I knew. But they were drinking and partying, and I wasn't ready for it. Probation and parole would come by and I would be in trouble. I thought this program was what I needed, so I went and asked her to take me back. I made it work for myself, instead of just doing what I want to do.* Bennett had hired him on as a trustee. Now he had enough money to start a bank account.

Mr. M. felt he had been prepared for reentry in prison. He had received classes in Reentry and Motivation for Change. In these programs he had learned about the Reentry Housing Program. One thing that bothered him was knowing he was going to have a hard time getting out from under his felony conviction. But a counselor told him "You can't have that attitude when you get out. You have to try to instill some hope before you get out. People will respond to the hopelessness."

Mr. M. had a strong feeling this time that he needed to make reentry work for him: *I always ran into my troubles. But I'm thirty-five years old. I have kids. I can't continue to do this. I grew tired. There were too many choices. I had never heard about a program like this. I could see how Ms. Bennett was interacting with us. Nobody else care. I decided to help her help us. I haven't had issues here. There are lots of things in the environment, but here, I can be what I need to be.*

Bennett added, *When he came to us, he was very bitter. But when he came back, I asked him, "Can you be a trustee?" I saw something in him. I knew he was bitter and angry, but he didn't break rules. He was so humble when he came back, I had to give him another chance. He was not acting like I owed him something. We had another housing trustee at that time, and I didn't want him because he was sly, cheating. But Mr. M. spoke up so eloquently, I couldn't believe he was the same person. He had to grow. He sees potential in all the men here too.*

Mr. M. remained highly sensitive to what he perceived as social stigmatizing. He told us he had asked Bennett not to try to combine the men from the two apartments anymore for group meetings: *Walking from this unit to that unit I seen the looks people in this area were giving us. It makes me feel a certain way. They might not notice it but I notice it. So I don't want them to look at us that way. It's always good to be cautious in life. We're all human, we all make mistakes. But I want them to see us like we live in an apartment complex just like they do. We're civilians now. We're here. We're neighbors.*

Another man, Mr. I., small, muscular, who had arrived only the week before, proudly told us he had come out of prison with a job doing car detailing at a nearby carwash seven days a week. Ms. Bennett asked him what had made the change in his attitude from last week, when confronted with her rules, he had said, "I don't think I want this. I feel like I am in prison."

After he thought he had served his entire sentence and had been out for three years, Mr. I had been returned to prison for another year due to a bureaucratic error in calculating the time he had to serve on various sentences. During his jail sentence five years ago and then the three years out that followed, he had been able to stay clean, which gave him confidence that he could continue on that path after this return to incarceration. Although he said he was not a talking man, Mr. I. engaged in an extended soliloquy in response to Bennett's question that continues to echo for us because it combines so many of the themes that haunt reentry and incarceration itself— including childhood trauma, systemic deprivation, violence, recidivism, insight, hubris, hope.

When you come back to society, you are laden. When you come back into this world, you might not feel yourself to be filthy but you got to prove yourself to people back in this world. They gonna to give you that look. They gonna size you up and see if they can trust you in certain manners or if they can talk to you. You got to prove yourself to society. This is a challenge. I've always been a person, I don't work from challenges.

I've learned through life there are a lot of meanings to the definition of a man. Age don't make you a man. Maturity, responsibilities, and the way you carry yourself every day, that's what makes you a man. That what people look at. They don't look at your age. You can be forty-five year old but still be a child because the maturity of your mind is still in a child state. You have to understand where you are in life. I done went through the trenches. I done came from the dirt. I been locked up for murder. I been locked up for aggravated assault. I been locked up for armed robbery. I been locked up for trafficking cocaine. (Not trafficking, Bennett demurred.)

I'm thirty-six. I been to prison five times. So, for me, what really made me say, "Go ahead, give it a try?" My eight kids, they look up to me. No matter how many times I been locked up. No matter how many times I been in jail. So if I want them to see something different, that mean that in me I have to swallow some things, bottle them up, right from the start. I wanted to run [when this last sentence came up]. But, I got a bigger picture inside of me now. Five years ago I lived right through jail. I left and lived right for three years. When I figured out that I can come out here, stay free, still look good, still make money, still do all the things that everybody else is doing, that change you.

A lot of people they are afraid of change. They are scared of what that change will bring. A lot of us have been doing so much drugs so long that we afraid if we make the change. When I left last time I made a promise to myself, not to nobody else: I'm going to make sure that from that day they let me out that every step I take be <u>outside</u> of a wall.

Because I done spent since the age of thirteen <u>behind</u> these walls. I lost my fifteen year-old son to the streets, now he's doing twenty years. When that happen it's a lot of stuff. . . . You pray to God, you ask God to show you something, you ask God to give you signs, allow you to see things that you need to see to help you guide yourself. A lot of what we pray and we read of his Word we don't understand. So I come to a point where I began to understand.

I stopped worrying about where everybody else thought of me, which way I move, how I talk, how I walk, that don't matter because God don't worry about me. The only thing He worry about is me doing what I need to do to better myself to show my righteousness to Him. For me, it just became a point where I got tired. A lot of people say I'm tired of this, I'm tired of that, but they actions, they actions don't follow up they words. You can say anything you want out your mouth, but if you don't put an action behind what you say, you just talking.

I try not to get talking. I try to prove to myself that I know I can be better. I know what I can do, I know the steps I need to take, I know the way I need to go. I know if I need to go back. I know if I need to go forward. Because God always shows me every morning: This is your agenda—period. If you do this, you don't worry about that. Because if you do this, that other is no longer you. I tell a lot of people, like my family—I don't get along with my family—I tell them, if you look at my past, you will never see my future.

What helped me see the future? Me. Me and God. I relied on no one else. The only person I had who would have helped me do that was my granmomma and she died a couple of years ago. When I lost my granmomma, part of me said, "Now it's time." You go through life and you play like a basketball game but when those times come and you really want to change, believe me, you will humble yourself. I brought myself down to a little child. That first night, I would have gone out of here, but I humbled myself, I brought myself back down to the dirt from where God brought me. I humbled myself. I said, "I'm going to make this work for me. I'm not going to work for anybody else. I need to work for me." I need to prove to myself I can do it and just keep moving. If I make myself, then maybe I can go to this brother and talk with him and help.

My children. These are the absolute most important thing for me. I grew up without a mom or a daddy. I always made my bed. When I had kids, I said, whatever I'm going through, I'm always going to be there for my kids. Because I look at it like this. There's no child that ask to be brought into the world. That means that it is our responsibility to take care of them. I don't want no nother man raising my kids, teaching my kids how to do right, what needs to be done. Because I look at it—you're not going to teach them what I'm going to teach, because what I teach it going to come from my soul. You're going to tell them just to get them out of your face. But I'm going to show them out of love.

I got a family member that help me. Like I told my family member, I don't do this for you all. I don't do it for me. I don't do it for my family. I'm doing this for my kids. If it it's not for them, it doesn't make sense. Because I look at it, I've lived, I've lived. I've done everything I wanted to do and more to be thirty-six years old. So I'm trying to do everything I need to do for my kids because nobody knows when God's going to call us home. So what I'm doing now, I'm planning. Planning, putting things in movement. The job I got it ain't the best. I've only been there three days and I'm about to be promoted, so I already—

"That's the first time he talked!" exclaimed Bennett.

\\5//

COMMUNITY-BASED REENTRY PROGRAMS

BASICS AND RE-ENTRY COALITION, INC.

We were interested in learning more about existing, community-based groups that had focused on reentry before the recent reforms. We were especially interested in what motivated and sustained the commitment of the people central to this work. Both the Georgia Bar Association's BASICS program and the Re-Entry Coalition, Inc. in Carrollton seemed to have an intrinsic energy that promised longevity.

BASICS: MICHELLE MENIFEE

I AM somebody.

The BASICS *(Bar Association Support to Improve Correctional Services)* effort started over forty years ago in response to a challenge from Supreme Court Chief Justice Warren Burger to attorneys to take a more active role in reducing recidivism rates, or, as Michelle Menifee put it, "to explore ways to give back to the incarcerated." Originally twenty-two state Bar Associations began programs. Started in 1976, Georgia's program is the only one still in existence, in large part because of the late Ed Menifee's dedication as its program director, a position now ably filled by his widow, Michelle Jordan Menifee.

When he was asked to start the BASICS program, Ed Menifee, graduate of Tuskegee and a Vietnam veteran, had already begun a successful social program in Atlanta, the Southwest Atlanta Youth Business Organization (SWAYBO), that focused on fostering business, finance, and entrepreneurial skills in youth ages twelve to eighteen. Reading about his work in the local paper, the Georgia Bar Association asked him if he thought he could develop something similar for people reentering after incarceration. Given the employment constraints placed on people with felonies, his focus on entrepreneurialism was a good fit. Before working with BASICS or meeting her husband, Michelle, with a degree in criminal justice, had independently begun her own non-profit, Stepping Beyond, that worked with women returning from prison. It focused on providing basic necessities and helping re-accustom women to a world that had often changed dramatically in their absence.

The ten-week *World of Work* course puts an emphasis on financial literacy, career planning, and the soft skills needed to seek and sustain employment. The course is offered at transitional and diversion centers to individuals within a year of release. All the instructors have college educations, often advanced degrees.

The official program description describes the mission of the BASICS program to be to "aid and steer inmates in the direction of self-rehabilitation." Michele Menifee, as would her husband, puts it differently: *You go in and teach and motivate and plant seeds of hope. People are just depressed, in despair. When you go in and tell them they are special, remind them who they really are, something changes. Oftentimes in this world we're reaching for those things way up there, and what we need is right here. Its one of those simple concepts but so profound: Give someone the basic tools and remind them of how special they are—and they start believing it and they go out and prove it to themselves, to their families, their communities.*

Michele Menifee emphasized the importance of creating realistic expectations in the people in the program, and also what it means to work—the exertion to achieve a task. This involves defining work as chosen, rather than as slavery—and not consistently predicting failure. "There is no way people are *always* going to count you out," she told her classes. She felt that the most important first step was to build people up so that they have the confidence to make that exertion—and the changes that come with it. Then the other steps would come as well: *I never ask them what they did. My focus is on where we are going. Everyone has a different story. But so much is learned behavior, based on survival. They were taught to go in and take from a store. It was a way of life.* She laughed as she repeated one of Ed Menifee's favorite quotes: *If you are sincere about change, you must change your playmates, playground, and playthings.* Then, shaking her head, another: *Never under-estimate the power of the made up mind.*

Because of Ed Menifee's interest in economic development, the BASICS program includes, like SWAYBO, a social justice and economic empowerment dimension that can develop naturally. Michelle Menifee explained: *We do a class dealing with economic development. Sounds really broad, but if you teach someone that means bringing more training to your community, that means shopping centers, just buying into your educational system. "So, you mean to tell me I live on the south side of town and I'm always saying I'm going over here on the north side to shop and to eat, that I'm not helping my community grow?" "Yes, you're taking taxes over to the other side—that helps them improve their infrastructure. . . . That's why we see the Mercedes dealer over in Buckhead and the used car lot over in Bankhead." "Oh, is this why I shouldn't throw trash: no developers will come?" That is impactful. People are going back with a different mindset. I think we've gotten great results.*

The program has graduated over 10,000 participants in its forty years: 75% of people maintain their jobs or are promoted after their release, and there is only a 15% recidivism rate in this group.

We attended two BASICS graduations, in 2014 and 2015, at Metro Transitional Center, when it was a woman's facility. Menifee spoke about the importance of these graduations for reframing our understanding of individuals who have been incarcerated, a process she thinks often takes place at these graduations, even for members of the State Bar: *People often see inmates, based on what they see on television, as incorrigibles. They don't want them back. But with students who have gone through the program, when the people here at the graduation hear them talking intelligently and speaking from the heart, they get a chance to see them in a different light. Then I think society is willing to give them another chance. It's the same with the state bar, the attorneys, the justice system: If they see you trying, putting forward an effort—It's something about a norm, when people are sincere, you can tell the difference. Just having those different groups witness the transformation in itself makes society more accepting of those coming out. People are able to embrace the change. It is not by happenstance that people now are willing to take this question off employment applications. It means we want to humanize these individuals.*

Menifee sees this process as a mutual transformation, involving significant changes on the parts of the women returning as well. One of those changes is being able to see themselves as having caused harm. It is a process that it is natural to want to sidestep: *It takes awhile for someone to get to that humbled point. It's like: "Oh, I'm not even dealing with that, that's <u>behind</u> me." But when you can embrace the fact that you need to be forgiven for what you've done and that whatever that forgiveness looks like—it may be forgiveness with your higher power, it may be forgiveness with the family, or the victims—you need to embrace that and see what needs to take place in order to right the wrong. It* *means saying I know what I have done is wrong: It has offended someone, someone has been victimized, someone has been hurt. You almost need to make a U-turn and go back and start afresh. When you are forgiven and are able to forgive yourself, that right there is a breath of fresh air.*

At the end of each graduation ceremony, led by Menifee, all the women in their graduation gowns affirmed, loudly and repeatedly, "I *am* somebody. I *am* somebody." The echoes of Jesse Jackson's use of the phrase decades earlier, with its emphasis on intrinsic dignity and the long, sustained and sustaining commitment to black empowerment, were everywhere. The impact on the audience, made up of family members and friends, was intensely moving.

Menifee also noticed the disorienting effect that the care she showed the women during the classes had on the correctional officers. She described an interesting dynamic that shows the complex ways incarceration shapes everyone involved: *We go in and they [the correctional officers] are lovely people. They're good to me. But they carry their frustrations out on the inmates. It's a group they know they can talk down to and verbally abuse and get away with it. One guard said to me, "Why do <u>they</u> get all the attention? Why do <u>they</u> get all the treatment? You bring toys up here for their children. We have children too." I wanted to say, "Oh, you're frustrated. You're not able to see that this person is coming back to your neighborhood."*

We do the chant, "I am somebody special," after the classes, and I've witnessed when the ladies leave class a guard may get in their faces. I say, "Just hold your peace." I think it comes along with that role—that the guards need to know there's a line of distinction there, that it has to do with their self-worth. I'm always nice, I bring donuts to the ladies and remind them to share with the guards. The ladies object sometimes, but I insist.

Menifee said, explaining her long-term commitment to this work: *I don't want to give up. My frustration comes from wanting to do more and needing more resources. If I could I would teach classes all year long or more classes throughout the state. It is a simple concept, but so profound. You give someone the basic tools, you tell them how special they are, and encourage them to go out and prove it to themselves. <u>Changing lives and mindsets.</u> I live for this. I love the energy. It's like when a baby learns to walk, talk, those Aha! moments. Seeing a mother who has given up hope for her daughter coming to graduation and saying, "I never thought I would see my child do something." Seeing a child see his mother in this way. These changes of attitude are heart changes.*

RE-ENTRY COALITION, INC.

BOB JACKSON, TOMMIE CATO, NARVIS FARRIS, NORMAN SIMMS
We saw reentry as an issue of civil rights.

We drove to Carrollton, Georgia, on the far west of the state, to meet and talk with the founding members of the Carrollton Re-Entry Coalition, one of the oldest community-initiated reentry groups in Georgia, which differs from other reentry coalitions with its emphasis on reentry as a question of racial equity. We met in an attractive white bungalow near the city hall, which had been donated to them by the city. The mayor of Carrollton, James Garner, had served on the Board of Parole and also as Commissioner of Corrections during its most punitive period from 1995 to 2000. He seemed, however, supportive of this local reentry effort.

The three founding members of the coalition were all active members of NAACP. Narvis Farris, a former deputy sheriff in Carrollton, and Norman Simms were both presidents of the Carrollton chapter of the NAACP and Bob Jackson was a local member who had become a state-wide coordinator. All of them were working on NAACP Legal Redress, and it was in this capacity that Farris was being asked for help with reentry. In late 2003, Farris noticed that not only in Carrollton but across the state men were going back and forth to prison. He was beginning to field many requests from families for information and assistance.

Bob Jackson, the director of the coalition and its spokesperson, described it this way: *Phone calls were coming in from wives, girlfriends, mothers, grandmothers complaining that they couldn't understand why this recycling was going on. If men went to prison they were supposed to come back out and go to work. The harassment was another thing. Mothers calling up and saying, "He didn't do anything and they just came and picked him up. Said he violated probation. He ain't got a job, he can't pay his restitution. They know that." Chief said we had an issue and we needed to take a look at it and see what we could possibly bring to the NAACP to help them help us handle this on a larger scale.*

After studying the issue for six months, they decided to get in touch with the Department of Corrections. They met with A.J. Sabree, newly charged with Reentry, who told them that they needed to start developing a relationship with local authorities, that they would get nowhere without local buy-in, which they proceeded to obtain. "We met the assistant mayor, the city manager, sheriff, the secondary line of command, the county commissioner, the social clubs—Kiwanis, Lions, and talked to them. Churches was not friendly then and are not friendly now. "

The more they looked at the issue, the clearer they became that this was a civil rights issue: *We were going to work it through NAACP legal redress. As we looked back at all the issues concerning the civil rights movement, we began to see that it is a new form of civil rights: housing, voting, jobs, employment, education, probation/parole (fees, obligations, revocations). The concerns under second chance correlate with civil rights so much so that now we would say the face of racism and discrimination is reentry. It was called civil rights, but it is now called reentry. You have guys working certain jobs in the prison, and when they come out, they cannot get those same jobs because they have a record. Whether you have a record or you don't, it's still the same fight. It's worse if you have a record.*

Believing their program had broader application across the state they thought that they would work with the state NAACP, with its 109 state branches. However, their relationship with the NAACP was fraught. The state NAACP did not want to be associated with reentry and, some years after the coalition's founding, objected to having their organization included in the reentry coalition's name. The state NAACP even threatened to shut down the Carrollton branch. The NAACP Re-entry Coalition had to re-name itself Re-entry Coalition, Inc. and apply again for 501c status. But by then they were so well established in the community and in the corrections and supervision communities that "The mayor, the sheriff, and the prosecutor all stood behind us." Their local Walmart offered them a large grant they were unable to accept because they hadn't yet re-established non-profit status. They retained their social justice frame.

On the other hand, they also began to have a strong feeling for the broad social resistance to reentry, within the black community as well: *The NAACP overall, at both national and state levels, was not for it. It allowed us to see how hard-nosed the system really was about helping disadvantaged people. Some people say theoretically I want to help, but only to the benefit of them. But the reality is it isn't about them, it is about the people in need. That's all we were doing—trying to help the people with this revolving door, because we saw that it IS racism and it is hard to deny it.*

The coalition's relationship to various other groups engaged in the new reform efforts was edgy as well. For example, the social outreach efforts of the Governor's Office of Transition and Entry (GOTSR) they found were a one-way street. They felt that they had shared their planning paper with

GOTSR as it got started up and that they were seeing, without adequate acknowledgment, some of their own ideas at play in the plan that GOTSR developed, especially the ideas around scaling up. More importantly, they felt that GOTSR's efforts undermined the motivation of community-originated groups. Jackson said, *They want us to be their extension. If they do come here, it's because they're trying to implement or enhance something they want to do. When we said we're all volunteer, they said, "Woah, you've been here twelve years and you're volunteers?" That's a blow to them.*

The idea that people might start their own coalitions and do so very intentionally on a purely volunteer basis deprived GOTSR of the justification for the leadership role they wanted. Jackson described the tensions, and his own solutions, this way: *The state can't do it. The board room is filled with paper and high ideas, but the work is done on the ground. Jay Neal [the director of GOTSR] knew it when he rolled it out. He said, this is not set up for you to get us to do your program. Well, WE said that. We ain't looking for you. Matter of fact, we want you to do what WE do. That would make everybody happy. That's where some of the confusion around the state came from. First thing that come out of everybody's mouth: "Where the money?" Ain't no money. You have to create your own money. The state is actually asking for our help, all that community supervision wants to do, they're asking us in the community to help do that. If the community won't do it, it won't be done. They tried that with the Department of Corrections. But prisons kept exploding. Communities kept waiting on government. The church is the most important element—everyone is there—government, business, civic. If you can get the church, you can get everybody.*

However, the reality is churches remain deeply ambivalent about reentry. The coalition discussed this continued social resistance. It wasn't that people were unaware of the issue, indeed pastors would call or come to them because they had a family member who needed help, but they did not talk about it in the church. Simms, explained: *You look at the black churches, and my sense is that the thought is you've got to be saved and once you're saved, all this stuff will go away. They strive on come to Christ, like all those things will then pass away, but they don't. They know what I do, but do they come by and say, Can we help? They don't seek to find out. The Bible explicitly says, "If I was hungry, If I was imprisoned"—it should be easy.*

Jackson pointed out the powerful denial at work: *All the communities are saturated with churches. One out of thirteen people in this state is in prison or under probation or parole, and you have a church of 1300 . . . do the math. We're sitting here talking about how to get churches involved and churches have agreed to not let a sex offender live near my church. That's deep. Think about it. Because if the pastors got together and fought that, that restriction would not exist.*

There were several dimensions of the coalition's work on the ground that they felt made them distinctive. First, they were completely volunteer. Also they were a service provider—they responded to real needs in real time. They didn't cherry-pick their cases, indeed, preferred the complex ones, for example working with sex offenders and mental health. They weren't time-limited in the services they provided. Someone could return to their program years later. Jackson summed it up this way: *My thing is service. We deliver customer service. This program was designed to have an open door policy. We respond to the need when the call comes. A lot of agencies, if it's 4 o'clock or 5, they'll say call me tomorrow. No appointment here. We open at 9, we close at 5, but our phones are 24/7 so they can always call. We know crimes occur after hours and sometimes they just need somebody to talk to. You never know how effective that call was.*

Once you enter, you're always part of the program. You don't pay anything to come or to stay here. Although some are mandated by courts/probation, we want to maintain that openness even if the judge says, you have to go. Our program is there when you need it and to the degree that you need it.

It was important to each of them that they did this work without any thought of financial return. They felt that having people work on a volunteer basis had important ramifications for how their available monies were spent, that they were more likely to invest it in the men and women who came to them than those who also saw that money as providing their own salary. Again Jackson explained: *We're not about the fluff. Nobody in this room after twelve years received a dime. We took money out of our pockets. We do it because it just feels right. I've been a champion for fighting for poor and disadvantaged people all my life and there is no difference here. I haven't suffered or lost nothing. I took a three-year sabbatical to work here and get this thing up and going, and I ain't miss a beat. I know what it takes. We don't have people coming in here to pick up a check, because it ain't here. No check here. When you come in here, it's because your heart tells you to come here. We all know that.*

We didn't set out to get approval. We don't look to the community to endorse us. We look at the community to respect the work we do. You don't have to champion us or put our names on a billboard. Just pat us on the back if you can—step out of the way if you can't. And the money doesn't count. When you have it in your mind you are doing the work and it's God's work you know that He'll provide. You know what needs to be done, you know how to do it, so you do it. If someone like Jay Neal never says, "Hey guys you've done a great job," we'll still be doing what we're doing.

Tommie Cato became an important addition to the core group. She shared the volunteer orientation, and also brought in two important bodies of experience: *Other than being a servant, I am a returning citizen. When I was sentenced the judge was saying, "This is not a criminal offense." And my pastor was standing there and he said, "It's something God wants you to do and you are going to be a blessing to somebody." And I thought, "This man just said two years in prison, how am I going to be a help to anybody?" But prior to that I had been a probation officer and I could see for a fact that in prison you were never told about what help was available getting out. So I wrote my pastor that when I got out I wanted to help people know what help was available to them.*

When I saw in the paper that they were opening a reentry, I called and told them I wanted to come and volunteer. Mr. Jackson asked what I can do and I told him I wanted to be able to tell people and show them how to go about getting the resources you eligible for. I tell anybody my heart and my soul is in helping people. All my work has been in social services. That is what I do and I get joy doing it. We don't just tell them to go to DFACS, we try to give them a name of somebody and a time. DFACS, probation, mental health, the director of the Salvation Army, all these social services in Carroll County, everybody knows my name. Even when I come back, they never treated me as if I had been in prison. I can call any of the organizations. Jackson had met them, but I had <u>worked</u> with them.

Their understanding of the central needs of returning citizens was drawn from what they saw and heard frequently. One recurrent issue was the financial pressure of reentry, and the failure of Probation and Parole to understand how that contributes to recidivism. [Changes at the Department of Community Supervision since our interview have provided community supervision some flexibility in reducing or redistributing various economic pressures.] *The parole and probation officers out in the field, if they would respect the guys for the problems they have, show them and guide them as opposed to, in their word, "lock them up." Child support is a growing, growing problem. In fact it is one of the biggest reasons for recidivism. Some of these guys go down under the radar to keep from child support. We have a number of cases where people go to work, we find them a job, we put them to work, and they get behind on their child support. They try to keep up, but they have it set up so when they get paid,* *the child support take over half the check. They expecting a $300-$400 check, and when they get it, they have $20-30. The guy say, what the heck. What am I working for? So that set him underground, under the radar. Then they're going to arrest them because they are in arrears. It makes no sense. They can't produce anything locked up.*

They felt that collateral consequences for the community as well as the individual were not adequately considered at every step in the prosecution process: *Judges, prosecutors need to know how these remedies affect the person, the community. Will the community have to pay for these fifteen-year probation times? Will he have a drivers' license? Will he be able to work? Where will he be able to work? A lot is going on behind the door that we don't know about.*

Another issue were collateral consequences of charges that were not prosecuted but not expunged: *We just got through working with a guy today. Never been to prison, but how many charges does he have? Rape, two aggravated assaults. These have never been adjudicated. But if you pull his docket, that's the first you see—rape, aggravated assault, aggravated assault. These are two index crimes: they only go away if they are expunged. They don't go away unless you work on it and have the wherewithal to do that. Unless you do, the first thing someone is going to see if they arrest him or do a background check are those charges.*

They talked about cases that they loved to take on, emphasizing that an effective response needed to be highly specific to the actual circumstances. *There are not that many really bad people. The rest of them are just lost. They are mental health or they need drug rehab. What makes Carrollton unique? We walk a guy from A to Z. He stays with us, we are going to walk him through. And we stay on it until we get it. We love complicated cases. We want everything brought to us. We don't want you just because your case is pretty. We want them ugly situations. Because that is what teaches us about what needs to be fixed in the system. Those are the things that we want to challenge. No cherry picking here.*

One of the more challenging cases involved finding housing for two seventeen-year-old sex offenders recently released from the Department of Juvenile Justice, who were forbidden by law from living with their families as long as there were younger children in the house. One of these boys had been imprisoned since he was thirteen. They found them bicycles to ride to and from their offices daily to look for work. One of them, because he was slick, ended up back in prison. But one wonders how you can expect a seventeen year old imprisoned since thirteen to create a meaningful life from scratch without any family contact or context, especially burdened with all the lasting collateral limitations placed on sex offenders.

What really stood out in these cases was the state in which people were released from prison and the way the coalition became involved because of a desperate call from the correctional or community supervision system itself. These cases were often located in other cities than Carrollton—for example Douglasville or Atlanta, about an hour away. One case involved a probation officer calling to ask for help with a man released without food or housing a day after a serious ice storm. The probation officer had called them because he was not allowed to pay for food or housing out of pocket. He did not share that the man was paraplegic. The coalition found him a hotel room, luckily on the first floor, and paid for a couple of days lodging *because we wanted to have some time to work with the guy. We got him some food. He loved to talk. He was a happy guy. Self-sustaining. That made it easier. We got to like the guy.* They found a place for him to live for a month and located a TV, blanket, pots and pans. Then, with some funding from a local agency, they found a placement for him in a homeless shelter with reentry services.

Another call came from Central Prison in Macon on a Friday night, informing them a man who had been released from prison that afternoon was now on a bus to Atlanta. He had been in prison for ten years, and would have ten years of probation to follow. He needed to report to the Atlanta probation office within 72 hours. But the sheriff in Atlanta didn't want to accept him, perhaps because of his mental health status, and wanted to ship him back to Macon. The man had been released without medication. With some consultation back and forth with Macon and with the help of the director of the Atlanta Recovery Center, the man was admitted to Grady Hospital, where it required three days for him to stabilize. The director of Atlanta Recovery Center, which offers transitional housing, then hired him, helping him meet the employment provisions of his probation.

Certainly, the coalition's decision not to cherry pick its cases works to the benefit of the state—and to that of the men reentering. But it may not work to the benefit of the society in general unless the conditions that lead to such lapses are addressed. Since the time of this interview, there have been new efforts in Corrections to have reentry plans for everyone leaving prison, which they supposedly double check several times before someone leaves. We can hope the frequency of calls like this may be less.

These cases perhaps explain the enthusiasm the coalition showed for the classes they were providing in the Carroll County Prison, a state prison housed in a county facility. The coalition wanted to help create a more graduated experience for people coming out, to foster, in that popular reentry phrase, *a seamless transition*. They offered a two-week class where they brought in officers from Probation and Parole to talk about what men could expect under supervision. The men were surprised, for example, to hear the chief tell them that they could have one dirty urine, so they should be careful to tell their officer if they were going to test positive, for example on their birthday, so supervision wouldn't waste resources testing them. Of course, the chief emphasized, if they didn't tell them, or it happened more than once, the consequences would be very different. When the men left prison, they now would have faces to associate with supervision expectations, have experienced a graduation, and would have, as Cato emphasized, the names and numbers of real people they could call.

When asked what they thought made the most difference in the lives of the people who came to them for help, Cato emphasized self-esteem, accountability, and constancy: *It irks me when someone says, "I can't. I'm a convicted felon." One girl and her sister, they were like joined at the hips, and they came to our Thursday discussion. I told them to stop saying that, and they said, "That's all good for you to talk about Ms. Cato. You ain't never been to prison." I went out and pulled up my sheet and showed it to them. That child went over to Carrollton Tech the next day and enrolled and got her GED and got a job, got away from her sister. The newspaper did a front-page spread on her.*

Simms returned to the idea of family reunification: *It comes back to the families. If you can reconnect them back—they have been away so long. It takes time to adjust back to normal life. If they can adjust and become taxpayers like you and I, if we can get them a job and they can do the things that people in a community do. If I see young men and women back and doing positive things that we helped initiate, where the light went on about reentry and they go out and tell someone else, that's success.*

Getting other people in the larger public to see the value in what they were doing was slower coming. Cato described a conversation she had with a woman with a landscaping business who asked her why she should hire someone with a criminal background when there were people she could hire without them. Cato's response, which made her laugh in retrospect, was, "Well, for one thing, you might be their next victim!" The landscaper called up later to see if they had someone who could come to work.

\6/

TRANSITION CENTERS & EARLY EMPLOYMENT

We know that we get better results with reentry if an individual progresses through a supervised transitional process, especially one that promotes employment. Such transitional programs clearly work—in Georgia successful participation increases the chances of avoiding a return to prison by up to a third, according to the Department of Corrections (DOC).

As we heard over and over, one of the biggest challenges facing people leaving prison is employment. Georgia has thirteen Transitional Centers (TC) operating throughout the state, two of which are for incarcerated females. This provides space for a total of around 2,700 people at a given time, a small percentage of those who are incarcerated as well as of those who would like to be placed in a TC. A primary purpose of the TCs is to allow the offender to work in the community while living under the discipline of the center. We interviewed the warden of the Atlanta TC, the employment coordinator at another TC, employers who regularly hire people transitioning from prison, and some of those employees to understand better the challenges and benefits of spending time with one foot in and one foot out of prison.

MAKING THE TRANSITION

During the participants' first four to six weeks, they remain at the center, both as part of the transition process itself as well as to provide time for the staff to become acquainted with them and assess their readiness to work in the community. As Warden Steven Perkins of the Atlanta Transitional Center explained: *All of the staff from counselors to security is monitoring whether the individual is ready. You can be sure that they will not go out of the center if they are not ready—whether they have the discipline to go out that door, arrive at their job on time, fulfill their work assignment, and return to the center at the appointed time without being seduced by the temptations that would surround them.*

This early period also provides time to ensure that the participant has completed the practical requirements needed prior to their release. These generally are steps that are initiated while in prison but not necessarily completed prior to the person's transfer to the TC. For example, everyone needs a Social Security card in order to work and some form of identification to function in society. It might appear a minimal expectation for DOC to ensure that all inmates obtain these prior to their release or transfer to a TC but that has not always been the case. However, improving performance in this has been a major preoccupation of Georgia's recent reform process. It should also be noted that the failings have not always been DOC's but sometimes those of other agencies with which it must coordinate, from local Society Security offices to agencies in other states, for example, for inmates born outside of Georgia.

Another function of the first weeks at the TC is to provide life skill classes to participants, especially to fill gaps in what they did not receive while in prison. As Warden Perkins pointed out, residents receive some preparation every day for the reality that soon: *you are going to be in the public. But, if you come here with the mentality of what you had to do to survive in prison, you are not going to make it here. This is a community-based facility and for you to be here you have to act like you are living in the community.*

Since some participants had limited or even no employment prior to their incarceration, they often lack the most basic knowledge about gaining work and expected on-the-job behavior. David Croft, the employment coordinator at Phillips TC, offered the example of Ron, who had no work experience prior to his fifteen years of prison. Ron was placed at a chicken plant but on his first day failed to check in with the human resources manager as he had been told to do. Consequently, he was reported to Croft as a no-show escapee. Given what Croft knew of Ron, this didn't seem right. He went to the plant and found Ron, still hard at work after sixteen hours on the line—without a break. Ron said he had just followed the other workers in and started working and kept working because he did not want to lose his job. Croft is now extra careful to emphasize these first-day work procedures with all of his participants.

TC residents are paid a full wage but have limited control over what they receive. Their check is sent to the TC, which deducts room and board expenses. If the offender still owes fines, fees, or restitution, more is deducted for those payments. After receiving a small allowance, the remainder is put away in savings that the participant receives upon leaving the TC. The saved amount can be considerable given that the typical work release period lasts six to nine months, sometimes longer, giving the returning citizen a very helpful grubstake to ease the first months of their reintegration.

TC residents have the option of keeping their job following their release. However, many were placed away from their hometowns to which they will want to return. Still, we did talk to some TC participants who decided on their release to remain in place. Even a low-wage job at a chicken plant, if a secure job, is valuable for someone with a criminal record.

Part of the TC employment coordinator's job is to cultivate relationships with potential employers. The better the economy and the tighter job markets, the easier this becomes. In the fall of 2015 Croft was consistently placing close to 100% of all of Phillips's TC residents, receiving more calls from prospective employers than he could fill. In contrast, a year and a half before he had about 80% placed, leaving a number of residents pounding the pavement themselves to find jobs.

Located about an hour north of Atlanta, the majority of the Phillips TC placements were at warehouses, chicken plants, and landscaping companies. Very few were at fast food restaurants, which in Atlanta were frequent employers for TC residents. Not surprisingly for a growing metropolitan area, another frequent job was construction. In the fall of 2013 the Atlanta TC was working with fifty-six different employers. As Warden Perkins noted, "we are in the middle of Atlanta so our guys can branch out and go anywhere to get work." Consequently, his phone was burning up every day with family members calling him to see how their imprisoned relations could get a placement there.

Perkins had worked in corrections since his graduation from a small historically black college in Oklahoma. As he moved up the career ladder in Georgia his positions were always in facilities with a greater emphasis on preparation for successful reentry than usually found in regular prisons. This rehabilitative focus seemed to suit him well. As he emphasized: *once you have a person incarcerated, the best thing is to equip them for when they get back out into society as opposed to lock them up and not offer them anything.* He added that he told new residents: *this is a blessing to have a situation like this. You made some bad choices . . . but you are still a person like I am. But you made bad choices. This is a time that you can correct the bad choices that you made.*

However, Perkins stressed that transitional centers "have a non-negotiable mission: protect the public, that is number one." The ultimate worry of officials, of course, is that a resident on work release might abscond or, worse, get caught committing a new crime. Controversies about such programs break to the surface intermittently around the country. Critics of these programs seem to be overlooking the reality that someone on a work release is less likely to recidivate than someone released without any supervision or assistance.

The biggest problem that Warden Perkins could remember at the Atlanta TC with neighbors was complaints about blowing leaves too early in the morning. Neighbors confirm the absence of problems. Residents and businesses had formed a group to monitor what they regarded as the high levels of crime in the area and to liaise with police. A 2013 Midtown Ponce Security Alliance web posting noted that after keeping a close watch on the TC for ten years, "we just don't have any dangerous or even problematic situations involving this place to report to you." Instead, their concern was formerly imprisoned individuals who had completed their sentences without going through any kind of rehabilitative programs. Now back at their old street corners and other hangouts, they were again pursuing "a life of street drugs and the criminal activity going along with it."

The successful program completion rate at Atlanta TC runs around 70 to 80%. In significant ways it is more than that. Warden Perkins used the example of a former resident, Sam, who staff predicted would fail out of the program because of the obvious "bad attitude" with which he arrived, complete with facial tattoos. In their initial interview the warden asked, "You have family here?" and Sam responded with something sarcastic. Perkins then told him to look out the window where a young woman was passing by on a skateboard. "How many times did you see that in prison?" Perkins asked him. Sam admitted that of course in prison he didn't even have a window to look out. Then Perkins advised him, "Look this is a different environment man, you've got to leave that behind." Perkins related to us that as the "weeks went by, he was a totally different individual. He had been in one of the most notorious gangs in prison but he came and did well." Eventually Sam did hit trouble and was returned to prison. But, upon his release he got back in touch with Warden Perkins, receiving his help on both housing and employment.

David Croft of Phillips TC made the same point about expanding the definition of success. He offered the example of Mike, who was terminated by his employer after only four months for losing his temper on the job. But Mike had been incarcerated at the age of thirteen. Entering the work release program at twenty-three, he had never worked in his life. Given that background, Croft told Mike, "'you made a mistake but you were successful. You got to remember that next time." Another example he cited was Ray, who lasted ten months at his job as a forklift driver before he was fired. Ray had accidentally scraped a door. He told his supervisor, who told him not to tell anyone. But one day the manager came by, saw the door, and asked who did it. Ray confessed that he did it and was fired. Croft explained, "I would call that success too. He did the right thing and he was well liked out there."

WORKING AT THE POULTRY PLANT

The purpose of inmate work-release programs is to help ex-offenders reintegrate into society but they exist because they are also of value to low-wage employers. As Croft pointed out, as the economy strengthens, employers of manual labor struggle finding employees who are willing to work.

The problem for low-wage employers became acute in the mid-2000s when the federal government began cracking down on the employment of undocumented workers. When we interviewed former DOC Commissioner Gen. James Donald, the example he gave was Georgia's important chicken industry. The federal crackdown came at a time when Donald was looking for ways that inmates could work. One of the poultry industry leaders met with then Gov. Sonny Perdue with Donald also in attendance, asking the governor for help, saying, "'I am about to lose my business.'" Perdue then turned to Donald, who replied that he could give them two hundred workers the next day. The placement of TC residents soon expanded at that plant and then to others in the area and then throughout the state. Donald ensured that they received the same (low) pay as other workers. As a result, there were TC workers "getting out with $5,000, $10,000 in their pockets."

We were provided with another perspective of the program's origins from Mark Bland, corporate director of human resources at Claxton Poultry. The poultry industry had been actively lobbying the state government to institute such a program even before the crackdown given the shortage of labor it faced. Fortunately for Claxton Poultry, there was a state prison that included a transitional center just about fifteen miles down the road. Even more fortunately, Smith TC was soon relocated to Claxton right across the street from the poultry company. When we talked with Bland, Claxton Poultry had been working with the TC for about ten years. With close to two thousand employees, about 160 were TC residents. Perhaps another three or four hundred employees were on parole or probation, largely people from the area rather than TC residents who stayed after their release.

Throughout our conversation Bland emphasized the similar treatment of the "transitionals" and the regular employees. The transitionals wore no special clothing or anything else that would distinguish them. That meant their co-workers and even supervisors did not necessarily know their status. They started at the same entry-level jobs, doing the same work as anyone else. They got the same pay as co-workers at the same levels as well as the same benefits, which at Claxton included an on-site health clinic staffed with medical personnel and offering inexpensive prescription drugs. The hope was that upon their release they would stay; Bland estimated that perhaps up to 20% might. He mentioned one former TC resident who continued to rise through the ranks and was a manager of supervisors at the time of our interview.

The similarities extended to problem behavior. Bland noted that people asked him if the transitionals didn't worry him but his response was "not a bit," indeed, "they are not much different from my regular plant population," adding, "I respect them just as I do anyone else." Violence was rare—employees knew that the police would be immediately called and transitionals knew they would be sent back to prison. Still, disciplinary problems at the plant were frequent. Bland acknowledged that he probably terminated people more frequently than at other types of companies. Drug and alcohol use on the job was problematic (his bookshelves were topped with confiscated bottles, some quite large). Bland did mention one area where transitionals were different: "they have been locked up and all of a sudden they have 400 or 500 women . . . so that is a problem on a daily basis, especially at night." On the other side, he pointed out, "a lot of these ladies, they know these guys have been in there and they are starting to accumulate some money. Boy they have them some girl friends." He had noted at the beginning of the interview that some transitionals leave with savings up to $10,000.

The relationship with the transition center was not always smooth, a subject that Bland had discussed more than once with the DOC commissioner. TC workers at the plant were expected to be on the job for a minimum of six months, which Bland saw as minimally viable for the company but sometimes his TC workers were released early. They were also supposed to be physically capable of the work and willing to accept this job. Neither were always true.

Even with the workers from the transitional center, maintaining an adequate workforce was a constant challenge. Brand saw about three-quarters of his employees as "good dependable people who come to work everyday," but the rest were constantly churning over. These were usually younger workers, often with no prior work experience and perhaps not very fit. He acknowledged that the environment could be overwhelming at first: wet and cold, noisy, lots of other workers, "a tremendous amount of birds back and forth" (some 440,000 arrive at the plant to be killed each day), and a ten-hour shift standing on concrete. (We would also add the smell of the antiseptics used, which hit us as we approached the plant and were still with us hours after we left.) Bland said that he had told the company, "if there is a piece of machinery that can do the work, regardless of the cost, you need to buy it."

LANDSCAPING

The landscaping industry is another frequent employer of transitional center residents. Chris Watkins, a hiring manager for a large landscaping company in the Atlanta area, told us that he too faced "a very serious challenge with securing good reliable labor." Having once worked as a TC mental health counselor himself (a job that he loved but the center closed), Watkins decided to try hiring from the Phillips TC. He asked that his company's name not be identified because of the associated stigma—something that made him mad because he felt "it should be seen as a positive thing that we are doing this." The program did have the backing of his company's owner. Gov. Nathan Deal made it clear to the owner, a long-time friend, that he was counting on companies like this to make reentry work. Watkins had already started the program when he got the word that "we need to make this happen." Incarceration was not a concern for his company's hiring. Their position was: "as long as your past does not affect your day-to-day performance then it is none of our business."

Landscaping is hard work. The crews worked four ten-hour days a week, outside in the heat and cold. About 70% of the regular hires stayed with the company but at the time of the interview less than 40% of those hired from the TC. Watkins did interview TC prospects intensively but had found it hard to determine who would work out—although that usually became clear within the first two weeks. Watkins mentioned two workers, both close to that mark, who had tested positive for drugs and were terminated because of the company's drug-free policy. One of the men was from the local area and if he had stayed with the company after his TC release, he would have been making about $15 an hour. We heard repeatedly of the easy availability of illegal drugs of all types in both TCs and prisons. It "drives me nuts," Watkins said. To him transitional centers were where there should be the most intense oversight. "This is where substance abuse should be stamped out—but is not."

Another major difficulty was transportation. David Croft, the employment coordinator at Phillips, admitted that there had been major problems with past private companies that had the contract to transport residents to and from their places of employment (there is no viable public transit in the area). He blamed the last transit company's "blasé attitude"— they are "just inmates"—with losing many jobs for his residents.

Watkins at the landscaping company agreed that the new transportation company was a notable improvement and liked that they hired drivers who were previously incarcerated. Still, the company had a limited number of vans, a limited number of drivers, and many stops. Residents, then, were paying out of their own wages for inefficient transportation that might drop them off very early and pick them up very late. It was an improvement, though, over prior waits of two or even three hours.

There appeared to be no overt conflicts between the regular landscaping crew and those from the TC, but Watkins did observe some of the regulars felt superior to the TC workers, which undermined morale. Watkin's policy was to not divulge which workers were from the TC but "it is impossible to keep that away from the rest of the crew." The TC workers "arrive at the same time, in donated clothes, DOC boots, and have the same packaged lunch with DOC printed on the milk cartons." There were racial differences too. About two-thirds of the regulars were Hispanic, the TC workers were overwhelmingly African American. On the regular crew it was the Hispanics who were "the hardest working guys that we've got" compared to the blacks and whites. Consequently, the majority of his crew managers were Hispanic as were most of those who did the specialized labor.

FACTORY WORK

A different dynamic prevailed among workers at Murray Plastics in northwest Georgia in Gainesville, in no small part because the majority had a criminal record and many were still residents of transition centers and halfway houses (HWH). The owner and plant manager made no distinction between employees with or without a record and expected their workers to do the same. What mattered instead was work ethic and integrity. The six employees that we talked with individually were grateful for the second chance they had been offered. That opportunity was not just employment but also the possibility of advancement—at the time of our interviews the first shift leader, front office manager, and accounts manager all had started at entry level with criminal records and worked their way up.

The third-generation owner of the small family business, Bill Hall, and his plant manager, Denis Dubus, were frank that the low entry-level wage that they pay would have to be substantially increased without the availability of TC and HWH residents. On the other hand, they contended that with higher payrolls they would not be able to compete. The company was a custom plastic injection molder. It is precisely the kind of low-skill manufacturing that has been leaving the U.S. for years for countries where low-skill labor is dirt cheap.

Murray Plastics often retained its employees after their release, in contrast to some other employers of TC labor that, as characterized by Dubus, take the position that "they are convicts, who cares? They are being punished, use them and abuse and throw them away and get another one." Hall also mentioned a company that terminated employees when they were released from the TC. Uncertain as to the reason, he surmised that it might be that while at the TC the workers were dependable because the TC ensured that they show up, have trustworthy transportation, and are drug tested.

Some years ago Murray Plastics hired from a local probation diversion center but it closed. Then they obtained many workers among HWH residents. They learned about the transition centers from one of their employees who had spent time at Arrendale, a TC for females located a little south of Gainesville. Eventually, they heard about the men's TC at Phillips. However, the initial contact was made by a Phillips resident who walked in the door—and was hired. At the time of our September 2015 interviews more than three-quarters of the forty or so employees were past or current residents of centers (TC or HWH).

Two of the employees we interviewed, Vanessa and Ryan, were among those who would not be staying at the company upon their release. Not from the area, they saw their lives as resuming elsewhere. Vanessa was one month shy of completing a ten-and-a-half-year imprisonment for armed robbery and kidnapping. She sought placement at a TC so she could have recent work experience on her resume when she sought employment after her release. A resident at Arrendale TC at the time of our interview, she had worked at Murray for almost a year as a machine operator. During the years of her imprisonment, her mother had been raising her two children in southern Georgia, which was where she was heading upon her release. She had not been able to see any of them during the entirety of her incarceration.

Ryan was arrested during his first year in college when he attempted his first drug sale: Adderall. He was fortunate. The judge postponed his sentencing until after completion of a six-month residency in a drug and alcohol treatment center. Residents were expected to pay their room and board by working at a job that they found (and by cooking and cleaning). Having no prior work experience, finding a job proved difficult. After four or five weeks of walking throughout the city from company to company, Ryan took a job at a chicken plant but soon quit, finding the work "dreary and disgusting." ("There are three conveyer belts and they hang dead chickens on them that travel around over head dripping water on you.") A fellow resident told him about Murray where he was offered a job the day he knocked on the door—in fact, he was invited to start right then and he was relieved to get a delay until the next day. Ryan's hope was that the judge would be satisfied with his performance and allow him to return to his college in southeastern Georgia. He would take with him, he said, both a newly developed work ethic and ability to interact with people from different backgrounds (some of his co-residents had been in prison for up to twenty years).

The other employees interviewed—Duane, Frank, Cristy and Pam—were residents in the broader Gainesville region at the time of their arrests (all on drug charges). Two were already long-term Murray employees at the time of the interviews and the other two expected to remain as well. All were grateful for the "second chance" atmosphere of the company, especially the opportunity to move up to positions of greater responsibility based on their demonstrated ability. Indeed, two of them had once run their own companies.

Duane, now in his fifties, had spent his life in construction, owning his own company for a period of time. He lost that and more as his life spiraled down with drug use. He served time in a county jail (after he had already gotten clean on his own) and then at a prison work camp, which he liked better because working was "better than sitting in a cell . . . you feel better about yourself when working" (and the food was better too, he added). He started at Murray working the machines but soon was placed in charge of shipping and receiving, appreciating the trust he was given to work without supervision. After three and a half years in that position he was then promoted to accounts manager. As such he was part of a six-person council that met regularly with owner Bill Hall to discuss the operations and future of the company. "We know the final decision is upon that man but we will have the discussion and he listens," he said. Duane doesn't earn "nearly the money that I used to make" but was appreciative to be working for "a really good company."

Noting that he had "been in trouble all of his life," Frank started selling drugs around the age of thirteen and served his first sentence at fifteen for insurance fraud and arson. Eventually, though, he owned his own heating and air company, along with thirteen rental properties, but was still selling drugs. Following his arrest, his plea bargain put him in a rehabilitation center for six months and then on probation. At forty-one he had been a machine operator at Murray for a little under a year, most of that time while a resident at the rehab center. Since his release he had been living with his mother and his fifteen-year-old son. In his own words, Frank had been humbled. For a man who had been accustomed "to having good money" he was living at a different scale now, but was "proud of where I am today."

Cristy also tumbled from a comfortable life due to drug use and a related drug conviction, but the underlying cause was tragedy. Happily married for twenty years with a house, multiple cars, and three children, one day she came out of the shower to find her husband dead from a heart attack. Someone offered her some meth to help with her grief and "it got me from that day." Within six months she was arrested, placed in drug court, failed out, and sent to prison for eighteen months. Her last three months were at the Arrendale TC, which placed her at Murray where she had worked for fourteen months when we talked. Like so many others she was frustrated by the background check barrier to many jobs and apartments and by the loss of her right to own a gun. Having been a school bus driver, she had a commercial driver's license but "nobody is going to hire me." In contrast, Murray Plastics had given her opportunities that other places wouldn't and allowed her to start and finish her day early so that she could meet her daughters' school bus. At times her work was tedious but it could also be challenging and "it keeps me busy and I enjoy it." She too expressed pride in "the woman I have become, of the mother I have become."

Pam was another casualty of the meth plague that hit rural and small town Georgia. Now she was Murray's first shift supervisor, ran the quality department and was soon to become the company's quality manager. She was introduced to meth by a boyfriend, who she left at twenty, moving back in with her parents. Eventually she was using with her mother and, following her mother's death, with her aunt. They were arrested a day apart: "being in jail with my own family, that was enough for me." Her jail time was short, but she was a convicted felon. Consequently it took her time to find a job. She found Murray through the Department of Labor and "that's when doors opened." At the beginning she worried about what would happen when her probation officer checked up on her at work, but a coworker reassured her that everyone there was on probation.

As a leader, Pam often drew on her own story, believing that her testimony might help other transitioning workers. If she saw that a "person is not really that interested in working but instead only thinking about when they would get out, I would tell them, 'You need to focus. You need to take care of you. Do you want to be back there?'" And then she would advise: "When you get out you need to get a job, you need to get yourself stable." Some times she gave the other workers hugs, even though her boss didn't approve: "I think if you show them love and care that they will appreciate it more and maybe one day they will go, 'you know what, Pam was right.'" She concluded, "I can't save the world but if I can help a few people, one day here, one day there, that's really cool." Of herself, she said, "I am straight, I am clean, I have a beautiful three-year-old daughter. I have a brand new car outside, have my own place. I am quite proud of myself."

Murray Plastics is a for-profit business. Workers are expected to perform and if not they are let go. Expectations and accountability are important dimensions of reentry as they are in most aspects of life. But so too are second chances. Plant Manager Dubus effectively summarized their viewpoint, one that other employers would do well to adopt: *I tell everyone who walks in the door, "I don't care where you have been or what you have done, that is your issue. Here the only thing we care about is your work ethic and productivity. You prove that and we will grow you, we will grow you right along with us." It doesn't matter if they just came out of college or if they are the worst criminal you have ever met because deep down we believe that people are people. Same as you and I.*

CALL CENTER PLUS SERVICES

Georgia CALLS provided a different model of working with reentering people, one that was so comprehensive that under current conditions it could only reach a very small percentage of those who would benefit. Although in the end it was not viable, the effort still offers a compelling model of what inspired people can accomplish, one that points us in an important direction as we as a society become more serious about public safety grounded in the effective reintegration of the previously incarcerated.

At the heart of the operation was a call center. The catalyst for Georgia CALLS was Jay Reeder, a socially conscious entrepreneur who operated a for-profit call center, VoiceNation Live. Reeder had been working with a program serving Atlanta's homeless. Realizing that many of the homeless had been previously incarcerated, Reeder sought a way that he might be able to offer employment to at least some people facing reentry challenges. His idea was to start Georgia CALLS as a staffing agency to the parent company. The workers would be paid the same as at VoiceNation. Georgia CALLS would be paid a premium, which then allowed it to support its program staff and the services they provided. He brought in his long-time friend Mark Mobley, a pastor and local public official, as its executive director.

As Mobley explained to us, the participants's daily seven plus hours of work was supplemented by two hours of courses. The overall facility devoted a surprisingly large part of its space to a common room/eating area painted with bright colors and posted with affirmative sayings. It was well stocked with donated food from a food bank that was available to participants for breakfast when they arrived and snacking throughout the day. A hot lunch was prepared for them at no cost. Outside there was a small area for smoking, shooting baskets, and a picnic table under trees, a space particularly enjoyed by those who lived in the confines of a transitional center.

From it's beginning in Fall 2014, Georgia CALLS worked with the Phillips TC. In the beginning all of the participants came from the TC but it later broadened its reach to people who had been out of prison for up to a year. Part of the reason was the mismatch between the requirements of a call center with the skill levels of the average person transitioning out of imprisonment. With training they needed to be proficient at typing. They also needed to be able to communicate clearly and effectively with customers calling in to VoiceNation's some 3,000 different clients.

Throughout our conversation Mobley emphasized the centrality of attitudinal/thinking change for successful reentry and therefore for the program itself. Here the seamless integration of the call center work and the overall program was apparent. It was not uncommon for customers calling customer service to become angered quickly or even to be already angry when they called. Many of the participants came from backgrounds that stressed that when you are pushed, you pushed back. The Georgia CALLS program emphasized that "just because they are angry does not mean that you have to be." *You have the power to decide,* as Mobley explained. He added, *To see men and women exert that kind of control when in the past they have not . . . . That attitude change is what we are after.*

Such lessons were reinforced daily in the two sets of classes taken by all participants throughout the first year of the program. The first was a spiritual development course. The other class was about life skills broadly understood. There were five sets of topics, ranging from money management and decision-making skills to anger management and forgiveness.

Mobley interviewed all potential participants, determining not only if they had adequate skills (or could be brought up to the necessary levels in a reasonable time) but also whether they appeared to have sufficient "desire to make this change." He estimated that about half of the people he interviewed lacked the necessary skill levels, appropriate motivation, or their lives were in too much turmoil. Still, within the first few months of participation about half dropped out of the program: *their life is in such turmoil they couldn't concentrate and just literally walk out the door, not because they are upset with us or with the job, but they just can't keep their focus because they are overwhelmed— including some of the most skilled people that we have brought in.*

Georgia CALLS did have staff that worked with participants on the practical challenges of daily life. The program was willing to adjust schedules to accommodate court dates, visits with community corrections officers, etc. But once again transportation issues loomed large. This was not a problem for the workers coming from the TC but it often was for the others. Given the facility's location in the suburbs north of Atlanta, there was no meaningful public transit. Rides were not always reliable, and cheap cars break down. One participant drove an hour and half each way because he really liked the program but had to drop out because of car problems.

In one of the most moving portions of our conversation, Mobley described interviewing a young man from the transitional center, imprisoned since he was thirteen: *He now had the opportunity to work for us but he did not have the skill level. It was so far below that there was no way I could have trained him. To tell him no was one of the hardest things I have ever had to do in my life. I am going to start businesses that he could work at. I am going to figure out how to do it.* That is an important challenge for all of us.

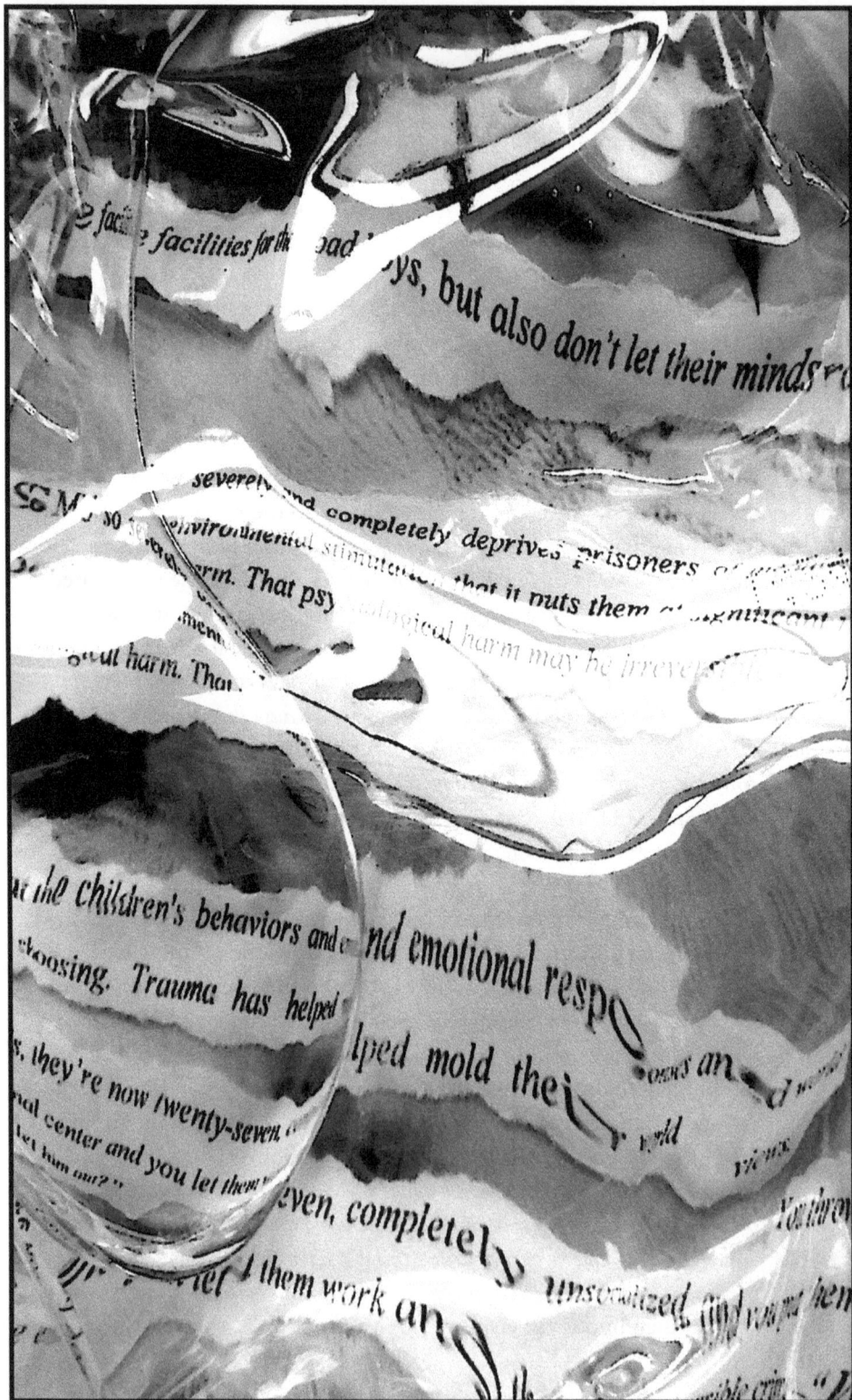

e facilities for the *bad boys*, but also don't let their minds...

M... so severely and completely deprives prisoners o...environmental stimulation that it puts them at significant... rm. That psychological harm may be irreversible...

out harm. That...

...he children's behaviors and emotional resp...choosing. Trauma has helped mold the...r old...

s, they're now twenty-seven...nal center and you let them...even, completely unsocialized...let them work and...

V

PUZZLE PIECES OF REFORM

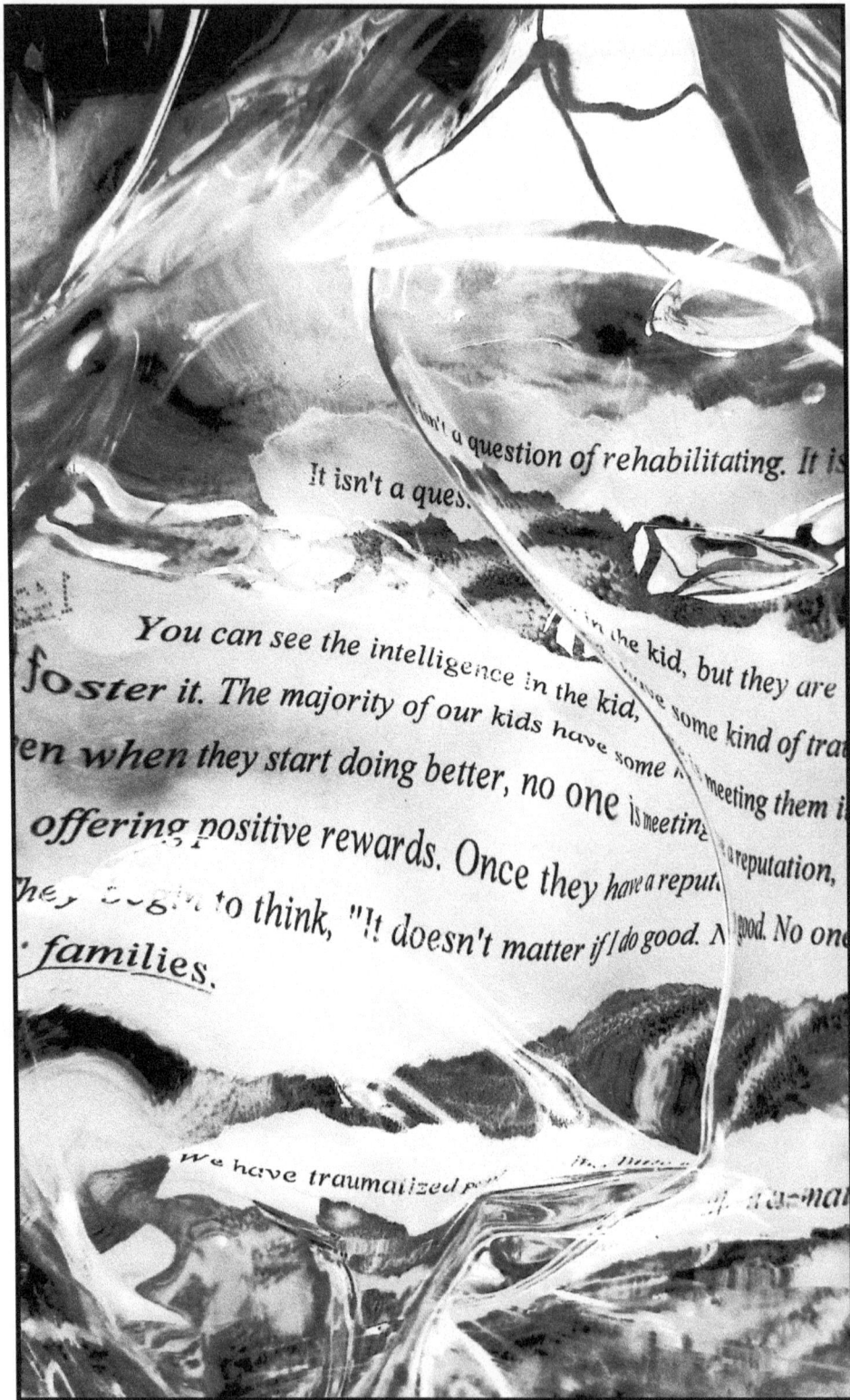

...'t a question of rehabilitating. It is...

It isn't a ques...

...the kid, but they are...

You can see the intelligence in the kid, ...some...some kind of tra...

foster it. The majority of our kids have some ...meeting them i...

...en when they start doing better, no one is meeting ...a reputation,

offering positive rewards. Once they have a reput...

...ey ...g... to think, "It doesn't matter if I do good. N...good. No one...

families.

We have traumatized ...

\1⁄

PROSECUTORS, PUNISHMENT & REENTRY

Prosecutors are widely portrayed as both the least constrained actors in the criminal justice system and also the least understood by the public. As elected officials, prosecutors should be publicly accountable, but in fact they act with very little oversight.[1] A recent scholarly overview of the relevant literature concludes that prosecutors are "quite possibly the most pressing challenge in American criminal justice," and that there is broad agreement that the power they now wield should be reviewed and limited.[2]

We should not have been surprised, then, that we had such difficulty securing interviews with district attorneys anywhere on the staff chart. We had similar difficulties throughout the enforcement side of the criminal justice system, in great contrast to our experience elsewhere. But unlike police chiefs and prison wardens, state and county district attorneys in forty-five of the states, including Georgia, are elected officials.

Consequently, we are grateful to the three district attorneys (one active and two former) who did talk with us. Indeed, because of the breadth of their careers, collectively these conversations gave us a lived sense of core changes in the criminal justice system in Georgia and the country as a whole over the past four decades, a period that includes the harshness of the 1990s laws and the more recent movement toward diversion and reentry.

PROSECUTORIAL ACCOUNTABILITY AND RACE

Robert Keller, when we talked to him, was in a reflective mood. He was at the end of a long and distinguished career in the Georgia legal system, having served for more than twenty-seven years as the district attorney in Clayton County, just south of Atlanta and home to the busiest airport in the country, Hartsfield-Jackson. He then served a seven-year term on the Georgia Board of Pardons and Paroles, and was, at the time we talked, the assistant director of the new Governor's Office of Transition, Support, and Reentry.

Keller grew up in a small town in southern Alabama. Upon graduating from Emory Law School, he settled in Clayton County. After a few years each as an assistant district attorney and in private practice, he was appointed district attorney in 1977 when the position opened. When he left office in 2004 he was the longest serving DA in Georgia at that time (which has 159 counties).

As district attorney, Keller was a strong prosecutor and also an adept politician, with a relaxed, accessible demeanor which for years helped him adapt to a county that rapidly changed its demographic composition from an affluent, almost completely white, suburb of Atlanta with highways named for Herman Talmadge, to a poor, predominantly African-American population whose residents often moved in to escape troubled areas in Atlanta.

Keller's sensitivity and skill at working with these demographic changes is exemplified by a case where a group of white youths were arrested after attempting to burn down the local offices of the NAACP. On the surface this would appear to be a racially motivated crime. Defense attorneys maintained otherwise, explaining that the fire accelerant that the boys carried was intended for the home of a friend—they were going to set his door on fire. However, he wasn't home so they left and walking by the NAACP building tried using it there without premeditation. Keller brought in the NAACP leaders to talk with the defense attorneys and then asked them, as a group, to make their recommendation about appropriate criminal charges. With their buy-in, he then made the decision to bring lesser charges so that the youth would be tried as juveniles rather than adults.

PROSECUTORS AND ELECTIONS

Eventually, the demographic changes caught up with Keller. His first challenger in the 2004 Democratic primary, Jewel Scott, an African-American candidate swamped Keller by a two-to-one margin (with a third candidate taking another 10% of the vote). Other white incumbents were defeated as well. The defeat was hard for Keller since he believed his opponent was minimally qualified for the office while he had been a good and fair prosecutor, one for whom race had never factored into his prosecutorial behavior. It helped when a good friend called him the next day remarking, "Keller, you have been district attorney for twenty-seven and half years and you could barely get 30% of the vote? You must have been the worst district attorney Clayton County ever had." Keller told us, "That was all I needed to hear" and years later the two of them would still laugh about the exchange.

Scott's tenure proved to be controversial, in part because of some questionable actions on her part as DA and in part due to scandals involving her and her politically ambitious husband. She lost her bid for re-election in 2008 at the same time her husband lost in his attempt to unseat the county's chief executive. The incumbent executive, also African American, had created a multiracial coalition that included an alliance with a white female juvenile court judge (and former assistant DA under Keller) who successfully defeated Jewel Scott.[3]

It is exceedingly rare for two district attorneys in succession to lose their reelection bids—in 85% of the races nationwide they are unopposed. Given the advantages of incumbency, on those infrequent occasions when DAs are challenged they are victorious about two-thirds of the time both in primaries and general elections.[4] Regardless of who wins, elected state and local prosecutors countrywide are almost always white (95% in 2014) and almost invariably male (79% white male). Indeed, two-thirds of the states in 2014 still had *no* elected black prosecutors. Only 1% were, like Scott, minority women.[5]

SUGGESTED REFORMS

If elections are the primary mechanism by which we hold prosecutors accountable, then our electoral system needs to be restructured both so that district attorneys lose more often and so that more people of color are elected as chief prosecutor. One suggestion deserving serious consideration would create multiple prosecutorial districts in larger, more diverse counties, for example, separating denser urban centers and more affluent suburbs. As one proponent explains, "Each of the prosecutors in the new smaller districts would deliver a different blend of enforcement priorities, intrusions, expenditures, and public safety, customized to the preferences of their own communities."[6]

A parallel suggested set of reforms that would affect prosecutors involves juries. First, juries in larger cities would not be selected citywide but rather from smaller, more neighborhood-based zones, that is "a jury of one's peers." This, as Harvard Law professor William J. Stuntz explained, "would empower the black jurors [who] . . . need more power over the fate of the young men in their communities."[7] Second would be to reduce the number of peremptory challenges by which potential jurors are dismissed. As one close observer of criminal justice in Georgia told us, it is still too easy for prosecutors to eliminate potential jurors on a racial basis while claiming other reasons. This is a particular problem for communities where a high percentage of families have members with a criminal record and this association is then used to strike the potential juror.[8] Stuntz acknowledges that the combined effect of these two changes might make obtaining convictions harder but, the system is already stacked in the government's favor. In the end, Stuntz argues, "If a prosecutor cannot convince a dozen residents of a high-crime neighborhood that one of their neighbors should be punished, punishment is probably unwise and could well be unjust."[9]

We might fear that these decentralizing measures would result in dangerous criminals being freed by permissive neighbors. What this overlooks is that while these neighbors might want to curtail rampant mass incarceration, at the same time they do want to be safe. Indeed, the people most likely to be victimized by crime are not affluent suburbanites but residents of communities of concentrated disadvantage. It is African Americans who are most afraid to walk through their neighborhood alone at night; surveys consistently show a difference of 10% or more compared to whites.[10] In the face of the heroin and then crack epidemics it was many of these same communities, such as in Washington D.C. and New York City, that gave strong support to the laws lengthening the penalties for drug-related crimes.[11] Today with the pendulum having swung toward reform, there is often little black/white difference on specific criminal reform questions.[12]

RACE AND JURIES

These issues concerning race, juries, and prosecutorial advantage are sharply highlighted by one of the most prominent cases occurring during Keller's tenure as Clayton County DA. In 1983 Keller succeeded in convicting Calvin C. Johnson Jr. for rape, for which he received a life sentence at the age of twenty-five. From Keller's perspective, he had succeeded during cross-examination in undermining the credibility of Johnson's claims of innocence. However, perhaps what most clinched the jury's verdict, he suggested, was the victim's actions. During her testimony she was visibly under duress. Upon leaving the stand and crossing in front of Johnson's table, this petite woman leapt out at the much larger man.

Johnson had better luck years later after DNA testing became available and especially once the Innocence Project took on his case. When the judge in the case retired and all the evidence stored in his office was being thrown away, the clerk informed Keller's office. Keller sent over two investigators who found the rape kit from Johnson's trial in the trashcan. When they called Keller asking what to do with it, he decided they would save it, although there was no legal requirement that they do so. It sat on the shelf until Johnson learned about DNA testing and contacted Keller's office to see if they still had the kit.

After several years of delays and mishaps, the DNA was finally tested and exonerated Johnson. Fortunately too, unlike far too many prosecutors elsewhere, Keller did not oppose turning the kit over to be tested or challenge the results. Upon Johnson's release after sixteen years of false imprisonment, his family having exhausted its resources seeking his freedom, Keller shook his hand and wished him well.[13] Subsequently, the two have appeared together speaking about the importance of evidence preservation.

Johnson is black, the rape victim was white. The all-white jury convicted him in forty-five minutes, rejecting his testimony and that of his four supporting witnesses but believing the victim, who had picked him out of a set of photos but could not identify him in a line up. A few weeks later Johnson also stood trial in Atlanta for a rape case with many similar features. In that case, with a racially mixed jury, he was found innocent.[14]

PLEA BARGAINING AND MANDATORY MINIMUMS

J. Tom Morgan served fourteen years as district attorney of DeKalb County. Like Clayton, DeKalb lies adjacent to Fulton County, which contains most of the city of Atlanta. Also like Clayton, DeKalb's population grew first from white flight from the city, then from African-American flight, and now by a growing presence of immigrants from around the world. Currently the county has a slight African-American majority, a reversal from the slight white majority of 1990.

Morgan grew up in south Georgia in the city of Albany and graduated from the University of Georgia Law school. For nine years he worked as an assistant DA in DeKalb, most of that time focusing on prosecuting crimes against children, the first prosecutor in the state with that specialization. These cases ranged from sexual and physical abuse to murder. The work was grueling, especially as the number of child homicides grew. In 1992 Morgan was elected district attorney, serving until he stepped down in 2004 to enter private practice.

DRACONIAN CRIMINAL JUSTICE LAWS

It was during the 1990s, as we have noted earlier, that much of the most draconian legislation that reduced parole, lengthened sentences, and instituted mandatory minimums was passed throughout the country, including in Georgia. According to Morgan, up until then in Georgia the maximum sentence a juvenile could be given for any crime was five years, including for murder. At the time there were "some really horrible gang murders" and a sense that their frequency was increasing, so prosecutors went to then Governor Zell Miller to ask that defendants in juvenile murder cases be tried automatically as adults. "Be careful what you ask for," Morgan said in retrospect. Miller gave them that and much more. The Juvenile Justice Reform Act of 1994 (SB 440) not only mandated that youths age thirteen to seventeen who committed murder come under the jurisdiction of adult courts but also defendants in six other crimes. Collectively known as "the seven deadly sins," conviction would carry an automatic mandatory minimum sentence of ten years without the possibility of parole.

In their review of a case, prosecutors did have the discretion to send cases back to the juvenile courts. Morgan explained that he personally would make the decision about whether to try a child as an adult, choices which he regarded, along with the death penalty, as the toughest decisions he had to make as district attorney: "I was elected to make such decisions." For example, in cases of armed robbery, the most frequent of the seven deadlies, he would prosecute the juvenile who carried the gun as an adult. If other minors were involved, he would consider the circumstances and whether they were willing to provide evidence against the person holding the gun. Kevin, whose story we shared earlier when discussing the lost decade of SB 440 juveniles, was one of the first youths Morgan charged as an adult.

Morgan continued to believe that trying juveniles accused of murder as adults was appropriate policy. But otherwise he thought the change was a mistake: *Juveniles when they come back, their life is pretty much destroyed. That's why it so hard to sentence a fifteen year old to ten years in prison without parole. They've lost the formative years of their life behind bars.* A public defender who represented many of these minors, Ruth McMullin, amplified this point, noting that this period up to about age twenty-four is crucial for the development of our reasoning faculties and that we are putting these youths in prison where they spend all of their time with others who have made the same bad decisions. Concerning the effect of incarceration itself, Morgan said bluntly, *I don't think there is any reform in prison. After you have served ten years in prison, you don't have a chance.* In contrast, Keller from Clayton County mentioned two cases to us where he decided that the defendants would be charged as juveniles rather than adults. Making good on the break they were given, both went on to become attorneys themselves.

In 1995 Georgia's instituted mandatory minimums for adults with SB 441. This was part of the "truth in sentencing" movement sweeping the country, based on the belief that criminal behavior would be better deterred by the knowledge that full—and lengthy—sentences would be served. Indeed, the Violent Crime Control and Law Enforcement Act of 1994 conditioned certain federal grants to states on their adoption of truth-in-sentencing provisions.[15] As Gov. Miller explained, he was putting an end to a system that "seems better at letting criminals go, instead of keeping criminals locked away serving their time." Along with the mandatory minimum sentencing discussed earlier, Miller's "Two strikes and you are gone" provision was the most severe in the nation.[16] By 2018 a third of Georgia's prison population had been sentenced under these laws.[17]

Just to make sure judges got the message, the governor sent out a letter to all judges across the state, Judge Michael Hancock told us, reminding them that they had no discretion in terms of imposing the mandatory minimum. According to Bob Keller, before 1995 people convicted of the most serious crimes in Georgia served an average of seven years, but following these laws, the average grew to seventeen years. More broadly, the average sentence served by prisoners released in 2000 was eight years, in 2017 it was more than twelve years.[18]

The Issue of Discretion

A big part of what drove the truth-in-sentencing movement was the issue of discretion as employed by prosecutors, judges, and parole boards. But this cut in two very different ways. The mood of the times was getting tough on crime, from Bill Clinton in the White House to Miller in the Georgia state house. For the get-toughers the problem was criminal justice officials with too much discretion that they were using to minimize the amount of time served by offenders.

However, for other advocates of the change the problem was the unfairness of the great variability in the sentences received by people committing the same crime with similar records but with different prosecutors and judges.

The justice system of the United States is amazingly fragmented. For example, in Georgia there are forty-nine different judicial circuits. As Keller gained seniority he served on a statewide sentencing reform commission. Both then and later on the Parole Board, constraining this variability in sentencing and in granting parole was an important objective for him. After his career as a prosecutor, Morgan became a defense attorney with almost all of his clients under twenty-five. He pointed out to us the unfair variation that can exist between often lighter sentences for offenders in metropolitan areas where there is much crime—and harsh sentences not appropriate to the crime in smaller counties where "a severe crime can be the crime of the century." He found the charges against his private clients, which often involve drugs and/ or alcohol, varied significantly depending on the prosecutor.

Limiting racial variations in sentencing was, somewhat surprisingly, another justification for these laws. Paul L. Howard Jr., elected in 1997 as the first African-American district attorney in Georgia and still serving Fulton County and Atlanta, has voiced his support of mandatory minimums. He wrote in 2013, "Black defendants are at least 30 percent more likely to be in prison for the same crime. Whenever the judges are allowed to sentence at their discretion, the disparity increases. That's why I believe it's important that everyone who commits a similar crime should receive a similar sentence. There is racial disparity. One of the best ways to avoid it is to make the sentences the same."[19]

Recent evidence from Wisconsin provides validation of Howard's point about discretion, here involving prosecution of misdemeanor offenses. An extensive analysis of statewide data found significant racial disparities in cases dropped, dismissed, or reduced. For example, comparing defendants with no criminal histories, whites were 25% more likely than blacks to have their charges dropped.[20] Or, to take one step further back, white kids' "dismissal" occurs when they were not arrested in the first place, as Atlanta defense attorney Ryan Locke put it to us.

Truth in sentencing has definitely limited the discretion of judges and in important respects that of prosecutors. However, at the same time in other very significant aspects, mandatory minimum sentencing has greatly enhanced the power of prosecutors. This is because of the way they have affected the dynamics of plea bargaining between prosecutors and defendants.

Dynamics of Plea Bargaining

Mass incarceration first of all requires an even larger process of mass arrests since many of those arrested will not be charged, convicted, and incarcerated. As more and more defendants have deluged courthouses, the judicial system has increasingly bogged down. Everyone is overworked: public defenders, prosecutors, and judges. Trials consume scarce time and resources. If the defendant agrees to plead guilty to the charges proposed by the prosecutor and accepts the associated punishment then a trial is avoided.

It should be clear why the incentive structure for prosecutors and judges would encourage settling cases without a trial through plea bargaining.[21] But what about for defendants? These incentives must be substantial because about 95% of all cases are settled this way.[22] Invariably the deal offered by prosecutors reduces the charges and punishment that the defendant would face if the case were to go to trial. For the guilty defendant, then, the incentive is clear. But we also have substantial evidence of innocent defendants pleading guilty.

According to two recent books by law professors examining misdemeanor charges, the specific reasons vary but essentially result from the calculation by defendants that the continuing costs (in a broad sense) of fighting the charges outweighed the perceived costs of the guilty plea.[23] Atlanta attorney Locke explained to us that in his experience a client waiting in jail would always take a guilty plea rather than continue waiting in jail for a trial. For those not in jail, they might plead guilty because they are tired of returning time and again to court only to have their case postponed when they can ill afford to miss work or arrange for child care.

Prosecutors routinely overcharge defendants, especially at the felony level. They do this because they can then use removing these charges as bargaining chips in their interactions with the defendant. It is important to emphasize that prosecutors have full discretion (i.e., no oversight outside of their office) in determining how much to charge and how much to bargain away.[24]

The dynamic is stacked against the defendant even more when mandatory minimum charges are involved or two- or three-strike automatic life sentences. What do you do if the plea bargain strips away such charges but they remain if going to trial? As law professor Angela J. Davis explains, "the stakes are often too high for a defendant to exercise his constitutional right to trial, regardless of the weakness of the prosecutor's plea offer."[25] The evidence is clear. At the federal level prior to the institution of mandatory minimums, 15 to 20% of cases went to trial but since then the percentage keeps falling, in 2015 down to 3%.[26]

By one authoritative account these tougher sentencing policies account for most of the increase in mass incarceration.[27] At the federal level about one half of the increase is due to more severe sentencing of drug offenders but at the state level that accounts for only about one fifth of the increase. For the states, the most important driver has been harsher treatment of violent offenses. Another would be sex offenses. Former DeKalb district attorney Robert L. James, Jr. gave us this example. For certain sex offenses the minimum was ten years. If an innocent person were offered a plea carrying a five-year sentence, they might take the risk of going to trial. But later the minimum was changed to twenty-five years. Even if innocent, who would take that risk if offered five years?

Two examples of the dynamics involved in such cases were related to us by former DeKalb public defenders. The first involved a fourteen year old being tried as an adult for a sexual assault on a young child. According to the public defender, Laila Kelly, they first had to sit through the trial of another juvenile being charged as an adult and defended by a private attorney. When the first defendant lost, the mother of her client started wailing and insisted to her son that he take the plea still on the table for four years. If he too were convicted he would receive a ten-year sentence. He said that for him it made no difference. He was innocent. If convicted he would kill himself, as he would if he took the plea. Fortunately, Kelly had enough time to investigate and challenge the evidence. He was found innocent. Two of the jurors told Kelly they couldn't believe that her client had been charged in the first place.

The second case had the opposite outcome. As explained to us by Ruth McMullin, a man in his fifties was accused by his thirteen-year-old stepdaughter of raping her. The man claimed he was innocent and McMullin was convinced that he was telling the truth, in part because the girl's testimony was not credible to her. The prosecution offered a plea of two years in prison. Maintaining his innocence, he went to trial, lost, and went to prison for life. From that point on, McMullin used the case with subsequent clients to illustrate the risks they would run in going to trial when lengthy sentences were involved.

Severe Consequences with Little Gain

The ultimate tragedy of mandatory minimums is that, just like with all lengthy sentences, they do little to enhance public safety. They have little effect on crime rates.[28] Instead, according to legal scholar Michael Tonry, these laws "shift discretion from judges to prosecutors . . . fail to acknowledge salient differences between cases, and often punish minor offenders more harshly than anyone involved believes is warranted."[29] Is it any wonder, then, that surveys find that they are disliked by large majorities of judges, defense counsel, and probation officers (with prosecutors more evenly divided).[30]

Judges have a moral and legal obligation to judge each case on a case by case basis, insisted Judge Gregory A. Adams, who at the time we interviewed him was the Chief Superior Court Judge for DeKalb County. However, mandatory sentencing often tied his hands where he believed judicial discretion was called for. He used the example of a juvenile robbing another juvenile of his tennis shoes using a BB gun or even a water pistol. Under Georgia law this is armed robbery. If the district attorney were to make this charge, the juvenile would be tried as an adult and if convicted would receive a minimum ten-year sentence. In this case Judge Adams would have preferred the option to hold the youth accountable but punish with a lesser sentence. *Judges have the experience and wisdom to be able to distinguish the individuals who are truly dangerous from those who can be properly held accountable through lesser forms of punishment,* he concluded.

Finally, there is evidence that when the public confronts these issues directly as opposed to abstractly, they do not support the lengthy sentences now called for by the law and associated sentencing guidelines. One federal district judge hearing a child pornography case asked jurors to record what they thought would be an appropriate sentence. When he later looked at the results he found that the sentence he gave based on federal guidelines was almost five times higher than what the jurors thought appropriate. Expanding the study with the cooperation of other judges to twenty-two other cases, the average sentence recommended by jurors was about one-fifth that of the median guideline suggestion.[31]

Addressing mandatory sentences is one crucial area where the criminal justice reform process in Georgia has fallen far short. We know from conversations with members of the Georgia Criminal Justice Reform Council (GCJRC) and from statements made at public meetings that at least some of the reformers recognize the damage done by mandatory minimums and the need for change. A small step in that direction led to legislation in 2013 allowing judges to deviate from the constraints for some drug offenses but only with the concurrence of both defense and prosecutor. Following from a recommendation in the 2016 GCJRC report, a subcommittee was established to look further into the issues but its mandate excluded the seven deadly sins.[32] As the life of the Council expired with the election of a new governor in 2018, no further progress had been made except for a recommendation in its final report encouraging continuing consideration of the issue.

REVERSING MASS INCARCERATION

Given the crucial role of prosecutors in expanding mass incarceration in the United States, rolling incarceration back to rates more in line with other major democracies—and even our own not too distant past—requires change in the fundamental orientation of prosecutors. Invariably successful candidates for district attorney until recent years ran campaigns centered on being the toughest on crime of all contenders. Today's reformers still need to provide such assurances but they have a broader agenda. This is reflected in the general platform describe as Fair and Just Prosecution now being taken up by various progressive prosecutors around the country, including in Georgia. For example there is Scott Colom, a young African American who defeated an incumbent in northeast Mississippi, who pledged, in the words of a reporter, "to lock fewer people up, stop treating drug addiction as a crime, and expand rehab services."[33]

Larry Krasner, who was elected in Philadelphia in November 2017, is among the most prominent of the progressive candidates in recent years to have won their race for district attorney in large cities and counties around the country. Krasner's career had been as a public defender and as a civil rights attorney; before winning he had never prosecuted a case. Rather than the "tough on crime" rhetoric of the normal candidate for chief prosecutor, Krasner promised to institute reforms to reduce mass incarceration in his city, which had the highest rate of the ten largest cities in the country. His reform agenda received substantial attention nationwide.

The last two district attorneys in our home county of DeKalb have had a similar progressive orientation: Robert D. James, Jr., who served six years beginning in late 2010, followed by Sherry Boston who defeated him in 2016. We interviewed James and his director of diversion programs, Kaleema Thomas. In addition, we observed him in various public forums over several

---

Philadelphia DA Larry Krasner's Progressive Reforms[34]

In February 2018 Philadelphia District Attorney Larry Krasner announced a series of major reforms for his office. They include the following:

❖ *Decline certain charges. This includes possession and buying of marijuana as well as prostitution when the sex worker has two or fewer prior convictions.*

❖ *Charge some other offenses at lower levels where they can be handled more promptly and with less incarceration. Specifically, in cases of retail theft of under $500 when the defendant has no or few prior convictions, punishment would be limited to no more than 90 days incarceration and fines of up to $250, along with paying full restitution.*

❖ *Divert more with "an eye toward achieving accountability and justice while avoiding convictions where appropriate."*

❖ *Actively work to expand participation in re-entry programs.*

❖ *Plea offers for most crimes (but not major crimes) should be below those suggested by the state sentencing guidelines and where those recommendations are for less than two years, the plea offer should rely more on house arrest, probation, and alternative sentences.*

❖ *At sentencing state on the record the benefits and costs of the sentence recommended. In Philadelphia, the estimated cost of one year of incarceration ranges between $42,000 and $60,000, enough to cover the salary of a beginning teacher or police officer, and more than the total income of the city's average family ($41,000).*

❖ *Request shorter probationary sentences.*

❖ *A positive drug test for marijuana should not normally be considered a violation of probation or parole.*

---

years, including the annual Faith Leaders Conference James co-sponsored with the county sheriff. This conference provided informational talks with various members of the prosecutor's office as well as tours of the county jail, morgue, police department, and police academy.

Like the prior DAs we interviewed, James grew up in an educated middle-class family. But unlike them, it was in a later period and as an African American. As a teenager he witnessed first hand the impact of the crack epidemic on the small town not far south of Nashville where he grew up. America as he lived it "changed right before my eyes." He had friends who began using and selling crack, who were arrested, and imprisoned, as well as others who were shot and murdered. He had family members who went from advanced placement classes to selling crack to felony convictions and imprisonment to being in their 30s and 40s and unable to get jobs.

James explained to us that by the time he received his law degree from Georgia State University in Atlanta in 1999, it was clear to him that "we had lost the war on drugs, that it was time for a more intelligent way to go about it instead of trying to incarcerate our way out." It was also clear to him that the country had been over-incarcerating African-American men and women.

Pre-Trial Diversion

After a stint as an assistant district attorney in one of metro Atlanta's smaller counties, James was elected DeKalb County solicitor-general in 2007, that is, the prosecutor for criminal misdemeanor offenses. In both that position and subsequently as district attorney, he expanded the type of pre-trial diversion programs that have become more frequent, especially for lower risk offenders of less serious crimes. At the felony level, pretrial diversion was limited to first-time offenders whose crime was nonviolent and non-aggressive. Successful completion of the program of classes, drug testing, community service, and probation resulted in the dismissal of the case.[35] Participation in Georgia's diversion programs by law must have the concurrence of victims.

James's first significant effort to extend beyond conventional diversion came in 2008 with Jobs Not Jail (JNJ), which he started as solicitor-general and then carried over into his tenure as DA. James told us that the inspiration for the program came when the state labor commissioner asked an audience to tell him the difference in the incarceration rates of employed black men and employed white men. The answer: none.

James said that his highest priority as prosecutor was addressing recidivism, especially among youthful offenders. First, he took pride in substantially reducing the number of juveniles that were tried as adults. They would still be held accountable but through the juvenile system (former public defenders Kelly and McMullin praised this reduction to us as well). Given his responsibility as district attorney to protect public safety, James did not hesitate to prosecute and see the convicted sent to prison where he believed it was appropriate. At the same time, throughout our interview he called for more study and discussion about how sentencing and incarceration can better enhance public safety instead of too often sending away bad people and having them return even worse. What do we need to be doing, he asked, to make sure that the armed robber becomes, for example, a plumber?

Second, young offenders (17-24) were the focus of the two programs that he emphasized. In the beginning JNJ diverted first-time offenders of serious misdemeanors into a year-long program of education and job/life skills training, along with job placement. When he moved to the district attorney's office the program focused on those with felony charges. Unlike general pre-trial diversion programs, this was based on the accountability court model. Like drug courts, for example, a judge in regular court sessions held participants accountable for their compliance and progress.

DIVERSION ON STEROIDS FOR YOUTH

The next step was the development of the Anti-Recidivism Court (ARC). Although again directed at young first-time felony offenders, the intended participants in ARC were assessed to be at high risk of re-offending due to compounding background factors such as family dysfunction, school suspensions, and indigency. At the same time, they were assessed as having sufficient capacity to complete what James emphasized was a very demanding program. Participants included lower-level drug dealers but not bigger dealers or those with armed offenses. Given the greater recidivism risks of this population, all the dimensions of the prior JNJ program were enhanced in ARC, for example, much tighter supervision (including ankle monitors) and more frequent court appearances. "Essentially, the message is we control your lives," James said. "This is diversion on steroids."

The program was indeed demanding. At the time of our interview, thirty-eight had successfully completed but twenty-four had exited (the current class had another thirty-two participants). The key determinant seemed to be readiness. The participant had to be willing to make the life style changes necessary to succeed in the program. For some the catch was the curfew—9 p.m. every night for the duration of a program lasting a minimum of a year. For others it was marijuana. Virtually every participant tested positive for marijuana as they began the program. They were given some weeks to get with the drug-free program. If it appeared that they had addiction problems, they were offered the alternative of drug court. But for some neither option was better than dropping out and taking a chance with their sentence. At that point James's office would recommend against probation because they had failed their second chance opportunity.

James emphasized that for those who were committed he was willing to supply extra resources to help them succeed. That might mean extra support to help meet their educational needs. He also contracted with a private company to manage their probation, providing two officers dedicated exclusively to ARC as members of the team. James's office covered the probation fees for participants who were indigent (most of them).

Some critics do not like diversion programs, especially not those like ARC that extend extra resources to assist offenders, describing them as "hug a thug." For these critics, James would stress the monetary savings associated with diversion (for ARC, a quarter the cost of jail) and the contributions to public safety. For James the original impetus for these programs was the importance of decent employment for reducing crime, incarceration, and recidivism. At one forum, James stressed the importance of employers being willing to offer jobs to people with criminal offenses, then moved beyond exhortation to modeling, announcing to great applause that he was offering two ARC graduates paid internships in his office. At a later forum one of them announced he had turned the opportunity into a paid position.

FAIR AND JUST PROSECUTION

Procedural justice focuses on the importance of having a system that feels fair to all participants in it, guilty and innocent. In our interview, James stressed the importance of fair and respectful treatment of defendants from first contact with the police through the rest of the criminal justice process. Perceived unfair treatment can affect attitudes for years to come. As an African American, he said he had had his own bad experiences but the impact was less intense as a middle-class person than it would be for a poor person. Respect for poor young African-American males is huge, he pointed out, because self-respect is about all they have: "They need to be treated the same way we treat our own children, our nephews and nieces."

This growing emphasis on procedural justice is seen in the recent election of progressive prosecutors across the country and the development of networks to bring them together. Most notable is Fair and Just Prosecution (FJP), which was formed after the 2016 elections not only to facilitate connection but also to provide training and other resources.[36] Among the newly elected reformist prosecutors who have endorsed FJP's principles are Philadelphia's Larry Krasner and DeKalb County's Sherry Boston. The organization's vision is to work with these prosecutors to promote "a justice system grounded in fairness, equity, compassion, and fiscal responsibility."[37] A central objective is to help prosecutors reduce incarceration rates, the subject of a recent FJP report. Their recommendations include making diversion the rule, charging with restraint and plea bargaining fairly, trying to end cash bail, encouraging the treatment rather than criminalization of mental illness and drug addiction, not trying kids as adults, de-emphasizing misdemeanors, shrinking probation and parole, and promoting restorative justice.[38]

The policies and practices of prosecutors also have enormous consequences for communities and therefore on the view that communities have about the fairness of the entire criminal justice system. As the FJP report points out, prosecutors "can use their discretion to improve the overall fairness and efficacy of the criminal justice system and champion priorities that improve the safety and well-being of our communities." To do so, "Fairness is paramount. It helps achieve the mission of public safety by building trust, which in turn aids police and prosecutors in solving crime." To this end, the project's report offers eleven recommendations to prosecutors. These include changing office culture and practice to make it more equitable and accountable; addressing racial disparity; increased sharing of information with the defense and playing fair with forensic evidence; holding police accountable; expunging and sealing criminal records; working to end the death penalty; and calculating the cost of incarceration.

Bringing Public Defenders to Parity

To these two sets of excellent recommendations we would add three others. The first comes from John Pfaff, the author of probably the most influential book of the last decade on the role of the prosecutor in expanding mass incarceration. Among the many reforms he suggests, Pfaff highlights adequately funding public defenders as perhaps "the most effective way to regulate prosecutors."

Georgia's experience of recent decades makes the point particularly well. Prior to a major reform in 2003 each county individually determined how it would comply with the Supreme Court's mandate in its historic *Gideon v. Wainwright* decision of 1963 and subsequent decisions that indigent defendants must be supplied with counsel in any case with the possibility of imprisonment as punishment. Decades later Greene County (located halfway between Atlanta and Augusta) still relied on a part-time lawyer selected by lowest cost and without a county supplied office. This defender had a public workload double the nationally recommended maximum (along with his private practice), pled 99% of his cases, and after seventeen years appeared to observer Amy Bach "exhausted—by the job and the system."[39]

This scandalous situation was not Greene County's alone. The Atlanta-based Southern Center for Human Rights (SCHR) sued similar counties, which also brought increased media attention. The state bar association took up the issue as did eventually the chief justice of the state Supreme Court and finally the legislature. In 2003 the Georgia Indigent Defense Act became law, establishing a statewide public defender program. Major improvements followed but significant problems remain. As the SCHR points out, "Public defenders carry crushing caseloads, lack the investigative and expert assistance they need to represent their clients effectively, and are pressured to represent defendants with conflicting interests."[40]

Crushing caseloads is a frequent characterization of the public defender situation throughout the country, along with insufficient salaries, especially when compared to prosecutors. It is hard to establish, though, just how bad the situation is. The widely cited standard for an acceptable caseload was established back in 1973 but not on the basis of any research and by one authoritative account were undoubtedly set too high.[41] That standard for public offenders handling misdemeanor cases is 400 a year. Recent reports concerning the core Atlanta county of Fulton cite defenders carrying from 500 up to 1000 cases. The seventeen staff attorneys have only two desks to share along with their phones. Some have waited years for a work laptop; others are still waiting.[42] This is despite the fact that under Governor Deal there was a 25% increase in state funding of the program in real dollars from 2011 through 2017.[43]

Some of the prosecutor/defender disparity has been the result of federal priorities. During the peak of the war on drugs, Georgia's police and prosecutors received almost $18 million in federal funding from 1985 to 1990. During this period the number of drug cases filed in DeKalb County increased tenfold, as did the workload of public defenders; however, there were no federal funds going to Georgia's public defenders.[44]

Atlanta defense attorney Ryan Locke told us that many of the clients who hire him were first represented by a public defender. When they tell him they want a "real lawyer" (having obtained funds from family and/or friends) he explains that previously he had been a public defender and retains great respect for those doing that work. However, he acknowledges that there is a difference. The constant for public defenders everywhere is "too many cases and not enough time." As a private attorney he can give clients more time. That might include going beyond working directly on the case to providing the personal time with the client who needs extra reassurance or repeated explanations.

There remains substantial variation between counties in the adequacy of their public defender programs. Some contract with the state to run their offices; others, such as DeKalb County, run their own offices and supplement the funding received from the state. In our interview with Claudia Saari, the head of DeKalb's public defenders office, she indicated that their average misdemeanor caseload was 375. The national norm for felony caseloads is 150, the DeKalb average was 170. However, because these are averages, that means some defenders were carrying loads above that. Similarly with salaries, she said that some of the public defenders had parity with prosecutors but others did not. One former member of her staff who we interviewed said she had gone without a salary increase for seven years before she resigned. For support services, parity was even further away—prosecutors have secretaries, public defenders do not. They all should have county-supplied electronic tablets to easily carry between office and courtroom but many did not. As Saari concluded, achieving parity across these dimensions "would be huge."

The rest of the story of the public defender in Greene County further confirms the importance of adequately funding these offices. The defender ended his contract with the county and eventually ended up on the staff in Houston County (just below Macon), which at the time was "widely considered one of the best, if not the best" public defenders office in Georgia. In his prior impossible situation he had been "slipshod and ineffective," in Bach's account, but in his new setting "he'd become competent and successful," providing another example "that systems often shape the individual."[45]

Given the crushing workloads and low salaries facing many public defenders, it is not surprising that burnout is a frequent theme when this occupation is discussed. The public defenders with whom we spoke all cited those cases where they felt that they made a significant contribution to the positive outcome for their clients as giving them a major morale boost, sometimes a long lasting one. On the other side, there were the cases where it was hard not to be dragged back down. As one public defender said to us, "how many times can you have the same conversation with a forty-five-year-old crackhead that you have already represented multiple times?"

Experience as Defense Counsel for Prosecutors and Judges

Our second additional recommendation comes from U.S. District Court Judge Jed S. Rackoff, who would require prosecutors at both the state and federal levels to spend part of their time serving as defense counsel for indigent defendants under the supervision of the legal aid supervisor (his suggestion is six months out of every three years). Rackoff explains, " I can think of no other step more likely to make prosecutors aware of the great power they possess or the need to temper it with other considerations."[46]

In our conversation with former DeKalb district attorney J. Tom Morgan he made a similar suggestion, although as defense counsel more generally rather than specific to indigent defense. He also suggested what is our third recommendation: that judges should have had prior experience as both prosecutors and defense counsel. Currently judges are much more likely to have had prosecutorial rather than defense experience. A big step forward would be the selection of candidates with experience as defense counsel. Even better would be, as Morgan recommends, both sets of experiences.

Group Impact of Prosecutors and Public Defenders

Finally, it is important to indicate that both prosecutors and public defenders have important collective roles beyond their work on individual cases. Prosecutor associations are among the most powerful actors when it comes to criminal justice reform. Because the recent reform process in Georgia operated on a consensus basis among major stakeholders, it gave groups willing to use that leverage substantial influence. Clearly the Prosecuting Attorneys' Council of Georgia was a major brake on the reform process on a number of occasions. As just one example, the GCJRC considered a minor change to mandatory minimums in January 2017. The representative of the prosecutors' council voiced opposition during the discussion. The GCJRC's vote was unanimous except for the vote of the member who was a district attorney. Council chair Carey Miller then tabled the recommendation because "what we do is collaborative and unanimous." Analysts have found the same throughout the country. As Udi Ofer, director of the Campaign for Smart Justice at the American Civil Liberties Union, points out, "In state after state, we've seen DA associations hold back reforms that are supported by Democrats and Republicans alike."[47]

Nowhere have we seen public defender associations playing a similarly influential role. Perhaps with greater parity across the board with prosecutors that day will come. Meanwhile, DeKalb's Claudia Saari explained with pride the more general role that public defenders do play while "fighting for the underdog:" *We keep the government in check. We make sure that everything is done fairly. We bring integrity to the criminal justice system by making sure everyone [police, prosecutors, judges] is doing everything right. We are making sure that rights are not being trampled.*

COMPLETING THE CIRCLE

The day we spoke with Clayton County's Robert Keller, he was musing on the conversation he had just had with someone returning from prison after thirty years. Now that he was released, the returning citizen wanted to know if he could adopt someone he had befriended in prison, so that this younger man might benefit after his death. As he suggested there might be other legal ways besides adoption to ensure that the protege benefited, Keller found himself wondering if providing legal advice and assistance to men returning from prison might be a way of completing the circle of justice in his own career. He had never, he acknowledged, really thought about reentry very much as a prosecutor. Clearly, it was intrinsic to the decisions he made in his seven-year service on the Georgia Parole Board. But, to actively and directly engage in the results of those decisions he made as part of the parole board and as a prosecutor would be a different matter. Definitely something to ponder. As it is for all of us. Few of us will ever be a prosecutor or parole board member but those who are act in our name. We too, then, bear some responsibility for the consequences of their decisions.

Endnotes
1. See, for example, A.J. Davis, *Arbitrary Justice: The Power of the American Prosecutor.* Oxford University Press, 2007, p. 8; B. Forst. "Prosecution." In *Crime and Public Policy*, ed. J. Q. Wilson and J. Petersilia. Oxford University Press, 2011, pp. 438, 449; M. Gottschalk. *Caught: The Prison State and the Lockdown of American Politics.* Princeton University Press, 2015, p. 266.
2. D. A. Sklansky. "The Problems with Prosecutors." *Annual Review of Criminology.* (2018): 452-53.
3. D. Silliman, "District attorney, husband sued for $1 million," *Clayton News-Daily.* 29 Apr 2008; "A victory for the adults in the room," *Atlanta Journal-Constitution [AJC].* 10 Aug 2008.

4. J. F. Pfaff. *Locked In: The True Causes of Mass Incarceration—and How to Achieve Real Reform*. Basic Books, 2017, p. 141.

5. N. Fandos, "A Study Documents the Paucity of Black Elected Prosecutors: Zero in Most States," *New York Times [NYT]*. 7 Jul 2015.

6. R.F. Wright. "Elected Prosecutors and Police Accountability." In *Policing the Black Man: Arrest, Prosecution, and Imprisonment*, ed. A. J. Davis. Vintage Books, p. 250; also see Pfaff, *Locked In*, p. 215.

7. W.J. Stuntz. *The Collapse of American Criminal Justice*. Harvard University Press, 2011, p. 304.

8. Interview with Marissa McCall Dodson.

9. Stuntz. *Collapse*, p. 304.

10. J. Fisher-Rowe and J. Thukral, eds. 2014. *An Overview of Public Opinion and Discourse on Criminal Justice Issues*. The Opportunity Agenda, p. 16.

11. See, respectively, J. Forman Jr. *Locking up Our Own: Crime and Punishment in Black America*. Farrar, Straus and Giroux, 2017; and M.J. Fortner. *Black Silent Majority: The Rockefeller Drug Laws and the Politics of Punishment*. Harvard University Press, 2015.

12. See, for example, the survey results in Morning Consult Tracking Poll, September 2016. 160812_crosstabs_Vox_v1_AP.0.

13. C.C. Johnson Jr. with G. Hampikian. *Exit to Freedom*. University of Georgia Press, 2003. Johnson's co-author acknowledged Keller for personally answering his questions and giving him complete access to all relevant records (p. 285).

14. David Firestone, " DNA Test Brings Freedom," *NYT.* 16 June 1999.

15. S. Raphael and M. A. Stoll. *Why Are So Many Americans in Prison?* Russell Sage Foundation, 2013; also see M. Tonry, "The Mostly Unintended Effects of Mandatory Penalties: Two Centuries of Consistent Findings." *Crime and Justice.* 38, 1 (2009): 65-114; and J. Travis, B. Western, and S. Redburn, eds. *The Growth of Incarceration in the United States*. National Research Council, 2014, pp. 71-97.

16. C. R. Seabolt, "Criminal Procedure—Sentence and Punishment: Provide That Persons Who Are Convicted of Certain Serious Violent Felonies." *Georgia State University Law Review* 11, 1 (1994): 158-65.

17. American Civil Liberties Union, "Blueprint *for* Smart Justice." 2018, p. 9.

18. ACLU, "Blueprint," p. 8.

19. Paul Howard, "On the Record," *AJC.* 24 Feb 2013.

20. J. R. Borchetta and A. Fontier, "When Race Tips the Scales in Plea Bargaining," *The Marshall Project*. 23 Oct 2017.

21. R. E. Barkow, Rachel Elise. *Prisoners of Politics: Breaking the Cycle of Mass Incarceration*. Harvard University Press, 2019 S. Bibas, "Plea Bargaining's Role in Wrongful Convictions." In *Examining Wrongful Convictions: Stepping Back, Moving Forward*, ed. A. D. Redlich et al., 157-67. Carolina Academic Press, 2014; and Davis, *Arbitrary Justice,* pp. 46-47.

22. Pfaff. *Locked In*, p. 132.

23. I. Kohler-Hausmann. *Misdemeanorland: Criminal Courts and Social Control in*

an Age of Broken Windows Policing. Princeton University Press, 2018; A. Natapoff. *Punishment without Crime: How Our Massive Misdemeanor System Traps the Innocent and Makes America More Unequal.* Basic Books, 2018.

24. Davis, *Arbitrary Justice,* p. 31.

25. Davis, *Arbitrary Justice,* p. 57.

26. J. S. Rakoff, "Why Prosecutors Rule the Criminal Justice System—and What Can Be Done About It." *Northwestern University Law Review* 111, 6 (2017), p. 1432.

27. Raphael 2013: 70-89.

28. Travis, Western, Redburn, *Growth of Incarceration,* pp. 83, 131.

29. Tonry, "Mostly Unintended Effects, pp. 81-82.

30. Tonry, "Mostly Unintended Effects, pp. 81-82.

31. M. Tonry. *Sentencing Fragments: Penal Reform in America, 1975-2025.* Oxford University Press, 2016, p. 32. *Report of the Georgia Council on Criminal Justice Reform—2016,* pp. 53-54.

33. N. Tabor, "What If Prosecutors Wanted to Keep People *out* of Prison?" *New York.* 27 Mar 2018.

34. "Philadelphia DA Larry Krasner's Revolutionary Memo," document linked from Shaun King, "Philadelphia DA Larry Krasner Promised a Criminal Justice Revolution," *The Intercept.* 20 Mar 2018.

35. For an evaluation finding positive outcomes for diversion programs see M. Rempel et al. "NIJ's Multisite Evaluation of Prosecutor-Led Diversion Programs: Strategies, Impacts, and Cost-Effectiveness." Center for Court Innovation, 2018.

36. Matt Ferner, "If You Want To Totally Change America's Criminal Justice System, You Need A Plan," *HuffPost.* 29 May 2018.

37. Fair and Just Prosecution, "FJP at a Glance."

38. E. Bazelon et al. 21 Principles for the 21st Century Prosecutor. Brennan Center, 2018.

39. A. Bach. *Ordinary Injustice: How American Holds Court.* Metropolitan Books, 2009, p. 17.

40. Southern Center for Human Rights, "Right to Counsel;" Bach, *Ordinary Injustice* , pp. 41-62.

41. B. Furst, "A Fair Fight: Achieving Indigent Defense Resource Parity." Brennan Center for Justice, 2019, p. 8.

42. Southern Center for Human Rights, "Problems at Fulton County State and Magistrate Court Public Defender Office Are Brought To Light." 13 Jul 2018.

43. S. J. Totonchi, "Fulfilling Promises: Celebrating the First Decade of Georgia's Public Defender System," *Georgia Bar Journal.* June 2016: 22-25.

44. D. Baum, *Smoke and Mirrors: The War on Drugs and the Politics of Failure.* Little, Brown, 1996, pp. 304-05.

45. Bach, *Ordinary* Injustice, pp. 70, 74.

46. Rackoff, "Why Prosecutors Rule," p. 1436.

47. Quoted in J. Pishko, "Prosecutors Are Banding Together to Prevent Criminal-Justice Reform," *The Nation.* 18 Oct 2017.

\2/

JUVENILE JUSTICE
LESS IS BEST

In 2012, as part of its criminal justice reform, the Georgia legislature passed HB 242, designed to reduce the number of juveniles sentenced to juvenile jails or prisons. Its main reforms were to stop the detention of juveniles for status offenses, such as truancy and runaways; to create two classes of felonies depending on the severity of the crime; to provide more funding for community-based services; and to create a legal designation, Children in Need of Services (CHINS), for at-risk children who had not been adjudicated as delinquent (for example, the truants and runaways no longer being detained), making them eligible for prevention programs. In line with these legislative reforms and often instigating them, juvenile court judges are creating innovative diversion courts that are increasing community-based supervision. These changes have reduced the number of juveniles incarcerated in the troubled Georgia juvenile prison system, prisons ranked as some of the worst in the country, reduced their level of recidivism, and provided more educational options. However, in the youth jails and prisons the level of inmate on inmate and inmate and staff violence remain high and racial disparity remains significant.

JUVENILE COURTS

The juvenile court structure in Georgia includes locally funded courts, known as independent courts, in thirteen urban counties; these courts provide their own intake and community supervision services. The Department of Juvenile Justice (DJJ) provides these services to the other state juvenile courts. (Some independent courts rely on DJJ for some community supervision services.) DJJ provides secure detention for all the juvenile courts through their youth jails, the Regional Youth Detention Centers (RYDCs), and their prisons, the Youth Detention Centers (YDCs). DJJ is responsible for aftercare and reentry services for children when they leave their secure facilities.

CLAYTON JUVENILE COURT

Clayton County Juvenile Court, an independent court, has had a strong spokesman and determined change agent in its chief judge, Steven Teske, who played a key role in the modifications of the juvenile criminal code that were part of HB 242. These reforms were preceded by over a decade of reform activity within the Clayton Juvenile Court itself. Working closely with the Annie E. Casey Foundation's Juvenile Detention Alternatives Initiative (JDAI) since 2001, the Clayton Court has emphasized the importance of accountability courts and mediation in resolving delinquency issues in ways that do not condemn children to prison unnecessarily. In 2015, the long-term success of Clayton's program led to JDAI duplication efforts in the other state juvenile courts. The statistics for Clayton Juvenile Court are very encouraging, for example, a 75% drop in the daily population in detention, a 41% decline in length of stay, a 70% decline in commitments to the Department of Juvenile Justice detention centers, from 122 in 2002 to 12 in 2018.

Colin Slay, now the director of juvenile court operations, provided us with a very lucid historical review of the changes in the Clayton Juvenile Court. Slay, who has been involved with the court since 1998, was trained in the Casey Foundation's Applied Leadership program and has been involved in taking JDAI to state scale. He was a probation officer before the changes took place in the early 2000s, and described what it was like at that point: *There was a lot of burnout and turnover. They were locking kids up for technical violations, for not finishing an essay. In the back of our minds, we were all wondering if what we were doing was right. Some kids were coming in over and over. They had these boot camps. Zell Miller, the governor, was a marine but he'd been a wayward child, and the camps had worked for him. The kids did well at them because they were structured and consistent, but when they came home, they were right back at it. There was no attention paid to the home environment, where there wasn't that level of supervision.*

Probation was really frustrating. The school resource officers, when they came in, had no additional training on adolescent development or mental health. Laws about not disrupting public schools that were meant for adults were applied to kids. There were seven or eight probation officers, and they spent four hours every Wednesday on dispositions, kind of de facto probation. It was cookie cutter. Kids had to write an essay, do community service, pay restitution, receive drug and alcohol counseling, receive a psych evaluation. It was all dictated from the bench. Officers had case loads of 85 to 120 kids. There were no assessments, no risk classifications. You couldn't even put out fires, there were too many cases. They would lock kids up for not writing an essay. The detention capacity was 60 but it was not uncommon to have 120 kids in there. You would have thought there would be outcry from the community, but the juvenile system is mysterious to most people.

One of the most important and successful attempts at reducing criminal justice involvement for juveniles in Clayton County was Teske's work in 2003 to reduce the school-to-prison pipeline. The introduction of school resource officers in 1994 had the effect within a year of increasing the number of juvenile complaints 1,200%, which severely stressed the capacity of the court, as Slay described. Teske who had come to juvenile justice by way of parole, where he had been a field officer and chief in South Fulton, placed an emphasis on data-oriented approaches, in particular the need to develop a validated risk and need assessment that, in Slay's term, "allowed us to guard the front door." One aim was to separate low-risk offenders who needed to be diverted, from higher-risk offenders who needed more stringent control. The court began to develop Balanced and Restorative Justice (BARJ) diversionary approaches, which then allowed staff to focus more intensively on children who were genuinely at risk. There was community outcry at this, because people thought children were being let off too easily.

To address this resistance, in 2003 Teske, with the support of then Chief Juvenile Judge Karlton Van Banke, used a little known section of the juvenile code to require community stakeholders, including the schools, the police, and the court, to convene to create a community risk reduction program. The result was the School Referral Reduction Program, which identified four delinquent offenses that would no longer be referred to the court but would be dealt with in a graduated way, moving from warnings to educational parent-child workshops. Since this program was implemented, there has been a 90% reduction in misdemeanor complaints from the schools. When we talked with him, Teske proudly demonstrated charts of the inverse trends that were observable after these efforts, high school graduation rates rising as criminal prosecutions fell.

RESTORATIVE JUSTICE

We met with the diversion program supervisor, Tabatha Barker, and a probation officer and counselor closely involved in various balanced and restorative justice options the court offers, including mediation or informal adjustments. Barker gave us a diversion walk through: *Let's say we have a kid who has a little marijuana at school. Drugs in a school zone is a felony. The court officer will screen the family, give them a copy of their rights, provide them with an attorney. If the kid says he did it, we will do a brief assessment, ask some general questions. The real question here is what is in the best interest of the kid. Should the sanction take place in the courtroom or informally? Our bias is to keep it informal. Often the parents will tell us, "He needs to learn his lesson. Let him see the judge." We try to explain why that isn't an option.*

We want to keep the diversion simple, with a three to six months time limit. We'll refer a kid to an educational workshop, perhaps to counseling—either through the school system, mentoring, or an individualized educational program. We'll create an agreement and have the child and the parents sign it. A big part of our job is educating parents on their responsibilities. Many of them don't understand they have legal responsibilities to their children. When we tell them this, they often really don't want to hear it. They want to use the judicial system as punishment. Parents have to be involved in any informal contract. We know by the time they leave whether they will stay on it. Some parents feel <u>they</u> are being punished. Programs require parents' attendance. We get talk back, but that changes when they experience the workshop

We do a lot of coaching, advising with the parents. We talk about felony convictions, the magnitude of the consequences. We have to educate a lot about mental health, especially in the African-American community. Tell parents they need to meet their children where they really are. With girls, there is a lot of PTSD, sexual abuse. So we do a <u>lot</u> of talking, and providing resources. There is no cut off with what we do.

The probation officer, Stacy Weaver, talked about the difficulty of trying to encourage change, especially with juveniles who are so enmeshed in environments that they can't change, certainly not alone: *It is a struggle. You can see the intelligence in the kid, but they are in an environment that doesn't foster it. The majority of our kids have some kind of trauma. There is a lack of hope. Even when they start doing better, no one is meeting them in their story, in the small steps, offering positive rewards. Once they have a reputation, it is difficult to change it. They begin to think, "It doesn't matter if I do good. No one will notice it." You have to raise <u>families</u>. When I came in in 1999, it was "lock them up." Kids would be sent to boot camps, and they would do great there, but* *then they would come back and within no time were right back where they were. That was why we started focusing on the whole family unit, mother, grandmother, uncles, therapists, school—to try and bring them all along, show the change, create a reward for it.*

They were strategic in what they chose to enforce. If a child didn't complete an essay or pay a probation fee, he wouldn't be referred up to the court, but if he committed additional offenses, for example received a drug charge, then he would be. In terms of deciding what conditions were going to be imposed, they said that the court as a whole shared the internal rule, "If we wouldn't do it to our own child, we won't do it to any child here."

ALTERNATIVES TO DETENTION: F.A.S.T.

A major emphasis of the reforms has been to reduce the number of children who enter detention and also the length of time they are held in detention. To that end, Clayton Juvenile Court has a Finding Alternatives for Safety and Treatment (F.A.S.T.) panel that meets three mornings a week to review the cases of children detained within the last 48 hours in the Department of Juvenile Justice Regional Youth Detention Center (RYDC), the juvenile jail, to see if they can find alternative detention measures. These panels are made up of representatives of the school system, DFACS, Behavioral Health, the DA's Office, and trained community volunteers. Parents attend as well.

We attended one of these meetings and what we were most impressed by was how working with juveniles inevitably involves you in complex social systems and social conditions, and also with precarious, struggling, often loving families. In the meeting we attended, we heard from a distraught and over-worked mother, who owned and drove her own truck, a sixteen-foot flatbed she built for local hauling. She had recently moved to Clayton County. Her two younger children travelled with her in her truck. But her older son, Alex, was skipping school, hanging with other unruly kids, being recruited by gang members, and using drugs. He hid drugs in the legs of his bed, his eyes were always bloodshot. She had called the sheriff herself because she was concerned about drug dealing in the neighborhood.

She had been in an abusive relationship with this son's father when she was nineteen and the father was thirty-five. The father had a criminal record. Alex had witnessed the domestic violence. She had separated when Alex was very young. She and her children had been living with her parents, but Alex had become rude and aggressive and her father, who was on chemo for cancer, couldn't tolerate the aggression. "When he disrespects me and my parents, my *womb* hurts," she said. She didn't feel she could guarantee that Alex would stay home if he were released from detention—or that she could supervise him effectively. The committee decided that they would tell the judge, who would see him that afternoon, to keep him in detention, then see if they could put him on housebound supervision, with a monitor, and develop some wrap-around services that included a psychological evaluation, especially to assess whether he was modeling violence that he had witnessed early in his life. They considered him a flight risk—not a risk to the community or himself, but thought he was a threat to his family.

The next child discussed, Ryan, had divorced parents who lived in the same city. The mother had drug issues and was in a methadone clinic. She had remarried, and Ryan and his stepfather didn't get along. Ryan said his stepfather used drugs with his mother, that his mother was not honest about her attendance at the methadone clinic. There were two younger brothers. When Ryan was not in school, he smoked pot. He was in Functional Family Therapy (FFT), and in a mentoring program. The FFT with the mother didn't work. "She is a fast talker and makes you think she's serious, but she isn't," said one of the court staff.

Ryan had gone to live with his father, who lived with Ryan's paternal grandmother. The father seemed the more responsible parent, although he had been incarcerated a year ago. He had a job on an off-shore oil rig. After an incident with the step-father, Ryan was told to keep away from his mother's house, but because there was no supervision and he lived within walking distance, "he do what he want to do." The mother had legal custody and didn't want to give up her legal benefits. The grandmother and father were both positive about Ryan. The grandmother said "in *our* household, he is a joy to be around." The father and grandmother thought with only three people in the household adequate supervision would be possible. The father worked three weeks off shore and then had two weeks home. The grandmother felt she could supervise when her son was away. The father was trying to get some services in place for Ryan. Ryan was sixteen and in ninth grade and not doing well. He wanted to go into Job Corps, get a GED, and learn a trade. There seemed to be some doubt from others on the panel that there was actually space for him in Job Corps at present. DJJ reminded everyone that they detained only if the juvenile was a threat to self, family, or community, or a flight risk, which did not seem the case here. Ryan would be released to his father.

SECOND CHANCE COURT

One distinctive feature of Clayton Juvenile Court is its active support of a Second Chance Court. This is a high intensity accountability court for juveniles who have been convicted of a designated Class A felony, a violent crime with mandatory sentences of between ten and twenty years if they were tried as adults. However, their cases had been sent back to juvenile court for adjudication. Most of them were convicted of aggravated assault, armed robbery or burglary. They were all facing five years in juvenile prison if they didn't succeed in Second Chance Court. The year we observed, the number of boys attending the court ranged from six and fourteen. Most were between the ages of fourteen and seventeen.

When talking with the DA for the juvenile court, Chris Montgomery, he pointed out that the court was highly collegial. He shared all information with the public defender to ensure that they found the best solution for each child. "I'm here for the kids too. I'm here for justice, not prosecution." He was a strong advocate for the Second Chance Court, but with boys he thought might not be able to sustain its strict supervision, he would often recommend that they accept a plea of two years incarceration, rather than face the five they would receive if they couldn't complete the Second Chance Court program.

It was not clear that the boys always grasped the dedication of the court or the severity of the consequences they were trying to protect them from. Nor was it always clear that working with them as a group helped them recognize the seriousness of their misconduct. In general, they seemed in court like very normal, high energy teenagers. Many of them had substance abuse issues. Some of them were doing well in school, sometimes on a gifted track, and others were struggling, going to various alternative schools.

They were carefully supervised by two dedicated probation officers, received group cognitive behavior counseling, were drug tested weekly, had a curfew, their school attendance was monitored, and they had to wear an ankle monitor for the first six months—longer depending on their compliance. Both Judge Teske and Judge Bobby Simmons were actively involved in this court. All the boys met together with the two judges and the probation officers every Tuesday evening. At some point the judges, wanting to encourage social presentation skills, instituted a tie night, when everyone had to come dressed for a job interview. The boys were encouraged to think about college. The disappointment of the judges and the probation officers was palpable when one of the boys so carefully mentored and monitored committed a new offense.

We talked at length with the two probation officers, Venson Jones and Dean Hix, who worked for the Second Chance Court, along with their supervisor, Kendra Stevens. They each came from different backgrounds and brought in different perspectives, but their dedication was similar: Hix was originally a youth minister; Jones had a twenty-year career in the U.S. Army; Stevens was a criminal justice major in college and had worked in juvenile probation both in Texas and at this court.

Jones observed that working with these boys was similar to working with the young recruits he trained as a sergeant in the Army, just that there were fewer resources with which to meet their needs. He saw his job as providing discipline, counseling and development and leadership skills. He found that he had to learn to focus on one dimension at a time, to understand what a major change it was for one of the juveniles to get out of alternative school and go to a regular school. He thought that what he did was like planting seeds, sometimes they took, sometimes they didn't. He felt that it worked better when he worked one-on-one with the juveniles, that as a group they could harden.

All three of the probation officers expressed their frustration working with other institutional systems that seemed to feel that these boys were expendable and didn't share their own commitment to change. Hix said, "Schools, for example, will tell us, 'You are working to fix this one kid and we have a thousand—and this one with his behaviors is taking thirty kids with him.'"

Stevens echoed: "I'm so frustrated working with other systems that can't see how they could change. They have no desire to assist or help—they just want to get rid of the kid. That's not an option for us."

"There are mothers who say, 'Just take him,'" Jones said.

"They're wondering where is that adorable child I had once. Now he is sixteen and out committing crimes," Hix added with a laugh.

"Many of them are single parents, working, raising themselves. They're struggling," Stevens said with a sigh.

They each felt the work they did, even if it seemed invisible to the juveniles themselves, was important. They didn't actually believe that the boys were indifferent although they often appeared so. Stevens said, "I don't believe they want to be convicted, incarcerated, but they feel it is *inevitable*, that it is not that big a deal, and that it is *expected* of them. They don't see their lives going in any other direction."

"When they get caught, they are afraid. What we have to do is transfer that fear to before they act," Jones observed.

Hix expanded on this: *I think they need to shift from fear to internalization of values—but that takes time and maturity. If you can just get them through these years, they will be fine. They need to be learning from their mistakes. They just don't get how irrevocable some of these consequences can be. You see kids trying to get in the Army or Navy, and they can't. Then they begin to realize the lasting part. They really live in a very small world here. It's all peer influence, thug mentality. They feel stigma with the ankle monitoring, and also a bit of status.*

In the court sessions, the two judges had very different styles. Teske, who had been a parole officer, emphasized personal relationship. These boys could always call on him for a recommendation for a job. He tended to exhort, not unusual with judges, so sessions where he was present sometimes had the feel of a classroom or a church. Simmons was generally less talkative—and less tolerant. As an African American, he had a keen sense of the systemic and cultural challenges these boys faced.

Simmons' commitment to the court grew from his background: *I grew up in rural southern Arkansas. When I was growing up, I had a neighbor from Wisconsin. He had a big influence on me. Even to the way he talked. I borrowed it. He would always tell me how important education was. We would take sticks and do multiplication tables in the dirt yard and he would say, "My friend," he always talked like that, "My friend, remember education is something no one can take away from you." My first day in magistrate court, I had a fifteen year old, a sixteen year old, a seventeen year old. Armed robbery. Murder. I thought, no way I want to be here. I don't want <u>them</u> to be here and <u>I</u> don't want to be here.*

One court session when Simmons was the only judge present, he spoke at unusual length about his aspirations for the boys and his awareness of the challenges they faced. It was summer, and he was encouraging the boys to stay up with their school work. He suggested that they look at the Khan Academy, which offers free online video tutorials in math. He began there, but his discussion expanded to a larger meditation on social mobility, countering racial prejudice, and making strategic choices.

Don't allow the math problems to scare you. But if you learn the approach, it will help you. Other kids, their parents are helping them. They've been prepping over the summer so they get the jump on you. But you get the jump on them. School can be fun, but it can be a boogie if you don't know the answers. If you can play basketball and know the rules, if you can play chess, checkers, cards and learn the rules, you can win. You can win in school too. It's all about knowing the rules.

But if you don't know the fundamentals, you can't learn anything. What's at stake? If you get good grades, you can get a scholarship. You won't owe $100,000 when you get out. Our incentive, us poor folks, is "You may have a jump on me but I'm going to catch you—and I'm going to break that tape." You may be running in that race a little behind right now, but that doesn't mean you're not going to catch up.

Simmons was explicit about the behavioral changes that needed to take place to give these boys a chance to catch up. A very important ability, perhaps the most important, was to know what matters to *others* in a larger society that these boys had almost no contact with except inside this court.

There's a time and a place for everything. You need to know when to turn it on and turn it off. It's how you survive in the world and here in this court. Personally, I expect to see gradual changes in you that you make of your own accord. What we're saying to you is what is required by society to be successful. How do we decide what is appropriate? When the majority say it's appropriate.

Don't let prejudices let you stay in a vacuum. Don't allow anyone to tell you where you are, where you belong. Dress for success, for what you want to be, for how people perceive you. Didn't you read about that boy—got killed just because people think young black men always carrying? Images are always associated with certain types of activities, people associate a person with that type of activity. There are people in suits that are robbing us and not going to jail. But nobody suspects them because you don't see them going to jail.

But you have to look at the statistics. What percent of the population is black? 12%. So if someone says, the person who committed a crime is black, that reduces the pool of suspects. Then you take the hairdo—twists, dreadlocks. That narrows the pool further: to what 90% of black boys would wear. In the end, the police put in all of it—dreadlocks, baggy pants, gold grill. So then they don't have to look around a lot. Black boys don't necessarily do more crimes, they get caught more. There are TV cameras everywhere, and this dress creates an image that stands out.

So whether you straight as an arrow, if you fit the description, they don't worry about what kind of person you are, your personality. They just look at you and say, "He one of those." You walk in for job looking like that, your application go in the trash can.

But if you go in with the look they want, they'll hire you. Malcolm, did you see that movie? Muslims, you could spot them anywhere—bow ties, sharp suits, shoes shined. There was a difference. Whatever you want to be, you look carefully at the people doing that job. What do those people look like? What type of education did they get? Do it. You can't go in being completely different from what they want and expect to get a job.

If you want to be rapper, you need to be that way in one crowd. Turn it off in another.

In another session, Teske made many of the same points. This was a tie night. Jones, the probation officer, had asked Teske to explain again to the boys what it meant to "turn it on and turn it off." This was particularly important because that week a member of Second Chance Court, unable to abide by the terms of his supervision, was being sent to prison to serve five years. Teske gave his own examples: *What you're doing now determines what you'll look like at thirty. When you drop out of school, the odds go sky high you'll end up in prison. So turn it on, then turn it off. My clothes are turning it on tonight. What does Steve Teske wear on his day off? Tattoos and earrings. Beyond the robe, I'm still a human being. But not like Jeremy, where turning it on and turning it off has to do with crime. I work out at LA Fitness with lawyers and accountants. When the Super Bowl is on, there is a lot of swearing. But you will never hear these men utter those words outside that locker room. Outside they turn it on because it is about their jobs and making money.*

In retrospect, one particular July evening at Second Chance Court stood out as encapsulating both the great promise and the tensions of this intensive attempt at diversion and redirection. On that evening, several family members were present at the court to honor the accomplishments of some of the boys in the court. There was a large cake on a table in the center of the room which read *Congratulations, William.* Jones, the probation officer, quietly removed the price tag and discussed with the other probation officer, Hix, when the pizzas might arrive. William sat at a table with his mother, a strikingly beautiful woman, and the court chaplain. The boys in the court sat at other tables, as did four members of another family. Everyone had dressed for the occasion, Simmons sitting at a table beside the door, was wearing an elegant gray suit and white sweater.

Teske arrived a little late, also looking a little dressier than usual. He said he was looking forward to this evening because he was discouraged, having had to commit several boys to juvenile prison in the past week, and it felt good to be able to celebrate something. He walked over and inspected the cake, then went to William and told him they would end the evening with the cake, but right now he wanted to give him a man hug. This made the third juvenile judge, Deitra Burney-Butler, crack up.

The evening began with all the boys standing and Hix saying what each of them had been doing that week, stressing accomplishments. One boy had been in a YMCA swimming program and had been asked to stay on and help other students. Two boys, rising juniors, Antavious and Deon, had been attending Atlanta Tech's leadership program and visiting college campuses. Tairon had been finishing up all his classes and tonight would have his ankle monitor removed. Hix flourished an orange screwdriver.

Deon spoke about the leadership program and visiting college campuses and what it felt like to think he could go there too. Antavious, who was often quiet, almost sullen in expression, spoke up. What he liked about the program was that "it separates the men from the boys." Hix complimented Antavious for how well he had handled the disappointment that had accompanied their trip to the Governor's Mansion. The bus had been stopped because someone had stolen a key. Everyone was taken off the bus and held there. There was no visit. Hix emphasized that it was the *way* Antavious had responded to this disappointment that felt especially promising. Teske then elaborated on the importance of acting as a group, which meant that you also took the punishment as a group, but then seemed to jump tracks, or take an alternative perspective on the situation, remarking on how these young men had been taught not to snitch, but *was* it snitching to say, "Take responsibility for your own actions and their consequences." In other words, was it snitching to man up?

Tairon, who was going to graduate from ankle monitoring, was unusually reserved. Jones shared with us that he thought something was not right with Tairon this evening, that usually he was open. He thought maybe Tairon was having family problems. When Teske began to turn to William and the cake, Hix reminded him that there was another celebration this evening, the removal of Tairon's ankle monitor.

"So what did you have to do to get that monitor removed?" Teske asked Tairon.

"Follow the rules," Tairon answered promptly.

"He get that taken off, he still got rules to follow," Tairon's father, seated with his wife and parents at another table spoke up gruffly. "He live in my house, he follow my rules."

Teske, a little taken aback, recouped and shifted from Tairon's self-discipline and individual accomplishment to his potential for obedience. "Are you going to follow the rules in your father's house?"

"Got no choice," Tairon muttered.

"He don't, I want that monitor right back on. I be sending him right back to you," Tairon's father said. Jones, sitting beside us, squirmed at the lost opportunity.

Teske gamely rode this wave. How would Tairon like it if his father said that the only reason he fed and housed him was because the law said he had to? "It's like you saying the only reason you follow the rules is because you got no choice. It showed a lack of respect. I'm fifty-three, do you think I have the freedom to do anything I want?"

Teske looked around at all the boys, who shifted uncomfortably, lowered their eyes. "No way. You have relationships; you have to meet the expectations. My wife tells me she expects me to be home at seven for dinner, I've *got* to be there."

The whole room turned, with relief, to William. Teske talked about John Wayne in *The Quiet Man*, and praised William for also being quiet and full of substance. When Hix was asked to share William's story, he began, "William made the decision to change before he ever came to Second Chance Court." Jones praises William's superior performance in Youth Challenge, a demanding program for at-risk youth run by the National Guard, where William had earned his corporal stripes. Judge Simmons added, "You don't need that ankle monitor anymore, son. You have an inner one." William's mother also spoke about how proud she was of her son. Hix singled out how responsibly William behaved with his younger brother, always walking him home from school. A photo was taken with William and the two judges. Teske reminded William that graduation didn't mean good-bye. William could call on the probation officers if he needed help. "I decide what they do. They have salaries that let them be there for you. Just like when they went down to Macon to watch you graduate."

Later, we talked with each of the boys. Tairon, his father having left (with probation officer Jones chasing after him), was more his typical effervescent self. He was proud of finishing his classes. He would turn seventeen in two days and would become a father in three weeks. He was very excited about fatherhood.

William broke his usual silence when spoken with privately. He felt finishing Second Chance Court was a big accomplishment. "I had determination," he said, "so I was pretty sure I could do it, but it wasn't easy." He had loved Youth Challenge, especially the discipline. "I don't think I was suited to high school," he said. But now he had, as Jones had encouraged the boys, a plan and was beginning to put it into motion. He wanted to work in heating and air, get a certificate, work for a company, then have a business of his own. He was interning with his uncle, a contractor, that summer, then applying to technical school for the fall.

Antavious, who had attended the leadership academy, was equally inspired. "I never thought of college, but I go to these campuses and I'm thinking I can do this." When asked to explain his comment about separating the boys from the men, he explained, "Boys don't take responsibility. They do what they want. They don't think about consequences. They say they *could* have—"

"But they don't go ahead and *do* it," added Deon.

When asked if they were sharing their newfound interest in college with their friends, Deon responded, "You got to cut away from them." Antavious agreed, "I don't see my old group. I broke with them." But when asked if they had any idea of other people in their schools they might be able to share these new goals with, both of them looked away, the old opaqueness returning.

Four years later, thinking about Antavious's enthusiasm, we checked the internet to see if we might find notice of him going to college. However, we found, instead, a heartbreaking newspaper article from 2017 describing his bullet-ridden body, a poignant photo on the funeral home page showed him just before puberty.

NEWTON JUVENILE COURT

When we met with Newton Juvenile Court's Chief Judge Sheri Roberts and Judge Lisa Mantz in 2015, the court was deeply involved in a pilot program to improve services to dual status youth, those who were involved with both the delinquency and the child-welfare sides of the court. Almost 60% of the children seen in their court fell in this category. These children are at much greater risk of truancy and delinquency, more likely to be detained and to spend more time in detention, and have higher rates of recidivism. Many of these youth would fall under the new CHINS (Children In Need of Services) category created through SB 242. For this pilot, the juvenile court in Newton was receiving guidance from the Robert Kennedy Foundation and financial support from the MacArthur Foundation. We talked at some length with Roberts about their initiative and other diversion programs developed by the court and also observed Mantz in a meeting with the drug court staff and presiding over a bi-monthly session of the drug court. This court with all female judges had a different tone than the Clayton Juvenile Court, with a more explicit emphasis on welfare and more attention paid to extended family systems.

DUAL STATUS COURT

Several elements of Roberts' varied professional background influenced her approach. She had worked for a decade as a lawyer for the Department of Family and Child Services (DFACS) and from this developed a strong commitment to increasing the communication and coordination between agencies in order to address the needs of children seen by the court. She also had an MBA, and her business background supported her strong continuous use of data to identify and respond to trends and to evaluate effectiveness. A lifetime resident of the county, she had observed its rapid growth and demographic shift, like Clayton a decade earlier, to majority-minority, with a concomitant increase in the need for services and an increasing racial disparity in both delinquency and welfare rates.

Juvenile judges are appointed, not elected, which allows them to be more programmatically adventurous if they are progressive. Roberts, like Teske, took advantage of this to push changes she thought important. She too used her power as a judge to convene relevant stakeholders, in this case behavioral health, DFACS, police, schools, and DJJ, in order to refine the processes by which they defined and responded to dual-status youth. Along with finding ways to unify services, they set a broader goal of identifying these youth and providing them with services as early as possible. What they found was that truancy was the most common offense committed by dual-status youth. They also discovered that child molestation or sexual battery, particularly at an early age, was a relatively rare but important indicator as well. They created a mapping process that allowed all participants, families as well, to see how different institutions were involved at different stages in the process. They also established a broader social context in which to consider these at-risk children, which included a multisystem family meeting for those who were identified.

Newton Juvenile Court relied on DJJ to provide some services. Although reluctant to send children to long-term detention, they did make use of DJJ's assistance in finding other out-of-home placements as well as using their probation services. On their own, they created an Evening Reporting Center as an alternative to pre-trial detention, as well as a program for boys who were suspended from school so they could continue their studies. When they discovered that girls were becoming more justice involved and that they responded poorly to probation, they created a special program for them, Girl Steps. Roberts said, "I was seeing more girls in court and they drive us crazy. They do more self-harming behavior. Summers were a particular problem." The program offers group counseling, parenting classes, and mentoring. Each session, Roberts invited the girls and their parents to her home. She has found that diversion programs work when parents are involved. "We want to empower parents to be proactive with the schools, to help parents *be* parents." Roberts reliance on data led her to cut an abstinence program, "It was just not realistic with my kids. We had twelve and thirteen year olds who were pregnant." She replaced it with classes on pregnancy and sexual responsibility.

Drug Court

The need to take a systems approach was evident when visiting the drug court administered by Judge Lisa Mantz. (Mantz later left to be come an Assistant Deputy Commissioner at DJJ, but the drug court remains active.) At the staff meeting that preceded the court session, Mantz and the drug court staff discussed the status of parents in as much detail as that of the children. By the time Mantz met with the parents and children in court, she would usually have a solution to offer. For example, one mother who left for work very early left the pill her son needed to take out on the counter, but he wouldn't take it. The drug court staff offered to give it to him. Another boy's mother had gone into drug treatment without telling her son she was leaving, so he was staying with his grandparents. His father was trying to help, but as one staff member noted, "He has to spread his time around. He has lots of baby mamas." This boy was angry and non-compliant. In court, Mantz, listening to the mother, quite young herself, explain her own need for treatment, would tell him, "You can't control what your mom does but you do have to claim your own stuff. Mom, thank you for being honest, that's a big thing." Another boy, dual-status, had a father on meth and alcohol and would need to be removed from his home, separated from his parents and his twin brother. Depending on the placement, he might not be able to be part of the drug court. Mantz considered whether he would ever see the value in what she had done.

The concerns of the staff were broad reaching. They discussed the boys' school work as well as their progress in the drug program, how they responded to community service, one boy's talent for singing, sex education, the dynamics of the group and where and how they might intervene both on a tendency to glorify drugs and also to bully certain members. The approach of the staff and judge was holistic. Mantz herself had a strong interest in nutrition and stress and noted that easily addressed vitamin deficiencies were associated with various behavioral issues—so why not address the possibility with a simple multivitamin a day? Influenced by Bessel van der Kolk's work on trauma, she also encouraged participants to take yoga and find other ways to become mindful. One staff member described the latest yoga position that the boys were practicing.

In formal court, however, Mantz was clear and very brief in her comments to the boys and their families. She said later that studies showed that no one listened if you spoke more than five minutes, so she took special care to be as brief and direct as possible. She was always careful to praise something about both the child and the parent as well as establish behavioral guidelines.

What stood out in these meetings was the level of care that was being provided to these boys. When asked if they thought the youth had any sense of the scale of the work and resources being directed at them, the general feeling was no, neither the boys nor their parents did—but the work was still valuable for their well-being and the well-being of the larger community. Many of the boys would prefer to be on probation, Mantz said. However, they were unaware that the level of services they were being provided was greater than what they would receive through DJJ or would be able to afford on their own. One staff member added, "Community agencies see the value. The County Commissioners, DFACS, DJJ. Any person you might meet on the square." Mantz said, "I was at the store the other day and when someone mentioned I was a juvenile judge, a woman said, 'I think you have the noblest job.'" There was general laughter.

DOUGLAS FAMILY COURT AND DJJ: COMPLEX TRAUMA

We had an interest in how the growing evidence on the consequences of complex trauma, especially on child development, was influencing juvenile justice and spoke about this with both Judge Peggy Walker of the Douglas County Juvenile Court in Douglasville and with Dr. Christy Doyle, director of behavioral services at DJJ.

JUDGE PEGGY WALKER

Walker had become a major advocate for incorporating trauma-informed responses within the judiciary and had given workshops on the subject to judges all around the state. She thought all judges needed to be educated on the behavioral and mental consequences of complex trauma, common in children raised in difficult circumstances, in order to adequately evaluate and respond to a child's behavior. Her focus was on what promoted resiliency in a child and in a family.

Walker said that when she began to focus on juvenile justice, she had quickly realized that you couldn't change delinquency by looking at it in isolation. You had to take into consideration abuse and neglect, poverty and domestic violence, addiction and mental health. She began working full-time as a juvenile judge in the 1990s, when juveniles as super-predators were a media issue and Georgia passed its severe juvenile crime laws. "Now research shows that punitive wasn't productive—it *enhanced* their criminality. Now we're looking at this as a community, trying to limit secure detention to a very small percentage of the cases."

She was struck by the consequences of parental mental health on child welfare, describing how in the 1980s with deinstitutionalization, people with severe mental illness—psychotic or bipolar or schizophrenic—would leave the court with their children without any support. They would raise their children in difficult settings, inconsistently, and the child would react with bad behavior. "The court can't charge an ill parent. It's a tightrope. They may have burned all their bridges. There is always the potential for suicide."

Walker sought and received federal funding for the Family Drug Treatment Program, which is for parents with substance abuse or mental health problems who have infants and toddlers. The court continues now with state and county funding. It has a dual focus—on the well-being of the child as well as the parent, integrating concepts from both drug and dependency courts.

Walker emphasized the need to be able to listen to behavior as well as speech: *If people don't develop, behavior is their language. To make an accurate trauma assessment, you must understand the origin of behavior. For example, I had a child who was coming into court every week on technical violations, but it was because he needed the contact with us. His mother was on meth and he couldn't tell. You have to look at body language like choosing words. If someone is always looking at another family member for permission to speak, there may be family violence. If children are brought in for abuse or neglect, it is easy to miss addiction, domestic violence, sexual assault.*

A major concern for Walker was how to bring in support *before* you reached crisis points, like removing a child. Was there a way to keep children safely in their homes by bringing in enough supportive services? Could we become better at recognizing the risk for homicide, suicide, domestic violence? Move away from group homes for teens because they increased the risk of delinquency and sexual abuse and exploitation? Could we find ways to improve the educational consequences for children removed from school, by intensive case management or day reporting? Most importantly, she asked herself, *Could we stop sanctioning every little thing and start rewarding the appropriate thing—the one that would help them change? How little kindness these families have experienced, how little recognition. There is no positive reinforcement.*

Walker said that her focus on trauma had changed how she practiced: *I have more compassion. I am more thoughtful about my words and actions so I don't create more trauma.* She had a wonderful phrase for what she thought was the essential skillset for both probation and child welfare, *the gift of engagement*, to be able to connect, build trust, motivate.

Dr. Christy Doyle

Christy Doyle is responsible for developing mental health policies for DJJ. She began her career as a journalist but then earned a degree as a licensed clinical social worker. She was always interested in forensic mental health but brought into it the partnering concept of social work: "No one likes to think of themselves as helpless," she observed. She went on to get a doctorate in law and policy because she realized "without good policy you can't have good practice."

Doyle observed that most of the response in corrections was reaction instead of prevention. It also tended to see a child in a vacuum: *But a kid is just a piece of a family system. No matter how healthy he is, he goes home to what he goes home to. We had a kid in a long-term residential substance abuse program. He got his GED. He was in a good place. He was very attached to his mom. He had used drugs with his mom, and now he wanted to help his mom. He called her as he was preparing for release and asked her, "Can you not use when I'm around?" His mother said, "It's my house. I'll use whenever I want." There was another mother who responded to her son's sexual abuse of his sister by asking, "Where is she going to learn about sex without a family member to teach her?" That's what we're sending kids back to. Parents who have no guidance to offer.*

Doyle talked about the high prevalence of trauma among the juveniles in detention: *The ACES (Adverse Childhood Experiences Scale) threshold for poor outcomes is four, but the average kid in DJJ has six to nine. Ninety percent of the kids have experienced at least one traumatic event. The majority have experienced multiple events. So have their parents. So its normalized. We have traumatized people raising little traumatized people.*

However, Doyle did not see this assessment as defining, she saw it as an invitation to do things differently, to address the most important consequence of trauma: the belief the world is not a safe place and you can't trust people. She also pointed out that it is difficult, but essential, to separate out trauma-induced behaviors and normal adolescent behavior: *Adolescents are by nature impulsive and experimental. The best and brightest exhibit some of these behaviors, they're developmentally appropriate. But you need to tease out the impact of complex trauma, the existence of antisocial personality. Our kids are often so marginalized socially, by age, color, criminal offense, mental illness as well. And you need to create the opportunity to make safe mistakes.*

In her own life, Doyle had had much personal practice with making these discernments and opportunities. Over the years, she and her husband had fostered fourteen boys between the ages of eleven and seventeen, adopting two, having long-term relationships with those they didn't adopt. Several of them had some level of juvenile justice involvement.

Doyle felt it was important to educate correctional officers on trauma, that the correctional impulse is to push back: *They don't understand that the children's behaviors and emotional responses and world views are not of their choosing. Trauma has helped mold their world views. In corrections it is easy to see their behaviors as volitional; they lack the realization that some of this is not as much in their control as they think. As with substance abuse, emotional and social development stop with trauma. A fourteen year old who looks twenty-five* *can have the social competence of a ten year old. They can be emotionally young but socially precocious. Sometimes you look at someone and think, four or five, that seems right. It isn't a question of rehabilitating. It is about <u>habilitating</u>. You can't assume some basic competencies and life skills—something as basic as brushing your teeth, washing.*

She described officers' responses to training on trauma and on the use of incentives as positive. She was also very positive about a course on trauma and mindfulness they were using with juveniles themselves called *SPARCS: Structured Psychotherapy for Adolescents Responding to Chronic Stress.* The course provided information on the various effects of chronic stress/complex trauma, including its impact on affect and impulse regulation, attention and consciousness, self-perception, relationships with others, somatization, and systems of meaning. More importantly it provided means for the juveniles to begin to control some of the effects of trauma that most impede them socially, especially affect regulation and attention. A four-session version of the course was being used in the RYDCs, the juvenile jails. The phrase SOS was being used regularly. It was a signal that the individual needed to Slow Down-Orient-Self Check.

One reason that Doyle liked the course was that it avoided labels, like trauma, while giving the adolescents a much needed sense of agency: *No one has to say, "I'm traumatized." Instead they can respond to the question, "What have you experienced?" For many the only emotion they know is mad—not guilty, disappointed.*

She saw this focus on the experience, not the label, as useful as well because the label *traumatized* implied victimization and that was a concept girls were more willing to internalize than boys. The boys were more comfortable internalizing the label *victimizer.* To accept this different perspective, "I have been affected," signified a dramatic shift in worldview, one those around the boy might not readily accept either. *Once the worldview changes, you no longer fit into the system. But family dynamics are such that they want to keep themselves in familiar equilibrium, even if it has a poor outcome.*

Doyle saw this training as giving them *master skills that would help them sustain a relationship, providing a new language of feelings, and giving them opportunities to build relationships with staff by practicing these skills.* Already she was hearing officers say, *You need an SOS.* But more importantly the boys were realizing they had some crucial agency, they could make choices that changed their inner world and the world around them as well.

However, it is hard to reconcile the rehabilitation—or habilitation—envisioned in the conversation with Christine Doyle with various descriptions of life inside DJJ facilities.

DEPARTMENT OF JUVENILE JUSTICE

CITIZENS' ACADEMY: A BIRD'S EYE PERSPECTIVE

The Department of Juvenile Justice was one of our more problematic experiences—especially the dissonance between the way in which its activities were explained and promoted in its first six-week Citizens' Academy, where its troubled history and its recent devastating audits went unacknowledged, as well as with the in-the-trenches experiences shared with us by DJJ prison guards.

The Citizens' Academy was a six-week program DJJ designed to introduce interested people to the various activities of the department. This included presentations on upper administration and legal affairs and court and probation officers; visiting various juvenile courts, prisons and jails; and more presentations on efforts to address sex trafficking, compliance with the federal Prison Rape Elimination Act (PREA) requirements to reduce the number of sexual assaults in prison, the credentialed school system responsible for educating the children in the prisons, behavioral health, and reentry initiatives. Both juvenile courts we visited with the Citizens' Academy, Clayton and Newton, we also observed independently.

There was high energy and buy-in by the administrative staff for this first Citizens' Academy, which was championed by then director of DJJ, Avery Niles. DJJ had experienced many changes of leadership after Albert Murray's effective six-year term as commissioner ended in 2010. Murray, the longest serving DJJ commissioner, had come to the department after a long multi-state career in juvenile corrections, and had overseen the last years of the federal government's eleven-year oversight of DJJ because of over-crowding and abuse. His tenure was followed by five commissioners between 2010 and 2012. So, by 2014, Niles's two-year tenure was already distinguished by its longevity. In 2019, Niles would be abruptly fired for falsifying his resume with an associate's degree.

Appointed by Nathan Deal, most of Niles's experience had been in law enforcement, and this academy was modeled on those often used by police and sheriff's departments to reach and interact with their local communities. The hope was that the people who attended would become strong advocates for the department. The people we attended with included several who had known the previous director, Albert Murray, as well as a mother whose son had benefited from his time in prison, and a man who served as a court watcher for his community in the Fulton County Juvenile Court, making sure that the young delinquents in his neighborhood were being adequately dealt with. He finished the program intent on developing a mentoring program to help with reentry.

Our response to the well-organized program was colored by earlier interviews we had held with capable, experienced, and thoroughly burnt out prison guards whose description of their work conditions bore no relationship to what we were seeing on our tours. We also, within the second week of the academy, had been taken aside by someone at DJJ and told that our presence in the Citizens' Academy had been brought up and discussed among the various department heads, in particular how we might be "managed."

The last day of the program, when Niles asked if anyone had questions, we brought up various troubling realities described in a recent state audit of DJJ security staffing and asked why none of these issues had been mentioned during our six weeks together. To be effective advocates for the department—and there were many dimensions of their programs well worth advocating for—we, as citizens, needed to be trusted with the whole picture, we said. For example, the 2014 audit looked at the reasons for 49% annual turnover rate for correctional staff. Staff morale was low because of the turnover of leadership, the perception that advancement was unfairly determined, the extremely low salaries with little hope of advancement, enforced overtime that was compensated only by comp time that was impossible to claim because of the enforced overtime, and the level of violence in the facilities. Auditors suggested people advancing to officer status be tested for reading level as a way of improving selection criteria. This had improved officer retention and competency at the Department of Corrections. Sexual assault was a concern. In 2013, Paulding RYDC, had ranked second *in the nation* for the level of sexual victimization and Eastman YDC had ranked fourth. These findings were supported by PREA reports listing sustained high levels of sexual assault and harassment, including a disturbing number of staff on inmate molestations. The level of youth recidivism was also high, around 65%, as was the racial imbalance in Georgia's juvenile prisons. We wondered if he could speak to any of those issues. Niles looked blank, then quickly changed the subject.

Niles had opened the first session of the Citizens' Academy, by saying, *We're taking a proactive approach. We are encouraging you to come into the system and look. We invite you to challenge the system to make sure we do what we are supposed to do. It is easier to build stronger children than it is to repair broken men and women. Challenge us on our facts.* Although that intention was not realized in our last question and answer period in the Citizens' Academy doesn't negate its importance: We do need to challenge the system, and we need to see where it is succeeding as well as where it is not.

It is important to recognize that the trend nationally and in Georgia on juvenile justice is positive. Nationally, juvenile incarceration rates have fallen dramatically in the last two decades, including in Georgia. Between 1997 and 2011, Georgia's commitment rate declined by 68%, one of the five states with the greatest declines.[1] This decline has continued. Far more adjudicated youth are being kept in at-home placements. At the beginning of 2019, the number of juveniles on DJJ probation was 10,526 (87% of them under at-home or in-the-community supervision), while the admissions to RYDCs was 8,378, down from 14,160 in 2013, and the YDC admissions were 430, down from 633 in 2013.[2] Three-year recidivism rates now hover at 36-37%.[3]

The final report of the Georgia Council on Criminal Justice Reform when identifying areas of success for juvenile justice reform, cited the 36% decline in secure confinement and nearly 50% decline in total commitments, as well as the adoption of validated assessment instruments to help judges make better decisions about whether to detain a juvenile before trial and where they should be placed after conviction. It also emphasized the reform's success in providing grants to help under-resourced communities provide more community-based alternatives to juvenile incarceration, for example, providing validated cognitive and behavioral programs, like Multisystemic Therapy, Thinking for a Change, and Aggression Replacement.

Within DJJ there have also been positive developments. It is now several years into the accreditation process with the American Correctional Association. There is a renewed emphasis on education and on reentry. DJJ is its own accredited state school system, with twenty-nine year-round schools that provide a high school diploma. In addition, in the last few years, the educational emphasis has expanded to provide academic and technical skills opportunities from high school and beyond through the Career, Technical, and Agricultural Education program that supports the academic program with real world skills and applications, providing experience in horticulture, construction, automobile maintenance, welding, forklift and culinary arts, computer skills, and law and government. The Graduate Education Program focuses on transition and reentry, helping develop soft skills, assistance with standardized tests, and also providing access through a program called e-Core to twenty-six online college level courses accepted in the Georgia university system.

However, various significant issues remain. There is marked racial disparity in the juvenile justice population. African-American youth are 5.6 times more likely to be incarcerated than white youth.[4] This disparity begins at referral, with black youth being at least twice as likely as white youth to be referred to a juvenile court, the disproportions after that point are less, but are cumulative, so by the time you reach commitment the differences are much higher. A recent report on Disproportionate Minority Contact in Georgia estimated that if one were to address this issue of disproportion at the point of referral, the practical implications would be great: in a large urban county like Fulton it would mean that in 2006, 5,668 fewer youth in Fulton county would have been referred to a juvenile court, in 2014, 3,369 fewer, numbers that reflect both the overall decline in justice-involved youth and the persistent racial disproportion.

The level of violence in Georgia DJJ jails and prisons is deeply disturbing and has been for years. The DJJ 2014 Annual Report includes statistics for youth-on-youth and youth-on-staff assaults from 2012-2014: For the YDCs, there were 2,938 youth-on-youth assaults and 1,331 youth-on-staff assaults, while youth-on-youth violence in the RYDCs was over twice as high. The 2016 PREA report details 1,494 youth-on-youth and 205 staff-on-youth allegations of sexual violence, from harassment to assault from 2013-2016. Since then, even with a substantially reduced number of inmates, assaults have increased, although sexual violence seems of have reduced. Between 2015 and 2018 in the seven YDCs, there were 3,400 youth-on-youth physical assaults, 150 youth-on-youth sexual assaults, 1,400 youth-on-staff assaults. There were also 1,600 misconduct allegations against officers.[5]

Perhaps the most troubling of all the problems with the juvenile prisons is the level of turnover, especially of juvenile corrections officers, who make up over 30% of the DJJ workforce and have the most direct and sustained contact with the youth in facilities. In 2014, the audit identified serious problems with correctional officer retention, citing a 49% turnover rate. Since then, turnover statistics for correctional officers have dramatically worsened. In 2016 there was a 101% turnover rate in first year correctional officers.[6] In 2018, the turnover rate for correctional officers was 84%, a rise of 44%.[7] The turnover for the department overall had risen by 42%. It is impossible to see how one can create a safe environment for the youth adjudicated to this system or for the officers necessary to staff it with this level of turnover.

Another issue is the qualifications of the DJJ Commissioner. Niles spent several decades in the Hall County Sheriff's Office, rising to be warden of the county work camp of fifty prison inmates. He had relatively little education, no experience running a large corrections agency or experience with the distinctive needs of troubled juveniles. His replacement, Tyrone Oliver, also with a long career in a county sheriff's office, was most recently police chief and deputy city manager in Social Circle, population 4,479. He also has had no experience administering a large, complex organization dedicated to troubled juveniles. Given the long-term and deeply ingrained problems in DJJ, it is unclear why there is no attempt to bring in someone with extensive administrative experience in corrections and with expert knowledge of the distinct challenges of addressing the needs of delinquent juveniles, a system that to be effective must have a much stronger grounding in rehabilitation than in control.

DJJ: GROUND-LEVEL VIEW
Delia & Neisha

Our interviews with the two frustrated prison guards, Delia and Neisha, surprisingly, gave us the most reason for hope in this very troubled system. They both worked in RYDCs, the juvenile jails, where youth are held before trial. Delia, on extended disability leave from DJJ because of a work-related injury, led a large prison ministry at her church and was an active jail chaplain. She had in various other jobs—Job Corps, daycare, respite foster care, and group homes—worked with the same at-risk juvenile population: "kids on probation, homeless, with some kind of mental disability."

Neisha, a DJJ lieutenant then on administrative leave, had become interested in juvenile justice while growing up in Detroit because her own brothers were in and out of detention centers "and I wanted to know if what they told me about them was true." She saw many of the children in DJJ as leading lives like her own, trying to care for their younger siblings. Working at thirteen, a mother at sixteen, raised in the projects, she was not, she said firmly, "a product of them. I had a praying great-grandmother who cared for me. I never wanted to disappoint her. It is where your mindset is that matters."

Both Delia and Neisha were mothers, and their attitude toward the young people they supervised was founded on tough love. They understood that some of the children returned to prison because it was their safe place. Delia explained, *There are some kids who come back because they love us. They trespass just enough to come back. For some it is like a daycare center. They don't see it as real detention.* On the other hand, some as young as twelve years old did it to gain status on the street. Others recidivated because *They're going right back into the environment. There's no change. If those pieces were in place, the kid might have a chance.*

In their own lives, they walked their talk. Neisha, when her son was getting in trouble as an adolescent, had two officers she knew pick her son up and keep him in jail for two days: *He never knew I had him picked up. But he got hisself together.* Several times, mothers and fathers brought their children to her at the RYDC to perform a similar service—and she had obliged: *You have to get to their level. They never act up afterwards. They aren't bad kids, their parents just gave them everything.*

They felt that the five weeks training they received in the late 1990s to become officers was limited in many ways, that the only real criteria you had to meet was "to be crazy enough to want to do it." The training felt quite militarized, with a lot of marching, and, although it did cover policies and procedures, it laid a heavy stress on what take-down tactics were permissible with juveniles. Now, they noted, martial arts had taken over from bear hugs and kicking behind knees. Now they twisted hands or noses, kicked a shin, used the nerve behind the ear to bring a person down. They felt restraint was important. "Some people have hurt kids bad. Not necessarily intentionally. The kids were out of control." What was really necessary they both said, was to build rapport, then you could regain control of the environment.

"Protect and serve" was the motto they lived by, which meant, to begin with, "checking the rooms every fifteen minutes to make sure they're alive, someone hasn't hanged themselves or been sexually assaulted." Escort them off the unit. See that they were in classes because many of them didn't go to school on the outside. But what protect and serve meant with angry, acting-out adolescents, many much bigger than they were, was not always clear.

The greatest reward of their jobs was the relationships they were sometimes able to build with the young offenders. Delia said: *They know they have to go back on the streets, or on to prison. But you can still have an impact. We had people in the midst of riots, and we could de-escalate. We told them, you lucky to have us as your officers. We were no holds barred. We stayed on their tails. They saw we weren't there to mistreat them. We met their families. They never retaliated against us when they met us on the street.*

Neisha added: *One young man came up and told me, "You used to keep me on lockdown all the time." I told him, "I didn't have fear of you there, and I don't have fear of you now." Lots of officers are scared of them, and the kids know and they pop off on those officers. I've always been a fighter. I'll do my job but I will protect myself. You have to be unafraid to fight. Kids see that.*

Both Delia and Neisha talked about the tension between the chronic low staffing and rapid turnover and procedural rules that were impossible to obey because of that low staffing. The officer to inmate ratio was sometimes as high as 40 to 1. In these cases, one had no choice but to leave your post unattended if another guard, ignoring safety policy, put herself in a position where she were being attacked—even if that choice led to an official reprimand or demotion. But if that reprimand was designed to cover-up the chronic staff shortage and the unsustainability of the protocol, then the decision felt greatly unfair—especially for a job that paid only $30,000 after thirteen years and two promotions. (Since we talked with them law enforcement salaries across the state have been raised 20%, so that starting salaries are now about $28,000).

They were blunt in their assessment of DJJ: *It needs to be blown off the map. They need a whole new mentality. No more cliques. No more competition. They need to change everything from scratch: how they hire people, what their goals are.*

Various improvements they suggested were to change the employment criteria, discounting a single drug arrest, so that more men could apply, and to have counselors provide actual face-to-face services for youth, not just talking with them over the phone.

The change in offenders' attitudes they felt would make the greatest difference: *Getting them to believe that they can be a better person than their crime or their family. If someone keeps telling you you'll never be nothing, you begin to believe it.*

Delia and Neisha's views resonate with those of James Gilligan, the forensic psychiatrist who effectively reduced the level of violence in several prisons in Massachusetts, whose suggestions about how to address violence in adult prisons, are even more appropriate for changing the conditions in juvenile ones, prisons whose inmates will definitely return to live with us:

> *Prisons themselves could actually start preventing violence, rather than stimulating it, if we took everyone out of them, demolished the buildings, and replaced them with a new and different kind of institution—namely, a locked, secure residential college, whose purpose and functions would be educational and therapeutic, not punitive. It would make sense to organize such a facility as a therapeutic community, with a full range of treatments for substance abuse and any other medical and mental health services needed to help the individual heal the damage that deformed his character and stunted his humanity.*
>
> *If it seems utopian to replace prisons with schools, let me remind you that prisons already are schools and always have been—except that they are schools in crime and violence, in humiliation, degradation, brutalization and exploitation, not in peace and love and dignity.*[8]

Endnotes

1. Pew Trusts, "Public Attitudes on the Juvenile Justice System in Georgia," 5 Mar 2013.
2. Georgia Department of Juvenile Justice [DJJ], "Quick Facts 2019."
3. DJJ, "Recidivism Report 2018."
4. Sentencing Project, "Black Disparities in Youth in Youth Incarceration: African Americans 5x More Likely than Whites to be Held," 2017.
5. A. Judd, "Deadly consequences: Murder case exposes a system's failings. Juvenile Justice In Georgia, Part 1," *The Atlanta Journal-Constitution.* 10 Nov 2019.
6. DJJ, "Strategic Plan FY 2018-2021."
7. DJJ, "Annual Report 2018."
8. J. Gilligan, *Preventing Violence.* Thames & Hudson, 2001, pp. 117-18.

Additional Sources

Juvenile Courts

"Clayton Juvenile Court: Juvenile Detention Alternatives Initiative."
Slay, Colin. "Clayton County's JDAI Journey."
Slay, Colin. "Guarding the Front Door."
"Annual Report FY19, Juvenile Court of Clayton County."

Department of Juvenile Justice
"Annual Reports," 2013-2020.
"Quick Fact Sheets," 2018-2019.
    "FY 2014 Through 2017 Strategic Plan."
    "2018-2021 Strategic Plan."
    "PREA Annual Reports," 2016-2018
    "2018 Recidivism Report (January 2019 Update)."
    "2011 Recidivism Report."
S. Gonzales et al., "Disproportionate Minority Contact in Georgia's Juvenile Justice System: A Three-Prong Approach to Analyzing DMC in Georgia." Georgia Criminal Justice Coordinating Council, 2018.
G. Griffin, "Department of Juvenile Justice Security Staffing." Georgia Department of Audits and Accounts, Performance Audit Report No.13-16, 2014.

DJJ Prison Conditions
A. Judd, "Deadly consequences: Murder case exposes a system's failings. Juvenile Justice In Georgia, Part 1," *The Atlanta Journal-Constitution*. 10 Nov 2019.
M. Lee, "In Georgia, Sex Abuse Allegations Cloud Progress of Juvenile Justice Reform," *Juvenile Justice Information Exchange* [JJIE]. 17 July 2013.
J. Swift, "Georgia Closing Juvenile Prison With Nation's Highest Rate of Sexual Victimization." *JIE*. 29 Oct 2013.

Juvenile Justice Reform
Applied Research Services. "Pathways to Desistance: A Comprehensive Analysis of Juvenile to Adult Criminal Careers." Georgia Criminal Justice Coordinating Council, 2017.
Georgia Criminal Justice Reform Council Reports, 2011-2018.
"Georgia Juvenile Justice Incentive Grant Program: Executive Summary 2018, Georgia Criminal Justice Coordinating Council.
Pew Trusts, "Georgia's 2013 Juvenile Justice Reform: New Policies to Reduce Secure Confinement, Costs, and Recidivism."
R.A. Mendel, "No Place for Kids: The Case for Reducing Juvenile Incarceration." Annie E. Casey Foundation, 2011.

Comparative Statistics
"Georgia Juvenile Justice," Juvenile Justice Geography, Policy, Practices & Statistics. Office of Juvenile Justice and Delinquency Prevention, "Statistical Briefing Book."
W. Sawyer, "Youth Confinement: The Whole Pie 2019." Prison Policy Initiative.

ʼ3ʼ

ADDICTION, MENTAL HEALTH, ACCOUNTABILITY

It was graduation day in the DeKalb County Drug Court in metropolitan Atlanta. Isaiah, a tall, thin middle-aged man, was called up before Judge Tangela M. Barrie. Pronouncing him "a great example of perseverance and change," the judge laid out his record: an addict with over fifty arrests, he now had been clean and sober for six hundred days. The judge turned on her phone and "I Believe" sang forth. Isaiah wept as his fellow participants and the audience honored his achievement with prolonged applause. The judge beamed. Collecting himself, Isaiah spoke with calm dignity, acknowledging the long years when whatever he had to do to support his addiction, "I was going to do it." Finally accepting that he needed help, he entered the stringent two-year program. He ended by thanking individually many of those who had supported him, including the sheriff and the court recorder. The two men seated in the jury box in orange jumpsuits and headed back to jail, who earlier had projected attitudes alternating between indifference and defiance, followed Isaiah's graduation triumph with the same joy as the rest of us.

The session's second graduate, Cynthia, stood proudly before the judge and audience to the refrain of "her feet on the ground, head in the clouds." Her turnaround had been substantial as well. Arrested more than twenty times, Cynthia was now clean and sober for 640 days, maintaining employment for the first time in her life, and on her way to obtaining a GED. Noting that for this graduation she was wearing a cap and gown for the first time in her life, she added, "I wish my mother could see me now." But she did have many other friends and family in the audience celebrating her accomplishment. Judge Barrie ended the graduation ceremony addressing them directly, appreciating their support for Cynthia and pointing out how important continuing that support would be to her future. The judge then handed the two graduates her judicial order withdrawing their convictions and probation, along with their program completion certificates.

This was the only one of the four drug courts sessions we attended where the judge played music, but we did attend a session in Hall County in northeastern Georgia that was highlighted by a beautiful duet performance. Participants had been told to devise a small piece about recovery. This pair decided on a song. Part of the impact was visual—the alto lead was younger, short and wiry. The man providing a doo-wap backup and falsetto refrain was towering and bulky. The blend in every sense was gorgeous.

Drug courts are a recent innovation—the first was started in Miami in 1989. The model proved attractive. An "astounding" exponential growth soon followed with more than eight hundred in operation (or gearing up) by 2000 and around 3400 in 2015.[1] Practices vary widely between and within states, with individual judges enjoying wide latitude. This makes generalization difficult as well as questionable practices possible.

As drug courts succeeded, this model expanded into other areas, notably for mentally ill people involved with the criminal justice system. With the expansion of these different forms of accountability courts, professional organizations developed at state and national levels and along with them sets of best practices promoted by training sessions and incentivized by grants. A particularly important step occurred in 1997 when the relevant office of the U.S. Department of Justice published the ten key components of good drug court programs.[2] At the state level, Georgia has been at the forefront in recent years in the development and oversight of accountability court standards.

There are severe limits, however, to the capacity of accountability courts to handle the immense volume of potential clients enmeshed in the U.S. criminal justice system. As a consequence of decades of the "war on drugs," by 2005 about a half a million people were incarcerated in the United States on any given day for a drug offense.[3] The discussion of the accountability court model that follows concludes with the necessity of far broader changes in how we as a society respond to the law-breaking related to substance abuse.

DRUG COURTS

Positive reinforcement is at the heart of the drug court model. Participants are called before the judge to answer questions about their progress, receiving praise for whatever steps forward they have taken. Some might be given a candy bar, others a certificate. Even when they fall back, sanctions are often applied with an upbeat message. Hall County Judge Jason Deal in the session we observed told a participant who had been maintaining a good record (fourteen months sober, a job, and back in school) but was now being sanctioned for a violation with a night in jail that it was just a "glitch" and he could complete the sanction with ease, even "standing on your head." Another participant with a bigger set of violations was sentenced to jail for a week. Expressing his disappointment over the violations, nonetheless Judge Deal encouraged the participant as he was handcuffed and taken off to jail to "shake it off and keep going."

This is not your usual courtroom, and drug courts do have their critics. Despite the presence of important supporters of such accountability courts on the Georgia Council on Criminal Justice Reform, strong recommendations were stifled in its first report by critical members, such as then District Attorney David McDade of Douglas County. Described as a "vociferous opponent of easing up on drug offenders," McDade argued that placing offenders on probation "decriminalizes drug possession."[4] Others criticize the approach taken in the courtroom. Chief Superior Court Judge Walter Matthews of Floyd County, for example, claimed that drug court "is more suited for a counselor than a judge," objecting to the practice of "a judge sitting in a courtroom patting people on the head and giving them trinkets and gifts because they went a week without using methamphetamine or cocaine."[5]

Deal admitted that he too was once a skeptic, telling us, "You hear about them clapping and handing out candy bars and you wonder what kind of crazy stuff is that." When he was the district attorney, he would occasionally sit in on drug court sessions presided over by the judge he would eventually replace in that role. He described the experience that got him to really take notice.

A participant was taking his turn before the judge: *He's got the slouch on, his pants are dragging, he is doing the shuffle and I think, That guy is going to jail. The judge said, "When you first started drug court you went to jail every week, you were in jail more times than you were out, you didn't have a job, you didn't pay your child support but lately things have been turning around, you have been doing better."*

And the guy said, "Well, that's right judge."

"Tell me why things have turned around."

And the guy said, "You know judge, I started going to church and I figured that I needed to do better." And I am thinking, "Yeah, everybody gets religion when they get in trouble." And he says, "My kids, I had to do better by my kids." And I think, "Everybody says that before going to jail." And then he turned around and looked at all the people in drug court and he said, "I know you all are counting on me to do better so I try to do better because I know you are counting on me."

EFFECTIVE SANCTIONS

Criticisms about the drug court model tend to fade with experience of their actual operation and in the face of the mounting evidence that they work. Positive reinforcement is just one side of the drug court formula. The other is sanctions. When participants violate the terms of their program they face graduated sanctions that are applied "regularly, consistently, and promptly."[6] The DeKalb Drug Court (DKDC), as a typical model, follows an elaborate matrix that specifies, for example, eight hours of community service the first time someone misses a court session, but three days in custody the second time and ten days in custody the third time.[7] It is all about "restoring consequences to action," DKDC Director Liam Harbry explained to us. Even in jail the program does not stop. Participants continue with their lessons and homework and are visited by their counselors. Particular attention is given to having them analyze "the warning signs that got you back into trouble."

Another important aspect of drug court sanctioning is that it is virtually immediate, especially in contrast to the usual judicial process. With the regular system, six months might pass before an arraignment notice is received for a possession charge, maybe nine months before the case is processed. *That is not very effective for changing behavior, so much time has passed,* Deal observed. *Here, if you mess up on Tuesday you are going to see me on Friday.*

Harbry also contrasted drug courts with community-based treatment programs, which are less effective for the drug dependent because "showing up is the problem for them and they don't stop using." Drug courts, in contrast, "can use the authority of the court to keep them engaged in treatment for a long period of time." In the earlier phases of the program, it's this external authority and the sanctions for noncompliance that keeps participants on track. Over time, though, Harbry emphasized, *what you see is that it internalizes. The treatment is actually settling in, they are understanding the curriculum, they are learning to manage their addiction challenges, address some of their criminal behavior, criminal thinking.* With this change the probabilities of success escalate, culminating in testimonies such as one we heard by a DKDC graduate at an event we attended: "Soon I will be five years clean. People can change, I prove it."[8]

HOW DRUG COURTS OPERATE

To enter a drug court, a participant has been both arrested and has acknowledged a drug dependence problem. To DKDC Clinical Coordinator

Shannon Morgan, criminality and drug dependence are often connected in ways beyond crime to support one's drug habit. She pointed to the enjoyment of the adrenaline rush of risky behavior as one connection often not addressed in conventional treatment programs: *If you go to the twelve-step meetings they are not only talking about their addiction but also the crimes they have committed. They go hand in hand, drugs and alcohol and crime. Consequently, drug dependent offenders need to learn not only how not to use but also to learn how to deal with those triggering things, the rush of getting money.*

Drug courts vary in how they handle their participants. Some are diverted prior to trial into their drug court program; in others, they enter a guilty plea but sentencing is deferred; a third path occurs after conviction and sentencing, which are then suspended pending program outcomes. With successful program completion the charge in the first two cases is normally dismissed; in the third, the sentence is modified.

The usual program follows a therapeutic model rather than the typical adversarial court arrangement. Both the prosecution and the defense sit together as part of the team working with the participant. For example, when we sat in on the team meeting held prior to the Hall County Drug Court session, Deal presided from a small table, sitting alongside representatives from the district attorney, public defender, and probation offices, the director of the drug court program, and several of its counselors. Representatives from several other county offices attended part of the meeting, at times crowding the small room. The situation of each participant was discussed individually, the tone very much one of "we are here to work together to help this participant succeed." However, success depends on participant honesty and compliance. The probation officer was adept at using Facebook to find participants posting selfies when attending events after their curfew. Similarly, drug screen urine tests are given frequently, randomly, and always supervised. DKDC's Morgan told us: *Our biggest thing over anything else in drug court is honesty. We will work with you if you relapse, if you fall back into old behaviors . . . but dishonesty . . . it is showing that you are not really wanting to do this.*

The essential principle is that participants are consistently held accountable for their behavior. Accountability is overseen by all of the team members, but at the center is the relationship between the participant and the judge. What was clear to us in observing drug court sessions has been verified by one of the most important national studies of them. The MADCE evaluation of two dozen courts across the nation, including Hall and Fulton

Counties in Georgia, found that participants' attitudes toward the judge is the most important correlation with the desired reduction in criminal behavior and drug use.[9]

Speaking to this point, Morgan told us that before starting drug court her clients *hate everybody involved with the court house, they hate the judge. They are so nervous the first time about going to talk in front of the judge because their experience with people who have been sitting up there in that robe has not been positive.* However, through their drug court experience with supportive judges and other people who work for the government, "it changes them . . . changes their perceptions." Parallel changes occurred with the three police officers who were part of the drug court team. They told Morgan that working so closely with offenders in this context changed how they conducted the rest of their police work.

Participants early in their program might appear before the judge every week, later it might be monthly. Best practices has the judge interacting at least three or four minutes with each participant, offering praise freely where it is appropriate and sanctions when called for. In the DKDC session that we attended with Judge Courtney L. Johnson presiding, she focused her attention on what participants were learning in the cognitive-behavioral course all were required to take concerning emotional regulation. One young male told the judge that he had not realized that emotions could act as triggers of unwise behaviors. Another, perhaps a decade older, confessed that "in my previous life I didn't even know about emotions." A third man of about the same age when asked by Johnson what was the emotion hardest for him to deal with, replied that it was anger, adding that he was learning that "I'm entitled to have the emotion but I don't have to act on it." A number of the participants told the judge that they were working on "replacement thoughts," that when they caught themselves entertaining a risky thought they could replace it with a more positive thought. Often the judge would ask them for an example. A man perhaps in his forties said he had recently received a call from an ex-friend trying to lure him back into the old lifestyle. Instead, he focused his attention on the positive aspects of his current life in the recovery house.

Our impression from the give-and-take between the judge and participants was that real learning indeed was taking place. In some cases, though, answers felt rote. We were reassured by both Harbry and Morgan that this was not unexpected and with time and repetition, understanding deepens. Relevant to many aspects of the program, there is truth in the adage, "fake it until you make it."

When Morgan interviewed prospective participants she was honest with them. "I tell them if you don't want to change, if you don't want to do the work, then don't do drug court because it is hard." She divided prospectives into two groups, those who were sincerely ready to do what is necessary and those with the attitude, "I'll get through this and still do what I want to do." She warned them that the second approach wouldn't work because "we are too involved with your life for too long." If the non-committed nonetheless entered, soon they were saying to themselves, "Oh my God, what have I done?!" Morgan split these participants again into two groups. At some point some might get motivated to change and move over into the committed-to-make-it-work group, but the second group was headed toward termination.

DRUG COURT EFFECTIVENESS

Drug courts have been studied enough that it has been clearly established that their track record is better than the alternatives. The MADCE nationwide evaluation of two-dozen courts found that participants still involved in their programs after eighteen months "reported less drug use, less criminal activity, were more likely to be in school or employed, and were less likely to be depressed."[10] For the DeKalb court, successful program completion (which would be twenty-four months) has varied between 65 and 75%.[11]

Not returning to jail or prison is another critical indicator of success. Nationally, recidivism is reduced an average of 26% by drug court programs, with the most successful courts featuring reductions of 35 to 40% (such as DKDC). In addition to reduced recidivism, graduates also show big reductions in drug use and criminal activity.[12] It is also important to emphasize that when someone does not make it through drug court, that participation might still aid recovery later.

It is certainly well established that accountability courts are cost-effective. As DeKalb's Harbry told us, "the money part is a no brainer." The daily cost of housing someone in the county jail runs around $57 but at the drug court "we are able to produce results that are lasting and effective for less than half" that cost—which is similar to what national studies find.[13] Furthermore, unlike the typical inmate upon release, the drug program graduate leaves, as Harbry noted, with "the skills necessary to maintain his sobriety and his recovery for the rest of his life."

Some critics contend that the success of the drug court model is overstated because courts tend to cherry pick the low-hanging fruit, meaning they limit eligibility to offenders with the lowest risk of reoffending.[14] This critique overlooks the political realities of starting programs like drug courts, especially in more conservative areas with strong law-and-order orientations. For example, Deal acknowledged that both in his county, and Georgia more generally, "initially the only way you could get any acceptance was to start off with people with very few convictions." His predecessor in Hall County at the beginning limited the program to just first offenders or those with only one prior felony. Eligibility expansion proceeded cautiously. Deal initiated a drug court in neighboring Dawson County in 2006. With a population around only 22,000, the court load was light, inviting expansion. The opportunity came with an offender "who was perfect" for the program but had two prior convictions. Deal got the district attorney to allow the person into the program and then *slowly but surely we brought in folks who did not qualify under our normal rules and saw that they were doing as well if not better than the other folks, and the public hasn't risen up so we were able to say it is working.*

Originally the court was limited only to those charged with drug possession or, if the district attorney agreed, possession with intent to sell. Over time limitations loosened to take people with drug dependence issues but whose charges were non-drug related, such as forgery, assuming both the district attorney and the victim agreed. Still, public perception and support remain a concern. For example, the program would not admit someone charged with residential burglary. After all, as Deal pointed out, "somebody breaks into your house and you run into them at Sears the next day, that would be a little traumatic." Nonetheless, he has had young people appear in regular court before him for armed robbery of whom he said: *It would be much more effective for them and the state to have them in some type of intensive accountability court where they went to school, worked a job, somebody was watching over them instead of sending them to prison to learn how to be hardened criminals.*

With the increasing participant numbers and the differing needs of the two groups, Hall County split the program in 2013 into two tracks, the original drug court (with 135 participants in 2016) and the newer felony probation track (59 participants). In addition, as Deal noted, "we are really trying to keep them a little bit separate because the science says you should not mix high-risk with low-risk offenders" because of potential negative influences on the low-risk. As of mid-2016, the Hall County programs had graduated 574 participants with another 139 in Dawson County.[15]

HIGH-RISK URBAN PARTICIPANTS

Political realities differ in metropolitan counties. The DeKalb County program, for example, began with high-risk, high-need offenders, although still excluding offenders arrested for selling drugs, committing a violent crime, or classified as sex offenders (restrictions often dictated by state and federal statutes). Later it added an additional track for medium-risk participants. Its evolution, then, was the opposite of much smaller, more rural Hall County. As Melissa Manrow of the Sheriff's Department explained, the original program "was designed for hard-core users, it had no space for someone working a 9 to 5 job," for somebody who was in trouble but their family and employer would take them back.

Observing court sessions for the two tracks, the differences were striking. Participants in Track One (high-risk, high-needs) were overwhelmingly African-American males, many of whom seemed to lack resources. Their average age appeared substantially higher than for Track Two, which was more racially diverse, with many also appearing to be economically comfortable. Shannon Morgan verified the observation—a recent study indicated Track One participants were about 85% African American and 90% male. Their dominant drug was invariably crack cocaine. Track Two participants were younger, more racially diverse, and using a range of drugs—meth, heroin, other opiates and pain pills, in addition to crack. Heroin use was definitely on the rise, especially with younger people. It is relevant to note here that all three of the DeKalb judges either observed or interviewed for this section are African American, as was the district attorney, the chief of the Sheriff's Department, and the heads of the county government and school district. The overall county population is 54% black, 33% white.

By definition the high-risk/needs population is going to be challenging to work with. As Manrow graphically described a not-uncommon participant: *We get the guy who has been smoking crack for twenty-five years, he has been living under a bridge, he has been eating out of a garbage can, he has been stealing whatever he could get his hands on. He was so much more likely to end up dead under a bridge than in recovery and sober.*

Despite these challenges, a number of the people we spoke with expressed greater satisfaction—and even ease—in working with the higher risk participants. As Deal explained: *They've been to prison, they know what it is like. They lost everything, they burned every bridge, and so they really don't make excuses very much. God save you from a nineteen-year-old kid with a substance abuse problem and mental health issues, they're impossible. (I remember being twenty: you think you are bullet proof.) But if you get a guy who is thirty-five who has been in prison half his adult life, he knows what you are talking about, he wants to stop, he just doesn't know how. The folks who have lots of history do well if you can get enough support for them to allow them to succeed.*

DKDC's Morgan also highlighted practical reasons for the differences. The high-risk participants "are very scheduled." During their first four months they are at the program from 8:30 in the morning until late in the afternoon when they then return straight to their recovery residence. The lower-risk Track Two participants are intended to be working during the day and if not, spending the time job searching "but that can often be pretty leisurely." They come in for two-and-a-half-hour group meetings two times a week but otherwise the evenings are theirs. With "more time on their hands they find it a little bit easier to get involved" in the behaviors the program seeks to change.

Manrow added socio-economic status to the distinction: *The folks from backgrounds of privilege have gotten chance after chance. But, the people coming from background of disadvantage and neglect don't get many chances. When they get one, they take it. We had privileged folks from all races that had a real hard time and we had abused people of all races who said this is a chance and I am going to seize it.*

The evidence on the characteristics of participants most likely to succeed in drug court programs suggests a mix of those found among these two tracks. The national MADCE evaluation discovered that program retention at eighteen months was highest among older, more mature participants with a primary drug other than marijuana. Also predictive of success was being employed or in school at the start of the program. When offenders with violent histories were allowed to participate, their substance use declined as much as it did with other offenders and their criminal activity even more. However, participants held back by mental illness were less successful.[16]

MENTAL HEALTH AND JUSTICE

Unfortunately, many offenders have mental health problems, many of whom self-medicate with drugs and or alcohol. About 40% of people with mental illness at some point in their life will be incarcerated.[17] The best estimate is that a little over half of state prison inmates have a mental health problem as do close to two-thirds of local jail inmates.[18] Among those jail inmates whose mental illness is serious, more than 70% have a co-occurring substance abuse disorder.[19]

As in many metropolitan areas, the DeKalb County Jail, "for the lack of a better term, is the largest mental hospital in the state," as Melissa Manrow put it. On any given day at the jail, she indicated, about five hundred prisoners take psychiatric medications. Unlike a true mental hospital, though, psychiatric care is limited to stabilization. It is not the function of a jail to provide therapeutic care nor are such resources available. Still, "the sad part," as Alisa Roth wrote about a program she lauded at the jail in adjacent Fulton County, was that "for many of these men, this may be the best mental health care they get."[20] And even within the Fulton system others get far worse treatment. Recently a federal judge declared conditions in the county's jail for mentally ill women as "repulsive." In particular, the judge cited the jail's filthy conditions and use of prolonged periods of solitary confinement.[21]

If an inmate's condition surpasses the stabilization capacity of a Georgia jail's staff, they are to be sent to the regional state mental health hospital—one of five located throughout the state. However, there are not that many beds available, according to Manrow. For those who are sent to the hospital, they receive broader therapeutic treatment but only to the point where they are assessed as mentally competent to stand trial or serve their sentences if already convicted.

We spoke to several defense attorneys, both public and private, with substantial experience representing clients with mental health issues. The complexity of this representation became particularly clear in our conversation with Constancia Davis. The clients themselves might have little insight into their best interest because of distorted thinking from their mental illness. Families might have more insight, but if the problems have been chronic, they often get worn down. Indeed, families are often the ones who called police because of their fears that a person might harm themself or someone else and they have nowhere else to turn. Their reasoning is usually that at least in jail the person would be safe.[22] In New York City the police department estimated in 2015 that it responded to more than four hundred mental health calls *every day*.[23]

However, the police might not find sufficient cause for arrest and the results can be tragic. Former DeKalb County District Attorney Robert James in a talk we heard gave the example of one case he prosecuted. A mother called the police several times about her mentally ill and abusive son, but on arrival they never found sufficient cause to arrest him. One day he snapped, killing his mother and two of his siblings.[24]

Davis explained that her job as the adult client's defense attorney is to advocate for their legal rights. However, this might not coincide with what might appear to be the mentally ill client's best overall interests. Should the client wish to go to trial then that is the course the attorney would pursue, even if it would appear that the client would be a better candidate for hospital admission. If, in contrast, the client were not to resist an incompetency hearing, this would open them to the possibility of a hospitalization lasting longer than the prison sentence they might have received, perhaps even substantially longer.

At the time we spoke about these issues with Claudia Saari, the head of DeKalb County's public defenders office, that office was the only one in the state with a special unit devoted to mental health cases. The unit had two lawyers and four social workers dedicated to working with these clients. Most centrally, this meant legal representation with the goal of getting judicial agreement, where appropriate, for a range of alternatives to prison, from a diversion program to at a day-reporting center to hospitalization. Meanwhile, the social workers assisted families to secure services and resources needed to help the client avoid returning to the criminal justice system.

MENTAL HEALTH COURTS

Following the success of drug courts, mental health courts also have been spreading across the country since first established in 1997. A 2016 count found over three hundred in operation. Evidence is also accumulating on their effectiveness. One of the most thorough and most recent evaluations found the recidivism rate for graduates after three years was one-third that of those who were not able to complete their program. Even for those who did recidivate, the severity of their crime was less the longer they had stayed in the program.[25] Consequently, these courts save money, by one estimate over $6 for every $1 dollar invested.[26]

In Georgia 57% of its 159 counties now have mental health courts, with the southern half of the state the least covered. Here too Hall County is an innovator. One of Judge Deal's colleagues started in 2004 a court for criminal defendants whose offenses are linked to their mental health issues. In 2014 a separate track was added just for veterans, following another nationwide treatment innovation.[27]

ELIGIBILITY CHALLENGES: The objective of mental health courts is to help the client to complete the program successfully, which results in the dismissal of the charges they face. However, the mental illness of some defendants is too severe for them to be a viable program candidate. Conversely, the prosecutor might not be persuaded that mental illness is relevant to the case. Another constraint pointed out to us by Constancia Davis is that in some courts impulse control disorder diagnoses such as kleptomania are not included within their eligibility criteria.

Offenders with a violent charge are typically excluded from participation in all accountability courts. This exclusion made sense when these treatment courts were new and building acceptance. Now that they are broadly accepted, this barrier is worth re-examination, especially in the case of mental health courts. As Davis pointed out, sometimes the person is having a delusional episode, perhaps from a failure to take their medication, and out of fear strikes whoever might be trying to restrain them, be that a caregiver or perhaps the police. If they cause bruises they are subject to battery charges, which would make them ineligible in many counties for diversion.

HOUSING AND ELIGIBILITY: Bureaucratic factors can also be an obstacle when someone is arrested in one county but lives in another. Davis found this most likely to be a problem with suburban counties that will only accept their own residents in their treatment programs. The offender might be willing to relocate to the county where they have been charged but these are the same counties with less affordable housing as well as minimal public transportation. More generally, Davis indicated that housing is a constant problem. You might be able to find treatment for a client, "but if they don't have a safe supervised place to stay with transportation, it can be a nightmare." [Claudia Saari also stressed to us that finding housing for poorer mental health clients is "a huge problem."]

These housing difficulties also contribute nationally to prolonged incarceration for the mentally ill. Along with the lack of community programs to provide services and supervision for offenders with mental illness, parole boards are more likely to deny them parole than other offenders so that they serve a greater proportion of their maximum sentences.[28]

Mental Health & Addiction Issues

Finally, there is again the dual diagnosis issue, the frequent co-occurrence of substance abuse disorder with mental illness. In some of the counties where we observed, as well as in some others where Davis worked, the individual with a dual diagnosis will not be taken into their drug or mental health treatment courts. Here again Hall County stands out for its willingness to work with this group.

Coordination between the drug and mental health courts concerning these defendants, Deal told us, is an art. There are some prospective participants that the drug court does not want to admit "because we think they have too much mental health for us" but similarly the mental health court "doesn't want to take them because they think they have too much substance abuse for them. . . . Folks get stuck out in the cold, there is not a good solution for them." Consequently, the judge thinks it would be good to have a hybrid court for defendants with dual-diagnoses.

Opioid-addicted offenders are another problem needing greater flexibility and perhaps another hybrid court, whether mental health issues are involved or not. Specialists in opioid addiction insist that the evidence is clear that far better results are obtained through a treatment program that includes strictly regulated but indefinite maintenance doses of opioid medication such as methadone or buprenorphine. Most importantly, "cold turkey" withdrawal leaves the addict with heightened vulnerability to overdose and death should they reuse—as has been happening throughout the country in large numbers in recent years. However, only a third of drug courts nationwide allow opioid maintenance treatment and it would be a rare jail that would allow a participant serving a short jail stay as a drug court sanction to continue with their therapeutic opioid use.[29]

Deal, for one, agreed with this view. He told us that in Hall County "we have a pretty good system for dealing with people with meth and crack cocaine" but his impression was that their program was not as effective with people addicted to heroin. The experts, he acknowledged, advise medically assisted treatment. The problem is that in regular drug court, "I say to my folks that you can't use anything, you can't drink." Furthermore, the maintenance drugs like methadone are also subject to abuse. The solution then would be a separate track for handling opioid addiction. However, finding the judicial time and the resources is problematic. Deal had not seen heroin as a problem in his region until the two or three years before we talked but it was now growing and "kids are dying with it." He pointed out that "meth will kill you but it will kill you slow. You don't die from overdosing" as you do with opioids.

PROMOTING ACCOUNTABILITY COURTS

Promoting accountability courts was a major feature of criminal justice reform in Georgia under the leadership of Governor Nathan Deal. As we sought to understand the origins of the governor's strong commitment to criminal justice reform, invariably the people we interviewed highlighted his experience with the drug court presided over by his son (Judge Deal himself downplayed his importance). The governor's primary vehicle for advancing the reform agenda was the Georgia Criminal Justice Reform Council (see Chapter 5).

From the beginning the Reform Council's co-chair and driving force was Michael P. Boggs. When serving as a Superior Court Judge, Boggs established one of the first drug courts in the southern half of the state. He told us that he had grown frustrated with the lack of sentencing options for offenders for whom substance abuse was a root cause of their offenses. As he pointed out, "I just decided that sending folks to prison and getting them out and putting them on probation and revoking them and sending them back to prison when we were never really addressing the underlying root cause of their criminal conduct was really probably not the best business model." He was aware of the drug court alternative since one was functioning in a neighboring circuit. "So I researched the propriety of drug courts and spent quite a bit of time talking to judges in the state who were running drug courts." Given limited county financial resources in his area, he "bootstrapped together" successful grant applications to the U.S. Department of Justice to get the program running. Wanting "to try to see if it would work to help save some folks," he found that the drug court did, making it "the most satisfying thing I have ever done as I did as a judge."

The Reform Council's first report provided a good explanation of the potential for accountability courts in Georgia, pointing out that "most individuals sentenced to prison are drug and property offenders . . . [with their] average length of stay behind bars more than tripled between 1990 and 2010." Yet, most were evaluated as having a lower risk to reoffend. Many, then, would be good candidates for accountability courts but the thirty-three accountability courts at the time served less than half of the state's counties and only about 3,000 offenders.[30] Significant recommendations, however, were stymied by lack of consensus on the Council. Nonetheless, the governor did commit $10 million of increased funding for these courts in his next budget.[31] Through FY2017 the state reinvested in accountability courts through grants to local programs more than $113 million.[32]

As the Reform Council's life was extended by Governor Deal's executive order its membership altered substantially as well. Most importantly, the Council's leading critic of drug courts left and Judge Deal was added (he told us he did not lobby for the position, rather others encouraged his addition). From that point accountability courts were a central features of criminal justice reform in Georgia. By early 2014 the state had 105 accountability courts, according to the governor's office, enrolling more than 4,100 offenders, many of whom "would likely be in prison without this alternative."[33] Four years later there were 149 accountability courts with at least one in each of the state's 49 judicial circuits. By FY2017 these courts served a total of about 8,900 participants.[34]

Accountability Standards

Establishing accountability court standards and holding judges to them has been an important part of the Georgia reform process. Any doubts about the need for such measures should have been removed with the *This America Life* March 2011 broadcast about the tyrannical behavior of Superior Court Judge Amanda Williams of Glynn County, located on the coast south of Savannah. Following the damning evidence presented by the radio program of her abusive treatment of drug court participants, such as indefinite incarceration, the state's Judicial Qualifications Commission initiated an investigation. Following the release of its equally damning report, a former state Supreme Court chief justice was appointed to pursue ethics charges. Shortly after, Judge Williams resigned.[35]

At the recommendation of the Reform Council, the Accountability Court Committee of the Judicial Council of Georgia (which represents the state's trial and appellate judges) defined standards and mandatory practices for the courts as well as created a certification and review process to ensure compliance.[36] A further step was taken in 2014 when the state legislature created the Council of Accountability Court Judges of Georgia (CACJ) to continue this work. This put Georgia in the forefront nationally as the first state to undertake this innovation. The initial chair of the council's executive committee was Judge Deal.[37] In early 2016 the CACJ issued a revised set of standards for each type of accountability court, a very thorough document totaling eighty pages.[38] The authorizing legislation also gave the council teeth: to receive state funding accountability courts must meet its certification standards.[39]

There also appears to be strong networks of support among drug courts staffs. At the time we talked DeKalb's Shannon Morgan, for example, was doing most of the training for the state on the assessment tool that courts use to establish the level of risk of each new program participant. Appropriate use of such tools is part of the certification standards and providing such training is one way the state promotes compliance and thereby well-functioning courts.

EXPANDING THE MODEL

And the accountability model continues to expand. A recent innovation has been Family Treatment Courts, which serve both children and parents when parents lose custody due to substance abuse. It is estimated that about 40% of foster care placements in Georgia in recent years have been due to heroin addiction. The goal of these courts is to promote parent recovery so that the family can be reunited. Based on Reform Council recommendations, SB 174 in 2017 strengthened these courts and their expansion, in particular by authorizing funding part-time juvenile judges for that purpose.[40]

Despite the many successes of accountability courts, numerous observers question just how useful this model is for meaningful criminal justice reform. The fundamental problem is one of scale. Around 2011, for example, the number of seriously drug-involved offenders in the country was thirty times greater than the number of participants in drug court programs.[41]

Judge Deal acknowledged that with more time and money the Hall County program could expand to include more offenders, something he would like to do. The limit for him, though, is time: *I don't think physically there is another time that I could do it. There is only so much judge time. You can throw more money but that doesn't create more hours in the day for the judges. We are all running as hard as we can.*

BROADER REFORM NEEDED

The spread of accountability courts have helped us as a society to think more clearly about the relationship between drug dependence and crime.

As we explore more fully the implications of viewing drug dependence as a public health issue and not one of criminal behavior, our understanding of what constitutes a crime in this area and what is an appropriate sentence both shrink. When implemented as broad policy changes, the magnitude of our reentry challenges would shrink immensely as well.

Prison admission rates for drug offenses at the state level increased ten-fold for the three decades ending in 2010.[42] The most frequent arrest in the United States is for marijuana possession. After almost a half of century of the war on drugs, marijuana remains "nearly ubiquitous in inner-city neighborhoods, as well as on college campuses."[43] Few of these college students are busted for their joints but many inner-city minority youths are arrested on a daily basis, leaving them with a life-long record and all of the many reentry obstacles that entails. No one should be in jail for possession of a drug that is less dangerous than alcohol.[44]

Indeed, to be really serious about the relationship between drugs and crime, the center of our attention should be alcohol. [45] As we are reminded, "more crimes, and especially violent crimes, are committed under the influence of alcohol than under the influence of all illicit drugs combined."[46] This is particularly true for murder when one half of those convicted of homicide in 1989 were using alcohol at the time but less than 6% were on other drugs.[47]

The use of and especially dependence on harder drugs should be regarded as public health issues and, as with marijuana, not as a reason for incarceration. [48] A survey of state and federal inmates in 2004 found about half "met the psychiatric criteria for drug dependence or abuse."[49] In Georgia in the late 1990s, three-quarters of the prison population was estimated to have a history of substance abuse. In Atlanta the same proportion of people arrested for new crimes tested positive for cocaine.[50]

Incarceration does not even cut off access to drug use. Our interviews confirmed again and again the widespread availability of drugs in prisons and jails.[51] Yet less than 15% nationally receive any drug treatment while incarcerated.[52] The treatment that is available often does not draw on the best available evidence of what does work. When more than two-thirds of treatment centers and clinics still do not offer the medicines that have the best treatment results it is even less likely that jails and prisons will. [53]

The evidence is clear that disproportionate sentences have done little to keep the public safe because deterrence does not work in drug markets. Cocaine prices actually fell more than two-thirds (even adjusting for inflation) across a quarter century when the ratio of both arrests and prisoners to the amount of cocaine sold increased at least ten-fold.[54] The explanation is simple: imprisoning a burglar will prevent more burglary, but "taking . . . drug dealers off the streets does not directly prevent drug selling" because there are many others ready to take their place.[55]

Nonetheless, we continue to give mandatory minimum prison terms of five, ten, twenty, or even more years to small-time street dealers—sentences "more severe than punishments received by many people convicted of robbery, rape, or aggravated assault."[56] Finding that only 14% of federal drug offenders had played an important role in drug trafficking, the congressionally-mandated Chuck Colson Task Force on Federal Corrections recommended that serious consideration be given to relying on alternatives to incarceration for lower-level trafficking offenses.[57] These alternatives could include accountability courts and probation using "swift and certain sanctions."[58]

Many drug users are incarcerated for nonviolent small-scale property crimes to support their expensive habits. A viable alternative drawing on European approaches is suggested by legal scholar Michael Tonry. For these types of crimes "the defendant is offered the opportunity to resolve the case by accepting the financial or community punishment they would have received if convicted." There is no guilty plea. There is no bargaining. If the defendant were assessed as drug dependent then the offer could include mandatory treatment.[59]

Adoption of these and other measures would also be an important step toward addressing one of the most serious injustices of the U.S. system, which is the significant discrimination against African-American citizens in prosecuting the war on drugs. Blacks use illegal drugs less than do whites, with the exception of crack cocaine.[60] The evidence is also clear that blacks do not sell drugs more often than do whites. Yet, in recent years blacks have been three to four times more likely to be arrested for drug offenses than are whites, and this disparity is actually down from the late 1980s when the difference was six-fold.[61] Following arrest on drug charges, African Americans are more likely to be convicted and then more likely to be incarcerated.[62] The cumulative effect of this discrimination can be severe. When combined with the draconian laws passed during the height of the war on drugs, the result in Georgia was that 419 of the 423 prisoners serving life sentences under the repeat offender drug laws were black and most had sold less than $50 worth of drugs.[63]

Societal attitudes toward addiction to illegal drugs are beginning to turn away from incarceration toward a public health perspective, in no small part because 90% of new heroin users in the past decade were white and often middle-class. As one legal scholar points out, "had this compassion existed for African-Americans caught up in addiction and the behaviors it produces, the devastating impact of mass incarceration upon entire communities would never have happened."[64]

The Georgia Reform Council was able to chip away at some of these policies—but only some. Important changes in the law it successfully proposed included, in 2013, allowing judges under certain circumstances to depart from mandatory minimums for trafficking offenses and, in 2016, providing parole eligibility for some repeat possession offenders for whom it had been denied.[65] Boggs explained in a newspaper interview:

> *The council believed that these sentences were fundamentally inequitable and immoral, particularly when compared to the fact that many convicted serious violent offenders in Georgia are eligible for parole consideration at some point during their sentence. . . . While these nonviolent drug offenders had earned their way into the prison system, they should, under appropriate circumstances, be afforded an opportunity to earn their way out.*[66]

CONCLUSION

One of the nine members of the Colson Task Force on Federal Corrections was Jay Neal, who has been one of the strongest proponents of criminal justice reform in Georgia. He first dealt with addiction issues as a pastor for twenty-five years in his small rural community in the state's northwestern corner. His involvement with a local residential treatment center and especially with the men from the center who attended his church was a big part of what moved him from a belief that substance abuse was a matter of weak will and morals to one of biochemistry. As he told us, originally he had believed that the drug and alcohol abusers *did not care enough about their families to quit doing what they were doing and take care of their families.* Then he began to understand it differently as he saw *big strong men broken down in tears, broken by the way they had failed their spouses, broken by the way they had failed their children, wanting more than anything to be the husband their wife needed and the father their children needed yet continuing to struggle with addiction.* During the same period he attended a national conference on addiction where he looked at brain scans. *I saw the chemical changes that take place and I began to realize that those men did not choose how their minds would respond to the substance.*

When Neal entered the State House in 2005 he worked on substance abuse legislation that would reduce the criminal sanctions on what he now considered an illness. In 2010 he had the opportunity to attend a national conference on sentencing and corrections and once again his preconceived notions, now on punishment, gave way "to evidence-based sentencing based on the risks and needs of the individuals." In the following years as one of the prominent leaders of the Georgia criminal justice reform effort, Neal promoting the view concerning drug dependent offenders, as he stated to us, that *we need to hold them accountable for their criminal behaviors but do it in such a way that instead of punishing them and locking them up with the criminally minded, we're holding them accountable while providing for them the treatment they need to be able to get beyond their addiction so that they can become productive, pro-social members of the community, taking care of their families, working a job, paying their taxes.*

ENDNOTES

1. E. J. Miller, "Embracing Addiction: Drug Courts and the False Promise of Judicial Interventionism." *Ohio State Law Journal* 65 (2004): 1479-576; Office of Justice Programs, "Drug Courts," U.S. Department of Justice. June 2015.

2. S. B. Rossman, et al. *The Multi-Site Adult Drug Court Evaluation: The Drug Court Experience.* Urban Institute, 2011, p. 14.

3. P. Reuter, ed. *Understanding the Demand for Illegal Drugs.* National Academies Press, 2010, p. 89.

4. B. Rankin and C. Teegardin, "Georgia Rethinks its Prison Stance," *Atlanta Journal-Constitution [AJC].* 3 Jan 2012.

5. B. Rankin and C. Teegardin, "Drug Court: Saving money, Saving Lives," *AJC.* 4 Mar 2012.

6. W. P. Guastaferro and L. E. Daigle. "Linking Noncompliant Behaviors and Programmatic Responses: The Use of Graduated Sanctions in a Felony-Level Drug Court." *Journal of Drug Issues* 42, 4 (2012), p. 397.

7. Guastaferro and Daigle, "Linking," pp. 415-416.

8. Presentation by Tracy M. at "Jobs Not Jail: A Call To Action," DeKalb County District Attorney's Office. 13 Apr 2016.

9. Rossman, et al., *Multi-Site,* p. 95. For a dissenting view, see Miller, "Embracing

Addiction."

10. Rossman, et al., *Multi-Site*, p. 110.

11. Presentation by DKDC Director Fredericka Dent at "Jobs Not Jail."

12. W. R. Kelly, *Criminal Justice at the Crossroads: Transforming Crime and Punishment.* Columbia University Press, 2015, pp. 180, 277.

13. Reuter, *Understanding*, p. 74.

14. M. Szalavitz, "How America Overdosed on Drug Courts." *PacificStandard.* 18 May 2015.

15. Council of Accountability Court Judges of Georgia. *Newsletter.* July 2016, p. 2.

16. Rossman, *Multi-Site*, p. 109.

17. Kelly, *Criminal Justice*, p. 189.

18. W. R. Kelly, R. Pitman, and W. Streusand, *From Retribution to Public Safety: Disruptive Innovation of American Criminal Justice.* Rowman & Littlefield, 2017, p. 54.

19. J. Travis, B. Western, and S. Redburn, eds. *The Growth of Incarceration in the United States.* National Research Council, 2014, p. 207.

20. A. Roth, *Insane: America's Criminal Treatment of Mental Illness.* Basic Books, 2018, p. 192.

21. B. Rankin, "Fulton Must Improve Jail Conditions for Ill Women," *AJC.* 24 Jul 2019.

22. V. A. Hiday and P. J. Burns. "Mental Illness and the Criminal Justice System." In *A Handbook for the Study of Mental Health*, ed. T. L. Scheid and T. N. Brown. Cambridge University Press, 2010, pp. 480-81.

23. Roth, *Insane*, p. 234.

24. M. Niesse, "Man pleads guilty to killing 3 family members," *AJC.* 24 Nov 2014. A similar tragedy in Seattle was the subject of a Pulitzer Prize winning feature article later expanded into a book: E. Sanders, *While the City Slept: A Love Lost to Violence and a Young Man's Descent into Madness.* Viking, 2016.

25. J.S. Costopoulos and B. L. Wellman. "The Effectiveness of One Mental Health Court: Overcoming Criminal History." *Psychological Injury and Law* 10 3 (2017): 254-263.

26. Kelly, Pitman, and Streusand, *From Retribution*, p. 167.

27. B. Edelman, "Veterans Treatment Courts: A Second Chance For Vets Who Have Lost Their Way." U.S. National Institute of Corrections, 2016.

28. Hiday and Burns, "Mental Illness," p. 493.

29. Szalavitz, "How America Overdosed."

30. *Report of the Special Council on Criminal Justice Reform for Georgians—2011*, pp. 9-10.

31. A. G. Sheinin and B. Rankin, "Deal signs bill revamping many criminal sentences," *AJC.* 2 May 2012.

32. *Report of the Georgia Council on Criminal Justice Reform [GCCJR]—2018*, p 20.

33. "Governor Nathan Deal: Office of the Governor: Priorities." Downloaded 14 Aug 2015.

34. *GCCJR—2018*, p. 20.

35. This American Life. "Very Tough Love," National Public Radio. 25 Mar 2011; O. Montoya, "Judge To Resign Amid Ethics Probe," *Georgia Public Broadcasting.* 20 Dec 2011; also see 03 Jun 2015.

36. Judicial Council of Georgia, "Judicial Council Approves Standards for Accountability Courts."

37. Council of Accountability Court Judges of Georgia [CACJG], "Newsletter," September 2015.

38. CACJG, "Standards for Georgia Accountability Courts." 7 Jan 2016.

39. CACJG, "Newsletter." December 2015.

40. *GCCJR—2017*, p. 34.

41. D. A. Boyum, J. P. Caulkins, and M. A. R. Kleiman. "Drugs, Crime, and Public Policy." In *Crime and Public Policy.* Eds. J. Q. Wilson and J. Petersilia. Oxford University Press, 2011, p. 386.

42. Travis, Western, and Redburn, *The Growth of Incarceration*, p. 68; S. Raphael and M. A. Stoll, *Why Are So Many Americans in Prison?* Russell Sage Foundation, 2013, pp. 38, 60.

43. J. J. Fader, *Falling Back: Incarceration and Transitions to Adulthood among Urban Youth.* Rutgers University Press, 2013, p. 71.

44. P. M. Boffey, "What Science Says About Marijuana," *New York Times Editorial Series.* 30 Jul 2014.

45. Boyum, Caulkins, and Kleiman. "Drugs, Crime," pp. 379-380.

46. M. A. R. Kleiman, *When Brute Force Fails: How to Have Less Crime and Less Punishment.* Princeton University Press, 2009, p. 153.

47. D. Baum, *Smoke and Mirrors: The War on Drugs and the Politics of Failure.* Little, Brown, 1996: 265.

48. See the example of Switzerland. T. Wainwright, *Narconomics: How To Run a Cartel.* Public Affairs, 2016, p. 253.

49. Reuter, *Understanding*, p. 72; C. Vestal, "Helping Drug-Addicted Inmates Break the Cycle," Pew Charitable Trusts. 13 Jan 2016.

50. M. Light, "Georgia's Criminal Justice System at a Crossroads: Tough Laws, Smart Decisions," Georgia Public Policy Foundation. 1 Mar 1999.

51. As A. Hattery and E. Smith point out, "Every ex-offender we have ever talked to . . . put it this way: 'Anything you have on the outside you have on the inside.' This holds true for access to sex, drugs, and virtually everything else." *Prisoner Reentry and Social Capital: The Long Road to Reintegration.* Lexington Books, 2010. p. 35.

52. Kelly, *Criminal Justice*, p. 179.

53. C. Vestal, "In Drug Epidemic, Resistance to Medication Costs Lives," Pew Charitable Trusts. 11 Jan 2016; C. Moraff, "Why Drug Rehab Is Outdated, Expensive, and Deadly," *The Daily Beast.* 09 May 2016.

54. Kleiman, *When Brute Force Fails*, p. 156.

55. Kleiman, *When Brute Force Fails*, p. 155. M. Tonry, "The Mostly Unintended Effects of Mandatory Penalties: Two Centuries of Consistent Findings." *Crime and Justice* 38, 1 (2009), p. 102.

56. Travis, Western, and Redburn, *The Growth of Incarceration*, p. 88.

57. CCTF. *Transforming Prisons, Restoring Lives: Final Recommendations of the Charles Colson Task Force on Federal Corrections.* Urban Institute, 2016, p. 12.

58. CCTF, *Transforming Prisons*, p. 23, 25. Also see, J. E. Kennedy, I. Unah, and K. Wahlersw. "Sharks and Minnows in the War on Drugs: A Study of Quantity, Race and Drug Type in Drug Arrests." *UC Davis Law Review* 53 (2018): 729-801.

59. M. Tonry, *Sentencing Fragments: Penal Reform in America, 1975-2025.* Oxford University Press, 2016, p. 22.

60. M. Tonry, *Punishing Race: A Continuing American Dilemma.* Oxford University Press, 2011, pp. 28-29, 60; K. L. Alexander, D. R. Entwisle and L. S. Olson, *The Long Shadow: Family Background, Disadvantaged Urban Youth, and the Transition to Adulthood.* Russell Sage, 2014, p. 151.

61. Travis, Western, and Redburn, *The Growth of Incarceration*, p. 60.

62. Tonry, *Punishing Race*, p. 70; Kennedy, Unah, and Wahlersw. "Sharks and Minnows."

63. C. Teegardin and B. Rankin, "Georgia's bold step: rethinking prison sentences," *AJC.* 22 Aug 2015.

64. Kimberlé Williams Crenshaw quoted in K. Q. Seelye, "In Heroin Crisis, White Families Seek Gentler War on Drugs," *New York Times.* 30 Oct 2015.

65. The relevant legislation is HB 349 in 2013 and SB 367 in 2016.

66. Teegardin and Rankin, "Georgia's bold step."

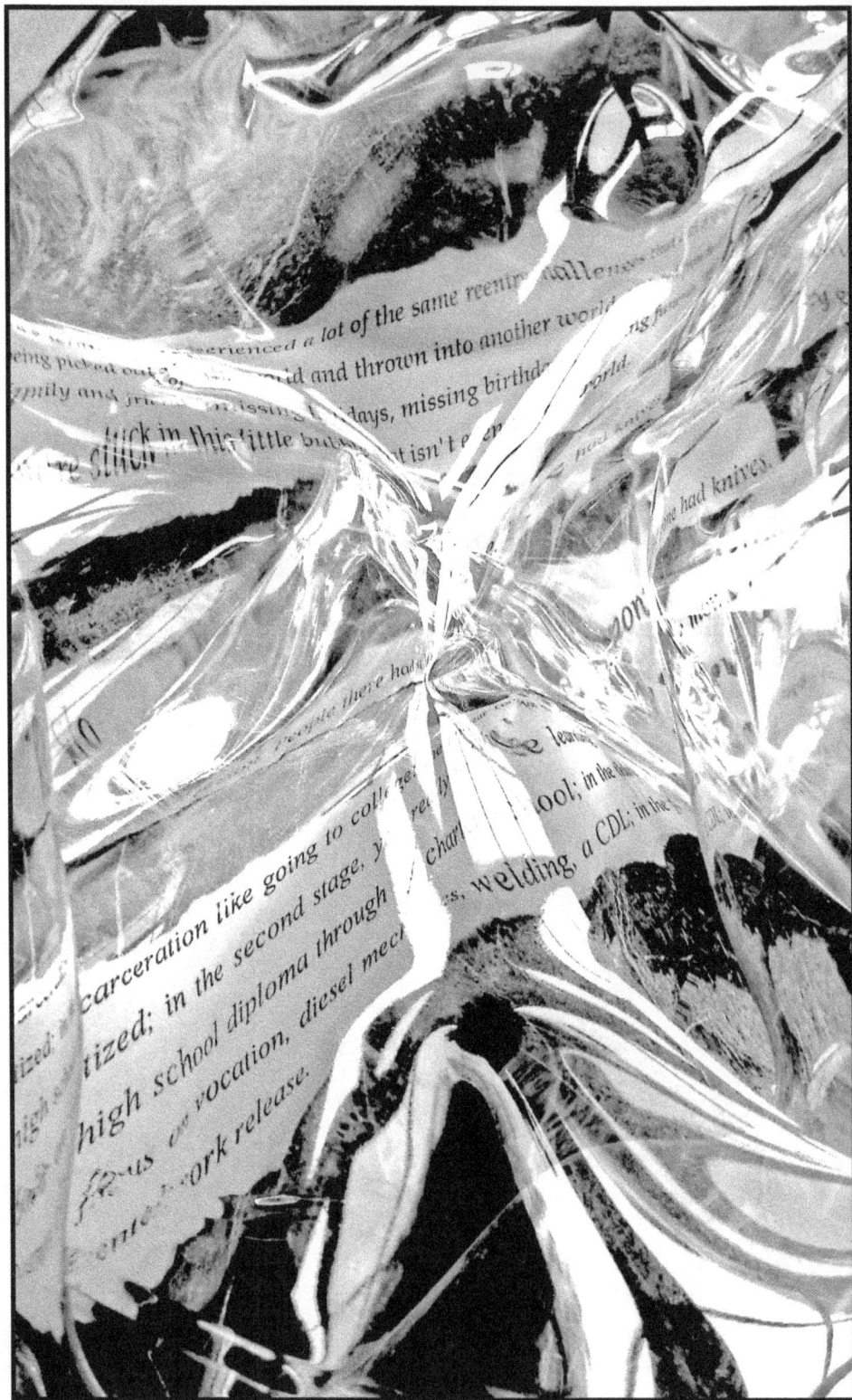

...experienced a lot of the same reentry challenges that...

...being picked out of... world and thrown into another world...

...family and fri... missing... days, missing birthd... world...

...stuck in this little bu... it isn't even...

...one had knives

...carceration like going to coll...

...tized; in the second stage, y... reach... charl... ool; in the...

...high school diploma through...

...us or vocation, diesel mec... es, welding, a CDL; in the...

...enter work release.

\4/

CORRECTIONS
WHAT DOES REENTRY HAVE TO DO WITH IT?

In this chapter we survey some of the challenges in the Georgia prison system as it actively embraces reentry while its prison population simultaneously, and intentionally, becomes proportionately more violent and its prisons harder.

The Georgia Department of Corrections (DOC) was in general unresponsive to our requests for interviews, even when individual staff members clearly expressed an openness to speak with us. The few interviews we conducted took months to arrange and were closely monitored by PR staff. Eventually, we did speak with Warden Steven Perkins of the Atlanta Transitional Center along with Susan Shlaer and Chaplain Susan Bishop at Arrendale prison. We visited both of these institutions to hold these conversations. However, we found it much easier to communicate with recently retired personnel, especially those involved in the earliest efforts to introduce reentry and reintroduce programming into the prisons. They remained committed to the importance of reentry and were eager to share their experiences. The interviews included conversations with three retired commissioners, Allen Ault, James Donald, and Brian Owens. We talked as well with the director of reentry services during much of that period, A.J. Sabree, and the legislative liaison for Corrections, B.J. Blair, with whom he closely collaborated on community outreach, especially with employers, as well as with Katrinka Glass, who was in charge of risk reduction services, which introduced much of the cognitive-behavioral change programming and substance abuse counseling into the prisons. We have followed the changes in emphasis and practice since Owens' tenure through DOC's annual reports, which are easily accessed—as well as through the substance of various lawsuits filed against the DOC by the Southern Center for Human Rights, the most diligent watchdog of the Georgia prison system.

REENTRY: SEAMLESS TRANSITION OR 90-DEGREE TURN

In the 1990s, Georgia chased the federal dollars given to expand prison capacity to keep pace with its rapidly growing prison population. In 1985, it had a prison population of 16,401, by 1994, it had doubled to 33,175. Georgia's Board of Pardons and Paroles in 1993, even before the most restrictive sentencing laws were passed, announced proudly that it was now able to stop its emergency release of prisoners, which they had done to avoid the federal over-crowding lawsuits that were filed against the other southern states. They were now free to build more prisons *and* reduce parole:

While other states are limited by court order or agreement as to how many inmates their prisons can hold, Georgia is increasing the number of prisoners while simultaneously reducing the number of releases. While the average time served for most offenses in other states is shrinking, offenders in Georgia are finding that they are serving more time.[1]

Much of this growth was financed by federal VOITIS (Violent Offender Incarceration/Truth in Sentencing) incentives—of which Georgia had received $82,211,036. By 2004, the prison population was 48,009.

However, national priorities began to reverse in 2000 when Attorney General Janet Reno started to emphasize the importance of reentry. She spoke passionately, compassionately, and pragmatically: "We are not going to end the culture of violence until we address this problem, the problem of prisoner reentry." During her watch as attorney general, she had been part of one of the most punitive periods in criminal justice and was beginning to observe, with concern, the broader social consequences of having imprisoned so many under harsh mandatory minimums. What she said then, still holds today.

They come into prison with rage, with a sense that they have been treated unfairly. They come into prison as dropouts or illiterate. They come into prison without life skills, without a job or an anticipated job. They come in with so little chance of getting off on the right foot, unless we do it the right way.

While in the prison they get new problems foisted on them, hate, they come to look at life as simply a matter of survival, and then with all these problems, they come out in too many instances without too much supervision and they come back to the very fragile communities from once they came.[2]

Now, following Reno's appeal, federal incentives turned toward reentry, and Georgia took advantage of those dollars as well. Because its prison population had grown so much, Georgia was the focus of three national reentry initiatives, from the National Institute of Corrections, the U.S. Department of Justice, (through the Serious and Violent Offender Re-entry Initiative (SAVORI), and the National Governor's Association, which they combined into one project: The Georgia Reentry Impact Project (GRIP). The Urban Institute also produced a comprehensive report on Georgia Reentry in 2004.[3] The strategies developed in those years still shape state reentry efforts and are well summarized in A.J. Sabree's article, "Georgia Reentry: A Transformation in Correctional Philosophy."[4]

However, even with its decade and a half of reentry activities and its recent eight-year criminal justice reform efforts, Georgia's prison population has continued to climb, although at a slower rate. Admissions have fallen by 17.37% between 2012 and 2019, from 21,402 to 17,693, but releases have decreased as well, from 19,623 to 18,030. In 2019 its inmate population was 53,216—still one of the highest in the nation. The racial disparity in 2019 was 59.8% black to 35.9% white, almost identical to what it was in 1978, but down from the 66% black in 2002. The proportion of violent offenders to nonviolent offenders within prisons has continued to grow, from 45% of the prison population in 2004 to 67.8% in 2019, and the number of gang-related offenders has grown by 156.5% between 2012 and 2019, from 5,609 to 14,386.

Annual reports now detail the rise in violence and suicides, escapes and assaults, the number of shakedowns for contraband, the drone detection systems, the work of the digital forensics unit. Outside observers also report on the levels of violence. The number of suicides in the past few years is about twice what would be expected in a prison population of this size. The 2019 annual report states that 20% of offenders have mental health diagnoses and that they have implemented Special Mental Health Treatment Units for people with severe persistent mental illness with a history of assault.

The amount of contraband gathered throughout the prisons is substantial, for example, in April and May 2019, 11,000 items were seized with the help of Tactical Squads and K9 units. These included 1,469 cell phones, 2,830 homemade weapons, 9,487 grams of marijuana, 2,695 grams of meth, and 3,586 syringes. Twenty-two shakedowns in nine of the thirty-four state prisons that quarter detected another 1,639 items. The 2019 year-end total of contraband seized for the whole system included $6,152,265, 5.75 kilos of heroin, 2,759 kilos of marijuana, and 148 kilos of methamphetamine.

In 2016, forty-six current and former prison guards were arrested in a federal sting operation for accepting bribes and smuggling contraband to inmates.[5] Our conversations with inmates indicated that this was common, and that the explanation was simple: money. In 2016, the only state in the country with lower starting salary for correctional officers was Mississippi. Educational requirements are minimal, a GED. The pay of Georgia corrections officers now ranks a few states above Mississippi with the 2017 state-wide raise for law enforcement officers. A starting correctional officer now makes $27,936; one at a close or special mission prison, $31,040. A behavioral health counselor 2 enters at $29,399, with a masters degree. A deputy warden with a GED and two years of supervisory experience can begin at $58,233.

In addition, the number of correctional staff is falling. In 2019, there were only 4,668 correctional officers for 53,216 inmates, compared to 6,794 officers to 52,704 inmates in 2011. In 2019, the turnover rate for correctional officers was 42%, with a vacancy rate of 21%. Because there is such difficulty finding addiction counselors, prison staff are trained and certified to serve these functions. Staff are also being trained for mental health and suicide awareness.

The medical system at DOC has been the object of numerous lawsuits, paying out over $3 million in settlements for negligence or malpractice in 2018 alone. Its psychological services are even worse. A recent review of the Special Management Unit (SMU) at the Georgia Diagnostic and Classification Prison, known as Jackson, often called the flagship of Georgia's prisons, was described by the prison authority Craig Haney in these terms:

> . . . one of the harshest and most draconian such facilities I have seen in operation anywhere in the country. . . . The conditions, practices, and procedures to which prisoners in the SMU are subjected are not only draconian in nature but are dangerous in effect. That is, the Georgia SMU so severely and completely deprives prisoners of meaningful social contact and positive environmental stimulation that it puts them at significant risk of very serious psychological harm. That psychological harm may be irreversible and even fatal.[6]

Men have been kept in cells that are 7 x 13.5 feet with no natural light for up to seven years with no sources of intellectual or sensory stimulation, allowed out of their cells only to exercise for an hour in metal cages the same size as their cells. The only objects in their cells are a bed and toilet and, sometimes, a shower spigot. The window to the outside is covered with a metal plate, the window to the hallway is covered too. The most frequent duration of imprisonment there has been three to four years. Many of the men are seriously mentally ill. Of the forty-three men released in 2015-16, twenty-six left because their sentences ended, in other words, they were released directly into the community. A settlement with the Southern Center for Human Rights in 2018 now limits the amount of time someone can be kept in these conditions to two years, requires regular review, and permits access to sensory and intellectual stimulation such as tablets, email, music.

When we talk about reentry, all these statistics and conditions are part of what we mean. Reentry also means the positive results that are primarily associated with the return of educational and vocational programming to the system since 2016. There have been expanded efforts to provide high school equivalency diplomas to inmates under twenty-one through charter schools; and GEDs to other inmates, along with library services. In the last three years, over 8,000 inmates have earned GEDs. Forty different career and technical education programs are now offered through the system in coordination with Technical College System of Georgia. Inmates have responded very positively to these greater opportunities. Enrollment in the Career, Technical and Higher Education program grew from a monthly average of 3,749 in 2017 to 7,468 in 2019, with successful program completions rising from 6,090 to 18,659. With the help of a Second Chance Pell Pilot, 200 offenders have been able to enroll in accredited college classes as well. Volunteering, which ran about 8,000 during the tenures of Donald and Owens, fell to about 3,000 but has risen again to about 5,400 with the certification of 1,369 new volunteers.

Standard operating procedures are now in place that require that staff participate throughout an individual's imprisonment in facilitating reentry readiness, ensuring that they have a reentry plan in place, that the necessary identification documents are ready for them when they leave, whether they move into community supervision or max out. DOC has focused attention on getting documents needed for reentry, drivers' licenses, secure identity cards, birth certificates, and Social Security cards. An important practical step has been to create a documents repository of identification documents that are accessible to DCS and the Department of Labor as well. In 2019, the repository received over 23,000 birth certificates/Social Security cards for offenders being released, and well as 6,717 drivers' licenses or IDs.

Inmates are provided with a twenty-five page reentry skills handbook titled, "Reentry begins with you," designed to help them create their own personalized reentry plan, complete with a model job application form. Given the average reading level and work history of people leaving Georgia prisons, its level of detail seems optimistic. This booklet is available on the DOC and DCS websites.

THE COMMISSIONERS' VIEWS

The process by which the department arrived at this point that includes both clear reforms, which can improve reentry, and extensive hardening, which can make reentry more difficult, has been intentional and hard won. We talked with two of the retired commissioners most central to the effort of introducing reentry into the prison system as a sustained concern, General James Donald and Brian Owens, after they had left the department. Both went over to serve on the Board of Pardons and Paroles after their terms as commissioner. Together they had a sustained eleven years leading the Department of Corrections (Donald for three and Owens for eight)—an unusually long period of consistent leadership for this organization.

JAMES DONALD
CLARIFY THE MISSION

General James Donald was the first African American to lead the DOC. He said that when a woman asked him how he felt leading a prison system where 66% of those incarcerated were African American, he answered, "It probably makes me work harder." Although Donald himself would point to his efficiency as his greatest gift to corrections, what we feel Donald brought into the system, perhaps unintentionally, was an ability to see and respond to the men in prison as fully human. Chaplain Susan Bishop described how she felt a shiver run down her spine when she heard Donald refer to the inmates as "the sons and daughters of Georgia." She had never heard anyone speak of them that way. When this was shared with him years later, he mentioned that with the increase in white prosecution for drug crimes, now it was clear that it was *everybody's* sons and daughters we were talking about.

General Donald came from a family with a strong commitment to civil rights: his oldest brother Cleveland was the second African American to graduate from Old Miss, soon followed by their brother John, then by James Donald himself. Their father had served in the Army in World War II, and Donald joined ROTC as soon as he turned eighteen. He joined because "the military accepted us unequivocally." It had a clear structure, a clear mission, and was a genuine meritocracy, values that Donald would bring into corrections. Indeed the first thing you see in the annual reports from his tenure is a list of core values that reflect him and also his military training: Loyalty, duty, respect, selfless service, honor, integrity, personal courage.

Donald also brought in from the military a clear sense of the importance of having a career path. He, like Owens after him, worked to improve the professional qualifications of personnel, which were relatively low. He provided a 2% bonus for getting an associates degree, a 5% bonus for getting a bachelors. He began to require that wardens get a BA. He was clear that little or nothing would get done if you did not have the loyalty of your troops and he made a point of being in the field several days a week: *If you take care of the staff, the mission will be done. I never left a prison without talking to staff. As a leader you need to be there. You've got to talk to the troops, be in their heads.* He approached inmates the same way: *You look inmates in the eye in every prison. You know what to look for if you are talking and _listening_ to them.*

Before coming into corrections, General Donald had specialized in base realignment and closure, especially of bases in the Pacific and Asia. His expertise in this area was one of the reasons he was selected for the position in corrections. At that point, Georgia had built itself up to one hundred prisons, many of them smaller two-hundred-bed prisons situated in various parts of rural Georgia. These small prisons were politically popular, providing stable employment in economically distressed areas, but were inefficient to run. Donald eventually closed forty of them despite resistance from state legislators. He ran into similar resistance from the large firms that had a monopoly on prison commissaries when he opened them up for competitive bidding.

One distinction Donald made early, and one that, as he noted, seemed immediately to take hold in other areas but not in Georgia, was the difference between "those we are afraid of and those we are mad at." He strongly encouraged different responses to the two: *I pretty much coined this phrase and then it took off like wild fire. If we are afraid of them, then I support locking them up and indeed throwing away the key. But if we are just mad at them because they have a drug issue and they have been burglarizing our houses and wreaking havoc in the communities, there ought to be alternative ways of treating them. Now that got picked up, it was in the _Washington Post_, all over, but I did not hear it in*

Georgia. I would watch my colleagues cringe in law enforcement when I would say that. They were not embracing it—but when Governor Deal came in here and started saying the same thing, oh, it was like, my God, where have you been!

Donald was a strong advocate of the new Day Reporting Centers as an effective alternative sentencing response to those we are mad at. What he liked most about these centers was that they kept individuals in the community and lowered recidivism: *The goal was to treat the problem not the symptom. If a guy is acting out and having problems, why are we taking him from his family, his community, his support, his children that are now going to be cast into a welfare situation because he was smoking dope or using some meth? In most cases he has a job. We take him out of that job, putting him behind the wire for sixty or ninety days, and he comes back, his job is gone, his kids are on welfare, it just didn't make sense. This day reporting center allowed him to keep his job, work in the community. We put them in metropolitan areas, in high crime areas, where the people live. So he could catch the bus, but he was required to report there every morning, and every other morning we would drug test him. When he first got there we put him into some intensive programming to deal with his addiction. When we compared the recidivism rate for somebody coming out of the prison system and someone graduating from this program, it was like night and day. Coming out of prison, recidivism was like 27% recidivism over the first three years, 65% over a lifetime. But from the Day Reporting Center it was like 7%.*

A pragmatist, Donald saw employment as key to reentry: "The fastest way to rehabilitate someone is to get the guy a job." Consequently, he was proud of how he began to match transitional centers to large employers in difficult industries to staff, like poultry processing. In 2007, when Crider Poultry lost two-thirds of its work force to ICE raids, Donald, meeting with Governor Deal and the owner Billy Crider offered to immediately fill the gap with inmate labor: *Billy comes, "Gov, I don't know what I am going to do, I am about to lose my business, and you know when I lose my business all those mom and pop chicken houses down the road, they lose their businesses too. Governor, I am hurting. You've got to help me, these feds had done me wrong."*

What we did, is, we changed the mission of the detention center that was in the community they were in. We moved out all of those inmates that had long terms left, and we moved in all the inmates who were transitioning home and needed a job. In the first year alone Billy Crowder paid into inmate accounts $14 million, in the first year of plucking chickens, cutting them up, all of that. They loved it, because they had a guarantee, if the guy didn't want to work, then we *sent him back to prison. But who is not going to work? Because Billy was paying them $8 an hour, his Hispanic laborers, and I made sure he paid our guys the same pay, and an extra dollar if they showed up. The next week, after we got it up in operation, the folks down in Claxton Poultry heard about it and they called me in down there and said we got to have one, so we did the same thing there.*

Drawing on his military experience, Donald saw his job as identifying the core mission of the organization and sticking to it, relying on other groups to do the others subsidiary missions, preferably at no direct cost. In the case of DOC, the mission was the cost-effective, efficient running of prisons. He encouraged privatization because these private companies assumed the cost of building the prisons and also of pension plans for the employees. (Two of the for-profit prisons, Riverbend and Coffee, have regularly been mentioned to us by inmates and people working in reentry as the cleanest and most effective ones in the Georgia system.)

He viewed faith-based prison volunteers primarily in this light: "8,000 volunteers we pay nothing to serve God." Faith and character dorms were a way of increasing the quality of incarceration through positive peer influence, which involved no extra programming or labor costs. To some extent he viewed day reporting and work-release in the same way—reentry too. Recidivism was costly and directly affected the core mission.

Donald, in his push toward professionalism, also militarized DOC, creating highly armed CERT teams to go into prisons to look for contraband, or to reassert order. These were negatively portrayed in the National Geographic video series, *Hard Times*, although Donald strongly defended them. He did acknowledge that transparency, including the use of cameras, was key, and that self-criticism was especially difficult in the military, and in corrections, and needed to be actively encouraged by those in command.

BRIAN OWENS
SEAMLESS TRANSITION— REFINING THE ASSEMBLY LINE

Brian Owens has an intellectual interest in criminal justice, but emphasized that he did not come from a family that valued education, so whether it was his own interest or his family's disinterest that was unusual could alternate depending on the company he was in. He did, however, return often to the importance of education for changing your chances in life. It helped with the big picture, which was what intrigued him. When he entered parole, he became interested in theory and found himself working on a theory of parole that would combine and apply social learning, routine opportunities (suitable target, motivation, lack of capable guardianship), and deterrence theories. Like many in parole, he rose by working in demanding South Fulton. Later, when talking about challenges of reentry he returned to this experience, especially the importance of environment: *I learned quickly as a parole officer I would rather have a lifer as my client compared to some twenty-two-year-old drug slinger, young, uneducated, raised in poverty, raised in projects. I was amazed that anybody twenty-five years ago could make it out of the projects, everything was stacked against you. There were no other adults around who were pro-social.*

When Jim Wetherington moved from chair of the Parole Board to become commissioner of Corrections in 1999, Owens moved with him. He was handed the Friday report, a weekly report of about thirty pages of statistics, with the suggestion that he become expert in a particular area. So, he became expert in prison statistics. Responsible for doing prison population predictions, he ended up speaking frequently with governors and legislators who were now objecting to the growth because the cost was becoming apparent.

What Owens was proudest of were his achievements that emphasized the big picture but also took care of the micro. From projections he turned his attention to how to make the entry process into the prisons more efficient: *There are approximately 70,000 felon cases a year in GA, with about 49,000 with felony probation and the rest incarcerated. Forty-nine judicial circuits, a little over two hundred Superior Court judges, not using the same sentencing guidelines and with different cultures, with Georgia having probably the widest sentencing guidelines of any state, and similar offenses get very different sentences. For example, if you break into a shed and steal, your sentence could go from probation in Atlanta, where its not seen as a big deal, to twenty years in farm country. Which means no predictability in the prison population. Getting good data is very important for getting some certainty, predictability. We were receiving 21,000 sentencing packages, handwritten, just five years ago. Most systems were like that. Seventy clerks working in the office. But in the technological world it is all about speed.*

We broke down the whole system into all the steps, looking at it and asking, "How can we speed up each of these steps?" We mathematically modeled it. 140+ county jails with inmates waiting to come into the state system. The delays in processing were costing the state $25 million a year. So what can we do to speed it *up?* Then *it was taking two or three months to get from jail to the diagnostic center and another two months to get to prison. This was a great success: my last year as commissioner we paid county jails zero.*

In much of his time at Corrections, Owens methodically implemented the major recommendations developed by the Georgia Reentry Impact Project, all of which involved improving the collection, analysis, and dissemination of data. The most important of these for reentry was the development of COMPAS (Correctional Offender Management Profiling for Alternative Sanctions), which was needed in order to establish an inmate's risk/need/responsivity classification. During our conversation, Owens went to his computer to show how the system could help him now in his parole decisions. The program automatically determined what courses and treatment an inmate would need to receive before leaving prison to address his dominant risk factors, such as substance abuse, educational deficits, mental health. It also identified any potential problems with reentry, for example, not having housing, family support, having sex offender limitations. It kept a record of an inmate's entire prison history, disciplinary reports, changes in risk status. This was the program that provided Melanie Barker, the prison in-reach specialist in community supervision, the information she needed to develop the reentry plans for high-risk releases.

The phrase *seamless transition* used by Janet Reno in 2000, and still reused as a mantra in almost any discussion about the institutional goals of reentry, can also be visualized, as Owens seemed to, as a well-working assembly line. Indeed, he had talked with people in industry to see how they refined efficiency: *Today all sentencing documents are standardized and electronic, received from the courts by Corrections within twenty-four hours of sentencing. Now inmates get to diagnostics within fifteen days, and then from there to prison within fifteen days. Programming matches risks and needs. Every time an entry is made on the offender, the assessment automatically updates. You can be in a medium-security prison and wake up with your risk reassigned.*

Owens also likened the incarceration process to going to college: *Prosecutors have a key role: some 90-95% of cases are pled. With an average sentence of about sixty months, thirty months will be served on average. So you can look at incarceration like going to college: the first year (or nine months) you're getting acclimatized; in the second stage, you really start the learning process, you get a GED or a high school diploma through the charter school; in the third year, you're a junior and focus on vocation, diesel mechanics, welding, a CDL; in the fourth year, it's transition center, work release. Just work release alone reduces recidivism 11%.* What Owens left out was that transition centers only have the capacity to house 12% of the number of people released each year. This problem of scarcity, sometimes mentioned, sometimes not, qualified many of the improvements being set in place.

While Donald felt that employment was especially important for reentry, Owens was influential in getting the faith and character dorms started in prisons. He expanded the program to different prisons, including making one prison, Walker, a faith and character prison. In these dorms and prison, inmates spend two years in the program, then either transition out of the prison system or continue their incarceration in another prison. Programming is provided by volunteers or by participants themselves. Owens was also influential in getting New Orleans Baptist Seminary programming into the prisons—again on a volunteer basis, at no cost to Corrections.

Two areas of programming that Owens felt were especially important, indeed they were the only non-volunteer programming in the prisons during the 2000s, were cognitive-behavioral and substance abuse treatment—in part because these were the only ones that met the evidence-based criteria needed for legitimacy. These classes also addressed what are considered the major criminogenic factors, "stinking thinking" and addiction. In general, except for substance abuse treatment, prisoners only received programming in their last year or eighteen months, and only based on their risk level. Many of the men we talked to who had been imprisoned after 1994 on mandatory minimums had received no programming throughout their incarceration. If there was vocational training, they were limited to one course a sentence, and it was seen as a coup to be able in one way or another to maneuver the system enough to be able to train in two skills.

One area that clearly concerned Owens was mental health and substance abuse. He was strongly supportive of Katrinka Glass's effort to increase the number and professional training of substance abuse counselors, of which there were very few in the state as a whole, by partnering with Mercer University. Corrections financially subsidized the training. He was also practical about trying to get adequate mental health services. Finding that few mental health professionals wanted to work in prisons, he encouraged officers who already had that interest to make it their focus: *Once a person with mental illness gets in the system, they can never escape the system. That's why we put mental health counselors in every probation office, did the mental health and drug courts, integrated treatment facilities, expanded day reporting centers, and day center lites in rural areas—to try to keep them from being engaged in the hard criminal justice system. Let's work on the disease in the community rather than the symptom, which is crime. The disease is addiction and mental illness. The crime is what they commit. We used to lump everybody together and you all go to prisons. In rural areas, they don't have the resources to treat, so they put people in prison. But if you put resources down there, the judges will do something different, and they are now.*

When he was preparing to move from second in command to first, Owens was offered the services of a leadership coach, a turn-around specialist. The coach emphasized to Owens that leaders think about people and processes. In Corrections, Owens amended, it is people, processes, and infrastructure. These became his favored categories for analyzing his management strategies and accomplishments.

Owens's first actions when he became commissioner were to improve the educational qualifications of staff: *Believe it or not, when I took over as commissioner, you didn't even have to have a high school diploma to be a warden. What company, like Jackson, has 600 employees, a $35 million budget and your CEO is a high school graduate?* In his first term, he mandated wardens earn a BA within four years; in his second term, he raised requirements to an MA.

Attending to processes often involved responding to the unintended consequences of various laws and policies, consequences that often depended on scale: *It seems very easy, if I just add a year or two years, or a mandatory two years on this particular offense, that's not going to affect a big prison system of 65,000 inmates and a 1.2 billion dollar budget, but it does. Anytime you multiply by 25,000 a year, which is your prison admissions, it has a big impact either negatively or positively.*

A particular concern in this way were mandatory minimums and the challenge this group posed: *Seven deadly sinners, young men typically, who come in on armed robbery are a totally different problem from the college degree model. Seventeen year olds don't do crimes by themselves, so you don't get one, you get four, you get the lookout guy, the one just driving along smoking dope, you get the driver, and the one with the gun. When I was there, we had 9,000 deadly sins. They've got nothing to benefit them if they go along with the system. They are going do to their ten years to the door no matter how well they behave.*

We got a law passed that the commissioner could put seven deadly sins inmates in transitional centers for their last twelve months. That is a huge risk for the commissioner if they were to commit another crime. I voted yes in 1994 on the seven deadly sins, but ten years later I felt like a fool—so I felt an obligation to try to change it a little bit. So my way to change it as a commissioner was to put some seven deadlies in a transitional center. All downside for me personally, you understand. You throw one of these kids, they're now twenty-seven, completely unsocialized, and you put them in a transitional center and you let them work and they commit a horrible crime—"Well why did you let him out?" But from a policy perspective it was the right thing to do. A favorite quote of mine is from Tennyson: "Knowledge comes but wisdom lingers." Once I got a little more wise, I realized that law was bad and I could affect it by the transitional centers.

One important consequence of the criminal justice reforms was the movement to decrease the number of nonviolent offenders committed to prisons: *Now only 7% are coming in for nonviolent offenses—which I think is good policy but it means you have to change your people, processes, and infrastructure. I saw criminal justice reform happening but didn't know that shift would be as drastic as going from 27% nonviolent down to 7%.*

This shift in population meant that they needed to start concentrating on the gangs they were bringing into prison, or that were originating in prison, which are a major source of within-prison violence: *The two major gangs are the Goodfellas and the Ghostface Gangsters. The Goodfellas—seven brothers, believe it or not, started it. They got caught. They knew they were going to jail. They got so brazen that they would put GF on their cheekbones. They started a protection racket at the Fulton jail: you join the Goodfellas and whatever prison you get sent to, we'll protect you when you're there. That's where the Hays problem started. We didn't see that one coming, but we reacted to it. I think I'm currently still being sued because I locked every Goodfellas down. I just stopped it. And if they could prove they were not part of the gang, I let them out, and I let them back out into the system one by one. They're the ones making the shanks, doing the extortion.*

And the other group is the Ghostface Gangsters. They are a very vicious white group that actually started in the prison system and now has tentacles on the outside. When you hear about the people calling from prison—"I'm so and so and I'm going to beat your son unless you send me a thousand dollars, here's a picture of him"—typically the son is in on it. So they run extortion and hits in the Georgia prison system. Those are the dangerous ones, so you have got to have good intel. That's another thing we did was create a unit of six to eight professionals who did nothing but work intelligence.

Gangs are even more of a concern now several years later. Gangs are now called, in corrections jargon, security threat groups, or STGs. In 2019, gang members, numbering 14,386, were 27% of the prison population. Of the eight gangs identified, Bloods (4,686), Gangster Disciples (4,051), Crips (1,373), and Ghostface Gangsters (1,164) had the greatest membership. DOC is imbedding "gang professionals" in twenty-eight prisons and also starting a pilot Identity Reformation program, a support group for gang-affiliated offenders in Hancock Prison, one of its evidence-based prisons.

For infrastructure, Owen's interest was in the hardening of many of the facilities, especially in maximum security: *Infrastructure is the most expensive to change. But when you have Ghostface Gangsters or Goodfellas that are constantly at war with each other on the streets of Atlanta—and they are coming in as seventeen year olds with a ten, fifteen, or twenty-year sentence—you better have the infrastructure to be able to hold them. So we started on hardening. Very expensive. Remember Corrections has three billion dollars worth of infrastructure. So we started from the inside of the cell out and from the outside of the fence in. I'm not giving anything away because the inmates know it now. We took our close security prisons, which hold our bad actors, we have eight of them, and we stripped everything out of the cell. We took the beds that used to be just bunk beds, we took real heavy grade steel and bolted them to the walls. Heater vents, heavy duty. Light fixtures, heavy duty. Got rid of porcelain commodes, put in stainless steel commodes. Put in totally new locking mechanisms. Totally new technology. Don't give them the opportunity to make a shank. We completed by my term all the close security facilities. More capital dollars, bonds, than ever before. But the governor gave us the capital. He would rather have spent it on schools, but he knew what was going on in the prison system—we were getting tougher inmates.*

When asked about the Special Management Units (SMUs), especially the incarceration of specific inmates who had been in there for four or more years, Owens insisted that programming was available, justified the use of use of handcuffs and being shackled to a desk during programming as evidence-based, and insisted that people could work their way out in eighteen months to two years if they just followed procedures.

It's not really like what you're reading. Some advocates want you to believe that. They have a television in there, or they may. There's a shower in there. It's not like Florence, Colorado, the federal high max. And every day, if you behave, you come out for programming. And we start you in a module which is basically steel, and they are stacked in a semi-circle, because these are dangerous guys. There are only 200 of them in the whole prison system out of 50,000. These are the killers of staff and of inmates, high ranking gang members, dangerous inmates. When you get to high max, you are given instructions on how you can work your way out. So after you serve six months where you are let out every day, but you are escorted to a rec pen, then we start programming you, cognitive, research-based programming. Everything the system does is evidence-based, not like the old days. Those days are gone. Start out in a module, then you graduate to an old school desk set up attached to the floor. You're in handcuffs, so you can't hurt anybody. Then you graduate to just handcuffs. Then by the time you graduate everything, you're downgraded and moved to different facility and general population. Which is the way you can work yourself out. It takes eighteen months to two years. Now some people never leave High Max, ever, ever. They are just too dangerous. And they refuse programming. Well, that's on them. There is a way you can work your way out. That's only 200 beds of 50,000.

Owens included programming as one of the processes that needed attention, even in lockdown: *So you harden the prison system, you make sure you have educated wardens, and constantly look at your processes. Like high max. So instead of locking up Little B [see below] for two years without programming, we said. All right, if you behave you get television, but we're going to control the channels. We're going to put tablets in our lock beds, where you can get educational materials and even emails (we look at them before they get out). Even in lockdown we put them in there. Harden up these facilities for these bad boys, but also don't let their minds rot.*

However, three years later, all these sources of stimulation Owens mentioned were absent for many of the people that Haney observed and were reintroduced only by the legal settlement. Little B, who at age thirteen had been sentenced to adult prison in 1997, at the height of the predator child/tough on crime era, had already been in High Max for over four years, by some accounts labeled a gang member only because he urged a work slowdown to protest work and prison conditions.[7]

Owens felt Governor Deal, with his dedication to reentry and criminal justice reform, had followed the same strategy of getting the right people in to drive criminal justice reform processes and institutionalize change through legislation in a way that it would make it much harder for the pendulum to shift back. Similarly, Owens used data systems to institutionalize certain kinds of change and cross-agency communication. The Scribe program, for example, makes all the information in corrections available to probation officers, while standard operating procedures for reentry all rely on COMPAS information, especially the TAP plans that follow an individual from the day he enters Jackson Diagnostic through to community supervision or max out.

Owens, like many people with a community supervision background, saw early prevention as key: *Do all you want with prisons and community supervision, but you have got to get them between third and eighth grade—every penny you invest between third and twelfth grade is going to pay for itself in criminal justice costs avoided. Reading at third grade is predictive.*

He described how he had paid attention to a program begun at Southwire in West Georgia, the company that participated in the earlier Take 5 program administered by Sabree, which hired returning citizens. Southwire dropped out of Take 5 but in 2007 independently developed a program, Twelve for Life, in partnership with the local high school, to help prevent prison entry. The school had very high dropout rates. Southwire built a warehouse and moved their safest processes to it and offered the school district employment for students at highest risk of dropping out—on the condition that they stayed in school. Owens took a similar approach to the local high school near Tift College in central Georgia, where DOC administrative offices are located, bringing in a number of high school students in danger of dropping out to work in the offices, with the same educational conditions.

Owens thought in general people had no idea how very complex prison operations are: *Good-hearted, well-intentioned people think they know how to fix the criminal justice system, but the criminal justice system like any other profession on the surface looks easy, but it is a <u>complicated</u> business with many constituents: eighteen members of the board, 136 members of General Assembly, all the DAs, all the judges, the governor and his staff, <u>and they are all your boss</u>. Because we are <u>all</u> experts in criminal justice. The biggest challenge is the sheer complexity of it.*

He was clear that prisons are essentially about control and that expectations of transparency or accountability need to conform to that reality: *The mission of a prison system is to hold prisoners and to keep them away from society. That is mission number one of any prison anywhere. Nine thousand faith-based volunteers, that is transparency. Having professionals going in to do programming, that is transparency. A comprehensive audit system to make sure there are no abuses, one that media can get through open records, that is transparency.*

He used another language to ground his own complex responses: *I am of the philosophy that prison is punishment, losing your freedom is punishment;*

being in prison itself should not be. Every person is a child of God, every inmate, and should be treated as so. I believe that to my core. I read someplace that if you could bring back leaders of the nineteenth century and asked them their greatest policy failure as a nation, certainly it was slavery; I got thinking about it for the twentieth century and it is mass incarceration. I have another core belief: It didn't happen on purpose, there isn't a prison-industrial complex, instead lots of unintended consequences. That is our biggest sin.

HOMER BRYSON, GREGORY DOZIER, TIMOTHY C. WARD
HARDENING PRISONS & EXPANDING REENTRY

From 2015 to 2020, there were three DOC commissioners, Homer Bryson, Gregory Dozier, and Timothy C. Ward. Bryson came from the Department of Natural Resources, in particular park management, and lasted a year, then became director of Georgia Emergency Management and the Homeland Security Agency. Dozier, an effective career bureaucrat who worked as an assistant commissioner to both Owens and Bryson after heading the Department of Motor Vehicles, left to become the state's chief financial officer in Governor Kemp's new administration, and is now commissioner of the Technical College System of Georgia. Ward has spent his entire professional career in DOC, moving up from prison guard to counselor to warden to assistant commissioner of facilities.

As the numbers that opened this chapter show, the public focus of DOC during the last few years, as seen in its annual reports, has been on its substantial, expanding accomplishments with reentry. However, during this time problems with gangs, contraband and violence have increased, and the prisons have been substantially hardened, contributing to the physical conditions described by Haney. Staff retention and quality are a serious problem.

COMMON SENSE REFORM: CAN IT APPLY TO GEORGIA?

It doesn't cost much to treat people with respect. . . . It doesn't cost that much to care.
Janet Reno

Two progressive practitioners have particularly influenced our thinking about incarceration and reentry: Dennis Luther and Dora Schriro. We encountered Luther's *28 Beliefs About the Treatment of Inmates* early in our reading, and Dora Schriro's award winning Getting Ready program and the establishment of a "Parallel Universe" in the Arizona Department of Corrections toward the end of our writing (following up on something Brian Owens said in his interview). Both of these successful practitioners have influenced us because their suggestions are at the same time radical and just common sense.

LUTHER: 28 BELIEFS

Luther was a progressive warden of a federal prison in the 1990s, just before the get-tough-on-crime backlash. In the six years he spent as warden at McKean Federal Correctional Institution there were no escapes, murders, or suicides and only three serious assaults against staff and six against inmates. Luther summarized his approach in his *28 Beliefs*.[8] The first of these was echoed by Owens: Inmates are sent to prison *as* punishment, not *for* punishment. In other words, after incarceration, the rest is reentry. This is the essence of his second belief, one that is simple and also world reversing: *Correctional workers have a _responsibility_ to ensure that inmates are returned to the community no more angry or hostile than when they were committed.* His other core belief was that staff must show, not tell, consistently modeling the respectful behavior that they want to see.

When these ideas were brought up with Owens, he mentioned that it was difficult, not to mention unrealistic, to think a single correctional guard could adequately model prosocial behavior for a hundred or two hundred inmates.

However, Luther's beliefs have formed the foundation of the strongly rehabilitative emphasis of the Oregon Department of Corrections, where staff/inmate interactions are a core part of their model. Oregon insists that part of the job of the correctional staff is to create a learning environment, where staff are expected to consistently practice the three Rs: act as role models, reinforce positive behaviors and redirect negative ones. This reciprocal real-world approach permeates their attitude toward work, which is compensated, and the emphasis on maintaining family ties. They refer to inmates as AICs, Adults in Custody. On their website they show photos of staff and AICs having lunch together, something that is difficult to imagine in a Georgia prison.

Schriro: Parallel Universe

Another very promising program took place in the Arizona Department of Corrections during the period when Dora Schriro was commissioner. Called Getting Ready, it's central idea, "a parallel universe," has the same shocking simplicity as Luther's leaving no angrier than when you came in. It is simply that the incentives in the prison system need to align with the incentive structure in the world outside the prison. "We operate our prisons like the real world as much as we can with similar rules, responsibilities, and rewards."[9] This was a shift that did not require additional funds, only a mind shift. The program focused on three facets of inmate life: school or work, structured self-improvement, and community betterment. The jobs that the world rewards, and the skills and education required for them, become the most important ones in the prison as well. The rules in the prison matched the rules in the outside world, behavior that wasn't criminal there wasn't criminal inside the prison. An interesting dimension of this program was its focus on victims, allowing prisoners to participate in various efforts to raise money for victim groups and in other ways begin to address society's need to see some efforts at restoration, something that is often missing in reentry efforts.

The phrase "parallel universe" began to show up in the Georgia graphic for its reentry handbook somewhere around 2014, but applied only to the transitional centers. What is important about Schriro's idea is that this parallel universe is not created, indeed it can't be created, in the last year or two of a ten, or twenty, or thirty-year sentence. It must be there from the beginning, not just as a promise and as an opportunity, but as a realized environment, one that reflects the values of the larger world.

Georgia prisons in the last ten years with the re-introduction of programming are beginning to create a parallel universe, especially with programming that has real world credentialing. However, that programming needs to take in real world constraints—if no one will hire someone with a criminal background to perform a particular skill, training in it while in prison breeds false hope.

Paying inmates real-world wages for real-world work is an important way of creating a parallel universe. Georgia is the only prison system in the country that does not pay inmates for work—whether in the prisons, in its prison industries, or for work in counties and municipalities, work which saves those entities millions of dollars. The only program for which there appears to be any kind of prisoner reimbursement, part of the federally subsidized prison industries enhancement program (PIE), involved producing 5,000 cuff ports "robust enough to withstand the rigors of prison life" for the South Carolina DOC to use to harden its prisons. This failure to compensate prisoners for the real-world work they do in real-world terms clearly creates a sense of exploitation on the part of inmates and has been the central grievance for several prison strikes. It is also a lost opportunity for the department to develop institutional trust. All work done by inmates in a prison should be compensated if we are to create a world-worthy continuum. A simple first step would be for all the municipalities in Georgia that make use of uncompensated prison labor and proudly announce the amount of money they have saved—for example Hall County, reform-minded Governor Nathan Deal's home county, which announced it had received $2.5 million in unpaid prison labor in 2013 alone—to equally proudly list by name and in prominent public view the names of each man and woman whose labor provided that subsidy. Given the refusal to compensate prison labor, DOC's $5 charge for inmate medical consults, especially during the 2020 pandemic, is unjustifiable and can only be seen as a surcharge on the families of inmates.

Lerman: The Modern Prison Paradox

It feels like a bifurcated approach is here to stay in Georgia prisons. As Owens pointed out, the prison population will continue to grow, and grow more violent, not because crime is increasing but because we are diverting some people from prison and keeping other people in for longer times. However, the moral justice of reentry is also here to stay, so reentry efforts will continue as well. The question is whether discussing reentry mainly in terms of the 40% of nonviolent inmates while at the same time creating a more punitive and deprived environments for the 60% (and growing) of inmates convicted of violent crimes, we are actually making ourselves safer. After twenty years in a "hardened" prison, what will *their* vision of society be, and their idea of right relationship with it?

Amy Lerman studies this phenomenon in her interesting and disturbing book *The Modern Prison Paradox,* which looks at the same process in California prisons. An important point she makes is that the people who are most vulnerable in this situation are those people in for a violent crime who are relatively low on the risk scale. They are the ones whose social modeling in the prison will be most adversely affected by increased hardening. Lerman describes the development of an alternative universe in the face of violence:

> *strategic social connections are formed, as individuals band together for mutual protection and exchange. However, the social ties forged in prison ultimately foster social norms that are anathema to broad-based, cooperative community engagement.[10]*

The tendency in Georgia to harshly punish crimes such as robberies and burglaries, crimes often done by juveniles or young men, sending them all to prison as a group for long periods, with few incentives to sustain prosocial behavior and many incentives not to, leads to the creation of a different kind of parallel universe, one that should concern us, one that we are actually seeing now that gangs of young men comprise nearly a third of the prison population.

This experience can be as damaging to the officers as it is to the inmates, as Lehrman writes:

> *Among correctional officers, as among inmates, the subjective experience of prison was characterized by intense and nearly constant concerns about physical violence, a sense that the public was both unaware and indifferent to their suffering, and a feeling that there was no one advocating for or protecting them.[11]*

We do need to ask: What will, really, make us safer as a society? Certainly not putting people through experiences that no one believes makes them better people and then releasing them, further damaged, to our care as a community. In 2019 Georgia Department of Corrections released 18,030 people with 16,251 dependents. As a society, who do we want those dependent children to be welcoming? As social psychologist Craig Haney wrote in *Reforming Punishment*, "recognizing the power of the prison context to so effectively shape behavior represents a strong argument in favor of making correctional environments as much like the free world as possible."

Perhaps it begins with something simple, to ask ourselves, and keep asking ourselves, what would I feel like if I or someone I hold dear were in this position, what would feel fair, responsible, hopeful? This attitude is at the heart of both Schriro's "Parallel Universe" and Luther's *28 Beliefs*. Maybe we can start by applying Luther's second belief to everyone: As a society it is our reponsibility to make sure people return from prison no angrier, and preferably more hopeful, than they were when they entered, whatever position they find themselves in: inmate, correctional officer, commissioner, chaplain, volunteer, family visitor.

Endnotes

1. State of Georgia Board of Pardons and Paroles. *Annual Report Fiscal Year 1993.*
2. United States Department of Justice. "Remarks of the Honorable Janet Reno on Reentry Court Initiative" John Jay College of Criminal Justice. 10 Feb 2000.
3. N. G. LaVigne and C. A. Mamalian. *Prisoner Reentry in Georgia.* Urban Institute, November 2004.
4. A. J. Sabree, "Georgia Reentry: A Transformation in Correctional Philosophy. *Corrections Today.* 1 Dec 2007: 80-86.
5. R. Cook, "46 Georgia prison guards sentenced for transporting drugs." *Atlanta Journal-Constitution* [AJC]. 16 Aug 2017.
6. "Expert Report and Declaration of Professor Craig Haney." U. S. District Court for the Middle District of Georgia, *Gumm v. Sellars.*
7. E. Brown, "Free Little B;" *The Condemnation of Little B.* Beacon Press, 2002.
8. D. Luther, "28 Beliefs About the Treatment of Inmates." *Connections to Corrections.* VI, 2 (2013), p. 11. Also see D. Holmstrom, "A Warden's Respect Unlocks a Prison." *Christian Science Monitor.* 21 Jul 1992; and R. Worth, "A Model Prison," *The Atlantic.* November 1995.
9. D. Schriro, "Getting Ready: How Arizona Has Created a 'Parallel Universe' for Inmates." National Institute of Justice. June 2009. Also see: Oregon Department of Corrections, "The Oregon Accountability Model" and "Correctional Case Management;" S. M. McCann, "Program Helps Prisoners Get Ready for Real Life," *Christian Science Monitor.* 31 Jul 2008; and M. Wilson, "Oregon Prison Industry Program Nets Record $28.5 Million as Prisoners Earn $1.25/Hour," *Prison Legal News.* April 2019.
10. A. E. Lerman, *The Modern Prison Paradox: Politics, Punishment, and Social Community.* Cambridge University Press, 2013. p.197.
11. C. Haney, *Reforming Punishment: Psychological Limits to the Pains of Imprisonment.* American Psychological Association, 2006, p. 308.

Additional Sources

Georgia Department of Corrections
DOC Annual Reports, 1999-2019
DOC Impact Reports
DOC Annual Statistical Reports
DOC Contraband Arrest Reports
DOC FACT SHEETS 2019
DOC Standard Operating Procedures: Reentry Pre- and Post-Release Planning, 2020
Georgia Department of Audits and Accounts, *"State Corrections and Community Officers: Requested Information on Salaries and Other Personnel Costs Special Examination."* 2013.
"Reentry Begins with You." Reentry Skills Handbook 2019

Georgia Prison Conditions
Solitary Confinement
Southern Center for Human Rights [SCHR], "Georgia Prisoners Reach Settlement to Reform One of the 'Harshest and Most Draconian' Solitary Confinement Units in the Nation." 9 Jan 2019.

Suicide & Medical
M. Blau, "Georgia's prisons face troubling rise in suicides. What are officials doing about it?" *The Telegraph.* 11 Aug 2019.

R. Cook, "Georgia sees another rash of inmate suicides." *AJC.* 27 Jun 2018.

D. Robbins, "Prison hospital doctor resigns, cites security, patient care concerns." *AJC.* 28 Jan 2018.

D. Robbins, "Deaths this year at Pulaski State Prison revive concerns that the state is failing to provide adequate medical care for its female inmates." *AJC.* 13 Dec 2019.

Violence
D. Reutter. "Violence, Security Lapses, and Media Attention Lead to Reforms at Georgia Prison." *Prison Legal News.* February 2014.

J. L. Smith. "Georgia Georgia's Hays State Prison sees exodus of guards; violence feared when inmate lockdown ends." *Chattanooga Times Free Press [CTFP] CTFP.* 30 Jun 2013.

J. L. Smith. "Lawsuit Filed In Killing of Hays State Prison Inmate." SCHR. 5 Sep 2013.

SCHR, "The Crisis of Violence in Georgia's Prisons." July 2014.

Corruption
R. Cook, "46 Georgia prison guards sentenced for transporting drugs," *AJC.* 16 Aug 2017.

Prison Wages
A. Crisp, Adam. "Georgia Inmates Strike In Fight For Pay." *CTFP.* 14 Dec 2010.

W. Sawyer, "How much do incarcerated people earn in each state?" *Prison Policy Initiative.* 10 Apr 2017.

S. Wheaton, "Prisoners Strike in Georgia," *New York Times.* 12 Dec 2010.

⟨5⟩

GEORGIA CRIMINAL JUSTICE REFORMS
HOW FAR WE HAVE COME, WHAT'S LEFT TO BE DONE

A decade ago Georgia sharply reversed course from being arguably the most punitive state in the union. Under Governor Nathan Deal, Georgia earned recognition as one of the states in the forefront of criminal justice reform, indeed, the title of an early 2015 *New Republic* article declared it "the country's most successful prison reform."[1] As indicators of this national role, other leaders of the state reform were appointed to the Chuck Colson Task Force mandated by Congress to recommend changes in federal corrections policy, the prestigious Harvard Executive Sessions, and the Board of Directors of the Council of State Governments Justice Center.

In this chapter we describe the major reforms of the Deal era after a quick review of the reforms of his recent predecessors. A third section highlights the most important factors that explain Georgia's accomplishments: economic pressures, evidence and networks, and leadership. As impressive as these many accomplishments have been, however, they fell far short of adequately addressing either the drivers of mass incarceration or the consequent reentry needs, as the concluding section will point out. Compounding these shortcomings have been the policies of the subsequent administration, one whose rhetoric is more akin to that of the "tough-on-crime" period and whose actions have pulled back from some of the Deal-era reforms, indeed, even eliminating some.

CRIMINAL JUSTICE PRIORITIES OF PRIOR GOVERNORS

There were a variety of criminal justice reform efforts in Georgia prior to the Deal administration, although certainly nothing as comprehensive or sustained. For example, Governor Jimmy Carter (1971-1975) created a Department of Offender Rehabilitation, combining prisons, parole, and probation under one roof, and attempting to reorient policy toward rehabilitation and community corrections.[2] Among the opponents of these changes were many guards and administrators within the new department.[3]

Much of Georgia's most punitive criminal justice legislation was adopted in the mid-1990s under another Democratic governor, Zell Miller (1991-99). Miller proudly took credit for having increased Georgia's prison capacity by 85% by the end of his term in order to accommodate the increasing incarceration that followed these new laws.[4] His Corrections commissioner was Wayne Garner, who was remembered for his declaration that one-third of Georgia's prisoners "ain't fit to kill and I'll be there to accommodate them." Garner was also known for his searches for contraband without advance warning to prison officials, with one of these raids in 1996 reputedly leaving so many prisoners beaten and injured that it was termed a "blood bath."[5]

When Roy Barnes became governor (1999-2003), he promptly replaced Garner with Jim Wetherington, a reform-minded former police chief and Board of Pardons and Paroles member. He pushed Corrections in a different direction, promoting halfway houses, diversion centers and minimum-security detention facilities for nonviolent offenders. He also sounded the alarm that increasing incarceration numbers and an escalating Corrections budget were jeopardizing other priorities, such as education and healthcare.[6]

Republicans took control of the state government with the election of conservative businessman Sonny Perdue (2003-2011). He replaced Wetherington with James Donald, a retired Army general, who served for the next five years. Gen. Donald is credited as the originator of the now frequently repeated distinction between "prisoners that we're afraid of" and "those that we're mad at," the point being that they should be handled differently.[7] For those in prison he emphasized the importance of finding them opportunities to work before their release. People in Corrections working on reentry found him to be a strong supporter of their efforts: "he loved everything we were doing and it just blossomed."[8]

Nonetheless, the drivers of mass incarceration in Georgia remained in place. Consequently, the numbers incarcerated rose 16% across Perdue's tenure. The other half of the challenge facing Deal as he gained the governor's office in January 2011 was the severe budget strain remaining from the economic crisis that hit the country in late 2008.

CRIMINAL JUSTICE REFORM UNDER GOVERNOR DEAL

In March 2011 the Georgia General Assembly passed HB 265,

establishing the Special Council on Criminal Justice Reform for Georgians as well as a Special Joint Committee to consider the council's recommendations in the following session. The heads of the three branches of government shared appointing the council's members. From the beginning the council was co-chaired by Michael P. Boggs, the only original member still serving when the council terminated at the end of Deal's tenure. HB 265 tasked the council to:

❖ *Address the growth of the state's prison population, contain corrections costs and increase efficiencies and effectiveness that result in better offender management;*

❖ *Improve public safety by reinvesting a portion of the savings into strategies that reduce crime and recidivism; and*

❖ *Hold offenders accountable by strengthening community-based supervision, sanctions and services.*[9]

The council was so successful at its initial work that its role was then institutionalized. In May 2012 Deal issued an executive order extending its life and then the following year HB 349 gave the council statutory existence for five more years, now named the Georgia Criminal Justice Reform Council. The annual pattern began with the council creating its agenda in consultation with the governor's office, investigating those issues, and issuing a report with its analysis and recommendations.[10] That report created the legislature's major criminal justice agenda as it went into session. Many of these recommendations were passed into law, often by an overwhelming margin. Those that were unsuccessful were often picked back up by the Reform Council for further consideration, support building, and re-recommendation.

One example of how the Reform Council often did its work was the process behind its 2016 recommendations to strengthen the state's First Offender Act, the law that allows first-time offenders in certain cases to avoid conviction and a public record following successful completion of their sentence. The council appointed a special study committee to address the matter, made up of a range of stakeholders such as prosecutors, criminal defense attorneys, court clerks, and law enforcement. The committee presented its recommendations to the Reform Council, which then adopted them as its recommendations to the General Assembly.[11]

The Reform Council also served as a vehicle for departments of the state government to recommend reforms to the legislature. As one example, a set of recommendations in the 2016 report to reduce driver's license suspensions in certain cases as unnecessarily punitive from a reentry perspective followed from a presentation by the Department of Driver Services that included those recommendations.[12] Having the proposal as part of the set of reforms proposed in the council's annual report enhanced the visibility and importance of the department's suggestion while having the department bring the original recommendation enhanced the legitimacy of the council's recommendation. Undoubtedly in many of such cases there had been prior informal collaboration between the council and the department in question.

The Reform Council's efforts focused on three general areas: adult reform, juvenile reform, and reentry. Although annual legislative action proceeded in the same sequence over the first three years, they can most effectively be discussed here by beginning with juvenile justice reform.

JUVENILE JUSTICE REFORM

Georgia spends a lot of money on juvenile justice—in some years more than a quarter of that spent on adult corrections. The Reform Council found that almost two-thirds of the Department of Juvenile Justice pre-reform budget was spent to operate out-of-home secure facilities.[13] As pointed out by Supreme Court Chief Justice Carol Hunstein (a council member in its first year), "Spending $91,000 a year to lock up a juvenile and getting 65% recidivism in return is not working. We can be smarter with taxpayer dollars. More importantly, we can produce a safer Georgia."[14] Also disturbing to the council was the finding that 53% of juveniles placed in 2011 in a non-secure residential facility, such as a group home, had only been adjudicated for a misdemeanor (or even in some cases a status offense, e.g., truants and runaways) with more than half assessed as low-risk.[15] The usual annual cost of these placements was $29,000 while the cost of community supervision of a child remaining in their home is only $3,000.[16]

Approved unanimously in 2013, HB 242 entirely rewrote the Georgia Juvenile Code, as mentioned in our earlier chapter on juvenile justice.[17] The path for such a comprehensive change had been prepared by advocacy groups and some legislators who had been pushing for years for these reforms. HB 242 embodied their mission, placing the relevant state officials under a new mandate: "to preserve and strengthen family relationships in order to allow each child to live in safety and security." These reforms, as indicated by the Reform Council, reflected developmentally appropriate approaches relying on evidence-based, cost-effective alternatives to incarceration. The objective was to ensure that "young offenders are treated in a way that is more morally appropriate, more judicially appropriate, and more economical for Georgia taxpayers."[18]

An essential objective was to redirect lower-risk offenders guilty of lesser charges to improved community supervision, create a category (CHINS) for children who were both deprived and delinquent, and no longer criminalize status offenses such as truancy or running away from home.[19] The legislature enhanced these policies in the following years at the Reform Council's recommendation. For example, SB 365 in 2014 further reformed procedures for placing juveniles in secure facilities, including bringing procedures sufficiently in line with federal guidelines so as to make the state eligible for federal funds to serve the needs of this population.[20]

Reform action was also taken at the executive level. In 2015 the Deal administration adopted the nation-wide Juvenile Detention Alternatives Initiative (JDAI) promoted by the Annie E. Casey foundation as the operational philosophy for juvenile justice in Georgia. Designed to help jurisdictions reduce reliance on secure detention, it was already used in the Clayton and Newton juvenile courts, as discussed earlier. State-wide implementation of JDAI began in 2017.[21]

In addition, the administration's Juvenile Justice Incentive Grant Program was dramatically successful in reducing actual commitments to secure facilities. In the first round of these nine-months grants, forty-nine participating counties averaged a dramatic 62% decline in commitments instead of the predicted 15%. As a consequence, two detention centers were closed and 1,122 youth served their sentences in their communities through evidence-based programs rather than in out-of home placements. The program was then expanded to sixty counties serving 70% of the state's at-risk youth.[22]

A major concern of juvenile justice reformers is the school-to-prison pipeline, that is, the criminalization of school disciplinary actions. The Reform Council took important steps in addressing the issue with recommendations that were incorporated in 2016's comprehensive criminal justice law, SB 367. The thrust of the reform was to minimize criminal justice system involvement in disciplinary actions that could best be handled by schools and families, with special attention to schools that employ school resource officers.[23]

The role of families was addressed more directly the following year in two major ways, both reflecting the directly expressed interest of Governor

Deal in the topic, himself once a juvenile court judge.[24] SB 174 strengthened Family Treatment Courts, like the one Judge Walker ran in Douglasville, which handle parents with substance abuse problems. SB 175 gave courts tools to pressure parents to more meaningfully involve themselves in holding their justice-involved juveniles to appropriate behavioral standards. Lack of compliance could lead to contempt of court charges—civil, not criminal, charges. As justification, the Reform Council pointed to research showing a direct relationship between parental involvement and delinquency.[25]

Adult Reform

In its first report, issued in late 2011, the Reform Council indicated that the length of the average time served in prison had tripled between 1990 and 2010 yet many of these prisoners were assessed as having a low risk to reoffend.[26] Alternative sentencing for people with substance abuse or mental health issues often had been impossible because the appropriate services and program were "either insufficient or unavailable in many areas of the state."[27] Inmates seeking similar services while incarcerated or even as part of their transition out of prison faced parallel obstacles. More than 1550 inmates were sitting in county jails at the time of the report waiting for space to open for them at either a Probation Detention Center or a Residential Substance Abuse Treatment Center.[28]

The Reform Council's recommendations provided the core of HB 1176, which passed into law in 2012 on unanimous votes. It contained many features but a primary objective was to reduce the number of nonviolent offenders sent to prison and reduce the time to be served while still upholding accountability for wrongdoing. For examples, the monetary threshold for a theft to be considered a felony was increased while graduated penalties were created for burglary, forgery, theft, and drug possession. The system of alternative sentencing through accountability courts, such as drug and mental health courts, was strengthened in several respects at the same time that the Deal administration committed $10 million of increased funding for them.[29]

These reforms did encounter opposition as they moved through council deliberation and then the legislative process. Some opposition proved to be a losing minority position, such as one Council member's strong objection to drug courts.[30] In other cases initial opponents were won over by incorporating into the legislation some of their key concerns. The leading example would be the Sheriff's Association, which was initially concerned that the reform would entail greater burdens for its members' counties. Their support was gained with measures that promised to speed the transfer of offenders from county to state responsibility.[31] For some years the state had run a big backlog of these transfers, both frustrating county sheriffs and adding to the Department of Correction's (DOC) budgetary woes. If after fifteen days prisoners had not been transferred from county jails to state prisons then the DOC had to pay for their upkeep yet for some years its appropriations dedicated to this purpose were less than half of the actual cost. Perhaps for both of these reasons, the great success the state has since achieved in ameliorating this problem featured prominently in reformers' reports and presentations, as well as in our interview with former DOC Commissioner Brian Owens.[32]

However, other Reform Council efforts stalled, most importantly, attempts to reform mandatory minimum sentences in the face of strong opposition by prosecutors, always a powerful force on criminal justice issues. In subsequent years the council remained unable to substantially address this issue though it was able to make minor recommendations that made it into law. In 2013 HB 349 restored some judicial discretion concerning mandatory minimum sentences for certain drug offenses, the intention being to ensure, in Deal's words, "that our prison resources are reserved for the 'kingpins' while the 'mules' are given a chance at reform."[33] Greater judicial discretion was also allowed in certain other limited areas involving sexual and violent crimes. In 2015 HB 328 opened the possibility of parole for low-risk nonviolent offenders on their fourth felony conviction who have served at least twelve years.[34] SB 367 the following year created the same possibility for less serious drug offenders.[35]

The Reform Council then undertook a more thorough assessment of other possible sentencing reforms during 2016-17. The major proposal to come forward from the relevant subcommittee of diverse stakeholders concerned augmented sentences being given to recidivist offenders. The basic question was how much time needed to pass for old offenses not to activate recidivism enhancement when sentenced for a new offense. For some southern states it was five years, for others it was ten. As a partial step in bringing Georgia more in line with nearby states, the proposal was that if ten years had passed then judges could decide whether to apply the recidivist statute in sentencing. The representative of the Prosecuting Attorney's Council, Chuck Spahos, objected, stating that these were career criminals and reiterating the importance of "truth in sentencing." Everyone on the council voted for the recommendation except for the district attorney member. Consequently, Co-Chair Carey A. Miller moved to table the proposal, pointing out that "what we do is collaborative and unanimous." The council concurred.[36]

Several other important Reform Council recommendations were successfully incorporated in 2016's SB 367, notably, expanding the types of accountability courts and increasing food stamps eligibility. The legislature agreed that the lifetime ban on food stamps for drug offenders should be ended. Like most states Georgia had followed the federal government ban instituted in 1996 but was now one of the last states to reverse course. There were also changes in how criminal records are dealt with, as discussed below.

Reentry Reform

Focused attention on reentry issues was a natural development for Georgia's criminal justice reform. Recidivism is a failure from many perspectives—public safety, financial, and humanitarian. Reintegration is a challenge.

Georgia's Prisoner Reentry Initiative (PRI) was launched in November 2013 by the Reform Council with the ambitious vision that every person "released from prison will have the tools and support needed to succeed in the community."[37] The objective was to develop a framework based on local-state collaboration to provide these services along with nongovernmental stakeholders. Notably, reformers stressed that reentry efforts were to be targeted not just during the transition period prior to and following release but must begin when incarceration itself begins, meaning a "seamless transition from the time they come in till the time they're discharged after completing supervision."[38] The implications of this commitment for corrections practices are enormous.

The reentry initiative and its framework were legitimated by SB 365, which was signed into law in April 2014 following almost unanimous legislative approval. At the time the estimate was about one-third of all parolees were being convicted of new crimes and ending up back in prison. As Deal stated as he signed the bill, "If we do not do what we can to make it possible for them to re-enter and be law-abiding citizens when they re-enter, then we have, in fact, increased the danger to all of us as Georgians."[39] Through the PRI and this legislation, the state was committing to helping "returning citizens" (as they are often called by reformers) to reintegrate into society, providing assistance to help with the primary limitations on education, employment, and housing.

On the executive side, Deal created the Governor's Office of Transition, Support and Reentry (GOTSR) by executive order in June 2013. GOTSR was mandated to provide the necessary leadership and coordination among the multiple governmental entities and nongovernmental stakeholders "to develop and execute a robust systematic reentry plan for Georgia offenders."[40] Development and implementation of this comprehensive reentry plan across 2015-17 was facilitated by winning almost $6 million in federal grants in 2014, augmented by $3 million in state funds.[41] The GA-PRI was described as a state/local partnership "led" by the Reform Council but "managed" by GOTSR.[42] The arrangement did not work out.

Reentry Reorganization

The work of parole and probation officers is crucial to the successful reentry and reintegration of those who have been incarcerated. Over the decades Georgia has experimented with different ways of organizing these officers. The structure Governor Deal inherited had them separated with probation field services under the Department of Corrections and parole field services under the supervision of the Board of Pardons and Paroles. Youthful offenders came under the separate supervisory system of the Department of Juvenile Justice. As Deal pointed out in his 2015 State of the State Address, the resulting lack of coordination was inefficient and ineffective. This fragmented system also meant that, as he noted, "On many occasions, one troubled family or neighborhood will deal with multiple agencies."[43]

Accordingly, the governor proposed in 2015 the creation of the Department of Community Supervision (DCS) "to eliminate redundancy and enhance communication" by bringing the field services of the three agencies under the same roof. The proposal was overwhelmingly approved by the General Assembly a few months later in HB 310. This legislation also attached GOTSR to DCS but with the reentry office retaining its budgetary independence. Later in the year they were fully integrated for the purpose, as Governor Deal explained, of "streamlining services, eliminating redundancies and enhancing communication throughout state government."[44] These organizational changes and associated reforms were discussed at length in the section on community supervision.

Misdemeanor Probation

HB 310 also dealt with misdemeanor probation issues, a hot topic in recent years in the state as well as nationally. Georgia leads the nation in its probation rate—by far—with most probationers poorer people, many having a difficult time paying their misdemeanor fines. About 80% of Georgia's misdemeanor probationers are supervised by private companies contracting with municipal and county governments. Controversies around this issue have received substantial attention in the state press, particularly the jailing of people behind in their payments, even for traffic fines. The issue was also addressed in Reform Council deliberations and its 2015 report.[45] This was a reform Deal particularly wanted, Co-Chair Boggs informed the Council, adding his own view that "no one should be revoked to jail for failure to pay fines." The Council's extensive set of recommendations was largely incorporated in HB 310.[46]

The Reform Council returned to misdemeanor bail in its final year, 2017-18, spurred on by continuing judicial activity challenging the constitutionality of state bail practices. Forming the basis for its recommendation was a report from the Judicial Council Ad Hoc Committee on Misdemeanor Bail Reform, which had representation from the various courts handling misdemeanor cases. The council also heard from advocacy groups and other stakeholders but its final recommendations fell short of what they proposed. Once again prosecutors were successful with their arguments, with their representative stating that "one size does not fit all" given the variations between counties and offenses and that judges, who are elected by the community and accountable to it, should be trusted.[47] As passed in May 2018, SB 407 did expand the possible use of citations instead of criminal charges, as well as requiring judges when setting bail to consider the defendant's financial status.[48] Indeed, the bill did go far enough to gain Governor Deal condemnation from a county sheriff, who charged, "This governor has done more for those who perpetrate crime than Lucifer and his demons combined."[49] However, another bill based on the Reform Council's recommendation to create a legislative study committee on bail reform failed to reach a floor vote. Around the same time, the city of Atlanta succeeded in going further in reform, eliminating cash bond requirements for indigent defendants in its municipal courts.[50]

FELONY PROBATION

The Reform Council also gave attention to the vast issue of felony probation. Georgia's very high rate has been created by both its heavy reliance on probation and the long duration of those sentences—an average more than double that of North Carolina. While thirty-two states cap probation at five years, about three-quarters of the felony probation population in Georgia exceed this threshold—even though almost half of them are assessed as having low to moderate risk of recidivism. Meanwhile, research indicates that more than three years of probation does little to promote desistance.[51]

The subcommittee that had studied this issue consisted of a broad cross-section of critical stakeholders. However, when it presented its recommendations, at least two important changes occurred. One was the removal of a recommendation supported by Co-Chair Boggs to establish a rebuttable presumption of indigency, allowing for a waiving of fees as had been done earlier for misdemeanor probation. It was tabled when Chuck Spahos, the district attorneys' representative, voiced opposition to the council. Spahos also succeeded in modifying the core recommendation that for a first or second conviction for nonviolent felony drug and property offenses there be a rebuttable presumption of a probation-only sentence. This would still allow prosecutors to object and with the judge's concurrence the sentence could still include incarceration. Nonetheless, Spahos strongly objected to including second convictions, which he claimed would cause heartburn among prosecutors. The council then agreed to limit its recommendation to just first convictions.[52] This was later watered down further in the General Assembly when it passed HB 174 in May 2017. This new law also included a softened version of the Reform Council's recommendation that probation for this category of offenders be limited to three years once all the conditions of their sentence were met. [53]

Record Expungement

The same dynamic was at work on another issue crucial to reentry—criminal record restriction/expungement. The Reform Council intermittently dealt with the issue of the public availability of offender records throughout its tenure but was unable to secure more than minor changes. Its biggest success in this area was with SB 367 in 2016 following the legislative rejection of its recommendations in the two prior years. However, the 2016 change applied only to the First Offender Act. But, as the council report pointed out, "the methods used to prevent first offenders from having a public record have been outpaced by technology and the expanded use of private companies that conduct background checks."[54] The importance of the issue should be clear from the perspective of facilitating reentry. Nonetheless, the council's task force on this issue was not able to arrive at a consensus, in part because of concerns expressed by Spahos, representing the state's district attorneys, that what happens in court is open to the public and therefore the record should be as well.[55] The new law allows individuals exonerated under the First Offender Act to petition to have their records restricted.[56]

The issue was revisited by the Reform Council in 2018 through a presentation by the Georgia Justice Project, which had been working on the issue for years. The thrust of its recommendations was to bring Georgia more in line with other southern states, based on consultations with a wide variety of stakeholders, from prosecutors to employers. Nonetheless, it was Co-Chair Boggs's sense of the council that it was not yet ready to vote on the matter and perhaps the better approach was to deal first with only misdemeanor charges.[57] This was the council's eventual recommendation, along with studying the possibility of extension to those with felony convictions. However, neither made it into law during the year.

A COMPREHENSIVE MASTER PLAN?

In retrospect one could imagine Georgia had been following a comprehensive plan laid out at the beginning of the Deal administration, given that the progression from one year's reform to the next seems so logical. However, that was not the case, although Boggs agreed that the progression was a natural one.[58] In the beginning, the agenda was limited to the immediate crisis at hand: increasing numbers of incarcerated predicted for an already overcrowded prison system at the point when there was a severe shortfall in state revenues. With its able handling of these immediate issues, the council gained the confidence of other political actors, accruing political capital. Clearly the reform model being pursued worked. The juvenile justice system was plagued by many problems but reformers had been stymied for years in their efforts at major change. It was a natural subject for the next round of deliberation as was reentry in the third year and then the organizational changes of the fourth. At this point, in our understanding, the Reform Council reached the limits of what some crucial stakeholders would accept. Consequently, subsequent recommendations were not as substantial in their scope, and action by the state legislature was even less so.

EXPLAINING THE REFORM PROCESS IN GEORGIA

Major criminal justice reform is not unique to Georgia. For southern states in particular, the reform initiated earlier by Texas has been an important example. Other states such as California, Illinois, Michigan, and Ohio stand out in the literature. In explaining these reforms several factors are prominent, which for convenience we will group together into two sets: economics, and evidence and networks. For understanding the Georgia case, it is critical to emphasize a third: leadership.

ECONOMICS

The economic crisis that slammed the U.S. in 2008 created severe fiscal crises across the nation. For FY2008 the Georgia budget had grown 6.9%. With the Great Recession and revenue shrinkage, for FY2009 appropriations were down 8% and for the following year another 9.7%.[59] Under such conditions no budget line could be sacred, including Corrections. However, prisons were already overcrowded and although crime rates were falling, recidivism rates were not. The Reform Council's 2011 report highlighted the predicament with Figure V. 1, a graphic that we include because it was featured in many presentations of the period.

Figure V. 1. Georgia Historical Prison Population & Baseline Projection

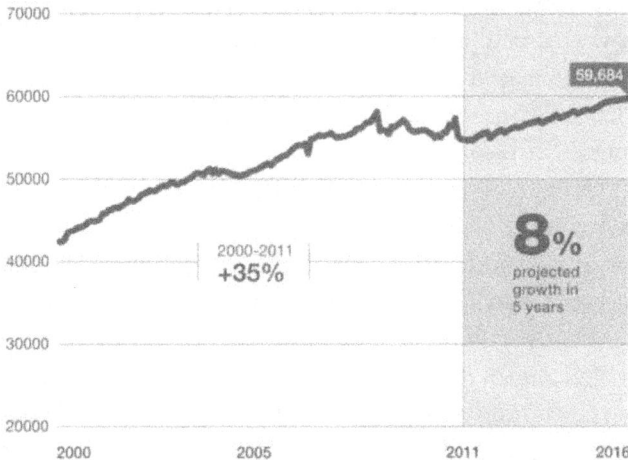

Source: Report of the Special Council on Criminal Justice Reform for Georgians—2011

As the report explained, with Georgia's prisons already at 107% of capacity and current trends predicting an 8% expansion in prison population, "the state faces the need to spend an additional $264 million over the next five years in order to expand capacity to meet the projected increase in population."[60] Instead of new construction, Georgia chose reform. These savings in the adult criminal justice area were mirrored in juvenile justice where the reforms instituted were projected to save about $85 million.[61] Much of these avoided costs went to easing the budget crunch. However, by the end of 2014 about $51 million of state funds were reinvested into criminal justice reform, especially accountability court expansion, an amount said to be "unmatched anywhere in the United States."[62] The triggering event of the fiscal crisis created by the recession, then, created a big opportunity for reform, one that was utilized.

EVIDENCE-BASED NETWORKS OF EXPERTISE

Grouped together here are three related policy determinants: declining crime rates, the growing body of evidence-based criminology, and the availability of national networks of expertise and support. All of these were cited repeatedly in our interviews. "Evidence-based practices" might be the most frequent of any phrase we heard, not just from academics and policy-makers but even from previously incarcerated people themselves now working in the reentry field. As the Reform Council co-chair for 2012-2016, Thomas Worthy, pointed out, in Georgia this is "a data-driven conversation."[63] And the data was clear: the excessive "get tough on crime" policies of past decades had not enhanced public safety; rather, sometimes they were even counterproductive. Worthy referred to this as "two or three decades of bad sentencing policies."[64] Georgia policy-makers also took note of the fact that "all 19 states that cut their imprisonment rates between 1999 and 2009 also experienced a decline in their crime rate."[65]

Crucial to bringing this national evidenced-based "developing consensus" to policy-makers in Georgia was the Pew Foundation and behind it the Justice Reinvestment Initiative (JRI) of the U.S. Department of Justice. Pew sponsored a small group of Georgian policy-makers to attend its national conference on sentencing and corrections reform in 2010. The group continued meeting on its return, expanding its membership to include leaders from each branch, providing the basis for the Special Council on Criminal Justice Reform. In this it was following the JRI model of a bipartisan, interbranch group of elected and state officials who would then engage critical stakeholders around criminal justice issues. The fundamental idea was that reforms could both enhance public safety and save money, with the savings reinvested back into reentry services and high crime neighborhoods, which would then lower crime.[66] As the council worked on its reform proposals, Pew's Public Safety Performance Project provided essential technical assistance as the JRI partner, including support drafting recommendations and conducting stakeholder education.[67]

When Georgia reformers moved to juvenile justice the following year technical assistance from the Annie E. Casey Foundation augmented the continuing support from Pew. Scholars from the Barton Child Law Center at the Emory School of Law shared their expertise over the years when the subject was juvenile justice.

Georgia's reentry initiative was also very successful in winning federal grants, probably in part because Georgia had been an eager adapter of many of the best practices accumulated and promoted by national experts at the National Prisoner Reentry Council and the National Institute of Corrections (NIC). In addition, in the prior decade Georgia received reentry technical assistance through a program sponsored by NIC and the National Governors' Association. This participation also required the state to develop and implement a comprehensive recidivism reduction plan when the Second Chance Act became national law in 2008. As Georgia developed its reentry framework, additional technical support was received from the Vera Institute for Justice, and after 2016 the Council of State Governments as its JRI partner, especially on probation reform. [68]

Also important, especially in the early stages, was the Right on Crime Initiative of the Texas Public Policy Foundation, which "advocates a corrections system that emphasizes accountability, personal responsibility, limited government and fiscal sustainability."[69] Under their guidance, a Georgia campaign was launched publicly in September 2011, working through the Georgia Public Policy Foundation (GPPF). These conservative groups provided Georgia not only evidence that the reform effort under Republican leadership in Texas was working but also political cover for politicians who might worry about being portrayed as soft on crime. The GPPF also forged alliances with liberal groups to facilitate bipartisan support for the initiative.[70]

Among the Atlanta-based criminal justice advocacy groups, two played significant roles throughout the reform process. The Georgia Justice Project (GJP) and the Southern Center for Human Rights (SCHR) were important stakeholders for the Reform Council's broad consultations. Furthermore, as the process advanced, relationships of credibility and trust developed between the council and the two organizations. Doug Ammar, GJP's director, and Marissa McCall Dodson, SCHR's public policy director, not only frequently testified before the council on the positions advocated by their organizations but were often members of its ad hoc working groups, indeed, on occasion made the presentation before the council on behalf of a working group.[71]

Numerous other groups played more limited but still important roles throughout the reform process. Sometimes ad hoc groups were created outside of the Reform Council but played a significant role through their recommendations given their influential membership (e.g., the Judicial Council on Bail Reform). The council also heard from grassroots organizations (e.g., Southerners on New Ground, a multi-racial LGBTQ group advocating on bail reform). Other organizations though not appearing before the council, followed its course closely over the years, keeping their memberships informed and encouraging their legislative lobbying when relevant. A prominent example was the Interfaith Children's Movement, whose monthly meetings we often attended. There were also numerous local groups throughout the state involved with criminal justice issues in their communities. A prominent example is Women on the Rise, a group largely of previously incarcerated women, that played a crucial role in getting Atlanta to end cash bail in its municipal courts and to close the city's detention center.

LEADERSHIP

The prior factors are insufficient to explain the pace-setting reforms that occurred in Georgia when they did. A necessary condition was that political leadership with both strong commitment and sufficient ability be in place. With such an extensive set of reforms, numerous individuals in Georgia played important leadership roles. In addition to Governor Deal, three other individuals were especially significant: Michael P. Boggs, Jay Neal, and Michael Nail.

NATHAN DEAL

Prior to his election as governor, Nathan Deal was a congressman serving a north Georgia constituency. Previously he had been an attorney, prosecutor, and juvenile judge. From the first day of his governorship he was an impassioned advocate of criminal justice reform and the redemptive possibilities of prisoners. As governor, Deal set and sustained the agenda, placed people of vision and competence into key positions, and facilitated the development of an effective reform process. Although he certainly saw the Georgia reform as embedded in solid conservative principles, he opened the state reform process to deep collaboration and guidance with outside groups often seen as having a more liberal agenda, the Pew Foundation being a primary example.

In addition to his role as administrative leader, Deal was an active public advocate for criminal justice reform and the importance of providing for the rehabilitation of offenders. Part of his effectiveness in this role stemmed from the obvious fact that for him these issues are not just pragmatic, they are also humanitarian in a deeply felt way. When the federal Colson Task Force met in 2015 with the Reform Council one of its members, Jim Liske, president and CEO of the Prison Fellowship Ministries, observed about the state's reform, "Yes, it's being driven by . . . budgets, but you don't get everybody on the same page unless you come to some heart issue and I think the leadership we see in Governor Deal is he's made this an issue of human dignity."[72]

It was not uncommon for reports to describe Deal as tearing up when he talked about reentry, something we witnessed ourselves at a state reentry conference in early 2014. For Deal these were not abstract policy questions but instead were about real people and their lives. For example, when he signed the adult reform bill into law he said, while fighting back tears, "To listen to the stories, to the lives that have been changed, the families who have been reunited and lives that have, quite frankly, been cast aside by the system that was in place, had a tremendous emotional effect on me."[73]

When we have asked in our interviews what people thought was the source of Deal's emotional commitment to criminal justice reform they invariably highlighted his personal experiences, especially with prisoners working in the governor's mansion and his attendance of graduation ceremonies at the drug court presided over by his son, Jason Deal, in their home county.

Gov. Deal often helped people who worked at the governor's mansion find jobs and is quoted as explaining:

I've had the opportunity to help some of them as they've left find a job. . . . They work hard. They appreciate the opportunity for a chance in life again. And those are the stories that don't often get told. . . . When you see people every day, you see how hard they work. And it becomes like a family member—you want to try to help them and I try to do that. . . . I tell them they can be an example. . . . The ones we have working there, we would trust them to do anything. And they have earned that trust.[74]

People we talked with who worked in the mansion or attended dinners there also described similar respectful behaviors—the governor addressed inmates by name and even chatted with them in a personal way (guests, though, often ignored them).

Expanding the role of accountability courts was at the core of the Deal administration reforms and discussing them provided some of the most poignant parts of the governor's speeches. For example, when he was a luncheon keynote speaker at a major Bipartisan Summit on Criminal Justice Reform held in Washington DC in March 2015 one journalist highlighted how moved Deal was when describing drug court graduations.[75] In explaining his father's commitment, Judge Jason Deal also drew attention to their life in a small town where the family has lived and worked for decades, including his mother as a schoolteacher. In such towns, a prosecutor or judge might very well have someone who was in Mrs. Deal's classroom appear before them in court, or someone who you dealt with in court greet you when you walked into a restaurant.[76]

Michael P. Boggs

Michael P. Boggs's leadership of the Reform Council was central to the success of the Georgia criminal justice reform process. Leadership in this situation required substantive mastery as well as the interpersonal and group facilitation skills necessary to move disparate interests and perspectives toward consensus. The overwhelming bipartisan support that the council's recommendations gained in the General Assembly was continuing testimony to Boggs's leadership abilities, along with that of the three individuals who served sequentially as his co-chairs. In addition, Boggs traveled widely throughout the country as an effective public advocate for criminal justice reform.

Boggs was a practicing attorney in southern Georgia when elected to the State House in 2000. Four years later he won office as a Superior Court judge. In that position he soon realized that substance abuse was behind many of his cases. An early drug court adopter, he recalled it as "the most satisfying thing that I did as a judge." He was a strong and effective advocate for accountability courts on the Reform Council, to which he was one of the judicial appointees at its inception. At the time of his appointment he had also been serving on the Judicial Council of Georgia's Standing Committee on Accountability Courts. In January 2012 Governor Deal appointed him to the Georgia Court of Appeals and then in December 2016 elevated him to the Supreme Court of Georgia, to which he won a six-year term in 2018. He also serves as the chair of the Board of Directors of the Council of State Governments Justice Center.[77]

When explaining the motives behind the various elements of the

Georgia reforms Boggs usually cited the financial savings and the public safety gains. He also referred often to their moral dimension, including in our interview, especially as it related to handling nonviolent offenders with more appropriate sentences, such as through accountability courts. Similarly, in discussing with reporters 2015's HB 328, which addressed the situation of long sentences without parole for drug offenders with multiple convictions, he declared, "The council believed that these sentences were fundamentally inequitable and immoral," referring to offenders whose fourth conviction might be for a small-time drug bust.

Jay Neal

Jay Neal is a good example of a strong conservative who could be persuaded by evidence to change long held beliefs when the two conflicted. He first dealt with addiction issues as a pastor, moving from a belief that substance abuse was a matter of weak will and morals to one of biochemistry. This led him to working with a recovery center and, when he entered the State House in 2005, to working on substance abuse legislation that would reduce the criminal sanctions for what he now considered an illness. One fortuitous connection to come out of this work was his collaboration with Adam Gelb, who was then with the Georgia Council for Drug Abuse but would later be the director of Pew's Public Safety Performance Project. Neal also developed a good working relationship with Misty Giles, a policy adviser to Governor Perdue with a strong interest in criminal justice reform. Giles wrote the grant for attendance at the 2010 Pew conference discussed earlier, choosing Neal to be part of the small group, with Gelb vouching for him with others at Pew who had concerns that Neal was not part of the House leadership.

With Deal's gubernatorial victory Neal was ready to go, promoting evidence-based criminal justice reform to the governor-elect and others, authoring the bill that created the Reform Council, and co-sponsoring the first year's reform bill, HB 1176.[78] As executive director of GOTSR he embraced the cause of reentry for returning citizens, speaking effectively of the need to reduce the many barriers facing their successful reintegration. Neal's service at GOTSR ended in October 2015 and he then became executive director of the state's Criminal Justice Coordinating Council. He was one of just nine people selected to serve on the Chuck Colson Task Force on Federal Corrections, active during 2015-16.[79]

Michael Nail

Once state officials supervising and/or providing services to the previously incarcerated were fragmented between four different agencies: Parole, Probation, GOTSR, and Juvenile Justice. Since 2015 they have all been gathered into the Department of Community Supervision (DCS), which has been led by Michael Nail since its inception. A strong advocate of evidence-based policies and practices, he is also an adept organizational change agent. Nail's involvement with the creation and development of DCS was covered in Section II.

Nail was one of the small group of Georgians who attended the 2010 Pew conference, which was a forerunner of the Reform Council. Later he was selected as one of twenty-nine members of the Executive Session on Community Corrections at the Harvard Kennedy School—co-sponsored by the National Institute of Justice and the Department of Justice—that was active during 2013-16. He remains an active practitioner and proponent of reform, for example, through his current involvement with Executives Transforming Probation and Parole (EXiT), which unites current and former community supervision executives to build a national movement to transform probation and parole.

CONCLUSION

Speaking to the Colson Task Force when it held hearings in Atlanta in 2015, Michael Boggs identified four integral components to Georgia's success: executive leadership, political will, collaboration and inclusiveness.[80] In our interview he also pointed to another key component: self-constraint. The Reform Council was keenly aware that the success of its recommendations depended on building trust among legislators: *They trust that we are not going to get them out on to a limb, either Democrats or Republicans, politically. They now understand that this is not an issue that is going to get them beat so we built that inner confidence in them that they can do this without political ramification. We have built up in them confidence to know that because our efforts are data driven, that this is not merely a mental exercise about what might work in Georgia but rather an exercise in how we might use that data to drive more thoughtful public policy reforms.*[81] The same confidence building also held for other stakeholders, such as law enforcement, prosecutors, and judges—not to mention the attentive public.

Georgia under the Deal administration implemented what is regarded as one of the most successful criminal justice reforms in the nation. However, it also fell far short of promoting many of the changes needed, including in areas that reformers expected to be addressed. Given that Georgia is a conservative-dominated state, it would be politically naive to argue that its pace of reform was too cautious. These political realities meant that reformers had to bide their time before taking on policies that have been major failures, including in both costs and public safety. A major case in point is mandatory minimum sentencing. As Boggs pointed out to the Colson Task Force, "I don't think we could have started with mandatory minimums. I mean we have to build political capital and political will."[82] His co-chair at the time, Thomas Worthy, added that even though everyone in the room knew mandatory minimum sentencing "is bad public policy," the Georgia reform process was taking "smaller step[s] to get people more politically comfortable with it so that when we come back around for the larger step you're not going to run into quite as much opposition from the law enforcement and prosecutorial communities."[83] Unfortunately, the life of the Reform Council was to expire before those larger steps could be taken, leaving it to its final report to recommend to the legislature and future governors that the issue be addressed.[84] Deal expressed the same hope as he left office.[85] At that point the state's overall prison population was 1.2% higher than when his term began (although still less than the 8% increase projected without the reforms).[86]

Some leading advocacy organizations argue for a much broader and deeper attack on mass incarceration. For example, the American Civil Liberties Union's Smart Justice Project has devised a plan that would cut incarceration in Georgia by 50% by 2025.[87] Doing so would free a huge sum that could be instead directed to other needs. However, to reach this dramatic goal would require reducing average time served by 70% in seven out of eight offense categories and 60% in the remaining.

The financial resources needed to fund the far-reaching criminal justice reforms that are still needed—not to mention to address the underlying social ills of concentrated disadvantage—are substantial, whether they are to be obtained by the ACLU's reinvestment strategy or by higher taxes. In addition, salaries need to be significantly increased in the Departments of Corrections and Juvenile Justice so that hiring standards can be elevated while staff turnover can be reduced. This is increasingly important because as alternative sentencing is put in place, the remaining incarcerated population is more challenging. Yet in our exploration of Georgia's criminal reform process we never encountered among its leaders a willingness to address in a meaningful way the prevailing constraints on financial resources. "No new taxes" remains the dominant sentiment and constraint.

In fact, the Republican governor elected in 2018, Brian Kemp, has proposed tax cuts instead. Meanwhile, Kemp's 2020 budget called for cutting funding for the public defender system, accountability courts, mental and dental health care and testing and vocational certification programs for the incarcerated—yet argued for budget increases for prosecutors and private prisons.[88] His major criminal justice initiative so far has been a tough-on-crime legislative package directed at gangs, a major feature of which was to expand the number of crimes for which juveniles could be tried as adults.[89] Governors change, priorities change. But progressive legislators and their advocacy group allies continue to work to keep their concerns also on the agenda—for example, by introducing their own reform bills—while remaining prepared for more propitious election results.

ENDNOTES

1. N. Shavin, "A Republican Governor Is Leading the Country's Most Successful Prison Reform," *New Republic.* 31 Mar 2015. Also see the Georgia sections in G. Berman and J. Adler. *Start Here: A Road Map to Reducing Mass Incarceration.* New Press, 2018; and D. Dagan and S. M. Teles. *Prison Break: Why Conservatives Turned against Mass Incarceration.* Oxford University Press, 2016.

2. Allen Ault interview.

3. B. S. Chilton, *Prisons under the Gavel: The Federal Court Takeover of Georgia Prisons.* Ohio State University Press, 1991.

4. S. Eby-Ebersole, ed. *Signed, Sealed, and Delivered: Highlights of the Miller Record.* Mercer University Press, 1999, p. 397.

5. T. Crawford, "The Business of Incarceration." *Georgia Trend.* May 2010.

6. "New corrections chief has progressive ideas for managing prisons," *Athens Banner-Herald.* 13 Oct 1999.

7. James Donald interview.

8. B.J. Blair interview.

9. Report of the Special Council on Criminal Justice Reform for Georgians—2011, p. 5.

10. Michael P. Boggs interview.

11. Report of the Georgia Council on Criminal Justice Reform [GCCJR]—2016, p. 20.

12. Report of the GCCJR—2016, p. 28-30.

13. Report of the Special Council—2012, p. 7.

14. Report of the GCCJR—2015, p. 13.

15. Report of the GCCJR—2012, p. 9.
16. Just Georgia, "What will the new Juvenile Code change?"
17. Report of the GCCJR—2014, p. 34.
18. Report of the GCCJR—2016, p. 33-35.
19. A detailed outline of the bill can be found in Just Georgia, "2013 Juvenile Justice Reform Legislation."
20. S. Bilimoria and R. Carver, "Juvenile Court Administration SB 365." *Georgia State University Law Review* 31, 1 (2014): #3.
21. Report of the GCCJR—2017, p. 47; 2018, p. 61.
22. Report of the GCCJR—2015, pp. 27-28.
23. Report of the GCCJR—2016, pp. 37-38; W. S. McPhillip, A. A. Palmer, and O. Snir. "SB 367—Comprehensive Reform for Offenders Entering, Proceeding through, and Leaving the Criminal Justice System." *Georgia State University Law Review* 33, 1 (2016): #10.
24. Authors' meeting notes, 25 January 2017; G. Bluestein, "Deal signs justice system changes to offer 'redemption' for ex-convicts," *Atlanta Journal-Constitution [AJC].* 09 May 2017.
25. Bluestein, "Deal Signs"; Report of the GCCJR—2017, p. 49.
26. Report of the Special Council—2011, p. 9.
27. Report of the Special Council—2011, p. 10.
28. Report of the Special Council—2011, p. 11.
29. A. G. Sheinin and B. Rankin, "Deal signs bill revamping many criminal sentences," *AJC.* 2 May 2012; M. Buice and T. Garcia. "Crimes and Offenses HB 1176." *Georgia State University Law Review* 29, 1 (2012): #15; Georgia Department of Corrections, "Sentencing Legislation."
30. When the GCCJR membership was altered the following year Douglas County District Attorney David McDade was no longer included.
31. H. Lempel, "Conversation with former Georgia State Representative Jay Neal about criminal justice reform," *GiveWell.* 15 Jan 2014, p. 4.
32. Report of the GCCJR—2015, p. 17; CCTF, *Georgia's Justice Reinvestment Initiative: Applying Lessons Learned to the Colson Task Force's Federal Reform Efforts* (Proceedings Transcript). 8 Sep 2015, pp. 6-7; Brian Owens interview.
33. Office of the Governor, "Deal signs second edition of criminal justice reform." 25 Apr 2013. Also see M. Klein, "Second Adult Criminal Justice Reform Bill Becomes Law." Georgia Public Policy Foundation, 25 Apr 2013.Web.
34. C. Teegardin and B. Rankin, "Georgia's bold step: rethinking prison sentences." *AJC.* 22 Aug 2015.
35. Report of the GCCJR—2016, p. 25-26; G. Bluestein, "Next steps in Georgia's criminal justice overhaul become law," *AJC.* 27 Apr 2016.
36. Authors' meeting notes, 25 Jan 2017.
37. Report of the GCCJR—2014, p. 16.
38. Then-GOTSR Executive Director Jay Neal, CCTF. *Georgia's Justice Reinvestment Initiative,* p. 12.

39. C. Sharec, "Deal signs criminal justice reform bill into law," *Gainesville Times*. 14 Apr 2014.

40. Office of the Governor, "Creating the Governor's Office of Transition, Support, and Reentry." 24 Jun 2013.

41. Report of the GCCJR—2014, p. 39.

42. Report of the GCCJR—2014, p. 23.

43. "Gov. Nathan Deal's 2015 State of the State address." *AJC*. 14 Jan 2015.

44. Office of the Governor, "Creating the Department of Community Supervision." 12 Jun 2015; "Deal streamlines agencies to enhance criminal justice reforms." 5 Oct 2015.

45. C. Teegardin and K. Torres, "Overhaul of Georgia's probation system gains final passage." *AJC*. 27 Mar 2015.

46. Authors' meeting notes, 28 Oct 2014; Report of the GCCJR—2015, pp. 21-26; P. A. Evans and C. M. Martin. ""HB 310—Penal Institutions: Community Supervision and Transition." *Georgia State University Law Review* 32, 1 (2015): #15.

47. This was the representative of the state's solicitors-general, who prosecute misdemeanor cases before the state courts. Authors' meeting notes, 28 Nov 2017, as well as 20 Sep 2017, 18 Dec 2017, and 19 Jan 2018.

48. M. T. Prabhu, "Georgia governor signs bail overhaul into law," *AJC*. 07 May 2018.

49. G. Bluestein, "Deal's cash bail proposal gets him a comparison to Lucifer." *AJC*, 15 Feb 2018.

50. R. Cook, "Atlanta mayor signs new ordinance changing cash bail system in a nod to the needy," *AJC*. 06 Feb 2018.

51. CSG Justice Center presentations at GCCJR meetings, 26 Jul 2016 and 11 Oct 2016.

52. Authors' meeting notes, 6 Nov 6, 2016.

53. A. J. Navratil and J. E. Hill. "SB 174—Probation and Early Release." *Georgia State University Law Review* 34, 1 (2017): #6, pp. 134-37.

54. Report of the GCCJR—2016, p. 20.

55. Authors' meeting notes, 2 Nov 2015.

56. McPhillip, Palmer, Snir, "SB 367."

57. Authors' meeting notes, 19 Jan 2018.

58. Michael Boggs interview.

59. Authors' calculation from the annual series, Georgia Office of Planning and Budget, *Budget in Brief*. The overall appropriation series is from *Budget in Brief: Amended Fiscal Year 2015 and Fiscal Year 2016*, p. 40.

60. Report of the Special Council—2011, p. 7.

61. Report of the GCCJR—2014, p. 12.

62. Report of the GCCJR—2015, p. 39. The 2017 report indicated $47 million through 2016 (p. 19) while the 2018 report gave no specific figure on reinvestment (p. 20).

63. CCTF. *Georgia's Justice Reinvestment Initiative*, p. 14.

64. CCTF. *Georgia's Justice Reinvestment Initiative*, p. 14.

65. Report of the Special Council—2011, p. 8.

66. N. LaVigne and et al., "Justice Reinvestment Initiative State Assessment Report. "Washington DC: Urban Institute, 2014, pp. 1-6.

67. Jay Neal interview; Lempel, "Conversation."

68. Report of the GCCJR—2014, pp. 15-18; The Council of State Governments Justice Center, "Georgia's Justice Reinvestment Approach: Strengthening Probation and Increasing Public Safety." July 2017.

69. K. McCutchen, "Tough on Crime, Smart on Criminal Justice Spending," Georgia Public Policy Foundation. 30 Sep 2011.

70. R. Lu, "Justice Reform: Georgia's Bipartisan Cinderella Story," *thefederalist.com*. 26 Mar 2015; M. Klein, "Getting Smart on Crime Puts Georgia Ahead," Georgia Public Policy Foundation. 12 Sep 2014.

71. Authors' meeting notes; Marissa McCall Dodson interview.

72. CCTF, *Georgia's Justice Reinvestment Initiative*, pp. 22-23.

73. A. G. Sheinin and B. Rankin, "Deal signs bill," *AJC*. 2 May 2012.

74. G. Bluestein, "Nathan Deal on the inmates in his midst," *AJC*. 30 Apr 2013. Also see, B. Rankin, "Nathan Deal's criminal justice reforms leave lasting legacy," *AJC*. 21 Dec 2018.

75. Shavin, "A Republican Governor."

76. Jason Deal interview.

77. Michael Boggs interview; Supreme Court of Georgia, "Justice Michael P. Boggs."

78. Jay Neal interview; Mary Margaret Oliver interview.

79. T. Gest, "Watts to Chair Task Force on Federal Prisons," *The Crime Report*. 9 Dec 2014.

80. CCTF, *Georgia's Justice Reinvestment Initiative*, pp. 9-10.

81. Michael Boggs interview.

82. CCTF, *Georgia's Justice Reinvestment Initiative*, p. 18.

83. CCTF, *Georgia's Justice Reinvestment Initiative*, pp. 17-18.

84. Report of the GCCJR—2018 report, pp. 66-68.

85. B. Rankin, "Nathan Deal's," *AJC*. 21 Dec 2018.

86."Year-end counts of inmates of the Georgia Prison System, 1925 to present," Department of Corrections.

87. ACLU. "Blueprint *for* Smart Justice." American Civil Liberties Union, 2018.

88. Marissa McCall Dodson, "Week 4—An update on the 2020 Legislative Session," Southern Center for Human Rights. 11 Feb 2020. Many of these cuts were resisted by the Republican-controlled legislature.

89. J. Sharpe, "Critics prevail in push for gang bill edit," *AJC*. 9 Mar 2020.

oncept was Pamperi...
and it was more...

...So, I'm out in...
...come a provider.

We ne... ...look more carefully at the stories
understa... ...Ne need to... ...erstand crime and justice. We need to collabor...
ones, mor... ...s, more complex, nuanced, compassionate ones that
for both... both the suff... ...ing of the victims of crime and the p...
change a... ...nge and co... ...uctive social contrib... ...he...
who have... ...have been... ...victed of crimes an... ...ed for...
that unde... ...understan... ...reality of both irreparable harm
capacity for... ...ity for remorse and change.

...e of power that was given to a young teen
...ith a firearm. And make a lot of money.
was a ja... ...sense of power...
...ntrol this room with a firea...
...eves he has it figured out.

VI

REVISIONING JUSTICE

\\\/ /

SHARING THE BURDEN: CLOSING THE CIRCLE

WHERE WE, COMMON CITIZENS, FIT IN

We've written this book primarily for people like us, concerned about the reality of mass incarceration and its corollary, mass reentry—but relatively untouched by them personally. We don't pretend to provide one, or many, tidy solutions. This has been a *listening* project. Its purpose has been to bring under one roof—or between the covers of a book—the good faith stories that people within our complex and adversarial criminal justice system rarely share directly with one another. We hope by doing so new stories can come into being, ones that you, as readers, can help create.

Mass incarceration, which has been demonstrably unequal in its racial and class impact, requires a deep rethinking of the purpose and consequences of our criminal justice system, a system we all, consciously or not, help create—and therefore one that we can change. What actions can we, ordinary, law-abiding people, take ourselves to begin to repair *our* social fabric?

What if we placed at the center of our assessment of the criminal justice system the acknowledgement that 95% of people who are incarcerated will return to live among us again as our co-workers, neighbors, family, and intimate partners? As a society, we want those who return to society to act in ways that respect our safety. We want them to be law-abiding and to use their abilities to contribute to their own development and to the well-being of their families and of the larger society. What if we used that expectation to shape our criminal justice system from beginning to end? What if we were quite clear that using constructive reintegration as our major metric, we are working in our *own* best interest?

Throughout this project, this core question informed our listening: *What would a criminal justice system that includes constructive reintegration as its responsibility, its <u>primary</u> goal, look like?*

We do believe that until constructive reintegration is introduced into our criminal justice system as a core measure of success, the system does not meet its essential fiduciary role—which is to make our society safer for *all* its members. After decades of mass incarceration, this completion of the *cycle* of justice is more important than ever. We also feel that we, as common concerned citizens, have an important, active role in assuring that this happens *in ways that meet our needs too*. How do we define *our* terms for trustworthiness—and help create the *conditions* in which those terms realistically can be met?

CENTRAL CONTRADICTIONS: A TRIANGULATED CONVERSATION

The real question here is how social trust*worthiness* is re-established after mass incarceration in a triangulated conversation. When individuals reenter after incarceration, they feel they have paid their debt to society— when, from society's view, they have not necessarily established their *social* trustworthiness. The state feels that having completed imprisonment, or community supervision, it has completed its responsibility and it is time for communities to weigh in with their resources. But communities often feel their own needs for safety have not been consulted.

This is the point where the very human consequences of crime and of our criminal justice system become apparent. *Almost no one believes that prison makes you better.* In fact, if you have spent decades in a violent, unprogrammed prison, associating only with other anti-social peers, people will, quite rightfully, feel you are *more* dangerous than when you went in. This is the *state's* injury to society—and it underlies many of the deeply stigmatizing responses the broader society has toward the formerly incarcerated and its distrust of the criminal justice system itself. The state has to take responsibility for the additional harm and danger it has created for the broader society by the conditions in which it has imprisoned—and the *inequitability* with which it has imprisoned. How is it going to undo, individual by individual, its dehumanizing choices—the excessive sentences, absence of programming, use of traumatizing practices of isolation? How is it going to make it safe for *us* to step up?

A company that agrees, at the request of the state, to hire ex-offenders cannot ensure their work-readiness—that is the responsibility of the state that has provided or withheld education and training while people were in prison. Employers and communities, as citizens, need to call the state to account.

Communities also want to see intentional behavioral and attitudinal change on the part of the ex-offender. What will persuade them to hire, to allow someone to live in proximity, is *not* the number of years they were exposed to a dehumanizing, traumatizing environment, years in which they were not gainfully employed, years in which resources flowed from their family to them rather than the other way around. Ex-offenders need to understand that they are rightfully being asked to personally establish through their own intentional, voluntary actions a firm base for social, not only institutional, trustworthiness. Part of trustworthiness for most of us is whether someone can *feel* the human, emotional cost of the harm they have done—not so they can feel guilt, rather so they will stop themselves from doing more harm. Remorse, not acknowledgement of legal culpability, re-establishes social trust. There is always an element of personal choice in crime, and a very real, specific and often irreparable human cost. Offenders need to own that.

Communities need to assume responsibility as well—for tolerating the often dehumanizing conditions of incarceration, as well as those well-known conditions that contribute to criminal behavior—poverty, lack of education, childhood deprivation and exposure to violence, unemployment, racial inequality, inadequate mental health care. What standard *should* we use to establish the individual trustworthiness and prosocial intent of someone imprisoned at fifteen for ten or twenty or thirty years, deprived much of that time of education, skills training, or models of positive social engagement?

Communities need to create realistic standards of reciprocity. We can't ask for self-sufficiency from people who are reentering if we won't employ them or allow them housing. We can't expect respect if we refuse to see them, too, as intrinsically valuable and capable of change. If we don't honor the distance they have had to cover.

As a society, as common citizens, we need to own the criminal justice system as a whole, from legislation through reentry, and evaluate it in terms of its capacity to make us *all* genuinely safer—not by writing off an inexcusably large and racially inequitable number of fellow citizens but by ensuring that those who do harm are held accountable and that our system of justice is held accountable *as well* to the redeeming possibility of growth and change—making sure the individuals they return to us are *less* angry and *more* capable of social contribution than when they went in. If this also requires that we participate in reforming the broad social conditions that promote and perpetuate criminal behavior, so be it. A recent report on crime victims' views on safety and justice found that the large majority of crime victims favor rehabilitation over punishment, preferring community-based supervision, mental health and substance abuse treatment, employment, and, especially, early prevention through investment in education and a focus on neighborhood safety rather than prosecution.[1]

LET'S GET SPECIFIC: WHERE WE CAN STEP UP

At the end of a book this long, there is a desire to sum up and solve. We don't feel inclined, let alone able, to do this. The reality of mass incarceration and mass reentry is too pervasive and unresolved, the challenges it poses too various. It needs all of us. We do however end with some specific suggestions for how we, as common citizens, might take a more active role in this triangulated conversation.

CROSS-IDENTIFICATION: GOOD FAITH LISTENING

What we take personally from all these hundreds of hours of conversation is the over-riding importance of good-faith listening, anywhere and everywhere in this complicated system, of listening for what inspires individual people, of trying to understand how they experience the *value* in their own lives, especially in the context of wrong-doing and punishment. People share this information most effectively through stories, stories we can enter into, return to together, taking different perspectives, understanding differently as our experience broadens, matures. Story allows us to move fluidly between psychological and sociological lenses and the kinds of thinking they each involve. When and why do we invoke individual responsibility, when do we invoke social conditions, as explanations—or excuses?

We come away from this listening project with a conviction that cross-identification is essential to finding genuine justice, that it balances our most dehumanizing, punitive drives, and provides a constant invitation to a more humane stance. It encourages us to understand harm and repair as relational, specific, contingent, faithful—and might help us all identify better criteria by which to evaluate our criminal justice system, categories like reintegration, safety, trustworthiness, hope. That conviction underlies many of the observations and suggestions we make here.

CRIMINAL JUSTICE SYSTEM: COMMUNITY OVERSIGHT

THE TWO FACES OF PROFESSIONALIZATION: EXPERT SILOS

Professionalization encourages the setting of clear standards of practice and defining a distinct knowledge base, both of which can improve performance and provide a sense of purpose and esteem. However, professionalization can also *decrease* social accountability and accessibility, and, eventually, social and institutional trust. Practitioners can become self-referential, loyal to the mindset of the group, and forget that professions exist to meet a social need, perform a *social* purpose and it is that need, that purpose from which they derive their real authority—and accountability.

In our criminal justice system, it is particularly easy to become self-absorbed and ignore that larger social contract. Both victims and offenders (and communities as well) can feel as if their needs for safety and justice are ignored by police, prosecutors and defense attorneys, judges, departments of correction, parole, community supervision. The procedures are opaque and elaborate, the language purposefully arcane, the sense of privilege high, the level of accountability low—and available only through the same self-referential system.

The legal scholar and judge Stephanos Bibas in his essay "Transparency and Participation in Criminal Procedure" describes how, as trials become rarer—almost all cases are resolved by pleas—our courts have become more and more opaque to us as common citizens.[2] This also makes the insiders who know how to work these arcane rules unaccountable to the outsiders—victims, defendants, common citizens—who don't have the same knowledge. This leads to a downward spiral where, because we can't see the *workings* of justice, we assume they don't exist, and respond by making harsher and harsher laws to account for what we're not seeing. The reality is that people will usually choose the more restorative option when presented with a choice at a trial. Encouraging greater citizen participation throughout the system, Bibas argues, "would force insiders to reckon with outsiders' perspectives, needs, and desires."

Reentry, especially after mass incarceration, is one place where this tension becomes acute. A system that has established its standing by being tough on crime cannot expect, as it changes its priorities, that the public will change theirs just as easily if it means that they will bear the brunt of that change. A real problem comes when a pragmatic *professional* decision—we simply can't afford to incarcerate so many—is presented to the public as a moral imperative: *You* need to open your hearts, pocketbooks, and employment rosters to make room for all these people we have put through experiences that will not make them better, more accomplished citizens. The result is a mélange of conflicting values that activate in unpredictable ways.

It is up to us to step in, define what we see as the real moral imperative—a safer and more just society for all of us—and begin to evaluate each of these professions by how much they are contributing to that goal.

Laws—Who Are They Written for?

One of the biggest challenges for citizens is to see law as not the final arbiter of justice but as *one* instrument—and a blunt and often deeply inadequate one—toward that end. To correct this simplification, we need to keep asking, individual by individual, what happened after the law was applied? Did our community become safer? Did we incorporate *return* as part of that safety? Did we *feel* the expanding implications of our decisions in terms of broader social or institutional trust on the part of the whole community?

Cory Beggs, coordinating chief for the South Fulton (Atlanta) DCS office, the largest in the state, shared his idea about what he calls middle-class bliss with a sense of frustration, and, perhaps, a little bit of nostalgia. "It's a bubble," he said. "But you don't know it until it is punctured." At that point, there can be a collapse of *all* institutional trust.

One way to try to preserve a bubble is stigma. We stigmatize what we don't want our world to hold. Another way is criminalizing. It is possible to see much of our criminal justice system as designed to establish and protect that middle-class bubble. The middle class has passed the laws that keep their life within the bounds they want it. We assume these laws will not affect us in a negative way, rather they will confirm our status and our way of life. However, as citizens, whether these laws are appropriate for the needs of the society *as a whole* is also our responsibility. As those who have most benefited from our legal system, we bear the greatest responsibility for seeing that it is just to all. The way that broader appropriateness is often discovered or assessed is when that bubble is punctured and those laws are applied to us and our loved ones.

A recent example in Georgia is a suggested law which would allow someone, like the white gun-rights legislator who wrote it, to brandish a gun without facing a felony aggravated assault charge. The legislator's rationale for the change in law is: "Just because I have a weapon on my person and I show that weapon, I should not be charged with a felony—a twenty-year felony—for simply brandishing my firearm in my attempt to de-escalate what I consider a situation where I felt threatened."[3] It is hard to imagine that he would accept the same reasoning, let alone the same behavior, from a black teenager who chose to "de-escalate" an argument with him in the same way.

If we take our criminal laws as a map of the world as we want it to be, who is the person the law is designed for? Who is it designed to control, stigmatize, define as *not us*? What is the social "steady state" and the ideal citizen these laws assume? Do they account for limited opportunities? Do they assume return? Have we effectively criminalized poverty, lack of education, addiction, despair, race? How would these laws look if those communities who have been inequitably punished were to rewrite them? How would they look if they were designed to protect those most vulnerable to criminality?

Law Enforcement—Whose Safety, Whose Control?

This book is extensive but not comprehensive. We did notice that the people least likely to talk with us about reentry were those who defined their professions as ones of enforcement or control: police, prosecutors, judges, corrections. One can't help wondering what would happen if those parts of the criminal justice system began to define themselves primarily as *public safety* officers and representatives, not *law enforcement*. How would their definition of their functions change, how would interactions with common, law-abiding but openly questioning citizens change? Most importantly, how would the systems *themselves* change? For these control dimensions of the criminal justice system are the ones where genuine reform is most critical—and where transparency, and feedback, is often most strongly resisted.

Sarah Geraghty and Melanie Velez from the Southern Center of Human Rights, in their article "Bringing Transparency and Accountability to Criminal Justice Institutions in the South" argue that in order to have a "nuanced and evidence-based public debate about the efficacy of our criminal justice system," we common citizens must have access to sufficient information from our courts, prisons, and jails to be able to assess their success and failures.[4] That nuanced debate is in *all* our best interest. Unilateral control, as Michael Nail points out, is not a relationship. Trust, especially institutional trust in a democratic country, requires voluntary reciprocal influence—in criminal justice as much or more than in any other dimension of our common life.

Owning & Transparency

To assess is one thing. To assume a broader responsibility for the situation in order to establish common-citizen metrics for success is another, more implicating step. Most of the suggestions we make here focus on *our* owning *our* criminal justice system, however uncomfortable that may feel. In many ways it is much easier to hand it off to professionals and then blame them. But if *our* safety as citizens is the ultimate justification *for* the system, then we need to step up, step in. This means we as citizens need to own the very real conditions we are sentencing people to, genuinely asking ourselves, *Will* these definitions of crime, these lengthy sentences, these prison conditions, really create the changes we want to see?

Law is a mental construct. Life isn't. It is our job to bring our full humanity into continuous connection with the criminal justice system, to show up, to *feel* for all those involved and to use this real world *affective* wisdom of ours to help create better metrics for success—for example reintegration, observable prosocial contributions, desistance—and better feedback loops, ones that allow each of these silos to receive information about the success of *their* actions in increasing *our* long-term safety using *our* terms for success.

We can begin to introduce *our* metrics of success into these self-referential systems by using *our* power to ask questions in public forums, to vote. For example, since district attorneys are locally elected, this means that as citizens we can question their practices at the local level, ask prosecutors how often they are elevating rather than reducing charges, whether they are looking at the size of racial, income, education differences in who is charged. We can ask our prosecutors to identify crime trends, especially in juveniles and young adults under twenty-five and find ways that these can be addressed that don't saddle these young people with burdensome criminal records. Instead of asking, *How many people did you charge and convict or plead out?* We can ask: *How many were you able to assist successfully in a second, or third, chance?* Communities can ask for both lower crime rates *and* lower and shorter incarceration rates and evaluate the success of their district attorneys on both measures.

The expectation of transparence in our institutions of control, genuine, collaborative transparence, can only take place if there is good faith listening on both sides. Police, prosecutors, judges, and corrections officials are public servants and should be held accountable in that way—do more to inform us, involve us, in creating conditions that *we* define as safe and just. But we also need to hold ourselves accountable for not wanting to know, for being willing to let someone else assume responsibility for meting out increasingly surreal punishment, for allowing our prison populations to become so vast, our prison conditions so *un*restorative, our legal system so complex and opaque.

If we, as citizens, were to directly observe prosecutors, police, judges, correctional and supervision officers in action, observe them as they conducted their work, see the world through their eyes, would *our* views also change? Would we develop a more nuanced understanding of what is required practically to create a system where constructive return is a real possibility? Would *our* metrics improve?

TIME

Across the decades and throughout the country there has been a dramatic inflation in sentences due to increasing lengths of mandatory minimum sentences and decreasing eligibility for parole. In addition we have applied these sentences to younger and younger people. In Georgia, people who were given life sentences after July 1, 2006 are not eligible for consideration for parole for thirty years (before 1995, eligibility began after seven years), those with consecutive life sentences are not eligible for sixty years. Only those serving life sentences for drug-related offenses are eligible for consideration after seven years. In Georgia, the current number of prisoners on life sentences is 1.8 times the number of prisoners in the whole system in 1970.[5] This is a national phenomenon. The sheer length of these sentences eliminates almost all incentives for reform.

They boggle our minds as well. When a judge tells three fifteen-year-old boys that their eighteen-year sentences "will pass sooner than you think," *we* need to ask what kind of thinking the judge is doing. Is it based on *felt* experience? Would eighteen years feel completely different if he, or his child, was the one marking the days off on a calendar? What are prosecutors thinking when they choose to charge a boy of seventeen with a sentence that carries a mandatory thirty years? What is going through a judge's mind if he adds another hundred years?

When we read about these sentences in the newspaper, do we go back to our own lives and ask ourselves, what did *I* do between the ages of seventeen and twenty-two, eighteen and twenty-eight, fifteen and forty, twenty-four and sixty—and factor into that sentence the range and depth of experiences that are being lost—from leaving home, finishing school, finding a job, finding a partner, having and raising children, losing our parents? Do we factor the effect of depriving people of these maturational experiences into our sense of punishment *and* into our expectations for reentry? If almost everyone incarcerated eventually returns to live among us, it is important to understand how we can, for our own best interests, make sure that the developmental clock, the one we need to expand our sense of loyalty and responsibility beyond ourselves and our immediate needs, keeps running. When we read about men who were wrongfully convicted who have spent twenty or more years in prison, our remorse makes the social cost of these sentences clear.[6]

Most research on the relation between length and or harshness of sentences indicates that longer sentences are associated with *increased* recidivism.[7] In our interviewing, we frequently heard from people that one of the first things they had to do to survive in prison was to forget about ever getting out and just concentrate on surviving in the environment they were in, where the rules of engagement bore little or no relationship to those of the society outside. This response was most common—and most damaging—with young men facing, before they were twenty, sentences of fifteen to twenty-five years. As Napolean at the Day Reporting Center, recently released from prison said, *Around a wolf, be a wolf. Around a sheep, be a sheep. I will defend myself if I need to. I'm still waiting to see what your next move going to be.*

Very few people are able to continue to work toward reward horizons that are longer than the years they have been alive, certainly with no regular social reinforcement. Indeed, these surreal sentences lend themselves to heroic stories of resistance and revenge, not to growing insight and re-evaluation. These stories may make good movies, but they don't make healthy relationships or communities—inside prison or outside it.

As a society we need to insist that the relationship between sentence length and desired result of imprisonment be specified and supported by evidence. Again, this may help clarify what the goal of punishment is and require that we relate it to our larger values as a society. For example, if we simply want to submit people to the harshest environment possible for the longest time possible for no purpose but to cause them harm, we need to say that.

Direct Experience with Corrections Conditions

All of us need to get real about the conditions we're subjecting people to when we incarcerate and how those conditions affect their ability to return to us as people we are *more* likely to accept as neighbors than when they went in. We suggest that all legislators on judiciary committees in charge of establishing sentences, superior court judges, and especially prosecuting attorneys should follow the example of Rick Raemisch, the commissioner of Corrections in Colorado who spent twenty hours in a super max cell, and spend at least two days and nights in a prison cell and a week on probation.[8] This is even more important for those directly involved in the imposition of those punishments, such as commissioners or wardens in corrections. We could go farther and say it should be a condition of those positions, the inverse of the golden rule. It means not going clothed in authority. It means wearing handcuffs and shackles. Hearing a door lock behind you. If you are too afraid to experience these conditions for two days, you should not be willing to sentence others to them for years. This also means directly experiencing the conditions of community supervision: ankle monitors, call-ins, fines, drug screens, people entering your home at all hours of the day or night. Again, if you are unwilling to experience this for a week, you should not be willing to sentence someone else to fifteen years of probation (a distressingly common circumstance in Georgia).

CORRECTIONS: WHAT'S IN A NAME?

The process of institutionalization involves stripping people of identity, reducing them to a single role: patient, private, intern, inmate. This can be seen in the process of taking away people's names as they enter the criminal justice system, calling them defendant, then giving them numbers in prison. Doing this invites dehumanization. A guard calling someone by a number and insisting that they call him by his role, officer, is able to disregard the rules that govern civilized behavior; it is an invitation to create a degraded, not a parallel universe. If we want people to be prosocial, it is important that we continue to use their names, rather than reducing them to items in our system of control. We suspect that where there are prosocial dynamics, names will always be in use.

This stripping away of identity is also typical of a rite of passage, the difference being that after a rite of passage people are given expanded social identities, often new names. As Anthony observed, prison is great at breaking a person down, the problem is it doesn't build you up again. This may be why it was so important to him that everyone in the prison always use his whole name, so he wouldn't be confused with the many other Anthonys in prison, so what was on him was on *him*—and why he became violent when someone called him inmate. It may also be one of the reasons why he has been quite successful in reentry, because he was able to knit his story together, be the active agent in it, assume responsibility for his choices. These are qualities we want to encourage.

Systematic Feedback Loops: The Wisdom of the Incarcerated

We suggest that those with the most direct knowledge of the effects of incarceration, the formerly incarcerated, be involved in the evaluation of its effectiveness. Incarceration, especially as practiced in the United States, is a harsh, often alienating and traumatic experience. It needs to *mean* something not only to the person experiencing it but to all of us if it is to have any positive social value. To ask people to reflect on their experience of incarceration and community supervision *as it impacts their ability and desire to reenter and constructively reintegrate in society* is one way of encouraging a sense of social responsibility and agency.

Standardly surveying individuals in prison or on community supervision and their families and correctional officers about what *they* think has or is helping individuals make changes, would give all the people in the institutions valuable, evidence-based information through a process that is in itself reflective of the change they want to see.

A questionnaire, which could be administered by the formerly incarcerated or common citizens to increase confidence, could be as simple as the following:

What experiences in prison helped you reenter?
What experiences in prison made it more difficult to reenter?
What changes in prison practices would make it easier to reenter well?

Regular surveying of this kind might challenge the unilateral control orientation of corrections institutions, but makes good sense if successful reentry and reintegration are *our* measure of success. Sustained desistance *is* based on an individual's understanding of his situation, we need to bring those differing evaluations in line with one another.

It is important for all of us to understand what, even in this most punitive period, *has* helped people to reenter effectively. For example, if inmates identify *peer* initiated activities as one of the most important aids for reentry, or disrespectful staff behavior as one of the most important impediments to developing a pro-social orientation, these should be taken into account in program development and staff training. It is not enough to ask these questions, it is also important to act on the answers.

COMMUNITY:
Using Our Informal Power To Define Wisely

Rethinking Stigma: Record Expungement

One the most significant barriers to reentry and reintegration after crime and punishment, one that *cannot* be addressed by systemic reform of the criminal justice system, is the intense social stigma broadly felt in the U.S. toward people with a criminal history, especially those with felonies. Stigma works as a preventative if the prevalence of an action is rare. However, in the U.S., we are releasing 700,000 people from prison *annually*, individuals who have high needs because of the reduction of services in prisons and often a valid distrust of the criminal justice system because of the pervasive and markedly unequal social impact of our criminal justice policies and practices.

Stigma may no longer work as a deterrent for crime, but it remains a powerful impediment to reentry, creating difficulties with employment, housing, education, vocational training, and community acceptance. Stigma and its collateral consequences are often more difficult to overcome than the sentence itself, indeed feel like an infinite sentence, or, more often, as if one is perpetually being retried for the same crime, as we have seen in the lives of Tony and Cynthia, who are still finding difficulty with housing thirty law-abiding and constructive years after his reentry.

In a time of mass incarceration, this blanket condemnation of anyone with a felony means that millions of people are being lost to us as contributing citizens. We all lose. In this regard, we need to rethink thoroughly the role of criminal records. It is estimated that 70 million to 100 million people, as much as a third of our population, have some kind of criminal record—from arrest through conviction. To stigmatize that number of people, particularly around employment, education, and housing is counter productive in the extreme.

Legal measures should be taken to enforce constraints on the use of records and also to ensure that the records are accurate. Members of our society should also not be allowed to profit economically from distributing them, including state agencies, especially without responsibility for their accuracy. We should also consider setting a limit to how long records exist—even if that may be difficult to do with the timeless memory of the internet. If not, there needs to be more thought about developing some kind of law that publicly releases people from collateral consequences, as is common in England after ten years free of crime. This "absolution" needs to be as broadly and prominently available as are criminal records. This is an act of reintegration that we as a *society* need to take as reparation for the injustice of mass incarceration.

Until then, we all need to begin to read and respond to those criminal records differently, asking ourselves when and why it is appropriate to consult them. When hiring, we need to identify what our requirements for trustworthiness are and ask ourselves whether any individual could ever satisfy them. We need to ask ourselves where realistic caution stops and indiscriminate stigma begins. It is fair to wonder, If not now, when? If not this person, then who?

VIOLENCE

Much of the conversation about reentry makes an automatic distinction between violent and nonviolent crime that needs to be unpacked in several ways because blanket social stigma against those convicted of violent felonies is greatest. Much white-collar crime creates havoc and real harm to people but because it doesn't directly harm them physically, we consider it of lesser social impact. Is this really true? Someone who attacks another with a water pistol or a brick can receive the same charge as someone using an assault rifle. Are these comparable?

Does refusing to return voting rights to individuals who have served time for violent crimes really make us safer as a society? If we want people to be active, constructive participants in our society after incarceration, they need to be able to participate fully in civic activities that give them a sense of agency. In particular, they have something important to add to our understanding of what does and does *not* facilitate successful reentry—and what might reduce crime itself. Why would we not want to learn from that?

Would we have as much violent crime if we did not make highly dangerous weapons so broadly available and if we did not do so with a broad social consensus that there are many occasions when self-protective violence is justified? If we made the restrictions on *justifiable* violence much stricter, would that change how we viewed people who have been convicted of violent crimes? As a society, we need to look carefully at how—and when—and with what groups we *normalize* the use of violence, not only who we charge but who we *don't* charge . . . and why.

REINTEGRATION CIRCLES: USING OUR SOCIAL CAPITAL

Departments of Corrections in several states, especially Minnesota and Vermont, have used volunteer Circles of Support and Accountability (COSA) to support and monitor sex offenders or other nonviolent offenders.[9] Ohio has used Citizens Circles to help support people meeting the terms of community supervision. Rev. Thurmond Tillman has thought of COSA as something that could be brought into practice in churches.

We have wondered whether something similar, Reintegration Circles, could be developed in communities completely independently of the criminal justice system, meeting a need later in the reintegration process, where the aim is establishing social trustworthiness and inclusion in the broader community. These groups could provide a counter-force to stigmatization, make room for another form of social restoration on the part of the larger community by having them share the challenges and rewards of reentry with the offender. Drawing in people from different positions in society, these groups could relieve the burden on the communities most devastated by crime and incarceration, who are often expected to be the ones to provide the social capital for reintegration.

The explicit commitment of these groups would be not only to mentor and support individuals as they develop their own plans for social repair—but also to serve as social references, attesting to the level of individual effort, identifying the social barriers faced, lifting up the achievements. Because the volunteers participating in these circles would know they were going to act as social references, they would need to be very honest about what was needed to persuasively demonstrate trustworthiness because *their* reputations, too, would be involved here. They would have a very strong personal incentive for encouraging the continued success of their reintegrating neighbor.

If the groups were socially diverse enough in education, race, class, and experience, the trustworthiness standards developed in the group would be more likely to speak to the wider community. These groups could create a relabeling process that should have value to employers as well, whose resistance to employing people with criminal records has to do as much or more with the fear of a negative social reaction as it does with fears of liability. The groups could also provide a support network for the reintegrating neighbor that is broader—and possibly more accepting—than their immediate community in which the harm they have done is still vivid. They can then bring their participation in this group back into their more immediate community as a demonstration of trustworthiness.

Everyone would be investing something precious here—their time, and good will, and hope—in an incremental process that can bring something more tangible and resilient into being; a safer and more collaborative society, a story that says, "I want and can *with your help* reintegrate in a way that makes me a trustworthy friend, neighbor, employee, citizen."

MASS INCARCERATION IS INERADICABLY PERSONAL
An Open Invitation

Mass incarceration is ineradicably personal.

Individual men and women go to prison, seldom innocently. Usually they have done real harm to other individuals, to themselves, to those who love them, and those they live among. Individuals all.

Individual women, men and children struggle to live on without them for years, await their return for years, struggle to reabsorb them for years. Individual people craft and vote for laws, arrest, jail, charge, defend, convict, imprison, release, supervise, employ or refuse to employ, rent to or refuse to rent to, forgive or refuse to forgive. Millions and millions of times over.

The sheer scale of each of these realities—the individual and the mass—threatens to overwhelm our imagination and our hearts. This dual reality can feel overwhelming or empowering or both simultaneously. What we *can't* do is let one reality numb us to the other.

Return is the point when these realities truly intersect. We're not asking anyone to take on a project as extensive as the one we have done, but we do invite you to begin to dismantle this troubling and undeniable reality of mass incarceration and mass reentry and reintegration, *one* choice at a time. Bureaucracy inures. So does mass. We *all* need to be at a deep level *un*accustomed. We *all* need to be active bystanders. Caring ones. It begins with repeatedly asking the simple question: If this were me or someone I loved dearly? . . . and trusting and *acting* upon our answers again, again, again, in good faith.

OUR JUSTICE CREDO

Real justice—making right, repairing social balance—is relational, specific, contingent, faithful.

It is relational: It restores social trust between individuals, between individuals and communities, between individuals and the state.

It is specific: Individuals commit specific acts of harm, and it is that specific damage that is in need of repair. We look for change in the specific area where harm was done. If someone steals, we want to hear them say, "I been done changed those behaviors. I never ever in my life thought about trying to rob another person. Or *looked* at another person like I wanted what he had. So I have *changed. For real.*"

It is contingent: Actions have impact and consequences that create, challenge, or destroy trust and social balance. If someone changes for the better, the actions that demonstrate that change need to create changes in *our* attitudes, behaviors and expectations just as fully as do changes for the worse.

It is faithful: We unapologetically *want* our better selves to triumph, individually and communally. We commit to that possibility as the more powerful and beneficial one.

Endnotes

1. Alliance for Safety and Justice. *Crime Survivors Speak: The First-Ever National Survey of Victims Views on Safety and Justice.* 2020, pp. 3-5.
2. S. Bibas, "Transparency and Participation in Criminal Procedure." *New York University Law Review* 81, 3 (2006), p. 961.
3. M. T. Prabhu, "Bill aiming to make it legal to brandish a gun advances" *Atlanta Journal-Constitution [AJC].* 03 Mar 2020.
4. S. Geraghty and M. Velez. "Bringing Transparency and Accountability to Criminal Justice Institutions in the South," *Stanford Law and Policy Review* 22:2 (2011): 455-488.
5. Sentencing Project, "People Serving Life Exceeds Entire Prison Population of 1970." February 2020.
6. Innocence Project, "Robert Clark Exonerated by DNA Evidence After 24 Years in Prison." 25 May 2007; J. Sharpe, "House OKs money for 3 overturned murder convictions," *AJC.* 16 Mar 2020.
7. J. Travis, B. Western, and S. Redburn, eds, *The Growth of Incarceration in the United States.* National Research Council, 2014, p.131.
8. Associated Press, "Colorado's Prison Director Spent One Night In Solitary Confinement—That's All It Took." 25 Feb 2014; R. Raemisch, "Why I Ended the Horror of Long-Term Solitary in Colorado's Prison," *ACLU.org.* 5 Dec 2018.
9. G. Bazemore and S. Maruna, "Restorative Justice in the Reentry Context: Building New Theory and Expanding the Evidence Base." *Victims and Offenders* 4 (2009): 375-384; K. J. Fox, "Redeeming Communities: Restorative Offender Reentry in a Risk-Centric Society." *Victims and Offenders* 7 (2012): 97-120.

What kind of a system do we create when we think of
who break laws as essentially different from us? What
attitude justify, what does it protect us against? What
this way do to our character as individuals and as a
and as a nation?

I woke up but it was too late. For once in my life
life I wanted to live. But I didn't think I was
desperate for a change. I thought they might
dropped murder charges on the guy who did it
thought of suicide. I'd rather die than do
think I was ever getting
thought they might see I was
es on the guy who did it and put in on me
rather die than do all that time

at the time, thirteen years old, get caught was
I never thought about if I got caught I alw
I was going never thought about if I got caught
ning caught going to be smart about it. I never, I can
caught at all, at all.

VII
ADDENDUM

\\\///

THE ARC OF OUR LISTENING

We started with the few people we did know in the criminal justice system. One of these, law professor Patrice Fulcher, as a young public defender had helped defend Michael "Little B" Lewis, a thirteen-year-old sentenced to life in prison for a murder there is credible doubt he committed. She recommended other public defenders associated with Gideon's Promise, who in turn recommended other public defenders and defense lawyers. We focused on lawyers who defended SB 440s, children thirteen to seventeen tried as adults.

Another group that was very open to us were African-American Muslims, lawyers and educators and imams and chaplains, who saw the need for our project. Chaplains were also very open to our interest, and we talked to official and volunteer prison chaplains, both Christian and Muslim. The chaplains and staff in the special programs office at DeKalb County Jail were very receptive.

The director of the local 9 to 5 campaign to Ban the Box, Marilynn Winn, herself a proud returned citizen was very open to us. At the same time, several community groups concerned with mass incarceration, The New Jim Crow and the Interfaith Children's Movement, formed and we attended some of their meetings.

We also began visiting courts. The progressive Clayton County Juvenile Court was very welcoming and we talked with judges, administrators, mediation staff and probation officers. Heather attended their Second Chance Court monthly for over a year. She also interviewed juvenile judges at two other juvenile courts. Later, she attended a six-week Citizen's Academy for the Department of Juvenile Justice and interviewed several guards and psychologists.

Charles focused on diversion courts, spent a day in Gainesville observing Judge Jason Deal's court and also spoke with administrators and counselors and observed both diversion and mental health courts in our home county.

Our project coincided with the years of a nationally significant criminal justice reform effort in Georgia under Governor Nathan Deal (2011-19).

Leading the process was the Georgia Council on Criminal Justice Reform. Charles attended many of its meetings through the end of its tenure in late 2018, interviewed its highly effective leader, Justice Michael P. Boggs, as well as legislators, judges and human rights lawyers involved in these reforms.

The state's reform effort in 2013 focused on developing reentry services. This involved creating a special governor's office for this purpose, which was rolling out a reentry program focused on high-risk offenders that was looking for community buy-in. We attended several large community meetings dedicated to that purpose, which introduced us both to people who had been formerly incarcerated and to the officials involved in their supervision.

We were very lucky at this point to connect with three people who greatly increased the scope and access we had inside the corrections community. At a community meeting, Heather met Robert Keller, a former district attorney and member of the state Parole Board, who was part of the newly developed office on reentry. He shared his own breadth of experience and, in turn, introduced her to Michael Nail, then executive director of Parole and now commissioner of the Department of Community Supervision, which was formed during this period to combine the community supervision services of both probation and parole. Nail provided Heather with extensive access to parole field officers, and, later, with equal access to probation. This access was invaluable in deepening our understanding of what is involved in reentry from institutional, community, and individual perspectives. It allowed Heather to talk at length with both urban and rural community supervision officers, with supervisors and top administrators, psychologists, community specialists and in-reach prison specialists, go on ride-alongs, attend victim-offender dialogue trainings, and talk with individuals currently under supervision. This book really wouldn't be possible without him.

The other person who provided us with invaluable support is A. J. Sabree, who worked for thirty years in the Georgia Department of Corrections as an imam, assistant director of chaplain services, and, finally, director of reentry services. His decades of experience gave us a felt history of corrections in Georgia, the origins and relative successes of various reentry efforts. He also helped found a support group made of formerly incarcerated men and women he had known during his time in Corrections and introduced us to these impressive individuals as well. Many of these men and women had been incarcerated for decades, so they had a depth of knowledge about prison conditions as well as the challenges of reentry. We attended meetings of the support group regularly for more than two years and interviewed many of its members.

Both Nail and Sabree provided us with a very special gift—*trust*—and made us acutely aware of its importance in a good faith listening project like this—especially in the criminal justice system. Trust, like distrust, is contagious. Because they trusted us, other people did as well. This has, in turn, allowed us to write as expansive and fundamentally hopeful a book as we have.

The Department of Corrections was not as open. However, we did receive, after much delay, permission to talk, under observation, with a chaplain, teacher, and the warden who oversaw three Atlanta transitional centers. We also, through the help of Sabree, were able to talk to a number of individuals, recently retired, who had worked actively on rehabilitation and reentry issues in corrections. We also talked with three retired commissioners of corrections, James Donald, Brian Owens, and Allen Ault, which gave us a feel for recent and past changes in the Department of Corrections.

Police and prosecutors were resistant, but our status as constituents helped us talk with both a current and retired district attorney in our home county. We also talked with local and school police officers.

We met with members of various community coalitions across the state, in Macon, Carrollton, and Savannah, which gave us a clearer sense of what motivates people in certain communities to come together and claim this issue as their own at the local level. Charles also talked with several employers who have actively employed people who are reentering.

Most importantly, we were graced by the trust, honesty, intelligence and wisdom of the many men and women who have shared their experiences of incarceration and reentry, as well as family members who have done the same. These are difficult experiences, ones that are hard to share, especially with strangers. These experiences were shared with the clear hope that understanding would increase acceptance and make reintegration a real possibility not only for them but for others like them. We share that hope and share their stories now in that spirit.

We were also aided by writers in other places who interviewed people on their reentry experiences. Sarah W. Bartlett in Vermont, founder of *writinginsideVT*, interviewed a number of women from Vermont's women's prison, and Eve Mills Nash conducted interviews in Canada.

\\\/\/

INDIVIDUALS INTERVIEWED
[Institutional titles at time of interview]

Gregory A. Adams, Chief Superior Court Judge, Stone Mountain Judicial Circuit
Fareed Ali, PIIC
Eve Mills Allen, Writer, New Brunswick, Canada
Sharon Almon, Community Coordinator, GA-PRI, DeKalb, Department of Community Supervision
Sarah Allred, Associate Professor of Sociology, Berry College
Thomas Andris, Parole Officer, South Metro, and Facilitator, Victim-Offender Dialogues, State Board of Pardons and Paroles
Allen Ault, Dean, College of Justice and Safety, Eastern Kentucky University, Former Commissioner of Corrections, Georgia, Mississippi, and Colorado
Angie Avery
Frank Baker, employee Murray Plastics, Gainesville
Kelly Barge, President, Level Ground
Tabatha Barker, Diversion and Program Services Coordinator, Clayton Juvenile Court
Melanie Barker, Prison In-Reach Coordinator, GA-PRI, Department of Community Supervision
Casey Barkley, Community Supervision Officer, LaFayette Field Office, Department of Community Supervision
Tamiko Barnes, GED Instructor, Special Programs, DeKalb County Jail
Christopher L. Barnett, Executive Director, Georgia Board of Pardons and Paroles
Sarah W. Bartlett, writinginsideVT
Cory Beggs, Coordinating Chief, Fulton, Atlanta, Georgia Department of Community Supervision
Charlie Bethel, Georgia State Senator; Member, Judiciary Non-Civil Committee
Xochitl Bervera, Founder, Racial Justice Action Center
Susan Bishop, Chaplain, Arrendale State Prison, Georgia Department of Corrections
B.J. Blair, Georgia Department of Corrections, Reentry Coordinator, retired
Mark Bland, Corporate Director of Human Resources, Claxton Poultry Farms
Michael Bobo, Chief Parole Officer, Jessup Parole Office, Georgia Department of Community Supervision
Michael P. Boggs, Justice, Georgia Court of Appeals; Co-Chair, Georgia Council on Criminal Justice Reform
George Braucht, Enhanced Supervision Program Manager, Governor's Office of Transition, Support and Reentry
Felicia Brown, Youth Specialist, Workforce Innovation & Opportunity Act, SIP

Donald Bryant, Star Corporal, Savannah Police, Savannah Impact Program

Gary Burts, Pastor, Lakewood Church of Hope

Dainhen Butler, Anger Management Consultant; PIIC

Roland Carlisle, 9 to 5 Reformed Citizens Committee

Gene Carswell, Board Member, Macon Reentry Coalition

Denise Carswell, Board Member, Macon Reentry Coalition

Henry Carter, Director, Atlanta Technical College AIM Program

Marcus Carter, LPC, Mental Health Counselor, Atlanta Community Impact Program, Georgia Department of Community Supervision

Jacqueline Casique

Tommie Cato, Assistant Director, Carrollton Re-Entry Coalition

Keir Chapple, Program Manager, Victim-Offender Dialogues, Georgia Board of Pardons and Paroles

Semaj Clark, Youth Ambassador, Brotherhood Crusade and student

Kevin Clay, CEO, Global Leadership Integrated

Joe Cobb, Peer Counselor, PIIC

Eric Cochling, Vice-President, Georgia Center for Opportunity

Tommy Conley, Coordinator, Youth Ministry, W.I.R.E.D., Berean Christian Church

Eric Dylan Crider, Community Supervision Officer, South Fulton, Department of Community Supervision

Curtis Crocker, Head Chaplain and Director of Special Programs, DeKalb County Jail

Faith Croskey, Senior Management Analyst, Savannah/Chatham Police, SIP

Crystal

Roderick Cunningham, Founder, Beverly Cunningham Outreach Program

Angela Daniels, CEO, A&D Consultant Services

Constancia Elena Davis, Attorney, Criminal Law

Nier Davis

Jason Deal, Superior Court Judge, Hall County

Tess Devino

Denis W. Dubus, Manufacturing Manager, Murray Plastics, Gainesville

Anthony Dillard, A.B.L.E.

Michael Dinkins, Director, Community Service, Probation, Georgia Department of Corrrections

D.L. Dixon, Sergeant, School Detective Section, Atlanta Police Department

Marissa McCall Dodson, Public Policy Director, Southern Center for Human Rights

James E. Donald, Maj. Gen. (ret); Former member Georgia Board of Pardons and Paroles and Commissioner, Georgia Department of Corrections

Christine Doyle, PhD, Director, Office of Behavioral Services, Georgia Department of Juvenile Justice

Eloise Edmonds, Writer, PIIC, WIT

Terry Eiland, PIIC

Ramona Famble, Lieutenant, Interim Director, Savannah Impact Program

Narvis Farris, Director of Operations, Carrollton Re-Entry Coalition
Kirra Fields, Accounting Technician, WIOA, Savannah Impact Program
Ernesto Ford, Captain, Investigative Commander, Chamblee Police Department
Kathryn Fox, PhD, Professor of Sociology, University of Vermont
Bill Franklin, Program Manager, Newton County Juvenile Intensive Drug Court
Patrice A. Fulcher, Associate Prof., John Marshal School of Law; Gideon's Promise
Linda Gamble, Director, Comprehensive Human Services; PIIC
Omar Gay
Sarah Geraghty, Senior Attorney, Southern Center for Human Rights
Odarie Gibbs, APO, Savannah/Chatham Police, Savannah Impact Program
Katrinka Glass, Director, Risk Reduction Services, Georgia Department of Corrections, Retired
Darice M. Good, Attorney, Criminal, Juvenile and Child Welfare Law
Bill Hall, Owner, Murray Plastics, Gainesville
Lynn Hamilton, Founder and Director, Mothers with Sons in Prison
Claire Hamilton, Lead Organizer, New South Network of War Resisters
Kinnetta Hamilton, Captain, Georgia Department of Community Supervision, District 5, Fulton County
Michael Hancock, Senior Superior Court Judge, Stone Mountain Judicial Circuit
Liam Harbry, Administrative Director, DeKalb County Drug Court
Thomas Hare, Assistant Chief, Stone Mountain Judicial Circuit, Georgia Department of Community Supervision
Lamario Harris, Governor's Office of Transition, Support and Reentry, Mentor Coordinator
Rashad Hasan, CEO, Thirty Movers
Betty Hasan-Amin
Cassandra Henderson, Youth Ministry and Prison Ministry, Ebenezer Baptist Church
Nolan Henderson, Manager, START Program, DeKalb County Jail
Jasmin Hill, Coordinating Chief, Stone Mountain Judicial Circuit, Georgia Department of Community Supervision
Dean Hix, M.Div., Juvenile Court Officer, Second Chance Court, Clayton Juvenile Court
Danny Horne, Chaplain, Department of Juvenile Justice, former Head Chaplain, Georgia Department of Corrections
Hazel C. Horne, Pastor, Jesus Christ Center of Truth
Omar Howard, Chaplain, Atlanta Transitional Center, GA Dept. of Corrections
Donna Hubbard, Director, Women at the Well Transition Center
Robert Jackson, Executive Director, Carrollton Re-Entry Coalition
Robert D. James, District Attorney, DeKalb County
Buster Johnson, Special Parole Officer, M.O.R.E., Smith Transitional Center, Georgia Department of Community Supervision
ShyRonda Johnson, Chaplain, DeKalb County Jail

Timeka Johnson, Community Supervision Officer, Georgia Department of Community Supervision

Venson Jones, Juvenile Court Officer, Second Chance Court, Clayton Juvenile Court

Amanda S. Jordan, District Director, District 5-Fulton County, Georgia Department of Community Supervision

Robert E. Keller, Deputy Director, Governor's Officer of Transition Support and Reentry; former Member, Georgia Board of Pardons and Paroles

Laila Kelly, Attorney, Criminal Defense, former Public Defender, DeKalb County

Sheila Key, Coordinator, Alternative Dispute Resolution, Clayton Juvenile Court

Shawn Kinzer, Corporal, Savannah/Chatham Police, Savannah Impact Program

Cynthia Kitchens, Reentry Specialist

Tony Kitchens, Reentry Specialist

Kevin Lane, Newton Conference Center, Economic Development Programs, Georgia Piedmont Technical College

Tim Lewis, Sergeant, Savannah/Chatham Police, Supervisor, Savannah Impact Program

Peggy Lieurance, Volunteer Educator, Georgia Department of Corrections

Ryan Locke, Attorney, Criminal, Juvenile and Family Law

Debby Anderson Lynn, RN

Melissa Manrow, Special Projects Coordinator, DeKalb County Sheriff's Office

Judge Lisa Mantz, Newton Juvenile Court

Kevin Mason, U.S. Probation, Macon Office and Macon Reentry Coalition

Arianne E. Mathe, Attorney, Juvenile and Family Law, former Public Defender, Hall County

Scott Maurer, Assistant Commissioner, Georgia Department of Community Supervision

Duane McClelland, employee Murray Plastics, Gainesville

Dubraye McDaniel, Founder, God Deliverers, PIIC

Michael McKinney, Claxton Poultry Farms

Ruth R. McMullin, Attorney, Criminal Defense Law, Juvenile and Family Law; former Public Defender, DeKalb County

Michelle Menifee, Coordinator, BASICS World of Work; Founder, Stepping Beyond

Lia Miller, Field Training Officer, Marietta Field Office, Department of Community Supervision

Mark Mobley, Executive Director, Georgia Calls, Buford

Christopher Montgomery, Clayton Juvenile Court Deputy Chief Assistant District Attorney

Crystal Moon, Hearing Examiner, State Board of Pardons and Paroles

Annie Moorman, Parole Officer, Conyers, State Board of Pardons and Paroles

Shannon Morgan, LCSW, Clinical Coordinator, DeKalb County Drug Court

J. Tom Morgan, Attorney, Criminal Defense Law; former District Attorney, DeKalb County

David Morrison, Director, Field Operations, State Board of Pardons and Paroles

Adil Muhammad, student
Furquan Muhammad, Imam, Masjid Al Mu'minun, Prison Chaplain
Sheila Murphy, Owner, Helping Hands
Michael Nail, Commissioner, Georgia Department of Community Supervision
Jay Neal, Executive Director, Governor's Office of Transition, Support and Reentry
Ryan Nelson, employee Murray Plastics, Gainesville
Barbara Neville, M.O.R.E. Program Manager, Georgia Department of Community
    Supervision
Cristy Norris, employee Murray Plastics, Gainesville
Paula O'Neal, Coordinating Chief, Dept. of Community Supervision, Savannah
Mary Margaret Oliver, Georgia State Representative; Member, Juvenile Justice/
    Judiciary Committees
Brian Owens, Member, State Board of Pardons and Paroles; Former Commissioner,
    Georgia Department of Corrections
Michael Owens, PhD, Associate Professor, Political Science, Emory University
Jerome Patillo, Associate Director, Comprehensive Human Services; PIIC
Steven L. Perkins, Warden, Metro Complex, Georgia Department of Corrections
Tairon Philpot, Singer, Hair Stylist
David Pointer, Writer
Charles Purvis, District Director, Georgia Department of Community Supervision
Brenda Rasheed, Chaplain, DeKalb County Jail
Intisar Rashid, Attorney and Lead Teacher, W.D. Mohammed High School
Raven
Nathan Reed, Computer Specialist
Deanie Reid
Michael Rich, PhD, Executive Director, Emory Center for Community Partnerships
Elaine B. Richardson, PhD, Director, Clinical Services-Mental Health, Department
    of Juvenile Justice
Sheri Roberts, Chief Judge Newton Juvenile Court
Shalandra Robertson, Director, Victim Services, Georgia Board of Pardons and
    Paroles
Lillian Robinson, Kairos Prison Ministry
Ivan Rouse, Case Manager, Georgia Works
Aura Russell, M.O.R.E., Georgia Department of Community Supervision
Claudia Saari, Director, DeKalb County Public Defenders Office; Gideon's Promise
A.J. Sabree, Director of Reentry Services, Georgia Department of Corrections,
    retired; Consultant Reentry Services, Department of Juvenile Justice
Pam Salcido, employee Murray Plastics, Gainesville
Yvonne Saunders-Brown, Founder, Gateway Training & Consulting, formerly
    Georgia Department of Corrections
Melanie Scarbrough, M.O.R.E. program, Phillips Transitional Center and Arrendale
    Transitional Center, Georgia Department of Community Supervision
Michael Schulte, Fellow, Georgia Center for Opportunity

Andrea Shelton, Founder, HeartBound Ministries
Susan Shlaer, Diagnostic Director, Arrendale State Prison, Georgia Department of
     Corrections
Tim Shuler, Independent contractor
Norman Simms, Board President, Carrollton Re-Entry Coalition
Bobby D. Simmons, Clayton Juvenile Court Judge
Pamela Simpson, Corporeal, Savannah/Chatham Police, Savannah Impact Program
Kevin Skidmore, President, Four Fourty Trucking
Colin Slay, Chief of Staff, Clayton Juvenile Court; Annie E. Casey Foundation,
     Applied Leadership Network
Beth Smith, Case Manager, Newton County Juvenile Intensive Drug Court
Coleman Smith, Lead Organizer, New South Network of War Resisters
Renee Snead, Operations Director, Governor's Office of Transition, Support, and
     Reentry
Charles Sperling, Director, STAND
Stacy
Kendra Stevens, Field Operations Supervisor, Clayton Juvenile Court
Jesse Stone, Georgia State Senator; Chair, Judiciary Non-Civil Committee
Diana Summers, Court Administrator, Newton County Juvenile Court
Kaleema A. Thomas, Director, Diversion Programs, DeKalb District Attorney's
     Office
Curt Thompson, Georgia State Senator; Secretary, Judiciary Non-Civil Committee
Thurmond N. Tillman, Pastor, First African Baptist Church, Savannah
Darren Tooson, Parole Officer, Gainesville, Georgia Department of Community
     Supervision
Vanessa Torrence, employee Murray Plastics, Gainesville
Erica Trotty
Nicki Vaughan, Assistant Director, Public Defenders Office, Hall County
Peggy H. Walker, Chief Judge, Douglas Juvenile Court
Paul Washington, Work Ventures Supervisor, Savannah Impact Program
Chris Watkins, Account Specialist, Landscaping
Stacy Weaver, Field Operations Supervisor, Clayton Juvenile Court
Irving White, Kirk Healing Center for the Homeless and Steering Team, Liberty
     County Prison Reentry Coalition
Napolean Whitehead
Robert Wilkerson, Counselor, Day Reporting Center, LaFayette Field Office,
     Department of Community Supervision
Cynthia Williams, Public Information, DeKalb County Sheriff's Office
Travis Williams, Attorney, Public Defender, Hall County; Gideon's Promise
Marilynn Winn, Women on the Rise, formerly Chapter Organizer 9 to 5
Aakeem Woodard, Founder, The Bridge

\\\///

SCHOLARS WHO HAVE MOST INFLUENCED US

MASS INCARCERATION & RACE

Alexander, Michelle. *The New Jim Crow: Mass Incarceration in the Age of Colorblindness, rev. ed.* New Press, 2012.
A thorough and compelling book that has succeeded more than any other in its intention to stimulate discussion about how a criminal justice system perpetuating racial hierarchy drives mass incarceration.

Clear, Todd R. and Natasha A. Frost. *The Punishment Imperative: The Rise and Failure of Mass Incarceration in America.* New York University Press, 2014.
Details the forces behind "the incarceration imperative" and its damaging consequences, especially for disadvantaged communities, as well as the reasons for increasing support for an alternative approach with concern for reentry at its center.

Davis, Angela J., ed. *Policing the Black Man: Arrest, Prosecution, Imprisonment.* Vintage, 2017.
This compilation provides a good summary of the major inequalities in the African-American experience with the criminal justice system. Many of the major thinkers on criminal justice reform and reentry contributed, including Bruce Western, Jeremy Travis, Bryan Stevenson, Tom Tyler. Very good review of the scope of the system—and where more citizen oversight would be useful.

Forman, James. *Locking Up Our Own: Crime and Punishment in Black America.* Farrar, Strous & Giroux. 2017.
A law professor and an opponent of mass incarceration, Forman explores why black communities supported and sometimes drove get-tough-on-crime legislation in the 1970s and 1980s.

Tonry, Michael. *Punishing Race: A Continuing American Dilemma.* Oxford University Press, 2011.
An internationally preeminent legal scholar, Tonry argues that even if laws that have seriously aggravated racial inequality were passed without that intent those consequences could and should have been predicted. The racial disparities of mass incarceration can be reduced more effectively by changing those laws rather than by trying to address racial inequality directly.

Travis, Jeremy, Bruce Western, and Steve Redburn, eds. *The Growth of Incarceration in the United States*. National Research Council, 2014.

The most thorough and reliable analysis available of the evidence on mass incarceration, from its causes to its consequences—for individuals, their families and communities, and society at large. The result of a major investigation by a large team of leading scholars through the National Research Council, the report also offers a number of recommendations both to reverse course and to address the damages that have been done.

Western, Bruce. *Punishment and Inequality in America*. Russell Sage, 2006.

The result of an eight-year project, this book provides an extensive quantitative analysis of the impact of mass incarceration on inequality, particularly racial inequality.

INCARCERATION

Cullen, Francis T, and Cheryl Lero Jonson. *Correctional Theory: Context and Consequences*. Sage, 2012.

The authors evaluate the major competing theories that have guided our correctional systems in light of what the best available evidence tells us. As they write, "Many offenders are within the grasp of the correctional system for years on end. If they leave our supervision with the same antisocial values, the same thinking errors, and the same social and psychological deficits, then shame on us."

Gilligan, James. *Preventing Violence*. Thames & Hudson, 2001.

A forensic psychiatrist, Gilligan served as the director for mental health of the Massachusetts prison system. His analysis of the origins of violence focuses on the aggressive basis of our conception of masculinity, especially the interactions between respect, shame and trauma. He provides good recommendations for violence prevention: reduce guns, increase childhood interventions, and provide therapy.

Haney, Craig. *Reforming Punishment: Psychological Limits to the Pains of Imprisonment*. American Psychological Association, 2006.

This noted social psychologist writes powerfully on the mental health consequences of imprisonment, especially on how imprisonment under harsh and overcrowded conditions for long terms can be counter-productive for successful reentry.

Lerman, Amy E. *The Modern Prison Paradox: Politics, Punishment, and Social Community*. Cambridge University Press, 2013.

This book examines the consequences for both guards and inmates of the intensification of control in prisons for higher-risk offenders. Both prisoners and guards feel isolated, alienated from any social power, and in a situation of basic survival. Lerman suggests prison education can create an alternate culture within prisons that makes trust and collaboration and community (inside and out) more possible.

Luther, Dennis: *28 Beliefs about Inmates.*
A highly successful warden at the McKean federal prison in the 1990s, Luther was able to dramatically reduce violence by modeling the behavior he would like to see. His *28 Beliefs* influenced the development of the Oregon Department of Corrections Accountability Model, which sees staff modeling of respectful prosocial behavior as a core part of their job.

COMMUNITY & FAMILY IMPACT

Anderson, Elijah. *Code of the Street: Decency, Violence, and the Moral Life of the Inner City.* Norton, 1999.
The classic explanation of the difference between "decent" and "street" cultures in impoverished inner cities by our leading street ethnographer. Anderson highlights the survival requirements of the street code, where respect (often through violence) is seen as the only remaining social capital. He describes the need for all families in the inner city to master street code for self-protection and the role of the school as the staging ground for street values.

Braman, Donald. *Doing Time on the Outside: Incarceration and Family Life in Urban America.* University of Michigan Press, 2007.
Focusing on an African-American area in Washington DC with high incarceration rates, the central goal of this book is to describe the effects of incarceration on family and community life. Based on over two hundred interviews conducted over three years, the book provides a very good feel for the complex experience of the family members of those who are incarcerated as well as the broader social impact of mass incarceration, given the absence of men.

Wakefield, Sara and Christopher Wildeman. *Children of the Prison Boom: Mass Incarceration and the Future of American Inequality.* Oxford University Press, 2014.
This book examines the impact of parental incarceration on their children, giving close attention to class and especially racial disparities, concluding that these disparities are so great that they are major aggravaters of intergenerational social inequality.

SOCIAL TRUST & CRIMINAL JUSTICE

Bibas, Stephanos. *The Machinery of Criminal Justice.* Oxford University Press, 2012.

The criminal justice system has become increasingly divorced from the public's ideas of justice, leaving victims, offenders, and the public increasingly dissatisfied, especially because of the reliance on plea bargaining. Bibas also emphasizes the importance of remorse—for defendants as well as victims.

Tyler, Tom R. and Yuen J. Huo. *Trust in the Law: Encouraging Public Cooperation with the Police and Courts.* Russell Sage, 2002.

This book draws on Tyler's earlier empirical work looking at how people involved with the justice system, particularly the police and the courts, evaluate fairness and competence. The authors highlight the importance of procedural justice (the feeling that the system is, for all participants, equally fair, respectful, and comprehensible) for creating and maintaining institutional trust. Tyler's work has influenced current movements for prosecutorial reform and also changes to supervision practice.

Lerman, Amy E. and Vesla M. Weaver. *Arresting Citizenship: The Democratic Consequences of American Crime Control.* University of Chicago Press, 2014.

Disadvantaged communities have far more encounters with police, courts, and prisons than do others. These pervasive contacts decrease the faith of "custodial citizens" in our political institutions as well as reducing their political participation, including for those not found guilty of any crime. Their argument is based on many interviews in three different cities.

Howard Zehr. *Changing Lenses: A New Focus for Crime and Justice.* Herald Press, 1990.

Probably the most influential proponent of restorative justice, the author suggests that instead of emphasizing a retributive definition of justice we should look to a restorative model based on the needs of victims and offenders to rebuild social trust.

CRIMINAL JUSTICE & REFORM

Davis, Angela J. *Arbitrary Justice: The Power of the American Prosecutor.* Oxford University Press, 2007.

This book provides a good analysis of the adverse consequences of the largely unconstrained power of the prosecutor in the U.S. criminal justice system, written by a law professor who also was a Washington DC public defender for a dozen years.

Gottschalk, Marie. *Caught: the Prison State and the Lockdown of American Politics.* Princeton University Press, 2015.

The author evaluates the dominant approaches to both reentry and to dismantling the carceral state, arguing that they fall short. Meaningful change requires addressing how we treat violent and sex offenders, bring the U.S. more inline with our European peers.

Kelly, William R. *The Future of Crime and Punishment: Smart Policies for Reducing Crime and Saving Money.* Rowman & Littlefield, 2016.

Written for the nonacademic and non-expert, this books elaborates the failures of over-criminalization and excessive punishment as well as many of the major reforms now commanding broad support intended to both reduce mass incarceration and crime, saving money in the process.

Pfaff, John F. *Locked In: The True Causes of Mass Incarceration—and How to Achieve Real Reform.* Basic Books, 2017.

The author, a law professor, proposes a broad set of reforms to substantially reduce the numbers incarcerated, especially in the area he regards as the primary cause of mass incarceration—tough-on-crime prosecutors operating with minimal meaningful checks on their authority.

Wilson, James Q. and Joan Petersilia, eds. *Crime and Public Policy.* Oxford University Press, 2011.

Comprehensive reviews of what is known on twenty crime-related subjects by the best thinkers on these topics representing a variety of viewpoints.

REENTRY & DESISTANCE

Fader, Jamie J. *Falling Back: Incarceration and Transitions to Adulthood among Urban Youth.* Rutgers University Press, 2013.

Between 2004 and 2007 the author followed through intensive participant observation and interviews fifteen black and Latino juveniles as they entered a reform school targeted toward youthful drug sellers and users and then afterward as they resumed life in their communities. Excellent analysis for the shortcomings of the reform school and the many challenges the juveniles confronted in their reentry.

Maruna, Shadd. *Making Good: How Ex-Convicts Reform and Rebuild Their Lives.* American Psychological Association, 2001.

One of Maruna's most significant contributions is insisting that we see the individual reentering as an intentional actor, not just a reactor, someone whose own interpretations of their experience influence how they change. Based on interviews comparing persistent offenders and successfully desisting ex-offenders, Maruna emphasizes the need of a redemption narrative for successful reentry, that is, someone needs to find within themselves the motivation to develop a coherent, prosocial identity and story. He also emphasizes how others can either assist or impede this prosocial relabeling. A prolific collaborator, he has extended these insights in numerous directions, from supervision practices to public opinion.

Petersilia, Joan. *When Prisoners Come Home: Parole and Prison Reentry.* Oxford University Press, 2003.
    Author of one of the earliest and most influential books on reentry, Petersilia, a criminologist, contributed significantly to the extensive reform of the California criminal justice system.

Schriro, Dora. "Getting Ready: How Arizona Has Created a 'Parallel Universe' for Inmates." National Institute of Justice. June 2009.
    While Director of the Arizona Department of Corrections, Schriro proposed and implemented a common-sense, incentive-focused approach. Its basic premise was simple: the more the value and reward structure of the world inside the prison resembles the world outside, the more prepared, and motivated, inmates will be for reentry. Like Luther, her successful efforts were limited by changes in political administrations and a return to a more punitive correctional philosophy.

Travis, Jeremy. *But They All Come Back: Facing the Challenges of Prisoner Reentry.* Urban Institute Press, 2005.
    This remains the preeminent book on reentry with its thorough coverage of all aspects, from the rise and fall of indeterminate sentencing, growth in incarceration, and extended reach of supervision to individual chapters on the policy challenges of reentry in the areas of public safety, families, work, public health, housing, civic identity, and community.

Western, Bruce. *Homeward: Life in the Year After Prison.* Russell Sage, 2018.
    The research team interviewed 122 men and women five times across the first year following their release from prison in Massachusetts. Written to be accessible to a general audience, the book provides a close view of the many challenges they and their families faced, particularly obstacles to employment and mental health and addiction issues. The book takes the perspective that successful transition means attaining a basic level of well-being consistent with community membership.

EDITORIAL NOTE

We've made a few editorial choices worth noting. First is our use of *we* for ourselves as authors. Although we did not generally conduct interviews together, we have both listened to all of them. We worked to our individual strengths in dividing up responsibilities. Heather, with her interest in narrative and social trust, did most of the interviewing among public defenders, district attorneys, chaplains, juvenile courts, community supervision, corrections, and families. Charles, with his academic background in political science, focused on legislative reforms, judges, accountability courts, employers and an extensive, in-depth review of the voluminous academic literature on mass incarceration and reentry. We both interviewed people returning from incarceration. The ideas we present are, in large measure, shared.

Our second choice has been to use only first names for people who were incarcerated and for members of their families. In some cases we chose to use pseudonyms. This is our choice. Only two people we spoke to requested anonymity. We have done this because it gives us a sense of greater freedom to share our responses—and also gives the people who have shared their stories with us the freedom to identify themselves only when and if they choose. We have not changed the details of their stories. We recognize that our telling of the life stories shared with us are just that, *our* tellings of these stories. It is also a reluctant acknowledgement of the power of formal and informal social sanctions on those who are reentering.

With people who spoke to us, however personally, in their official capacities, we use the more standard convention of referring to them by their last names. In the very few cases where we felt there might be institutional blowback, we used pseudonyms, as we also did with any juveniles. In all but a few cases, we are ignoring the Southern emphasis on formal address, something that was carefully respected by both officers and supervisees in community supervision and in most public and formal interactions, where people were carefully addressed as Mr. or Ms. or Officer.

We have lightly edited direct quotes from interviews for concision and clarity.

METHODOLOGICAL NOTES TO SECTION 2

FIGURE 5.

The racial/ethnic composition of the prison population is an estimate, especially for 1980 and 1990. The resource guide for the data used here from the National Corrections Reporting Program (NCRP) indicates that there was substantial variation between states in how they reported this information. In 1997 new regulations were published to standardize classification procedures. Federal agencies had until 2003 to adopt these procedures but they were not mandatory for the states. Nonetheless, most have adopted them (see NCRP Resource Guide). For 1978-1999 when the reported data for just blacks, Hispanics, and whites is summed the total is greater than that reported separately as the total number under jurisdiction, peaking at a 9% over count in 1992. From 2000 on this sum is less than the total number reported as under jurisdiction, the error, smaller than before, peaking at a 5% undercount in 2013. Adding into the calculation the "other" category is also problematic. For 1978-1998 there was an "unknown race" category that given its escalating numbers appears totally unreliable and was not counted here; the same treatment was given to "additional race" for 1999.

Returning to the larger categories, in 2000 the number of whites dropped by 11% but returned to a steady increase in the following years. Yet in 2000 the number of blacks and Hispanics is about the same as the prior year. The assumption made here is that the primary reason for the over-counting for the 1978-1999 period was a double-counting of some white Hispanics, with a drop in this practice registered in 2000 as classification practices improved. Accordingly, that year's 11% drop in white inmates was applied to the prior years. The effect of all of these adjustments (with "others" now added in as well) is that an over-count remains (except for a slight undercount in 1978) but it has been reduced to never more than 5% with a mean across 1979-2014 of 3%.

FIGURE 6.

Similar problems were not encountered with the Georgia data as with the national data on imprisonment by race, with the exception of obviously erroneous data for 2010; for that year data directly taken from the Georgia Department of Corrections website was used. Georgia's "other" category was assumed as the remainder after the other three categories were subtracted from total prisoners under jurisdiction.

FIGURES 7 & 8.

The best source of data on crime is the *Uniform Crime Report* prepared by the Federal Bureau of Investigation (FBI) from information submitted by agencies throughout the country. Most useful for our purposes here are separate violent and property crime indices. The FBI's Violent Crime Index pulls together four crimes: murder, rape, robbery, and aggravated assault. Although precise definitions of aggravated assault vary, for the FBI it is defined as "an unlawful attack by one person upon another for the purpose of inflicting severe or aggravated bodily injury. . . . usually accompanied by the use of a weapon or by other means likely to produce death or great bodily harm." The Property Crime Index is based on three crimes: burglary, larceny-theft, and motor vehicle theft. An easy way to understand the distinction between the three types of property crimes is that they all constitute theft but the first and third are more specific, with larceny then covering all other forms of theft. Burglary is theft with forceful entry. Robbery also is theft but it is distinguished as the forcible taking from another person and therefore is included under violent crimes.

⟨⟨⟨⟩⟩

ACKNOWLEDGEMENTS

We want to thank all the many people who gave so generously of their time and wisdom. Even if we did not directly quote or reference all the many people we talked with, our understanding of the issues involved in reentry were enriched by every conversation that we had and many of these stories continue to resonate with us. A few of the individuals whose stories were not included but who spent extensive time talking with us deserve special mention for their influence on our thinking: Allen Ault, Sarah Bartlett, Xochitl Bervera, B.J. Blair, Michael Bobo, George Braucht, Marcus Carter, Judy Catterton, Keir Chapple, Curtis Crocker, Roderick Cunningham, Captain Ernesto Ford, Patrice Fulcher, Darice Good, Amanda Jordan, Kevin Mason, Ruth McMullin, Lia Miller, Crystal Moon, Annie Moorman, Eve Mills Nash, Shalandra Robertson, Lillian Robinson, Susan Shlaer, Travis Williams.

We also want to give special thanks to our early readers, whose keen eyes and encouragement made this a much better book: Melanie Scarbrough, Buster Johnson, Colin Slay, Cory Beggs, Michael Nail, A.J. Sabree, Zoë Losada, Trevor Reich, Diane Jackson, Geanie Brown, Patrick Jackson.

In particular we are grateful to members of the Wising Up Writers Collective, who have kept the faith for this project for many years now: Kerry Langan, Michele Markarian, Kathleen Housley, Murali Kamma.

Photographs by Heather Tosteson.

\\\\//

AUTHORS

HEATHER TOSTESON is the author of six books of fiction and poetry, most recently the novel *The Philosophical Transactions of Maria van Leeuwenhoek, Antoni's Dochter*. She is also the author of *God Speaks My Language, Can You?*, the first Wising Up Listening Project, an exploration of the spiritual journeys of people of different faith traditions. Her work in public health focused on racism, social trust, and how belief systems develop and change. She has an MFA (UNC-Greensboro) and PhD in English and Creative Writing (Ohio University).

CHARLES D. BROCKETT has a PhD from UNC-Chapel Hill and is a recipient of several Fulbright and National Endowment for the Humanities awards. A retired political science professor, he has published extensively on Central America, including two well received books, *Political Movements and Violence in Central America* and *Land, Power, and Poverty: Agrarian Transformation and Political Conflict in Central America*, as well as numerous social science journal articles and book chapters. With Heather Tosteson, he is co-founder of Universal Table and Wising Up Press and co-editor of the Wising Up Anthologies.

DISCUSSION GUIDE
SHARING THE BURDEN OF REPAIR: Reentry After Mass Incarceration
www.universaltable.org

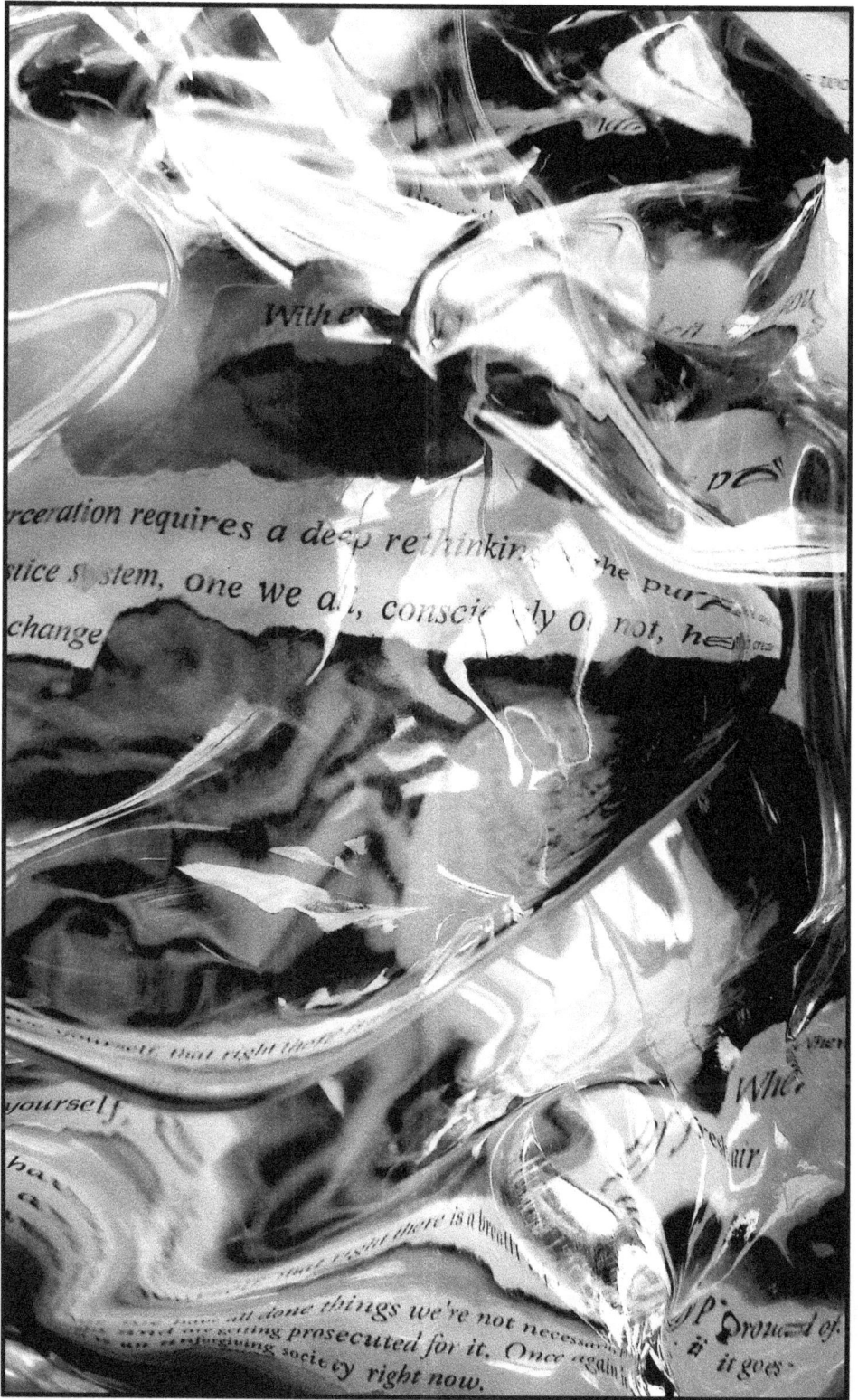

With e...

...rceration requires a deep rethinking... the pur...
...stice system, one we all, conscio...ly o... not, he...
...change

...yourself, that right there...

...yourself.

...ba...

...that right there is a breath...

...have all done things we're not necessaril...
...arted are getting prosecuted for it. Once again...
...are... forgiving society right now.

...proud of...
...it goes...

www.ingramcontent.com/pod-product-compliance
Lightning Source LLC
Chambersburg PA
CBHW020812270326
41928CB00006B/355